Managing a Nation
The Microcomputer Software Catalog

SECOND EDITION, FULLY REVISED AND UPDATED

Managing a Nation
The Microcomputer Software Catalog

EDITED BY

Gerald O. Barney

W. Brian Kreutzer

Martha J. Garrett

WITH CONTRIBUTIONS BY

Stephen J. Binhak
Margee M. Ensign
Richard Harwood
David Holland
Jennie M. Hommel
J. G. Krishnayya
Lynn A. Kurtz
Kenneth L. Kvamme

James W. Mercer
Norman Meyers
Peter J. Opdahl
Ann Elise Schneider
John D. Sterman
Alan M. Thorndike
Daniel Tunstall
Sheryl Wilkins

Routledge
Taylor & Francis Group

LONDON AND NEW YORK

First published 1985 by Westview Press

Published 2018 by Routledge
52 Vanderbilt Avenue, New York, NY 10017
2 Park Square, Milton Park, Abingdon, Oxon OX14 4RN

Routledge is an imprint of the Taylor & Francis Group, an informa business

A CIP catalog record for this book is available from the Library of Congress.
ISBN 0-8133-8297-1

ISBN 13: 978-0-367-01238-0 (hbk)

謹以本書獻給林自新

To Mr. Lin Zixin

whose search for microcomputer software
for use in his 21st Century Study of
the People's Republic of China led to
this book and whose energy, wisdom,
courage, and integrity inspired
us throughout its preparation.

Contents

Part One: Sectoral Software

Part Two: Integrated Models

Part Three: Tools

List of Figures

Chapter 18. Artificial Intelligence

Acknowledgments

In addition to thanking the many contributors to this book, we wish to acknowledge that the greatest contribution of all was made by the authors of the many software packages we have reviewed. Many thanks to all of you for your efforts in developing these programs, for your willingness to provide review copies, and for your answers to our many questions.

Our thanks also to the editors of *Simulation* for allowing us to reprint their review of modeling and simulation software in chapter 16. The information is copyrighted by *Simulation* and is reprinted here with permission.

Throughout this book there are references to individual items of commercial hardware and software. Because of the number of such references, it was not possible to acknowledge the registered trademarks individually, but the reader should know that all brands are registered trademarks of their respective holders.

Gerald O. Barney
W. Brian Kreutzer
Martha J. Garrett

Ordering Information

In each model review is a section called "Source," which gives the address of the source for the software reviewed. Telephone, telefax, and other numbers are included if available; these were current at the time the reviews were written. In many cases, the price of the software is also given. Prices are in U.S. dollars and are subject to change.

Addresses for institutions preparing and publishing data sources are given at the back of the chapter "Sources of Data." At the end of the chapter "Geographic Information Systems" is a listing of companies that manufacture or sell the software and hardware needed for such systems.

Potential buyers should contact the sources directly and request information about current prices, shipping costs, and acceptable means of payment.

The Institute for 21st Century Studies does not sell software.

About the Contributors

Gerald O. Barney is the founder and Executive Director of the Institute for 21st Century Studies. He directed the research for the U.S. Government's study, *The Global 2000 Report to the President*, and has published several books and numerous articles concerning global development, justice, environment, and security. He holds a Ph.D. from the University of Wisconsin in fusion energy physics.

Martha J. Garrett is the Institute's European Representative. After joining the Institute in 1986, she has devoted most of her attention to the training of national 21st Century Study teams and to their software needs and management problems. She holds a Ph.D. from the University of North Carolina in zoology with emphasis on ecology.

W. Brian Kreutzer was the Institute's principal researcher for *Managing a Nation* until 1988 when he moved to Cambridge, Massachusetts, to join Gould-Kreutzer Associates, Inc., as Vice President for Research and Development. He is a specialist in gaming interfaces for computer simulations. His degrees include computer science and information management.

Margee M. Ensign teaches the application of artificial intelligence methods to the field of international relations at the School of International Affairs, Columbia University. She prepared the chapter entitled "Artificial Intelligence: Present and Future Significance for Governments."

Kenneth L. Kvamme is an anthropologist with the Arizona State Museum at the University of Arizona. He is an expert on the application of geographic information systems in anthropology and prepared the chapter entitled "Geographic Information Systems."

John D. Sterman is Associate Professor of Management at the Sloan School of Management, Massachusetts Institute of Technology. He is an expert on the development of "corporate flight simulators," which are computer-based educational tools that simulate the performance of corporations over periods of several years. He prepared the chapter entitled "A Skeptic's Guide to Computer Models."

Daniel Tunstall is a Senior Associate at the World Resources Institute (WRI). He is a principal contributor to the WRI book series on world resource data. He prepared the chapter on "Sources of Data."

The following people contributed individual reviews or concepts for the book. J. G. Krishnayya is Director of the Systems Research Institute, Poona, India. James W. Mercer is an expert on water models and President of GeoTrans, Inc., in Herndon, Virginia. Norman Meyers is an international consultant on ecological matters, who resides in Oxford, England. Richard Harwood is a professor of crop and soil science at Michigan State University, East Lansing, Michigan. Alan M. Thorndike, an expert on the application of computers to politics, lives in Bellport, New York.

Contributors to the graphics, lay-out, drafting, and production of the book include Jennie M. Hommel, a Project Associate at the Institute; Lynn A. Kurtz, now a Project Associate at the American Trust for Agriculture in Poland; and Ann Elise Schneider, who was the Institute's Administrative Assistant.

Sheryl Wilkins, a Research Assistant with the Institute, helped search out models and draft reviews in the initial stage of the project. She then left the Institute to attend law school at Cornell University.

Stephen J. Binhak, David Holland, and Peter J. Opdahl, summer interns at the Institute, helped search for software and draft reviews.

Introduction

1. Introduction

Purpose

Managing a Nation: The Microcomputer Software Catalog is a collection of reviews of microcomputer programs of special relevance to those people around the world who are responsible for the management of the current and future affairs and business of their countries. Specifically, the book includes software that will be useful to teams carrying out national 21st Century Studies, to government ministers and other leaders making policy decisions, and to employees of the official agencies and private institutions that run national programs.

This book is a publication of the Institute for 21st Century Studies, an independent, non-profit, educational organization that provides training and other types of support for teams doing 21st Century Studies. Further information on the Institute is provided in the Appendix.

The Institute has defined a "21st Century Study" as an integrated, multisectoral investigation of the long-term future possibilities for the community under study—a city, a province, a nation, a region, or the world. (Also see Appendix.) Such projects are now being carried out in numerous countries and are producing significant benefits. An overview of the studies and reports from those in Mexico, Peru, and Costa Rica have been published in *Futures* (May, 1990; M. J. Garrett, guest editor). A more in-depth survey will be provided in *Studies for the 21st Century*, a forthcoming book edited by M. J. Garrett and G. O. Barney.

We at the Institute see the 21st Century Studies as potential catalysts to improve the quality of governance. The studies provide alternative scenarios of what countries might become, thereby stimulating thoughtful discussion about national futures. But even a national study of the highest quality will have only short-term influence unless it leads to improvements in official decision-making processes and management practices, both of which must be handled well if a country is to prosper. Thus, although our primary work is with 21st Century Studies themselves, we

recognize that they will have their impact primarily through consequent changes in governance, that is, in policy formulation and management practice.

Imagine, for example, that a 21st Century Study finds that a key challenge in the future of the nation will be providing adequate energy while protecting the environment. And imagine further that an official decision is made to give the energy-environment question high priority. Appropriate ministries must then carry out policy analysis to find a combination of energy sources that satisfies national energy needs, has minimal detrimental environmental effect, and is acceptable to the public. Then, even after the new energy plans and policies are in place, their execution will depend on good management practices such as the designing of an effective national electric grid.

Microcomputer software can help at each stage of this process. The 21st Century Studies often include comparisons between forecasts based on current trends and alternative scenarios. However, the task of building forecasts and scenarios that are internally consistent is a challenging one because of the wide range of sectors involved. Appropriate computer models can help immensely. Similarly, computer software can be very useful to analysts dealing with problems such as the most cost-effective way to reach a particular national goal. Finally, good-quality software can be invaluable in transforming policy decisions into well-managed programs.

History

This book has been in the making since 1981. At that time, Mr. Lin Zixin, then director of the Institute for Scientific and Technological Information of China, was heading the team carrying out the 21st Century Study for the People's Republic of China. As they worked, Mr. Lin and his team became aware that much of the analysis they wanted to do could best be handled with computer models. Their attempts to find appropriate software within the PRC were fruitless, however. Their search disclosed that such programs were not being used even within the national ministries.

Mr. Lin mentioned this problem to Dr. Gerald O. Barney, director of the Institute for 21st Century Studies. They agreed that, as part of its work, the Institute should collect microcomputer models that would be relevant to teams carrying out 21st Century Studies and to governments working to implement those studies.

In response to Mr. Lin's initial request and subsequent requests from other team leaders, the Institute staff began searching for software that would be helpful in national futures research, policy analysis, and governmental management. This work led to the publication of a small book entitled *Managing a Nation: The Software Sourcebook* (Barney and Wilkins 1986), which included reviews of fifty-two models. After four more years of searching, the Institute has a library of many hundreds of microcomputer programs—enough to fill three large filing cabinets. *Managing a Nation: The Microcomputer Software Catalog* reviews 127 of the best pieces from the total collection.

General Description

None of the programs here are general purpose software such as word-processing packages, spreadsheets, and databases, all of which tend to be widely reviewed, well advertised, and readily accessible. The programs that are included here are little known by comparison. They are seldom reviewed or advertised, and many are not even for sale commercially. This is not surprising, since many of them have very small potential markets. Consider, for example, a program designed for use by the head of a national ministry—the finance minister, perhaps. The potential worldwide market would be less than two hundred customers.

Much of the reviewed software comes from obscure sources. A few programs were written by students and published as parts of master's or doctoral theses. Some pieces were produced by small offices and minor bureaus within national governments and international organizations. Other pieces were created by small software companies. One set of models was built by the team doing the Peruvian 21st Century Study.

Each of the programs has been reviewed with two goals in mind: to give a useful general description of the software and to provide adequate technical information about it. Thus, the initial part of each review explains what the software does, who could benefit from using it, and what the benefits would be. The latter section of each review contains details regarding the modeling methodology, data requirements, programming language, theory and assumptions, and appropriate hardware.

Organization

Managing a Nation is divided into three parts. Part One reviews sectoral software, Part Two covers multisectoral and global models, and Part Three provides information to help users better understand and apply all kinds of computer models.

The sectoral models in Part One are collected into chapters on the following topics: agriculture; economy and industry; energy; environment and ecology; natural resources; politics; demography, health, and education; rural and urban development; national security; and transportation and communication. Most of these categories parallel the limited domains of government ministries, and most of these programs address relatively specific problems. Here are a few examples of the kind of software included:

LEAP is a national energy model that can be used in both industrialized and developing countries to evaluate alternative energy policies and programs.

Interactive Conservation Evaluation (ICE) is a program to help analyze alternative soil conservation measures for a wide range of soil conditions.

MINIECON is a dynamic macroeconomic model programmed on a spreadsheet; it can be fitted to any country and used to evaluate proposed economic policies.

CAMEO II is emergency management software that simulates a wide range of toxic chemical releases and can be used both for contingency planning and for managing operations during a chemical emergency.

Part Two of *Managing a Nation* includes both multisectoral national models and global models. The multisectoral national models synthesize many of the individual areas addressed in Part One. This integration is very important since virtually all public policy issues of importance cut across ministerial boundaries. Global models focus on a still higher level, providing an overview of the interactions among nations. Such models are of increasing importance, not only because of international relations and trade, but because of transnational environmental impacts and international migration. Two examples of Part Two models are:

STRATAGEM-1, a computer-managed board game, puts the players in ministerial roles and allows them to run a country for a simulated period of twenty to thirty years. The players quickly learn how interconnected apparently separate sectors really are.

GLOBUS, a global model of twenty-five national and regional submodels, explicitly represents the political interactions among countries.

Part Three is designed to help users derive full benefit from the programs in Parts One and Two and from other computer software as well. The first chapter, "A Skeptic's Guide to Computer Models," was written by Dr. John Sterman of the Massachusetts Institute of Technology. He points out certain critical questions that must be asked by all model users and especially by decision makers: "What is the purpose of the model? Is it appropriate for the issue we are addressing? What are the model's assumptions? What value judgments, both explicit and implicit, lie behind it?" Questions such as these can help assure that models are used appropriately and ethically in the governance process.

Data requirements are often considered the major limitation on the usefulness of software. In other words, potential users often dismiss a program not because of any inherent flaws, but because they doubt that they could find the data necessary to run the model. Actually, an enormous amount of data is available for all nations, in the form of statistics, maps, satellite images, and so forth. The second chapter of Part

Three provides a concise summary of the data sources especially relevant to national governance.

Several emerging technologies—geographic information systems, modeling languages, and artificial intelligence—show promise of many beneficial applications in governance. The Part Three chapters about these technologies review their status and suggest ways for interested officials to keep abreast of new developments.

The Further View: An Emerging Pattern

This book is like a mosaic. Up close we see just the individual pieces—the reviews. These are interesting in themselves, and each reader will find some that are especially noteworthy. But, if we step back and look at the whole collection, a pattern emerges. Seen in its entirety, this collection reveals that a new field has just come into being—the use of software to improve the quality of governance.

The widespread availability of microcomputers has produced an explosion of creative new software and models for government application. *Any* national government—developing or industrialized—can use this software. It does not require special personnel, such as system analysts or computer programmers. A competent staff person can be trained in a matter of weeks to use almost any of these programs. If needed, technical support is available for many of the programs. Most of them sell at modest prices and work on several types of inexpensive microcomputers.

But what can these pieces of software do? Why would a government want to acquire them? First, the programs provide structures for doing analysis and organizing data—structures that are well researched and in ready-to-use form. Secondly, the programs can accommodate large quantities of data and perform thousands of calculations quickly and reliably. Thirdly, the "what if" feature of many of the programs allows creation of many alternative scenarios in minimal time.

As a result of these characteristics, the programs allow users to concentrate on analysis and the results of analysis, rather than on arcane details of methodology and programming. In short, the programs can vastly increase the quality, efficiency, and productivity of a government.

An Unusual Opportunity for the Developing Countries

Microcomputers are one of a number of new technologies sweeping the world. The developing countries face real problems in applying many of the new technologies, however, since they require both high capital investment and a pool of highly trained technical personnel. Because of these requirements, such technologies are not likely to have a major beneficial influence on the developing world in the near future. (For an overall assessment of the problems faced by developing countries in applying new technologies and industrial management methods, see Sewell 1988 and Sewell, Tucker, and contributors 1988.)

The situation is strikingly different with computer technology, however. The early mainframe computers were available only to a relatively small number of people, most of whom worked in the industrialized countries. Today, however, computing power that cost hundreds of thousands and even millions of dollars a decade ago can be purchased in the form of microcomputers costing just hundreds of dollars.

What has happened to the hardware is only half the story. Similar progress has been going on in software. The development of sophisticated microcomputer software has been under way for three decades and has involved

billions of dollars of research. The resulting programs are more useful and more user friendly than programs of the past, and most are available at modest prices.

The result of these developments is that an important technology can be put to use right now by the governments of every nation. Thanks to the microcomputer revolution, a powerful piece of equipment has become available at prices that all countries can afford. And with the development of the kind of software reviewed in this book, an enormous set of effective tools has been placed in the hands of government leaders throughout the world.

This situation provides developing and newly-industrialized nations with an unusual opportunity. While it will take years of investment, research, experimentation, and training before some new technologies can be applied well in their countries, the new microcomputer hardware and software can be obtained and applied by them today. This technology is being used increasingly in most industrialized countries to improve the quality of leadership and the effectiveness of government agencies. The governments of the developing countries can do the same right now, taking advantage of software that can provide significant assistance in the tasks of organizing data, analyzing policies, considering alternatives, managing projects, and planning strategies. In other words, these programs can improve governance and help create the governmental environment needed for development.

The Future

The hardware and software available today is impressive enough to justify every national government giving this technology high priority. However, if reservations remain, a look at the future should dispel them. To get a sense of what software might be able to do in the future, we only have to look at the changes occurring in the hardware on which that software will run.

Almost all the programs described in this book run on microcomputers that are based on an Intel 8086 chip running at 4.77 MHz, with two 360 KB floppy disk drives and the 2.0 version of the DOS operating system. But such microcomputers were already available ten years ago! In other words, the microcomputer software now available for national governance

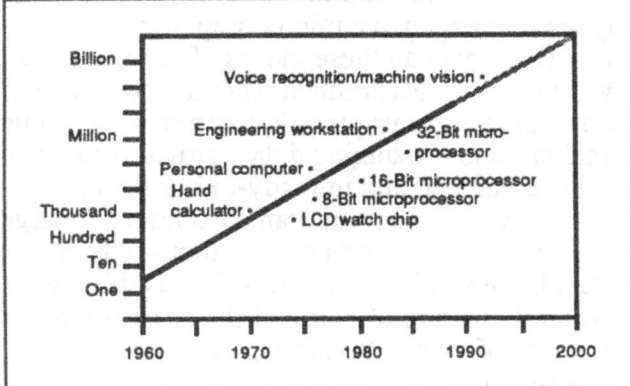

Figure 1-1: Growth in the number of transistors per microprocessor chip since the chip was first introduced in 1960. Source: After J. Marcoff, "The Chip at 30: Potential Still Vast," The New York Times, 14 September, 1988, p. D1.

is almost a decade behind advances in the hardware and does not come close to exploiting the capabilities of the current hardware.

The references for this chapter include numerous articles about current and expected developments in computer hardware (Markoff 1988a-b, 1989a-c; Scannel and LaPlante 1988; Clark 1988; Copeland 1989; Marshall 1989; Brownstein 1988, 1989; Krohn 1990a-b; Lewis 1988a-e; DeTray 1986; Dryden 1990; Hayes 1988; and Fisher 1988). The story they tell is an exciting one.

As shown in Figure 1-1, the power of microprocessors is increasing rapidly and is expected by industry experts to continue increasing for many years yet. Microprocessors that are expected to be available in 1992 will be able to perform 120 million instructions per second (MIPS). Industry leaders expect that, by the year 2000, microprocessors will operate at 250 MHz and will contain 100 million transistors. Intel Corporation has announced some details of the i786 chip, which it plans to release in the year 2000; the chip will include four tightly coupled, parallel processors, two vector processors, two megabytes of on-chip cache memory, and a digital video interface and will deliver 2000 MIPS.

The increasing power of computers is, however, only half of the story. The cost of executing a million instructions per second (MIPS), is declining steadily. (See Figure 1-2.)

The development of more powerful microprocessors and chips means that the microcomputers into which they are incorporated also have increased capabilities. When a VMSO5 processor board is inserted in IBM PS-2 model 80, this microcomputer becomes as powerful as an IBM 9370 Model 40 mainframe computer. Desk-top work station computers are approaching the capability of supercomputers that were at the cutting edge of the technology only five years ago. Desktop mainframes are under development that will use five chips—each measuring only a half-inch by a half-inch—that replicate the performance of the central processing units in IBM's 370 mainframe computers.

Another advance will increase yet further the performance of microcomputers. Most microcomputers today operate with microprocessors based on the Complex Instruction Set Computer (CISC) design.

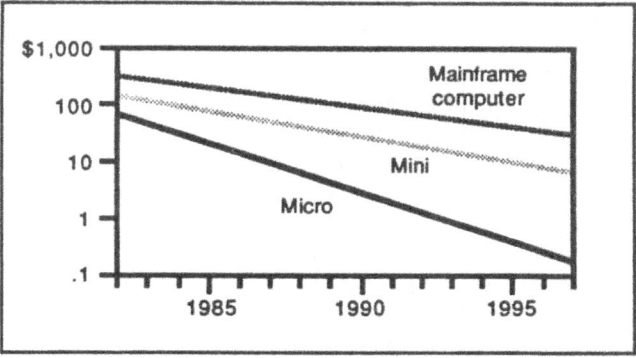

Figure 1-2: The falling cost of computational capability (measured in U.S. dollars per million instructions per second (MIPS)) for microcomputers, minicomputers, and mainframe computers. Source: After J. Marcoff, "The Chip at 30: Potential Still Vast," The New York Times, 14 September, 1988, p. D1.

Smaller, more powerful microprocessors based on the Reduced Instruction Set Computer (RISC) design, which increase dramatically the power of microcomputers (see Figure 1-3), are just beginning to enter the market.

Meanwhile, internal memory capacity is increasing at a similar rate. Microprocessors now available are able to manage up to four gigabytes (the equivalent of roughly forty thousand books) of physical memory and up to sixty-four terabytes (640 million books) of virtual memory. Current manufacturing technology has the potential to produce individual memory chips capable of storing 64 million bits of information, the equivalent of several encyclopedia volumes. New manufacturing technology based on X-rays is under development that will permit the storage of much more information per chip. Industry experts are predicting chips containing 1,000 million transistors by the year 2000.

External memory capacity is already enormous and is growing. Reliable two-inch disk drives, the size of a pack of cigarettes, can hold 100 megabytes of data. Compact Disk Read-only Memory (CD-ROM) now permits the storage on a single 4.72-inch disk of 550 megabytes of data (the equivalent of about five hundred books), with an access time of two to three seconds for any individual piece of data. The cost of producing CD-ROM disks has been dropping, and it is now possible to produce one for $3,000, rather than $30,000. High-capacity laser disks are being designed that will contain a combination of software, documentation, and necessary data.

Most impressive of all, computers are becoming much easier for people to use. Learning the basics of using any computer will become easier as operating systems become more nearly standard. Already an operating system exists that works the same way on computers sold by forty-four companies, including IBM and Digital. Graphic interfaces, first pioneered by Apple Computer Corporation, are becoming more common and will make it even easier for people to learn how to use software. Computers are even able now to tutor users with talking software ("soundware") made possible by digital signal processor (DSP) chips.

Computer tutoring will be even better in the future because of full motion interactive video. This technology is already available for microcomputers equipped with special parts and by the year 2000 will be an integral part of many microcomputer chips. Two-dimensional screen presentations may be replaced by stereoscopic three-dimensional images and models, which already can be produced with computer work stations.

Even programming will become easier. Object-oriented programming, which greatly increases productivity and compatibility, is already appearing. Also, compilers have been developed that automatically adapt programs written for a single processor so that the software can be handled by several processors working simultaneously.

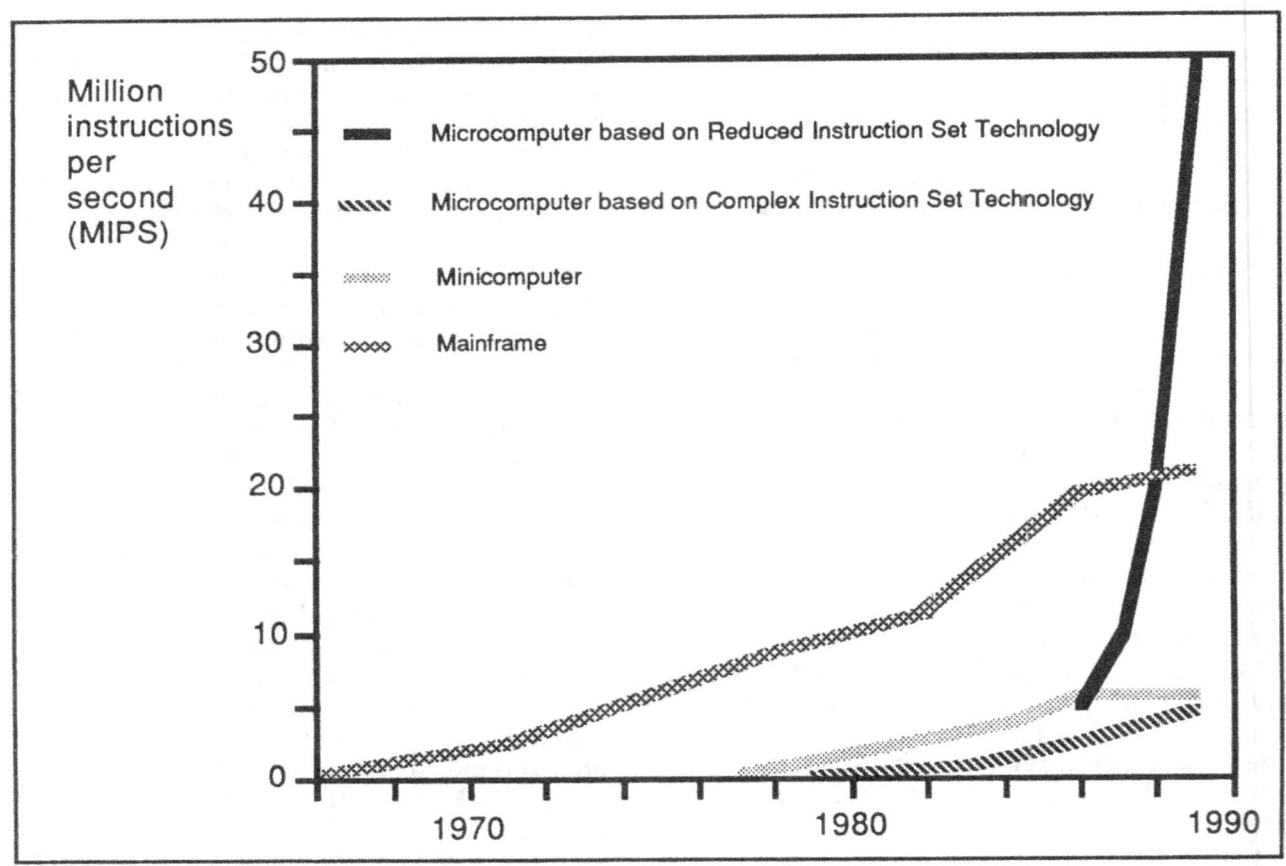

Figure 1-3: The changing performance characteristics of microcomputers based on RISC and CISC designs, minicomputers, and mainframes. Performance is measured in millions of instructions per second (MIPS) for a single processor. Source: After J. Marcoff, "In an Age When Tiny Is All, Big Computers are Hurting," The New York Times, 4 April, 1989, p. A1.

The role of the mainframe computer is also changing rapidly in response to the rush of microcomputer technology. In the most advanced applications, mainframes now act as powerful electronic librarians serving the information needs of smaller computers. Specialized servers based on a new generation of microprocessors may even displace mainframes from the librarian function.

The competition that microcomputers are giving even supercomputers is illustrated by events that occurred during the development of GLOBUS (Bremer 1987, pp. 799-801), a major new model described in our chapter on "Global Models." The GLOBUS Research Group was using a Cray X-MP supercomputer to develop the model, and runs required about three and a half minutes of Cray time. But the queue time to use the Cray, was four and a half hours, and as a result, progress on the project was slow. As an experiment, the team tried running GLOBUS on a microcomputer based on the Intel 80386 microprocessor, running at 16 MHz. Low precision tests ran in only a half hour, and full precision standard cases in four and a half hours—exactly the queue time to use the Cray! The GLOBUS Research Group abandoned the Cray for the microcomputer and increased substantially their rate of progress.

Factoring large numbers (useful in encrypting) is an area that traditionally has been an exclusion province of supercomputers. No more. Mathematicians at the University of Georgia used a network of 140 Zenith microcomputers to factor a 95-digit number (Cipra 1988). While large computers were used to factor the largest number to date (100 digits), the work at the University of Georgia demonstrates that it is the algorithm, not the size of the machines, that really matters.

Widening the Community of Knowledge

In the years ahead microcomputers are likely to have a significant influence on how nations and societies transmit knowledge from one generation to another. In considering the possibilities for societies, it is instructive to reflect on parallels between the widespread introduction of printing presses and the widespread introduction of microcomputers.

In *The Discoverers*, Daniel Boorstein (1983, pp. 480-556) presents a fascinating picture of the widespread effects that Gutenburg and his successors had on society. The invention of the movable-type press in the mid-1400s and the subsequent development of printing technology brought about myriad changes. Of course, the most obvious and immediate effect was that books were made accessible to a far wider audience than had previously benefited from them. As Boorstein puts it, the communities of knowledge widened. The rapidity and degree to which this occurred is hard to grasp. Before the printing press in the mid-1400s, estimates are that the number of books in Europe—all hand written, of course—numbered just in the thousands. By 1500 there were between ten and twenty million printed books on the continent.

But the influence of the printing press went beyond the dramatic increase in the number of books, because the books themselves began to have effects. Manuscript books, which were meant to be read only by the most educated, were almost always written in Latin and Greek. But publishers were aiming at a wider market, so books written in vernacular languages became commonplace, and translated works grew in acceptance. This popularization was one of the factors encouraging the development of modern European languages.

The enlarged public market also resulted in a growing demand for new books, and authorship was encouraged. Not only did the total number of books increase, but the number of titles exploded also. The very shape and format of books also changed in response to their growing use; they became portable, and page numbers and indexes were invented. Lending libraries, formerly off-limits to all but exclusive groups of subscribers, went public. Systems of education, social structures, even governments were affected. Boorstein quotes Thomas Carlyle on the subject, "He who first shortened the labor of copyists by the device of movable types was...creating a whole new democratic world."

The events that followed the widespread introduction of printing technology have many parallels in the developments being prompted by the widespread availability of microcomputers. The communities of knowledge are being widened again today. Twenty years ago few people on earth had access to a computer. Today, microcomputers are found in every country and are becoming common in some.

It is important to remember, of course, that printed books had powerful influence because they were effective means for transferring information and ideas. Microcomputers are amazing pieces of equipment, but by themselves they cannot serve this information-transfer role; they are, in effect, like empty books. The information is available, however, in the form of software.

For most of human history information has been shared verbally or through hand-written symbols. For the past five hundred years, it has been transferred through the printed word. Acquiring mastery of a particular field has involved the time-consuming process of reading and sorting through the information in many books, articles, and journals. Now, microcomputer software provides a new medium for transmitting information.

Appropriate, user friendly software can transmit many kinds of knowledge more efficiently than it can be transmitted by books. It can make a wealth of knowledge available in highly useful, versatile form. And with it, a person with only modest technical training can have access to the knowledge of many experts.

The microcomputer revolution is certain to affect libraries, just as the printing revolution did. Limited software libraries already exist; one of these, for example, is the International Ground Water Modeling Center, which has two locations: Holcomb Research Institute, Butler University, Indianapolis, IN 46208, USA; and TNO-DGV Institute of Applied Geoscience, P.O. Box 285, 2600 AG Delft, The Netherlands. Large, diverse collections are sure to be open to the public within a decade or two. People will be able to borrow microcomputer software on a particular topic from a library just as today they can borrow books on that topic. These libraries of software will have profound effects on the way information is transferred among people and between generations.

The Role of Software in Governance

The pieces reviewed in *Managing a Nation* are the kind of programs that will be found under "governance" in the software libraries of the future and in the software collections of governments. But software for managing a nation will have little effect, regardless of its quality, unless governments are prepared to use it and committed to using it to reach valid national goals.

Microcomputers and software are, of course, just tools, and like all tools, they can be employed to either good or evil purposes. The water-distribution program reviewed in this book can help government officials design water distribution systems that will provide adequate water to all of the citizens of their countries, but there is nothing to guarantee that the program will be used in this way. Where the water will go must be determined by the officials before they apply the program. Their decision will determine whether the program is used to supply water to everyone or just to the more privileged. The use of each and every computer program used in governance inevitably requires answers to political and ethical questions, questions that involve issues of conflict, justice, equity, and peace.

At the same time, even a government with the best of intentions cannot govern well unless its officials know what is going on in the country and what the people need. No country can prosper under a badly run government, regardless of the political intentions of that government. All national governments—in both developing and industrialized nations—need to be able to gauge the long-term strategic impacts of critical factors such as economic policies, large-scale development projects, and demographic trends. An efficient, well informed, and productive government is a basic need of every nation.

In the right hands, information technology can help fulfill this need and lead to improved governance. When a government is seriously committed, the right software can advance public welfare, economic development, and prosperity. It can be used to increase productivity in agriculture and industry, to make housing, education, and health care programs more effective, to provide energy more efficiently, to improve transportation and communication plans, to protect the environment and conserve natural resources, and even to analyze ways to improve national security while avoiding armed conflict.

A Program for Applying Software for Governance

For a nation to derive such benefits from the new microcomputer technology, four conditions must be met: (a) the top national leaders must support the idea; (b) officials at all levels of government and members of the team doing the national 21st Century Study must be willing to acquire the skills to apply the programs; (c) there must be good training programs available, not just to train current users but to prepare future ones; and (d) current hardware and software must be accessible.

The first two of these requirements can only be met by the people involved. The fourth requirement is being met in part by the revolution in microcomputers and the emergence of software for governance. The third requirement, training, is as important as the others, but it is not being addressed adequately by any government.

We believe that training programs on software for governance need to be oriented toward three audiences: top political leaders, professionals in governments and other national agencies, and educators. Thus, to be comprehensive, a training program must include these components: (a) overview courses for top officials responsible for national planning, development programs, 21st Century Studies, and other high-level policy decisions; (b) more in-depth courses for members of teams doing 21st Century Studies, employees from government ministries, and other persons who will apply the software to policy and management decisions; and (c) special courses for representatives from the Ministry of Education and institutions of higher education, designed to demonstrate how relevant software can be integrated into degree programs related to national governance, including public administration, political science, economics, operations research, city planning, public health, and management science.

In most countries, educating the top leaders will have to come first. It will be impossible to set up a strong training program unless the national leadership is convinced that software can make a real difference in governance. Most high-level political leaders just do not have the time to take a comprehensive course about how microcomputer software can be utilized effectively. What they have time for and what they need is a brief seminar that introduces them quickly to the new, powerful, inexpensive, easy-to-use tools available for every ministry of their government.

After the leadership is convinced, it should be possible to set up more detailed courses oriented to specific ministries and agencies and to groups such as national 21st Century Study teams. Each course should be designed to address the issues of concern for the participants and should include software that covers both the policy and management levels of governance.

The training program for educators should provide them with detailed information about how to introduce microcomputer technology, the powerful new intellectual tool of our time, into their professional curricula. Even modest changes in educational programs at universities could produce a steady steam of trained people capable of applying software to problems of policy analysis and management in both government and the private sector.

This brings us back to the fourth requirement, hardware and software. People trained in special courses or in university programs will be up-to-date on microcomputer technology for only a short time. Both hardware and software are going through rapid changes, and training provided today will be outdated within years. But truly effective analysis requires the best tools available for compiling data, analyzing policy, designing plans, and so forth.

Obviously, governments need a system to keep current on advances in both microcomputer hardware and microcomputer software relevant to governance. This book provides a contribution in this area, but effort is also needed at the national level. One approach might be for governments to establish national microcomputer resource centers, which would have responsibility for sharing information on new hardware, software, and data. Purchasing decisions, however, are probably best left to individual ministries and departments so as not to stifle the creativity that microcomputers are stimulating.

A Request for Help

The Institute intends to continue collecting information about software for use in managing nations. As you come across interesting, useful programs, let us know. If you create software yourself, please write to us about it. If possible, send us a review copy with complete documentation. Be sure to include information about how potential users can contact you and about the approximate price.

References

Barney, G. O. and Wilkins, S. 1986. *Managing a Nation: The Software Sourcebook*. Arlington, Va.: Global Studies Center.

Boorstein, Daniel, J. 1983. *The Discoverers*. New York: Random House.

Bremer, Stuart A., ed. 1987. *The GLOBUS Model*. Boulder, Colorado: Westview Press.

Brownstein, M. 1988. High-Capacity Floppies are Drives of the Future. *InfoWorld*, 12 September 1988, p. 27.

Brownstein, M. 1989. Intel i486 to Triple Performance of 386. *InfoWorld*, 3 April 1989, p. 1.

Clark, J. H. 1988. The Supercomputer Shrinks. *New York Times*, 26 February 1988, p. D1.

Cipra, Barry A. 1988. PCs Factor a "Most Wanted" Number. *Science*, 23 December 1988, pp. 1634-35.

Copeland, R. 1989. Intel, Prime To Develop ECL Version of i486. *InfoWorld*, 17 April 1989, p. 1.

DeTray, J. 1986. CD-ROM: A Curiosity No Longer. *CD-ROM Review*, 1 October 1986, p. 4.

Dryden, Patrick. 1990. Intel Charts CPU Evolution Through This Decade. *InfoWorld*, 26 March, 1990, p. 5.

Fisher, L. M. 1988. A New Approach to Programming. *New York Times*, 7 September 1988, p. D8.

Garrett, M. J., ed. National 21st Century Studies. *Futures*, May, 1990.

Garrett, M. J. and Barney, G. O., eds. *Studies for the 21st Century*, forthcoming.

Hayes, T. C. 1988. A.T.&T.'s Unix Is a Hit at Last, And Other Companies are Wary. *New York Times*, 24 February 1988, p. D8.

Krohn, N. 1990a. IBM's Five-Chip 370 Processor Could Lead to Desktop Mainframes. *InfoWorld*, 19 February 1990, p. 5.

_____. 1990b. CD ROM Publishing Arrives for the Little Guy. *InfoWorld*, 2 April, 1990, p. 22.

Lewis, P. H. 1988a. IBM Puts Its Cards on the Table. *New York Times*, 21 February 1988, p. F12.

_____. 1988b. 3-D Stereo: Get Out Your Glasses. *New York Times*, 17 April 1988, p. F15.

_____. 1988c. New Graphics Interface. *New York Times*, 1 November 1988, p. C10.

_____. 1988d. A Faster, Very Versatile Processor. *New York Times*, 6 November 1988, p. F9.

_____. 1988e. Bringing Realism to the Screen. *New York Times*, 22 November 1988, p. F9.

Markoff, J. 1988a. Shift to Simplicity Promises Big Advances in Computing. *New York Times*, 6 April 1988, p. A1.

_____. 1988b. The Chip at 30: Potential Still Vast. *New York Times*, 14 September 1988, p. D1.

_____. 1989a. A New Way to Speed Computers. *New York Times*, 31 May 1989, p. D6.

_____. 1989b. A System to Speed Airline Travel. *New York Times*, 6 September 1989, p. D1.

_____. 1989c. Personal Computers Gaining TV's Power of Image and Sound. *New York Times*, 12 September 1989, p. A1

Marshall, M. 1989. Intel 80586 to Contain 4 Million Transistors. *InfoWorld*, 21 August 1989, p. 1.

Scannel, E. and LaPlante, A. 1988. Products Benefit From MCA's Power. *InfoWorld*, 21 November 1988, p. 3.

Sewell, J. W. 1988. The Development Gap: Help the Third World Catch Up. *New York Times*, 22 May 1988, p. F3.

Sewell, J. W.; Tucker, S. K.; and contributors. 1988. *U.S. Policy and The Developing Countries: Growth, Exports, and Jobs in a Changing World Economy*. New Brunswick, N.J.: Transaction Books.

Part One: Sectoral Software

2. Agriculture

Introduction

Agricultural policy is one of the most difficult and important aspects of managing a nation. Food shortages or even increased food prices can threaten any government. To maintain adequate production, most governments have a variety of policies and programs that benefit farmers. In years of bad weather, the costs of these programs can make a major impact on the national treasury.

The formulation of sound agricultural policy is complicated by many major new developments. Food grains are fed not only to the human population but to an increasingly wide range of farm animals. Food grains are also being used to produce sweeteners (corn syrup) and fuels (alcohol). Inputs to agricultural production (fertilizers, pesticides, irrigation, cultivation, drying, and transportation) have made agriculture heavily dependent on fossil fuels and therefore also on the world energy prices. Genetic engineering is changing dramatically the plants and animals used in agriculture.

Given the complexity of the agricultural sector, it is fortunate indeed that much microcomputer software has been developed that can assist in the management of the agricultural sector of a nation's economy. The length of this chapter is an indication of the diversity of interesting and useful software now available. The following paragraphs provide an overview of the software reviewed here.

The Computerized System for Agricultural and Population Planning Assistance and Training (CAPPA) package from the U.N. Food and Agriculture Organization (FAO) provides a convenient starting point. CAPPA is a generic representation of the agricultural sector of a country's economy. It is much more, however, than just an agriculture sector model; integral to it are a demographic model and a macroeconomic model. CAPPA could, in fact, be included in the chapter on multisectoral models.

The Standard National [Agricultural] Model (SNM) was designed with objectives similar to those that motivated the development of CAPPA, but with an additional concern for the international consequences of national policies and programs. Like CAPPA, SNM is a generic national agricultural model integrated with a macroeconomic model of the non-agricultural sectors. Unlike CAPPA, however, the SNM system allows models to be linked together into a Basic Linked Network (BLN). This linkage provides a simple means of exploring the international implications of domestic policy changes in one or more nations and the implications for individual nations of changes in the global agricultural system. Detailed SNMs exist for three nations and one region; somewhat less detailed SNMs exist for fifteen other nations and one other region; relatively aggregate SNMs exist for thirteen regions that collectively make up the rest of the world.

CAPPA and SNM are both aimed at the development of a strong and dependable agriculture sector, but neither of these models is capable of addressing commodity cycles, a serious problem that plagues the agricultural sector of virtually every nation. These periods of boom and bust are caused by a variety of dynamic interacting properties of non-equilibrium commodity markets. The General Dynamic Commodity Cycle Model (GDCCM) provides a convenient and powerful tool with which to evaluate alternative policies and programs for damping these destructive cycles.

A disadvantage of all the models mentioned so far is that they deal in economic abstractions that are not tied to specific pieces of land. The Agro-Ecological Zone (AEZ) methodology provides an important link between economic analysis and soil and climate data for agro-ecological zones around the world. The AEZ model develops estimates of the sustainable yields of seventeen major crops under alternative technological inputs and then determines when population will reach the maximum that the area can feed sustainably from indigenous crops. While other methodologies can be used to make such comparisons, AEZ is unique in the degree to which it takes physical resources into account in projecting the changing balance between food needs and food production.

Ruminant livestock have always been an important part of the food system of all nations. These animals have the capacity to digest parts of plants that are indigestible for humans and to produce milk and meat that can contribute to the human diet. The ILCA Data Entry and Analysis System (IDEAS) provides a specialized database for herd management. Simulation of Production and Utilization of Rangelands (SPUR) is a pasture simulation model that can be used to evaluate alternative rangeland management policies that avoid deterioration from erosion and other effects of overgrazing.

Soil losses are one of the most serious threats to the sustainable development of societies around the world. The Interactive Conservation Evaluation (ICE) methodology provides a convenient means for evaluating the effectiveness and costs of alternative soil conservation measures.

FARMSIM, a program for evaluating agricultural projects proposed for development loans, has been used widely in Latin America. Its use should be discontinued. It perpetuates the practice of making agricultural development loans on the basis of short-term profit maximization with no consideration for sustainability issues. FARMSIM is included here as an object lesson on the importance of examining carefully the assumptions inherent in software to be used in national decision making.

The Farm Analysis Package (FARMAP) is a specialized database system designed to facilitate the entry, verification, and analysis of farm survey data. It can be used in either developing or industrialized countries and is a powerful tool for assembling basic data about the performance of and the constraints on farms throughout a nation.

Nations have faced food emergencies throughout history. Now, however, computers are providing powerful new tools in the fight against famine. The Famine Early Warning System (FEWS) takes satellite data and converts it into monthly reports that assess the prospects for drought and famine through the most

vulnerable parts of Africa. FEWS proved its effectiveness by providing advance warning of the 1988 Ethiopian famine, and as a result officials at the U.S. Agency for International Development (USAID) have decided to continue the FEWS program.

A supplement to FEWS is provided by the Food Needs and Availabilities Database and Estimation System (FNA System). This large, sophisticated spreadsheet integrates an enormous amount of economic and production data to project food needs for the poorest countries of the world two years in advance.

Every year, but especially in times of bad weather, it is important for farmers and agricultural officials to know how limited agricultural inputs can best be used. The Crop Estimation through Resource and Environment Synthesis (CERES) programs for maize, wheat, and other grains provide guidance on the best use of inputs for a given piece of land under a variety of circumstances.

To feed the populations of the future, leaders throughout the world are counting on great progress in agriculture. They expect agricultural research to increase yields and, at the same time, to reduce the dependence of agriculture on fossil fuels and eliminating farming practices that cause unsustainable environmental impacts. To meet these objectives, agricultural research has become a complex enterprise involving many disciplines.

One powerful tool that draws on these many disciplines is the crop model, which integrates all that has been learned about a particular type of crop plant. The model simulates the development of the plant, and differences between the model's output and field experiments are useful in developing research priorities. The crop model RICEMOD, reviewed in this chapter, could be the basis for development of other such models.

In all aspects of agricultural research on both plants and animals, there are many data analysis tasks that must be done if the maximum benefit is to be derived from the research. These analytical tasks are extremely time consuming however, if done manually. MSTAT is a low-cost, high-performance analytical support package designed specifically to facilitate the analysis of data from agricultural research.

Computerized System for Agricultural and Population Planning Assistance and Training (CAPPA)

Purpose

To facilitate the use of a multisectoral scenario approach to agricultural planning.

Description

CAPPA helps planners in the construction and appraisal of alternative scenarios for a nation's agricultural development over periods of up to fifty years.

Using CAPPA, planners can: (a) integrate population and labor force projections into their agricultural analyses; (b) assess trends in their nation's dependency on foreign food sources and take these trends into account in formulating agricultural strategies; (c) evaluate the effects of alternative agricultural policies on labor requirements, employment, and productivity; (d) perform nutritional analyses; and (e) consider the links between performance of the agricultural sector and rural-urban migration.

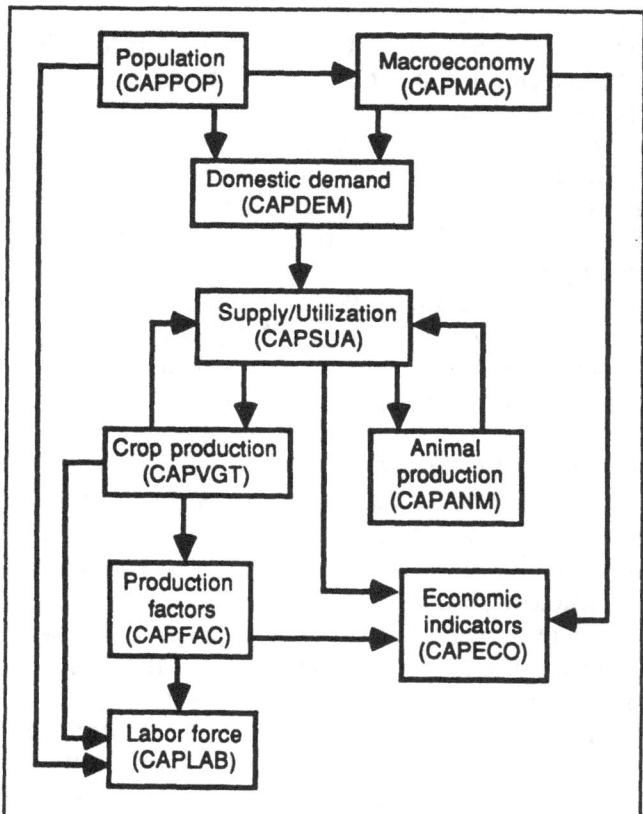

Figure 2-1: The CAPPA submodels and their principal interrelationships.

Theory and Assumptions

As illustrated in Figure 2-1, CAPPA is a set of interrelated partial simulation models, each of which is used in the construction of the scenario. The first step is a projection of domestic agricultural demand. The preliminary steps include projecting population and labor force at the horizon year of the scenario (population module), projecting macroeconomic variables (macroeconomy module), and projecting food and other demands for agricultural produce (domestic demand module). To avoid the considerable work involved in the preliminary steps, most users simply put in standard population and macroeconomic projections obtained from other institutions.

After the completion of the preliminary steps or the entry of standard projections, CAPPA leads planners through the specification and refinement of an agricultural development scenario. The steps in this process are: (a) setting domestic production and external trade objectives (supply/utilization module), (b) studying land development and land allocation requirements for the attainment of domestic production objectives (crop production module), (c) studying animal production systems and feed requirements (animal production module), (d) assessing input requirements and allotting labor requirements between human, animal, and mechanical energy (production factors module), (e) assessing employment implications (labor force module) and implications for economic indicators (economy module), and (f) revising various parts of the scenario based on evaluations of the components.

CAPPA stores a record of aggregate results for the scenarios in disk files. These files can be used to compare up to ten alternative scenarios.

CAPPA also facilitates the collection of relevant data. To help users get started, a database of default data can be obtained from FAO for many specific countries. For actual policy applications, the default data must be checked, revised, and updated. The CAPDAT program allows users to modify the data files. A special manual covering the preparation and modification of the database is planned.

Evaluation

For decades development planners have needed a tool to facilitate the planning of agriculture development. CAPPA is a helpful step in the right direction, but unfortunately the package does not go as far as it could to meet the needs of agricultural development planners.

FAO pointedly describes CAPPA as a training tool. A *training* tool, however, is not what is needed; what is needed is a *planning* tool. CAPPA could be a first-rate planning tool if a little more time and effort is put into its future development.

Neither CAPPA's software nor its documentation is of high quality. The software is difficult to use. Time-consuming iterations should be automated. The simulation models need to be strengthened; the only feedbacks they incorporate are those found in the accounting equations between the supply and utilization accounts and animal and crop production.

Documentation is available in both English and French. The English documentation we received needs major revisions by a competent technical writer. It is badly organized, and important bits of information are scattered about and difficult to find. Many sentences are difficult to understand because of the inadequate editing.

CAPPA is typically introduced to a country through workshops lasting one or two weeks. If the documentation were improved and the programs rewritten to make them more user friendly, the time needed to introduce CAPPA could be substantially reduced. Training would still be needed, but it could focus on developing an institutional structure for effective use of CAPPA, rather than on explaining how to work around the deficiencies of the software and documentation.

CAPPA has enormous potential for improving agricultural planning, but this potential will not be achieved without major improvements in the code and documentation.

Hardware and Software Requirements
   IBM PC/XT/AT or compatible. Requirements are 120 KB RAM, two floppy disk drives (or a hard disk and one floppy disk drive), Microsoft BASIC, and DOS 2.0 or above.

Source
   Chief, Development Policy Training and Research Service, Policy Analysis Division, Food and Agriculture Organization of the United Nations, Via delle Terme di Caracalla, 00100,

Rome, Italy; telephone: 57971; cable: FOODAGRI ROME; telex: 610181 FAO I.

Standard National [Agricultural] Model (SNM)

Purpose
   To analyze the consequences of domestic or international policy changes for a nation's domestic food situation.

Description
   The SNM is a generic model that can be (and has been) used to create country-specific agricultural models for either market or centrally planned economies. The structure of a typical country-specific model is illustrated in Figure 2-2. The purpose of the model is not to make forecasts or predictions but rather to explore the general consequences of alternative policies five to fifteen years into the future.

   The SNM was developed as a generic tool for producing a number of national agricultural models to be joined in a global system of agricultural models called the Basic Linked System (BLS). The BLS provides a worldwide market-clearing mechanism that balances exports and imports for all countries and establishes world prices for agricultural commodities. The BLS system of linked national models can be used to examine the international implications of national policy changes.

   Both BLS and SNM were developed as a part of the overall Food and Agricultural Program (FAP) at the International Institute for Applied Systems Analysis (IIASA).

Theory and Assumptions
   At its most basic level, the SNM is defined not by a methodology but by the set of protocols that a national model must satisfy if it is to link satisfactorily into the BLS.

   The most fundamental restriction laid down by the protocols results from the fact that the BLS must balance both the physical and financial flows of international trade. Therefore, national models must cover the whole economy, not just the agricultural sector. To meet this requirement at a minimum level, an SNM can represent the whole economy with only two sectors: agriculture and non-agriculture.

The agriculture sector produces nine commodities: wheat, rice, coarse grain, bovine and ovine meats, dairy products, other animal products, protein feeds, other food, and non-food agriculture. Agricultural commodities are designated in the model either for final human consumption as food and non-food or for animal consumption.

The non-agricultural sector produces a single commodity that is used variously as final human consumption, as an input to agricultural production, and as an investment good.

Land, labor, and capital are factors in the production of all commodities. The time required for production is represented by a one-year lag for both agricultural and non-agricultural commodities.

Beyond the requirement of a two-sector structure at the international trade level, the protocols require certain other technical conditions, namely, that all countries trade simultaneously once per year, and that consumption and trade for all countries equal the previous year's production (i.e., there are no inventories). The national models must be written in a version of FORTRAN compatible with that used in the BLS system, which is FORTRAN designed for the VAX computers produced by the Digital Equipment Corporation.

The national models must differ in structure if they are to address specific issues of interest to the nations they represent. The BLS permits such differences provided the basic protocols are met. In fact, most of the national models have greater sectoral detail than is required for linkage to the BLS. The national models also employ diverse methodologies: econometric modeling, non-linear programming, linear programming, and a hierarchy of linear programs.

The SNM structure was specially designed to facilitate the simulation of either a market or a centrally planned economy. The key to providing this flexibility is the option to relate the distribution of commodity output either to entitlements or to income resulting from production of the commodities. Through an appropriate choice of government policies on redistribution, trade, and production, it is possible to represent either a market or centrally planned economy.

When the BLS was developed at IIASA, it was expected that many nations would develop detailed national models that followed the

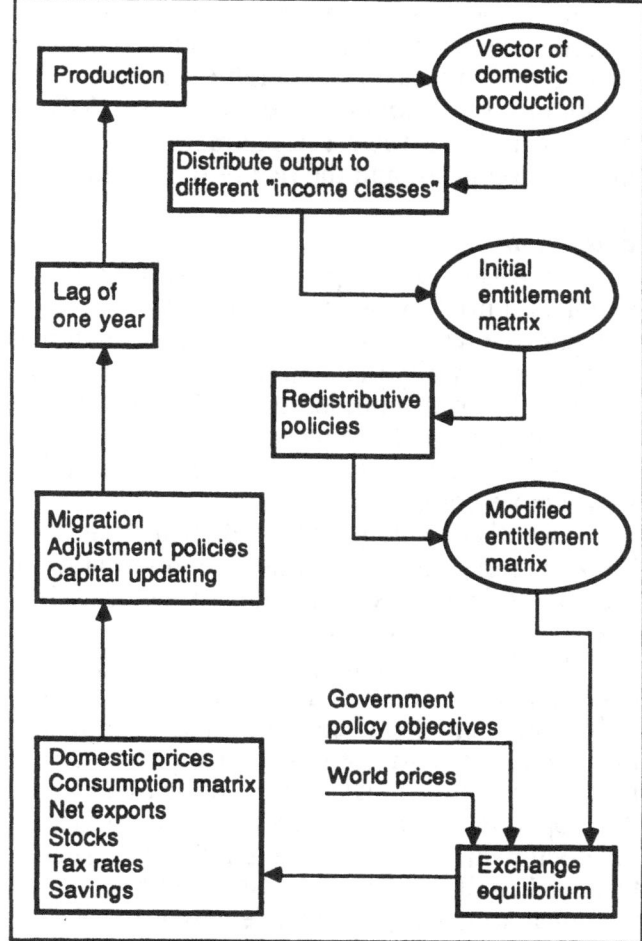

Figure 2-2: Structure of a typical national model developed with SNM.

protocols and could be linked into the system. In fact, however, only the United States, China, India, and the Council for Mutual Economic Assistance (CMEA) did so.

Because so few countries developed their own national models, it was necessary for the team at IIASA to develop national and regional modules to complete the global BLS. Two approaches were followed. Sixteen individual SNMs were prepared for Argentina, Australia, Austria, Brazil, Canada, Egypt, Indonesia, Japan, Kenya, Mexico, Nigeria, New Zealand, Pakistan, Thailand, Turkey, and the European Communities. The rest of the world was represented by fourteen residual country group models: African oil exporters, African medium income exporters, African low income exporters, African low income importers, Latin American high income exporters, Latin American high income importers, Latin American medium income countries, Southeast Asian high-medium exporters, Southeast Asian high-medium importers, Asian low income, Southwest Asian oil exporters, Southwest Asian medium-low income countries, and the rest of the world.

Evaluation

SNM is unique in providing a relatively simple, highly flexible, and relatively inexpensive way for linking agricultural national market or centrally planned models into a global system. The only competitor to SNM and BLS is Project Link at the Wharton School, University of Pennsylvania, and Project Link is vastly more complex and costly.

Two disadvantages of the BLS and the SNMs are the extremely simple representation of the non-agriculture sector and the total omission of environmental analysis.

Another disadvantage of an SNM is that installing and using it is not a trivial job. A well-trained mathematical economist and a computer programmer would need to work together for at least six months to install the generic SNM and develop a new national model from it. In fact, the documentation is insufficient for even such a team to install and apply the SNM without technical assistance from its developers.

Before investing in the elaboration of an SNM model, the leaders of a nation would be wise to assess the future of the BLS. The degree to which an individual SNM will be useful depends in large part on the extent to which nations support the BLS and adopt its protocols in their national agricultural models.

The world definitely needs something like the BLS, and efforts should be made to improve and strengthen it. One obvious drawback of the current program is that it is written in a *programming* language (FORTRAN). The whole effort might proceed further faster if BLS and SNM were rewritten in a *modeling* language for one of the more powerful microcomputers now available.

Hardware and Software Requirements

IBM AT or compatible, 640 KB RAM, hard disk and math coprocessor chip. A FORTRAN compiler compatible with the FORTRAN used on VAX computers produced by Digital Equipment Corporation.

Source

Director, Food and Agriculture Program, International Institute for Applied Systems Analysis, Schloss Laxenburg, A-2361 Laxenburg, Austria; telephone: (2236) 71-5-21; telex: 078137 IIASA A.

General Dynamic Commodity Cycle Model (GDCCM)

Purpose

To evaluate alternative policies and programs for the stabilization of the large and persistent variations in price and production rates that plague agricultural commodity producers around the world.

Description

The GDCCM is a dynamic model of the meat production sector of a national economy. The model can be calibrated to display the characteristic boom-and-bust cycles that characterize swine, chicken, and beef production in most countries. The model facilitates testing of alternative policies for stabilizing these destructive cycles. GDCCM was created by Dennis L. Meadows and its equations published in the book *The Dynamics of Commodity Production Cycles*.

Theory and Assumptions

GDCCM is based on non-equilibrium market theory. The assumptions underlying the "cobweb" of non-equilibrium market adjustment are expanded and refined into a dynamic, non-equilibrium model linking production, consumption, inventory, price, and inventory coverage policies. (See Figure 2-3.) The biological, physical, and psychological lags in the system are also incorporated into the model.

Evaluation

The validity of the GDCCM in simulating commodity cycles has been tested, and the results are reported in *The Dynamics of Commodity Production Cycles*. When data descriptive of hog production in the U.S. are used, the GDCCM exhibits the four-year cycle that plagues swine producers. When the parameters are changed to reflect these characteristics of the chicken system, the model displays the thirty-month cycle that has been observed in chicken production. Use of parameters characteristic of the cattle system results in the fifteen-year cycle characteristic of beef production.

The book describes alternative means of stabilizing commodity cycles (including buffer stock programs) and makes recommendations for stabilization programs at the national and international levels.

While GDCCM is relatively easy to install, use, and modify, some prior experience with system dynamics or agricultural economics is recommended.

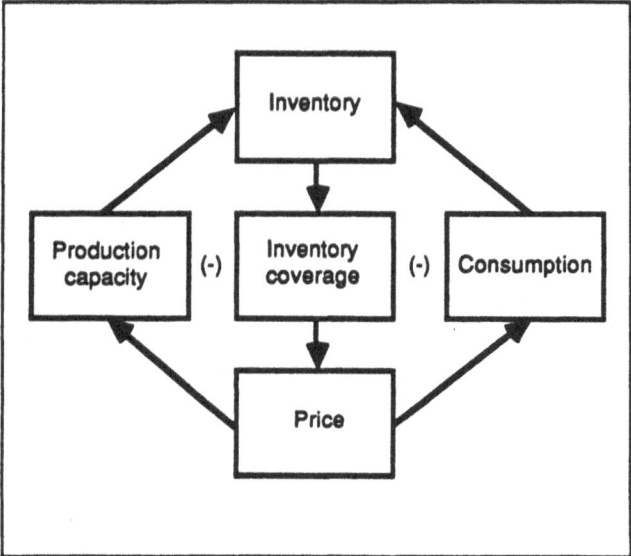

Figure 2-3: The two negative feedback loops that determine the dynamics of commodity production cycles.

Hardware and Software Requirements

IBM PC/XT/AT or compatible, 640 KB RAM, two floppy disk drives. Hark disk and math coprocessor chip recommended. Professional DYNAMO Plus or perhaps DYSMAP2. With some rewriting of the equations, the model could also be run on an Apple Macintosh with the STELLA simulation language.

Source

The model equations are provided in D. L. Meadows, *The Dynamics of Commodity Production Cycles* (Cambridge, Mass.: MIT Press, 1970). The address of the press is: MIT Press, Cambridge, MA 02139, USA.

Agro-Ecological Zone (AEZ) Methodology

Purpose

To make national or regional comparisons of future agricultural productive capacity and the food needs of the population.

Description

AEZ is a methodology for estimating the agricultural production that specific land areas can sustain under three levels of technological inputs. The methodology can also calculate the number of people a specific land area is able to support and project when the population will equal or exceed that number.

The AEZ Methodology can be used to answer the following questions:

How does the food and agricultural production potential in specific areas (within countries as well as within groups of countries) compare to the food requirements of the future populations of these areas?

How does the stable, sustainable level of production compare to these food requirements?

What alternative transition paths are available to reach desired levels of production?

What combinations of food-production techniques are sustainable and efficient?

What are the resource requirements of such techniques?

What are the policy implications—at the national, regional, and global levels—of sustainability?

The AEZ Methodology emerged from a series of projects begun in the 1960s at the U.N. Food and Agricultural Organization (FAO). These projects included: (a) a soil map of the world, (b) an international system for the classification of soil quality, and (c) a methodology for evaluating the sustainable production potential for eleven crops in specific agro-ecological zones throughout the developing world. The current version of AEZ was developed at the International Institute for Applied Systems Analysis (IIASA) with cooperation and funding from both FAO and UNFPA. In its current form it projects the number of people that a given land area will be able to support at a given level of technological inputs.

Theory and Assumptions

The AEZ Methodology (see Figure 2-4) utilizes two submodels: the crop production submodel and the demographic projection submodel. The crop production submodel, which projects an area's agricultural production potential, takes into account six factors for a given site: (a) type of the soil, (b) length of fallow time, (c) productivity losses due to erosion, (d) gains due to measures to mitigate the effects of soil degradation, (e) seed requirements, and (f) waste during planting and harvesting. The calculations are affected by the technological level assumed for the country.

Basic information used in the crop production submodel is supplied by the database on land reserves. This database is derived from two maps, a climatic map and the FAO/UNESCO map of world soils. The climatic map provides data on rainfall, maximum and minimum temperature, vapor pressure, wind speed, and duration of sunshine. The soil map provides data on soil type, moisture, phase, texture, and slope. An overlay of data from these two sources highlights areas where all conditions are suitable for agricultural production. Areas with similar soil and climatic conditions are marked as an agro-ecological cell. The production potential for seventeen of the most widely grown food crops is estimated for each cell.

One of the inputs required by the crop production model is an assumed level of agricultural technology. The user may choose from three levels, which are defined as follows: (a) low technology (traditional seeds, no fertilizer or chemicals, no soil conservation, and continuation of the presently grown mixture of crops on all potentially cultivable rain-fed land); (b) high technology (improved seeds, recommended fertilizers and chemicals, full soil conservation measures, and most productive cropping patterns on all potentially cultivable rain-fed land); and (c) intermediate technology (a mix of the low and high levels).

The demographic projection submodel produces population projections based on data for a base year, exogenously projected fertility and mortality rates, and assumptions concerning demographic policy.

The AEZ Methodology then calculates the adequacy of the projected food supply for meeting the needs of the projected population.

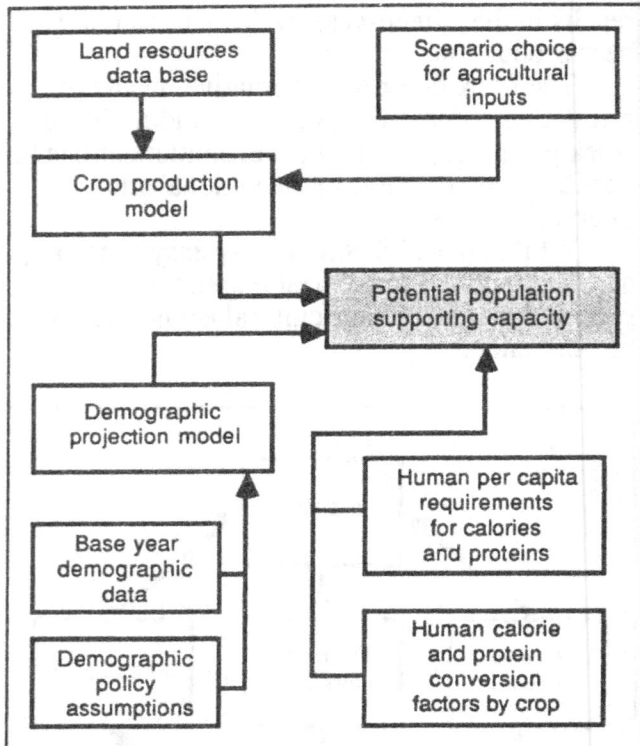

Figure 2-4: Schematic diagram of the AEZ Methodology.

The crop-production requirements of the projected population are calculated using per capita calorie requirements that are specific for the country's sex and age distribution and calorie and protein conversion factors that take into account the calorie and protein content of the seventeen crops. The food requirements are compared with the expected calorie production from both the irrigated and rain-fed agricultural areas. If the crop-production requirements of the projected population are less than the expected production, then the projected population level is regarded as being within the carrying capacity of the area.

Evaluation

AEZ is unique in its ability to integrate agronomic, climatological, economic, demographic, resource, and technological information into a single policy analysis model. This powerful tool addresses some enormously important issues of economic and agricultural development planning, and it stands in a class by itself.

This said, it must be added that AEZ needs improvement. The documentation should be improved. There should be an easy, orderly process for obtaining access to the model and database. An institutional commitment to maintaining and updating the soil map is needed.

Also, the assumptions behind the methodology raise a number of questions and should be re-examined. For example, the "rest periods" (sic) assumed to be needed between crops on some soils are substantially longer than the fallow periods that have been used successfully in some areas for centuries. Also, animals that consume crop by-products not digestible by humans are omitted from the model. These two assumptions probably lead to an underestimation of productivity.

Other assumptions probably lead to an overestimate of production. For example, the assumption that labor and surplus food can be freely moved among regions is open to question. So is the assumption that high levels of energy-intensive agricultural inputs will be available in the early twenty-first century. It is also questionable that high-input agriculture based on known technologies can be sustained without environmental deterioration.

Despite these shortcomings, the AEZ Methodology deals with critically important agricultural issues that cannot be addressed by any other policy analysis tool available today. AEZ is a major advance in agricultural analysis and deserves much further attention, support, and application.

Hardware and Software Requirements
IBM AT or compatible, 640 KB RAM, hard disk (40 MB or greater). FORTRAN compiler.

Source
Mr. G. M. Higgins, Director, Land and Water Development Division, Food and Agriculture Organization of the United Nations, Via delle Terme di Caracalla, 00100 Rome, Italy; or Mr. G. Fischer, Director, Food and Agriculture Program, International Institute for Applied Systems Analysis, Schloss Laxenburg, A-2361 Laxenburg, Austria; telephone: (2236) 71-5-21; telex: 078137 IIASAA.

ILCA Data Entry and Analysis System (IDEAS)

Purpose
To evaluate systematically and comprehensively the performance of a herd of livestock.

Description
IDEAS allows the user to: (a) maintain data on all important performance traits of a herd, such as reproduction, growth, and milk and wool production; (b) record climate, nutrition, and management information; and (c) access the data on individual animals.

The IDEAS was developed by the International Livestock Centre for Africa (ILCA).

Theory and Assumptions
IDEAS is composed of ten databases and a least squares analysis program. The databases are use to record detailed information about the herd, climate, individual animals, reproduction, weight, milk, wool, traction, health, and nutrition.

The package was developed with dBASE III. The least squares analysis function was developed with FORTRAN 77. Least squares analysis can be performed on: first parturienting, first parity reproduction, subsequent reproduction, weaning weight, survival rate to weaning, weight at any post-weaning age, survival rate to any post-weaning age, growth over any specified period, milk production, and maternal productivity.

Evaluation
IDEAS is a useful tool for anyone involved in the management of large herds of animals and can help in the formulation of logical management decisions. The program is menu driven and has been designed for ease of use. (See Figure 2-5.) For example, the main database—the herd details database—is linked to the other nine databases so data entered into the herd details database is automatically distributed to the other databases. Reports can be printed from any of the databases and in any combination needed for analysis. If IDEAS is used widely throughout a country, its standardized databases can form the basis for

comparative studies and for national policy formulation regarding livestock.

There are two volumes of documentation in both English and French. The documentation in English is well written and quite adequate. Furthermore, the International Livestock Centre for Africa will provide limited assistance for research and development applications of IDEAS in Africa.

Hardware and Software Requirements

IBM PC/XT/AT or compatibles, 512 KB or 640 KB RAM, floppy disk drive, hard disk (10 MB or larger), 80-column printer, MS-DOS or PC-DOS (version 2.0 or higher). IDEAS comes in two compiled versions depending on whether 512 KB or 640 KB of memory is available.

Source

Mr. J. Durkin, Computer Manager, International Livestock Centre for Africa, P.O. Box 5689, Addis Ababa, Ethiopia; cable: ILCA/Addis Ababa; telephone: 18-32-15; telex:

21207 ILCA ADDIS. The system is free to organizations funded by African governments. For others the price is US $800 for initial license plus an annual fee of US $200 to US $500, depending on location and type of organization.

Simulation of Production and Utilization of Rangelands (SPUR)

Purpose

To provide range planners and decision makers with a comprehensive rangeland simulation model for individual pastures and small basins.

Description

SPUR is an agricultural management tool for anticipating hydrologic, plant, and animal responses to environmental and management inputs and for assessing economic benefits of management decisions. It is not a tool for predicting the amount of production to be expected at the end of a particular summer, but rather a means of assessing the long-term (ten to twenty year) effects of alternative range management strategies.

Two versions of SPUR are available. The field-scale version can simulate the growth of up to seven plant species or functional groups. These species or functional groups can be grown on up to nine range sites within a grazing unit. The animal component of the field-scale version can be used to evaluate the effects of differentially grazing a pasture. The field-scale version provides pasture or allotment managers with a method to simulate both animal production and the growth and grazing of the major plant species.

The basin-scale version is more complex than the field-scale version. It provides a means of predicting quantities of run-off and sediment yield for basins of up to 2,500 hectares with up to twenty-seven hydrologic units (drainages adjacent to a channel).

The development of SPUR was begun in 1980 by members of the National Program Staff of the Agricultural Research Service, U.S. Department of Agriculture. The model components were drawn from a number of earlier models. The model was first written in FORTRAN IV on a VAX 11/750 computer; a microcomputer version was developed later.

ILCA's data entry and analysis system

Herd details - site code: <enter blank code to exit>

<enter XX for herd detail>

species:

Since no site code and species exist for the herd, an XX is entered for the site code and a C (meaning create) for the species. This leads to the appearance of the herd details menu where option 1 is selected.

Herd details

The options available are:

1) create a new herd
2) modify herd details
3) print herd details
4) delete a herd

0) return to initial screen

Please enter your choice:

Figure 2-5: Creating a new herd using the IDEAS program.

Theory and Assumptions

SPUR consists of five basic components: climate, hydrology, plants, animals (both domestic and wildlife), and economics.

The climate component requires the user to input daily precipitation, maximum and minimum air temperature, solar radiation, and wind run for the area under study. If only precipitation data are available, a *climate generator* will create consistent pseudodata for the four other climate variables.

The hydrology component uses the outputs of the climate component to calculate upland surface runoff volumes, peak flow, snow melt, upland sediment yield, channel stream flow and sediment, and a daily soil-water balance. The U.S. Soil Conservation Service curve number procedure is used to estimate surface runoff, and a modified universal soil loss equation is used to calculate soil losses.

The plant component uses net photosynthesis to calculate forage production. The user must provide data on the initial biomass, species photosynthesis, reparation rates, and nitrogen utilization. The plant component is based loosely on the Ecosystem Level Model (ELM) and Grassland Model by W. J. Parton et al. and J. K. Detling et al.

The animal component simulates the results of domestic livestock and wildlife grazing. The Texas A&M Beef model was used as the basis of SPUR's steer growth subroutine. This module requires the following inputs: time of grazing, diet supplements, growth and weight information, preferences for forage, and location.

The economic component uses the output from the animal component to perform a cost/benefit analysis on grazing practices, range improvements, and animal management options.

Evaluation

This is quite a useful model. Each sector is thoroughly documented in the 370-page user's manual, and a potential user should plan to spend a significant amount of time developing an understanding of this complex model. There is an enormous amount to be learned just from a careful reading of the manual, which is entitled *SPUR Simulation of Production and Utilization of Rangelands: Documentation and User Guide* (Agricultural Research Service, U.S. Department of Agriculture, 1987).

Hardware and Software Requirements

IBM PC/XT/AT or compatible, 640 KB RAM; hard disk and math coprocessor recommended.

Source

Request disks from: Mr. J. Ross Wight, Range Scientist, USDA, ARS-Pacific West Area, NW Watershed Research Center, 270 South Orchard, Boise, ID 83705, USA; Telephone: (208) 334-1363. Order the documentation cited above (ARS-63) from: National Technical Information Service, 5258 Port Royal Road, Springfield, VA 22161, USA. The software is free—while the supply lasts. The NTIS charges for the documentation.

Interactive Conservation Evaluation (ICE)

Purpose

To assist land users in the selection of least-cost soil conservation measures.

Description

ICE provides a framework for preparing cost/benefit analysis of alternative conservation measures. The goal is to simplify the process of evaluating and selecting among possible soil conservation measures for individual farms.

The Soil Conservation Service of the U.S. Department of Agriculture developed ICE in response to Title XII of the Food Security Act of 1985 and to meet the needs of other conservation programs. ICE is now being used by USDA field representatives both as an educational aid and as a software tool to help determine least-cost conservation solutions.

Theory and Assumptions

ICE is a framework for cost/benefit analysis. Several steps are involved in analyzing alternative conservation measures, and an orderly process (see Figure 2-6) is provided by ICE. To use the program, one must describe the area under study by providing the program with information on the dominant soil type and the major resource problems. Type of land use, acres cultivated, yield, net return, and the soil loss rate with no conservation must also be determined and specified.

The input data are of two types: fixed data (such as land use, mapping unit, etc.), and

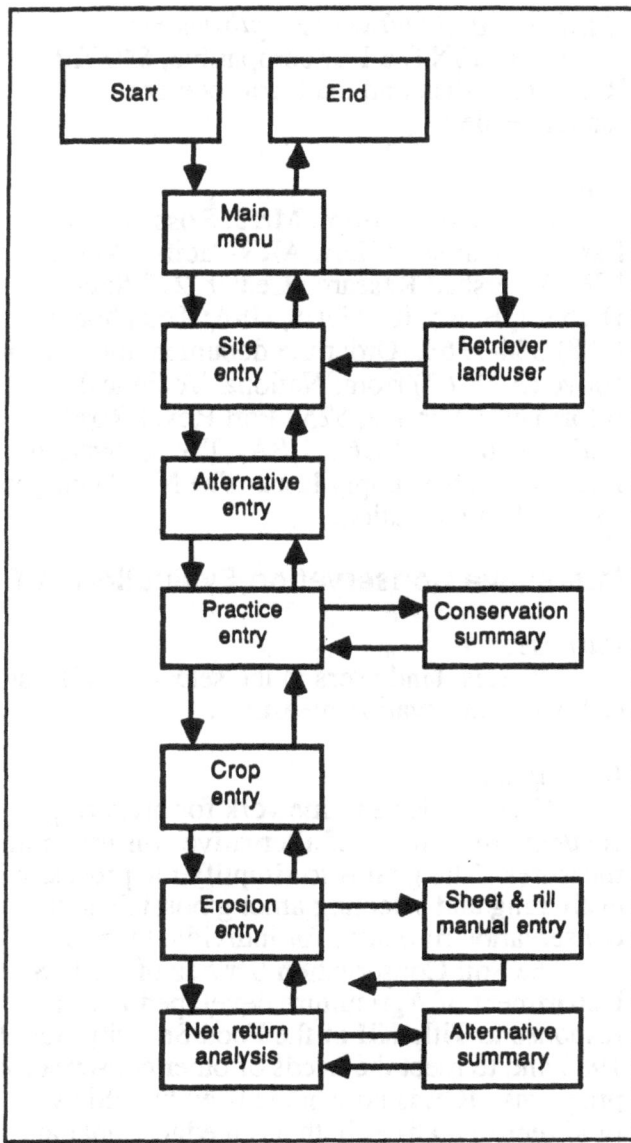

Figure 2-6: The processing flow used in ICE.

variable data (such as crops, practices and soil data).

The user must supply the model with daily weather data, standard soil characterization data (such as soil albedo, water content, and runoff information), and a variety of genetic inputs. The model is then able to produce the following output: yield information, biomass and leaf weight, number of ears produced, number of kernels per ear, water in the soil by layers, nitrogen in the soil by layers, mineralization information, and nitrogen uptake by the plant.

After the user chooses some "candidate" conservation measures, ICE ranks the alternative measures by cost. Three types of reports are produced: a conservation summary (flat rate schedule), a net return analysis, and a comparison of the alternatives with each other and with a no-conservation situation. The user can then choose the alternative that provides the best conservation at affordable costs.

Evaluation
This is a useful piece of software. It is menu driven and quite easy to use. Numerous help screens provide assistance as needed. The documentation is well written and contains an example application developed in detail.

Hardware and Software Requirements
IBM PC/XT/AT or compatible, DOS 2.0 or higher; or a FOCUS work station using the UNIX operating system.

Source
Mr. John H. Stierna, Agricultural Economist, Economic Division, Soil Conservation Service, U.S. Department of Agriculture, P.O. Box 2890, Washington, DC 20013, USA; telephone: (202) 447-6924. There is a nominal charge, subject to change.

FARMSIM

Purpose
To appraise farm development projects (water, land, roads, marketing, and so forth) by projecting cropping patterns, performing financial and income analyses, and providing economic analyses.

Description
The FARMSIM model is a microcomputer implementation of a methodology developed for the analysis of farm development projects. The model can be used for the economic analysis of any project in which the growing of field crops is facilitated in some way. Specifically, irrigation, flood control, land reclamation, agricultural credit, and other types of projects can all be designed and appraised with the aid of this model.

The accuracy of the economic analysis of such projects is highly dependent on a prediction of which crops farmers will choose to cultivate under the improved growing conditions. Prior to the development of FARMSIM, future cropping patterns were predicted rather arbitrarily. FARMSIM allows the analyst to consider systematically a wide range of economic factors that a farmer might consider in choosing crops.

Theory and Assumptions

FARMSIM uses an optimization method (linear programming) to simulate farmer's decisions. The farmer is assumed to make decisions that maximize income, subject to such constraints as possible crops, land area, water availability, labor, inputs, capital, and credit. The effects of departures from pure profit maximization, e.g., crops raised for home consumption, can be represented through maximum and/or minimum limits placed on the land areas devoted to individual crops. The model also assumes that returns (income/hectare for each crop) are constant and that farmers must take whatever price they are offered for their crops.

Credit is given special attention because limited credit may restrict cropping patterns. Two methods are used to account for the impact of limited availability of credit: (a) limiting the areas devoted to individual crops and (b) limiting the aggregate working capital to the total amount of credit available.

Exogenous input variables include, among others: possible crops, life span of non-annual crops, project capital, operating costs, value of production without project, constraints of land, duration of growing seasons, water availability, and the price, yield, and production costs of each crop.

Endogenous variables include shadow prices (extra income the farmer would gain if the constraint were loosened by one unit), the cropping pattern, physical production, gross and net revenue per hectare, production costs, availability and use of water, credit and other constrained inputs.

Evaluation

FARMSIM provides a convenient framework for preparing appraisals of farm development projects under the assumption that farmers should and do make cropping choices exclusively in an effort to maximize short-term profits. This assumption, however, needs to be questioned both for its validity and for its appropriateness in evaluating proposed projects.

The World Bank has come under severe criticism in recent years for a long history of funding projects that maximize short-term gains and severely damage or destroy the productive capacity of the land and environment in the long-term. The World Bank is now developing project analysis methods that explicitly take into account questions of sustainability. The regional banks, including the Inter-American Development Bank, have been slow to learn from the experience of the World Bank. The model has been used on approximately twenty major projects and has almost certainly contributed to the destructiveness of Latin American development projects funded by the IDB.

The fundamental problem with FARMSIM is that it represents an inappropriate approach toward project evaluation. What is needed is multicriterial analysis, not the linear programming on which FARSIM is based. Careful analysis of the resource and environmental implications of a given project are beyond this methodology.

Even linear programming could be applied more thoughtfully than is the case in FARMSIM. The model could at least be used to calculate some of the direct environmental consequences of the development project, such as the amounts of fertilizer that will enter local ground and surface water, and the amount of soil that will be lost. The possible use of FARMSIM for such purposes is not even mentioned in the document that presents guidelines for using the model.

Documentation is available in both English and Spanish. The English version we have reviewed is well done. The guidelines and technical volumes are each about two hundred pages in length. Together they provide both examples and technical detail. Additional assistance can be obtained from the IDB.

FARMSIM is one of the few analytical tools available for the evaluation of major development projects, and it is seriously inadequate for the task. A quick, low-cost improvement could be made by rewriting the 1981 guidelines document to discuss both the overall problem of assessing development projects and the specific but limited ways that FARMSIM can contribute to such assessment. A more important task, however, is the creation of a suitable multicriteria assessment tool that uses a more appropriate methodology and

incorporates long-term resource and
environmental considerations.

Hardware and Software Requirements
IBM PC/XT/AT or PS/2 or a compatible;
640 KB RAM hard disk or two floppy disk
drives; a math coprocessor chip. Hyper LINDO
linear programming package.

Source
Mr. Glenn Westley of the Inter-American
Development Bank; Washington, DC 20577,
USA; cable: INTAMBANK; telephone: (202)
623-2448. Hyper LINDO from: Lindo Systems,
Inc., P.O. Box 148231, Chicago, IL 60614, USA;
telephone: (312) 874-2524. FARMSIM is
available free of charge; Hyper LINDO is US
$1,500, subject to change.

Farm Analysis Package (FARMAP)

Purpose
To process survey data about farming
systems for use in guiding agricultural
development.

Description
FARMAP provides a convenient means of
recording and analyzing survey data concerning
farmers' present situation, including climatic
conditions, availability and quality of resources,
farming methods, production, incomes, and
family consumption, attitudes, and aspirations.
Potential uses of the package include:
assessing the effects of policy changes,
providing data for planning, preparing rural
investment projects, monitoring project
implementation, evaluating current and past
projects, developing extension
recommendations, and doing research on
farming systems.
FARMAP was developed to meet the unique
requirements of farm survey analysis. Field
workers use the software and microcomputers to
collect and enter the data in the survey districts.
Using the data-checking features of FARMAP,
the data can be verified and corrected locally.
Preliminary analysis also can be done locally and
given immediately to local officials. The
verified data are then sent to a central computer
for comprehensive processing and storage. A
professionally trained researcher can supervise
all steps of the operation.

Theory and Assumptions
FARMAP is a specialized database system
for storage, validation, and tabulation of farm
survey data. As illustrated in Figure 2-7, the
program uses four stages of processing: data
storage, data validation, data tabulation, and data
export for further processing.
During the data storage process the
following types of information can be recorded:
general survey area description, household
composition, land characteristics, cropping
pattern, livestock numbers, physical assets,
credit, stocks, resource flows, input use,
production, and household consumption.
Additional information specific to particular
surveys can also be incorporated readily. A
standard coding system allows easy exchange of
data sets and encourages secondary analysis of
stored data.
The data validation phase is particularly
important because farm survey data often
contains large numbers of errors. FARMAP data
verification options include checks on single
records, range checks on the magnitude of
inputs, and multirecord consistency checks.
FARMAP flags potential errors but makes
corrections only after being instructed to do so.
Both standard tabulation and advanced or
user-defined tabulation are available. Summary
tables for each farm, each crop or livestock

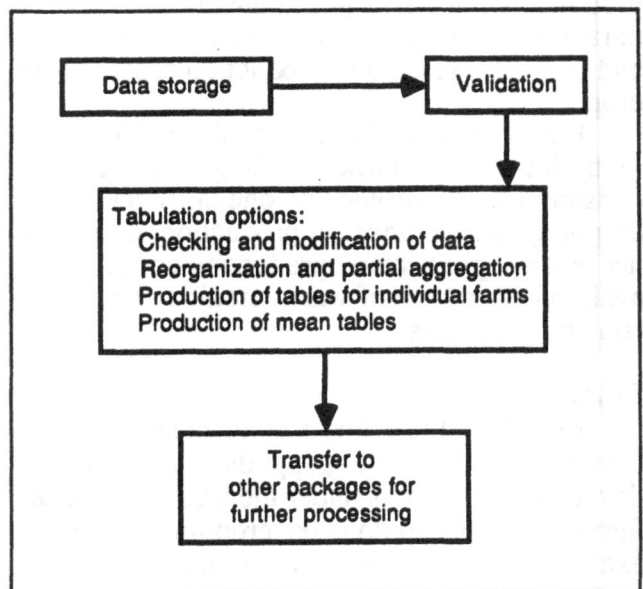

Figure 2-7: The four processing stages used in
FARMAP.

activity, and each plot of land on each farm are produced automatically unless suppressed by the user. There are also standard subtables covering household composition, land resources and land use, cropping pattern, animal resources, net worth, economics, cash-kind flow, and power use and type (human, machine, and animal).

Evaluation

FARMAP is a specialized, but very useful program. Its three most important features are local data entry and checking, standardized data categories, and ease of data transport to more powerful statistical analysis packages. The local data entry and checking should significantly increase the accuracy of survey data. The ability to perform partial analysis at the local level should provide quick feedback, thereby increasing local interest and cooperation. The standardized data categories should reduce the loss of useful data due to poorly defined codes and categories. The ease of data transport should increase the overall utility of survey research.

Because of its complexity and training requirements, FARMAP will be useful only to those projects that can afford the time and energy for applying it correctly. Analysts and programers must be trained for several weeks before they can install and maintain the program; prior experience in programming would be very helpful. Users require word processing and database management skills.

The FARMAP documentation is available only in English; it is extensive and technical. An audiovisual training program (including tapes, slides, transparencies, tutorial manuals, and diskettes) is being developed and should increase the number of potential users. Ideally, however, FARMAP should be rewritten to simplify its use and reduce the training needed.

Hardware and Software Requirements

IBM PC/XT/AT or compatible, 256 KB RAM, at least one floppy disk drive and a hard disk (at least 10 MB).

Source

Food and Agriculture Organization of the United Nations, Via delle Terme di Caracalla, 00100 Rome, Italy.

Famine Early Warning System (FEWS)

Purpose

To alert relief organizations and food donor governments to any incipient famine in Sahelian African countries.

Description

FEWS is a system of hardware and software that converts satellite data and field reports into maps (see Figure 2-8) that indicate areas in which crops are failing and famine is likely. It is being used at the U.S. Agency for International Development (USAID) to prepare monthly reports throughout the growing season for seven countries in Sahelian Africa—Mauritania, Mali, Chad, Sudan, Mozambique, and Ethiopia.

The technology developed for FEWS could be applied usefully by many countries in monitoring the conditions of their own crops during the growing season. The technology could also be used in managing forests. Famine relief organizations would also benefit by having independent FEWS facilities. Fortunately, FEWS is vastly less expensive than similar systems designed around mainframe computers.

Theory and Assumptions

FEWS uses microcomputers and related equipment to combine analysis of satellite imagery with information collected on the ground. The satellite data are recorded at a receiving station, where large computers perform various checks and generally clean up the data. Tapes of raw data or images are then made available to the FEWS team. An image processor is then used to analyze and present the images.

The image processing software is a key part of this overall system. The FEWS team developed a special image processor called IDA (image display and analysis) to meet the special needs of the FEWS system. IDA accepts any raster data set (e.g., LANDSAT and OLR data) with eight bits per point. At the FEWS project it is used daily to analyze NDVI (normalized difference vegetation index) images created by NASA (U.S. National Aeronautics and Space Administration) from data collected by NOAA (U.S. National Oceanic and Atmospheric Administration) using an AVHRR (advanced very high resolution radiometer) sensor.

IDA scales images, extracts parts of an image, and color-codes the data by assigning one of sixteen colors to each point in that image.

IDA can also overlay maps of several projections on the images. Smoothing and time series analysis can also be performed by IDA either on

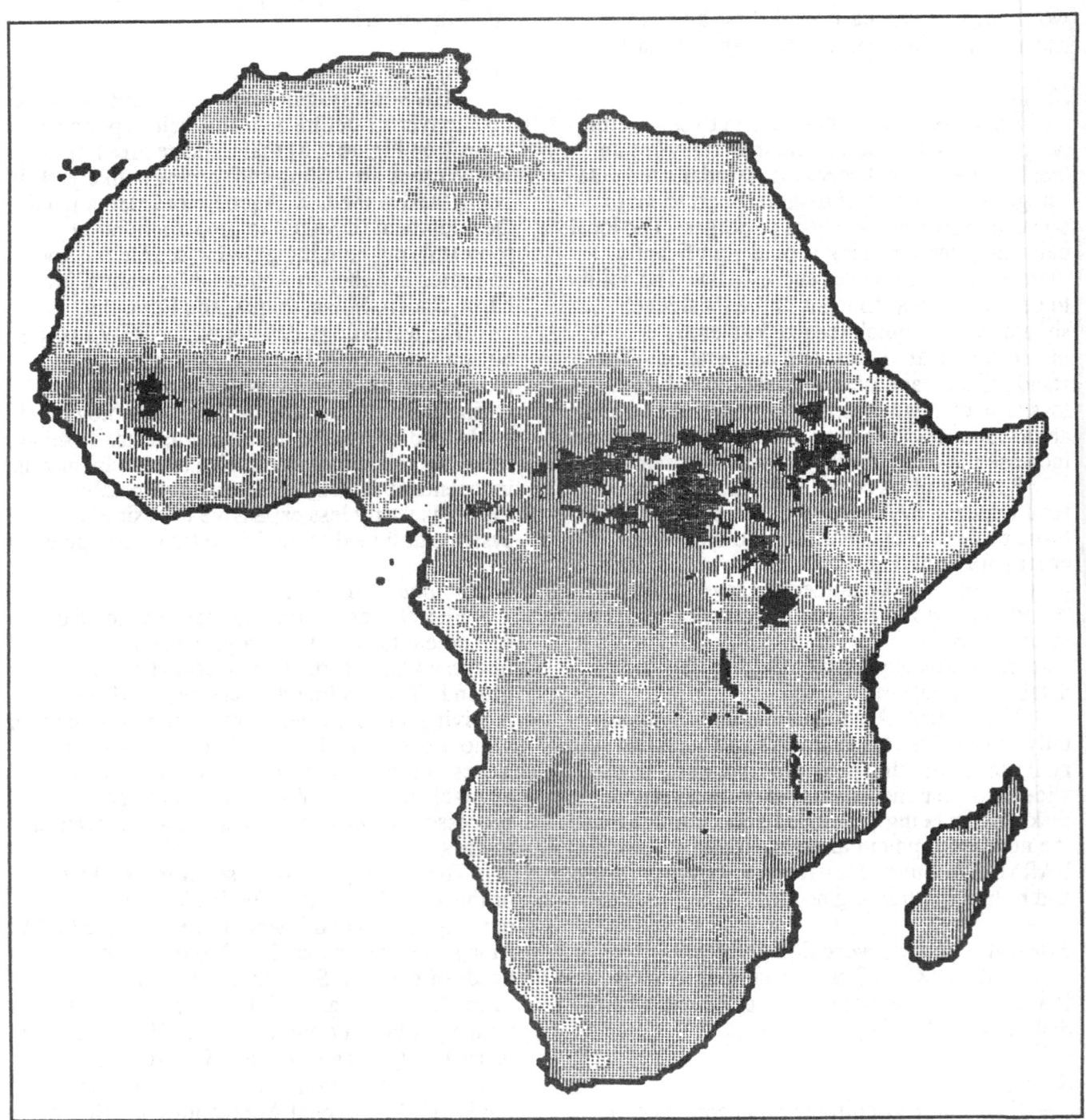

Figure 2-8: NDVI image of Africa for the period August 11-20, 1988. The image was prepared with IDA using NOAA AVHRR data processed at NASA Goddard.

each pixel or over a polygon (e.g., a country). Output from the system can be via a photograph of the image on the monitor, a color printer, a black and white printer, or a disk file.

Evaluation
FEWS is capable of delivering timely information that could be of tremendous benefit to many countries and to famine relief organizations. Any country could develop such a system for a relatively modest cost. Given the tapes available from NOAA, the computational requirements of a system can be met with inexpensive microcomputers. The IDA software can overlay political boundaries, rivers, vegetation, transportation networks, communication systems, and population distributions.

An "ideal" famine early warning system would be more precise then FEWS and would contain more detail. It would indicate where food shortages are developing, the number of people at risk, the amount of food needed, and when it needs to be delivered. To increase the precision and detail available from FEWS, USAID administrators have begun a five-year program of improvements.

Source
Information on replicating all or part of FEWS and obtaining data tapes can be obtained from: Mr. William Trayfors, U.S. Agency for International Development, AFR/TR/ PRO/FEWS, Washington, DC 20523, USA.

Information on IDA is available also from: Price, Williams and Associates, Inc., 8484 Georgia Avenue, Suite 400, Silver Spring, MD 29010, USA; telephone: (301) 565-9700; telex: 6715251 PRICEWM.

Other microcomputer-based image processors and their sources are:

ERDAS
ERDAS, Inc.
Advanced Technology Development Center
430 Tenth Street, NW, Suite N206
Atlanta, GA 30318, USA

MICROIMAGE
TERRA-MAR
2113 Landings Drive
Mountain View, CA 94043 USA

IDRISI
International Development Program
Clark University
950 Main Street
Worcester, MA 01610, USA

CHIPS
Kjeld Rasmussen
Institute of Geography
University of Copenhagen
Oster Voldgade 10, DK-1350
Copenhagen, Denmark

MICROPIPS and APPLEPIPS
The Telesys Group, Inc.
5455 Wingborne Court
Columbia, MD 21045, USA

Food Needs and Availabilities Database and Estimation System (FNA System)

Purpose
To forecast the food assistance needs of countries likely to need such assistance.

Description
The economic staff of the U.S. Department of Agriculture prepares forecasts of food needs for sixty-nine of the world's poorest nations countries. These forecasts, published annually in reports entitled *Food Needs and Availabilities* (*FNA*), are the bases for planning U.S. food exports, U.S. food assistance under Public Law 480, and relief activities of private U.S. relief organizations. The forecasts are prepared with a large spreadsheet program called the FNA System.

The FNA System is a sophisticated forecasting tool that could be useful to individual nations in assessing their food situation. The system could also be used by private food relief organizations to develop independent assessments of the food needs of countries they assist.

Theory and Assumptions
As illustrated in Figure 2-9, the forecast of food assistance needs is developed in five steps using a template on Lotus 1-2-3.

First, data on the supply and demand of basic foodstuffs is entered into the FNA System for each of the sixty-nine counties. Food processing and nutritional data are included for each commodity. Historical data on variables indicative of a country's ability to purchase food on the world market are also used.

In the second step, two-year forecasts are made for production of major commodities and for population. Total food requirements are computed by two methods, one based on status quo nutritional levels and the other based on the average per capita intake needed to achieve internationally accepted minimum daily requirements. Production is subtracted from total requirements to determine import requirements for each individual commodity. The individual commodities are then summed into one of four major commodity groups: grain equivalent, vegetable oils, pulses, and milk.

The third step involves making two-year forecasts for the balance of payments and for international debt. Commercial food imports in previous years are used in estimating the commercial import capacity. Forecasts of import prices are used to determine the quantity of food that can be obtained.

In the fourth step, the forecasted quantity of food imported commercially is subtracted from import requirements. The difference is additional food needs.

Finally, if stock information is available for the country, a stock adjustment is calculated using a procedure based on food security considerations.

All estimation and updating and most data storage are done within Lotus 1-2-3.

Evaluation

Forecasting the food needs of a country is an activity that potentially affects the lives of a large number of people, and it therefore deserves careful attention. This critical task was very difficult until the development of the powerful FNA System. Now private companies, government agencies, grain purchasing offices, relief agencies, and development groups can develop a timely picture of future developments in a country's food supply.

The spreadsheet contains a macromenu program that allows the user to: update selected

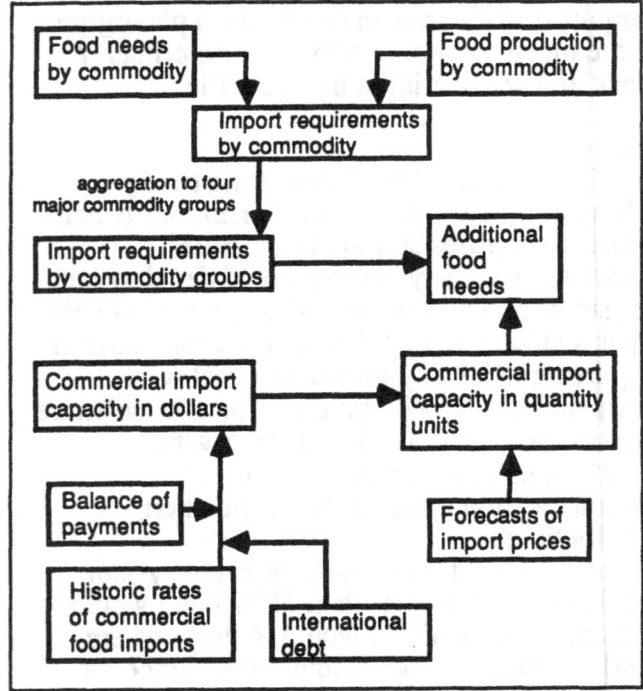

Figure 2-9: The structure of the FNA System.

portions of the spreadsheet, print all or part of the spreadsheet, graph preset portions of the data, backup key data, recover previously backed-up key data, prepare final output, and exit the menu. Many potential users who already have experience on Lotus 1-2-3 will be able to use this template with only minimal training.

The documentation, which is available only in English, is thorough and easily understood. The equations used are explained and their locations noted. Tips are given on what can and cannot be done with the equations.

Hardware and Software Requirements

IBM PC/XT/AT or compatible, two floppy disk drives, and Lotus 1-2-3. A hard disk and math coprocessor chip are recommended.

Source

Mr. Kelly White, U.S. Department of Agriculture, Economic Research Service/IED, 1301 New York Avenue NW, Room 728, Washington, DC 20005-4788, USA; telephone: (202) 786-1700.

Crop Estimation Through Resource and Environment Synthesis (CERES)-Maize

Purpose

To test quickly and easily a variety of different fertilization and irrigation schedules to maximize maize (corn) production from a given piece of land.

Description

There are two versions of the CERES-Maize model—the standard version and the nitrogen version. The standard version simulates the effects of weather, soil water, and cultivar on crop development and yield. The nitrogen version simulates the same things plus the effects of fertilization. The model can be used for short-term management decisions about crops, multi-year risk analysis for strategic planning, yield forecasting for large areas, and establishing priorities for research topics.

CERES-Maize was started by Dr. J. T. Ritchie at the Grassland, Soil, and Water Research Laboratory, in Temple, Texas. This laboratory is a part of the Agricultural Research Service of the U.S. Department of Agriculture. The model was completed and tested by Drs. C. A. Jones and J. R. Kiniry, also of the USDA-ARS.

Theory and Assumptions

CERES-Maize uses a variety of methodologies to produce its results. Among them are the Soil Conservation Service (SCS) curve number method for calculating water runoff and the Ritchie method for calculating soil evaporation.

The user must supply the model with daily weather data, standard soil characterization data (such as soil albedo, water content, and runoff information), and a variety of genetic inputs. The model will then produce the following outputs: yield, biomass and leaf weight, number of ears produced, number of kernels per ear, water in the soil by layers, nitrogen in the soil by layers, mineralization information, and nitrogen uptake by the plant.

Evaluation

CERES-Maize is a quick and easy way for a farmer or agricultural extension worker to determine when and to what extent to irrigate and/or fertilize a maize crop in order to maximize output. The model can be used by agronomists, teachers, extension service personnel, crop consultants, farmers, meteorologists, and agricultural engineers.

The program is relatively easy to learn and use and requires no specialized training. Running it is extremely easy: simply type the word CERES, provide the names of the parameter and the weather data files, and wait for the results. Since the program writes its output to data files, it is necessary to use a word or text processor to print them. The documentation is above average and includes details about all the equations and methodologies used.

One limitation of the model is that it was designed to simulate theoretically ideal growing conditions. As a result, the model does not deal with non-ideal factors such as weeds, insects, diseases, nutrient deficiencies (other than nitrogen deficiency), toxicities, and damaging weather.

The methodology used in CERES Maize has been applied to a number of other crops. CERES Wheat, for example, is well developed; information is available from Professor J. T. Ritchie, Michigan State University, Plant and Soil Science Building, East Lansing, MI 48824-1325, USA. Twelve CERES-style crop models are in preparation by Professor Gordon Tsuji, University of Hawaii, 2500 Dole Street, Krauss Hall, Room 20, Honolulu, HI 96822, USA.

Hardware and Software Requirements

IBM PC/XT/AT or compatible, 256 KB RAM, DOS 2.0 or higher. A math coprocessor chip is recommended.

Source

Dr. C. W. Richardson, Laboratory Director, USDA-ARS, Southern Plains Area, Grassland, Soil and Water Research Laboratory, P.O. Box 6112, Temple, TX 76503, USA; telephone: (817) 770-6500 or (817) 770-6600. The price is US $32.50

RICEMOD

Purpose

To simulate the growth of a rice crop as a means of integrating knowledge gained from research and establishing research priorities.

Description

RICEMOD is a crop simulation model developed to guide rice culture research at the International Rice Research Institute (IRRI). It was begun in 1979 as a tool for directing and providing feedback for research on rice culture. The model has evolved into a synthesis across disciplines of all that is known about the complex biochemical and biophysical systems interacting in a rice crop, from germination of the seeds to production of grain. The simulation requires as exogenous inputs daily information about solar radiation, maximum and minimum temperature, and day length. Model results are compared with field experiments. Discrepancies suggest areas for further investigation, thereby increasing the productivity of the research.

RICEMOD can be used to help guide rice research at other institutions or as a prototype model to guide research on other crops.

Theory and Assumptions

In RICEMOD, as in a rice plant, a photosynthetic product results from irradiation of leaves. The net amount of carbohydrate generated is determined by light intensity, leaf area, canopy shape, leaf thickness, and nitrogen content of the leaf blades. Part of the carbohydrate is used for respiration, the remainder being available for growth of the roots, culm and leaf sheath, leaf blades, and, after the vegetative stage, the panicle.

RICEMOD uses one approach to modeling plant development during the vegetative growth phase, and another approach after panicle initiation. During the vegetative phase, it is assumed that the relative percentages represented by the culm and leaf sheath, leaf blades, and roots are a function of the total population weight per unit area. After panicle initiation, a distribution factor (which changes as the plant grows) is used to regulate the simulated plant growth.

One of the major environmental factors affecting rice growth is adequacy of water in the root zone. As illustrated in Figure 2-10, RICEMOD simulates soil and crop water status as conditioned by soil water recharge and evaporation to the atmosphere. The model simulates root growth by taking into account density by soil layer, soil hydraulic and diffusivity parameters, soil evaporation, soil resistance to water movement, transpiration and leaf water potentials, root water extraction, and the soil water balance by layer in the profile. The effects of water stress on phenological development, leaf senescence, and carbohydrate partitioning are also included.

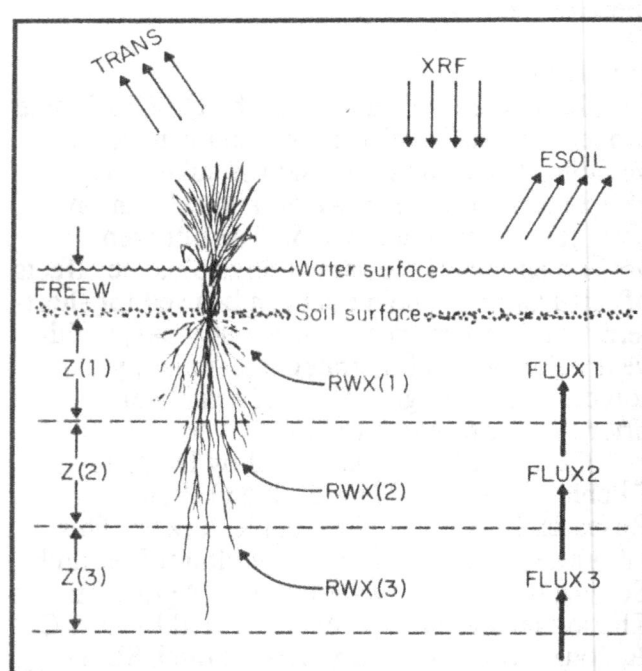

Figure 2-10: The many factors taken into account in RICEMOD's simulation of soil and crop water status.

Evaluation

As noted by the RICEMOD's authors, the ultimate simulation model for growth of rice crops should predict the growth of different varieties under any agroclimatic condition. RICEMOD is far from meeting this ideal. Several major simplifying assumptions have been made: (a) the crop is irrigated, and water stress does not limit its growth; (b) the crop is a homogeneous plant population of IR36, an improved, photoperiod-insensitive variety developed at IRRI; and (c) luxury levels of plant nutrients are present. Caution is required in applying the model beyond the conditions assumed.

In its present form, RICEMOD can be used to study the relative effects of radiation, leaf blade nitrogen content, respiration rate, and assimilate partitioning on rice plant growth. Reasonably accurate results are obtained using input of daily weather data.

The documentation is limited. Users will need to have a working knowledge of computers and an extensive knowledge of rice culture. Toward the end of the documentation, there is a bibliography of rice modeling literature. This literature could be useful in adapting the model to other varieties of rice or to other crops.

Hardware and Software Requirements
IBM PC/XT/AT or compatible, 160 KB RAM, floppy disk drive, and an 80-column printer. Or, TRS-80 Model 16/12, 64 KB RAM, CP/M-DOS, 8" disk drive, and an 80-column printer. FORTRAN IV or BASIC.

Source
Publications Office, International Rice Research Institute, P.O. Box 933, Manila, Philippines; telephone: 88-48-69 or 88-45-14; telex: 45365 RICE INST PM; cable: Ricefound Manila.

MSTAT

Purpose
To design, manage, and analyze agronomic experiments.

Description
MSTAT is an integrated microcomputer software program for support of agricultural research. The program can be used to design experiments for field or laboratory research and to manage the experiments. After the resultant data have been collected, MSTAT can be used to prepare descriptive and multivariant statistical analyses. Among the various parts of MSTAT are a plant breeding management program and modules for economic and seasonal analysis and for linear programming.

The program was developed with assistance of the Agricultural Economics Department of Michigan State University.

Theory and Assumptions
The MSTAT package includes thirty-eight different programs that can carry out a wide range of functions, such as maintaining and updating breeding records, assessing the stability of treatments over environmental ranges, and performing analyses for economic research. The programs can be divided into three categories: those that handle the recording of data, those that

perform various statistical analyses, and those that control output.

Among the programs designed for the handling of data are ones that: facilitate data entry from survey forms and other sources, sort data with up to fifteen levels of keys, compute histograms of data variables, group data values into categories, convert data using BASIC equations, and import and export ASCII files from databases and other sources.

MSTAT's statistical programs make possible a wide range of both simple and sophisticated analyses. The programs can be used to compute: summary statistics, means and totals, log (ED50), slope, intercept, separation of mean, Hotelling's T squared statistic, chi-square, coefficients for orthogonal polynomial equations, simple correlations and regressions, multiple regressions, and nonparametric statistics. There are also programs that perform: marginal returns analysis, hierarchical analysis of variance, one-way or two-way analysis of variance, lattice analysis of variance, multiple discriminant analysis, principal component analysis, non-orthogonal analysis of variance, factorial or split-plot analysis of variance, and with-and-between group regression analysis and ANOVA.

With the output control programs included with the MSTAT package, the user is able to: create scatter plots of any two variables; present probability values on the screen; print text, labels, and maps; print one or more curves on the same figure; and generate lattice/RD designs.

Evaluation
MSTAT is a powerful tool for increasing the productivity of agricultural research. It is menu driven, highly flexible, and interactive. MSTAT has been available for several years and is now being used by agricultural researchers, plant breeders, seed companies, and international research centers around the world. It is also being used in courses at many universities.

Productive agricultural research requires effective organization of the collection, management, and analyses of data.

MSTAT provides step-by-step programs for virtually every aspect of agricultural research.

The agricultural and economic research faculty at Michigan State University feels that this powerful program should be widely available, and as a result, the price of the software was set rather low initially and has not been increased. Given the power of this software and its modest price, this software should be utilized by every major agricultural research faculty worldwide.

Hardware and Software Requirements
Interpreted MSTAT: 64 KB RAM (or more), CP/M or MS-DOS operating system, Microsoft BASIC or GWBASIC or MBASIC, 80-character screen width. Compiled MSTAT: IBM PC/XT/AT or compatible, 256 KB RAM (or more). A printer is optional for most programs.

Source
MSTAT/Crop and Soil Sciences, Michigan State University, East Lansing, MI 48824, USA; telephone: (517) 353-1752; telex: 650-2247573 MCI. The price for the software, one manual, and basic license fee is US $300 for commercial organizations and US $100 for individuals, universities, and non-profit organizations. There are charges of US $25 for additional manuals, US $50 for a license fee for each additional machine, and US $25 for foreign air mail postage for each package (software and one manual).

3. Demography, Health, and Education

Introduction

Demographers were among the earliest users of computers. Their work, especially the numerical integration associated with population projections, required extensive amounts of computation and statistical analysis. The software reviewed here begins with some traditional demographic applications and progresses through some newer applications relating to health and education.

The professional demographer now has a full set of powerful analytical programs to use on a microcomputer. FIVFIV and SINSIN are highly respected, very flexible demographic projection models. A wide range of other tools for professional demography are available in the set of thirty-two programs called Microcomputer Programs for Demographic Analysis (MCPDA). These programs represent some of the finest software available for demographic analysis and are well suited both to the professional demographic needs of a nation's government and to the instructional needs of advanced university courses in demography.

For intermediate users who do not need the flexibility and complexity of professional-level programs, DEMPROJ may be a good choice. This software is relatively easy to use but still produces quality projections.

Migration and differences among subpopulations always present complications in demographic projections. Future Population allows the user to model three population groups (including migrating groups) simultaneously and then to integrate the models into an overall national or multinational picture.

One of the best available tools for investigating migration is the Integrated Multiregional Demographic Analysis Program (IMDAP), which projects population and migration flows in detail. Obtaining data on migration is difficult, and this package includes several programs for estimating the numbers needed to fill out a complete migration data set.

The Targets program provides a tool with which policy makers can analyze the size of a family-planning program needed to achieve specific, targeted demographic goals. DYNPLAN performs related functions and also analyzes the demographic consequences of various health programs.

Personal Choice was designed to assist in providing personalized counseling on contraceptive choice without requiring extensive amounts of time from scarce, expensive, health-care professionals. The program provides basic education on human reproduction and gathers information from the user that helps the health-care professional recommend a specific contraceptive method.

The Expert Diagnosis and Treatment Module (EDTM) goes a step beyond the support given by Personal Choice. EDTM uses artificial intelligence to provide a second opinion to mid-level health practitioners working in remote areas of developing countries where other professional assistance is simply not available. Given a patient's history and presenting symptoms, EDTM assists in identifying diseases and in deciding what treatments are appropriate and effective.

The AIDS Epidemic Model systematically organizes the available information on the spread of this disease and projects the numbers of people with various sexual preferences and drug-use habits who will contract the disease.

Regulator provides a user-friendly structure within which to apply risk-assessment methodology to the regulation of new, potentially dangerous, medical technologies. It can be used to evaluate a broad spectrum of regulating policies for a wide range of new technologies.

The Primary Education Tracking System (PETS) provides an orderly, disciplined, and inexpensive means to plan a nation's primary education system.

FIVFIV and SINSIN

Purpose
To provide policy-making officials with detailed demographic projections.

Description

FIVFIV makes population projections (forward or backward in time) for five-year cohorts at five-year intervals, showing distribution of the population by age and sex. SINSIN makes population projections for one-year cohorts at one-year intervals. SINSIN can also be used to calculate annual social and economic derivatives of the population projection. Both FIVFIV and SINSIN can be used to project either total population or subgroups such as civilian manpower.

FIVFIV and SINSIN were originally developed for use on a mainframe computer. Version 9.0 is fully adapted for use on a microcomputer and has a menu-driven entry program.

Theory and Assumptions

FIVFIV and SINSIN are most frequently used together with an economic model, as illustrated in Figure 3-1. FIVFIV and SINSIN use the cohort-component method. Fertility, mortality, and migration are separately taken into account. Six model life tables are available; four tables (North, South, East, and West) are based on the Coale-Demeny structure, and two tables (Far-East and South-Asia) are based on work by the Department of International Social and Economic Affairs of the United Nations. Required inputs include beginning population, mortality rate, fertility rates, sex ratio, migration rates or quantities, initial year, and adjustments for misreporting. Outputs include future population, mortality rates, fertility rates, and migration rates, all by age and sex.

Evaluation

FIVFIV and SINSIN are professional demographers' tools. They are highly respected and have been used in more than a hundred developing countries and population research centers. They provide a range of options and level of detail not available in most demographic programs.

The power of FIVFIV and SINSIN comes at a cost, however. These programs can be operated and their output interpreted by demographic experts only, and they require a substantial investment in time, energy, and equipment.

Population programs abound. If you do not need the power and detail of FIVFIV and

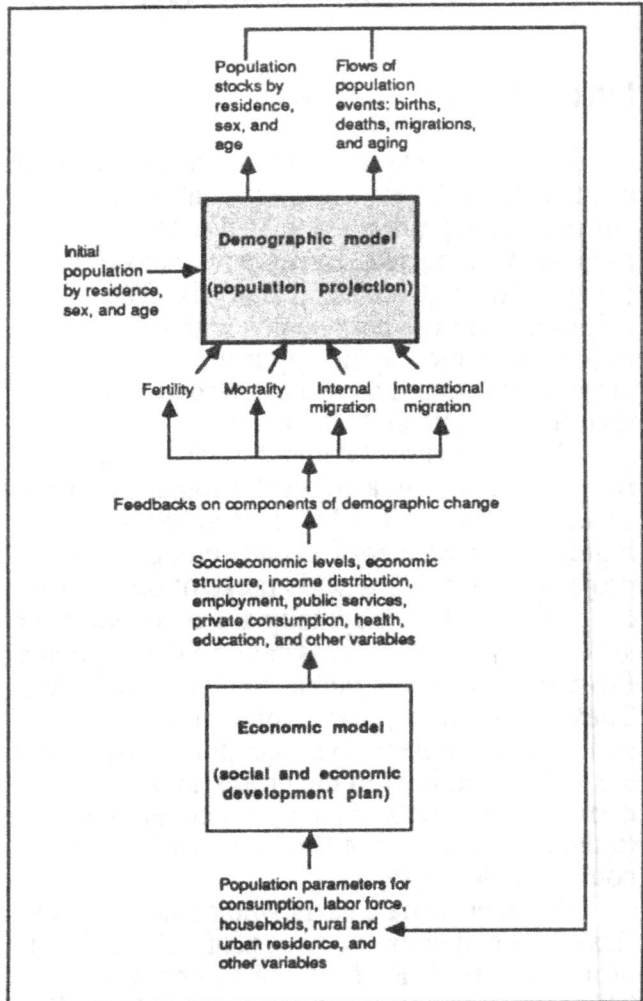

Figure 3-1: The use of FIVFIV or SINSIN with an economic model.

SINSIN, don't use them. They are much too difficult and detailed for applications other than the most detail-oriented policy decisions or the most precise demographic research.

The documentation, *Computational Methods for Population Projections: With Particular Reference to Development Planning*, is extremely dry, and requires knowledge of both demographics and computer programming. It contains instructions on how to deal with various special conditions such as unstable populations and misreporting. The first two-thirds of the manual was written for the original mainframe version of the program; the last third of the manual is a supplement written in 1987 to provide instructions for use of the microcomputer version.

Hardware and Software Requirements
    IBM PC/XT/AT or compatible, 256 KB RAM, at least one 360 KB floppy disk drive, a printer printing 120 characters per line; DOS 2.0 or later. Two floppy disk drives (or a hard disk and one floppy drive) and a math coprocessing chip are recommended.

Source
    Mr. Robert Sendek, Population Council, One Dag Hammarskjold Plaza, New York, NY 10017, USA; telephone: (212) 644-1300, telex: 234722 POCO UR; telefax: (212) 755-6052. The price is US $25.

Microcomputer Programs for Demographic Analysis (MCPDA)

Purpose
    To perform a wide range of tests and analyses on demographic data.

Description
    Microcomputer Programs for Demographic Analysis (MCPDA) is a set of tools for use by professional demographers. The package consists of a library of thirty-two related demographic programs. Each of the programs is designed to accomplish different tasks, ranging from calculating survival rates or intrinsic growth rates, to making linear or exponential interpolations. Because the programs can operate independently, the individual applications can be grouped on disks in combinations that will suit the user's needs.
    MCPDA is an adaptation for microcomputers of an earlier set of mainframe programs, Computer Programs for Demographic Analysis (CPDA), which was developed by the United States Bureau of the Census with support from the U.S. Agency for International Development. The Institute for Resource Development at Westinghouse converted CPDA to MCPDA and produced documentation for the microcomputer programs.

Theory and Assumptions
    In Appendix A of the MCPDA manual, the programs are divided into the following six categories according to their uses.

    (a) Curve Fitting, Smoothing, and Graduation. ABREV adjusts the number of age groups in a distribution to be the same as the number of age groups in the second distribution. BEERS separates grouped data into five parts. INTRP makes a linear or exponential interpolation between two values. MORNS ranks a given set of values and determines the median. SMOTH smooths a population distribution of five-year age groups. UNSMH smooths a population distribution in five-year age groups, except for the first two and last two five-year age groups, using a formula derived by the United Nations.
    (b) Evaluation. AGESX calculates age and sex rations for a population distribution by sex and five-year age groups. FWDRV adjusts age-sex distributions obtained from two population censuses taken ten years apart. IRDID compares the age distributions of two populations by calculating the Index of Relative Difference and the Index of Dissimilarity. PYRMD makes one or two age pyramids by sex from one or two age and sex population distributions, respectively. REVR5 updates, five years backward in time, each sex of a population distribution by five-year age groups. RVFWD obtains an estimate of the undernumeration of age group 0-4 in a population census, on the assumption that fertility has remained constant during the past ten to fifteen years.
    (c) Fertility. ADJFR calculates new age-specific fertility rates from a given set of age-specific fertility rates and a pattern of change. PFRAT estimates five-year age-specific fertility rates from survey or census information on the average number of children ever born per woman and a set or pattern of age-specific fertility rates. NRSFR calculates age-specific fertility rates, given a pattern of fertility rates, a life table, the net reproduction rate, and the proportion of female births to total births.
    (d) Mortality. BLT calculates a Coale-Demeny regional model life table for both sexes combined, given a life expectancy at birth for both sexes combined, a region (north, south, east, west) of the model life tables, and the sex ratio at birth. INCHM estimates the level of infant and child mortality, based on tabulations of the average number of children ever born and the average number of children surviving by age of mother. ELT calculates an abridged life table from age-specific mortality rates or the

probabilities of dying between exact ages x and x+5. LIFIT compares two sets of survival rates in five-year age groups from two different life tables, by calculating the differences between the two sets, by age. MLT calculates a regional model life table corresponding to a given life expectancy at birth, sex, and region using Coale-Demeny regression coefficients. MORDJ estimates a set of survival rates by five-year age groups for a particular level of life expectancy at birth, using a given set of survival rates from a life table and the life expectancy at birth from the life table. PKREG determines which regional pattern of survival rates in the Coale-Demeny regional model life tables has the smallest difference from a given pattern of survival rates for a particular sex. QXADJ estimates a set of values for the probability of dying between exact age x and x+5 for a particular level of life expectancy at birth, using a given set of such values from a life table and the life expectancy at birth from the life table. SRX10 calculates survival rates for open-ended age groups for a period of ten years (x and over surviving to x+10 and over) from two population distributions enumerated or estimated ten years apart. SURVI calculates survival rates by five-year age groups from two populations enumerated or estimated five, ten, or fifteen years apart. TWOCN estimates the life expectancy at birth, crude birth rate, and crude death rate from two populations by five-year age groups.

(e) Projections. PROJ5 projects a population distribution by sex and five-year age groups for a period of five years, using survival rates by five-year age groups for each sex, five-year age-specific fertility rates, and the number of migrants by sex and five-year age groups.

(f) Stable Population. ADJBG estimates the crude birth and death rates and the gross reproduction rate under quasi-stable population conditions. INTRT determines the intrinsic growth rate, given the female life table function in the childbearing ages and age-specific fertility rates based only on female births. INTSP estimates a stable population distribution and the life table pertaining to such a population, given the intrinsic growth rate and another stable population parameter. ONECN calculates stable or quasi-stable estimates of the crude birth and death rates from the age distribution and the rate of natural increase of a population. SPP

generates a stable population distribution and its parameters from one column of a life table and an intrinsic growth rate.

The manual gives detailed information about each of the above programs, including an explanation of the application's purpose, input data, methodology (complete with the relevant equations), and any special comments. Technical documentation, covering all aspects of set-up and operation for the programs is also provided. There is an extensive section on creating data files, which details the use of six editors (Edlin, IBM's Personal Editor, Volkswriter, Volkswriter Deluxe, Wordstar, and Lotus 1-2-3).

Evaluation

This is an important set of professional-level demographic programs for analysis of census data. The programs are well integrated, allowing the user to access any individual program with relative ease. The programs would be valuable both for every ministry concerned with the analysis of demographic data and for university departments teaching demography.

The format of all the MCPDA programs is uniform and easy to understand. Data presentation is also good, although making data files can be more or less tricky depending upon which editor is used.

Hardware and Software Requirements

IBM PC/XT/AT or compatible, 192 KB RAM, and two disk drives. A 132-column parallel or Epson compatible printer is recommended, but an 80-column printer (with compressed type) can be used. MS-DOS or PC-DOS (version 2.0 or higher), and a word processing package or editor that can create standard ASCII files.

Source

Institute for Resource Development, Westinghouse, P.O. Box 866, Columbia, MD 21044, USA.

DEMPROJ

Purpose

To allow for the easy entry and manipulation of demographic data and to provide population projections by age, sex, and region.

Description

DEMPROJ (ver. 2.51) develops projections for five-year cohorts by age, sex, and region. The projections are useful for development planning and may be made in five-year intervals for up to fifty years.

Theory and Assumptions

DEMPROJ is based on the cohort-component methodology. Exogenous variables include initial populations, total fertility rates, age specific fertility rates, model life tables, and migration rates.

Data is entered in a spreadsheet format with each entry in a separate cell. Two mathematical functions—multiply and interpolate—speed the data-entry process.

Projections may be viewed in three separate formats: line graphs, bar graphs, and tables of values. Printouts of any of the formats are available through an Epson-compatible printer. Projections and entered data may be saved for examination or reuse at a later date.

Input files made with DEMPROJ may be used as input for RAPID, Targets, or the EDSIM models. These models, respectively, display the effects of population factors on social and economic development, calculate the contraception use needed to attain desired fertility rates, and simulate the future needs for education facilities.

Evaluation

DEMPROJ is a menu-driven, interactive program for intermediate users, i.e., those who are not computer experts but need a demographic model that is methodologically solid. No prior computer experience is needed to run DEMPROJ. Context-sensitive help is always available. In addition to the analysis that can be done directly with DEMPROJ, other analyses are possible through its links with RAPID, TARGETS, and EDSIM.

Hardware and Software Requirements

IBM PC/XT/AT or compatible, 256 KB RAM, one floppy disk drive; DOS 2.0 or later.

Source

The Futures Group, 1101 Fourteenth Street NW, Washington, DC 20005, USA; telephone: (202) 347-8165.

Future Population

Purpose

To project population size and composition, births by mother's age, deaths by age, and number of migrants by age.

Description

Future Population is a demographic projection model for analysis and policy design. In addition to having the standard capabilities of most demographic projection models, Future Population can account for up to three population subgroups that have different demographic characteristics. If, for instance, a country contains distinct ethnic groups with different fertility patterns or death rates, the projections for these groups may be prepared separately and then combined to obtain the full national description. Or if part of a population is migrating to or from neighboring countries, the effects of migration can be projected.

Theory and Assumptions

Future Population uses the cohort-component methodology. After the data file is prepared, the computer estimates population size and age composition. The output is displayed in both tabular and chart form.

Most demographic data are published in age intervals of five years. Future Population can, through the use of a cubic spline function, disaggregate the five-year data into single-year intervals.

Evaluation

Future Population is easy to install and use. The documentation is clearly written. As the program is running, messages indicate which data are being analyzed and when the data are being "smoothed." Errors are reported through on-screen notices.

The data entry process is somewhat cumbersome. Population distribution, age-specific fertility rates, mortality rates, and estimates of migration must be prepared in a precisely prescribed format using a separate text editor or word processor. A self-contained data-entry capability with a series of prompts would be much more convenient.

Another minor problem with the program is that output is directed to a disk and must be printed subsequently with another program. To avoid a disruption of Future Population, one must be sure that there is enough free space on the disk for the output.

Hardware and Software Requirements
    IBM PC/AT/XT or compatible, two disk drives; a text editor capable of creating standard ASCII files.

Source
    NCSU Software, National Collegiate Software Clearinghouse, School of Humanities and Social Sciences, Box 8101, North Carolina State University, Raleigh, NC 27695, USA; telephone: (919) 737-3067. A decision on price is pending.

Integrated Multiregional Demographic Analysis Package (IMDAP)

Purpose
    To make national and subnational population projections by age and sex for either five-year or one-year intervals.

Description
    IMDAP is a system of demographic analysis programs centered around the Multiregional Population Projection (MPP) model. Unlike models based on the classical cohort-component methodology alone, MPP projects all subnational populations simultaneously and treats interregional migration in terms of direction streams, not just in terms of net migration. The simultaneous projection capability yields consistent results across all subnational regions, eliminating the need for ad hoc adjustments. The ability to track directional migration streams is especially useful for policy analysis, where—more often than not—the migration stream from region A to region B is of more interest than the number of net migrants in a region. MPP was designed for use under conditions of deficient and incomplete data and can be used both for developing and developed countries.
    The MPP model was first developed for a mainframe by Andrei Rogers and Frans Willekens. Later, Oleh Wolowyna, Senior Demographer at the Research Triangle Institute, transferred the original programs to microcomputers and adapted them to the specific needs of developing countries. The original

system of microcomputer programs was called Integrated Multiregional Population Projection (IMPP) Program; a new, expanded version is called Integrated Multiregional Demographic Analysis Package (IMDAP). This review is based on IMPP and on a fifteen-page paper describing IMDAP.

Theory and Assumptions
    Regional population projections require many more data than do nationally aggregated projections. This is especially true when interregional migration streams are also being projected by age and sex. Since most developing countries do not have such detailed data available, a capability to estimate such data using special demographic analysis programs is needed.
    To provide this capability, the MPP program was imbedded in a system of programs. (See Figure 3-2.) The individual programs have a common data structure for both input and output so that they can be used either separately or together.
    IMDAP comes on four disks. The first of these contains MPP, the core of the IMPP package. MPP is actually a group of three programs: UPDATE, PROJ, and TIMES.
    UPDATE reads the input data and prepares two output files for each sex, to be used by PROJ. PROJ utilizes an extension of the standard cohort-component method to project simultaneous regional populations and interregional migration flows. Using the output files of PROJ, TIMES generates a single output file containing the aggregated projections.
    Also included on the first disk is EDFILE, a data-entry editor specially designed for working with the IMPP system. It functions well and definitely makes the data-entry section of the program much easier.
    The second disk contains the Coale-Demeny and United Nations life tables and other data needed to make the whole system functional—including sample data for use when learning the system.
    The third disk contains four programs (LIFTB, MATCH, COMPAR, and BESTFT) that prepare data for the IMPP system. MATCH calculates United Nations or Coale-Demeny life tables or others based on user-supplied patterns of mortality. LIFTB uses a set of age-specific central death rates or age-specific probabilities

of dying to generate life tables. COMPAR compares empirical age-specific death rates (or age-specific probabilities of dying) to either United Nations or Coale-Demeny model life tables and produces indices of similarity. BESTFT finds one, two, or three components of the United Nations model life tables that best fit one or more probabilities of dying.

The final disk contains two programs entitled MAM and PREMAM. The purpose of MAM is to estimate data for incomplete two- and three-dimensional tables that would otherwise be unusable. It uses the multiproportional adjustment method and a log-linear model to estimate missing cells. PREAM is a data-presentation editor for MAM.

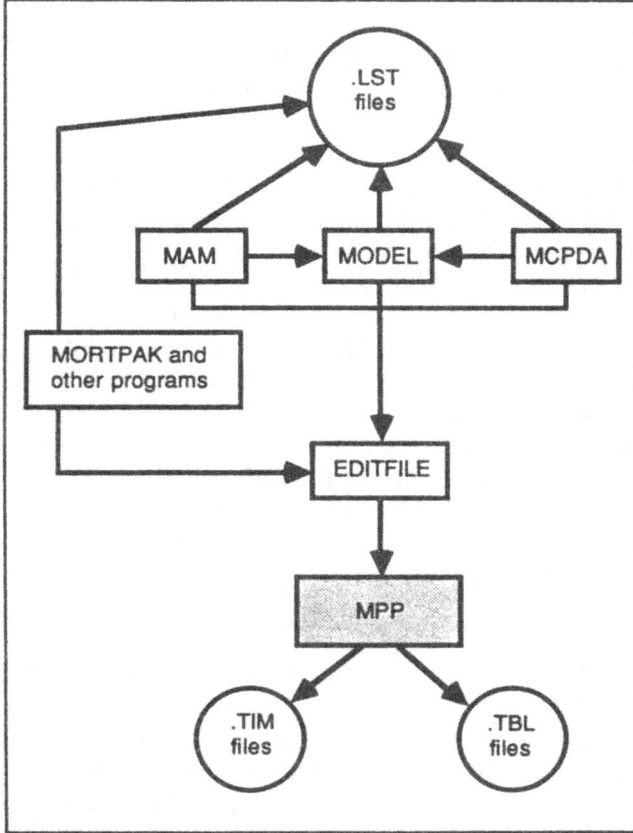

Figure 3-2: Structure into which the MPP program is integrated to form the Integrated Multiregional Demographic Analysis Package (IMDAP).

Evaluation
The current version of IMDAP has many good features, but it is still under development.

The version reviewed is difficult to use, and the manual is difficult to understand. Several parts are described as being "available soon."

The idea behind IMDAP—to integrate demographic analysis programs with support programs—is a great one. IMDAP would be especially useful if it incorporated the popular Microcomputer Programs for Demographic Analysis (MCPDA) discussed earlier in this chapter. According to the manual, however, the MCPDA programs have not been included in the latest version of IMDAP. The possibility of building in a capability for importing any subset of the database into Lotus 1-2-3 is also mentioned in the introduction to the documentation, but apparently this improvement has not yet been implemented.

Besides the problems of integration and completion, IMDAP suffers from inadequate testing of the programs themselves. The count (number of migrants) option for international migration needs to be corrected, the method for projecting single-year cohorts needs to be studied further, and the methodology for projecting the final age group needs to be improved and clarified.

Even those inadequacies could be circumvented if the user had adequate documentation, but the poor shape of the manual makes informed use of the models almost impossible. Of the forty pages dedicated to the MPP "core" of IMPP, twenty-four simply reproduce output of the three programs. Only three pages are actually devoted to descriptions of the programs and instructions on their use.

The IMDAP project is a large, complex undertaking that needs more time to mature. At present it is only useful to those demographic researchers who have plenty of time, patience, and computer experience. In its current condition, IMDAP is recommended only for professional demographers who happen to need its unique capabilities.

Hardware and Software Requirements
IBM PC/XT/AT or compatible with 512 KB, one floppy disk drive and a hard disk drive, math coprocessor; DOS 2.0.

Source
Center for Development Policy, Research Triangle Institute, P.O. Box 12194, Research Triangle Park, NC 27709, USA; telephone: (919)

541-7218; telex: 802509 RTI TPK; telefax: (919) 541-5985. The price has not yet been determined but is expected to be nominal.

Targets

Purpose

To estimate the number of people who will have to receive contraceptives and the fraction of those receiving contraceptives who will have to use the contraceptives if a family-planning program is to achieve a specific (targeted) decline in fertility by some specific future time.

Description

Many government leaders have concluded that reducing fertility rates is important to their nations' overall strategies for improving standards of living. As a result, these leaders have established family-planning programs aimed at increasing the use of contraceptives. The question then arises: If a reduction in fertility by x percent is desired in y years, how large does the family-planning effort have to be? Targets, written by John Bongaarts of the Population Council and John Stover of The Futures Group, answers this question.

Theory and Assumptions

There are seven factors that have been labeled by demographers as the proximate determinants of fertility: (a) marriage pattern, (b) contraceptive prevalence and effectiveness, (c) induced abortion, (d) postpartum infecundity, (e) frequency of intercourse, (f) spontaneous abortion, and (g) sterility. The first four proximate determinants have been shown to have, in general, the most important influence on fertility trends. Although the Targets documentation focuses on the four most influential proximate determinants, the program includes all seven, as shown in Figure 3-3.

The central equation of Targets relates the total fertility rate (TFR) at time t to the total fecundity rate (TF) through multiplicative indices of the proximate determinants. By various substitutions and rearrangements discussed in the Targets documentation, an equation is derived that determines the needed contraceptive prevalence among married women of reproductive age (MWRA) on the basis of: (a) the contraceptive prevalence among MWRA in the base year, (b) the contraceptive use-

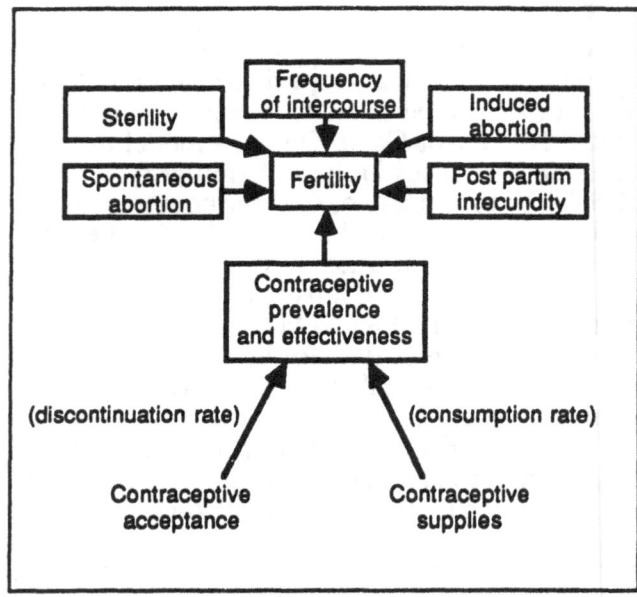

Figure 3-3: The relationships among principal variables used in the Targets program.

effectiveness in the first and later years, and (c) the proportional reduction desired in fertility from the initial to the target year. This basic equation underlying Targets takes into account all seven of the proximate determinants.

There are two versions of Targets: an age-aggregate (i.e., all ages together) version, and an age-specific version. The age-aggregate version is quite adequate for many applications but does introduce certain errors for long-term projections. The age-specific version is appropriate when highly accurate, long-term projections are needed.

Evaluation

Targets comes on two disks, one containing the age-aggregate version, and one the age-specific version. The aggregate version includes an option that allows the output of the RAPID model (see review in "Multisectoral National Models" chapter of this book) to be used as an input. A sample data set is also included with the disks, so the user can experiment with the program immediately.

The documentation included with the program is quite good. The manual provides over ninety pages of useful background information and detailed explanations of the model and its various elements. Many of the relevant equations are presented. One chapter is devoted to data entry for both the age-aggregate and age-specific models. One section details the information that will be needed during installation of the program.

It is very easy to install Targets on either floppy-disk or hard-disk systems. Data preparation and entry requires some knowledge of demographic terminology, but a thorough reading of the manual should clarify any questions. The actual process of entering data is straightforward. The program itself runs without problems and provides clear output in the form of tables or charts.

Hardware and Software Requirements

IBM PC/XT/AT or compatible, 256 KB RAM, at least one 360 KB floppy disk drive, printer, graphics adapter card.

Source

Mr. John Bongaarts, The Population Council, Center for Population Studies, One Dag Hammarskjold Plaza, New York, NY 10017, USA; telephone: (212) 644-1300; telex: 234722 POCO UR.

DYNPLAN

Purpose

To calculate the effects that specific health-care interventions and family-planning measures can be expected to have on the demography of a nation.

Description

It has long been known that both health programs and family-planning programs have significant demographic implications for a nation. Health programs reduce mortality rates and therefore, in time, increase the population. Family-planning programs reduce fertility and therefore, in time, reduce the population growth rate.

But the situation is more complex than that. Family-planning programs are usually effective only after families have the number of children desired. Desired family size tends to be large whenever infant mortality rates are high. If the desired family size is high, then family-planning programs are not effective. Thus, in these circumstances, health programs that reduce infant mortality rates often, in time, reduce fertility.

Most population programs do not disaggregate sufficiently to examine the demographic consequences of specific health programs and specific family-planning programs. DYNPLAN is an exception. The user inputs the data for various health intervention and family-planning alternatives, and the model calculates how these policy decisions affect the population for the next 100 years. Specific diseases, their effects on different age groups, and the effects of various programs on different age groups are all considered in detail.

DYNPLAN was written at the University of Michigan by Stan Berstein, George Simmons, and Wuk-Hee Hong. It was developed for and funded by the United States Agency for International Development as part of the RAPID II project.

Theory and Assumptions

Six data files must be prepared to apply DYNPLAN to a particular nation. These files are: DISDATA, DISEAS, CURE, PREVEN, COSTS, and POPLN.

The DISDATA file contains data on all the diseases that affect a country's population. The following data must be entered for the six different age groupings: annual rate per person, hospital visits per case, days lost without treatment, case fatality rate without treatment, proportion seeking care, days lost with treatment, and case fatality rate with treatment.

The DISEAS data file contains the diseases that are affected by health improvements programs. They are selected from the larger DISEAS data file.

The CURE data file contains detailed information on the diseases that are affected by the health improvement programs designed to cure people already infected with the target disease.

The PREVENT data file contains detailed information on the diseases that are targeted by the health improvement programs designed to prevent people from becoming infected by the disease.

The COST data file contains data on costs associated with each of the health improvement programs under consideration.

The POPLN data file contains data on the structure of the population.

The health policy data must be entered using DYNPLAN's data file management program; the family-planning data is entered interactively during the program's execution. The data contained in any of the data files can be viewed or changed using the data file management program.

The family-planning section of DYNPLAN is capable of analyzing four different contraceptive methods. The user must enter data about usage, effectiveness, budget considerations, and percent distribution by age-specific fertility rate.

The health sector of DYNPLAN includes up to three different curative programs and two preventive programs for disease control. A gradual reduction in the mortality rate due to industrialization, urbanization, and other modern development trends is also included.

There are four model life tables to choose from: Latin American pattern, a South Asian pattern, a Far Eastern pattern, and a general pattern.

There are a variety of different output options, including output to a disk file, from which the output can be analyzed further with a spreadsheet program.

Evaluation

DYNPLAN is an extremely good model. It has excellent documentation and is very easy to use.

DYNPLAN can be used as either a planning or an educational tool. As a planning tool, DYNPLAN gives a reasonable estimate of the resource and health-status consequences of different planned interventions. As an educational tool, DYNPLAN demonstrates the importance of cost analysis in selecting various health program alternatives, as well as identifying the major determinants of the health status of a nation.

Hardware and Software Requirements

IBM PC/XT/AT or compatible, 512 KB RAM, two floppy disk drives (hard disk is preferable), monochrome monitor, printer; DOS 2.0 or later.

Source

Mr. Stan Berstein, Department of Population and International Health, School of Public Health, University of Michigan, Ann Arbor, MI 48109, USA; telephone: (313) 763-3229. There

is a nominal fee to cover handling, postage, and disks.

Personal Choice: A Guide to the Selection of Birth Control

Purpose

To help health-care professionals provide quality birth control counseling.

Description

Personal Choice is a program to facilitate birth control counseling in a university setting. Students seeking a birth control method are asked to use the program before seeing a health-care professional. They follow instructions provided by the program and enter answers to questions.

The program presents information on the reproductive process and birth control and helps the user prepare the background information needed for birth control counseling by medical professionals. A particularly important part of this information has to do with the user's lifestyle and priority of needs. After all questions have been answered, the program explains alternative birth control methods that would meet the needs of the user. The health-care professional, relieved of the tasks of conducting the preliminary education and compiling the needs assessment, can focus on choosing the appropriate contraceptive method.

Personal Choice was written by Anne Andrade, a nurse practitioner with seven years of college health experience.

Theory and Assumptions

The birth control methods considered in Personal Choice are: birth control pills, condoms, the cervical cap, the diaphragm, the intrauterine device, the natural (rhythm) family-planning method, spermacidal materials, tubal ligation, and vasectomy. For each method, the program provides a description, illustrations, and an explanation of both the benefits and the dangers associated with the method.

Evaluation

Personal Choice is an impressive package. Its graphics are done well and are extremely instructive. The user interface is easy to follow and requires no computer experience or instruction to use.

Personal Choice has been successfully used on two campuses and has proven to be a welcomed asset in their health-care centers. The program helps determine the type of birth control that will satisfy the user's needs and also fit in with the user's lifestyle. Because both needs and lifestyle are considered, there is a good chance that users will be satisfied with the method chosen.

Personal Choice is not meant to be a stand-alone replacement for counseling by a health-care professional.

Although Personal Choice was written for a college situation, not for a family-planning clinic in a developing country, a modified version of the program might be helpful in other settings. With the current version, users must be able to read, but a synchronized audio tape might eliminate this requirement.

Hardware and Software Requirements

Apple Macintosh computer (128 KB RAM, minimum), or IBM PC/XT/AT or compatible with graphics adaptor.

Source

Ms. Anne M. Andrade, Brown University Health Service, P.O. Box 1928, Providence, RI 02912, USA; telephone: (401) 863-3475. The price is US $175. The package includes a site license that allows for duplicate copies of the disk, to be used exclusively on one campus.

Expert Diagnosis and Treatment Module (EDTM)

Purpose

To provide mid-level health practitioners in remote areas of developing countries with a second diagnostic opinion.

Description

The EDTM uses artificial intelligence methods to provide expert, on-the-spot, second opinions. It identifies prevalent health problems in the geographic area where it is being used, differentiates among symptomatically similar disorders, suggests confirming tests, and considers available treatment protocols.

When clinicians use EDTM, they receive a diagnosis and a prescribed treatment, along with suggestions about further tests that can be done to confirm the diagnosis and a listing of diseases

with similar presenting symptoms. An example of the output is illustrated in Figure 3-4.

Theory and Assumptions

EDTM is intended for use by clinical practitioners who have no access to human medical experts or computer experts. The artificial intelligence design used in EDTM has small boundaries and domains (a maximum of twenty diseases per systemic area), a rapid search capability, commands that are easily understood and executed (typically only a single function key), an expandable structure (for additional symptoms, diseases, and treatments), and a monotonic reasoning structure that forces definite conclusions about symptomatology and disallows hedging.

The EDTM consists of two separate parts: the reasoning mechanism (or inference engine) and the knowledge base on which the reasoning mechanism works.

The reasoning mechanism employs logic that leads users from symptoms to diagnosis to treatment. A frequency distribution is made for all symptoms of all diseases in the knowledge base. The most frequently encountered symptom is presented first. If the response is no, the next most frequently encountered symptom is presented. If the answer is yes, EDTM selects those diseases that have the acknowledged symptom as part of their array of descriptors, and a new frequency distribution is developed. The questioning continues until the derived pattern best fits one disease. The process rarely requires more than three minutes.

The knowledge base must be customized for a particular region of the world. Demonstration programs have been developed for the intestinal, respiratory, and skin complaints typical of many developing countries. Some diseases, notably hepatitis and malaria, can present complaints in several systemic areas and are therefore included in more than one demonstration program.

The intestinal complaint module provides a differential diagnosis for the following diseases: amebiasis, amebic abscess, bacillus cereus, food poisoning, botulism, campylobacter diarrhea, cholera, colestridium perfreingens, E. coli diarrhea, epidemic viral gastroenteritis, giardiasis, rotoviris, gastroenteritis, hepatitis, malaria, salmonellosis, staphylococcal food poisoning, typhoid, vibrio, parahaemolyticus, worms (roundworm and hookworm), and yersiniosis.

The respiratory complaint module provides a differential diagnosis for the following diseases: pneumocystitis pneumonia, mycoplasmal pneumonia, bacterial pneumonia, viral pneumonia, scrub typhus, Q fever, acute respiratory disease, common cold, tonsilitis or pharyngitis, influenza, malaria, hepatitis, and chlamydial pneumonia.

The skin complaint module provides a differential diagnosis for the following diseases: contact dermatitis, diaper rash, pustular dermatitis, atopic dermatitis, tinea capitis, tinea corporis, tinea unguium, tinea cruris, tinea pedis, tinea versicolor, urticaria, pediculosis, scabies, leprosy, candidiasis, varicella, cutaneous leishmaniasis, measles, rubella, verruca vulgaris, chanchroid, primary syphilis, secondary syphilis, and seborrheic dermatitis.

The knowledge base is developed by first matching symptoms and diseases using standard texts, field manuals, and other widely circulated documents. Clinicians with experience in developing countries then modify the pairing. Finally, experts from a particular region refine the matching.

Evaluation

Developing countries have specialized health-care problems and unique health-care delivery systems. While the physician/population ratio is approximately one per 700 in the developed countries, it is not unusual to find one physician per 70,000 in rural areas of developing countries.

Rural areas of African, Middle Eastern, South American, and some Far Eastern countries depend heavily upon paramedical personnel, mid-level practitioners and village health

```
INTESTINAL COMPLAINT WITH...
VOMITING
EXTREME WEAKNESS
MUCOUS IN THE STOOL
SHRUNKEN TONGUE
FAINT PULSE
*********************************
THIS PATTERN IS SUPPORTIVE OF...
E. COLI DIARRHEA
*********************************
*********************************
ALSO CONSIDER THE FOLLOWING DISEASES ...
(THE MOST LIKELY ALTERNATIVE DISEASE IS LISTED FIRST.)
SALMONELLOSIS
*********************************
....Begin fluid replacement promptly.....
Use sugar-added ORAL REHYDRATION SOLUTION
for oral use (5-7% of body weight) or
WHO DIARRHEA TREATMENT SOLUTION for I.V. use (8-10%
of body weight.)
....If feasible, confirm diagnosis.
....Culture stools.
....Advise improved personal hygiene and
seek common mode of transmission such as
contaminated water.
Figure XXX: Illustrations of the output from EDTM
```

Figure 3-4: Expert Diagnosis and Treatment Module (EDTM).

workers to provide health care. These individuals often are inadequately trained and experienced in diagnosing and prescribing treatment. They lack the resources and expertise to keep adequate medical and administrative records. The EDTM (plus the related software for record keeping and nutritional training) is an excellent new tool for meeting the unique needs of health care in developing countries.

Data entry is very simple. The function keys are used to respond to "yes or no" questions about the presence or absence of a symptom. Therefore little is required of the clinician other than a keen ability to determine what symptoms the patient is experiencing. The programs are menu-driven for ease of the novice user.

Many of the treatment suggestions involve drugs. EDTM includes a quick reference guide, which categorizes these drugs and names other drugs that are appropriate substitutes. Because EDTM is customized for a particular country or region, the most effective treatment plans and medications for the most prevalent diseases can be built into the software. It is a relatively simple matter to change the listing; the programs are written in BASIC (GWBASIC), and little programming skill is required to load, change, or save a program.

The intestinal diagnosis and treatment module is written to display and print, at the user's option, in English, French, Spanish, German, or Swahili.

There are at least two other organizations developing health care software for developing countries. These are Centre Mondial, Informatics and Human Resources, in Paris, France, and Wycliffe Bible Translators, JAARS Computer Services, in Waxhaw, North Carolina, USA.

Hardware and Software Requirements
The computer must be capable of running MBASIC programs under MS-DOS, providing hard copy output, and displaying ASCII text on an alphanumeric screen (4 lines by 40 columns, minimum). Storage medium may be diskette, microcassette, bubble memory, or removable ROM. An integrated word processing system is also recommended, but not required.

Source
Dr. Douglas R. Mackintosh, NCSI, Suite 400, 5205 Leesburg Pike, Falls Church, VA

22041, USA; telephone: (703) 671-3360. The price depends on the amount of customizing needed.

AIDS Epidemic Model

Purpose
To provide a means for testing and evaluating alternative policies and programs for slowing the spread of AIDS.

Description
The AIDS Epidemic Model is a dynamic simulation of the spread of the AIDS epidemic. The model calculates the chances of an uninfected person becoming infected through sexual intercourse with an HIV carrier or through sharing a needle with an infected drug user. It allows users to study the effects on the epidemic of alternative policies and programs. The model can simulate the implementation of a testing program, the use of sterile needles by drug addicts, and changes of sexual behavior. The model is of value to planners, hospital administrators, and educators.

The AIDS Epidemic Model was written by Dr. David J. Ahlgren, Mr. Alex C. Stein, and Mr. Peter A. Lyons.

Theory and Assumptions
The AIDS Epidemic Model (see Figure 3-5) divides the population into drug users and non-drug users and subdivides these categories into sexually active heterosexuals, male homosexuals, bisexuals, and intravenous drug users. The model treats female homosexuals like heterosexuals.

The model requires input data on the initial fractions of population that are uninfected, infected HIV carriers without symptoms and infected HIV carriers with symptoms. Other required inputs include the likelihood of HIV transmission through sexual and blood-blood contact and information on the policies to be evaluated.

The model assumes that HIV virus is transmitted only through sexual contacts among heterosexuals, bisexuals, and male homosexuals and by needle sharing of intravenous drug users. For each group, several probabilities are involved, including the average transmission probability per sexual contact, the number of

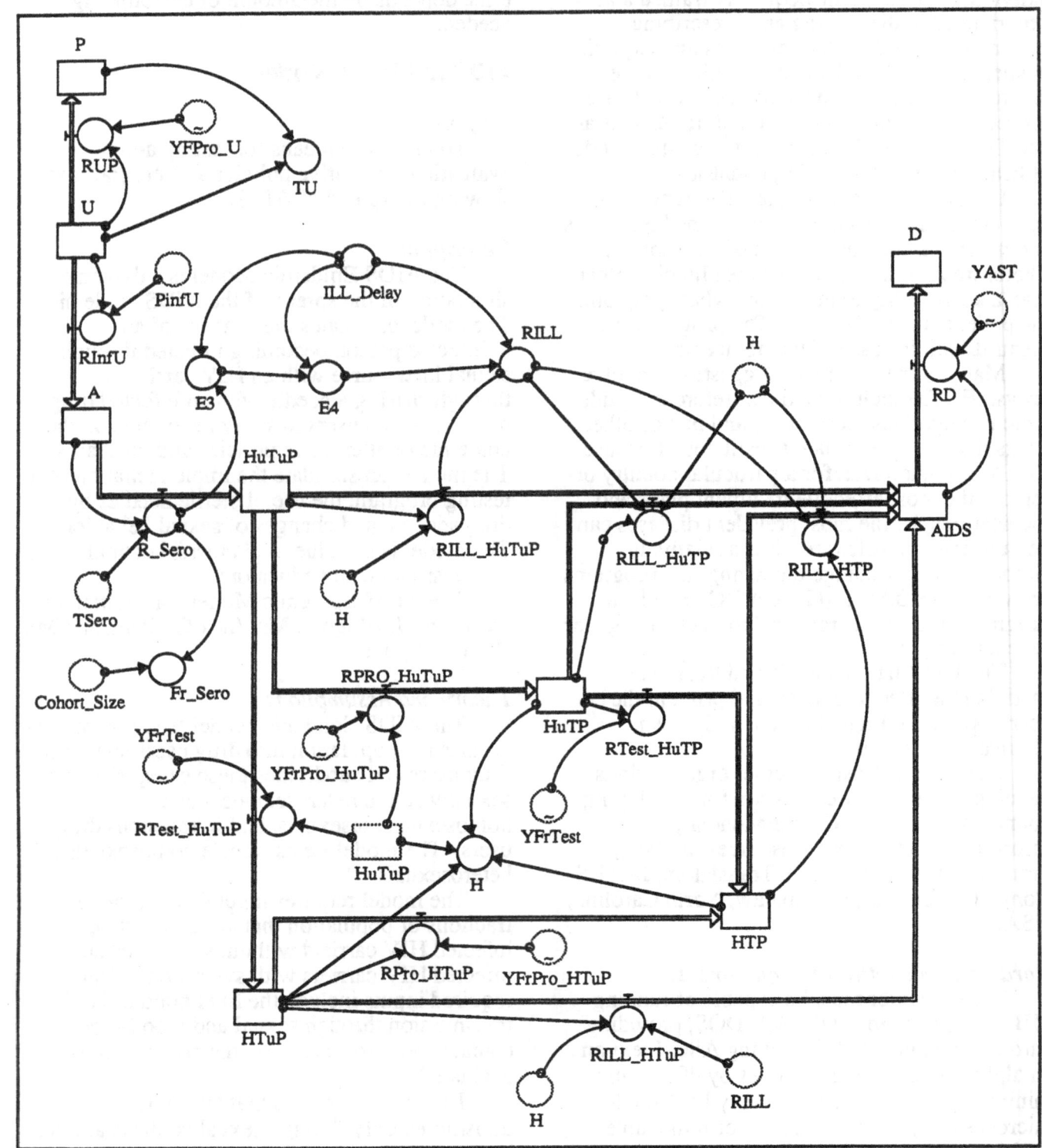

Figure 3-5: Template of the AIDS Epidemic Model.

new mates per year, and the average sexual contacts per year.

The output includes the number of infected and uninfected persons in the various population groups. The results can be viewed in graphical or tabular form. One can even watch the population levels change on the model's structure diagram.

Evaluation

The AIDS Epidemic Model should be very useful to policy makers concerned with health management and to groups providing AIDS education. The model not only allows for the testing of alternative policies and programs on the transmission of AIDS but also provides information on the dynamics involved in the spread of the disease.

It would be possible to modify the model so that female homosexuals are treated as a separate group. This modification would require a few additional equations.

Hardware and Software Requirements

Apple Macintosh microcomputer; the STELLA simulation program.

Source

Dr. David Ahlgren, Department of Engineering and Computer Science, Trinity College, Hartford, CT 06106, USA; telephone: (203) 297-2000.

REGULATOR

Purpose

To evaluate alternative strategies for the regulation of new, risky medical treatments.

Description

REGULATOR is a model of the various interacting factors involved in regulating the use of new, risky medical technology. It can be used as a laboratory for the evaluation and comparison of alternative regulatory strategies for new medical treatments over a simulated ten-year period. The parameters describing levels of harm associated with a treatment, length of time before harmful effects appear, and other characteristics of medical treatments can be modified independently so that regulatory strategies for a wide range of drugs or other technologies can be tested.

Theory and Assumptions

REGULATOR contains fifty parameters and twenty constants. It addresses the following considerations affecting the societal benefits from a new medical treatment: (a) the availability of the new treatment, (b) the number of patients eligible to receive the treatment, (c) the market share, i.e., percentage of those afflicted who are using the new treatment, (d) the perceived advantage of the treatment, (e) the awareness of possible harmful effects, and (f) any new reports of harmful effects,

For each run, REGULATOR allows the user to choose one of four regulatory policies. The first puts no restriction on the availability of the new technology. The second and third policies both delay availability initially, but whereas the second eventually allows the treatment to become fully available, the third policy continues to make distribution conditional on the perceived benefits of the treatment. Finally, there is a do-it-yourself option that allows the user full control of distribution.

Evaluation

REGULATOR is a useful new tool for investigating alternative risk management strategies in the field of medicine. There is a long-standing debate over whether it is better to be safe and delay the approval of new treatments or to be bold and allow the maximum number of people to reap the hoped-for benefits of a new technological development. With REGULATOR, one can simulate and evaluate alternative regulatory strategies over a ten-year period. All results are available graphically and in tabular form. In addition, an optional, animated, cause-and-effect display can be used to track the yearly consequences of any policy in a concise and understandable manner.

At this writing, the documentation provides background information on the model and on regulatory theories and describes some of the benefits and pitfalls of alternative regulatory strategies. It does so by leading the user through an example analysis based on the drug Clindamycin. Unfortunately, not all the equations used in the analysis are presented. Consequently it is impossible to understand the mathematical relationships used in the model.

The REGULATOR program itself runs smoothly, and the output presentation is clear. The model is simple to use, and the on-line documentation of the mechanics is quite thorough. The program's input requests are easy to understand, as are its displays of results. Documentation is lacking, however, on the theory, assumptions, and equations.

Hardware and Software Requirements
IBM-PC/XT/AT or compatible, 128 KB RAM, graphics board, color monitor; True BASIC.

Source
Dr. Jack Homer, System Dynamics Lab, Institute of Safety and Systems Management, University of Southern California, University Park, Los Angeles, CA 90089-0021, USA; telephone: (213) 743-4669. The price is US $100.

Primary Education Tracking System (PETS)

Purpose
To track and project national educational indicators for the primary level of education.

Description
The Primary Education Tracking System (PETS) is a tool for education planners and policy makers responsible for a national primary education system. With PETS it is possible to estimate current grade transition rates and to project future grade transition rates, student enrollments, and educational efficiency and productivity.

Theory and Assumptions
PETS uses a standard demographic model and the grade-transition methodology to develop its projections. The model consists of four modules that can be used independently or interactively.
The ESTIMATE module is used to estimate repetition, dropout, and enrollment rates. Input data include population by single-year age groups, age of entrance to the school system, current enrollment by grade, and current repeaters by grade. The output includes repetition rate by grade, dropout rate by grade, and new student enrollment rates.
PROJRATE projects future repetition, dropout, and enrollment rates under a specified

number of periods under various policies and programs. Inputs required include target repetition rate, target dropout rate, and outputs generated by ESTIMATE.
The EDPROJ module projects future enrollment for a specified number of periods. Inputs required include population by age, entrance rates for first grade, oldest legal school age, and the outputs from PROJRATE and EDPROJ. Outputs include enrollment by grade, gross enrollment rate, total enrollment, and total population of school ages.
The COHORT module estimates various measures of efficiency for the primary education system. The input required is the output of previous modules. The module projects the dropout-repeater history of a group of 1,000 students as they progress through the school system. The user can choose either to use fixed or varying dropout and repeater rates. Outputs include input-to-output ratios, graduates per 1,000 entrants, average years in school, number of on-time graduates, and other indicators.
The PETS modules are written in Turbo PASCAL. They are used in the HOST software environment, which is about as simple to use as Lotus 1-2-3 but permits more data-intensive applications than could easily be handled with Lotus 1-2-3.

Evaluation
PETS is a simple, easy-to-use software tool for national educational planners and decision makers. It requires only limited computer skills (some experience with HOST) and is fully documented in its user manual. The documentation is well written and explains clearly the use of the model and the methodology behind it.

Hardware and Software Requirements
IBM PC or compatible, DOS, 256 KB RAM, 3 MB of hard disk space, the HOST software, a math coprocessor chip, and a printer (optional).

Source
Both PETS and HOST are available from Research Triangle Institute, P.O. Box 12194, Research Triangle Park, NC 27709, USA.

4. Economy and Industry

Introduction

Economics has received the primary emphasis in national planning during recent decades. Leaders in most countries now recognize that a healthy future requires attention to more than just the economic aspects of development, but economics remains a matter of great concern and frustration, particularly because of the frequent failure of fiscal policies to produce the results expected. Economic theory and economic models are improving, however, and the software presented in this chapter can provide help to government ministers of trade, finance, and industry as they tackle their difficult tasks. Some of the programs are also relevant to business schools and to selected corporations, including small companies in developing nations.

The chapter begins with two programs related to foreign debt. As has been demonstrated all too frequently, it is very easy for a nation to become overextended with foreign debt. Two debt management systems, the CS-DRMS developed by the Commonwealth Secretariat and the DMFAS developed by the U.N. Conference on Trade and Development, now provide powerful, inexpensive tools with which ministers of finance can monitor and manage a nation's foreign debt.

Throughout the world, national leaders must work with a public that has only a limited understanding of the dynamics of an economy. This phenomenon becomes particularly important in a small country that has a high rate of political participation among its citizens; Iceland is an excellent example. To increase public understanding of the national economy, economists at the National Economic Institute of Iceland developed a dynamic macroeconomic model (MINIECON) on a spreadsheet. The model, which can easily be adapted to any other country, permits widespread and inexpensive dissemination of information that explains proposed economic policies—and their implication—in a way not possible previously. This model could also be useful to newspaper columnists in explaining economic developments in a nation.

Periodic swings in economic activity plague all industrial economies. The Dynamic Synthesis of Basic Macroeconomic Theory (DSBMT) model integrates the four approaches most widely used by economists in advising nations about how to stabilize these swings. Developed originally for the Canadian economy, the DSBMT model can be adapted to any nation. Since the DSBMT Model integrates all four of the most commonly used models, it is useful in reconciling conflicting advise from proponents of each.

While DSBMT is relatively complex (a tenth order differential equation), a much more complex model is needed to explain the many modes of behavior possible for a national economy. The System Dynamics National Model (SDNM) meets this need. It contains six sectors (capital goods, consumer goods, labor, households, finance, and government) and approximately twenty-five hundred equations. The SDNM displays the economic long wave (major depressions), the business cycle, and the overall growth of an economy. It can be used for research on any and all of these economic phenomena.

The System Dynamics National Model is too complex for teaching applications, and two simplified models have been developed to give students experience with two important modes of economic behavior. STRATAGEM-II simulates the economic long wave. Understanding Business Cycles (UBC) focuses on relatively short-term ups and downs of an economy.

Ministers of trade and finance must develop country risk assessments in considering alternative trade policies and agreements. They must also count on their countries' business leaders to perform country risk assessments when considering foreign plants and branches. The development of country risk assessments has tended to be a rather subjective process. Now, however, attempts are being made to add a measure of reproducibility and specificity to the process. The Expert Choice model is an example of one such effort.

Ministers of finance and trade must also count on their business schools to prepare well-trained business leaders. Running a business, like flying an airplane, requires experience. Now, just as there are flight simulators to train pilots, there are business simulators to train business professionals. BankExec/PC simulates several banks competing in a community; Business Simulator simulates other types of business activity.

For a nation to remain competitive in the world today, there are certain tools that its industries must learn to apply, including finite element analysis, electronic data interchange, and materials resource planning. Until recently the savings resulting from the use of finite element analysis in product design were available only to very large companies that could afford a large mainframe computer and expensive software. Now, however, microcomputer programs on finite element analysis (FEA) are available. Other useful microcomputer programs include QualEDI, for handling electronic data interchange of purchase orders and invoices, and Manufacturing Inventory System (MISys), for materials requirements planning in factories.

Commonwealth Secretariat Debt Recording and Management System (CS-DRMS)

Purpose
To record and analyze a nation's foreign debt and monitor other aspects of the use of loans and grants.

Description
The CS-DRMS computer software system facilitates the recording, analysis, and management of foreign debts. More specifically, the CS-DRMS software—according to the documentation—has the capability to do the following loan administration tasks: (a) maintain a complete inventory of all loans and grants and basic details of loan and grant agreements; (b) forecast debt service payments, both individually and in aggregate; (c) identify loans where debt service is in arrears and calculate penalty payments; (d) produce standard reports; (e) monitor loan and grant utilization, covering both

delays in the effectiveness of agreements and delays in disbursements and reimbursements; (f) maintain sinking fund contributions; (g) capture data on domestic loans and produce reports on a country's total debt; (h) capture data on lending to parastatal organizations; and (i) respond to specific enquiries.

The system can carryout the following loan management tasks: (a) provide information and reports on any group or class of loans; (b) capture exchange rate gains and losses in multi-currency loans; (c) carry out sensitivity analysis of the effects of interest rate and exchange rate variations; (d) test the implications of different volumes of new borrowing, based on different assumptions regarding currencies and repayment terms; (e) evaluate different loan offers; (f) evaluate different proposals for refinancing and rescheduling loans; and (g) use the output from CS-DRMS with exogenous economic data to project critical economic indicators.

CS-DRMS can produce a wide range of useful reports. Standard reports include the following: (a) single loan transaction report, (b) transactions to date report, (c) repayment terms summary report, (d) forecasting rules report, (e) projected debt service payments, (f) payments due report, (g) arrears notice report, (h) country report (for the *World Debt Tables* produced by the World Bank), (i) external debt outstanding report, and (j) debt indicator reports. In addition, special reports may be produced by using the database management system's report-writing facility.

CS-DRMS was developed by the Technical Analysis Group, Commonwealth Secretariat. Canada's International Development Research Centre (IDRC) contributed to the project.

Theory and Assumptions
CS-DRMS captures the basic loan particulars and transactions for both disbursements and service payments. The program automatically calculates loan balances and arrears of both principal repayments and interest payments. Aggregate figures are produced during monthly processing runs. The current balance of commitments, disbursements, and payments are kept for each loan record. Forecast figures are calculated in loan currency and compared with actual transactions as they occur. Aggregate figures are also stored in the local currency and in the user's selected base

currency. Interest and exchange rates are maintained separately for each base interest rate and currency.

CS-DRMS includes purpose-written data entry programs for forecasting and rescheduling rules governing future disbursements and repayments. In addition, CS-DRMS has an assumed disbursement profile facility, consisting of pre-defined profiles appropriate to typical uses of funds such as commodity assistance, projects, and programs. These profiles operate if the user chooses not to make direct estimates of disbursements.

CS-DRMS provides a set of tools for economic analyses, such as tests on the effects of future interest and exchange rate variations on debt service and evaluations of different rescheduling and borrowing scenarios.

Evaluation

CS-DRMS was first developed on an IBM PC XT and subsequently enhanced on an IBM PC AT running the PC-DOS operating system and on a Sperry PC-IT running the XENIX/UNIX operating system.

Although CS-DRMS is designed for use by a staff with little computer programming experience, a significant effort is needed to establish a suitable institutional environment for the use of CS-DRMS. The Commonwealth Secretariat can assist in this process, and one sub-regional resource center is being established at the Eastern Caribbean Central Bank.

CS-DRMS is being used in: Anguilla, Antigua and Barbuda, Barbados, Belize, Botswana, Cyprus, Dominica, Fiji, Grenada, Guyana, India, Jamaica, Lesotho, Maldives, Mauritius, Montserrat, Nigeria, Papua New Guinea, St. Kitts and Nevis, St. Vincent and the Grenadines, St. Lucia, Sri Lanka, Tanzania, Western Samoa.

Hardware and Software Requirements

IBM XT/AT with a hard disk (10 MB to 40 MB depending on the volume of loans) and 512 KB RAM; math coprocessor chip; a tape streamer unit; a 132-column printer; and voltage stabilizer. The system uses either DOS or the XENIX/UNIX operating system. It will run on multiuser machines under XENIX/UNIX. Users must also obtain Informix (a database management system) and the Lattice C language compiler.

Source

The Director, Technical Assistance Group, Commonwealth Fund for Technical Co-operation, Commonwealth Secretariat, Marlborough House, Pall Mall, London SW1Y 5HS, England; telephone: 01-839-3411; telex: 27678; telefax: 01-799-1507. The price for DS-DRMS depends on the specifics of the situation. The Informix database management system is available from: Informix Software, Inc., 4100 Bohannon Drive, Menlo Park, CA 94025, USA; telephone: (415) 926-6300; telefax: (415) 926-6593; telex: 361834.

Debt Monitoring and Financial Analysis System (DMFAS)

Purpose

To assist governments in the registration, monitoring, and analysis of external debt and other financial flows.

Description

The DMFAS fulfills the operational, statistical, and analytical needs of a wide variety of governmental users who have responsibilities for different aspects of debt management and external financial planning. It has been designed to support both macroeconomic sensitivity analysis and statistical analysis of the existing debt stock. Its principal functions are registration of new debts, monitoring of all debt, and analysis of the economic implications of debts. The system records the financial provisions of loan and grant agreements, the characteristics of the different parties or beneficiaries to the agreements, the utilization of the proceeds, and the relation of each agreement to other agreements. Transactions may be posted automatically to ledger accounts. By projecting debt-service payments by currency and by due dates, DMFAS can assist central banks in managing foreign exchange efficiently and in avoiding penalty interest charges for inadvertently late payments.

Theory and Assumptions

The DMFAS has seven major functions: (a) debt registration and recording of loans, (b) debt transaction accounting, (c) maintenance of reference files, (d) report preparation, (e) macroeconomic modeling and sensitivity analyses, (f) ensuring system security, and (g) provision of utility functions.

The module for debt registration and recording of loan terms is used to enter data on loan terms and schedules. This module also updates loan terms, schedules, and debt relations. Invalid and inconsistent entries are immediately recognized by the computer system, communicated to the user, and corrected on the spot.

The debt accounting module posts debt transactions, updates historical ledger data, updates loan ledger, and initializes each accounting period. The reports it provides facilitate the management of foreign exchange reserves.

Data that change frequently—e.g., interest and exchange rates—are kept up-to-date through maintenance of reference files. The content of these files is available to the user of the system in the form of separate reports.

A set of standard reports can be produced to support both debt management and investment decisions. These standard reports include registration certificates, reports on related clients, lists of loan terms in various orders, lists of clients in various orders, lists of loan relations, lists of rescheduling relations and terms, and reports required by the World Bank. In addition, DMFAS produces a variety of ledger accounting reports, debt-service projections, and utility reports.

The macroeconomic modeling and sensitivity analysis module is a menu-driven application of Lotus 1-2-3 designed to permit the user to test sensitivity and perform other forms of analysis. An interface procedure allows data to be passed directly from DMFAS debt files and from another balance-of-payments model, should one exist.

Part of DMFAS is devoted to guarding against unauthorized users and to the backing up and recovery of files.

Evaluation

The DMFAS is an extremely powerful and flexible tool for managing the financial affairs of a nation. It has been implemented both on personal computers and in mainframe environments. Little formal training or prior experience in the use of computers is required, since easy-to-follow screen displays guide the user step-by-step through the various facilities of the system. The DMFAS is available in English, French, and Spanish.

DMFAS is in use in eleven countries: Argentina, Bolivia, Costa Rica, Haiti, Liberia, Madagascar, Malaysia, Pakistan, Togo, Trinidad and Tobago, and Uganda.

Hardware and Software Requirements

IBM AT or compatible, 640 KB RAM, one floppy disk drive, a 20 MB hard disk, monitor, and printer. Optimally, a mainframe is used for primary data entry and storage, and microcomputers are used for data analysis, permitting the use of specialized software products available only for microcomputers.

Source

Chief, Technical Co-operation Service, U.N. Conference on Trade and Development, (UNCTAD), Palais des Nations, CH 1211 Geneva 10, Switzerland. The system is provided free to interested countries in the context of technical assistance projects financed by the United Nations Development Programme (UNDP) country programs.

MINIECON

Purpose

To illustrate the dynamic interrelationships among macroeconomic variables in a national economy.

Description

In a country like Iceland where there is widespread political participation involving the whole adult population, it is important that many people have a good grasp of the dynamics of the nation's macroeconomic performance. To increase such understanding, a spreadsheet model of the national macroeconomy was developed. The model illustrates the dynamic interrelationships among important macroeconomic variables and the functioning of the economy under different conditions. The model provides projections of private consumption, public consumption, investment, final domestic demand, exports, imports, gross domestic product, interest account, current account, gross national product, interest receipts from abroad, foreign debt, public debt, treasury revenue, and disposable income. Output can be in tabular or graphic form.

MINIECON was developed in 1985 by Dr. Thordur Fridjonsson at the National Economic Institute of Iceland. Later, Professor Thorkell Helgason and Bjarni Kristjansson adapted the model so it could run using Multiplan. Still later Einar Olafsson adapted MINIECON for use on Lotus 1-2-3.

Theory and Assumptions

MINIECON is a fourteen equation, general equilibrium model with dynamic feedback properties. Once the initial conditions and parameters are specified, the model will develop annual projections. The authors use the model for ten-year projections under various assumptions about the external environment and internal policies.

MINIECON was designed to represent the Icelandic economy, but it is inherently generic and can be used to represent any national economy. To apply the model to another economy, it is necessary to re-estimate (i.e., fit to historic experience) several parameters in the equations. These parameters relate to the equations for consumption investment, government expenditure, exports, imports, taxation, and income. Several exogenous inputs must also be provided in the form of a time series projection for the full period of the model run.

Evaluation

This is a wonderful educational tool that can even be used in some elementary policy analysis. Widespread use of MINIECON in countries around the world would substantially improve public understanding of national macroeconomic issues.

MINIECON is quite easy to use, especially for persons familiar with spreadsheets. Documentation is available in Icelandic and English. The English documentation is well written and appears to be a translation of the Icelandic. The equations for the model are given in clear detail. Guidance is provided in the documentation for applying the model to another national economy. Appendices provide step-by-step instructions for running the model and producing graphic output.

Hardware and Software Requirements

IBM PC/XT/AT or compatible; Lotus 1-2-3.

Source

Mr. Thordur Fridjonsson, National Economic Institute, Kalkofnsvegi 1, 150 Reykjavik, Iceland; telephone: (1) 69-9500.

Dynamic Synthesis of Basic Macroeconomic Theory (DSBMT)

Purpose

To provide, in a single dynamic model, a synthesis of the major theoretical macroeconomic models used by economists to provide advice on the management of the economies of nations and thereby to reduce disagreement among economists on economic policy.

Description

Even a casual reader of economic news will note that there is rarely agreement among economic advisors and that no matter what advice is followed, the economy, after six months, bears little resemblance to the situation that was foreseen by the economic advisors. "Politics" is often blamed. Political and personal motives are, in fact, often involved in the business of economic prognostication, but even with these aside, various economists do hold fundamentally different conceptions of how an economy operates.

Perhaps the widest gap is between economists who use static models and those who use dynamic models. Static models are derived from comparing descriptions of the economy in different static or equilibrium conditions. Since actual economies are never static or in equilibrium, static models are based from the outset on highly unrealistic assumptions. Nevertheless, they are very popular, perhaps because the mathematics of static analysis is much less demanding than that of dynamic analysis.

For many years advice on economic stabilization policy has been dominated by comparative statics models, which suggest that raising aggregate demand can restore full employment during economic downturns and that constraining aggregate demand can "cool an overheated economy." Economists who base their advice on these static models generally recommend countercyclic demand-management policies to stabilize the four-year business cycles that affect most industrial economies.

Over the past few decades, however, advances in mathematics, computers, and software have made the tasks of dynamic analysis quite straightforward. Several authors have developed dynamic economic models that do not suffer from the unrealistic assumptions of static models. These dynamic models suggest that conventional demand-management models may actually destabilize the business cycle. In other words, following advice derived from static models may actually increase problems of unemployment and inflation.

The developers of dynamic models have had little effect, however, on the thinking of economists or the managers of national economies. This limited influence can be traced in part to the simplicity of the dynamic models (usually second- or third-order difference equations) and to the fact that no one has explained satisfactorily the conflicting results from static and dynamic macroeconomic models.

The Dynamic Synthesis of Basic Macroeconomic Theory (DSBMT) model integrates the four models most commonly presented in macroeconomic courses on business cycles and stabilization policy. Two of the models are static; two, dynamic. The resulting DSBMT Model is a continuous-time, non-linear, dynamic simulation model of the U.S. economy. The model is sufficiently complex (tenth-order) to avoid simplistic assumptions of previous dynamic models, but simple enough to be easily applied to another country. The model also reconciles the previously conflicting results from static and dynamic models.

Theory and Assumptions

DSBMT integrates the salient processes of four macroeconomic models: (a) the multiplier-accelerator model developed by Paul A. Samuelson in 1939; (b) the "IS-LM" model published by J. R. Hicks in 1937 and developed further by his followers; (c) the aggregate supply-aggregate demand model published first by Rudiger Dornbush and Stanley Fisher in 1978 and now used in most books on macroeconomics; and (d) the inventory adjustment model published by Lloyd A. Metzler in 1941.

The DSBMT model consists of twenty-seven equations containing ten state variables (or stocks): income, inventory, employment, short-run expected demand, price, money stock, long-range expected demand, average output, capital, and lagged unemployment. The major interactions are illustrated in Figure 4-1.

There are three features of the model that should be noted. First, the model is written in continuous time, not discrete time, as were the original models of Samuelson and Metzler. The continuous-time format permits the use of smooth lag functions, whose dynamic properties do not depend on the size of the discrete time steps used in models written in discrete time.

Second, long-term growth dynamics has been omitted from the model. An implicit assumption is that the dynamics of growth and the dynamics of fluctuations are separable, i.e., that growth simply produces a trend in the theoretical operating point about which real economies fluctuate in dynamic disequilibrium.

Third, the model is "demand constrained." This means that supplies of labor and capital are not limited; either is available if required.

Evaluation

The DSBMT model is a significant achievement. The essential parts of four major macroeconomic theories have been brought together in a way that makes clear the contribution of each. The synthesized model provides a dynamic framework within which it is possible to explain and rationalize the conflicting views of the adherents to the four partial models.

DSBMT allows for the testing and evaluation of a wide range of stabilization policies. Among the policies that can be tested are the demand-stabilization policies aimed at raising demand when employment and output are low and lowering demand when employment and output are high. In particular, the model can test countercyclic transfer payments to consumers, countercyclic government spending, graduated income tax, countercyclic manipulation of the money stock, and countercyclic manipulation of money growth.

Analysis with the DSBMT model explains the apparent discrepancy between conclusions drawn with static and dynamic models. Countercyclic demand-management policies do stabilize the demand-driven cycle, as proponents of static models argue. Countercyclic policies also destabilize the business cycle, as proponents of simple dynamic models argue.

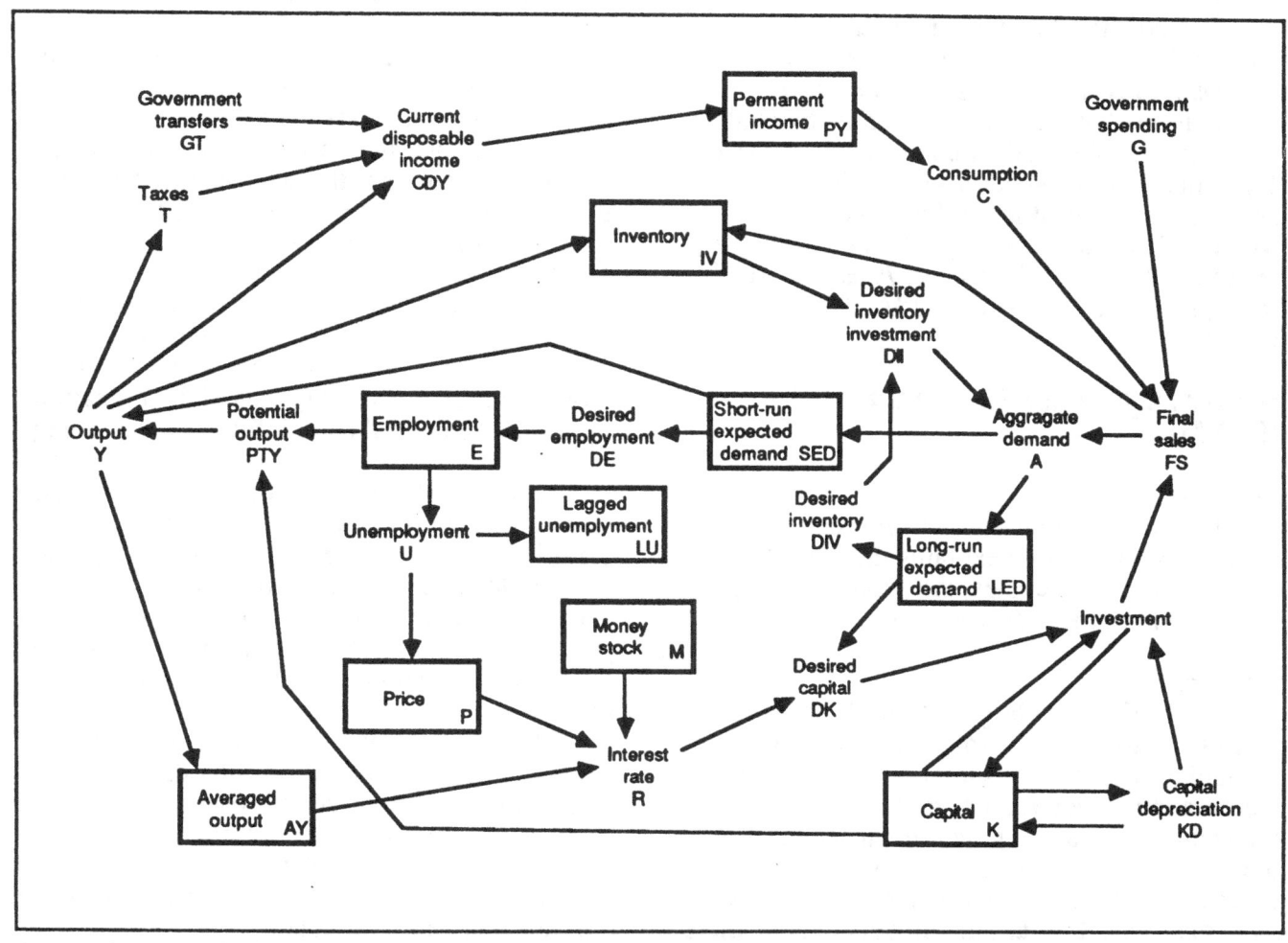

Figure 4-1: The major interactions in the Dynamic Synthesis of Basic Macroeconomic Theory (DSBMT) model.

The two results are reconciled by the discovery that the business cycle is caused by endogenous mechanisms that do not involve final demand. Variations in demand are important to a longer cycle created by a separate set of feedback relationships. The two cyclic models exist simultaneously in the same model, operating through relatively independent mechanisms.

The model can easily be made to represent other national economies. A relatively small number of parameters are needed for the twenty-seven equations, and these parameters can all be obtained from widely available sources of economic statistics. The model could be applied in many nations to evaluate conflicting advice from economic advisors.

DSBMT can also be used very effectively in a teaching environment. A wide range of policies can be tested by students in a short time. The transparent structure of the model encourages students to reflect on the structural origins of the dynamic behavior of economies.

Hardware and Software Requirements
IBM PC/XT/AT or compatible, 640K RAM, hard disk, printer. Color monitor recommended. Professional DYNAMO Plus or perhaps DYSMAP2. An Apple Macintosh using the STELLA language might also be a possibility, but the model's equations would need to be reformatted slightly.

Source

The equations and documentation for the DSBMT Model are provided in *A Dynamic Synthesis of Basic Macroeconomic Theory: Implications for Stabilization Policy*, by Nathan B. Forrester. To obtain a copy, write to: System Dynamics Group, Sloan School of Management, Massachusetts Institute of Technology, 50 Memorial Drive, Cambridge, MA 02139, USA, or to: Dr. Nathan B. Forrester, 79 East Barehill Road, Harvard, MA 01451, USA. The price is US $15.

System Dynamics National Model (SDNM)

Purpose

To provide a non-equilibrium model of a national economy that explains the underlying causes of business cycles, the economic long wave, inflation, and depressions.

Description

The SDNM is a large model. It has six sectors: a capital goods (plant and equipment) producing sector, a consumer goods producing sector, a labor sector, a household sector, a financial sector, and a government sector. Each sector contains, on average, seven blocks of equations, each of which contains about sixty-five equations. In total, the model contains more than twenty-five hundred equations.

The SDNM is a policy research model designed specifically to explore—in a single, unified model—the fundamental causes of depressions, inflations, business cycles, the economic long wave, growth, stagflation, government deficits, and the interaction of these economic phenomena.

The SDNM has been under development for more than a decade by the System Dynamics Group, Sloan School of Management, Massachusetts Institute of Technology (MIT).

Theory and Assumptions

To achieve their objectives, the members of the MIT System Dynamics Group chose a non-equilibrium formulation with structures containing delays, distorted information flows, markets cleared by more than just prices, and policies capable of amplifying effects. Feedback loops are the basic structural elements and the underlying cause of the model's dynamic behavior.

The six-sector structure (see Figure 4-2) of the model is a consequence of the original design objectives for the model. To allow examination of fiscal policy issues, a government sector is included to represent the activities of the local, state, and national governments. The governments impinge upon the economy by setting tax rates, collecting taxes, purchasing goods, hiring people, making transfer payments, and so forth. To allow analysis of monetary policy, the model's government sector includes money-supply growth targets and the operations by which the central bank influences the money supply.

The SDNM contains a financial sector that allows the government and other entities to participate in financial markets. Both supply and demand for financing are represented, including savings by the household and debt owed by both private borrowers and government. Interest rates are determined completely within the financial markets.

The model contains a representation of demand for goods and services by the household sector, so causes of price inflation can be studied. The household sector also determines how many people leave the household to earn wages in the market economy, so causes of wage inflation can be investigated.

A labor sector determines wages and the availability of labor through a labor market that mediates between the supply of people seeking work and the demand for employees. This sector is important in analyzing the causes of wage inflation.

Constraints on the ability to produce physical capital are important to the purposes of the SDNM. To allow investigation of how such constraints develop, the model represents the producing portion of the economy as two sectors: the sector producing capital goods (plants and equipment) and the consumer goods and services sector.

The six sectors are connected by five types of flows: physical flows (e.g., bricks), information flows corresponding to the physical flows (e.g., price, product availability, and orders), movement of people, financial flows (borrowing and payment), and information relating to the financial flows (e.g., interest rates and credit availability).

Evaluation

The System Dynamics National Model is the most comprehensive model of its kind. No other non-equilibrium model encompasses such a wide range of economic phenomena or attempts to simulate the long-term (up to two hundred years) economic behavior of a nation.

At this time, the model is useful only to a limited number of researchers. It is currently documented only in internal research reports and memoranda. Two books are in progress. By 1990 the books and the model should be available (at least in manuscript drafts) for policy research applications and teaching of advanced courses in economics.

Hardware and Software Requirements

A fast (20 MHz, minimum) microcomputer containing an Intel 80386 processor and math coprocessor chip; Professional DYNAMO Plus or perhaps DYSMAP2.

Source

Prof. Jay W. Forrester, Sloan School of Management, Massachusetts Institute of Technology, 50 Memorial Drive, Cambridge, MA 02139, USA; telephone: (617) 253-1571.

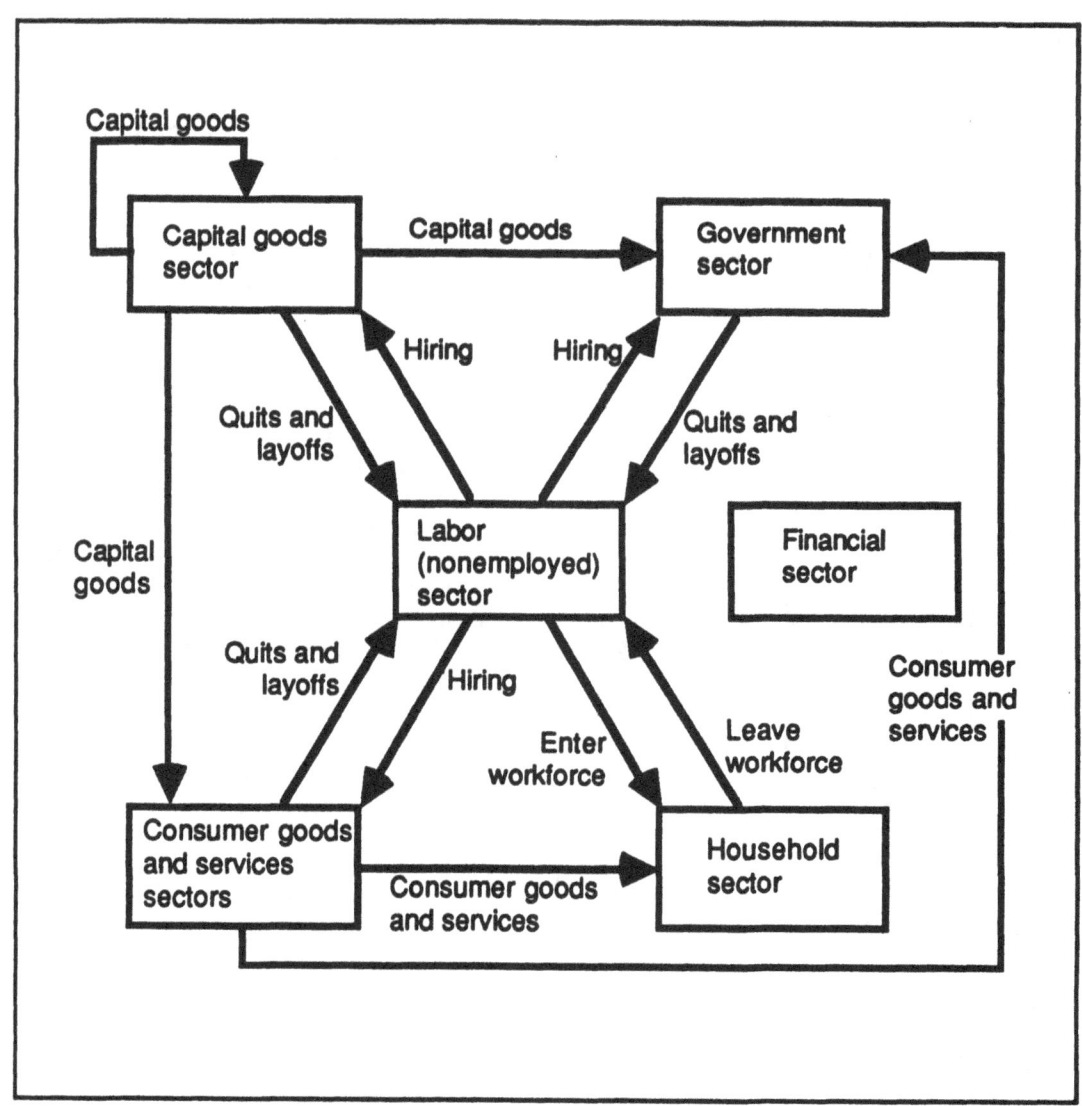

Figure 4-2: The principal physical flows among the sectors of the System Dynamics National Model (SDNM).

STRATAGEM-II

Purpose

To illustrate the basic causes of the "Kondratiev long wave," i.e., the approximately fifty-year cycle of economic prosperity and depression that is experienced by industrialized economies.

Description

STRATAGEM-II is an interactive computer simulation and board game based on a non-equilibrium, dynamic economic model. Part of the board layout is illustrated in Figure 4-3. The simulation is designed to help users understand the causes of the Kondratiev cycle—the long wave of economic prosperity and depression that plagues all economies.

The underlying model focuses on the capital investment decisions of individual firms. The

only exogenous input to the model is orders for capital placed by the capital sector, i.e., so-called self-ordering. The user inputs an order for capital goods; the computer returns a description of the economy two years later. The process is repeated thirty-five times for a seventy-year simulation game.

STRATAGEM-II was developed jointly by the International Institute for Applied Systems Analysis in Austria, the Resource Policy Center at Dartmouth College, and the System Dynamics Group at the Massachusetts Institute of Technology (MIT). Written by Professors John Sterman and Dennis Meadows, the model is a simplified version of the System Dynamics National Model (SDNM) which is described in the preceding review.

Theory and Assumptions

STRATAGEM-II is based on the theory that the self-ordering of capital in the capital sector is a fundamental cause of the over expansion of production capacity in the economy and thus also of the Kondratiev wave.

The basic assumptions include: (a) two fundamental industries exist in modern economies—the capital producers and the producers of consumer goods and services; (b) capital producers make their own equipment plus the plants and equipment needed by the consumer sector; and (c) goods producers sell primarily to the public.

Evaluation

This package illustrates that business management policies that seem logical for the short run may produce destabilization in the long run. The game also demonstrates how difficult it is to make optimal business decisions. Even given perfect information on the structure of the simulated economy, players generally must play two to four games before they develop business policies that avoid creating cyclic depressions in the economy. Given the fact that each game simulates 70 years, two to four rounds of play is the equivalent of 140 to 280 years of personal experience in managing an economy. Since no one has perfect information on the structure of the real economy, or 140 to 280 years in which to gain experience in managing a business in that economy, it should come as no surprise that business decisions in real businesses in the real economy are often less than optimal.

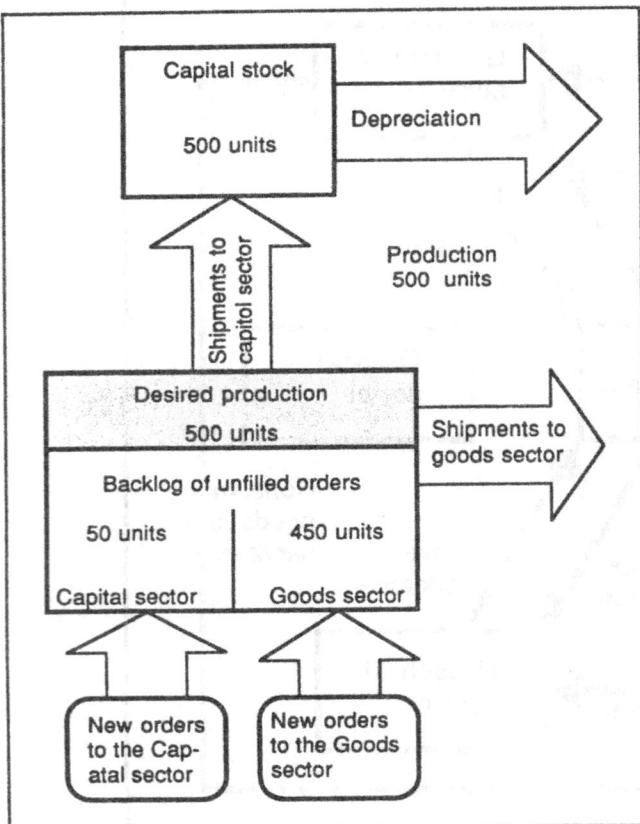

Figure 4-3: Part of the board layout for the STRATAGEM-II model. Configuration shown is for the initial (year 0) conditions.

Very clear directions are included in the user's guide. Professor Sterman has written two journal articles that provide additional assistance for the STRATAGEM-II user. "Testing Behavioral Simulation Models by Direct Experience" describes protocols for running and debriefing the game. "Misperceptions of Feedback in Dynamic Decision Making" discusses the results acquired from a large number of games played by many players. Both of the articles are available from Professor Sterman.

Formal training in using the game is not necessary. The game, documentation, and papers by Professor Sterman provide enough information for self-instruction.

STRATAGEM II was written as a management training game. However, the game works very well with a wide variety of individuals, including undergraduates, public administrators, systems analysts, and economists.

Hardware and Software Requirements
IBM PC or compatible, DOS, and at least 64 KB RAM. The color version requires a color monitor and board. A monochrome version is available.

Source
Prof. John D. Sterman, Sloan School of Management, Massachusetts Institute of Technology, 50 Memorial Drive, Cambridge, MA 02139, USA; telephone: (617) 253-1951.

Understanding Business Cycles (UBC)

Purpose
To provide an effective tool for introducing students to the business cycles in a national economy.

Description
The UBC materials are actually a course of instruction that includes several non-equilibrium models, explanatory information, exercises, solutions, and documentation. About ten hours of instruction and computer work with these materials would give students a solid understanding of the business cycle and of policies for reducing its damaging effects in an economy.

The UBC materials were prepared at the Sloan School of Management, MIT, by Professor John Sterman and his assistant Mr. Michael O'Brien.

Theory and Assumptions
The economies of all industrialized nations are plagued with business cycles—an irregular fluctuation in economic activity with peaks usually appearing at intervals of three to ten years. Business cycles contribute to a variety of economic problems including unemployment and business failures.

There are a number of theories of business cycles. Some argue that interactions between capital investment and consumer demand are the cause. Others point to the effects of monetary policy or to random shocks from outside the economy. Still others suggest an instability linked to the management of inventories and employment.

The UBC models progress in complexity. They allow students to consider alternative explanations of business cycles and to test the effectiveness of alternative policies in reducing the economic disruption caused by the cycles.

Evaluation
This is a terrific teaching tool. It not only gives students a clear understanding of a pervasive and damaging economic phenomenon, but also provides a non-threatening introduction to non-equilibrium economic models.

Hardware and Software Requirements
Apple Macintosh computer. The STELLA simulation language.

Source
Prof. John D. Sterman, Sloan School of Management, Massachusetts Institute of Technology, 50 Memorial Drive, Cambridge, MA 02139, USA; telephone: (617) 253-1951.

Expert Choice

Purpose
To provide a framework for analyzing the risk of doing banking business in a particular country.

Description

Bankers weigh a wide range of factors in assessing the risk of doing business in a particular country. Often such decisions are made on the basis of the subjective judgment of one person or the consensus of a small group. Some banks are now shifting to a more structured, disciplined, and analytical approach. Expert Choice is a tool to facilitate a more structured approach to country risk assessment. The program leads the user through a series of choices. An information screen is available at each node. The user makes judgments on a scale with six divisions: VGOOD, GOOD, FAIR, WEAK, POOR, XPOOR. The computer does the arithmetic of multiplying weighting factors and summing. The Expert Choice program was developed by the International Banking Division of the Royal Bank of Canada in collaboration with Topwalk Associates, Ltd.

Theory and Assumptions

The model is a collection of choice trees that are linked to country databases provided with the software. There are six trees in this structure: country economics, political risk factors, business sector, opportunity and capacity, country objectives, and marketing strategies. Each choice tree is divided into subchoices, some of which are subdivided even further. The country-economics choice tree asks the user to assess the economic risk to banking in the country under consideration. Users are led to consider the country's general economic setup, past record, present external debt, and the economic outlook.

The political-risk choice tree asks the users to assess the political risks for banking in this country. Users are led to consider political risks in relation to the country's government, society at large, and relations with other governments.

The business-sector choice tree asks the user to assess the business risks of banking in the country. The choice tree is subdivided into people, finance, rules, and competition.

The choice tree on opportunities and capacities asks the user to assess the extent to which an incremental change in the country limit meets the objectives of the user's bank. The amount of incremental change is determined from the previous three trees.

The country-objectives choice tree asks the user to prioritize objectives in the areas of return,

marketing position, network, and reduction of risks.

The final choice tree is concerned with market strategy. For each market strategy, it asks the user to determine the relative emphasis to be given to making loans, off balance sheet activities, service fee generation, and deposit gathering.

Evaluation

In principle, Expert Choice provides a measure of objectivity and explicitness to supplement the more subjective and personal expertise of the user. It requires the rating and weighing of each sector of each tree, and also encourages users to explain their reasoning. While the program provides a measure of order and reproducibility, country risk assessment, in reality, reduces to little more than a large number of subjective judgments weighted by subjective weighting factors. The simplicity of Expert Choice is obscured by the documentation, which is not clearly written. There is no summary of commands. Subprograms that do little more than ask the user to enter a number between zero and one are called "models." As simple as the program is, it could certainly be menu driven, but it isn't.

The documentation provides very little information on the contents of the database, but the example data screen for "Korea(s)" (sic) printed in the user's manual suggests the so-called data are rather general and discursive:

North Korea: Relations extremely hostile and tense. Seoul is considered vulnerable to attacks or infiltration from the North. Sporadic efforts to talk have produced no tangible results. North Korea also threatens the South in foreign countries (Rangoon massacre).

China: No formal relations, but the informal ones are improving. Trade is conducted through Hong Kong and, reportedly, is increasing.

Japan: Colonial overlords from 1905 until 1946, the Japanese are not considered to be friends. But, Japan has been the role model for Korea's post-war economic success. Also,

Japan is Korea's largest trading partner (both directions).

Hardware and Software Requirements
IBM PC/XT/AT; Lotus 1-2-3.

Source
Jack Zwick Associates, 1320 Old Chainbridge Road, Suite 350, McLean, VA 22101, USA; telephone: (703) 827-9000; telex: 650-3026942 MCI VW. The price is negotiable.

BankExec/PC

Purpose
To provide a realistic simulation of computing banks for use in training and development of banking professionals.

Description
BankExec/PC is used in training sessions for groups of fifteen to forty bank managers, directors, specialists, management trainees, and students in banking and finance courses. The training sessions: (a) provide an overview of the operations of a commercial bank in a competitive environment, (b) analyze different banking functions, (c) reinforce functional managerial skills, and (d) present an integrated approach to bank management.

During a typical training session, four or five participants per simulated bank compete against three to eight other banks in an imaginary community. The team members represent the bank managers, i.e., the chief executive officer, the lending officer, the investment officer, etc. The computer provides each team with detailed information on the status of the bank, which initially has assets of $500 million. The members of each team meet to assess the strengths and weaknesses of their bank's situation and to record the management decisions in a decision manual. The computer then processes the decisions of each competing bank, projects each bank's situation a quarter year later, and prints reports on each bank's new financial situation. Regulatory examinations may occur at any time. At the end of the one to two year period of operation, there is a stockholders' meeting.

Theory and Assumptions
BankExec/PC permits the competing banks to offer a significant number and diversity of products and services, including: (a) loans (wholesale and retail): a mix of fixed- and variable-rate loans, ranging from commercial to consumer types in up to fourteen categories. Loan commitment agreements are also possible. Mortgage loans produce service income; (b) investments: various options including treasury bills and bonds and securities purchases at par value; (c) deposits (retail): demand deposits and various savings instruments including fixed- and variable-rate savings certificates, NOW accounts, and money market accounts; (d) deposits (wholesale): demand deposits for business and corporate certificates of deposit; and (e) administrative: capital issues of common stock and debt, dividends on common stock, automatic purchase or sale of Federal Reserve funds to balance accounts, and the ability to borrow using repurchase agreements.

Evaluation
No country can afford to have its bank managers make major mistakes as a result of inexperience. BankSim provides useful training to bank managers and does so quickly and at no risk to real banks, real customers, and the real economy.

Hardware and Software Requirements
BankExec/PC operates on an IBM AT or compatible with 512 KB RAM, a hard disk, and math coprocessor chip. Minicomputer and mainframe versions are also available.

Source
Executive Education Division, American Bankers Association, 1120 Connecticut Avenue, NW, Washington, DC 20036, USA; telephone: (202) 663-5000. The user fee contract is US $2,000 for twenty participants; privileges for additional participants may be purchased at a rate of US $85 each.

Business Simulator

Purpose
To help future executives improve their decision-making skills as they introduce, market, finance, and develop a marketing opportunity.

Description

A user of Business Simulator assumes the role of chief executive officer (CEO) in a dynamic startup company. In this role, the user is responsible for tactical and strategic decisions that can either make the company a multinational success or bankrupt it. Decisions can be made in a variety of ways; the decision process recommended by the developers of Business Simulation is illustrated in Figure 4-4.

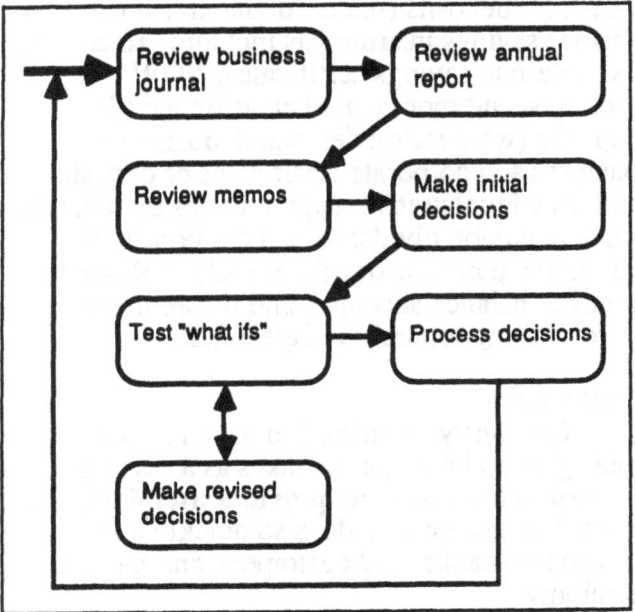

Figure 4-4: The decision making process recommended for use with Business Simulator.

The program leads the user through five progressively more difficult levels of decision making. As in the real world, the user's business includes a number of departments vying for budget dollars and attention. Also as in the real world, the goals of the departments sometimes conflict and make compromises necessary.

Business Simulator was designed at the University of Pennsylvania's Wharton School of Business. More than ten thousand MBA students and business executives from the largest U.S. corporations are reported to have trained with Business Simulator. The program is now marketed by Reality Technologies.

Theory and Assumptions

The model is organized into five parts: real world, consumers and investors, competitors,

expert analyst, and tutorial. Collectively these modules contain over three thousand equations.

The model operates as follows: (a) the real world module simulates "the business world" and determines such factors as growth, inflation, interest rates, and stock market strength; (b) the consumers and investors module provides purchasers for the user's products, stocks, and bonds; (c) the competitors module provides "business competitors" by analyzing the marketplace and making business decisions, which are based on strategies patterned after actual organizations and corporations; (d) the expert analyst module simulates the experts who evaluate the performance of businesses and, on the basis of their analyses, establish credit ratings and determine the attractiveness of industry stocks; and (e) the tutorial module provides a structured approach to learning lessons from Business Simulator.

Evaluation

The manual provides all the background material needed for the beginner to jump right in and for the more experienced user to make progressively more complex tactical and strategic business decisions.

The manual does not, however, provide an adequate description of the theory behind the simulation. Without a more adequate explanation of the theoretical foundation, there is little basis for evaluating the quality of the program.

Business Simulator is stimulating. It allows users to make mistakes that in the real world would topple their business. The tools employed during the execution of the program are the same tools business executives use in the real world: journals, spread sheets, and annual reports. The user's manual recommends a specific decision-making process for use with the Simulator and in real life. The manual asserts that if users apply this decision-making procedure consistently throughout their career, they will generally make the best decisions possible.

The simulation can be used by one person (competing with the computer) or by two people (perhaps you and your arch nemesis). Either way, Business Simulator is an enjoyable approach to develop business skills.

Hardware and Software Requirements
IBM PC/XT/AT or compatible, 256 KB RAM, two disk drives (one of which must read and write 360 KB floppy disks); DOS version 2.0 or higher. A color graphics card and a color monitor are recommended, but not required.

Source
Reality Technologies, 3624 Market Street, Philadelphia, PA 19104, USA; telephone: (215) 387-6055; telefax: (215) 387-2179. The price is US $99.

Finite Element Analysis (FEA) Programs

Purpose
To model a new product design and subject the design to a wide variety of tests prior to production of prototypes.

Description
There are now literally hundreds of materials that could be used in any product, and designers face an enormous task in selecting the materials and designs that will lead to an effective, durable, safe product at minimum price. Finite element analysis programs provide the means of testing a very wide range of designs even before prototypes are built.

Finite element analysis (FEA) programs were first developed by the U.S. National Aeronautics and Space Administration and are now used widely in industrialized economies around the world. In most industrialized countries, it is virtually impossible to purchase a major consumer product or ride in a car, train, boat, or airplane that has not been designed using FEA programs.

Theory and Assumptions
As the name implies, FEA programs model everything by breaking it down into small finite elements that are simple enough to be represented by specific mathematical equations. An example for an automobile bumper is provided in Figure 4-5. The equations—sometimes tens of thousands of them—are then combined into a complete mathematical model of the structure. Objects of virtually any shape and any number of components can be subjected to stress and thermal tests, both dynamic and static, before they are ever built.

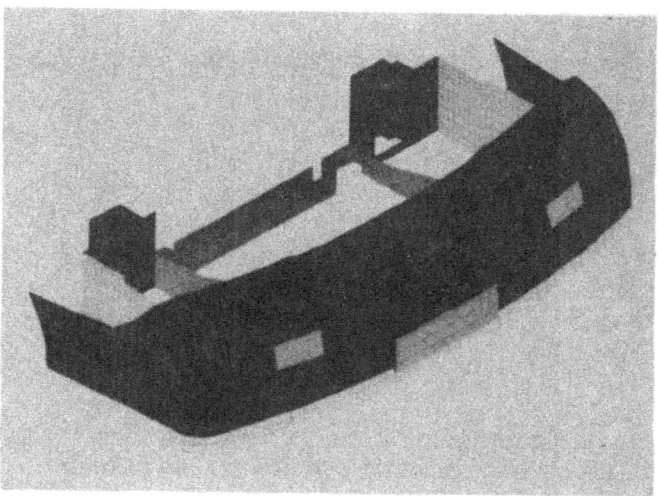

Figure 4-5: Design analysis of an automobile bumper prepared with the ANSYS Finite Element Analysis (FEA) Program. ANSYS display courtesy of Defiance-SMC.

Evaluation
Companies rely on FEA to save thousands of dollars and hundreds of hours in product development. The technique has important applications not only in product design, but also in manufacturing methods, process design, packaging, electronics, instrumentation, thermal devises, and thermal control.

Until recently FEA analysis required a large mainframe computer, but in recent years FEA programs have become available for microcomputers. The microcomputer versions can now do much of what the most advanced mainframe programs can do and at a small fraction of the price.

Any nation that aspires to an advanced industrialized economy should, as part of its development plan, be sure that industry leaders become familiar with FEA programs, especially those that operate on microcomputers. There are several sources of FEA software. Two companies that provide FEA software for microcomputers internationally are listed below.

Hardware and Software Requirements
IBM AT or compatible with a math coprocessor chip or one of the new microcomputers based on the Intel 80386 and 80387 chips. Mainframe versions of the programs are also available.

Sources

Swanson Analysis Systems, Inc., Johnson Road, P.O. Box 65, Houston, PA 15342-0065, USA; telephone: (412) 746-3304; telefax: (412) 746-9494. The MacNeal-Schwendler Corporation, 815 Colorado Boulevard, Los Angeles, CA 90411, USA; telephone: (213) 258-9111; telex 4720462 MSC; telefax: (213) 259-3838.

QualEDI

Purpose

To accelerate routine communications among businesses and simultaneously reduce costs.

Description

QualEDI is a microcomputer program to allow businesses to send routine documents to each other using electronic data interchange (EDI). In brief, EDI allows a wide range of specific business documents to be sent from one company's computer to another company's computer without the use of any paper. The process is illustrated in Figure 4-6.

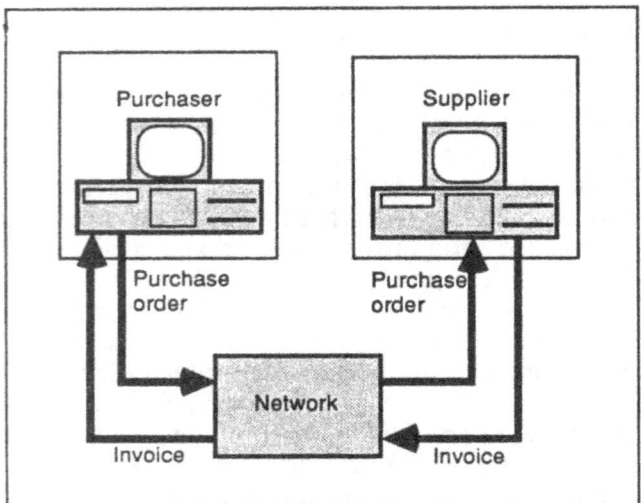

Figure 4-6: The process by which routine business documents are transferred between purchasers and suppliers using electronic data interchange (EDI) programs such as QualEDI.

The move toward EDI started about a decade ago in a few U.S. industries, including transportation, groceries, and pharmaceuticals.

In the early years, implementing EDI required a mainframe computer, software costing $50,000-$100,000, and months of effort. With the development of EDI standards and some microcomputer software, companies can now implement EDI within a week and at a total price of perhaps $10,000. As a result, EDI sales in the United States reached $35 million in 1987 and are projected to grow at 60% per year into the 1990s.

One of the keys to the success of EDI has been the development of relevant standard documents by the American National Standards Institute (ANSI). These standards provide for a terse, standardized format to be used in the electronic transmission of approximately 130 types of business documents, such as purchase orders, invoices, bills of lading, and so forth.

What ANSI did for EDI in the United States is now being done for all nations by the International Standards Organization (ISO), Central Section, 1, rue de Varenbe, Case Postale 56, CH-1211, Geneva, Switzerland. Although the international standards (called EDIFAC) are still evolving, a preliminary set has been published by ISO in its report ISO-9735.

Theory and Assumptions

QualEDI is a software package that allows a microcomputer to send and receive a wide range of documents to (and from) another computer (either micro or mainframe) in a form that can be understood and processed by the receiving computer. This permits purchase orders, for example, to be sent, received, and acted on without ever being printed or logged in.

QualEDI receives input information from a keyboard and stores it in a database. After extensive, automatic checking, the information is translated into the standard EDI format and transmitted by modem to another computer in another company. Electronic mail boxes are often used as the channel of communication. At the receiving end, QualEDI receives, checks, and stores the documents for further action. In addition, QualEDI has capabilities for print options, audit trails, backup, and recovery.

Evaluation

While there are some very large businesses in almost every nation, the bulk of the world's business is performed by relatively small firms that simply cannot afford mainframe EDI systems. However, these small firms face increasingly stiff competition from large firms that use EDI to cut costs and prices, in part by instituting just-in-time inventory methods. To remain competitive over the next decade, small-to medium-sized firms throughout the world will have to consider some form of EDI. QualEDI or some other microcomputer-based system may provide the capabilities needed (including formats for the standard international documents) at a very reasonable cost.

Hardware and Software Requirements

IBM PC/XT/AT or compatible, serial port, internal clock, 640 KB RAM, hard disk (10 MB or larger), monochrome monitor, 80-character printer.

Source

The APL Group, Inc., 644 Danbury Road, Wilton, CT 06897, USA; telephone: (203) 762-3933. The price of a multiple correspondent configuration is US $2,700; the price of a single correspondent configuration is US $1,650.

Manufacturing Inventory System (MISys)

Purpose

To provide small- to medium-sized manufacturers with some of the advantages of the materials requirements planning (MRP) done by large manufacturers.

Description

Maintaining an adequate inventory of parts and materials is a never-ending challenge to industrial managers. If outages occur, production is delayed or stopped. If large inventories are maintained, the inventory costs become prohibitive.

To handle this problem, large companies have invested heavily in materials requirements planning (MRP) systems. The software, training, reorganization, and equipment required, however, generally run to tens of thousands of dollars and involve many weeks of time. Manufacturers with annual sales on the order of a few million dollars cannot afford to make such a commitment.

MISys is designed to increase the competitive position and profitability of small manufacturing concerns with as few as ten to fifty employees. While MISys does not have the capabilities of full MRP system, it is a major step up from handling inventory decisions manually. MISys can produce purchase orders, bills of materials (itemized lists of the parts and materials needed in a finished product), and stock checks (reports on what parts, materials, and products are on hand). The functions performed by MISys are illustrated in Figure 4-7.

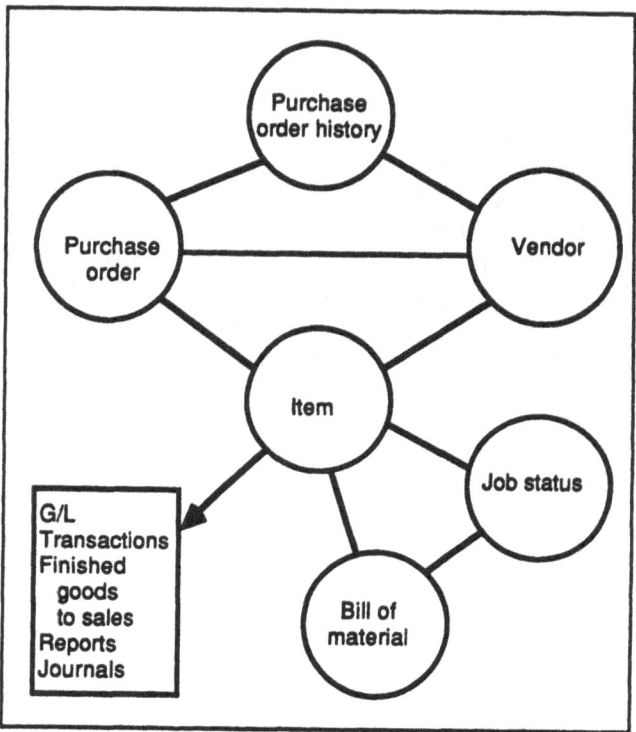

Figure 4-7: Relationships among the various functions performed by the Manufacturing Inventory System (MISys).

Theory and Assumptions

The central database in MISys consists of six interlinked files. They store information on individual inventory parts and materials, parts vendors, assemblies, purchase orders, purchase order histories, and job orders. Using the information in these files, MISys can produce the following reports: (a) stock reports: stock list and stock check, unused item report, shortage report, excess report, price variance report, item valuation report, activity report, and variance valuation report; (b) bill of material reports: assembly report, bill of material list, costed bill of material, where used report, assembly pick list; (c) purchase order reports: pre-order report, outstanding order report, overdue order report, purchase order history report; (d) vendor reports: vendor list, vendor product report, vendor performance report; and (e) job reports: job status report, job price report.

MISys also links to the accounting, financial, and marketing software produced by Computer Business Associates and to spreadsheets and databases via ASCII files.

Evaluation

Ministers of industry should be very interested in MISys and similar programs. In every nation there are large numbers of small- and medium-sized manufacturers who face stiff international competition. Advancing beyond manual inventory methods can improve the competitive positions of such firms. MISys and other MRP programs can smooth the flow of parts, labor, and products in a factory, thereby increasing the competitiveness of the industry and its contribution to the economy. The management philosophy at Microcomputer Specialists inspires confidence. The management wants to produce "appropriate" software, not big and expensive, but powerful enough to be effective. They also want satisfied customers, and to assure that they have no dissatisfied customers, they offer a money-back guarantee. This philosophy has paid off. There are now more than three thousand copies of MISys in use in the United States, Canada, United Kingdom, and Australia.

Hardware and Software Requirements

IBM AT or compatible, 640 KB RAM, 20 MB hard disk, printer. A local area network is recommended for relatively large factories.

Source

Microcomputer Specialists, Inc., 18 Lyman Street, Westboro, MA 01581, USA; telephone: (802) 457-4600 or (800) 833-1500.

5. Energy

Introduction

The economies of the world are driven by energy supplies, and the future of these supplies is in question. Most industrialized economies depend largely on petroleum energy supplies, and geologic studies of petroleum resources suggest that the global production of petroleum will peak around the year 2000. In economies of developing countries, the traditional sector depends largely on biomass resources, and the exploitation of these resources is proceeding in a way that is not sustainable in the long term. Coal is a widely available fossil fuel, but its combustion creates many problems, the most severe of which is probably carbon dioxide emissions and the associated greenhouse effect. Nuclear power does not produce carbon dioxide, but it generates radioactive wastes, involves the risk of serious accidents, and complicates the international management of nuclear weapons.

The models reviewed here are tools with which policymakers in both developing and industrialized nations can examine aspects of energy important to the future economic development and security of their countries. FOSSIL2, the primary energy policy model used by the United States over the past decade, allows the examination of a wide range of policy options for a large industrial economy. The model is particularly useful in analyzing the potential for energy conservation in the overall design of the energy sector of an economy. FOSSIL2 does not have a fuelwood sector, however, and is therefore of little use to developing countries in its present form.

The Long-Term Global Energy-Carbon Dioxide Model has many features similar to those in FOSSIL2 plus a sector that calculates carbon dioxide emissions. The Energy-Carbon Dioxide Model has been used in many studies but has not been examined or applied as extensively as FOSSIL2.

The Long-Range Energy Alternatives Planning System (LEAP) is designed especially for application in developing countries. It permits the analysis of all the major commercial fuels used in the modern sector as well as the biomass fuels used in the traditional sector. It is very easy to use, even for people who are inexperienced with computers and energy analysis. This model could also be useful to an industrialized nation; in some industrialized countries the contribution of fuelwood to the national energy budget is larger than that of nuclear power.

ENERPLAN is even easier to use than LEAP. This software is a powerful tool in the assembly of a national database on energy. As the data are developed, national energy balance sheets emerge almost automatically. ENERPLAN can also be used for the development of econometric models of the modern and traditional energy sectors, but LEAP would probably be a more useful tool of analysis.

The Charcoal Production Model (CHAR) attempts to deal with the economics of charcoal, a critically important component of traditional energy economics. While this model is inappropriate for use by an individual charcoal producer, it could be helpful in policy analysis provided that the environmentally destructive consequences of charcoal production and use were also addressed.

The Estimating Fossil Fuel Resources (EFFR) model addresses the question: "How long will oil resources last?" EFFR simulates the physical and economic processes involved in exploiting oil resources and applies to the simulation various analytical methods for estimating the total oil resource. Tests with the simulation show that the estimation methods most commonly used today significantly overestimate the size of the oil resource.

The BEYOND OIL model is a first attempt at developing an alternative approach to energy modeling. The model begins with estimates of ultimate recoverable resources, calculates the usable energy that theoretically can be derived from this resource, and finally estimates the economic output that this usable energy might provide. (The ECCO model in the "Multisectoral National Models" chapter approaches this issue from a somewhat different perspective.)

By any measure, electric power is a critically important segment of any nation's energy system. It is impossible to have a modern economy without access to electricity. On the other hand, conversion of other forms of energy to electricity is tremendously wasteful: typically two-thirds of the primary energy is lost as waste heat. The efficiency of a nation's electrical systems is therefore of great importance. Three programs reviewed here can be used to increase the efficiency of those systems. The Distribution System Analysis and Simulation (DSAS) model simulates the performance of an entire electrical distribution system and permits the analysis of how changes to the system would influence its efficiency. The Utility Fuel Inventory Model (UFIM) provides a means of minimizing the costs of fuel inventories held by power plants. The Transmission Line Optimization Program (TLOP) is a useful tool for the complex engineering task of maximizing the efficiency of electrical transmission lines.

FOSSIL2

Purpose

To evaluate alternative long-term energy policies for an industrialized nation.

Description

FOSSIL2 makes projections and evaluates alternative energy policies over the period from 1950 to 2020. The model was designed especially to address economic or supply disruptions associated with the transition from conventional fuels to alternative and renewable energy sources.

The U.S. Congress has passed legislation requiring the President to prepare, biennially, a National Energy Plan. The legislation requires that the plan have a thirty-year outlook and investigate a wide range of possible future energy conditions and developments. The FOSSIL2 model was developed specifically to perform this required long-term analysis. It has been the primary energy policy model used in the United States since 1979.

Theory and Assumptions

FOSSIL2 represents the national energy system as a complex socioeconomic system involving several interrelated feedbacks. For example, GNP, price, and availability are used to calculate demand; demand is used to calculate supply; supply is used to calculate price and availability; price and availability are then used to calculate a new GNP, and so on. Oil, gas, and coal resource depletions are simulated through a set of non-linear feedbacks in which conservation and fuel substitution are explicitly represented through lagged adjustment mechanisms.

As illustrated in Figure 5-1, the model is divided into two parts, one determining the demand for various fuels and the other representing their production. These two parts interact by exchanging information on fuel demand, availability, and price and using this information to balance supply and demand.

Supply is disaggregated by fuel type into four sectors: oil, gas, coal, and electricity. The four sectors interact when a production technology in one sector demands another fuel as either a feedstock or an energy input, e.g., when electric utilities require coal.

Each of the four fuels has three subsectors: a production subsector, which is divided into different production technologies; a financial subsector; and a supply/demand balance subsector. The financial subsector allocates a greater portion of the available investment funds to the production technology with the least marginal cost.

Major assumptions within the model include: (a) Demand is a function of GNP, the average energy price, and average energy availability; (b) energy availability is measured by a five-year moving average of the consumption/demand ratio; (c) in the supply sector, costs increase as production increases because it is less expensive to extract the initially discovered resources; (d) over the short run, producers can adjust supply through capacity utilization changes; (e) over the long run, supply can be adjusted through changes in production capacity financed by varying price and, therefore, profit levels; (f) energy demand will increase with economic growth.

The exogenous variables are listed in the documentation and include GNP, technology characteristics, imported oil and gas prices, and initial (1950) capital stocks.

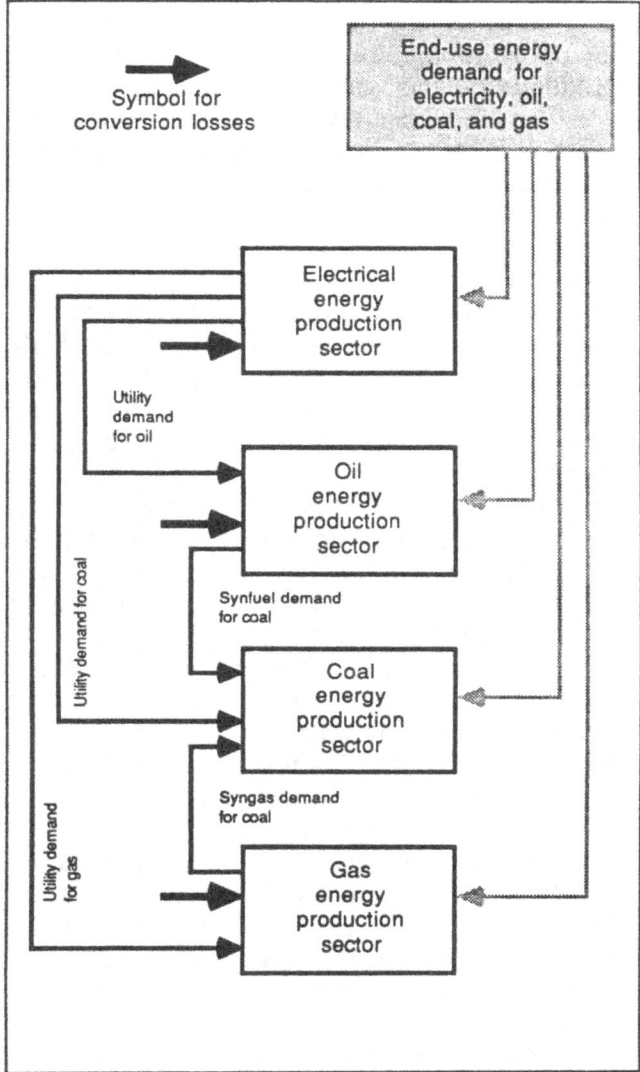

Figure 5-1: The basic structure of the FOSSIL2 energy model.

Evaluation

FOSSIL2 is an ideal model for use by the professional staff in a nation's energy ministry. It can test (in hours rather than weeks) virtually any energy policy proposal. The model can also be used for forecasting energy availability, demand, and prices.

The model has a structure that could be applied to most nations. A wide range of parameters would have to be changed to reflect the resources, economy, and policies of the specific nation, but this work could be completed by experienced staff in two to four months. Adaptation to a country with a centrally planned economy would require a bit more time but would be quite manageable. Adaptation to a developing country would require the addition of a fuelwood and traditional fuels sector. Applied Energy Services offers consulting services to users wishing to adapt the model or needing assistance in applying it.

FOSSIL2 can be used with exogenous projections of world energy prices or can be linked to the World Oil Model (WOIL) used by the U.S. Department of Energy to provide endogenous world oil prices.

FOSSIL2 is a mature, well-tested piece of software. It incorporates several million dollars worth of basic research about the fundamental interrelationships between energy and economies, and it has been tested and validated through a decade of policy analysis in the U.S. government and nine years of participation in Stanford University's Energy Modeling Forum (EMF). Participation in the EMF requires the analysis of a very wide range of scenarios that test every aspect of a model.

The documentation, which consists of three volumes plus an overview, is simple, clear, and well organized. Several flow diagrams and figures of the model's structure are provided. It is assumed that the user is familiar with energy terms, but very little technical language is utilized.

Hardware and Software Requirements

FOSSIL2 was developed on a mainframe computer using the DYNAMO compiler and has recently been converted to operate on a microcomputer using an Intel 80386 microprocessor chip running under OS/2 at 20 MHz and a beta site version of DYNAMO Huge. FOSSIL2 is too large to run under DOS with Professional DYNAMO Plus. FOSSIL2 runs in about fifty-five seconds on the microcomputer; the previous running time on an idle mainframe was twenty to fifty seconds and on a busy mainframe five to ten minutes.

Source

U.S. Department of Energy, Attention: Assistant Secretary for Policy and Evaluation, Office of Analytical Services, Washington, DC 20585, USA; or Mr. Roger F. Naill, Vice President, Applied Energy Services, 1001 North

19th Street, Arlington, VA 22209, USA; telephone: (703) 522-1315; telefax: (703) 528-4510. In late 1990, DYNAMO Huge will be available from: Pugh-Roberts Associates, Inc., 5 Lee Street, Cambridge, MA 02139, USA. The price is expected to be approximately US $4,000.

Long-Term Global Energy-Carbon Dioxide Model

Purpose
To make long-term global projections concerning energy utilization and carbon dioxide emissions from the energy sector.

Description
The Long-Term Global Energy-Carbon Dioxide Model integrates technological, economic, demographic, and geological factors to make projections to the year 2100 concerning global energy and carbon dioxide emissions. It can be used to study the interactions among energy output, energy price changes, population growth, labor productivity, energy supply, and energy tariffs—and the impact of all these variables on carbon dioxide emissions. The U.S. Environmental Protection Agency uses the model to investigate energy scenarios and their effect on carbon dioxide emissions.

The model computes energy demand for six major sources of energy in nine geographic regions. The energy sources are oil, gas, nuclear, solar, solids such as coal and biomass, and resource-constrained renewables such as hydroelectric power. The nine regions include: (a) the United States, (b) Western Europe and Canada, (c) Japan, Australia, and New Zealand, (d) the Soviet Union and Eastern Europe, (e) China and other Asian centrally planned economies, (f) the Mideast, (g) Africa, (h) Latin America, and (i) Southeast Asia. Carbon dioxide emissions are calculated for each fuel type in each region.

The model was written by Jae Edmonds and John Reilly for the U.S. Department of Energy, Office of Energy Research, Carbon Dioxide Research Division. It is available for either a mainframe computer or for IBM PC/XT/ATs and compatibles. The microcomputer version has several features not available on the mainframe version. The microcomputer version comes either compiled or in FORTRAN IV source code.

The provided database contains median values for key exogenous variables. There are thirty-nine adjustable exogenous variables, including population, growth rates, labor productivity, and synthetic fuel costs.

The model can take anywhere from thirty seconds to thirty minutes to run, depending on the specific assumptions and hardware configuration used.

Theory and Assumptions
As illustrated in Figure 5-2, the model is divided into four parts: a demand sector, which calculates the demand for each of the six major energy sources; a supply sector, which calculates the supply of the six major energy sources; an energy balance sector, which partially balances supply and demand in each global fuel market; and a carbon dioxide emissions section, which calculates the emissions by region and fuel type.

In calculating demand, the model considers population, labor productivity, economic activity, technological change, energy prices, and energy taxes and tariffs for each of the nine global regions. The calculations of energy supply take into account resource constraints, behavioral assumptions, and energy prices for each of the nine global regions considered.

The energy balance module brings energy supply and demand to a system-wide balance. This module uses a set of rules to reset energy prices iteratively until global energy markets balance within prespecified bounds. After an energy balance has been reached, the carbon dioxide emissions module applies appropriate carbon coefficients to the points in the energy flow where carbon is released.

Evaluation
This model is a powerful tool for examining how alternative energy policies will affect carbon dioxide emissions and the serious problem of global warming through the greenhouse effect. It allows the user to examine the long-term consequences of alternative strategies for meeting energy needs.

The model is an easy-to-use, menu-driven program and has excellent documentation. One caution, however: the data set provided with the computer code was developed as part of a study on the uncertainty associated with future emissions. For the original purposes of the

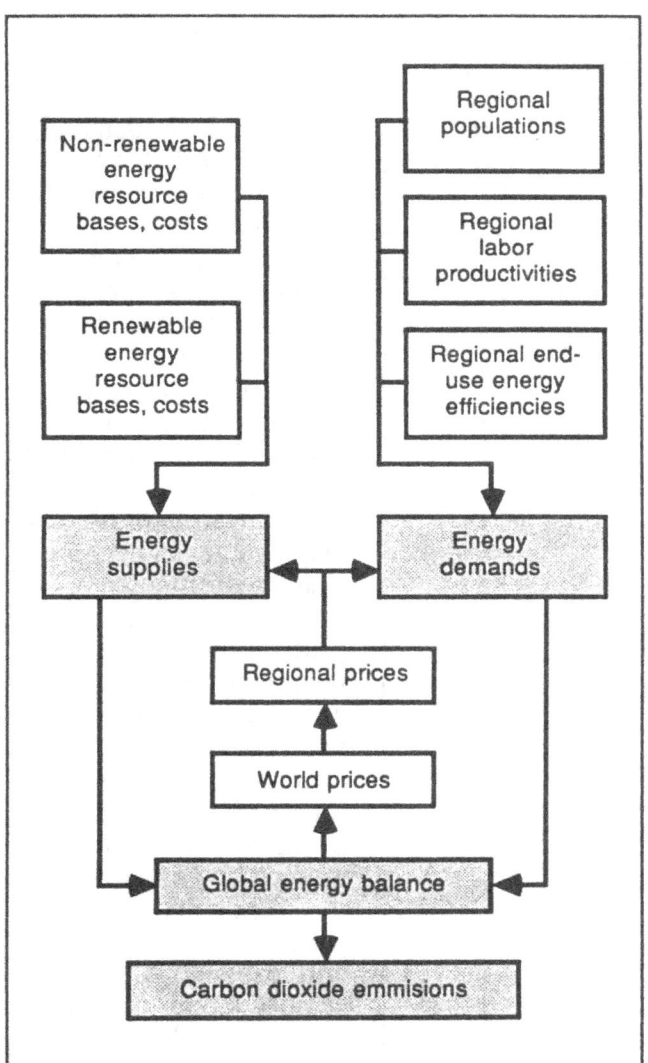

Figure 5-2: The overall structure of the Energy-Carbon Dioxide Model.

model, it was not necessary to ensure the accuracy of the regionally disaggregated pattern of energy supply around the world, and no attempt was made to do so. As a consequence, numerous regional anomalies appear in the data set provided with the code. The user should therefore revise the data set with figures that accurately reflect the regional patterns, particularly regional energy supplies, before using the model to calculate regionally disaggregated results.

Hardware and Software Requirements
   IBM PC/XT/AT, 520 KB RAM, color monitor, color graphics board.

Source
   Mr. Thomas A. Boden, Oak Ridge National Laboratory, P.O. Box X, Carbon Dioxide Information Analysis Center, Building 2001, Oak Ridge, TN 37831, USA; telephone: (615) 575-0390. The model is free.

Long Range Energy Alternatives Planning System (LEAP)

Purpose
   To provide a computerized framework for the evaluation of energy policy and planning options in developing countries.

Description
   LEAP is a flexible and accessible tool that enables energy planners and decision makers to identify and quantify the long-range implications of energy policy alternatives. It has three major functions: (a) to serve as an information bank and guide to data development for national energy accounts; (b) to function as an instrument for long-term projections of supply/demand configurations under alternative development scenarios; and (c) to provide a vehicle for identifying and evaluating policy and technology options regarding near and long-term supply/ demand balance, capital requirements, costs and benefits, and foreign exchange impacts.
   The fundamental goal of LEAP is to help developing countries to establish: (a) effective energy policy objectives, and (b) the program measures and investment strategy needed for achieving those objectives. Sufficient energy sources must be available for both the modern sectors, which generally rely primarily on commercial (often imported) fuels, and the traditional sectors, which continue to depend heavily on indigenous biomass energy. Policy initiatives and investment decisions must invariably be made under severe financial constraints; with the LEAP system, investment priorities can be identified in a timely and accurate manner.
   LEAP was created to manage data for the Kenyan Fuelwood project, an energy planning study conducted jointly by the Kenyan Ministry of Energy and the Beijer Institute of Sweden.

Since this first application, LEAP has been expanded into a comprehensive tool for managing energy planning. It is currently being used in several developing countries.

Theory and Assumptions

LEAP (see Figure 5-3) consists of seven interacting programs: three core energy forecasting programs, three macroprograms for related socioeconomic analyses, and one costing program for estimating the impacts of alternative energy scenarios.

The three core programs, namely demand, resource and transformation, provide the basic functions of energy accounting and forecasting. The demand program tracks the final fuel requirements by sector, subsector, end use, fuel, and device (e.g., kerosene stove.) The resource program projects production, availability, and utilization of biomass and changes in land use. The transformation program calculates the primary indigenous resources required to meet end-use demands, by taking into account the energy required for intermediate conversion processes as well as imports and exports.

While the core programs can be run alone with exogenous socioeconomic inputs, it is often desirable to have a consistent set of socioeconomic projections to accompany energy analyses. The three macroprograms—demographic, agriculture, and economic—develop socioeconomic projections that can be linked directly to the core programs. The demographic program, a cohort model, projects regional, urban, and rural population and households for alternative fertility and mortality scenarios. The agriculture program tracks agricultural commodity production, biomass

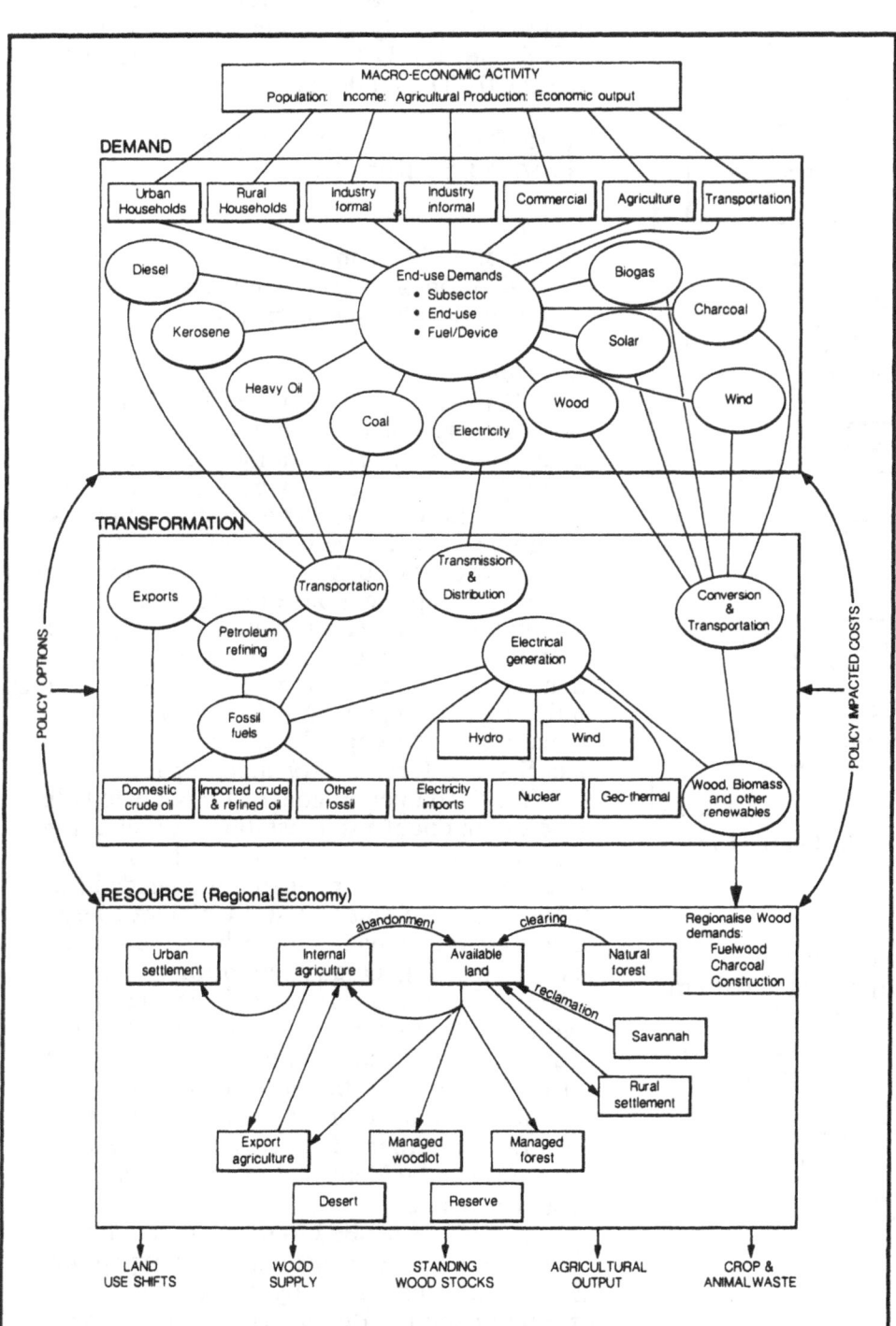

Figure 5-3: The general structure of the LEAP model.

wastes, and land allocations under user-specified assumptions regarding consumption and export targets, land availability, and agricultural productivity. The economic program develops national economic projections in terms of gross domestic product, sectoral outputs, income distribution, imports, and exports.

Evaluation

LEAP is an exceptionally well developed piece of software. Because of the modelers' belief that energy planning should be carried by local personnel within the appropriate government agency, the software has been written so that it requires no previous experience with computers. Menus appear on the screen to guide the user at every step. The user's manual is detailed and well written.

A separate handbook of data collection forms has been prepared, and the structure, theory, and assumptions behind the program are described thoroughly and clearly in a third volume.

Using LEAP, an analyst can develop national energy accounts and pictures of the future evolution of energy supply/demand balances with as much precision and detail as data availability permits. Furthermore, as the authors point out, lack of data should not preclude the use of LEAP. The system comes with background information from which estimates for almost any situation can be derived. These estimates can be replaced quickly and easily when more precise data become available. Thus LEAP also acts as a framework for development of a national energy database.

Hardware and Software Requirements

IBM PC/XT/AT or compatible, 640 KB RAM, one floppy disk drive, hard disk (10 MB or larger) and an Epson printer or compatible. DOS 3.0 or later.

Source

Dr. Paul O. Raskin, Stockholm Environment Institute-Boston, c/o Tellus Institute, 89 Broad Street, Boston, MA 02110, USA; telephone: (617) 426-5844, telex: 279926 ESRG BSN UR; telefax: (617) 426-7692; or Prof. G. T. Goodman, Stockholm Environment Institute,

Royal Swedish Academy of Sciences, Box 50005, S-104 05 Stockholm, Sweden; telephone: 46-8-72-30-260; telex: 17073 ROYACAD S.

ENERPLAN

Purpose

To perform basic energy analysis for a nation, province, or community.

Description

ENERPLAN (version 1.5) is a database framework and statistical package for use by energy planners at the national, provincial, or local level. It can be used as a database on energy and the economy or as a software tool for the development of energy balance tables. Planners with no previous computer experience can maintain databases, prepare energy balance tables, and produce tabular or graphic presentations of changing variables. More experienced planners can perform regression analyses, develop econometric models, run simulations, and explore the consequences of alternative energy policies and programs.

ENERPLAN was developed by the Tokyo Energy Analysis Group under the auspices of the United Nation's Department of Technical Co-operation for Development. The program was written by Yasuhiro Murota, Haruki Tscuhya, and Kohkichi Itoh. The documentation was edited by Bernard Rivers.

Theory and Assumptions

ENERPLAN is designed for use by planners having very different levels of experience with computers, statistics, and econometrics. The flow diagram is shown in Figure 5-4. For the relatively inexperienced, the program facilitates the entry of data into a database and the elementary manipulation of these data. The prestructured database covers most commercial energy forms and provides for a wide range of units of measurement. The database can include details of imports, domestic production, domestic consumption, and exports. Even an inexperienced planner can use the database to generate time series trends and energy balance tables showing net imports and exports of energy and to display these in either tabular or graphic form.

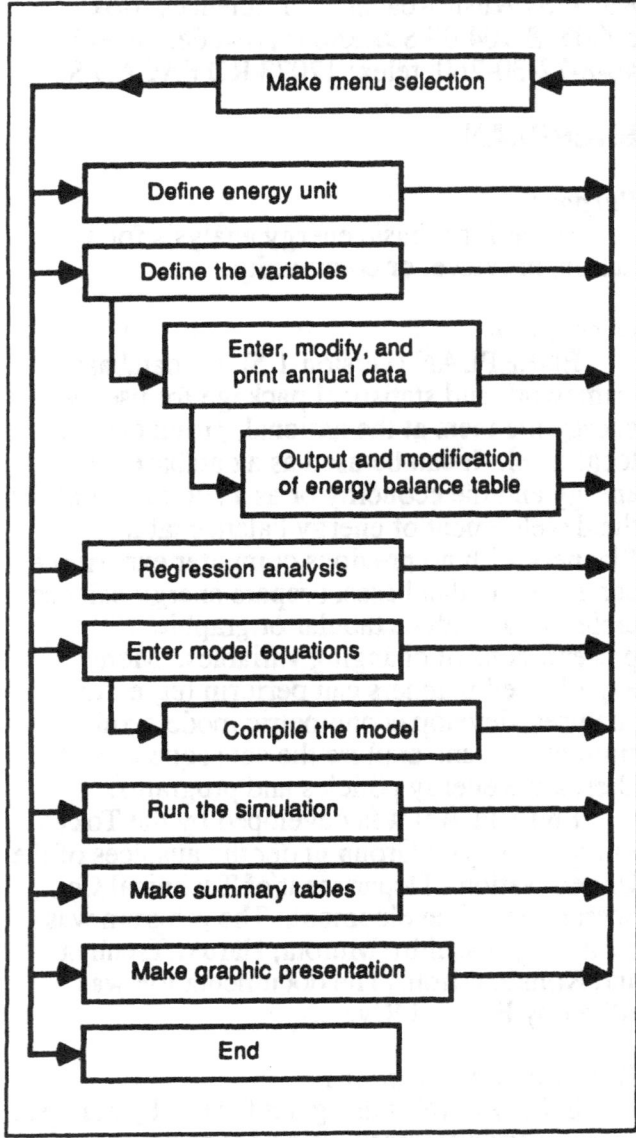

Figure 5-4: The flow diagram for ENERPLAN.

Planners more experienced with statistical procedures and econometric modeling methods can use the more powerful features of the program—regression analysis, projections of variables, economic and energy model development using econometric methods, and policy analysis. Instructions are provided for developing macroeconomic and energy models for the modern sector and for making appropriate linkages between these two models. A model of the traditional energy economy (wood, crop residues, dung, and so forth) is also included.

Evaluation

This is a nice piece of software. It is menu driven for ease of use. The documentation consists of photocopied pages of dot matrix print and includes few illustrations. It is not attractive, but it is very well organized and well edited. Even a planner with little or no computer experience could make productive use of this program given several months time and the necessary determination. A more experienced planner with a small support staff and good access to data could accomplish a great deal with ENERPLAN over the same period.

The program should also be of much interest to utilities and other energy suppliers and to university departments teaching public administration, resource management, economics, and public policy. There is much to be learned just from reading through the 200-page user's manual and examining available data.

Unfortunately, the program comes with an example of only one of the three types of models for which it is designed. A traditional fuels model is provided, but the designing of the modern-sector energy model and the economic model are left as exercises for the user. Many users would find it helpful if the package came complete with generic examples of all three types of models.

Hardware and Software Requirements

IBM PC/XT/AT or compatible, 256 KB RAM; two 360 KB floppy disk drives, or one 360 KB floppy disk drive and a hard disk; 80-column line printer, monochrome or graphics monitor.

Source

Mr. Nicky Beredjick, Director, National Resources and Energy Division, Department of Technical Cooperation for Development, United Nations, New York, NY 10017, USA; telephone: (212) 963-8764; cable: UNATIONS NEWYORK. The program is available free of charge to governments and universities upon request.

Charcoal Production Model (CHAR)

Purpose

To provide a tool for improving charcoal production in developing countries by calculating the financial returns to the local entrepreneur, taking into account the costs of all production factors.

Description

CHAR (version IIa) is designed to reduce the uncertainties in economic returns to small-scale charcoal producers by calculating in detail the expected rate of return. The model includes the costs of all production factors, including wood, equipment, and the transport of charcoal to market.

CHAR is intended to enhance general analysis techniques, projection analysis, and evaluation skills of managers of small-scale charcoal operations. The user's manual notes that the model has the additional advantage of introducing the use of spreadsheet software to these managers. The author of the manual suggests that once the spreadsheet methodology has been learned in this application, the manager of a small charcoal operation can develop other applications.

CHAR was developed by Energy/ Development International, Inc. (EDI), Washington, D.C., with funding from the U.S. Agency for International Development. Mr. Asif Shaikh of EDI reports that the model has been used fully only in Niger, where it contributed to an economic analysis of the possibility of making charcoal in a wood surplus area and shipping the charcoal to an area with market supply problems. Various offshoots of the model have been applied in Burkina Faso, Mali, and Zaire, he added.

Theory and Assumptions

Cost/benefit analysis is the methodology underlying CHAR, which is a Lotus 1-2-3 template. Inputs are entered via six data entry tables covering: (a) labor costs, (b) wood costs and moisture content, (c) equipment costs, (d) charcoal sales price, (e) administrative costs, and (f) transportation costs for both wood and charcoal. The results are displayed in two tables, one focusing on the cost/return ratio and the other on the ratio of wood inputs to coal outputs. The cost/return summary table provides costs of equipment, labor, administration, wood, and transportation and total cost by kilogram, ton, month, year, and kiln. Total costs, revenues, and profits are also given in detail, along with percent profit.

The quality of the wood and the quality of labor have been found to have a large influence on both the charcoal yield from a given weight of wood and the time needed to produce the charcoal. CHAR gives special attention to these factors by including the percent moisture in the wood and incorporating a labor remuneration scale linked to yields.

CHAR comes with a second template entitled BOGEY. It is used to calculate the optimum location for the charcoal production facility on the basis of wood and charcoal transportation costs. BOGEY assumes that consumers of wood and charcoal base their choice of fuel solely on the cost per unit of energy (gigajoule) delivered. Since transportation costs for a gigajoule of wood are much higher than for a gigajoule of charcoal, there is a distance from the market at which it is cost effective to convert wood to charcoal before transporting it to the market.

Evaluation

CHAR is menu driven and comes with a user's manual, which is available only in English at this time. The basics of Lotus 1-2-3 are explained for the inexperienced user, and an appendix of technical material is provided for the advanced user.

A major weakness in the manual is that the theory and equations underlying the model are not presented. Although the last several pages of the manual provide a listing of the formulas in each template cell, it would be a major task to determine the model's theoretical foundation from this listing.

CHAR was originally designed as a tool to help small-scale charcoal entrepreneurs run their businesses efficiently. It is unrealistic to suppose, however, that individual small-scale entrepreneurs in developing countries could afford the necessary microcomputer or would have access to the required data.

On the other hand, the model might be useful as a demonstration and planning device within a national or regional energy department. A good example is provided by the application of CHAR in Niger, where it was used to analyze the economic feasibility of a new charcoal production program. However, government officials considering alternative strategies in energy should beware of making decisions solely on the basis of CHAR, since the current version

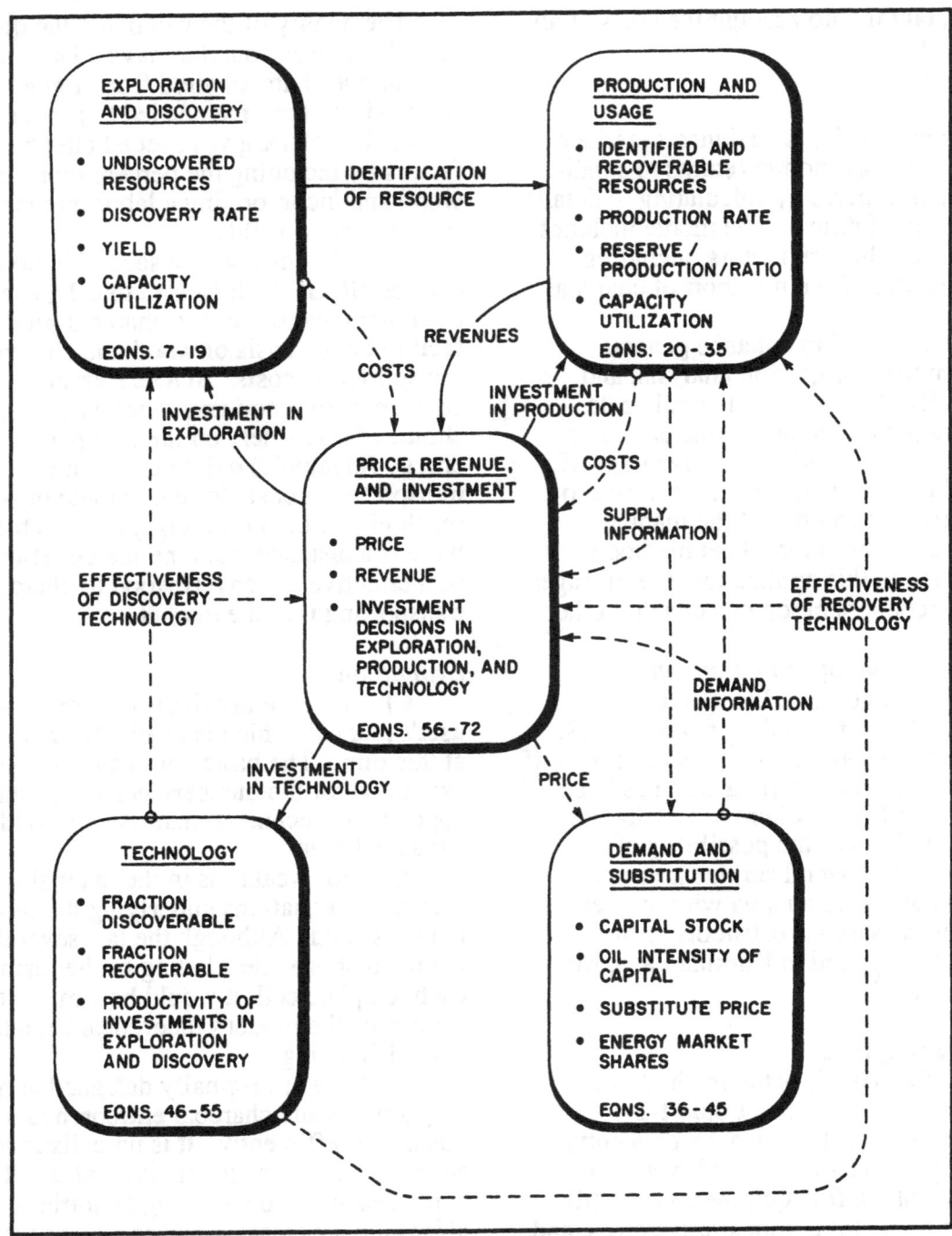

Figure 5-5: Overview of the Estimating Fossil Fuel Resources (EFFR) model.

of the software gives no consideration to the serious environmental costs of charcoal production and use.

Hardware and Software Requirements
    IBM PC/XT/AT or compatible with 640 KB, two disk drives, graphic card, Lotus 1-2-3, Release 2.0 or later.

Source
    Mr. Asif Shaikh, Energy/Development International, 1015 Eighteenth Street, Suite 802, Washington, DC 20036, USA; telephone (202) 822-8817.

Estimating Fossil Fuel Resources (EFFR)

Purpose

To simulate the global exploitation of oil resources and evaluate alternative resource-estimation techniques.

Description

EFFR is a dynamic simulation of the exploitation of oil resources. It is designed to test and evaluate different empirical methods for estimating the size of the remaining global (or national) petroleum resource.

Theory and Assumptions

Estimates of petroleum and natural gas resources have varied substantially, both over time and across estimation methods. EFFR (see Figure 5-5) addresses this problem by simulating the exploitation of the global petroleum resource and then testing alternative resource-estimation techniques by applying them to the synthetic data generated by the model. The tests indicate that the method developed by M. King Hubbert can generate an accurate estimate of petroleum resources as early as twenty years before the peak of production. On the other hand, the widely used geologic analogy method overestimates the true resource base over the full life cycle of the resource. The model and the tests are described in John Sterman and George Richardson, "Experiments to Evaluate Methods for Estimating Fossil Fuel Resources," *Journal of Forecasting*, 4 (1985): 197-226.

Evaluation

Every nation is faced with the problem of estimating its fuel and non-fuel resource bases, and a variety of forecasting methods exist. EFFR demonstrates that these various forecasting methods can be evaluated using modeling and synthetic data. It also provides an explicit, well-proven methodology for estimating oil reserves. A country-specific version of this model has also been developed for the United States; this country-specific version could be adapted to apply to other countries with relative ease.

Hardware and Software Requirements

IBM PC/XT/AT; Professional DYNAMO, or perhaps DYSMAP2.

Source

Prof. John D. Sterman, Sloan School of Management, Massachusetts Institute of Technology, 50 Memorial Drive, Cambridge, MA 02139, USA; telephone: (617) 253-1951.

BEYOND OIL

Purpose

To analyze how the physical limits to the availability of fuel may influence a national economy in the long term.

Description

In 1986 Carrying Capacity, Inc. published a book entitled *Beyond Oil: The Threat to Food and Fuel in the Coming Decades* (Cambridge, Mass.: Ballinger). This assessment of the U.S. energy and food economy is based on an energy accounting model, BEYOND OIL, developed by John Gever, Robert Kaufmann, David Skile, and Charles Vörösmarty at the Complex Systems Research Center, University of New Hampshire. The book and a separate executive summary have brought the BEYOND OIL model to the attention of large numbers of policy makers in the United States and other countries.

The BEYOND OIL model is a new tool for energy analysis. It attempts to do the opposite of what most energy models do in that it starts with oil resource estimates, then calculates the usable energy that theoretically might be made available from this resource, and finally estimates the economic output that this amount of energy can provide. Most energy models perform their calculations in reverse order, estimating first the desired economic output, then the required energy, and finally the necessary oil supply.

The BEYOND OIL model was programmed first on a mainframe. After the publication of the book, it was modified to operate on a microcomputer. The microcomputer version was designed so that it could be applied to any country.

Theory and Assumptions

The BEYOND OIL models (see Figure 5-6 for an example) are an effort to correct what the authors describe as a serious deficiency in neo-classical economic models, namely, the assumption that the supply and production of fuels and other natural resources are determined

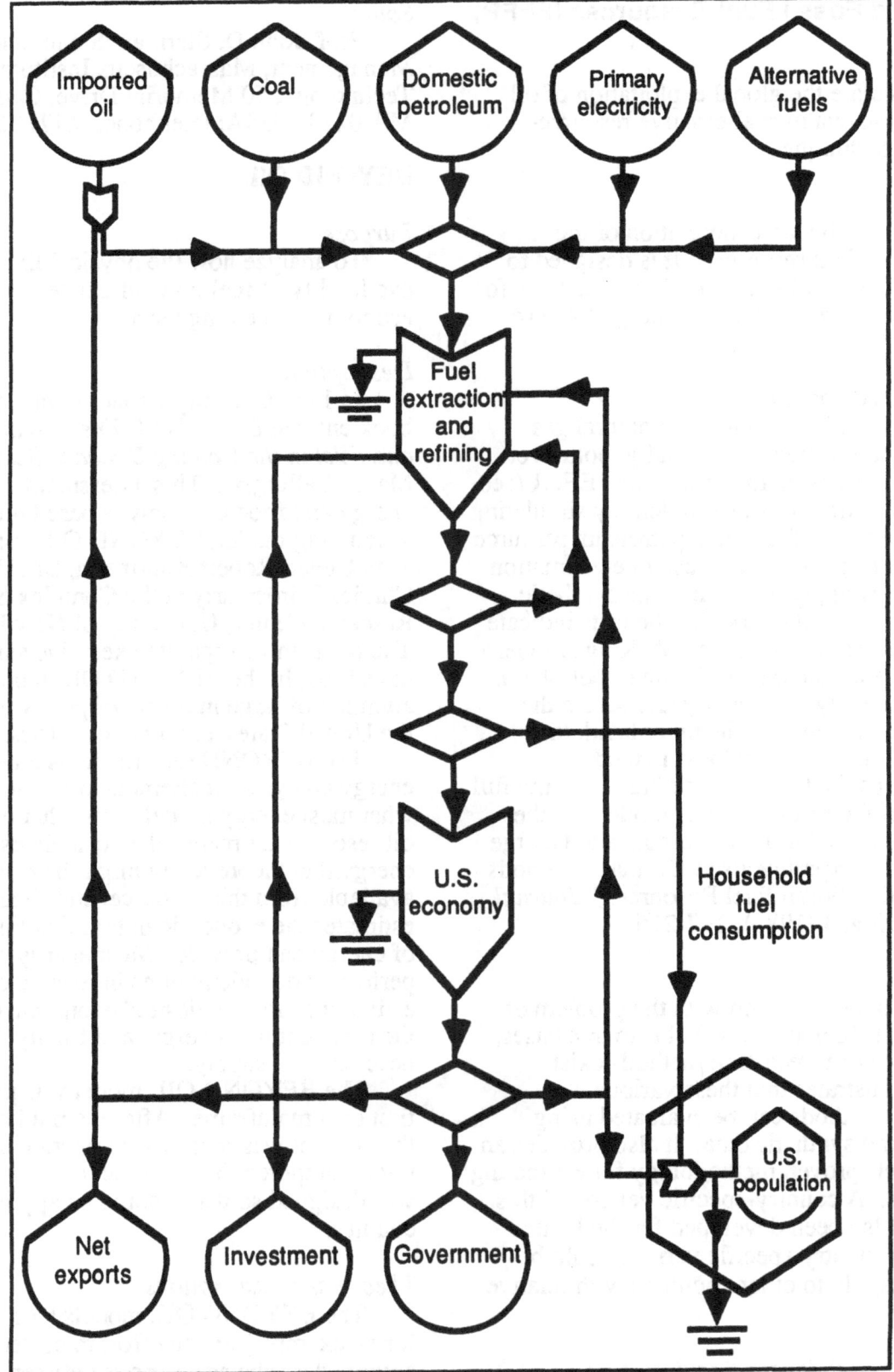

Figure 5-6: Simplified flow diagram of the BEYOND OIL model for the United States.

exclusively by prices and demand. While the model's authors recognize a continuing influence of price and demand, they argue that the laws of thermodynamics limit the amount of output an economy can generate with limited fuel resources of a given quality.

Evaluation

The microcomputer version of BEYOND OIL is, in the authors' words, "a first attempt" to provide to a wide audience a new tool for evaluating alternative national energy strategies. By this standard, the model is partially successful: it does provide a new tool. It is not, however, a model for a wide audience of inexperienced users. While simple in structure, this model is not easy to use or interpret properly. The input data must be prepared very carefully to produce a consistent and credible scenario, and subtle issues regarding the model's system boundaries and the assumption of no "radical change in energy supply or energy efficiency" must be understood.

BEYOND OIL has sometimes been referred to as a "net energy" model, i.e., a model that takes into account the energy that the energy industry consumes itself in order to provide energy for the rest of the economy. In fact, BEYOND OIL does not explicitly represent the energy consumed to produce energy. Instead, the authors employ arguments based on net energy considerations to justify the input figures, especially the initial resource estimates and the estimated price elasticities of supply. These estimates tend to be lower than those made by many other energy experts.

There are four documents relating to the model. The first and most essential is the user's manual, *The BEYOND OIL Model, (Microcomputer Version)*. The manual refers the user to parts of the book, *Beyond Oil*. A pamphlet entitled *Beyond Oil: A Summary Report* is also helpful, as is a 100-page collection of reviewers' comments on the model and responses by the model's authors.

Hardware and Software Requirements

Apple MacIntosh with 512 KB Ram and a disk drive for 800 KB (double-sided) disks and FORTRAN 77; or IBM PC/XT/AT or compatible, 512 KB RAM, and a hard disk (10 MB or more).

Source

The Macintosh and IBM/PC compatible versions of the model, the user's manual, *Beyond Oil*, the summary report, and the collection of reviewers' comments are available from: Carrying Capacity, Inc., 1325 G Street, NW, Suite 1003, Washington, DC 20005, USA.

Distribution System Analysis and Simulation (DSAS)

Purpose

To simulate the operation of an electric distribution system, especially operation at reduced voltage.

Description

The DSAS program simulates an electric distribution system in a very exact manner and analyzes the effects of reduced voltage on the energy consumption and losses in the system. The program reviewed, version 2.0, is capable of handling 500 buses with a maximum of 200 three-phase buses.

The DSAS program has been developed by the Electric Power Research Institute (EPRI) as part of its technical project entitled "Effects of Reduced Voltage on the Operation and Efficiency of Electric System."

Theory and Assumptions

The DSAS simulation is based on three-phase load flow algorithms rather than on the positive sequence methods generally used. Load behavior is simulated using the special EPRI load window model and load energy model instead of the conventional constant P and the Q load models. The EPRI transformer core loss model and load loss model are also employed. The mutual coupling effects between lines and to ground are included to reduce simulation error.

Evaluation

This model is a powerful electrical system simulator. Documentation is provided in two publications from EPRI: *Field Tests and Computer Code Development* (Electric Power Research Institute, 1984) and *User's Manual for DSAS* (Electric Power Research Institute, 1985). Order EPRI EL-3591, vol.1 and EL-3591-CCMP, vol.2.

Hardware and Software Requirements
    IBM PC/XT/AT and compatibles with 640
KB RAM. A math coprocessor chip is
recommended.

Source
    Manager, Software and Publications
Distribution, Electric Power Research Institute,
3412 Hillview Avenue, P.O. Box 10412, Palo
Alto, CA 94303, USA; telephone: (415) 855-
2000.

Utility Fuel Inventory Model (UFIM)

Purpose
    To assist a utility in balancing the cost of
holding fuel inventory against the cost of
running short of fuel.

Description
    The Utility Fuel Inventory Model (version
2.0) is based on alternative strategic inventory
policies—a set of seasonal inventory targets used
by the utility to determine order amounts. The
model translates these policies into expected
acquisition, holding, and shortage costs and
identifies the policy that entails the lowest
expected total costs. The model can take into
account seasonality, non-linear shortage costs,
and uncertain fuel deliveries and fuel burns. It
also can incorporate a variety of supply
disruptions in terms of their severity, warning,
and possible durations.
    UFIM can be applied to inventory problems
of both base load and cycling plants. It can be
used to develop inventory policies for individual
power plants or for a group of power plants that
burn a common fuel.

Theory and Assumptions
    The modeling approach used in UFIM is a
hybrid of stochastic simulations and dynamic
programming techniques. The core of the model
(see Figure 5-7) consists of three submodels:
disruption management, policy development,
and simulation.
    The disruption management submodel uses
input data on disruption characteristics to
calculate the expected costs of the various
possible disruptions as a function of the
inventory level at the disruption's onset.
    The policy development submodel uses
input data on normal-times demand, fuel prices,

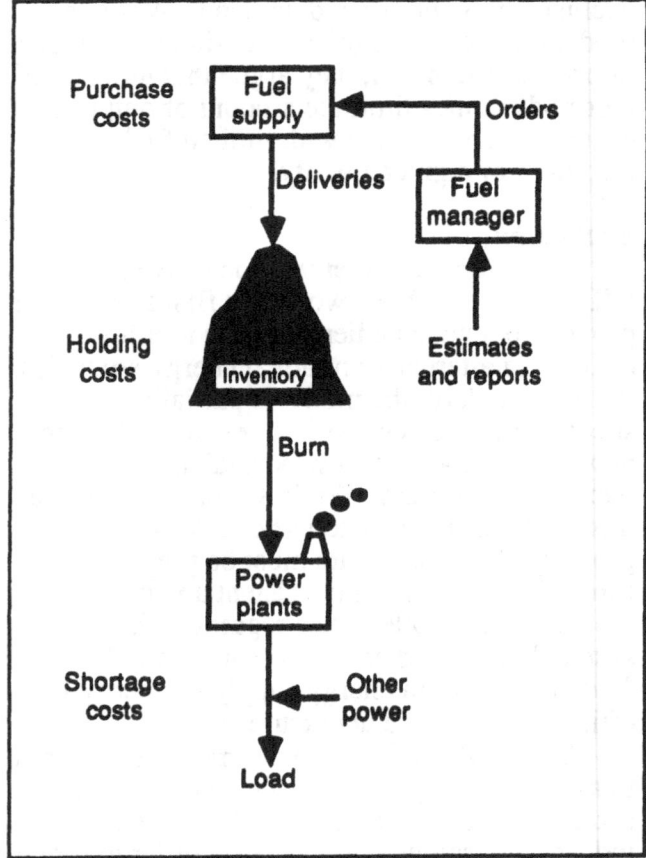

Figure 5-7: The elements represented in the Utility Fuel Inventory Model (UFIM).

holding costs and shortage costs, as well as the
expected disruption costs from the disruption
management submodel, to develop a baseline
inventory policy.
    The simulation submodel estimates the cost
of this baseline policy and of several similar
policies.

Evaluation
    Many countries face serious problems in
managing fuel inventories for electric power
plants. UFIM provides a useful tool for an
orderly assessment of future fuel inventory
needs.
    As a part of the validation process, EPRI
applied the model to two specific utility
situations. The first case study, involving
Consumers Power Company, focused on the
impact of winter weather on the utility's coal
inventory. The Tampa Electric Company case
study centered on an analysis of fuel supply
systems exposed to significant delivery lags.

UFIM comes with extensive documentation (EPRI EA-4766-CCM), which is entitled *Utility Fuel Inventory Model: Version 2.0*, (Electric Power Research Institute, 1986.) A videotaped lecture (EPRI PE85-01) on methodology for fuel inventory planning is also available.

Hardware and Software Requirements
    IBM-PC/XT/AT or compatible.

Source
    Manager, Software and Publications Distribution, Electric Power Research Institute, 3412 Hillview Avenue, P.O. Box 10412, Palo Alto, CA 94303, USA; telephone: (415) 855-2000.

Transmission Line Optimization Program (TLOP)

Purpose
    To provide an analytical tool for new electric power line design, uprating studies, evaluation of power transmission research, education, and generation of comparative cost data for planning or licensing.

Description
    When a utility begins planning a new transmission line, it needs to consider a large number of design options and to select from these options the combination of structure and conductor that results in the lowest cost. With the presently used manual technique, the engineer selects a particular structure and conductor and makes an initial engineering design. Many iterations using different structures and conductors are then carried out to determine the minimum-cost combination. This manual process is laborious and time-consuming and may actually overlook the lowest-cost combination of structure and conductor.
    The Electric Power Research Institute has developed a computer program that reduces the time and labor required to obtain an optimum design for any transmission line of conventional structure operating at any AC voltage between 115 kV and 550 kV.

Theory and Assumptions
    TLOP (version 1.4) approaches the design of a transmission line in terms of a system of interdependent environmental, structural, insulation, and economic design factors. Major variables considered (see Figure 5-8) are tower type, span length, and conductor system. Given combinations of user-specified design factors, TLOP calculates all costs and identifies the optimum design on the basis of either lowest lifetime cost or lowest initial cost. This same program can perform a sensitivity analysis to assess the cost impact of such varying parameters as loading criteria, electric field, or corona effects.

Evaluation
    TLOP is constructed around user menus and has extensive HELP files for all stages of program use. TLOP includes many useful subprograms needed by the line designer, including ones dealing with sag, tension, radio and audible noise, electric fields, and electric insulation clearances.
    The program comes with extensive documentation (EPRI EL-3592-CCM, revision 1) which is entitled *Transmission Line Design Optimization, TLOP Manuals* (Electric Power Research Institute, 1985.)

Hardware and Software Requirements
    IBM PC/XT/AT or compatible. Versions are also available for use on the Prime computer and on an IBM mainframe.

Source
    Manager, Software and Publications Distribution, Electric Power Research Institute, 3412 Hillview Avenue, P.O. Box 10412, Palo Alto, CA 94303, USA; telephone: (415) 855-2000.

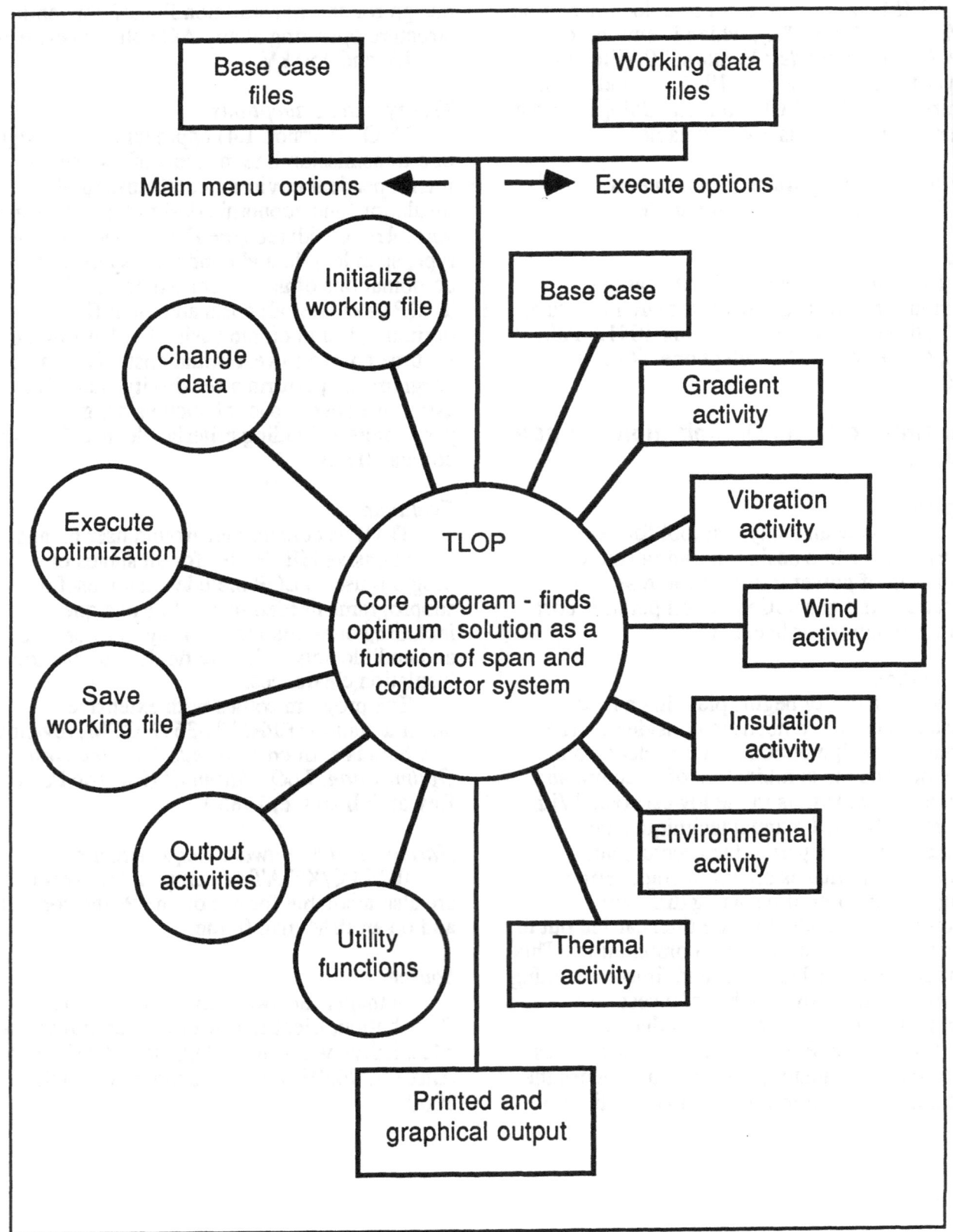

Figure 5-8: Functional flow chart for the TLOP model.

6. Environment and Ecology

Introduction

Since ecological awareness began to grow in the late 1960s, a wide range of environmental issues have attracted the attention and concern of policymakers. The software reviewed here and in other chapters touch on most of the major environmental issues under discussion today.

One of the most serious environmental threats to every nation is climatic change. Most climate models are too large for a microcomputer. The Atmospheric Greenhouse Model (AGM), however, is technically suitable for the exploration of a number of important global climate policy issues and yet operates on a microcomputer. The Long-Term Global Energy-Carbon Dioxide Model reviewed in the "Energy" chapter also has an environmental dimension directly related to atmospheric and climate change.

Perhaps the next most serious ecological problem on a global scale is the rapid loss of genetic resources. In virtually every nation, species are being lost annually (daily, in exceptional cases), and there usually is no awareness or understanding of how or when the losses occur. The Biological and Conservation Data (BCD) system provides a powerful tool for collecting data on endangered species and relating that data to the thousands of specific land-use decisions needed to protect the genetic resources of the planet. The Range, Livestock, and Wildlife model addresses the task of undertaking large-scale economic development in rural areas, while still protecting endangered species of wildlife.

Another major global environmental problem is the protection of soils from erosion. The model Range, Livestock, and Wildlife also speaks to this issue. Simulation of Production and Utilization of Rangelands (SPUR) reviewed in the "Agriculture" chapter examines range management and erosion in more detail. The Interactive Conservation Evaluation (ICE) methodology described in the same chapter analyzes soil losses from individual fields under alternative soil conservation practices.

Erosion not only destroys soils, but also damages water resources. The Enhanced Stream Water Quality Model (QUAL2E) allows water quality planners to simulate the hydrologic and water quality properties of streams and lakes under the impact of a wide range of pollutants from fields and other non-point sources as well as from point sources. The Model of Two-Dimensional Solute Transport and Dispersion in Groundwater (MOC) simulates the flow of pollutants to and within ground water resources. The Waterborne Toxic Risk Assessment Model (WTRISK) addresses water quality issues from the critically important aspect of toxic and hazardous pollutants.

A multifaceted and widespread environmental problem of special concern to many nations is acid deposition. Acid precipitation is generally thought to stem largely from the airborne products of coal combustion. The Acid Deposition (ADEPT) model provides a tool for evaluating alternative strategies for dealing with this problem.

Acidic material is just one of many classes of air pollutants. The thirty-three air pollution models in the User's Network for Applied Modeling of Air PollutionAir Pollution (UNAMAP) collection are capable of analyzing virtually every aspect of air pollution. The Complex Terrain Dispersion Model (CTDM) is a new, state-of-the-art model designed from the outset for use on microcomputers; it is one of the first air pollution models to address successfully the effects of hills on air flows and air quality.

The catastrophe that occurred in Bhopal, India, and many other accidents that were fortunately somewhat less disastrous have clearly signaled the need for better measures to cope with the accidental release of hazardous chemicals. The Computer Aided Management of Emergency Operations (CAMEO II) software can help by simulating a wide range of toxic chemical releases. It can be used both for contingency planning and for managing operations during an emergency.

People around the world have made many tragic mistakes with the pieces of equipment (often electrical) that contain toxic and hazardous materials. A huge number of these pieces of equipment are still in use. The Transformer/Capacitor Risk Management(TRIM) model provides a tool for systematically assessing the risks associated with the continued use of contaminated equipment and the costs of decontamination, replacement, and disposal.

There are many political problems associated with protecting the environment, and two models in the chapter on "Politics" deal with the political aspects of environmental management. The Estates Eutrophication Model is a political consensus-forming tool focused on interest groups concerned with alternative approaches to controlling eutrophication. EASY, the Environmental Assessment System, is another political consensus-forming tool with potential for application to a wide range of issues. In the form reviewed, EASY addresses the question of which technology for providing additional electricity to a nation would result in the least environmental impact.

Atmospheric Greenhouse Model (AGM)

Purpose
To analyze the consequences for the global climate of various scenarios regarding the production of carbon dioxide from fossil fuel combustion.

Description
AGM calculates atmospheric carbon dioxide concentrations and global mean temperature changes under alternative scenarios of carbon dioxide emissions from fossil fuel combustion. The model is first run to equilibrium with preindustrial values of all trace gases and then integrated from 1770 to 2200 using yearly values (historic and scenario) of carbon dioxide and trace gas emissions and/or concentrations. The scenarios may include cases with and without future restrictions on chloroflurocarbons and with various assumptions regarding future atmospheric concentrations of methane, nitrous oxide, and tropospheric ozone.

Theory and Assumptions
AGM consists of three coupled submodels on the carbon cycle, chloroflurocarbons (CFCs), and climate. The carbon cycle submodel uses a linearized impulse response function derived from the general circulation model developed by E. Maier-Reimer and K. Hasselman, with a correction to account for feedback between temperature and oceanic carbon dioxide partial pressure. The two-box CFC submodel, developed by T. Wigley, computes CFC concentrations from user-specified emission scenarios. The climate submodel is globally averaged and driven by the computed carbon dioxide and CFC concentrations as well as by exogenous inputs of methane, nitrous oxide, and tropospheric ozone concentrations.

The AGM uses historic rates of emissions of carbon dioxide from 1770 to present and scenarios for emissions in the future. Anthropogenic fossil fuel emissions are assumed to be zero prior to 1860, the beginning of the industrial era. Biospheric emissions of carbon dioxide are adopted from the historic reconstruction work of U. Siegenthaler and H. Oeschger.

Increases of methane and nitrous oxide are included using concentration scenarios from Wigley. Radiative heating due to carbon dioxide, methane, nitrous oxide and CFCs are computed using formulae from Wigley. In the absence of measures to limit the build-up of tropospheric ozone, radiative heating due to tropospheric ozone is assumed to be one-third that due to methane. Nitrous oxide and methane concentrations can be made to stabilize or start decreasing when carbon dioxide emissions begin decreasing. This possibility also applies to radiative heating from tropospheric ozone.

Evaluation
Anthropogenic changes in the global atmosphere and climate are among the most serious problems facing humankind today. The problems are complicated from both the scientific and political points of view, and they have not been well understood by average educated citizens around the world. One of the reasons for this limited understanding is that the relevant physical processes are so involved that only highly complex models on the very largest computers can describe them well, and few people have access to such computers and models.

The Atmospheric Greenhouse Model makes an important step toward encouraging wider understanding of global atmospheric and climatic problems. The model is simple enough to operate on a microcomputer, yet complex enough to explore seriously a wide range of policy scenarios.

At this time the AGM has no user's manual, but technical information is provided in the form of extensive comments inserted into the source code, which is written in FORTRAN 77. A limited description of the model will also be provided in a paper (publication pending).

Even though AGM is a relatively simple model by the standards of climatologists and atmospheric scientists, it is not for those who fear mathematics and computer science. Knowledge of FORTRAN is essential both for running the model and for understanding the technical comments in the model code.

This said, however, it must be emphasized that the model will be easily understood by anyone with a background in mathematics, science, and computers. The model could be very useful to a government's science advisor, for example, in explaining to leaders the national implications of the global climate changes taking place now as a result of anthropogenic alterations in the earth's atmosphere. AGM could also be very useful to university faculties teaching atmospheric science or climatology.

There is a need for a microcomputer-based climate model that is more user friendly and policy oriented than anything now available. Professor Harvey, the author of AGM, is considering revising it and two other atmospheric teaching models to make them more useful and meaningful to policymakers and average educated citizens. He would be interested to learn of other policy-oriented climate models for microcomputers.

Hardware and Software Requirements
IBM PC/XT/AT or compatible, 640 KB RAM. A FORTRAN 77 compiler.

Source
Prof. L. D. D. Harvey, Department of Geography, University of Toronto, 100 St. George Street, Toronto, Ontario M5S 1A1, Canada; telephone: (416) 978-2974; telefax: (416) 978-6729.

Biological and Conservation Data (BCD) System

Purpose
To provide an inexpensive, effective tool with which to inventory, rank, protect, and maintain endangered species.

Description
The BCD system, developed by the Nature Conservancy, is a relational database system designed to assist nations, provinces, and communities to identify unique and endangered species, take steps to protect the species, and track the future health and vitality of the species in the various locations where they are found. The BCD system can be used in support of a wide variety of conservation efforts, including the heritage programs undertaken by nations and provinces in cooperation with the Conservancy.

The BCD system is the product of eighteen years of experience in the protection of endangered species. The leadership of the Conservancy recognized at the outset that the effort needed to protect endangered species was vastly larger than the resources that were available. With this fact in mind, the Conservancy organized its program to: (a) identify scientifically and establish priorities for the many species needing protection, (b) maintain data on the exact geographic locations of the habitats in which endangered species are located, (c) organize the data in such a way that it can be quickly and effectively considered in land-acquisition and land-planning decisions, (d) seek means of acquiring or otherwise protecting specific parcels of land, and (e) monitor the conditions of the protected habitats and species.

The Conservancy's original set of databases operated on a Hewlett-Packard minicomputer. Careful, scientific thought went into its design. In 1985, the system design was updated and a microcomputer version was developed using dBASE III. Recently the microcomputer version of the BCD system has been converted to the Advanced Revelation (AREV) software, in part to take advantage of the multiple-valued fields, associations of multiple values, and variable-length fields provided by AREV. Since the amount of information to be recorded varies greatly from record to record, variable field lengths are essential if memory requirements are to be kept within manageable bounds.

Theory and Assumptions

The BCD system includes twenty-seven related, indexed files of data and information pertaining to biological and ecological element occurrences (locations), site and tract descriptions, protection agreements, legal requirements, and stewardship techniques. The twenty-seven files are organized under ten types: elements, element occurrences, sites, tracts, managed areas, projects, source abstract, contacts, action, and miscellaneous.

A wide range of reports can be produced with the BCD system, and the Conservancy has ready-made designs for some of the most useful reports: a "score card" element-ranking report, a site-tracking report, a site detail report, an element occurrence log sheet, a map margin sheet, and a summary report. The site-tracking report lists sites with their locational information, significance ratings and comments, and the tracts of land associated with each site along with status and comments. The site detail report lists each site with details on the tracts and the element occurrences on each tract.

Evaluation

Given the fact that there are an estimated three million species on the planet, it is clear that an effective program to protect endangered species requires the professional management of a very large amount of scientific, legal, economic, and geographic data. The BCD system is the only system capable of managing the data needed for an effective, site-specific, scientifically managed conservation program. (The International Union for the Conservation of Nature and Natural Resources in Gland, Switzerland, also has a database relating to endangered species, but its utility as a management tool is far more limited.)

Although the BCD system has very powerful capabilities, it is designed for use by people who have no previous computer experience. The system provides automatic vocabulary control, input pattern matching, conversion of data to the internal format, and display of output. A menu-driven application generator (see Figure 6-1) will assist in the creation of entry windows, report formats, data dictionaries, and other functions. Relational indices maintained by the system allow data entered in one file to be referenced automatically from other files. The twenty-seven databases are

so well interrelated that the user can flip from the entry screen for one file to that for another file with a single key stroke.

The Conservancy supports the BCD system with a 150-page users manual, training programs, and a staff that responds to telephone calls and correspondence. The software itself contains on-line help screens and is available in both English and Spanish. Development of a French version is in progress.

Hardware and Software Requirements

IBM/AT or compatible, 512 KB RAM (640

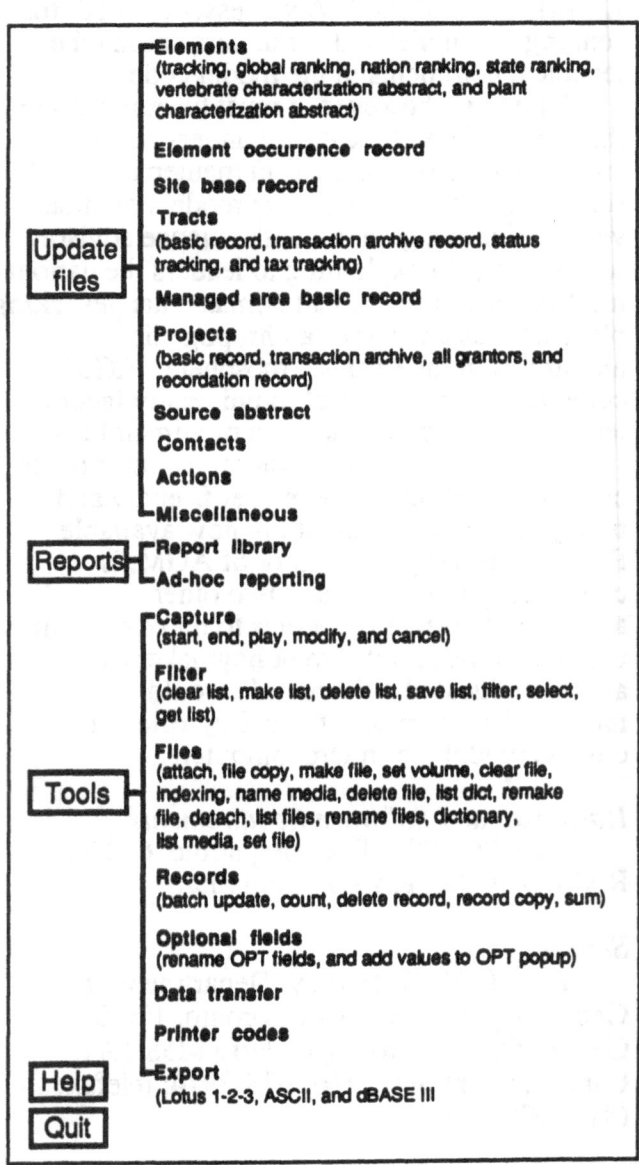

Figure 6-1: The menu-driven applications generator for the BCD system.

KB recommended) and a hard disk (40 MB recommended); DOS 3.1 or higher. The Advanced Revelation database software.

Source

The Nature Conservancy, Data Systems Divisions, 1815 North Lynn Street, Rosslyn, VA 22209, USA; telephone: (703) 841-5378; telex: 5106002960; telefax: (703) 841-1283. The price is negotiable. Purchase generally requires a cooperative agreement, licensing, and exchange of data. The price of the required Advanced Revelation database software is about US $500; it is available from: Revelation Technologies, Inc., 3633 136th Place, SE, Bellevue, WA 98006, USA; telephone: (206) 643-9898.

Range, Livestock, and Wildlife

Purpose

To help decision makers understand and evaluate policy alternatives for rangeland management.

Description

The Range, Livestock, and Wildlife model is focused on the sustainable use of rangeland. The model provides insights into the dynamics of range ecosystems as large as forty thousand hectares over periods of up to twenty-five years and facilitates the use of these insights in shaping the economic activities the range is expected to support.

The Range, Livestock, and Wildlife model was developed by Paul Faeth and Steve Berwick at the International Institute for Environment and Development (IIED), now part of WRI/IIED, with funding from the U.S. Agency for International Development. This model is one component of IIED's Integrated Planning Technology (IPT). The larger IPT framework includes interconnected models on land use, forestry, population, agriculture, socioeconomics, coastal resources, and range, livestock, and wildlife. The overall IPT methodology is addressed to the needs of project and research planners and involves much more than the models.

Theory and Assumptions

The Range, Livestock, and Wildlife model is the furthest advanced of the models that have been developed under the IPT approach. The

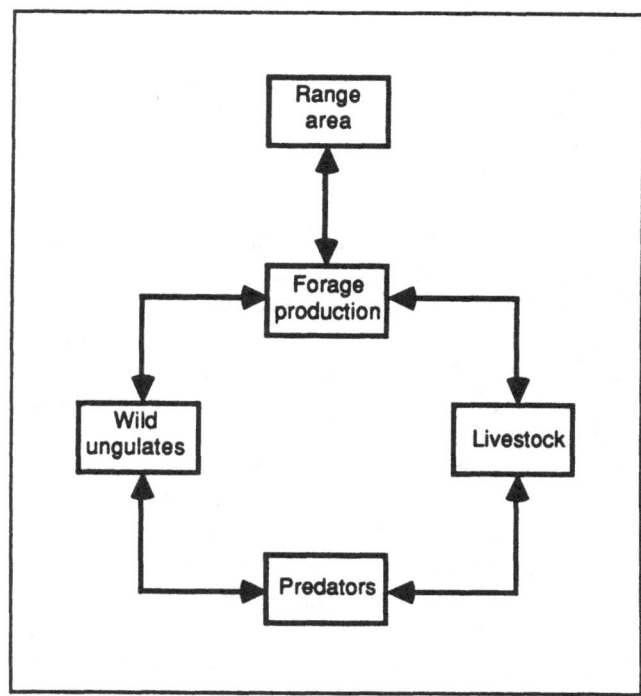

Figure 6-2: Linkages among the subsectors of the Range, Livestock, and Wildlife model.

model is a dynamic simulation and contains sectors devoted to range area, forage production, livestock, wild ungulates, and predators. (See Figure 6-2.) These five sectors are interlinked with more than 285 endogenous variables. Exogenous variables include precipitation, prices, human population growth rates, and the current density of animal stocks.

Evaluation

The program is incredibly easy to use. Anyone with a secondary education and access to a microcomputer could make use of the model.

One of the strengths of the IIED approach to model building is the modelers' consideration for the user. One way they show this consideration is by the inclusion of a glossary option under their main menu. The glossary provides definitions of specialized words, such as "herbaceous increaser," that are used in the model. This option is very helpful; the utility of models could be increased significantly if all model builders provided glossaries with their models.

At this writing the documentation, which is available only in English, is limited to flow diagrams and structure charts. While these are adequate to give a sense of the integrity of the model, more details are needed for an independent user. Fortunately, a book on the model is expected to be published by WRI/IIED in 1990. The book will present a compiled version of the model that has been adapted to commercial livestock and wildlife ranching in Africa and has been validated on the largest database available for this sector. With this book, the user's manual, and the disks, anyone familiar with how a range ecosystem functions (e.g., a rancher or a range scientist) could easily change the parameters to apply the model to range management in any part of the world.

The Range, Livestock, and Wildlife model is an excellent aid to decision making and an exceptional educational tool. It is recommended highly to anyone studying range management.

WRI/IIED also plans to publish a compiled version of its Forestry and Coastal Zone models sometime during the coming year.

Hardware and Software Requirements
IBM-PC/XT/AT or compatible with graphics card, MS-DOS 2.0 or higher. Although the model was developed with Professional DYNAMO Plus, the model comes compiled and does not require DYNAMO.

Source
Mr. Paul Faeth or Dr. Stephen Berwick, WRI/IIED, 1709 New York Avenue, NW, 7th Floor, Washington, DC 20006, USA; telephone: (202) 462-0900; telefax: (202) 638-0036; telex: 64414 WRIWAH. The price was not yet determined at the time of this review.

Enhanced Stream Water Quality Model (QUAL2E)

Purpose
To provide tools for water quality planning by simulating the behavior of the hydrologic and water quality components of a branching stream system or lake under the impact of a wide range of pollutants.

Description
QUAL2E is capable of simulating, in any combination, up to fifteen different water quality constituents: dissolved oxygen, biochemical oxygen demand, temperature, algae, organic nitrogen, ammonia, nitrite, nitrate, organic phosphorous, dissolved phosphorus, chloroforms, an arbitrary non-conservative constituent, and three arbitrary conservative constituents.

The model can be operated either as a steady-state or as a dynamic model. It can be used, for example, to study the impact of waste loads on in-stream water quality or to identify the magnitude and quality characteristics of non-point waste loads as part of a field-sampling program. It can also simulate the effects on water quality of diurnal variations in meteorological conditions and in algal growth and respiration.

QUAL2E gives both graphical and tabular output. Among other things, it can provide separate tables for each of the constitutes per computational element in each reach, i.e., similar stream section. It can produce these tables for each time increment requested.

The roots of this model go back to 1970 when the Texas Water Development Board designed QUAL1, a pioneering model of stream water quality. In 1972, the U.S. Environmental Protection Agency (EPA) based the development of the QUAL2 model on QUAL1. QUAL2 has now undergone thirteen years of additional revisions and modifications. The current (1985) model—QUAL2E, version 3.0—was developed under a cooperative agreement between the Department of Civil Engineering at Tufts University, the EPA's Center for Water Quality Modeling (CWQM), and the Environmental Research Laboratory in Athens, Georgia.

Theory and Assumptions
The basic equation solved by QUAL2E is the one dimensional advection-dispersion mass transport equation, which is numerically integrated over space and time for each water quality constituent. This equation includes the effects of sources, sinks, advection, dispersion, dilution, and constituent reactions and interactions.

Any branching, one-dimensional stream system can be simulated with QUAL2E. The stream is first divided into reaches, i.e., sections with similar hydraulic characteristics. Each reach has uniform hydraulic data, reaction rate coefficients, initial conditions, and incremental flows. For computational purposes, each reach is subdivided into smaller computational

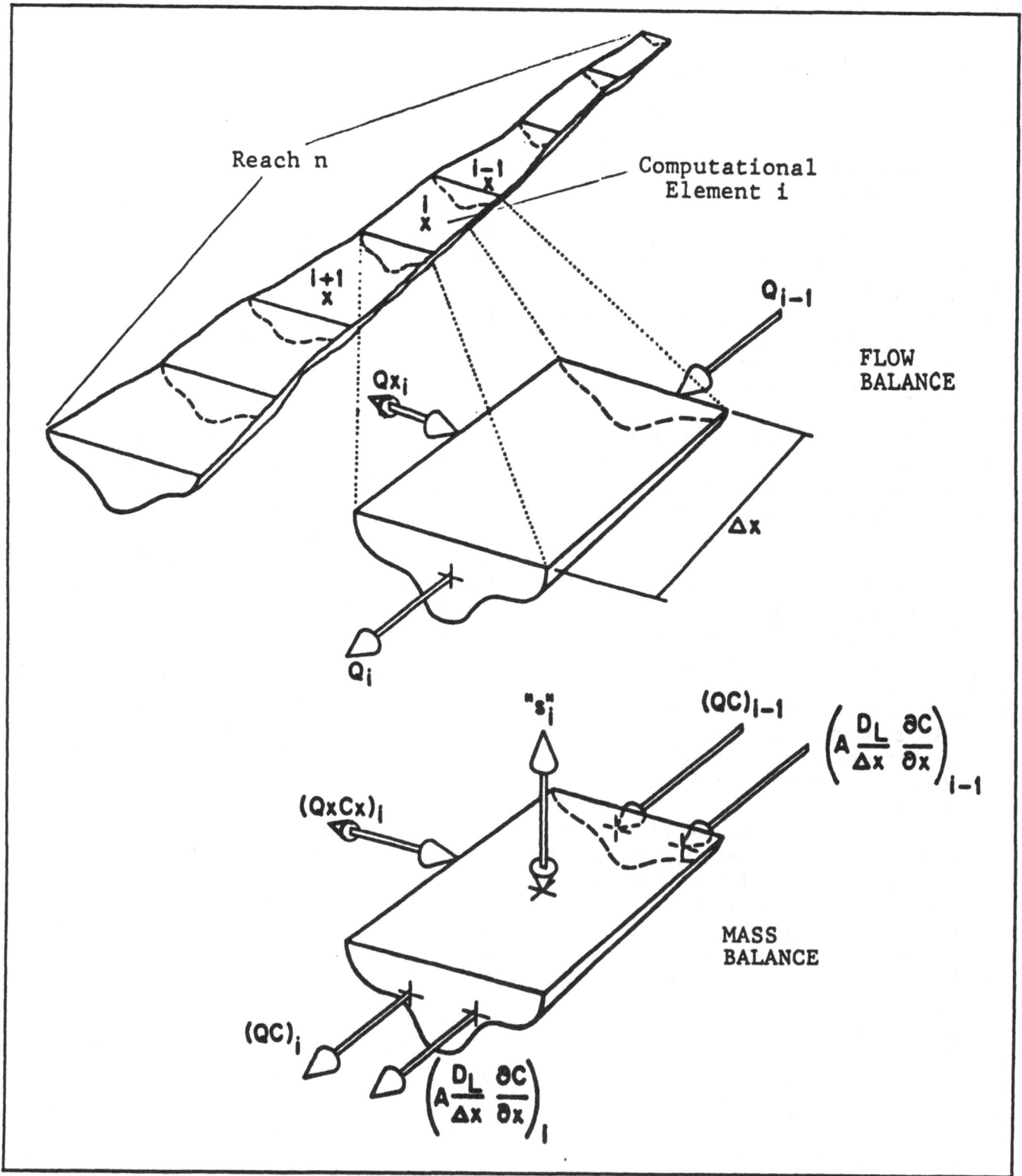

Figure 6-3: The discrete computational elements used in QUAL2E to represent a reach.

elements of equal length. (See Figure 6-3.) There are seven types of computational elements: a headwater element, a standard element, a junction element, an element just upstream from a junction, a waste input element, a withdrawal element, and a last element in system.

Uncertainty analysis can be performed with a modified version of the steady-state model called QUAL2EU. There are three uncertainty options available: sensitivity analysis, first-order error analysis, and Monte Carlo simulations. Using these capabilities, the user is able to assess the sensitivity of the output to uncertainties in the input data.

Both QUAL2E and QUAL2EU require significant amounts of data, and an interactive data preprocessor program, AQUAL2, has been developed to facilitate data preparation.

Evaluation

QUAL2E is one of the most widely used water quality models supported by the EPA or the U.S. Army Corps of Engineers. Anyone interested in water quality planning would benefit from this powerful model. The documentation is rather technical but effectively communicates the necessary information. The model is quite easy to install and, given the complexities of water quality analysis, reasonably simple to use.

QUAL2E has some dimensional limitations: a maximum of twenty-five reaches, no more than twenty computational elements per reach, no more than a total of 250 computational elements, a maximum of seven headwater elements, a maximum of six junction elements, and a maximum of twenty-five input and withdrawal elements.

These dimensional limitations could be eased through some additional programming using features of ANSI FORTRAN 77, which is the language in which QUAL2E is written.

Hardware and Software Requirements

IBM AT or compatible, math coprocessor chip; 256 KB RAM for QUAL2E, 512 KB RAM for QUAL2EU. DOS version 2.12 or higher, compiler for ANSI FORTRAN 77.

Source

Mr. David Disney, United States Environmental Protection Agency, Environmental Research Laboratory, Athens, Georgia 30613, USA; telephone: (404) 546-3123.

Model of Two-Dimensional Solute Transport and Dispersion in Groundwater (MOC)

Purpose

To stimulate groundwater flow and solute transport in one or two dimensions.

Description

MOC solves the groundwater flow equation by a finite-difference method. It then computes solute transport in the calculated flow field by the characteristics method. Both steady-state and transient flows can be calculated, and the aquifer may be heterogeneous and anisotropic. Forces resulting from differences in temperature or concentrations of dissolved solids are not considered.

Advective transport is computed by tracking particles; a finite-difference method is used after each step to treat dispersion, fluid sources and sinks, and velocity divergence. The code can accommodate injection and withdrawal wells, diffused leakage, and a variety of boundary and initial conditions. The modified version includes radioactive decay (but not formation of radioactive daughters) and equilibrium sorption.

The model was developed by L. F. Konikow and J. D. Bredehoeft of the U.S. Geological Survey. Modifications in MOC were made later by J. V. Tracy for the U.S. Nuclear Regulatory Commission.

Theory and Assumptions

MOC has two parts: the calculations of water flow and of solute transport. Water flow is calculated by computing the hydraulic-head field at each time step from a finite-difference approximation. The water velocity is calculated from the computed hydraulic-head gradient.

Solute transport is solved by the characteristics method. In this method, several particles are placed within each cell. In each time step, each particle is moved to a new position. An interim concentration within each cell is then calculated by averaging the concentrations corresponding to the particles that lie within the cell after being moved. The new concentration is computed by adjusting this interim concentration to account for dispersion, external fluid sources, and changes in saturated thickness. For the new version, the concentration is appropriately modified to account for sorption and/or decay.

The principal numerical approximations in MOC are the following: (a) time and space are discrete variables; (b) off-diagonal elements of the transmissivity tensor are neglected; (c) particle velocity is constant over each time step rather than following curved streamlines; (d) concentrations are averaged over a cell; (e) dispersion and recharge occur in "bursts" at the beginning of each time step rather than continuously; and (f) constant-head boundaries are approximated by zones of high leakance.

The following are the main assumptions: (a) Darcy's law is valid and hydraulic-head gradients are the only significant driving mechanism for fluid flow; (b) the porosity and hydraulic conductivity of the aquifer are constant with time, and porosity is uniform in space; (c) gradients of fluid density, viscosity, and temperature do not affect the velocity distribution;(d) the two-dimensional solute transport equation is valid; (e) sorption may be represented as equilibrium adsorption; (f) vertical variations in head and concentration are negligible; and (g) the aquifer is homogeneous and isotopic with respect to the coefficients of longitudinal and transverse dispersivity.

Evaluation

MOC is a thoroughly tested and documented model that would be well-suited for solving single-aquifer problems. Its high degree of acceptance makes it stand out among solute transport codes.

A principal disadvantage of MOC is that nodes must be placed in an equally spaced rectangular array. Also, it is restricted to equilibrium adsorption (either linear or non-linear).

A user's guide and various other forms of documentation are available.

Hardware and Software Requirements

The original program is written in FORTRAN IV and is compatible with many computers. It has been run successfully on Honeywell, IBM, DEC, Univac, and CDC computers. The revised program is written in FORTRAN 77 and, apparently, has run on IBM and CDC computers. A microcomputer version of the code is also available.

Source

A microcomputer version is available from: International Ground Water Modeling Center, Holcomb Research Institute, Butler University, Indianapolis, IN 46208, USA. The computer card deck of the original code can be obtained, at cost, from: Mr. Ralph N. Eicher, Chief, Office of Teleprocessing, 805 National Center, U.S. Geological Survey, Reston, VA 22092, USA.

Waterborne Toxic Risk Assessment Model (WTRISK)

Purpose

To estimate the risks of adverse human health effects from substances emitted into the air, surface water, soil, and ground water from a source such as a coal-fired power plant.

Description

WTRISK is a tool for the assessment of risks associated with the release of toxic chemicals, particularly into surface waters. The chemicals may have been emitted into the environment from a fossil-fuel power plant, for example, or from another source.

Theory and Assumptions

WTRISK employs a risk assessment methodology (see Figure 6-4) in which the inputs and outputs of independent mathematical models are linked to determine pollutant concentrations in all appropriate environmental media. The linked models simulate the emission of a potentially toxic substance, its transport and chemical transformation, the potential exposure of a nearby population, and the health effects of such exposure. On the basis of the resulting information about environmental concentrations, users can calculate exposure rates and combine them with regional population data and dose-response models to determine the probable incidence of chronic health effects in the area surrounding a power plant or some other source of toxic chemicals.

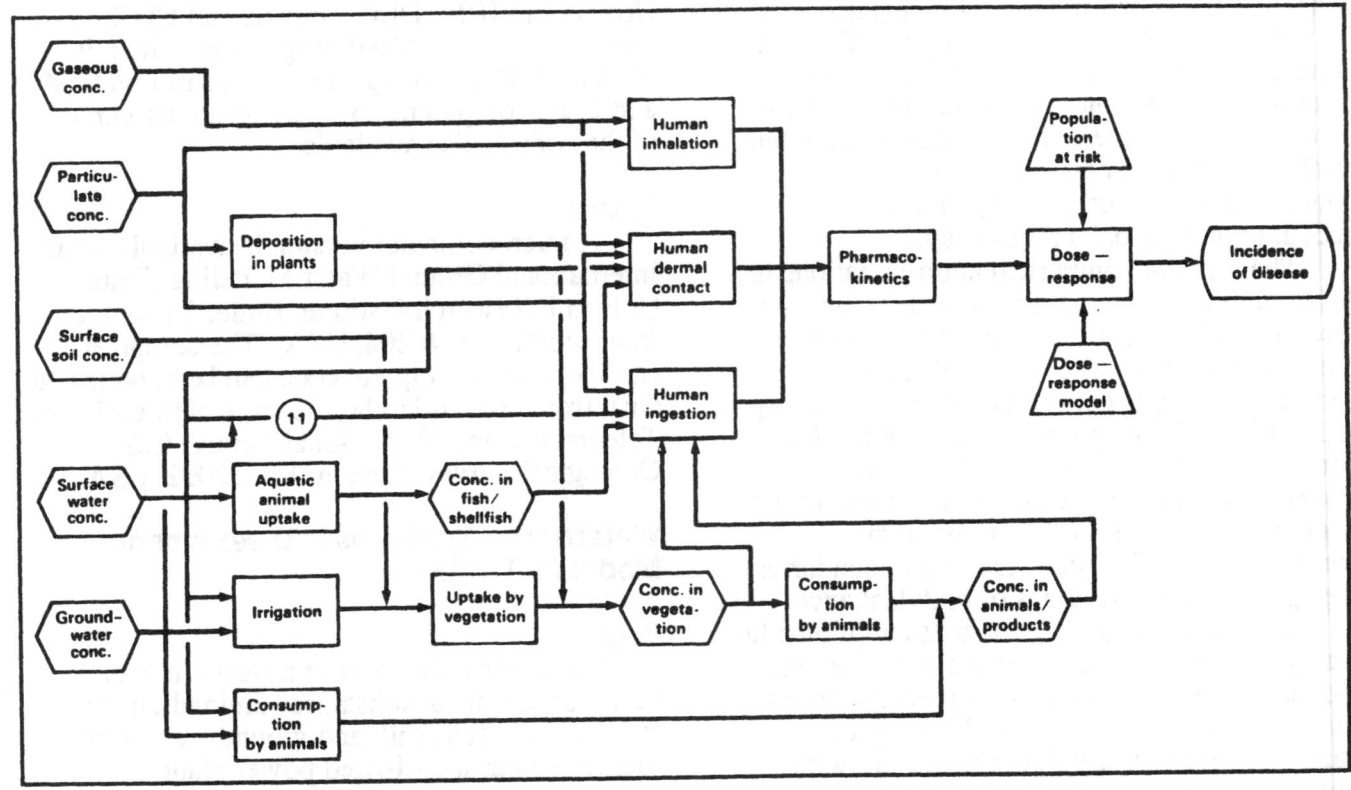

Figure 6-4: Part of the risk assessment framework used in WTRISK.

Evaluation

WTRISK is a flexible framework for risk assessment. The methodology emphasizes discharges to surface water but incorporates intermedia transfers among air, soil, and groundwater as well. The model is relatively user friendly, and even assists the user in estimating the source terms, i.e., the quantities of toxic chemicals emitted into the environment.

A technical report and a draft user's manual, "Water Emissions Risk Assessment Model (WTRISK) User's Manual," are available.

Hardware and Software Requirements
IBM PC/XT/AT or compatible.

Source

Manager, Software and Publications Distribution, Electric Power Research Institute, 3412 Hillview Avenue, P.O. Box 10412, Palo Alto, CA 94303, USA; telephone: (415) 855-2000.

Acid Deposition (ADEPT) Model

Purpose

To analyze alternative strategies for dealing with the problem of acid deposition.

Description

ADEPT is a decision framework for integrating available information and uncertainties about the consequences of alternative strategies for dealing with acid deposition. The program is tailored specifically for the comparison of strategies for acid-deposition control and mitigation. In addition, the program can be used to evaluate alternative research projects intended to resolve uncertainties in areas such as long-range transport and the ecological consequences of acid deposition.

Theory and Assumptions

The model reviewed, version 2.2, uses a decision tree framework showing the relationships among control strategies, mitigation measures, emissions at the sources, long-range transport, deposition, and ecological consequences. The decisions of interest include reductions in sulfur oxide and other emissions thought to be precursors of acid deposition, mitigation of acid deposition impacts through means such as liming of waterways and soils, and choice of strategies for research. As illustrated in Figure 6-5, there are three main submodels of the framework: the source submodel (emissions and control technologies); the transport and conversion submodel (long-range transport and chemical conversion in the atmosphere); and the receptor submodel (ecological impacts).

The software provides two versions of the decision tree model. The basic decision tree addresses decisions on emissions control and mitigation in the immediate future and a decade hence; it includes uncertainties in the long-range transport and ecological impacts. The research-emphasis decision tree addresses the effect of research funding on obtaining new information as the basis for future decisions.

Evaluation

To a greater or lesser extent, every nation is suffering from the effects of acid deposition. Analysis of alternative actions is a complex task. This program is a useful framework for systematizing the analysis of alternative strategies.

ADEPT is described in *Acid Deposition: Decision Framework*, vol. 1, *Description of Conceptual Framework and Decision Tree Models*, (Electric Power Research Institute). Volume 2 contains the equations for the model. A videotape on ADEPT is also available.

Hardware and Software Requirements

IBM-PC/XT/AT and compatibles, at least one 360 KB floppy disk drive. Recommended: two floppy disk drives, a math coprocessor chip, and Microsoft FORTRAN, version 3.1.

Source

Manager, Software and Publications Distribution, Electric Power Research Institute, 3412 Hillview Avenue, P.O. Box 10412, Palo Alto, CA 94303, USA; telephone: (415) 855-2000. Order EPRI report no. EA-2540, vol.1.

User's Network for Applied Modeling of Air Pollution (UNAMAP)

Purpose

To provide tools for analyzing the implications for air quality of a wide variety of possible development projects and programs and for assessing alternative air-pollution control regulations.

Description

The U.S. Environmental Protection Agency (EPA) is responsible for administering regulations for protecting the air quality in the United States. One of the major challenges

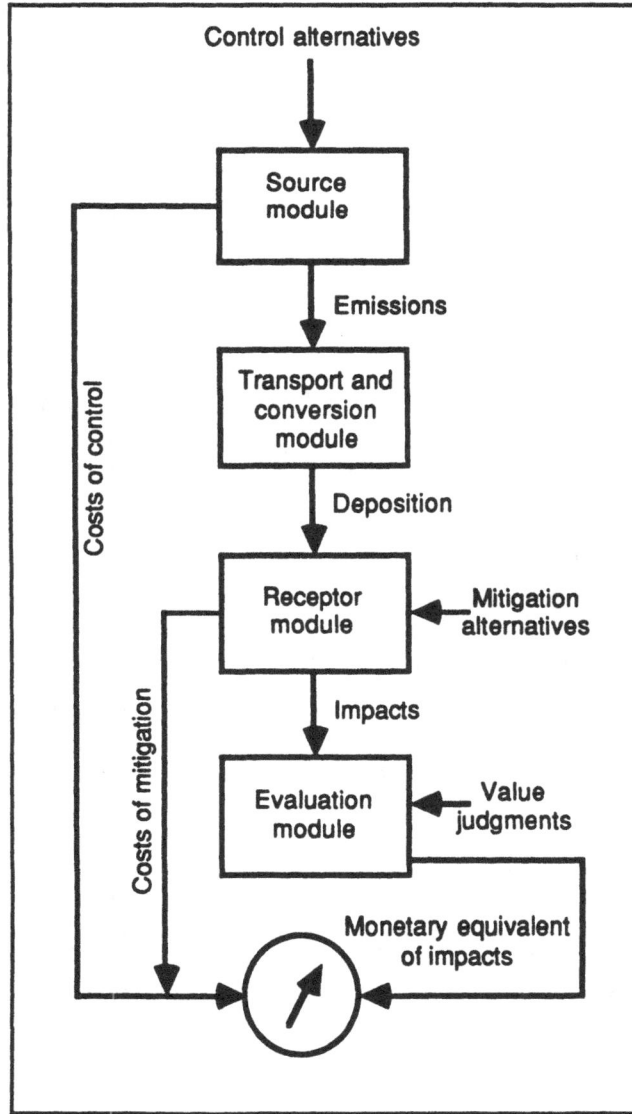

Figure 6-5: Overview of the Acid Deposition (ADEPT) decision framework.

facing EPA is relating rates of emissions of various pollutants to the resulting concentrations in the air.

Dispersion modeling is a method for estimating concentrations that result from discharges of substances. (See Figure 6-6.) While extensive field measurements are more accurate, dispersion modeling provides reasonably exact results and is far less expensive. For the cost of one or two field measurements, dispersion calculations can be made for hundreds or even thousands of locations.

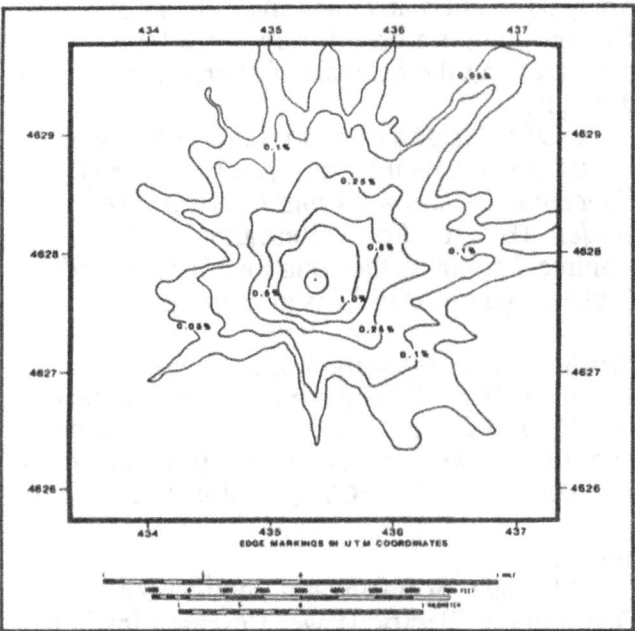

Figure 6-6: Isopleths of probabilities that concentrations will exceed 10 ppm for 1000 pound releases of chlorine over a 20-minute period.

Dispersion modeling is generally performed for one of three reasons. First, it can help to optimize the investment in air-pollution control equipment as well as determine suitable stack heights. Second, it can provide estimates of the consequences of accidental toxic gas releases. Third, it may be required by regulatory authorities as a condition for granting a permit. In the United States, most dispersion modeling is performed for the last reason.

Over the past twenty years, the U.S. EPA has developed and identified a series of dispersion models that it recommends. These models are made available through the EPA-sponsored User's Network for Applied Modeling of Air Pollution (UNAMAP), which sells a collection of recommended models through the National Technical Information Service (NTIS). The current collection (version 6) is called UNAMAP6.

There are thirty-three models in UNAMAP6. Described below are some of the most widely used models:

CALINE3 calculates carbon monoxide concentrations near highways and arterial streets.

CDM-2.0 (Climatological Dispersion Model) determines long-term quasi-stable pollutant concentrations.

CRSTER estimates ground-level concentrations resulting from up to nineteen collated, elevated stack-emissions.

ISCLT (Industrial Source Complex Long-Term) is a steady-state Gaussian plume model that can be used to calculate long-term pollutant concentrations from an industrial source complex.

ISCST (Industrial Source Complex Short-Term) is a steady-state Gaussian plume model which can be used to calculate short-term pollutant concentrations from an industrial source complex.

RAM is a short-term Gaussian steady-state algorithm for estimating concentrations of stable pollutants; it has been applied frequently in urban areas.

RAMMET is a program that processes hourly meteorological data for use with several dispersion models.

Theory and Assumptions
The theory and assumptions underlying UNAMAP6 models are far too complex to be discussed here. Readers interested in the details of specific models should contact the U.S. Environmental Protection Agency (see source paragraph below for address) to obtain the thirteen-page brochure, *Description of UNAMAP (version 6)*.

Evaluation

The UNAMAP6 set of air pollution models is probably the finest collection of such models available. Any nation without a comparable set of air pollution models should consider obtaining and applying the UNAMAP6 models.

The UNAMAP6 models are available on magnetic tape from the U.S. National Technical Information Service (NTIS), but in this form they operate only on mainframe computers.

Fortunately several companies and consultants have purchased the UNAMAP6 models and adapted them for use on microcomputers. The microcomputer versions have a core program identical to the mainframe versions but in addition have helpful menus, data entry aids, and other useful features. They are generally much more user friendly than the original mainframe versions. In addition, some of the companies supplying the microcomputer versions also provide consulting services, weather data (needed with most models), and training.

Hardware and Software Requirements

The hardware and software requirements vary with the specific model and supplier. In most cases, an IBM AT or compatible with a math coprocessor chip is adequate.

Source

The microcomputer versions of individual models are available from several companies. One such company is: Trinity Consultants, Inc., 100 North Central Expressway, Suite 600, Richardson, TX 75080, USA; telephone: (214) 234-8567; telex 265193 TRNTY UR. The price varies by model and supplier.

The whole set of mainframe versions of the models and the individual manuals (both technical and user's) can be obtained from: Computer Products, National Technical Information Service, 5285 Port Royal Road, Springfield, VA 22161, USA; telephone: (206) 487-4650. Order PB 86-222 361/AS. The price is US $1285, subject to change.

Complex Terrain Dispersion Model (CTDM)

Purpose

To calculate air pollution contractions for various pollutants discharged into the environment by a smokestack near complex terrain.

Description

CTDM is a refined plume dispersion model for elevated point sources near complex terrain. It contains algorithms that are suitable for neutral and stably stratified flows.

CTDM is a significant advance over previous air pollution models, which were not able to deal with the effects of complex terrain on the dispersion of a plume. Also, CTDM is the first major air pollution model developed by EPA that was designed from the outset to be operable on a microcomputer.

Theory and Assumptions

The CTDM package (see Figure 6-7) consists of six component programs: (a) the Complex Terrain Dispersion Model, (b) a terrain preprocessor, (c) a meteorological preprocessor, (d) a receptor coordinate generator, (e) a graphical concentration display program, and (f) an interactive program that allows the user to modify model inputs easily and run CTDM in a case-study mode.

The central feature of the CTDM methodology is its use of a critical dividing-streamline height (H-crit) to separate the flow in the vicinity of a hill into two layers. Flow in the upper layer has sufficient kinetic energy to pass over the top of the hill, while streamlines in the lower layer are constrained to flow in a horizontal plane around the hill. Two separate components of CTDM compute ground-level concentrations resulting from plume material in each of these flows: LIFT handles the flow above H-crit, and WRAP handles the flow below H-crit. Hourly profiles of wind and temperature measurements are used by CTDM to compute plume rise, the value of H-crit, and the Froude number above H-crit. The profiles of turbulence data are used to compute extent of dispersion of the plume at various heights.

CTDM requires considerable detail in meteorological input data and terrain information. Preprocessors specifically designed for CTDM are included for both types of input data.

Evaluation

While CTDM contains algorithms that are suitable for neutral and stably stratified flows,

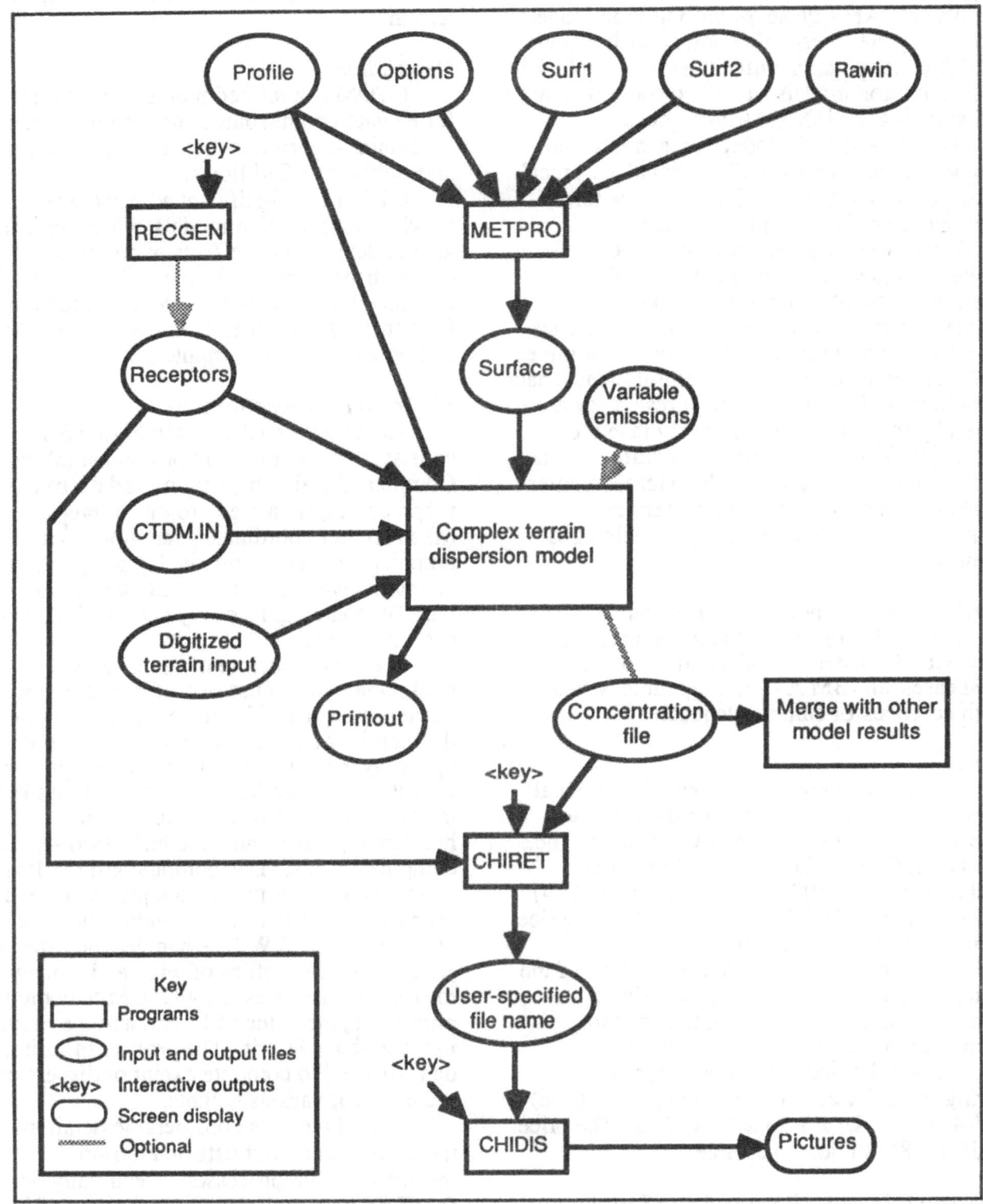

Figure 6-7: Interactions among the components of the CTDM system.

the sequential hourly data sets that are frequently used for impact assessments also contain hours characterized by unstable conditions. The development and evaluation of modules to account for these unstable conditions are presently underway within the Meteorology and Assessment Division of the EPA Atmospheric Sciences Research Laboratory.

Hardware and Software Requirements
All the programs, except the three graphics programs, PLOTCON, RECGEN and CHIDIS, are written in FORTRAN 77 and require no special hardware except a math coprocessor chip. The graphics programs are written in BASIC. The largest program, CTDM, requires about 240 KB of RAM. A text editor is needed to prepare input files. The interactive set-up program, SETUP, is a FORTRAN program based on PC/MS-DOS file manipulation commands; however, with minor modifications, SETUP could be made to run on other systems. The concentration display post processor is designed for EGA or CGA monitors.

Source
Both the model and user support are available from: Ms. Donna Burns, U.S. Environmental Protection Agency, Atmospheric Sciences Research Laboratory, Research Triangle Park, NC 27711, USA; telephone: (919) 541-1321.

Computer Aided Management of Emergency Operations (CAMEO II)

Purpose
To help local planning committees prepare for emergencies created by the release of hazardous chemicals into the air.

Description
CAMEO was developed jointly by the National Oceanic and Atmospheric Administration and the U.S. Environmental Protection Agency to help federal, state, and local governments and industry comply with Title III of the Superfund Amendments and Reauthorization Act of 1986. This act assigns four responsibilities to local governments and private industries regarding hazardous chemicals: emergency planning, emergency notification, community right to know, toxic

chemical release reporting. CAMEO II provides assistance in each of these areas.

Theory and Assumptions
CAMEO II is composed of seventeen databases, a mapping facility, an air dispersion model, and linkages to other external communications and mapping programs all contained within a Hypercard framework. One of the databases provides response information and handling recommendations for 2,629 chemicals.

One of the many impressive features of the program is a chemical code breaker. With this feature users can search the chemical database even if they have only partial information on the released hazardous material. For example, they may have only half of the Chemical Abstracts Service (CAS) registration number and a third of the chemical formula if identifying placards are partially destroyed in an explosion or fire. The code breaker program permits users to search the database for all of the chemicals having the known partial descriptors. Following the search, CAMEO II presents the physical properties of the hazardous materials that match the partial description. The released material can probably be identified then on the basis of observable physical characteristics.

Once the name of the chemical is known, CAMEO II can provide data on the health hazards, fire and non-fire hazards, first aid measures, fire fighting strategies, and protective clothing requirements.

CAMEO II also has an air dispersion model and mapping capabilities to determine how and where the chemical will spread. The air dispersion model is a Gaussian puff model and has extremely good graphic capabilities.

Handling a chemical spill is not the only use of CAMEO II. The model can also be utilized in the emergency planning process. With it, a user can create a series of interrelated maps that are tied to the chemical databases. These could include maps of facilities storing specific hazardous chemicals (see Figure 6-8), maps indicating the transport of hazardous chemicals, and maps of hospitals, senior citizens' homes, and other sites where people would require special help evacuating the area in case of chemical spills.

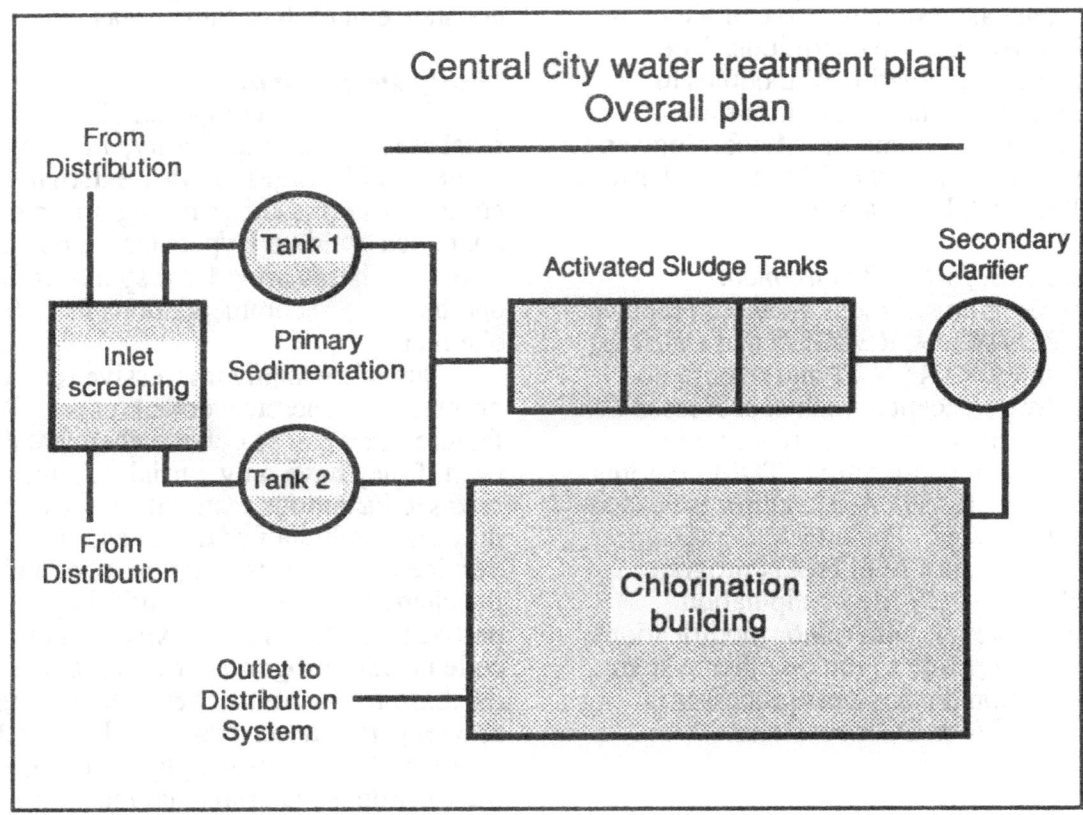

Figure 6-8: Sample building drawing that can be made using CAMEO II.

The user can also do both vulnerability and risk screening and vulnerability and risk scenario modeling using CAMEO II to produce worst and realistic case scenarios of hazardous chemicals spills.

Evaluation

All of the CAMEO II databases are interconnected and the framework used to interconnect them makes this program very easy to use. The documentation is excellent. It is written in a style that is easy to understand and does not assume extensive computer expertise. CAMEO II is one of the best computer software tools we have seen.

Hardware and Software Requirements

Apple Macintosh Plus, SE, or II computer, hard disk (minimum 11 MB of free space), Apple computer's Finder version 6.0, and System version 4.2 or higher, Hypercard 1.1 and its

home stack, an object oriented drawing program, and a painting program that can open MacPaint documents.

Source

Ms. Jane Snider, U.S. Department of Commerce, National Oceanic and Atmospheric Administration, Hazardous Materials Response Branch (N/OMA34), 11400 Rockville Pike, Rockville, MD 20852, USA; telephone: (301) 443-8933. The price had not yet been determined at the time of this review.

Transformer/Capacitor Risk Management (TRIM)

Purpose

To evaluate alternative utility actions and regulatory policies concerning electric equipment containing polychlorinated biphenols (PCBs).

Description

Since the late 1970s, the U.S. Environmental Protection Agency (EPA) has regulated utility equipment containing polychlorinated biphenyls (PCBs) under the Toxic Substances Control Act. Dielectric fluid composed largely or solely of PCBs is currently used by U.S. utilities in over thirty thousand large electric transformers and in several million capacitors. In addition, several million mineral oil transformers are potentially contaminated with small amounts of PCBs.

EPA regulations initiated in 1984 addressed risks from fires involving PCB-containing equipment. The primary concern in PCB fires is the formation of polychlorinated dibenzo-p-dioxins (PCDDs) and polychlorinated dibenzofurans (PCDFs)—potentially much more toxic than PCBs—as combustion by-products. Because of the possible danger to the public and workers from such fires and the large economic stakes involved in removing existing equipment, there is a need for an analytic tool to evaluate the effectiveness of policies to reduce risks.

TRIM describes the mechanisms by which PCB-containing electrical equipment could pose health or environmental risks. The model represents elements of concern in regulating PCBs, including an inventory of equipment over time; frequency of incidents involving release of PCBs, PCDFs, and PCDDs; quantities released; amount of human exposure; and human health effects. Economic considerations represented include costs of replacing equipment and of cleaning up after release incidents. The regulatory options that may be studied include phase-out programs, retrofitting, risk reduction measures, or combinations of the above. The dielectric fluids that may be investigated include askarel, contaminated oil, mineral oil, and silicone or other substitutes for PCB fluid.

Theory and Assumptions

TRIM includes two key components: a decision tree and a deterministic model. The decision tree represents the interaction of the principal regulatory decision with critical uncertainties that can have a major impact on the ultimate outcomes. Both near-term decisions and longer-range decisions subsequent to the development of new information can be included.

The deterministic model (see Figure 6-9) traces the potential impacts of PCBs from their use in electrical equipment, through release due to accidents or other incidents and resulting potential human and environmental exposure, to any ensuing health or environmental effects. The deterministic model is composed of six submodels representing equipment use and replacement, spills and other incidents, human exposure, human health effects, environmental exposure, and environmental effects.

Evaluation

While TRIM was developed for application in the United States, the model can be used

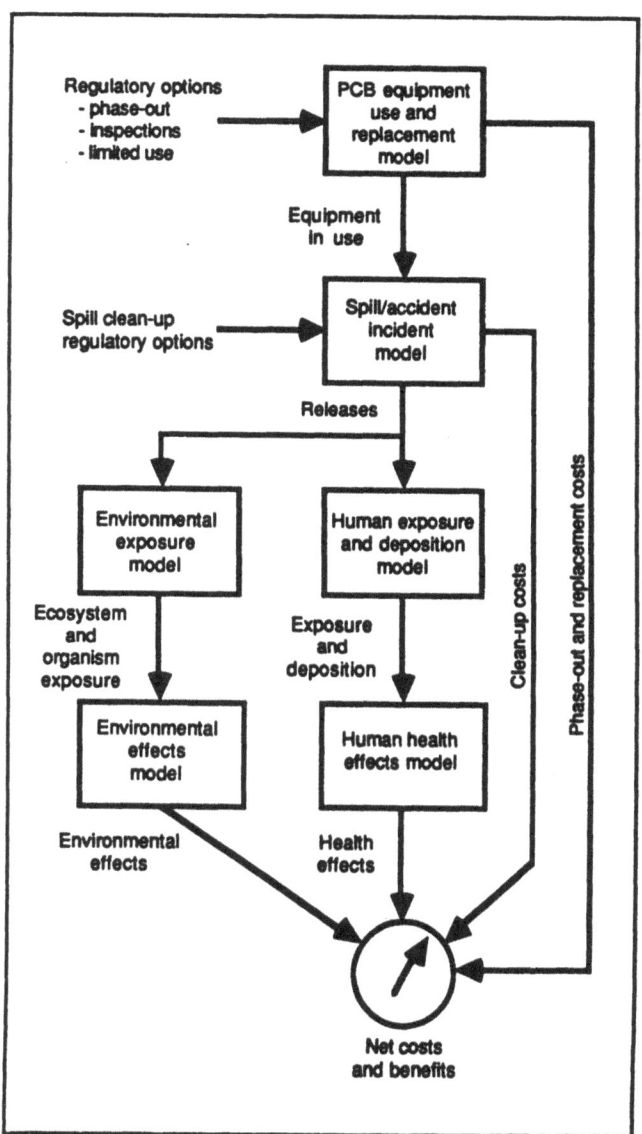

Figure 6-9: Relationships among the components of the TRIM deterministic model.

anywhere. Nations around the world face the identical problem—limiting public and worker exposure to PCBs and their more toxic combustion products. Analyses performed with TRIM can provide a basis in any nation for improved understanding and insight into the costs and benefits of alternative regulatory actions. TRIM can also be used by provincial agencies and other interested parties—e.g., a specific utility—to analyze the PCB problem on a sub-national scale.

While utility concerns were the original motivation for the development of TRIM, the model can be readily applied to non-utility equipment types that contain PCBs or other related chemicals that may present health hazards.

Hardware and Software Requirements
IBM PC/XT/AT or compatible.
Recommended: 640 KB RAM and a math coprocessor chip.

Source
Manager, Software and Publications Distribution, Electric Power Research Institute, 3412 Hillview Avenue, P.O. Box 10412, Palo Alto, CA 94303, USA; telephone: (415) 855-2000.

7. Natural Resources

Introduction

A nation's long-term development and security depend greatly on the management of natural resources. In this chapter we focus on three: water, forests, and fisheries. No country can prosper if its water resources are neglected. Healthy forests are also needed, to provide vital wood products, fuel, control of run-off, habitat for wildlife and endangered species, and recreational benefits. Fisheries are an important source of protein in diets of every nation. Yet, despite their importance these resources are being misused throughout the world. Water is polluted, forests are being destroyed, and fisheries are threatened. The following programs can help nations looking for better ways to manage these precious resources.

The management of freshwater supplies involves the management of riverbasins. This is a critical and complex task, since everything that occurs in a riverbasin is interlinked. That is why there are so many political tensions along national boundaries that cut across river basins: the interests of the up-stream and down-stream populations are often in conflict. Now HEC-1, a very powerful tool for the hydraulic analysis of an entire riverbasin, is available in a microcomputer version. The Irrigation Development Model (IRRIGM) provides an important advance in integrated analysis of the economic, agricultural, demographic, ecologic, and hydraulic development of a river basin. Because it addresses such a wide range of issues (including extension and credit programs), IRRIGM has a high potential for improving the long-term benefits derived from large irrigation projects.

Another important part of water management is the provision of safe drinking water and the sanitary disposal of sewage wastes. The Microcomputer Programs for Improved Planning and Design For Water Supply and Waste Disposal Systems (WSWDS) is a well-designed program for planning, improving, and maintaining water and sewage systems in developing countries. The Water Supply Simulation Model (WSSM) addresses related issues in the context of industrialized nations.

In both developing and industrialized nations there is a continuing need to forecast urban water usage for comparison with expected water supplies. Water Use Forecasting (WATFORE) performs this function very effectively.

Nations everywhere are becoming increasingly concerned about the recharge and pollution of aquifers from which vital water is pumped. Until recently three-dimensional groundwater models could only be run on mainframe computers. The Modular Three-Dimensional Groundwater Flow Model (MOD3D) provides, at a relatively modest cost, tremendous new assistance in the protection and maintenance of groundwater.

From the earliest of civilizations, canals have been important means of transportation for goods and water. The design, management, and operation of canals is, however, very complicated. Now, the Utah State University Hydraulic Model (CANALS) provides an inexpensive means of analyzing the functioning of complex canal systems.

A wide range of microcomputer software is now available for managing forests of many kinds. Only one forest-management program, The Woodsman's Ideal Growth Projection System (TWIGS), is reviewed here. References to many others can be found in "Catalogs, Books, and Newsletters."

While fuelwood plantations are a minor resource compared to forests, in many nations they are now being started and are providing important benefits. BIOCUT provides a convenient means of planning and managing the business aspects of these plantations.

Fire presents a major threat to fuelwood plantations and forests alike. [Fire] BEHAVE is a forest fire simulation program that can be used for training, research, and emergency planning, and even for directing fire-fighting efforts.

Trees in urban areas provide fuelwood in many countries and aesthetic benefits in all. Maintenance of an urban forest is, however, an expensive task. The program Tree Manager can significantly increase the productivity and quality of urban tree management.

Sport fishing and the associated business it generates can provide a very positive stimulus to a region's economy. The development of a successful sport fishing industry, however, requires careful, integrated management of the region's forests and fisheries. The Fishery Management Model for the Rio Grande Basin (RIOFISH), developed to improve angling sport fishing in the Rio Grande river, is a framework for considering the wide range of factors affecting river fishing. While this model has many features that relate specifically to the Rio Grande, its general structure could easily be adapted for use elsewhere.

Fish hatchery operations have unique and complex data storage and computational challenges. The Computerized Hatchery Optimization Program (CHOP) is a useful way to increase productivity in hatchery operations.

Effective management of fisheries relies on accurate estimates of fish populations, but making these estimates is a challenging task. Two programs, [Fish] Population Estimate and MicroFish, provide help.

A nation's fisheries can never be managed effectively unless there is widespread public understanding of the dynamics of fisheries resources and political support for wise management policies. Fish Banks, Ltd. is a highly effective way to teach the fundamentals of fisheries management to groups of all ages—and have a party at the same time.

HEC-1

Purpose
To stimulate the rise and fall of a river following precipitation.

Description
The HEC-1 model simulates the surface runoff response of a river basin to precipitation by representing the basin as an interconnected system of hydrologic and hydraulic components. Each component models an aspect of the overall precipitation and run-off process within a portion of the basin, commonly referred to as a subbasin. A component may represent a surface runoff entity, a stream channel, or a reservoir. Representation of a component requires a set of

parameters that specify the particular characteristics of the component and mathematical relations that describe the physical processes. The result of the modeling process is the computation of streamflow hydrographs at desired locations in the river basin.

HEC-1 was developed by Leo R. Beard at the Hydrologic Engineering Center in 1967 and has since undergone a number of updates and modifications. The microcomputer version was developed in 1984.

Theory and Assumptions
The stream network model component is the foundation of the entire program. It represents a river basin as an interconnected system of hydrologic and hydraulic components and has the capacity to calculate flood hydrographs at designated locations in a river basin. (See Figure 7-1.)

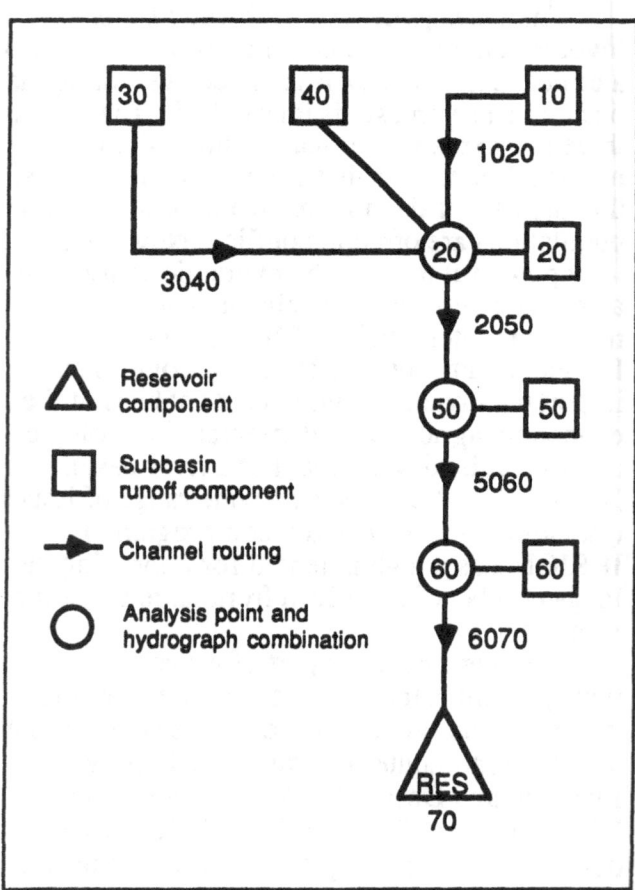

Figure 7-1: A river basin represented as a stream network for analysis with HEC-1.

The other seven components all depend on the stream network model and have more specific and specialized functions. The land surface runoff component represents the movement of water over the land surface and in stream channels. The river routing component represents flood plane movement in a river channel. The combined river routing and subbasin runoff components represent the intricacies of rainfall runoff and stream routing problems. The reservoir component represents the storage-outflow characteristics of a reservoir, lake, detention pond, highway culvert, etc. The diversion component represents channel diversion, stream bifurcations, or any other transfer of the flow of water. The pump component simulates the use of pumping plants that lift runoff out of low-lying ponding areas. The hydrograph transformations provide a capability to alter computed flows based on user-defined criteria.

Evaluation

HEC-1 is not a quick, easy answer to all water problems. Large numbers of inputs are required, and capable staff are needed to collect the data. A large volume of output is produced from the model, and a competent staff is needed to interpret and apply this output.

There are certain limitations in the HEC-1 model. Simulations are limited to a single storm because the model makes no provision for changes of soil moisture during the period between storms. Although the model results are expressed in terms of discharge rather than in terms of flood stages, output can be converted to stages on the basis of a user-specified rating curve. Stream flow routings are performed by hydrologic routing methods and do not reflect the full St. Venant equations; this means that the model should not be used for very flat river slopes. Reservoir routings are based on the modified Puls techniques, which are not appropriate where reservoir gates are operated to reduce flooding at downstream locations.

This said, however, HEC-1 can be of much help in water flow management for a wide range of river basins. Any agency concerned with river management that does not have an equivalent or superior model available would do well to consider acquiring HEC-1.

Hardware and Software Requirements

IBM AT or compatible, 512 KB RAM, MS-DOS, hard disk.

Source

U.S. Army Corp of Engineers, The Hydrologic Engineering Center, 609 Second Street, Davis, CA 95616, USA. The model is currently free, but the situation may change.

Irrigation Development Model (IRRIGM)

Purpose

To facilitate the design, implementation, and management of a large irrigation project in a developing country by simulating the system and measuring the relative cost and effectiveness of alternative actions.

Description

IRRIGM simulates an irrigation system and its interaction with the surrounding agricultural economy. The model deals with all three of the components of a typical irrigation project, namely, the physical irrigation system, the extension service program, and the credit program. The design of the physical system is taken largely as a given. The model focuses primarily on the maintenance, extension, and credit programs as policy variables having a major impact on the success of irrigation development projects. The model is particularly helpful in identifying the key factors that determine the long-term cost and effectiveness of the system.

Paul Faeth wrote IRRIGM as a part of a master's thesis at Dartmouth College. He then moved to the U.S. Department of Agriculture, where he applied and refined the model.

Theory and Assumptions

IRRIGM is partitioned into four sectors: (a) the biological and physical processes sector, (b) the design, implementation, and maintenance sector, (c) the farm socioeconomic sector, and (d) the project components sector. Each sector is influenced, directly and indirectly, by the other sectors. (See Figure 7-2.)

The biological and physical processes sector simulates crop growth and crop storage. This sector specifically represents seed technology, soil water, fertility, vegetation, soil nitrogen, and family food stocks.

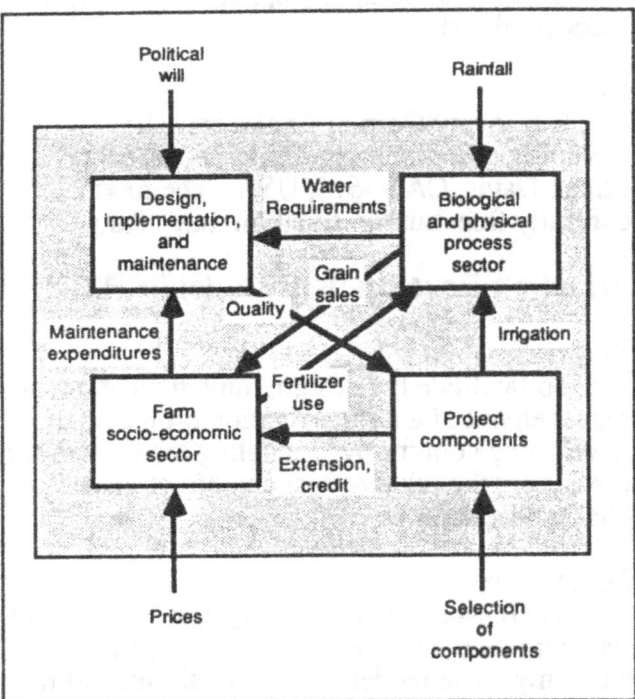

Figure 7-2: Conceptual overview of IRRIGM.

The project design, implementation, and maintenance sector simulates the sociopolitical pressures that influence the quality of design, construction, and maintenance. This sector specifically represents the incentives to collect information on the pace and quality of construction, on the work to be completed, and on the work completed to acceptable standards.

The farm socioeconomics sector models credit, extension services, and other factors related to the farmers' ability to increase their agricultural production and the incentives for them to do so. Among the details included in the sector are the farmers' cash on hand, savings, expenses (fertilizer, maintenance, etc.), loan payments, and perceived risks.

The project components sector models the irrigation system, which is designed in advance, and two policy variables, the extension and credit programs. The stored irrigation water, the standing water, and the soil water are specifically represented.

Evaluation

IRRIGM is a complex, integrated model of an irrigation project. All four sectors interact

dynamically. The model is flexible enough to be applied to a wide range of projects from the design phase to implementation. In its generic form, the model could be used effectively in courses on economic development.

Application to a specific project would require some modifications to make the model correspond to the situation. While the model modifications would be relatively simple, it would be a good investment to arrange for some assistance from Mr. Faeth.

Hardware and Software Requirements

IBM PC/XT/AT or compatible 640 KB RAM, hard disk, printer; Professional DYNAMO Plus or perhaps DYSMAP2.

Source

The theory of the model and a listing of the equations are provided in a master's thesis, "An Analysis of Factors Determining the Cost Effectiveness of Irrigation Projects in Developing Countries" (Dartmouth College, November 1983). Instructions on using the model are provided in "A User's Manual for the Irrigation Development Model (IRRIGM)—Microcomputer Version" (draft of December 1983). These two papers and a disk containing the model are available from: Mr. Paul Faeth, WRI/IIED, 1709 New York Avenue, NW, 7th Floor, Washington, DC 20006, USA; telephone: (202) 462-0900; telex: 64414 WRIWASH; telefax: (202) 638-0036.

A description of the application of the model to a specific policy issue is provided in *Determinants of Performance of Irrigation Projects in Developing Countries* (Washington, DC: International Economics Division, Economic Research Service, USDA, 1984), which is available from: Government Printing Office, 710 North Capital Street, Washington, DC 20402, USA. Order GPO stock no. 1984-460-941:20003-ERS.

Microcomputer Programs for Improved Planning and Design for Water Supply and Waste Disposal Systems (WSWDS)

Purpose

To analyze the costs and benefits of alternative designs of water distribution networks and gravity sewer systems.

Description

The WSWDS programs can perform a wide range of tasks related to water management. The overall goal of this package is to determine the most efficient and economical design for water distribution networks and sanitary sewage systems. More specific applications include designing the most efficient layout for pipes in a water distribution system and calculating the costs of water management projects.

The WSWDS system was created by the World Bank Interregional Project as a contribution to the International Drinking Water Supply Decade.

Theory and Assumptions

The WSWDS package is composed of ten distinct programs, which are grouped into four functions: network design, financial screening, statistical analysis, and supplementary programs. Most of the programs are written in BASIC; one is written in FORTRAN.

Four network design programs (BRANCH, LOOP, SEWER, and FLOW) help determine the best layout of a pipe network. BRANCH finds the least expensive design of branched water distribution networks using the Hazen-Williams flow equation. LOOP works with looped networks and is based on the Hardy-Cross analysis. SEWER is used to design either small bore or conventional sewer systems using the Manning flow equation. FLOW simulates water flows in looped distribution networks; it uses a variation of the Newton-Raphson method supplemented with either the Hazen-Williams or Manning flow equation.

A financial screening function is provided by the program SCREENS, which calculates the construction and annual costs of a proposed design. While this program can help assess the financial feasibility of a project, final financial decisions should, of course, take social and other considerations into account.

The statistical analysis function is provided by REGRESS, a multiple linear regression program. It estimates the best linear model of data provided by the user and provides for data transformations and outputs. In addition, the program calculates parameter estimates, correlation coefficients, prediction and confidence intervals, and residuals.

Four supplementary programs complete the package. HEADLOSS is a small BASIC program that assesses the capacity of a branched water distribution network. It calculates the friction loss in a single pipeline using the Hazen-Williams equation. MINTREE determines the shortest path connecting the junctions of a water distribution network. Although it does not always generate the optimal layout of the primary network, it can help in identifying a general structure for a looped distribution system. LINPROG optimizes linear functions subject to linear constraints using a general linear programming algorithm. NELDER optimizes problems with unconstrained variables using a general non-linear algorithm based on the Nelder and Mead algorithm.

Evaluation

In general, this package is thorough and well-designed, and it does what it is supposed to do without creating undue difficulties. The individual programs work very well with each other.

The manual (in English only) is thorough, professional, well structured, clear, and helpful. It discusses each of the system's programs in understandable terms with plenty of examples and helpful sample run-throughs. The manual also explains how to access the data used in the sample sessions.

The input and output are straightforward. A large amount of input data is required. Output from all of the programs in this package is readable and detailed. The user can send the information to a printer, the screen, or a disk file.

WSWDS has had quite widespread testing and evaluation. It has been distributed to numerous universities, government agencies, and training institutions and has become quite popular.

WSWDS is intended for use by engineering instructors and their students, and users must already know the basics of hydrology and engineering. The purpose of the manual is not to teach the user how to develop water distribution systems, but rather to show the user how to run the WSWDS program.

Technical help is available to developing countries or organizations working in those countries. Inquiries should be made to the address below.

Hardware and Software Requirements

IBM PC/XT/AT or compatible, 256 KB RAM, two disk drives, and a printer; BASICA or equivalent. Both Hercules graphics adapter and a math coprocessor chip are supported.

Source

TheWorld Bank, Water Supply and Urban Development Department, Attention: Kurt Carnemark, 1818 H Street, NW, Washington, DC 20433, USA. Request: *Microcomputer Programs for Improved Planning and Design for Water Supply and Waste Disposal Systems.*

Water Supply Simulation Model (WSSM)

Purpose

To help evaluate the physical and economic characteristics of a water supply system.

Description

The Water Supply Simulation Model (WSSM) was developed by the U.S. Environmental Protection Agency. The program integrates the various economic, demographic, and hydraulic considerations that water utilities might use in evaluating alternative water supply delivery systems. The model represents a water delivery system as a series of demand nodes (individual households, industries, treatment plants, junctions, storage tanks, etc.) connected by links.

Thus, to use WSSM it is necessary to describe in link-node form the water delivery system being evaluated. This description is made relative to a base map and involves providing WSSM with the physical, spatial, demand, and cost characteristics of each link and node. These characteristics include such data as pipe lengths, types, diameters, elevations, and so forth. These data are then entered into the file establishment module.

Theory and Assumptions

The WSSM consists of seven different modules. (See Figure 7-3.) The establishment module creates and checks the link and node data files. These files contain cross references between links and node files, location of nodes, and attributes such as type, material, and demand. The display, listing, and editing modules are used to verify the contents of the node and linkage files and to make the

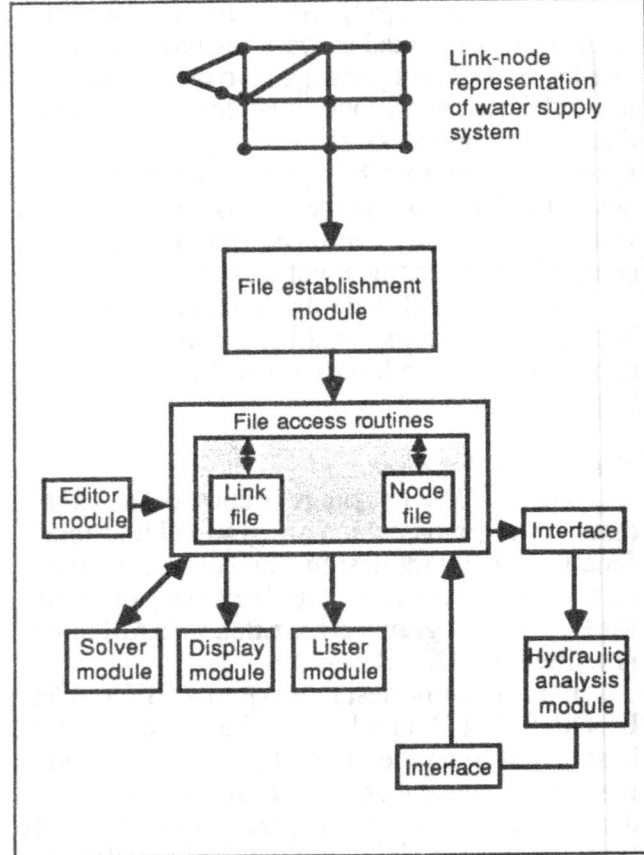

Figure 7-3: The basic structure of the Water Supply Simulation Model (WSSM).

appropriate corrections. The hydraulic module uses WATSIM, a nonproprietary hydraulic model, to calculate steady-state hydraulic flow and pressure from given demands throughout the network. The solver module determines the travel time from any source to a node. The input-output module manages the inputs and outputs.

WSSM produces two types of output. The first is a display of the node elevations and linkage flows. The second is a schematic display of the cost per 1,000 gallons of water delivered through the system. By simulating the system with and without a new addition, it is possible to determine how the change will affect the cost of supplying water to each of the various demand nodes.

Evaluation

The WSSM software is technically advanced but not exactly user friendly. The documentation, which comes on two disks, is extensive but requires technical knowledge of hydrology and computers. Two technical articles on the model's use are also required. A more user-friendly version is under development.

It should be emphasized that the WSSM software provides a methodology for understanding water supply network data, not answers to broad, general design questions. The software can simulate a water supply system; how the output should be applied depends very much on the specific questions of concern.

Much expense and effort has gone into developing and validating WSSM. The model has been tested in New Vienna, Ohio; Cincinnati, Ohio; Kenton County, Kentucky; and Tampa, Florida.

The applications of the WSSM are not limited to water delivery systems. Any delivery system that can be characterized as a distribution network overlaid on some spatial distribution of supply and demand can be simulated using the model.

Hardware and Software Requirements
WSSM was developed originally for mainframe computers using Standard FORTRAN. A user-friendly version for IBM PC/XT/AT and compatibles is now available.

Source
U.S. Environmental Protection Agency, Office of Research and Development, Water Engineering Research Laboratory, Attention: Dr. James A. Goodrich, Environmental Scientist, Systems and Cost Evaluation Staff, Drinking Water Research Division, Cincinnati, OH 45268, USA; or Dr. Richard M. Males, RMM Technical Services, Inc., 3319 Eastside Avenue, Cincinnati, OH 45208, USA; telephone (513) 569-7605. The price varies, depending on circumstances; write for details.

Water Use Forecasting (WATFORE)

Purpose
To forecast daily urban water use.

Description
WATFORE is a computer software system for forecasting daily municipal water demands. In addition, WATFORE can be used for impact analysis of alternative water conservation programs, yield studies on water supply reservoirs, and water rights adjudication.

Application requires several years of local water-use, rainfall, and temperature data for use in calibrating several coefficients. The calibration process involves careful consideration of local conditions and the spatial variability of rainfall.

WATFORE was developed by Dr. David R. Maidment and his research team at the Department of Civil Engineering, University of Texas, Austin.

Theory and Assumptions
WATFORE is a time-series, statistical model. It requires that the user input data on the daily total combined pumpage of a city's water treatment plants, daily maximum air temperature, and daily rainfall totals for a historic period. Estimates of temperatures (available from weather forecasting services) are needed for the forecast period.

WATFORE graphic and tabular outputs include: potential use due to seasonal variables, water use due to the impact of rainfall, water use due to temperature excess, water use due to previous forecast errors, forecasted water used, forecast error, and percent error in forecasts.

Evaluation
WATFORE is a generic model that can be applied with reasonable ease in many different cities. The user's manual is brief, but adequate.

WATFORE has a proven track record. It is currently being used by a number of cities (Corpus Christi, Texas; Longview, Texas; San Antonio, Texas; Edmonton, Alberta; and San Diego, California) as an operational forecasting and planning tool. It is also used by the Metropolitan Water District of Southern California to predict the system-wide demand for bulk water deliveries and long-distance water transfers.

Hardware and Software Requirements
IBM PC/XT/AT or compatibles, color graphics adapter; Microsoft Quick BASIC 3.0 or later. An AT class machine and a hard disk are recommended, but not required.

Source
The software, documentation, and calibration services are available from: Dr. Allie

Blair, IRRISCO, Inc., P.O. Box 4403-128, Austin, TX 78765, USA; telephone: (512) 452-8336. The price depends on the services needed; write for details.

Modular Three-Dimensional Groundwater Flow Model (MOD3D)

Purpose
   To simulate groundwater flow in three dimensions.

Description
   MOD3D simulates two- or three-dimensional flow in a porous medium, which may be heterogeneous and anisotropic and have irregular boundaries. The uppermost hydrologic unit may have a free surface. All other layers are confined or may convert between confined and unconfined. The stresses considered are wells, evapotranspiration, and recharge from precipitation.
   One or more layers of nodes may be used to simulate each hydrogeologic unit. If it is reasonable to assume that storage is negligible in a confining bed and that horizontal components of flow can be neglected, the effects of vertical flow through a confining bed can be incorporated into the vertical conductance terms that connect adjacent aquifers.

Theory and Assumptions
   The equation describing the three-dimensional movement of groundwater through porous earth material is solved using a finite-difference approximation and assuming a constant density flow field. The dependent variable is hydraulic head. Flow can be either steady or transient.
   To solve the flow equation, the region is subdivided into blocks in which the medium properties are assumed to be uniform. The continuous derivatives are replaced by finite-difference approximations for the derivatives at a point (the node at the center of the block). The result is N equations in N unknowns (head values at the nodes), where N is the number of blocks representing the porous medium.
   The program provides for the use of either of two interactive matrix techniques to solve the set of simultaneous finite-difference equations. These are the strongly implicit procedure (SIP)

and the slice successive over-relaxation (SSOR). The major assumptions are as follows: (a) Darcy's law is valid, and hydraulic-head gradients are the only significant driving mechanism for fluid flow; (b) the porosity and hydraulic conductivity are constant with time; (c) gradients of fluid density, viscosity, and temperature do not affect the velocity distribution; (d) hydraulic conductivity principal components are aligned with Cartesian coordinate system; and (e) resaturation of grid blocks upon dewatering is not permitted.

Evaluation
   MOD3D, a code written by the U.S. Geological Survey (USGS), uses a modular programming structure that eases modification of the code. The program was written to require a minimum amount of modification to run on most computers.
   Because of the modular programming structure, separate modules for various types of boundary conditions and source terms exist. The code is capable of eliminating modules dealing with boundary conditions and source terms that are not used in a particular simulation; this capability reduces computer memory requirements. Separate modules are included to simulate effects of recharge, evapotranspiration, wells, leakage from rivers, drains, and head dependent flux.
   Input procedures have been generalized, allowing each type of model input data to be stored and read from separate external files. Variable formatting allows input data arrays to be read in any format without modification of the program.
   Because of the model's recent advent, published field applications are limited, but much of its logic is derived from an earlier USGS three-dimensional groundwater flow model. Documentation is provided in M. G. McDonald and A. W. Harbaugh, *A Modular Three-Dimensional Ground-Water Flow Model* (USGS, 1984).

Hardware and Software Requirements
   MOD3D was programmed in FORTRAN 66 and has been run without modification on numerous computers, including IBM, CDC, DEC, Cray, Prime, Amdahl, and Univac. The documentation provides instructions for

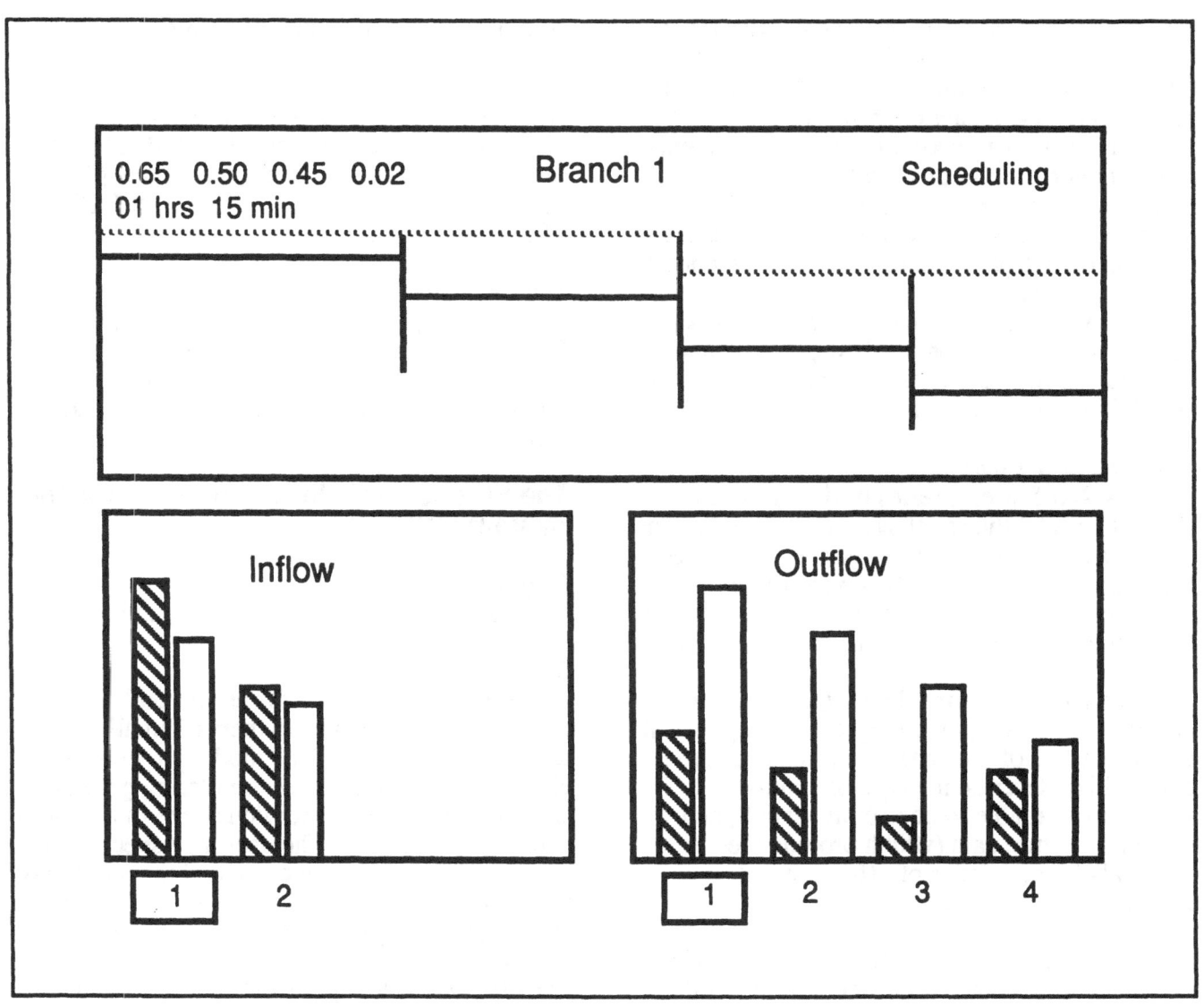

Figure 7-4: CANALS graphics screen display with outflow bars.

conversion to FORTRAN 77. A microcomputer version of the code is available.

Source

The microcomputer version is available from: International Ground Water Modeling Center, Holcomb Research Institute, Butler University, Indianapolis, IN 46208, USA.

The documentation for MOD3D cited above (Open File Report 83-875) and a magnetic tape of the computer program can be obtained, at cost, by requesting it from: Chief Hydrologist, U.S. Geological Survey, WRD, 411 National Center, 12201 Sunrise Valley Drive, Reston, VA 22092, USA.

Utah State University Hydraulic Model (CANALS)

Purpose

To perform hydrodynamic simulation of water flow in canals.

Description

This simulation model can be used in the planning phase to evaluate alternative canal designs and in the operations phase to help calculate the necessary control structure settings for maintaining water levels. It can also be used in the training of canal operators.

The model can simulate canals with up to four branches, each of which can consist of nine reaches with up to nine turnouts per reach. The model can be simulated in five-minute increments with a maximum of 150 increments. Even longer simulations can be made by saving results and starting a new run. The model produces output that describes flow levels, flow rates, and control structure setting for any point in the canal system.

CANALS was written by Gary P. Merkley to help in the operation, analysis, design, and operator training of canal systems. It is written in PASCAL for the microcomputer.

Theory and Assumptions

CANALS uses a series of linkages and nodes to model the canal system. The nodes and linkages are represented by a set of simultaneous St. Venant equations. Solutions to these equations provide the momentum and continuity for each node of the canal's reaches. (See Figure 7-4.)

The model requires three types of input: configuration data (which represent the physical characteristics of the canal); control structure data (which describe the type of control structures available to control the canal), and turnout structure data (which provide the physical characteristics of off-line canal structures that affect the flow of water downstream).

The model can be operated in three modes. The manual mode allows user operation of the control structures from the keyboard. The presetting and control structure mode allows the user to create a data file that will provide the control structure settings for each five-minute interval of the computer run. The gate scheduling mode automatically operates the control structures with the aim of maintaining operational water levels in every reach of the system.

Evaluation

The CANALS model requires no special computer expertise or training. It does, however, assume that the user has an understanding of the basic principles of open channel hydraulics.

The documentation of CANALS is very good. Forms for field data collection are included that simplify the input process. An appendix entitled "What can go wrong"

summarizes possible stumbling blocks and the strategies to overcome them.

Hardware and Software Requirements

IBM AT or compatible, 640 KB RAM, EGA (enhanced graphics adapter) card, Intel 80287 coprocessor chip, hard disk drive; MS-DOS 3.1, Microsoft PASCAL 3.31.

Source

Mr. Gary P. Merkley, Agriculture and Irrigation Engineering, Utah State University, Logan, UT 84322-4105, USA. There is a nominal fee to cover materials, postage, and handling.

The Woodsman's Ideal Growth Projection System (TWIGS)

Purpose

To project future yields for a small forest.

Description

TWIGS is intended for use by both consulting foresters and owners of small woodland properties. The model projects future yields by incrementally accumulating growth and mortality of each individual tree in a stand over a growth cycle. The user may specify the number of years in each cycle and the number of cycles to project forward. At the end of each growth cycle, ingrowth may be simulated by adding trees to a stand. The TWIGS system also provides extensive options for analyzing the biological and economic effect of stand management activities.

Theory and Assumptions

TWIGS projects the growth of individual trees (or groups of trees) on the basis of an initial tree list. This list can be actual stand data or tree frequencies generated for a normal or Weibull distribution by diameter class. Required inputs for a tree list based on actual data are: U.S. Forest Service species code, diameter at the base and height (dbh), trees per acre, tree status (live, cut, or dead), and tree class (acceptable, undesirable, or cull). The model includes parameters for thirty species of trees. It treats each woodland area as a local system dependent on the particular species growing there, the climate, the soil, and the human management practices, which can include a wide variety of

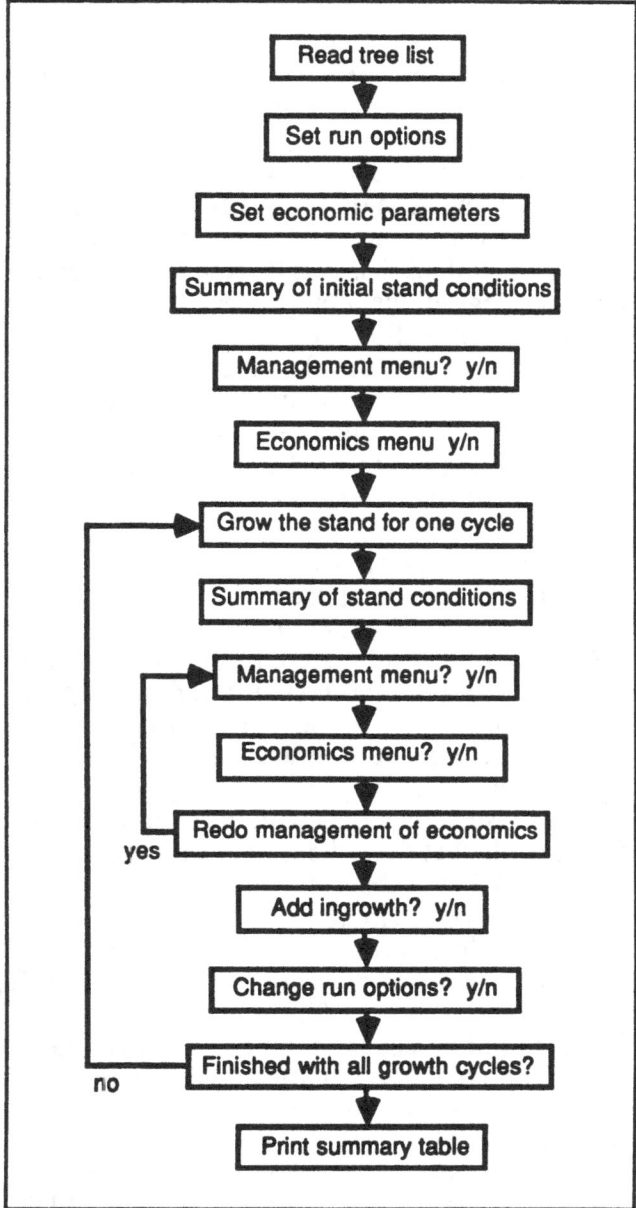

Figure 7-5: The flowchart for TWIGS.

cutting and thinning options. Output from the model includes estimates of sawtimber and fuelwood volumes.

Evaluation
    TWIGS is a complex, sophisticated program. (See Figure 7-5.) The source code listing is about seventy pages of PASCAL statements.
    The program is well planned, well executed, and well tested. The program, as it comes, applies only to forests in a relatively small part

of the United States. However, with appropriate modifications and adjustments, the program could be applied to forests anywhere in the world. In some cases the necessary modifications and adjustments would require extensive data collection and field research.

Hardware and Software Requirements
    IBM PC/XT/AT or compatible, 192 KB RAM, two disk drives, MS or PC-DOS 1.1 or later; or Apple II, 64K RAM, two disk drives, and Apple PASCAL.

Source
    Mr. Gary J. Brand, U.S. Forest Service, North Central Forest Experiment Station, 1992 Folwell Avenue, St. Paul, MN 55108, USA; telephone: (612) 649-5170. The price is US $45.

BIOCUT

Purpose
    To assess the economic viability of alternative designs and management strategies for wood energy plantations.

Description
    BIOCUT is a small-business simulation model. It is designed to facilitate the systematic investigation of the economics of an energy plantation supplying fuelwood or wood energy feedstocks. The model provides estimates of net returns and minimum required product prices and is useful in identifying the best plantation design and management alternatives.
    BIOCUT can be run in either a continuous or a pulse mode. In the continuous mode, only a fraction of the available area is planted each year, thus assuring a continuous supply of trees of harvestable age each year. In the pulsed mode, the total available area is planted the first year so that all trees mature at the same time.
    BIOCUT was developed by Oak Ridge National Laboratory in an effort to make its mainframe model, FIRSTCUT, available for on-site economic analysis.

Theory and Assumptions
    BIOCUT consists of four computational subroutines. COMPUT calculates yearly information on the financial status of the plantation, which is assessed in terms of cash flow, net present value, discounted average cost,

internal rate of return, and benefit/cost ratio. PLANT computes the plantation life cycle. RISK performs the risk analysis for net present value, using a probability distribution for the costs and revenues. REPORT outputs the yearly financial results, including the net present value, the discounted average cost, the internal rates of return, and the benefit/cost ratio.

Evaluation

One of the first things a user notices about BIOCUT is that there are almost no endogenous variables in this model, but a very large number of exogenous variables. As a result, a large amount of data is required. Inputs are needed on plantation scenario activities, economic parameters, plantation established activities, operation and maintenance activities, and harvesting, processing, and transportation. Since there are no default values for the required data, the user faces a very large input task.

On the other hand, BIOCUT can be used effectively both in highly capital-intensive areas and in highly labor-intensive areas because of the flexibility achieved by the extensive data requirements. This is, therefore, a model that can be applied widely with good results.

The BIOCUT documentation is provided in S. Das et al., *BIOCUT: A Microcomputer Based Economic Evaluation System for Wood Energy Plantations*. It is well written and comprehensive. The source code (in PASCAL) and the underlying equations are included.

Hardware and Software Requirements

IBM PC/XT/AT or compatible, 256 KB RAM; DOS (version 2.0 or later), and PASCAL.

Source

Order documentation cited above (ORNL/TM-9576) from: National Technical Information Service, U.S. Department of Commerce, 5285 Port Royal Road, Springfield, VA 22161, USA.

[Fire] BEHAVE

Purpose

To model the available fuel within a forest and to predict the behavior of forest fires.

Description

BEHAVE is a fuel and fire simulation model that can be used in conducting research, developing plans, educating foresters, and fighting actual fires.

In order for BEHAVE to provide an accurate simulation of a forest fire, the fuel supply present within the forest must be modeled in some detail. BEHAVE therefore includes a fuel subprogram that complements the main BEHAVE simulation programs.

BEHAVE was developed by the U.S. Forest Service at its Intermountain Fire Sciences Laboratory. The original model was for a minicomputer, but in 1984 it was modified to run both on mainframes and on microcomputers.

Theory and Assumptions

BEHAVE is composed of a FUEL subsystem and a BURN subsystem. (See Figure 7-6.) The FUEL subsystem models the endemic fuel of the particular forest area under study. It is composed of two routines: NEWMDL (a fuel model development program) and TSTMDL (a fuel model test and adjustment program). The FUEL subsystem comes with thirteen predefined fuel models that describe many common forests.

The BURN subsystem contains the programs used to simulate the behavior of a forest fire. In addition to FIRE1 (the main program), there are six modules: SITE, DIRECT, SIZE, CONTAIN, SPOT, and DISPATCH. SITE is used to calculate direction of maximum spread, rate of spread, flame length, fireline intensity, heat per unit area, reaction intensity, and effective wind speed. DIRECT is much like SITE except that it is less detailed; it makes rough estimates of the factors projected by SITE when detailed site-specific information is unavailable. SIZE can take the output of either DIRECT or SITE and calculate the area and perimeter of the fire. CONTAIN is used to estimate the equipment and personnel needed to contain the forest fire, to estimate the control line construction rate needed to control the fire, and to project the ultimate burned area. SPOT calculates the maximum distances fire brands can travel to start spot fires. DISPATCH links DIRECT, SIZE, and CONTAIN to provide a fire-fighting model that operates on the information likely to be available to a dispatcher.

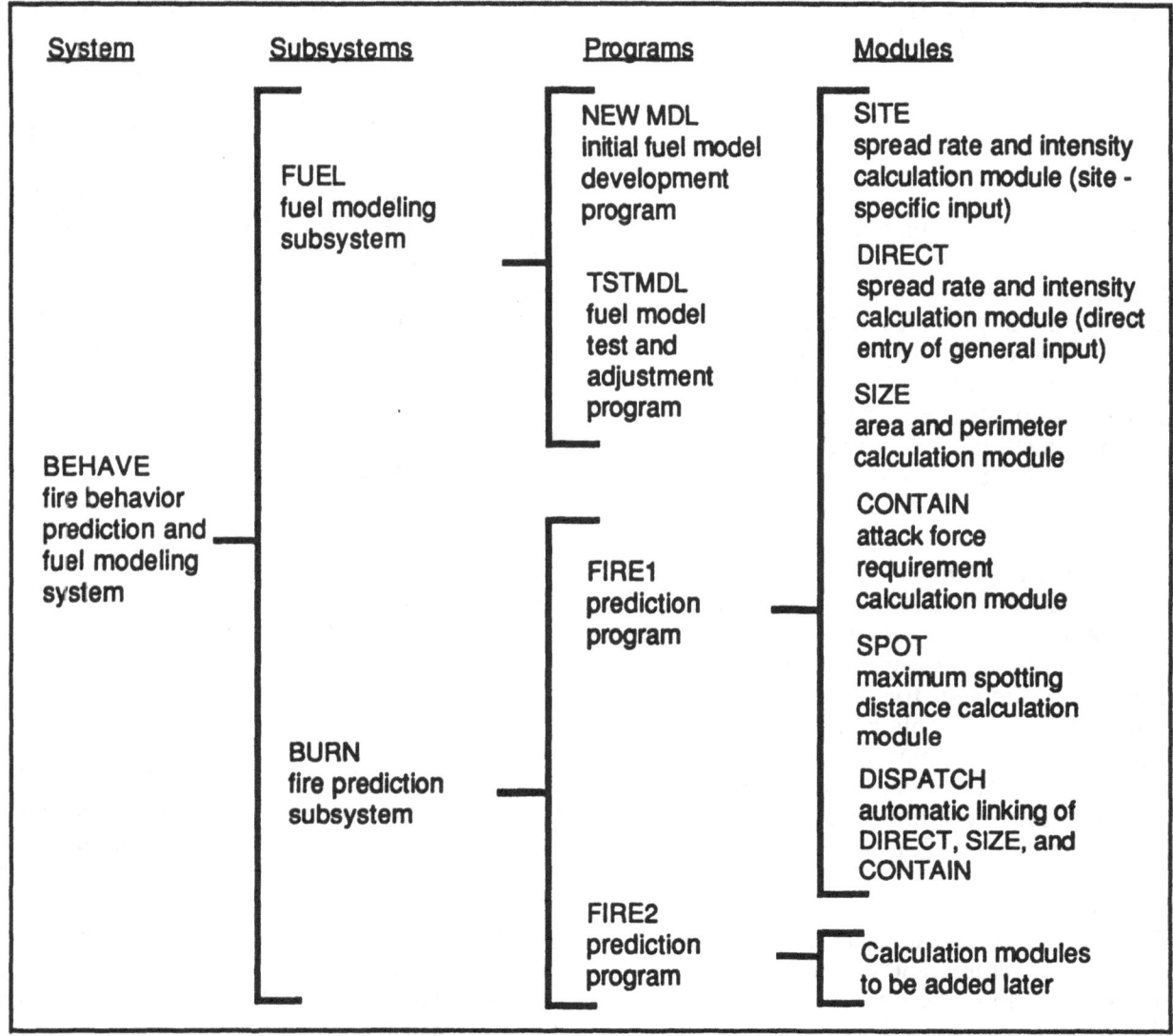

Figure 7-6: The BEHAVE system, consisting of the FUEL and BURN subsystems.

Evaluation

BEHAVE is an excellent model. It is so highly respected that the Aviation and Fire Management division of the U.S. Forest Service has chosen BEHAVE as the national fire-behavior simulation system.

There are two manuals for BEHAVE, one for the FUEL subsystem and one for the BURN subsystem. They are both well written and well illustrated.

Two microcomputer versions of BEHAVE are available. MICRO BEHAVE is a no-frills version of BEHAVE in compiled FORTRAN. PC BEHAVE has a wide range of user-friendly features, such as pop-up and bounce bar menus, windows, and on-line context-sensitive pop-up help screens. Its program has been rewritten in the C programming language.

Hardware and Software Requirements

For MICRO BEHAVE: IBM PC/XT/AT or compatible, 360 KB RAM, two floppy disk drives, and a printer. A math coprocessor chip is recommended. For PC BEHAVE: IBM PC/XT/AT or compatible, 256 KB RAM, two floppy disk drives, and a printer. DOS 2.0 or later. A math coprocessor is recommended.

Source

For MICRO BEHAVE: Forest Resources Systems Institute (FORS), 122 Helton Court, Florence, AL 35630, USA; telephone: (205) 767-0250. The price is US $15. For PC BEHAVE:

Microfire, Box 9243, Missoula, MT 59807, USA; telephone: (406) 728-7720. The price is US $250.

Tree Manager

Purpose

To facilitate the management of urban trees.

Description

Tree Manager provides an easy method for maintaining a tree inventory for a city. This software can be used in allocating tree-care resources, making budgets, preparing projections, developing justifications, and decreasing accidents and liability insurance costs.

Theory and Assumptions

Tree Manager is a specialized database program developed with dBase III. Three types of data are stored: tree information by site, work performed, and requests for service.

The three types of data can be accessed individually or in combination. Statistical analyses and projections can be made with all or parts of the data. Work orders and inspection records can be produced automatically.

Evaluation

Tree Manager can facilitate all aspects of urban tree management and can increase the efficiency of urban tree care.

The program is menu driven and very easy to use and understand. No special computer expertise is required. The documentation is good. The software is supported by ACRT for a year after the initial purchase.

The secret to making Tree Manager pay off is not just in learning to push the right keys, but rather in creating a management structure that results in a steady, high-quality data stream being entered into the computer. ACRT can provide consultation and assistance in organizing an agency to utilize the software effectively.

Hardware and Software Requirements

IBM AT or compatible; dBASE III Plus

Source

Dr. Elizabeth L. Buchanan, Vice President, ACRT, Inc., 152 East Main Street, P.O. Box

219, Kent, OH 44240-0219, USA. The price of the program is US $4,700 and up.

Alternative, less costly programs may be available. For a review of other software for the management of urban forests, see E. T. Smiley: "Urban Forest Management Computer Software: A Buyer's Guide" (Paper delivered at the Third National Urban Forestry Conference, Orlando, Florida, December 7-11, 1986). The proceedings are available from: American Forestry Association, P.O. Box 2000, Attention: Proceedings, Washington, D.C. 20013, USA; telephone: (800) 368-5748.

Fishery Management Model for the Rio Grande Basin (RIOFISH)

Purpose

To explore the effects on angler fishing of alternative management scenarios.

Description

RIOFISH is a management tool for comparison of alternative strategies for the management and enhancement of angler fishing in both mainstream reservoirs and connecting waters. It was designed to answer such questions as where fish management attention should be concentrated, what long-term harvest and stocking strategies are most suitable, where water can be redistributed to improve angling, and which flow redistributions will encourage more spawning.

The model was developed by New Mexico State University in response to a 1982 report that identified a potential for a sizable increase in regional income from improved angler fishing in the Rio Grande basin.

Theory and Assumptions

RIOFISH contains hydrologic, biologic, and socioeconomic submodels. (See Figure 7-7.) The hydrologic submodel uses time series data to project water levels, nutrient concentrations, light penetration, and temperature. The biologic submodel, a process model, projects the effects of variations in light, nutrients, temperature, water level and other factors on fish biomass. The economic submodel uses regression techniques to estimate angler fishing days, economic benefit to anglers, and the income and employment generated in the basin.

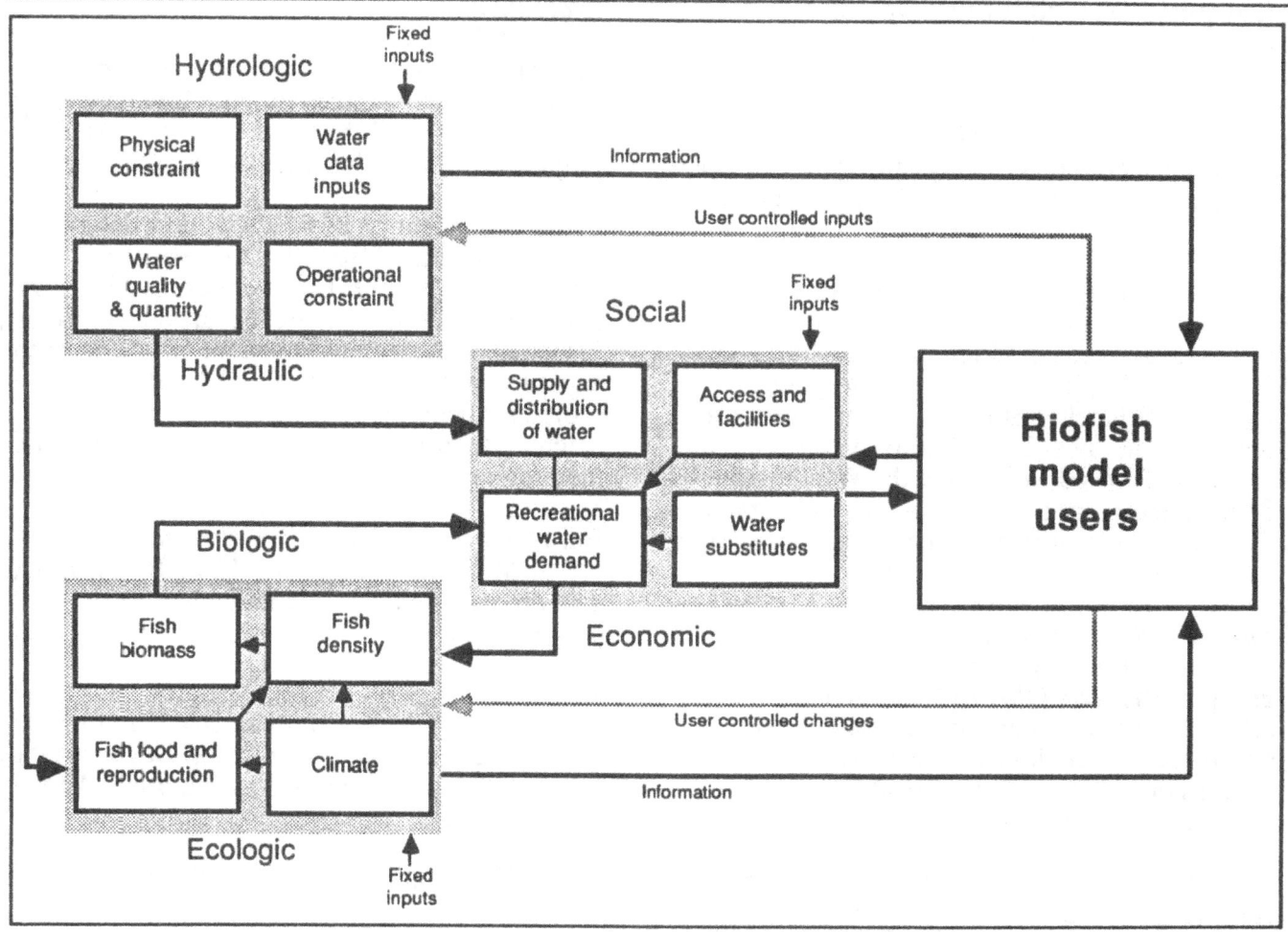

Figure 7-7: The linkages among the hydrologic, biotic, and socioeconomic submodels of RIOFISH and the model's users.

RIOFISH provides users with an appreciation of how the hydraulic, biologic, and economic subsectors interact with one another and how a change in one area will affect the others.

Evaluation

RIOFISH is a powerful management tool. Anyone interested in sport fishery management or in fishery education could benefit from its use. The user's manual is adequate. The technical manual is excellent and could be used as a beginner's text book in ecological modeling.

The one disadvantage of RIOFISH for use in other river basins is that the model has many features that are unique to the Rio Grande basin. Nonetheless, this model would be an excellent

starting point for the development of a fishery model for another river basin.

Hardware and Software Requirements

IBM PC/XT/AT or compatible, 512 KB RAM, hard disk, monochrome monitor, and printer; DOS 2.1 or later. Math coprocessor chip recommended, but not required.

Source

Ms. Susan B. Bolin, Department of Civil Engineering, New Mexico State University, Box 3CE, Las Cruces, NM 88003, USA; telephone: (505) 647-3512. There are two versions of RIOFISH, a FORTRAN version and a user-friendly APL version. Both are free in compiled form. Source code may be made available to research teams on a case-by-case basis.

Computerized Hatchery Optimization Program (CHOP)

Purpose

To improve and standardize documentation on all aspects of fish rearing through the creation and maintenance of an aquicultural database.

Description

CHOP is a specialized set of data base and computational programs designed for storage, retrieval, and manipulation of aquicultural data. It is an excellent, versatile set of programs suitable for hatcheries management, aquicultural research, and other biological research situations.

CHOP was developed at the Washington State Department of Game for use within their own fisheries programs. It has been successfully used there for a number of years.

Theory and Assumptions

The CHOP programs are organized in three groups. The six COMPACT programs combine data collection, production forecasting, and optimization techniques. These programs allow for the computation of the means, standard deviations, and ranges for user-defined intervals from CHOP data files.

The four K-Factor programs are used for collecting data for evaluation of the computerized hatching program, providing a means to evaluate pond populations, providing storage and retrieval of hatchery production data on a pond-by-pond basis, and projecting fish growth and feeding rates.

Lotus 1-2-3 templates have been developed to store pond and lot mortalities, biomass, and feed records, to provide fish disease treatment dosages by type of treatment and pond type, and to calculate the daily amount of food to feed fish at varying water temperatures in cold weather.

Data entered include: the hatchery code, species of fish, length, weight, the broodstock code, the year the majority of eggs were taken, the pond number, the type of pond, pond dimensions, volume, inflow, outflow, pond populations, total mortality for the period, and the number of fish planted or moved.

One very nice feature allows the creation of worksheets that may be transported to Lotus 1-2-3. The Lotus 1-2-3 option allows the user to carry out quite complicated manipulations of the data.

Evaluation

CHOP is extremely user friendly, has extensive error-checking procedures, and produces well-organized output. The data entry procedure is straightforward. The manual (in English only) contains a step-by-step example application.

The application of CHOP is described in *The Computerized Hatchery Optimization Program (CHOP): First Year Results (Phase I)* from the Washington State Department of Game, Fisheries Management Division. This document explains the objectives of CHOP, details the program's benefits, and includes a complete hatchery report generated with the assistance of the program.

Hardware and Software Requirements

IBM or compatible with 128 KB RAM, two disk drives, DOS 2.0 or later, and an Epson printer.

Source

Mr. Don Chase, Computerized Hatchery Optimization Project, Washington Department of Game, 600 North Capitol Way, Olympia, WA 98504, USA.

[Fish] Population Estimate (FPE)

Purpose

To estimate fish populations from known quantities of fish that are periodically captured and tagged.

Description

[Fish] Population Estimate (FPE), a small, Applesoft BASIC program, calculates fish populations from user-supplied data on fish that have been caught, tagged, released, and recaptured. The program was developed by Leo Schlunz at the Iowa Conservation Commission.

Theory and Assumptions

The FPE can employ any one of four different equations to estimate the fish population. The Peterson equation for estimating fish populations is usually used. The Schnable, the Chapman-modified Schnable, and the Schumacher-Eschmeyer variants are also available through the program's menu. All of the equations are taken or derived from *Computation and Interpretation of Biological Statistics of Fish Populations* by W. E. Ricker.

Data entry is very straightforward. Data are required on the number of fish caught, marked, and recaptured. The program automatically saves successive runs on a disk for printing and comparison of the results. The estimated fish populations depend exclusively on user input; it does not involve environmental factors such as nutrient levels or pond volume.

Evaluation

[Fish] Population Estimate is solidly designed and can simplify complex calculations and data management for fish hatcheries and fishery research programs. The manual (in English only) is short and concise, like the program itself. It provides all the information necessary to run the program and handle various problems. The underlying equations are described briefly, but the theoretical details are not presented.

A print routine for the Epson RX-80 is included within the FPE program. It is possible to use other printers, but to do so requires changes in the program.

Hardware and Software Requirements

Apple II with 48 KB RAM, Applesoft in ROM, a single disk drive for basic applications or two drives for advanced applications.

Source

Mr. Leo R. Schlunz, Fisheries Research Biologist, Chariton Research Station, Red Hawk State Park, R.R. 1, Box 209, Chariton, IA 50049-9775, USA.

MicroFish

Purpose

To help analyze data about fish capture from streams and estimate the time and expense associated with removal-depletion sampling using electrofishing gear.

Description

MicroFish was developed by John S. Van Deventer and William S. Platts of the Forestry Sciences Laboratory. It was originally introduced as the Fisheries Population and Statistical Package (FPSP) in 1985 and has since undergone a number of modifications and revisions.

Theory and Assumptions

MicroFish consists of three types of programs: the statistical package (which analyzes data on fish capture from streams), the sample size programs (which calculate the number of electrofishing passes required for the population estimates to have the level of precision desired), and the interactive program (which calculates the maximum-likelihood population estimates from the fish sampling data).

To use MicroFish, the user must provide it with two types of input: a file that contains fish names and corresponding numeric codes and a fish-capture data file. A third required input file consists of control parameters. However, since the defaults contained in this file suffice for most runs, the user normally will not have to be concerned with it.

The MicroFish statistical package takes this input and produces maximum-likelihood population estimates, total catches, capture probabilities, lengths, weights, condition factors, biomass; it also calculates relative percentages, standard errors, and confidence intervals by standard statistical methodologies.

MicroFish sample size programs back-calculates maximum-likelihood precision for user-specified ranges of population estimates, catchability, and number of electrofishing passes.

The results of these programs can be viewed in tables or in database format.

Evaluation

MicroFish is an easy-to-use fish database statistical package and would be useful to those individuals concerned with population estimates of various fish species in the streams for which they are responsible.

Hardware and Software Requirements

IBM PC/XT/AT or compatible, DOS 2.0 or higher, and BASIC.

Source

Mr. John S. Van Deventer, Forestry Sciences Laboratory, 316 E. Myrtle Street, Boise, ID 83702, USA. The package is free.

Fish Banks, Ltd.

Purpose

To teach the basic principles behind the sustainable management of a nation's marine fishery resources.

Description

Fish Banks, Ltd. is a computer simulation and board game dealing with the interactions between a nation's fish banks and a number of competing fishing companies. Up to ten teams can play. Each team assumes the role of the top management of one of the country's principal fishing companies. The teams all begin with equal fleets of ships and equal bank accounts. The teams make annual decisions on whether to buy or sell ships and on where to fish. The game leader enters the teams' decisions into the computer, which calculates conditions a year later. The goal for each competing team is to amass the greatest wealth by the end of the game.

Fish Banks, Ltd. was written by Dennis L. Meadows, Thomas Fiddaman, and Diana Shannon, all of whom are associated with the International Network of Resource Information Centers (INRIC).

Theory and Assumptions

Fish Banks, Ltd. focuses on three important factors determining the dynamics of any nation's fishing industry: the companies' bank balances, the size of the companies' fleets, and the size of the country's fish stocks.

Figure 7-8 illustrates the principal linkages among the variables in the model. The companies' bank balances are determined by their revenues less their expenses. Revenue is generated by selling fish, selling ships, and earning interest. Expenses are incurred by buying new or used ships, paying operating and maintenance costs, and paying interest on loans.

The nation's fisheries are divided into three areas: deep-sea fisheries, smaller coastal fisheries, and harbor fisheries. The choice of the area fished determines in part the amount of fish available to catch. Total national catch is determined by the number of ships, the weather, and the effectiveness of the ships. The effectiveness of the ships is determined by the fish stocks, which, in turn, are determined by the fish regeneration rate.

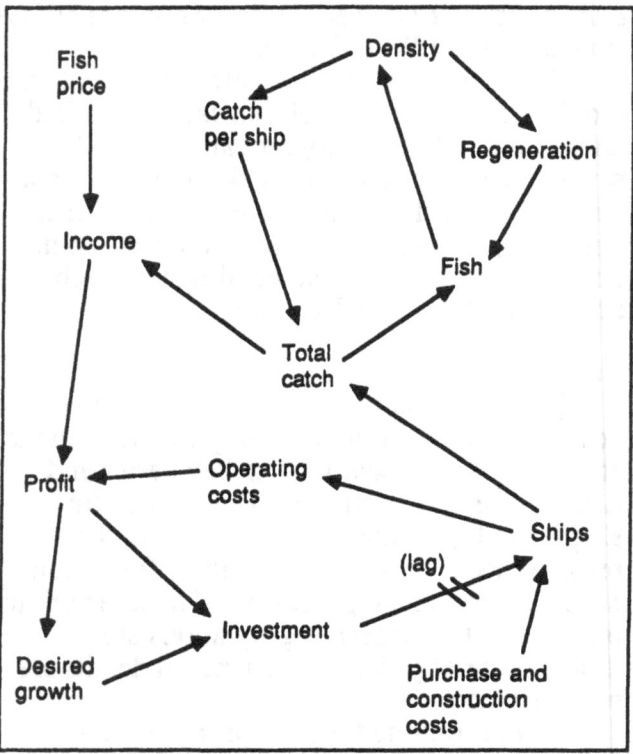

Figure 7-8: Principal linkages among variables in Fish Banks, Ltd.

Evaluation

Fish Banks, Ltd. is an effective educational tool for teaching the basics of managing a nation's fishery resource. It is both highly instructive and highly entertaining. The model can be used to increase political understanding of important public policy issues in any country having fresh or salt water fisheries. It is appropriate for groups of between five and thirty people and has been used successfully with twelve-year-olds and with U.N. officials. While it is relatively simple to administer, leaders must prepare carefully in advance if the game is to be a good experience for the participants.

The model is essentially a sophisticated version of the famous "tragedy of the commons" described by Garrett Hardin. It is easy for all of the teams, acting in their individual best interests, to destroy the fish banks and everyone's source of income. The lessons taught by the game are interesting to the players and relevant to any country involved in fisheries.

The documentation is easy to understand and includes a number of helpful graphics. Pages designed to be photocopied onto projection slides for the opening and closing briefings are included. In fact, all materials that are destroyed, lost, or used up in the course of a game can be replaced with photocopies from the manual. The documentation also includes a second, more complex version of the game for more advanced players.

Hardware and Software Requirements

IBM PC/XT/AT or compatible, or Apple Macintosh, or NEC-PC 8201A, or any other microcomputer capable of running a BASIC program of about six hundred lines. The model is written using only simple BASIC commands, so it can be used with a wide range of BASIC compilers on a wide range of microcomputers.

Source

Prof. Dennis L. Meadows, Institute for Policy and Social Science Research, Murkland Hall, University of New Hampshire, Durham, NH 03824, USA; telephone: (603) 862-2186.

8. National Security

Introduction

Too often security for a nation is thought to involve only weapons, military force, and the ability to do violence to others. Much more is involved. The word *security* means freedom from danger, fear, and anxiety. By extension, *national security* means freedom from danger, fear, and anxiety for a nation—for a people. National security, properly understood, includes not only military security against foreign invasion but also food security, economic security, domestic order, educational security, old age security, environmental security, and natural disaster security.

The models reviewed here are not as broad in their definition of security as we would have liked. There is too much emphasis on the purely military aspects of security. Also, there is really nothing at all dealing with the domestic disorders and civil wars that plague many nations. Collectively, however, the models reviewed extend the concept of security well beyond weapons.

Dunnigan's spreadsheet war games, Theater Combat Simulation (TCM) and Cost/Benefit Model (CBM), and the Theater Analysis Model (TAM) focus largely on weapons and military security. But the Low Intensity Conflict (LIC) Gaming System brings in a number of other aspects of security: drugs, corruption, employment, food, education, and economic development. Balance of Power illustrates the wide range of political and other factors involved in maintaining security—or at least avoiding war—in a bipolar world armed with nuclear weapons.

The developers of both the Low Intensity Conflict Gaming System and Balance of Power have included the phenomena of superpowers intervening in the affairs of other nations in ways that seem to condone such activities. The morality—and even the effectiveness—of such activities, however, is open to serious question. For a brief review of the problems that one superpower (the United States) has created for

itself by secretly interfering in the affairs of other nations, see B. Moyers, *The Secret Government* (Washington, D.C.: Seven Locks Press, 1988).

Nuclear Crash: The U.S. Economy After Small Nuclear Attacks provides a tool for assessing the destructiveness of even a "small" nuclear war on an industrialized economy. The Resolution of Capacity Shortfalls (ROCS) model provides a means for estimating the economic dislocations that would attend a conventional conflict or a national emergency of some other type. ARMS4 illustrates how, in an arms race, another nation's sense of security becomes an important determinant of a country's own national security.

Theater Combat Simulation (TCM) and Cost/Benefit Model (CBM)

In his well-known book *How to Make War* (New York: William Morrow and Company, 1983), James F. Dunnigan writes that he derives his perspective from his parents' "love of learning and hatred of weapons" and explains that his purpose is to "remove some of the obscurity and destroy a few of the myths" surrounding warfare so that people will understand that "in reality, warfare is never worth the cost."

Dunnigan, a world-renowned expert on war, has distilled his knowledge of war simulation into two powerful spreadsheets. One is Theater Combat Simulation (TCM). The other is the Cost/Benefit Model (CBM) for evaluating various weapon systems and munitions.

Both models operate on Lotus 1-2-3 and come with an unclassified database describing the current European Central Front (CENTAG plus the lower part of NORTAG). The user can edit the database, as well as any of the procedures and algorithms, to represent a conflict situation anywhere on the planet.

Purpose of the Theater Combat Model (TCM)
To enable the user to determine the impact of combat decisions on a theater-wide scale.

Description of TCM

All divisions, brigades, and headquarters (inclusive of their support units) are included in the order-of-battle database, which has been compiled from open sources. All or any part of the units in the order-of-battle database may be used. The user may mark each unit with a code denoting its place in the mobilization scheme for each side. The battle routines will use this mobilization in conducting the combat. The combat value of all mobilized units on each side is combined to conduct force-on-force engagements.

The user has access to all combat parameters, which take into account force posture, intensity, tactical advantage, and surprise. New weapons, or any other factor that can influence the outcome of the battle, can be introduced as additional combat value in a general sense through an override procedure. They also can be added by adjusting the combat capability of individual units.

Theory and Assumptions of TCM

The description of each unit in the order of battle includes manpower plus three indicators representing effectiveness in the areas of equipment, training, and leadership. Combat power is calculated by multiplying the number of men in the unit by the three indicators.

Adjusted combat power is calculated by applying modifying parameters to the raw combat power total. The parameters can increase or decrease combat power depending on how favorably or unfavorably the force is arrayed on the battlefield. The following combat modifiers have been built into the model: posture, attacking or defending, intensity, tactical advantage, surprise, and attrition.

Purpose of the Munitions Cost/Benefit Model (CBM)

To enable the user to compare the cost-effectiveness of various munitions in different combat scenarios.

Description of CBM

The model includes three modular functions for specific purposes. The weapon cost module itemizes the total life cycle cost of weapons. The weapon lethality module calculates a weapon's lethality over its estimated combat life.

The weapons mix module calculates the weapons mix.

CBM comes with an unclassified database for the NATO and Warsaw pact forces. The database can be modified to represent other forces.

Theory and Assumptions of CBM

CBM assumes that the efficiency of a weapon system in destroying other weapon systems is a combination of how effectively it destroys enemy weapon systems, how long it survives to do this, and how its cost compares to the cost of the weapon systems it destroys. It assumes that pure cost-effectiveness is not of paramount importance for a war extending beyond the initial stock of weapons. For such wars, the key factor is the cost of the weapon as a fraction of the national productive capacity.

Evaluation of TCM and CBM

These are impressive models. They allow the user to evaluate a wide range of different conditions, weapons, and tactics in the context of the current Central European Front. With a bit more effort these models can be addressed to different forces in other parts of the world.

Both TCM and CBM are written in Lotus 1-2-3 and have a simple and friendly appearance. A wide range of parameters can be changed quickly, easily, and without serious risk of error by modifying the database. There are even special model-specific menus, an unusually user-friendly feature for spreadsheets.

Despite the friendly appearance, fairly detailed knowledge of Lotus 1-2-3 is required to use TCM. The previous version of the model was written in Symphony, and the conversion to Lotus 1-2-3 was not perfect. Several cells contain error messages that must be corrected before the model can be used.

While it is also possible to modify the algorithms of the model, a word of caution is in order here. The language used by most spreadsheet programs to enable users to write macroinstructions is easy to learn, but users can easily get into trouble with it. It is advisable that users become thoroughly familiar with both Lotus 1-2-3 and the details of these models before attempting to change any of the algorithms in the macroinstructions. The simple appearance of TCM and CBM is deceptive. Their algorithms are complex, and an inexperienced user who attempts changes outside the relatively risk-free environment of the model's databases is asking for big trouble.

The documentation, which comes on the disks in an ASCII file, is technically adequate to allow a person knowledgeable in Lotus 1-2-3 to use the models. It is not well written, however, and reads like a quick first draft.

Dunnigan's spreadsheets provide users with a powerful set of war-gaming tools. With a good knowledge of Lotus 1-2-3, a user could apply the models to the European Central Front. With a bit more knowledge of weapons and war-gaming methods, one could apply the models' algorithms to another conflict situation. Modification of the algorithms themselves, however, is a major research undertaking unlikely to produce reliable results for anyone but war-gaming experts.

Probably the best use of Dunnigan's models is in teaching war gaming. The theory behind these and other war simulations is explained in Dunnigan's book *The Complete War Games Handbook* (New York: Morrow, 1980). Most of the data needed to use the models is included in his book *How to Make War* (New York: Morrow, 1988). Dunnigan's books, together with his spreadsheets, provide a comprehensive, in-depth, unclassified overview of the modern methods of warfare analysis.

Hardware and Software Requirements
IBM PC/XT/AT or compatible, 640 KB RAM, printer, and a graphics monitor. Lotus 1-2-3.

Source
Mr. James F. Dunnigan, 328 West 19th Street, New York, NY 10011, USA; or, since the models are in the public domain, anyone who has the models. To receive free copies from Mr. Dunnigan, send him two 5.25-inch, 360 KB floppy disks (formatted) and a self-addressed disk mailer with necessary U.S. postage.

Theater Analysis Model (TAM)

Purpose
To simulate air, land, and sea combat in a theater or smaller area of conflict.

Description
TAM is actually two models: a theater-level, air-land campaign model and a detailed air-naval

engagement model. The models run independently, but the user can reflect the results of either model in the inputs to the other. Both models apply primarily to conventional weapons but could be applied to situations involving nuclear weapons. Both allow the user to manipulate input conditions, databases, and environmental variables from within the TAM operating environment.

The air-land campaign model simulates air-land battles from battalion to corps level. The user chooses opposing ground unit formations and missions, as well as environmental factors that affect a battle. Air units are tasked according to mission and the specific ground units, if any, that they support. Model output includes attrition, movement of the forward edge of the battle area (FEBA), troop cohesion, and serviceability of facilities such as airfields and installations for command, control, and communication.

The naval engagement model allows the user to set up individual engagements involving any number and type of aircraft, ships, submarines, ground defenses, and targets. It allows a user to examine in detail the planning of individual missions or battles.

The development of TAM was funded by the U.S. Office of Net Assessments. The model has been used both by the Organization of the Joint Chiefs of Staff and by NATO.

Theory and Assumptions
The TAM air-land campaign model (see Figure 8-1) is a time-stepped simulation that calculates attrition and movement on the basis of expected kill and movement rates. The length of the time step is adjustable, eight hours being typical. Some randomness can be introduced into the simulations to represent the unexpected events that often occur in warfare.

Ground units are represented by armor, artillery, infantry, and air-defense combat strengths, as derived from static firepower scores. The combat power of ground units is modified to reflect formation, command and control effectiveness, force cohesion, terrain, and weather. The modified combat powers are used to determine force ratios in each combat sector, and the force ratios are used to calculate attrition and movement.

Air units are characterized by the number and type of aircraft in the unit. Each aircraft

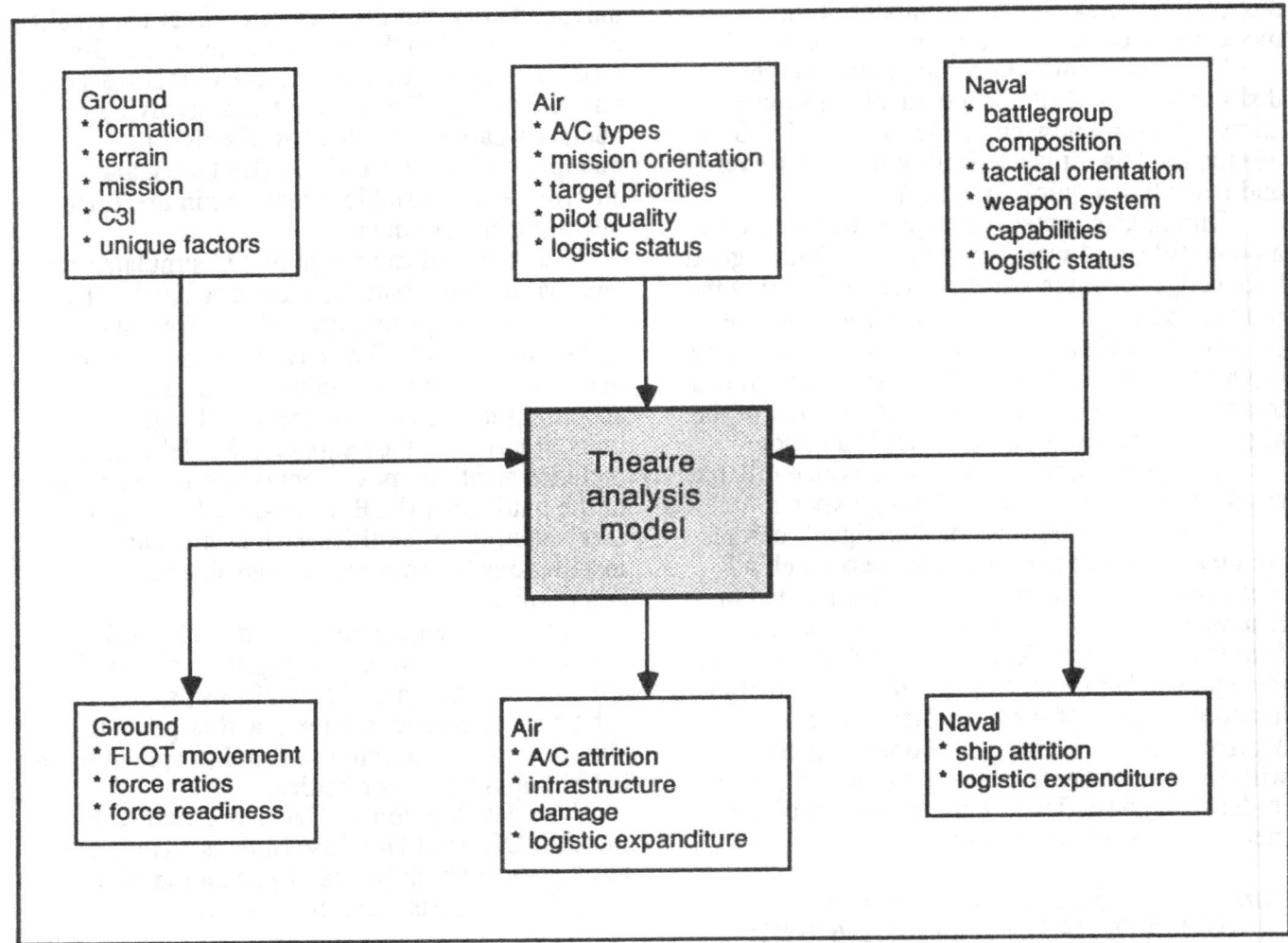

Figure 8-1: Inputs to and outputs from the Theater Analysis Model (TAM).

type represented in the model has a relative capability in the following mission areas: defensive counter-air, escort, offensive counter-air, interdiction, close air support, defense suppression, and electronic warfare. Each squadron is tasked to fly one or more missions for each eight-hour period. The model captures the dynamics of the air war through a series of difference equations that describe the effects of missions and the attrition of the aircraft. The ground and air war simulations are also linked through these equations as, for example, when aircraft hit ground units and critical targets, and when ground units shoot down aircraft.

The TAM naval engagement model is an event-driven simulation that steps through the various phases of air and naval engagements,

adjudicating each stage on the basis of calculated probabilities of detection, engagement, and kill. A hierarchical menu structure is used to define the forces, the roles of individual platforms in the force, and the environment.

For each type of event, probabilities of detection, engagement, and kill are calculated on the basis of the relative capabilities of the platforms involved. For instance, the probability of detection is calculated by comparing the searchers' detection rating to the targets' stealth rating.

The engagement model steps through each phase of the engagement, tracks the status of each platform in a force, and reports the final results. The results of individual scenarios can be saved in a computer file for comparison with those from other scenarios.

Evaluation

One objective of the TAM development project was to create models for people who have limited computer skills. As a result, the models are relatively easy to use.

The TAM system of menus facilitates the preparation of the input database. For example, the input database for an application involving division-sized ground units, squadron-sized air units, twenty airfields, air defenses, and a typical number of other important facilities can be constructed by a novice user in perhaps a week and by a trained analyst in one day.

The TAM models come on two disks: one for the air-land campaign model, and one for the air-naval engagement model. Both models are written in the Ada programming language. An additional disk is needed for data. The documentation is only in draft form at the time of this writing.

Hardware and Software Requirements

IBM PC/XT/AT or compatible, 640 KB RAM, and a math coprocessor. DOS 2.1 or higher. A compiler for the Ada programming language.

Source

Booz, Allen, and Hamilton, Inc., 1725 Jefferson Davis Highway, Suite 1100, Arlington, VA 22202, USA; telephone: (703) 769-7700. The pricing policy had not yet been determined at the time of this review.

Low Intensity Conflict (LIC) Gaming System

Purpose

To provide a research tool for analyzing the policies of nations involved in low-intensity combat and an educational tool for teaching the nuances of low-intensity combat situations.

Description

The LIC Gaming System can be used to examine insurgency, counterinsurgency, terrorism, terrorism counteraction, peace keeping, peacetime contingency operations, and anti-drug operations, anywhere in the world. The system deals with the political, military, economic, social, and psychological aspects of low-intensity conflict. It can be used from the perspective of the subject country's government forces, of the insurgency forces, or of an intervening nation. LIC raises many ethical and moral problems, particularly when used from the perspective of an intervening nation.

The game puts players in the positions of key decision makers. Players must allocate scarce resources and make trade-offs between conflicting objectives. The controller collects the players' action decisions after each round of play and enters them into the computer. The controller also provides the computer with some subjective inputs to ensure that the situation is correctly represented. The computer analyzes the players' decisions and provides results for the players to use in the next round of play.

The LIC Gaming System exists in two versions. One version has been fitted to general circumstances in Latin America. With relatively little effort it can be applied to an insurgency versus counterinsurgency situation in any specific Latin American country. The other version is generic and, with a bit more effort, can be modified to apply to any country in the world.

Development of the LIC Gaming System was sponsored by the War Gaming and Simulation Center of the U.S. National Defense University.

Theory and Assumptions

The heart of the LIC Gaming System (see Figure 8-2) is the model or adjudication tool. The model is a collection of data and algorithms arranged in modules corresponding to general classes of low-intensity conflict, e.g., peace keeping, insurgency versus counterinsurgency, and drug operations.

The players' action decisions are inputs to the model. Given these inputs, plus data on the players' assets and the current state of the country, the model simulates the political and military effects of actions. These effects may include changes in the social, economic, and political state of the subject country and changes in the internal politics of any intervening countries. Simulated results are returned to the players for use in developing the next round of action decisions.

The model is not intended to be predictive or absolute. The goal is only to indicate the

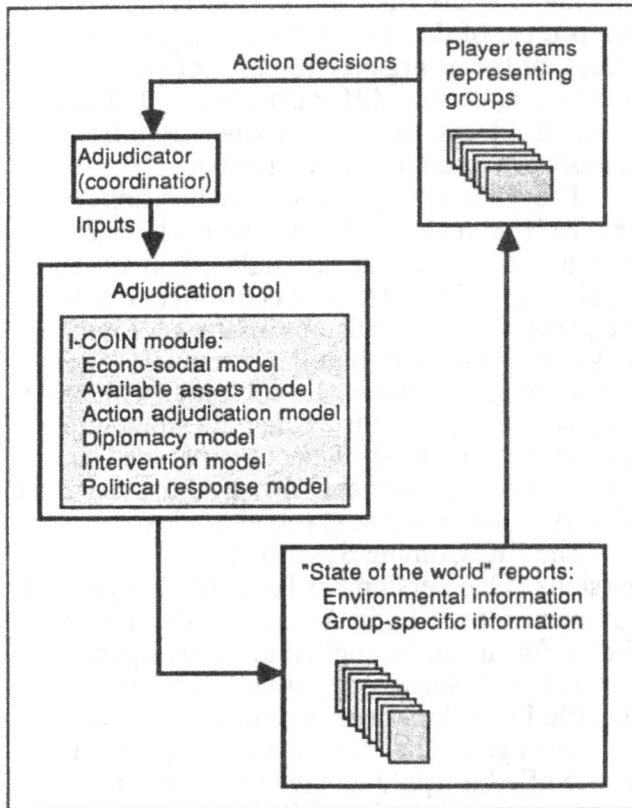

Figure 8-2: Overall architecture and information flow for the Low Intensity Conflict (LIC) Gaming System.

general direction and order of magnitude of cause-and-effect relationships.

Evaluation

The LIC Gaming System provides an innovative method to analyze low-intensity conflict problems and teach policymakers and military officers the key elements and relationships of low-intensity conflict, in general or in relation to current instabilities in specific regions. By exposing players to relevant situations and the consequences of alternative decisions, the gaming system teaches the complex interrelationships of low-intensity conflict.

Documentation includes gaming manuals and data handbooks. Effective use of the LIC Gaming System requires careful study of these materials. The controller, (or user, in a policy or planning application), must be familiar with the model, input rules, and application guidelines.

Hardware and Software Requirements

Apple Macintosh SE or II, or an IBM AT or compatible. Microsoft Excel.

Source

National Defense University, War Gaming and Simulation Center, Washington, DC 20319, USA; or, Booz, Allen and Hamilton, Inc., 1725 Jefferson Davis Highway, Suite 1100, Arlington, VA 22202, USA.

Balance of Power

Purpose

To simulate the global geopolitical power struggle between the United States and the Soviet Union.

Description

Balance of Power, which raises many moral and ethical questions, is based on a simplified model of modern global politics. The program assumes a bipolar world in which the United States and the Soviet Union are the superpower nations. The rest of the world is represented in the model by sixty other countries, which are essentially pawns that react constantly to policy decisions of the Soviet and American leadership. The objective of both superpower nations is to broaden their spheres of influence as much as possible without pushing too far and instigating a nuclear holocaust.

Theory and Assumptions

The game works on the premise that all countries vary in their level of stability, internal security, importance to global politics, and allegiance to one of the superpowers. Superpowers view the countries of the world along a continuum. The position of a nation on this continuum depends on how much the superpower desires a political shift there and how feasible it is for the superpower to interfere. The extent to which superpowers can manipulate circumstances within a given nation is governed by the ability of that nation's current leadership to control internal affairs. When a country falls within a particular range on the continuum, the superpower will move to influence it.

Each superpower gains prestige points by installing favorable governments in places of hostile regimes and successfully courting uncommitted countries to align with it. At the end of a simulated eight-year period, the country with the higher amount of prestige wins—if there has not been a nuclear war.

The United States and the Soviet Union can choose from a varied menu of policy options to help influence events and, in the process, change a government's political leaning and philosophy. These options include: (a) military aid to governments (weapons but not troops), (b) aid to insurgents, (c) intervention for the government or the insurgents (troops), (d) economic aid, (e) destabilization (sending in the CIA or the KGB), (f) signing a treaty, and (g) diplomatic pressure.

All of these policy options are subject to certain limitations that add realism to the game. There are budgetary restrictions (you can't give away what you don't have), diplomatic restrictions (not all nations will be willing to take a particular superpower's help), and physical restrictions (the logistics of any operation must be feasible).

Policy decisions in Balance of Power have broad secondary effects that reach beyond the country being targeted. For instance, if a superpower pours money and arms into countries and is generally willing to use force, it will elicit a similar global approach from its adversary. Such a tough policy will also scare smaller nations and probably cause a few to jump under the aggressive superpower's influence. The model is designed to reward the superpower that combines a willingness to fight and to stand firm with the intelligence to back down where appropriate.

Evaluation

With Balance of Power, Chris Crawford has created an interesting and provocative simulation that effectively utilizes the Macintosh's many capabilities. The graphics, which include a realistic map of the world and a number of charts, are superb. The game operates smoothly and intuitively. To work with or receive information about a specific country, you just point with the mouse to its place on the map and click.

The program's documentation is well written and provides clear instructions for working the game. The manual also presents some of the theory behind the international relations concepts that the game addresses. Just reading the materials that come with the program is likely to be informative, and playing the game will definitely prove educational. A massive amount of information is available for each of the sixty-two countries in the model, including a vast quantity of economic and social data that are immediately accessible on the screen. While some of the data have been estimated, they are quite realistic, as is the simulation itself.

There are things missing from the model, most notably, the rise of Japanese economic and military power, the emerging multipolar nature of world affairs, the influence of drugs and illegal immigration on the United States, the economic and ethnic dislocations in the Soviet Union, the possibility that the Soviet Union and Eastern Europe could undergo major political and economic changes, changes in trade relations, and the recognition that every country reacts to much more than just the actions of the superpowers. Nevertheless, Balance of Power is an excellent representation of the global political and military competition among superpowers that characterized world affairs for the past several decades.

Hardware and Software Requirements

Apple Macintosh computer, 128 KB RAM, and a mouse.

Source

Mindscape Inc., 3444 Dundee Road, Northbrook, IL 60062, USA.

Nuclear Crash: The U.S. Economy After Small Nuclear Attacks

Purpose

To study nuclear bottleneck attacks on the United States and especially the time required for the U.S. economy to recover from such attacks.

Description

Nuclear Crash is a large model (thousands of equations), that provides a dynamic simulation of the response of the U.S. economy to *bottleneck* nuclear attacks. Such attacks involve only 1 to 2 percent of the Soviet strategic arsenal, but they target key economic sectors, the destruction of which may affect the whole economy. The petroleum sector (production, refining, and distribution) emerges in the model as the ideal sector for a bottleneck nuclear attack.

The authors of the model conclude that effective deterrence can be achieved with a much smaller number of warheads than either superpower now possesses. They also argue that a strategic defense system must be essentially leakproof, since even a small number of warheads can devastate an economy through ripple effects.

The Nuclear Crash model was prepared by M. Anjali Sastry, Joseph J. Romm, and Kosta Tsipis under the Program in Science and Technology for International Security at the Massachusetts Institute of Technology. Nuclear Crash is based on an earlier model developed by Pugh-Roberts Associates for the U.S. Federal Emergency Management Agency (FEMA).

Theory and Assumptions

Nuclear Crash is a dynamic economic model in which parts of strategic sectors can be disabled to simulate the effects of a nuclear attack. The number of weapons required to achieve a given level of destruction is estimated by calculating industrial concentration curves from a detailed, commercially available, industrial location database. These curves give the fraction of an industry's capacity destroyed as a function of the number of nuclear weapons detonated.

Evaluation

Nuclear war is a prospect that cannot be ruled out for increasing numbers of nations. Accounts of Hiroshima and Nagasaki provide hints of what nuclear weapons can do. However, modern nuclear weapons are so much more powerful than those used by the United States on Japan that past experience is of limited help in understanding the devastation that a nuclear war would produce today. Simulation models are essential, therefore, for comprehending the threat posed by nuclear war.

Nuclear Crash is one of several models simulating the consequences of nuclear war. All such models reflect the enormous uncertainties that still exist, due to the fortunate scarcity of relevant data, about the effects of nuclear weapons on human settlements. This model makes an important contribution by modeling more effectively than previous models the time required for capital-producing industries to rebuild capital plants and equipment destroyed by such weapons.

Nuclear Crash has been the subject of some political controversy. For a short introduction to the debate see W. J. Broad, "Economic Collapse Tied to Atom War: Computer Analysis at Odds With Government's View," *New York Times*, June 1, 1987, p. A1.

Like any model, Nuclear Crash can be criticized. The documentation does not provide the equations and simulation specifications needed to reproduce the analysis. Demonstration of the model's historical fit is casual. More details of the decision structure assumed in the production sector would be helpful. In calculating blast damage, the model ignores the synergistic effects of electromagnetic pulse, firestorms from multiple detonations, and radioactive fallout from ground bursts.

Nonetheless, the dynamic, disequilibrium structure of Nuclear Crash sets a new standard for modeling of post-attack situations. The model builders have taken great pains to consider conservation of material, energy, and people in stock-and-flow networks, to develop robustness in extreme conditions, and to test parameter sensitivity.

The Nuclear Crash model should be of interest to leaders throughout the world for what it has to say about the vulnerability of a large industrial economy. The model could be revised to represent other types of countries, making it of broader interest to researchers and policymakers in foreign policy, security, emergency preparedness, and related fields. The documentation alone makes an excellent study tool for students of modeling methods, engineering, technology, society, and ethics.

Hardware and Software Requirements

IBM AT or compatible with a math coprocessor chip, color monitor, DOS 2.1 or greater. Professional DYNAMO Plus or possibly DYSMAP2.

Source

Documentation entitled *Nuclear Crash: The U.S. Economy After Small Nuclear Attacks* and a disk containing the model may be obtained from: Professor Kosta Tsipis, Program in Science and Technology for International Security, Massachusetts Institute of Technology, 20A-011, Cambridge, MA 02139, USA; or Alexander Pugh, Pugh-Roberts Associates, 5 Lee Street, Cambridge, MA 02139, USA.

Resolution of Capacity Shortfalls (ROCS)

Purpose

To address industrial mobilization issues for an extended conventional conflict.

Description

ROCS was designed to identify industries that have insufficient production capacity to provide for the increased demand that would occur in the event of an extended (three-year) conventional conflict. The model also defines alternatives for dealing with the shortfalls and calculates the costs of those alternatives.

Theory and Assumptions

The ROCS model uses input-output methodology. The economy is disaggregated into 115 sectors that fall into the general categories of ordnance industries, primary metals, aircraft and missile equipment, textiles and apparel, lumber and wood, and electronics.

The inputs include personal spending, purchases of new and replacement plants and equipment, exports, defense spending, federal non-defense spending, and state and local government purchases.

The outputs that can be produced for alternative policy options include: (a) emergency production capacity, (b) output, (c) shortfalls, (d) capital investments, (e) cutbacks of civilian imports, (f) exports, (g) imports, (h) resolution of shortfalls, (i) civilian cutbacks for all industrials, and (j) substitute investments.

Evaluation

ROCS should be useful to government officials responsible for developing contingency plans. In addition to its application in a prolonged war, ROCS can be utilized in simulating the industrial shortfalls that result from a wide range of national emergencies arising from other causes.

The documentation is good and includes many sample outputs.

The model's data requirements are extensive. For ROCS to be effective in an actual national emergency, data should be collected, prepared, and entered prior to the emergency.

Hardware and Software Requirements

IBM PC/XT/AT or compatible, 500 KB RAM.

Source

Mr. E. Lawrence Salkin, Federal Emergency Management Agency, Washington, D.C. 20472, USA; telephone: (201) 646-3603.

ARMS4

Purpose

To investigate how two countries can each maintain an adequate feeling of security and, at the same time, avoid a potentially destabilizing escalation in the numbers and power of their weapons.

Description

ARMS4 is a system dynamics model of the arms race, developed by Professor Jay W. Forrester and the System Dynamics Group at the Massachusetts Institute of Technology (MIT). The idea for ARMS4 came out of a trip that Forrester took to Moscow in 1983 to discuss how system dynamics could be applied to social problems. The Soviets were interested in exploring the forces underlying the escalation of weapons construction. Upon returning from that trip, Forrester worked together with members of the MIT System Dynamics Group and local political scientists to develop the ARMS4 model.

Theory and Assumptions

The ARMS4 model consists of a unified structure (see Figure 8-3) involving two countries. The goal for each country is to maintain a level of arms consistent with its own national security objectives. These objectives are, in turn, influenced by the national perception of the level of arms of the opposing country.

Increases in military capability improve a country's sense of security, but they also diminish the sense of security in the adversary nation. If the adversary nation responds by increasing its armaments, a self-reinforcing escalation—an arms race—can develop.

The model user can adjust parameters that reflect a number of psychological, technical, and political factors. One adjustable parameter, for example, is a country's tendency to overestimate the strength of other nations and underestimate its own. By adjusting parameters one at a time, users can search out plausible and rational defense policies.

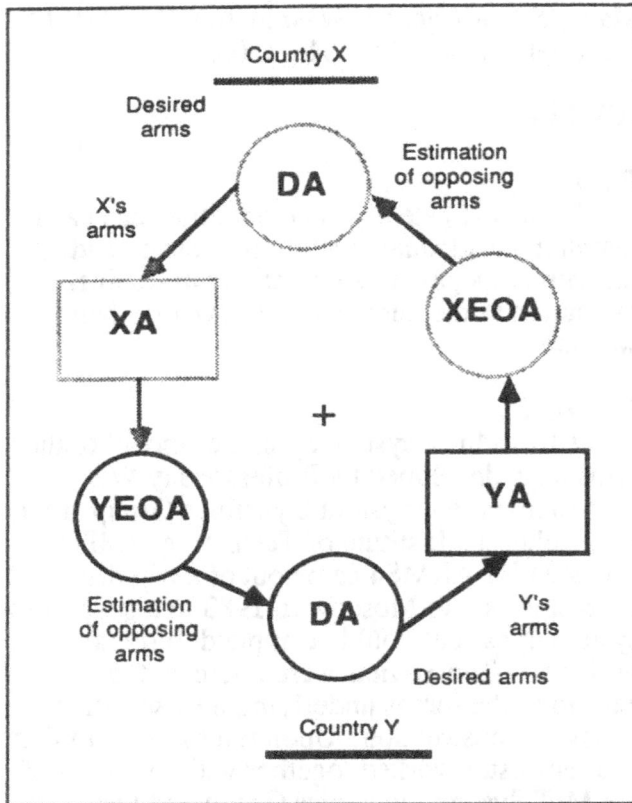

Country X

Desired arms

X's arms

DA

Estimation of opposing arms

XA

XEOA

+

YEOA

DA

YA

Estimation of opposing arms

Y's arms

Desired arms

Country Y

Figure 8-3: The structure of the primary positive feedback loop driving the ARMS4 model.

a variety of policies and thereby to develop an intuitive understanding of the field. It quickly becomes apparent to users that some policies seem rational but actually can accelerate the build-up of arms and decrease the security of both sides.

In 1919 Lewis Richardson developed a simple model of the political dynamics of an arms race. (See RICHDEMO in the "Politics" chapter.) Although there are some underlying similarities between Richardson's model and Forrester's, Forrester did not know of Richardson's work until after the development of ARMS4.

Neither ARMS4 nor the Richardson model represent in any detail what President Eisenhower called "the military industrial complex." This is unfortunate since these complexes are a major driving force in the dynamics of an arms race. William McNeill's *Pursuit of Power* (Chicago: University of Chicago, 1982) is a valuable resource in understanding their contribution. McNeill, a global-systems historian, points out that the feedback relationships governing the arms race and the military industrial complex began to evolve as early as C.E. 1000. He traces the development of these relationships from that point to modern times. An expansion of ARMS4 to include McNeill's insights would make an important contribution to world security.

Versions of ARMS4 are available in DYNAMO and BASIC. The BASIC version is mostly menu driven and comes with a step-by-step user's guide that includes sample simulations. The DYNAMO version requires somewhat more knowledge of modeling and is well suited to a research environment.

Evaluation

This model is a powerful tool for illustrating how technology, psychology, and politics interact in an arms race. It is also useful in identifying high-leverage policies, revealing inconsistencies in mental models, integrating theories, and improving communication on the topic of defense policies.

ARMS4 does not make detailed numeric analyses, such as the number of missiles each side should build, nor does it provide measures of who is "ahead" in the real arms race. The model is meant only to increase understanding of the underlying dynamics of the arms race. The focus is on identifying points of potential influence in the interconnected vicious circles that lead to armament build-ups. ARMS4 is probably the best tool available for this purpose.

ARMS4 makes a strong impact on most people who are exposed to it. The interactiveness of the model allows users to test

Hardware and Software Requirements

IBM PC/XT/AT or compatible, 640 KB RAM, two floppy disk drives, and BASIC. For research, Professional DYNAMO Plus or possibly DYSMAP2. The model could also be rewritten for STELLA on an Apple Macintosh.

Source

System Dynamics Group, Sloan School of Management, Massachusetts Institute of Technology, 50 Memorial Drive, Cambridge, MA 02139, USA; telephone: (617) 253-1578.

9. Politics

Introduction

Microcomputers are beginning to have an impact on diverse aspects of political processes, including elections. There are, for example, a wide range of specialized programs now for the scheduling, budgeting, and fund-raising tasks of a political campaign. Computerized voting machines have been introduced that greatly accelerate the tabulation process, although, like older methods, they are still vulnerable to tampering.

This chapter looks at another application of computers to politics, namely the use of software in understanding political situations and in reaching consensus about potentially divisive issues. One of the most interesting of such software tools is the Environmental Assessment System (EASY). It is a tool that mediators can use when helping develop a consensus on issues about which there is simultaneous disagreement over facts, consequences, and priorities. The EASY methodology has been applied successfully in debates on how best to expand a nation's electric power facilities, and it could be applied to many other types of issues.

The Estates Eutrophication Model was developed for similar consensus-reaching purposes, but the methodology is quite different from that of EASY. The Estates model was instrumental in resolving a heated political controversy in the Netherlands on alternative approaches to the problem of eutrophication.

Inter-Nation Simulation II allows students to assume roles as heads of state. The students make decisions affecting other nations, and the model simulates the global consequences. This model has been used with thousands of students at many institutions, including some of the military academies of the U.S. armed forces.

Two of the models reviewed here simulate the power transfers and violence that sometimes accompany the growth of developing countries. Users of Third World Simulation attempt to take power in a simulated developing country and, if successful, attempt to lead the country to development. The opportunities for change after taking power are greatly influenced by the tactics used to gain power. The Developing Nation model addresses the political aspects of the development process, especially the way in which violence and repression can emerge. It can be used either for education or research.

Two other models concern the political and social processes through which societies adopt a new idea. In the Diffusion Game, users must choose from several different tactics to promote a new idea among the citizens of a small town in a developing country. NEWIDEA is a dynamic simulation of the consequences of alternative strategies that an interest group might use in promoting the adoption of a new idea by a nation.

The Presidential Election Game and Simulation represents a U.S. presidential campaign. It quickly and effectively introduces students to some of the complex, strategic decisions that U.S. presidential candidates must make.

Three models focus on the political interactions among groups of people. RICHDEMO presents the famous Richardson model, which is the mathematical foundation for virtually all modern arms-race models. Prisoner's Dilemma presents the classic political and psychological problem of two isolated people who can help each other but, in doing so, may hurt themselves. The Tragedy of the Commons model presents the fundamental problem of regulating the use of a resource shared in common.

Readers interested in political models should also see the review of GLOBUS in "Global Models." The generic national model used in GLOBUS has an explicit representation of domestic politics. Furthermore, the GLOBUS global framework includes an explicit representation of international politics.

Environmental Assessment System (EASY)

Purpose

To provide a flexible decision support system for political decisions involving multiple decision makers and complex issues, such as the environment.

Description

EASY is the work of Ron Janssen and Wim Hafkamp, both of whom are experts in decision theory. They wanted to develop a practical tool to help societies make good decisions on difficult problems. The difficulties that societies have making good decisions on environmental issues attracted their attention, and they demonstrated their tool first on an environmental issue, namely the selection by a nation of a power generation alternative that is "most sound" environmentally.

The application of EASY is not, however, restricted to environmental issues. It is a computer-based system designed to facilitate the formation of consensus among groups of decision makers on difficult political issues. It is addressed particularly to questions about which more than one criterion can and should be considered in evaluating the available alternatives. The system processes cause-effect relationships in real world phenomena to produce impact analyses and evaluates alternatives at each link of the cause-effect chains on the basis of user preference.

In applying their tool to a nation's choice of power generation alternatives, Janssen and Hafkamp observed that decisions are difficult because interest groups and other parties are in conflict on many points simultaneously. To begin with, they are in conflict over objectives and interests, including: (a) general objectives, e.g., economic development, employment, environmental quality, sustainability; (b) attributes of objectives, e.g., for environmental quality: acidification, radiation, noise, safety risks; (c) interests of present and future generations; and (d) regional interests, i.e., the geographic distribution of the results of the objectives. Furthermore, these groups disagree over definitions, technical and economic data, hypotheses, and theories and models regarding the effects of alternative policies on the various objectives.

Under these circumstances, the very procedures traditionally used for decision making are disputed. For example, cost-benefit analysis usually fails to resolve environmental issues because many of the explicit and implicit assumptions required for cost-benefit analysis are rejected from the start by one or more of the parties involved.

Janssen and Hafkamp concluded that a new tool was needed for decision making in the 21st century. The tool had to facilitate not only traditional cost-benefit analysis, but also multicriteria analysis and multiobjective analysis. Furthermore, the new tool had to facilitate communication, mediation, and negotiation. EASY was the result.

Theory and Assumptions

In its initial application, The Environmental Assessment System (EASY) is a computer-based decision support system that assists decision makers, interest groups, and concerned parties in the assessment of the environmental effects of alternative means of electric power generation. EASY can be used to compare individual generation systems (nuclear, coal, gas, oil, wind, and so forth) and combinations of systems on the basis of their environmental effects.

The EASY analysis proceeds in two dimensions simultaneously. In one dimension physical and ecological cause-effect relationships are traced through first and second orders. In the second dimension, the preference weights of the interested parties are applied to the alternatives to lead to evaluative assessments. This two-dimensional approach to the analysis makes it possible to separate scientific arguments on cause-effect relationships from arguments related to individual preferences and policy priorities.

The analysis of the chains of physical cause-effect relationships starts with the emissions matrix. In this matrix, measures of eight types of emissions, two types of solid waste, three types of land use, and two indicators of risk are listed for various types of electricity generation (nuclear, coal, gas, syngas, oil, synfuel, hydro, and wind) and for various combinations of these. Distributional information is then applied to obtain current ambient concentrations. Ambient concentrations are related to threshold values to develop measures of ecological effects.

The analysis of preferences begins when the decision makers assign their personal weighting criteria to various ecological effects. EASY makes this process, in fact, easy. Users are simply asked to order the effects according to importance, e.g., acidification is more important than photochemical pollution, or vice versa. The net result might be, for example, as follows: Acidification > photochemical pollution > solid waste > risk > greenhouse effect > other effects. The weighting criteria are then applied to all systems to produce the appraisal matrix, which is illustrated in Figure 9-1.

Finally, EASY combines the analysis of chains of physical cause-effect relations with the analysis of preferences. The result is a ranking of the candidate systems. In this way the system makes the consequences of preferences and priorities explicit and apparent.

Evaluation

EASY is a captivating program. Anyone who has ever been frustrated by an unfocused, angry, inconclusive debate over a political issue will immediately perceive the utility of the program.

One of EASY's most impressive capabilities is its ability to help a decision maker who has doubts about the relevance or accuracy of some of the facts, processes, choices, and assumptions being used in the decision-making process. If one has new data or new ideas, it is simple to move back a stage or two and enter this information into the system. EASY instantly recalculates the final rankings.

With EASY as a mediating tool, it is possible to separate scientific arguments on cause-effect relationships from arguments related to individual preferences and different policy priorities. One can then focus the

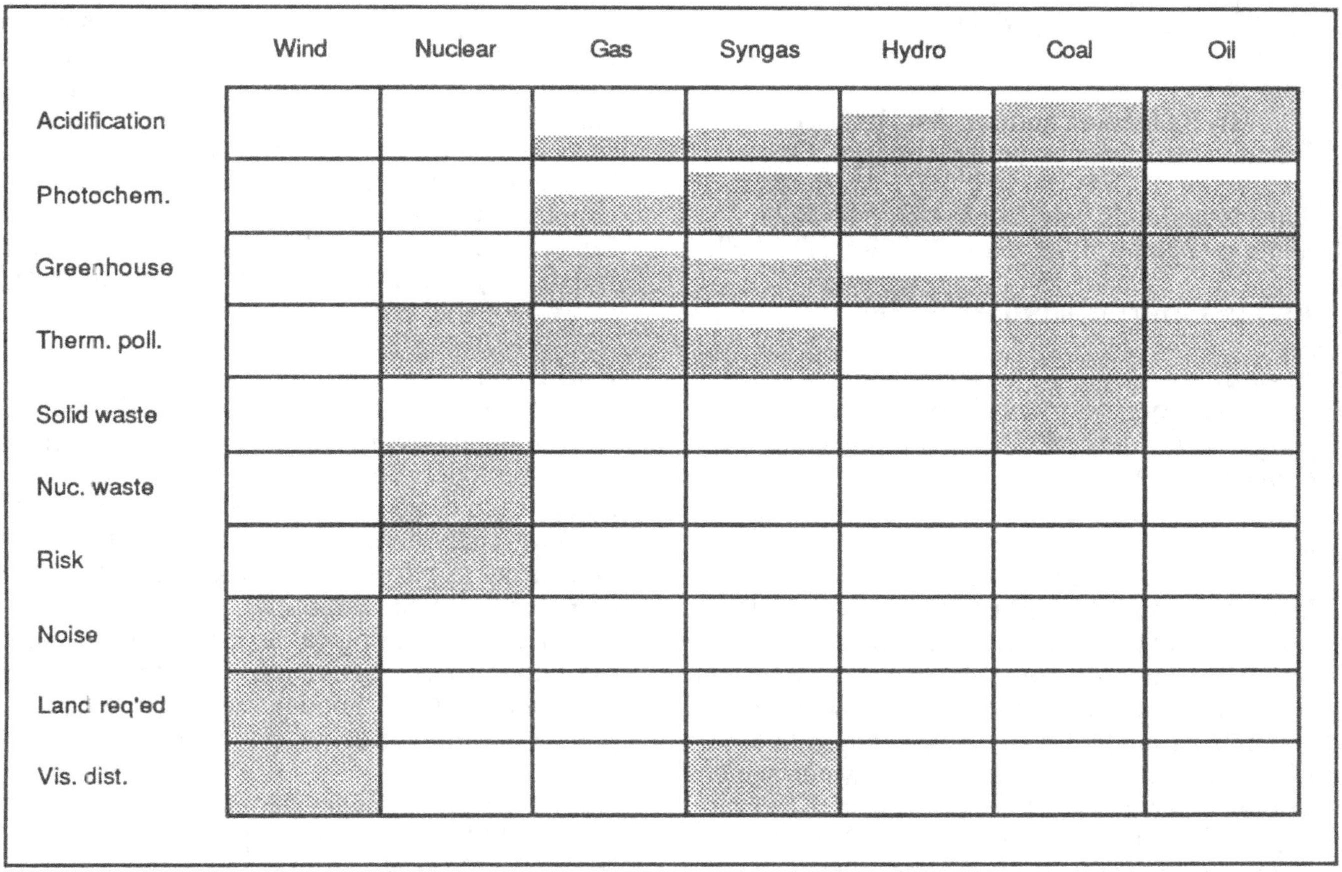

	Wind	Nuclear	Gas	Syngas	Hydro	Coal	Oil
Acidification			▓	▓	▓	▓	▓
Photochem.			▓	▓	▓		▓
Greenhouse			▓	▓	▓	▓	▓
Therm. poll.		▓	▓	▓		▓	▓
Solid waste						▓	
Nuc. waste		▓					
Risk		▓					
Noise	▓						
Land req'ed	▓						
Vis. dist.	▓			▓			

Figure 9-1: Graphical presentation of the sorted appraisal matrix produced by the Environmental Assessment System (EASY).

discussion on the specific points of disagreement, and in many cases these can be resolved. Differences may remain, but the area of disagreement probably will have been reduced significantly. Once the so-called solution space has been reduced, different preferences and priorities may in fact lead to the same ranking of alternatives.

EASY is unlikely to resolve all of the world's conflicts, but it has potential for cutting through large amounts of irrelevant disagreement. This done, the debate can focus on resolving key points.

It should be remembered that the methodology underlying EASY can be applied in a wide range of conflicts and is not limited to conflicts over environmental issues. This tool deserves much more attention than it has received to date.

Hardware and Software Requirements
IBM PC/XT/AT or compatible, 512 KB RAM, one floppy disk drive, and a Hercules graphics card or compatible.

Source
Mr. R. Janssen and Mr. W. Hafkamp, Institute for Environment and Energy, Free University, P.O. Box 7161, 1007 Amsterdam, The Netherlands; telephone: (20) 548-3827; telefax: (20) 44-5056; telex: 10399 INTVU NL.

Estates Eutrophication Model

Purpose
To analyze alternative policies and programs for the control of eutrophication in a country or region.

Description
The Estates Model describes the processes leading to eutrophication of surface waters in an imaginary region, which could represent a province or a small country. The surface waters have an inflow and outflow, both of which can be adjusted in the model. A sewer system carries off residential and industrial waste water, which is treated at a sewage treatment plant. The non-urban land is used for agriculture. The cattle farming areas are a source of phosphate pollution, both by leaching and by run-off.

The model simulates four approaches to controlling eutrophication: (a) reduction of phosphates in detergents, (b) tertiary treatment of sewage, (c) control of surface run-off from agricultural lands, and (d) control of phosphates entering the region from neighboring countries or regions. Each of these approaches has significant costs for different groups in the population.

The model was developed and applied originally in the Netherlands during an intense public debate over how to control eutrophication. Strong and vocal interest groups (estates) had formed seeking to avoid any approach that would burden their own estate with additional costs. Little exchange of information or serious dialogue was taking place among the estates. When the Estates Model was introduced into this difficult political situation, it contributed greatly to improved communication, a thoughtful and effective resolution of the debate, and effective action.

Theory and Assumptions
The model is based on the system dynamics methodology. Both the ecological processes and the four estates are represented in feedback loops. (See Figure 9-2.) Each estate has a control unit that is sensitive to costs (real and imagined) and to cultural and political issues. The four controlling estates, however, are not coupled with each other and are not subject to direct external control. The goal is to achieve a satisfactory water quality at acceptable costs and in a reasonable time.

Evaluation
The Estates Eutrophication Model is a fascinating hybrid of an ecological model and a political model. Its structure and logic are quickly and easily understood by diverse groups. It allows individuals to organize and interrelate a wide array of information pertaining to a complex problem with social, political, economic, and ecological aspects. The modelers have done an impressive job—not only with the formulation of their model, but also with their participation in the actual policy debate.

Hardware and Software Requirements
IBM PC/XT/AT or compatible and Professional DYNAMO Plus or perhaps DYSMAP2. Or with some rewriting of the equations, an Apple Macintosh and STELLA.

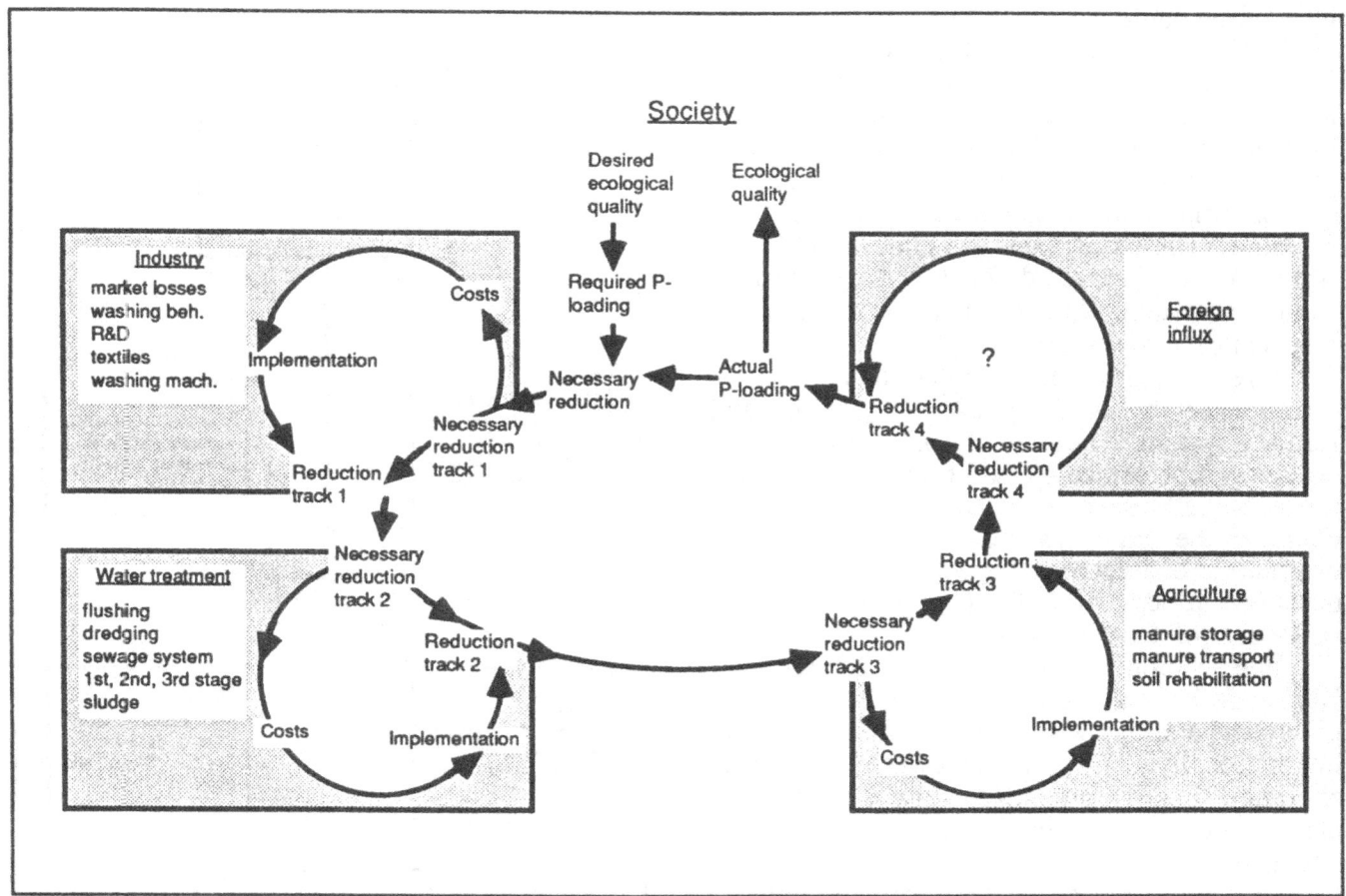

Figure 9-2: Estates Eutrophication Model.

Source

The equations for the model are reported in R. O. Beijdorff et al., "System Analysis of the Dutch Phosphate Policy", (Paper presented at the Royal Dutch Chemical Society Phosphate Policy Symposium, Wageningen, The Netherlands, March 1984). The paper and more elaborate versions of the model are available from: Foundation for Applied Ecology, Oorgat 2, 1135 CR Edam, The Netherlands; telephone: (02993) 72039. The price varies with the application and circumstances.

Inter-Nation Simulation II

Purpose

To simulate international decision making by assuming the role of executive-level government officials, who interact under different scenarios with representatives of other nations.

Description

Inter-Nation Simulation II is an interactive computer simulation of the international system. The core of the program is the role-playing game, which involves between fifteen and fifty people, who are divided into groups representing different countries.

Six officers are needed for each country, and there can be as many countries as necessary to accommodate the group size. Each country has a head of state, an official domestic advisor, a foreign policy advisor, a foreign affairs diplomat, a domestic opposition leader, and an intelligence research officer.

Each simulation is divided into a briefing session, a trial period, a series of decision periods, and a final debriefing session. The entire process is supervised by a game leader, who determines the issues addressed and the pace of the game.

The game leader can either choose a scenario from the set of ready-made situations or create a new one. Each scenario presents a set of problems to be solved during the course of the game; the best ones are designed to illustrate one or more important concepts in international relations. The participants can choose to go to war if their differences defined by the scenario cannot be settled, or they can decide to make and respect peaceful settlements.

Every country in the simulation is distinguished by its own political, economic, and military system. The state of each of these sectors is represented by different indicators that are set initially but can be changed over the course of the game. The political system, for example, is characterized by an indicator called decision latitude. High decision latitude is the equivalent of a dictatorship.

Inter-Nation Simulation II runs in rounds. During each round, countries decide what their policy and strategy will be both domestically and internationally. The computer offers a range for alterations in government spending, and the players decide the direction and extent of alterations.

During the game, two "publications" are distributed after each round of decisions—the *World Times* and the *Intelligence Report*. Both are controlled by the game leader and are based on messages and information sent among the different nations during play.

During each decision period there is a conference of the foreign affairs diplomats and also a forum called the International Organization, which is something like the United Nations. The conference and forum are designed to allow international communication.

The length of a particular game is flexible. Generally, players can have as many decision periods as they want, but typically the problems are solved after a while, and the game lags. The documentation notes that about four decision periods usually cover the necessary ground.

The original version of Inter-Nation Simulation II was developed by the renowned political scientist and modeler Professor Harold Guetzkow and his colleague Cleo H. Cherryholmes. The microcomputer version of the model was developed by Professor Bahram Farzanegan and his colleague Ronald Parker.

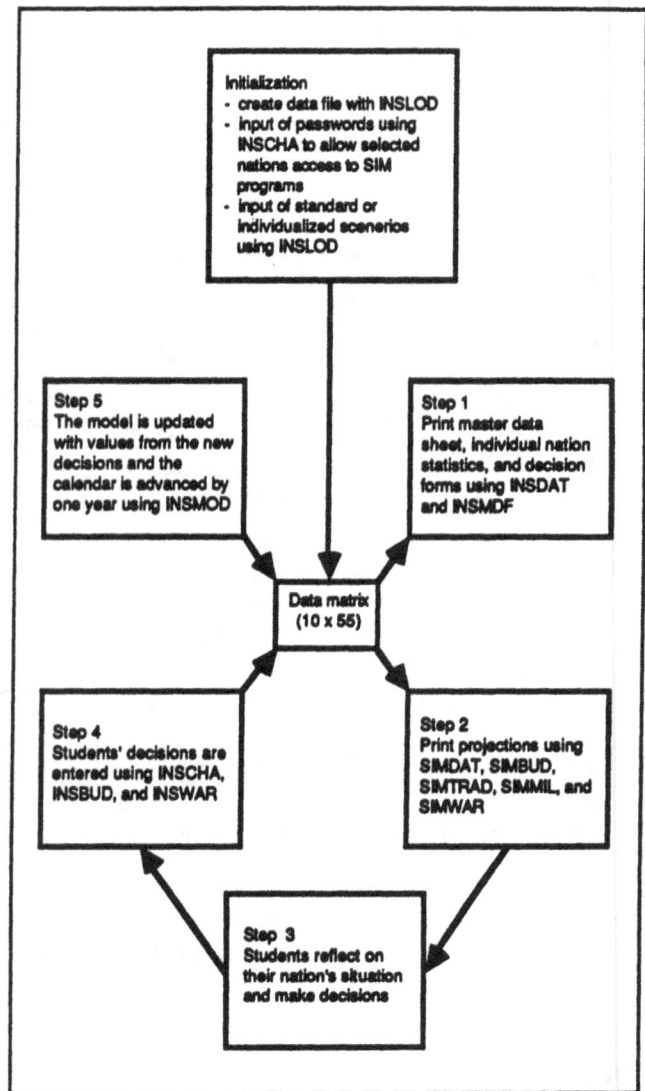

Figure 9-3: The initialization and five-step process used in Inter-Nation Simulation II.

Theory and Assumptions

The several submodels and their interrelationships are illustrated in Figure 9-3. The package includes a number of programs that perform necessary administrative functions. One program allows the game leader, by entering a password, to gain access to the simulation programs. Another program is used to enter the players' decisions. Another prints handouts for the players. Yet another is used to modify data in the control data file, which is a ten by fifty-five matrix.

The package also contains five programs that simulate the students' decisions and print projections showing the consequences of those decisions. Four of these cover trade, the budget, military, and war, while the fifth prepares data for the others.

Evaluation

Inter-Nation Simulation II is an excellent, simple model of international affairs. While players must work within the context of the model, it is not a rigid framework. They can concentrate on solving problems and analyzing interaction among the countries, while the computer facilitates the process by performing the necessary calculations.

The model concentrates on political, military, and trade matters and does not address some of the more complex international economic issues; these issues are subsumed by larger concepts. For instance, exchange rates are not specifically represented but are included among factors determining trade agreements and activity. Furthermore, since the model is designed to educate users on major interaction patterns among nations, the lack of certain details is not important in the overall scheme.

A major deficiency of the game, however, is the omission of global environmental issues. At a time when nations are actively considering agreements to limit the combustion of fossil fuels to decrease carbon dioxide emissions and avoid global climate changes, such matters need to be included in inter-nation simulations.

The success of the game is highly dependent on the skill and preparation of the game leader. The program is not complicated, but a few days are needed to learn the game well. It is probably best for a new leader to play the game a few times among friends before attempting it with a formal group. Also, leaders should run the model a few times with the preprogrammed situations before attempting customized versions.

The documentation is quite well written. The instructions make the programs easy to use.

Hardware and Software Requirements

Apple II/IIe/II+, IBM PC/AT/XT, or compatible; printer.

Source

NCSU Software Department, School of Humanities and Social Sciences, Box 8101, North Carolina State University, Raleigh, NC 27695, USA; telephone: (919) 739-3067.

Third World Simulation

Purpose

To simulate power transfers in a Third World nation.

Description

Third World Simulation is an educational tool designed to simulate the political and power struggles that sometimes occur in Third World nations. The objective of the players is to take control of the government and exercise power in a way that benefits the country's peasants.

The model was developed by Professors Douglas V. Porpora and Donald Stevens of Drexel University.

Theory and Assumptions

There are two phases to the game: first taking control and then exercising power.

The first phase is complicated by the fact that the country is initially under the control of a dictator about whom the players know little. The first task, therefore, is to learn about the dictator by taking action and seeing how he responds.

The dictators represented in the model are of two types, those who will fight to the death and those who will flee the country if faced with armed opposition. Some of the dictators employ death squads, fix elections, and bribe their opponents.

After developing a sense of the personality of the dictator, players can choose among various tactics to take power: election, coup d'etat, demonstration, general strike, urban insurrection, rural guerilla warfare, or foreign invasion. Each tactic has different effects on the support the aspirant to power can muster from peasants, domestic capitalists, foreign capitalists, landed oligarchy, urban workers, small-shop keepers, urban professionals, and students.

After taking power, players have several areas in which they can improve the life of the peasants: the infant mortality rate, the literacy rate, per capita caloric consumption, and other quality-of-life measurements. The ability of the new leader to effect change is determined by the support available. If power was obtained through a coup or election, much power is still held by the army and the oligarchy, and only limited changes can be made to help the peasants. If power was obtained through a revolution, the army is under the leader's control, but the oligarchy and multinational capitalists are not. A prolonged revolution drives up the national debt, limiting financial options after the takeover.

Evaluation

Third World Simulation is intended to introduce students to the complexities of Third World power struggles, and it achieves this end quite well.

While the documentation is not very detailed, it is sufficient for a new user to run the simulation. It is seriously inadequate, however, in explaining the details of how the model actually works. No equations or flow diagrams are provided. The user is simply presented with a so-called black box model.

The model is being revised, and better documentation is expected. The utility of this interesting model should be increased greatly by this improvement.

Hardware and Software Requirements

Apple Macintosh computer.

Source

Prof. Douglas V. Porpora, Department of Psychology, Sociology and Anthropology, Drexel University, Philadelphia, PA 19104, USA; telephone: (215) 895-2404; telefax: (215) 895-1414. A price will be set when the new version of the model is available.

Developing Nation

Purpose

To provide a model of the dynamics of violence in the development process and to address the question: "How can development occur without violence or repression?"

Description

Developing Nation is a dynamic simulation of approximately fifty years in the evolution of a developing country. The model is different from many other development models in that it includes an explicit representation of the sociopolitical factors that are generally assumed to be the underlying causes of violence. The model also includes representations of the costs—economic and otherwise—of violence.

The model was developed by Professor John M. Richardson, Jr. at American University in Washington, D.C.

Theory and Assumptions

Developing Nation contains three sectors: population, government, and economy. (See Figure 9-4.) The model contains nine level (or stock or state) variables and approximately ninety equations.

The population sector consists of a relatively standard dynamic population model plus an economic variable (demand for consumption goods) and two political indices (satisfaction and dissatisfaction). While violence is initiated by random events, the levels of satisfaction and dissatisfaction determine the potential for violence. Increased levels of development, measured by personal consumption per capita, reduce death rates and lagged birth rates and increase the productivity of the labor force.

The government sector receives revenues from the economic sector and allocates them to its security establishment and to human services. Decreased allocation to human services generate political pressures to increase the allocation. The national security establishment also generates political pressure to increase its budget. Its influence increases in turbulent times and also as its size increases. Repressive government policies limit the expression of demands and the outbreak of violence. When violence does occur, the strength of the security force is a factor in determining the intensity and duration of the violence. The government can be the recipient of foreign aid, which can be allocated to consumption, investment, human services, or national security.

The economy sector generates output and allocates it in response to demands, dividing it among consumption, allocations to government, and savings. The internal dynamics of the model affect the relative weight of these priorities. When violence breaks out, productive capital can be destroyed, thus reducing output. Labor productivity is affected by the levels of satisfaction and dissatisfaction and by the level of development.

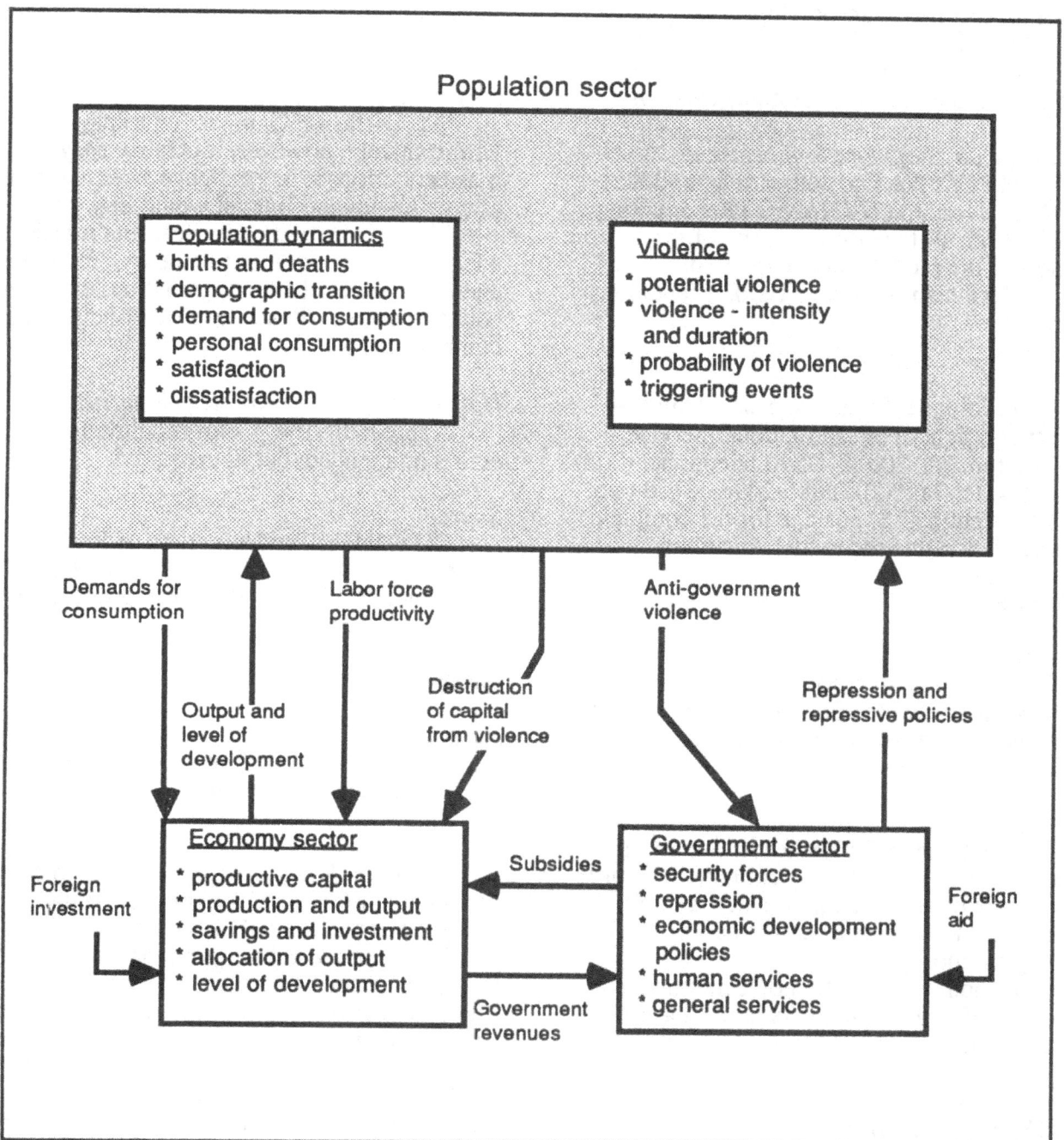

Figure 9-4: Developing Nation.

Evaluation

Violence in the course of development has been tragic and costly, yet little attention has been devoted to understanding the dynamic causes of violence and ways to avoid it. Developing Nation provides a functional model in this important area. In developing and evaluating the model, Professor Richardson has assembled statistical data on violence in many Third World countries. While Developing Nation cannot provide precise predictions of probable violence in any particular country, its relative simplicity makes it an excellent teaching tool. Various useful adaptations could be made to the model. It could be parameterized to represent specific countries, and disaggregated versions could be used to address issues in education, rural and urban balance, income disparity, and ethnic and religious tensions.

Hardware and Software Requirements
    IBM PC/XT/AT or compatible, 640 KB RAM; Professional DYNAMO Plus or perhaps DYSMAP2. With some rewriting of the equations, the model could also be run on an Apple Macintosh with the STELLA modeling language.

Source
    Prof. John M. Richardson, Jr., American University, School of International Service, Washington, DC 20016, USA; telephone: (202) 885-1694; telefax: (202) 885-2494. Send two disks and return U.S. postage for the complete documentation and the model equations.

Diffusion Game

Purpose
    To introduce users to alternative methods of publicizing a new idea or innovation and have them discover the optimum order and combination of these methods.

Description
    The setting for the Diffusion Game is a typical town in a developing country. The user has the task of convincing 70 percent of the population in one year or less to accept a new farming technology.
    This model was written by Christopher Lovelock, Harvard University, and Charles Weinberg, University of British Columbia.

Theory and Assumptions
    The town has four means of communication: a newspaper, a radio station, a meeting hall, and private discussions with leaders. Each of these methods of communication varies in effectiveness and in preparation time required. The order in which the methods of communications are used influences their effectiveness. For instance, radio and newspaper publicity before a demonstration increases the effectiveness of the demonstration. Information on the relative effectiveness of alternative means of communications can be obtained during the

game. The objective is to find a strategy that is maximally effective in convincing the population to accept the new technology.

Evaluation
    The Diffusion Game is fun to play. Unfortunately, however, it is fairly easy to master and looses its challenge after two or three plays. An advanced level would help greatly.
    The documentation is clear, but it lacks an adequate explanation of the theory behind the exercise. With a better explanation, the model could be used to illustrate basic principles of communication.

Hardware and Software Requirements
    Apple II/IIe/II+. Color monitor and printer are recommended, but not required.

Source
    CONDUIT, The University of Iowa, Oakdale Campus, Iowa City, Iowa 52242, USA; telephone: (319) 335-4100. The price of the game is US $55.

NEWIDEA

Purpose
    To provide a model of social change induced by social movements.

Description
    NEWIDEA is a dynamic simulation over a period of approximately sixty years of the interactions and mutual influences between a political or social action group promoting a new idea and the society of which the group is a part. The model is addressed primarily to the normal situation in which the true utility of a new idea cannot be gauged accurately until after its full implementation, and uncertainties consequently exist as to both the costs and benefits of adopting the idea. By changing parameters, the user can study various dynamic patterns of acceptance and rejection that result from different circumstances.
    In its presented form, the model represents an industrialized society in which an interest group is promoting "environmental concern," i.e., an ecologically sound relationship between human activities and the biosphere. The members of the environmental action group hold that action must be taken now; their opponents

hold that action can be delayed until the advantages become more apparent. The validity of either position can be assessed only through experience.

NEWIDEA simulates the consequences of alternative approaches that the environmentalists might use in transmitting their new idea to the society. If they do nothing, societal acceptance of the new idea comes only slowly and at high cost. If an environmental group forms and presses for acceptance of the new idea, change begins sooner, but resistance—a backlash—develops. If effort is devoted to increasing the commitment of the group members, there is short-term improvement counterbalanced by increased resistance to change. Intensive early publicity leads to overwhelmingly active resistance and delays acceptance significantly.

Many of the model runs indicate that quick aggressive action is counterproductive and leads to an "immune" response by the public. However, early concentrated activity of this sort generates social debate and also provides valuable experience for the group. A gradual, gentle approach that may appear optimal actually results in backlash also, in this case from public boredom with the issue.

Under another strategy, the action group devotes a large amount of time and energy on a few recruits to increase their effectiveness and insure against their reversion to the old views. This strategy works quite well within the model.

Theory and Assumptions
NEWIDEA was not developed from a statistical database, but from the collective knowledge and experience of a group of advisors, all of whom had been involved in action groups promoting new ideas. The model went through twelve major revisions; all of the versions before the final one were rejected because one or more advisors had experiences contrary to the model.

The final model is a twelfth-order differential equation describing eleven interrelated feedback loops involving numerous non-linearities. Approximately a third of the variables describe the state of the action group; half describe the state of the society; and the remainder represent the idea, which changes over time.

Evaluation
NEWIDEA cannot be used to make detailed predictions about the acceptance of innovative ideas. However, it can serve as an excellent training tool to teach students—or recruits to action groups—the dynamic phenomena involved in social acceptance of a new idea.

Hardware and Software Requirements
IBM PC/XT/AT or compatible with 640 KB RAM, hard disk, color monitor; Professional DYNAMO Plus or perhaps DYSMAP2. With some rewriting of the equations, the model could also be used on an Apple Macintosh computer with the STELLA simulation software.

Source
The equations for NEWIDEA are presented in J. Randers, "Conceptualizing Dynamic Models of Social Systems: Lessons from a Study of Social Change" (Massachusetts Institute of Technology, 1973), which is available from Massachusetts Institute of Technology, Thesis Reproduction Center, Cambridge, MA 02139, USA. The price is US $50.

Presidential Election Game and Simulation

Purpose
To simulate a presidential campaign in the United States.

Description
Presidential Election Game and Simulation represents the process of running for president in the United States. In the game, the candidate who wins a particular state is awarded the Electoral College votes associated with that state, which is the process actually used in U.S. presidential elections. At the end of the campaign, the candidate with the most electoral votes wins.

The user is given a budget of seventy hours and $100,000 for each week of the election and instructed to allocate the resources among the fifty states. At the end of each round, which represents a week, the computer generates a color map of the United States that shows the candidates' relative standings in each state at the end of the round. The length of the campaign is decided by the user at the beginning of the game.

Theory and Assumptions

In the game, the outcome of each round is determined in a two-step process. First, the computer compares the political position of the candidates with the political feelings of the state in question. Second, these comparisons are weighted by the computer in proportion to the amount of time and money each candidate spends in the state in question.

The player's political position is determined at the outset by a questionnaire. The questionnaire asks players to give their approval rating of different national policies and political figures. The players are also asked to rank the country's attitude toward their party's ideology and to indicate their sense of the importance of campaigning time and expenditures to election results. Each state's actual political preference is set in the model to correspond to the averaged position of the state's congressmen on the issues.

Evaluation

This is a very interesting simulation of the electoral process, and it illustrates a number of important points. For example, the candidates in the game quickly learn that they have insufficient time to campaign throughout the country.

Actually, the game lets players reach an unrealistic amount of the country within the time available. It allows users to spend the full seventy hours shaking hands and giving speeches in the different states, but it places no restrictions on which states can be included in a tour, as if travel required no time. Furthermore, time for other demands—television interviews, staff meetings, or fulfilling the responsibilities of a current political office—is not deducted from the time available for campaigning.

The model could be improved in several other ways. Given the importance of television in campaigning, the model needs a way of accounting for it. The model should also distinguish between the incumbent and challenger candidates, since they have different time constraints and different campaigning opportunities.

The model is also flawed by its assumptions that if the country were predominantly Democratic (liberal), it would never elect a Republican (conservative) president. Recent experience shows that this is not the case.

Overall, however, this is a good, simple model. It is easy to use and the documentation is clear. If a constructive discussion period follows the simulation, the model could be an excellent educational tool.

Hardware and Software Requirements

Apple II/IIe/II+ or an IBM PC/AT/XT or compatible with a graphics card. A printer is useful, but not required.

Source

National Collegiate Software, Duke University Press, 6697 College Station, Durham, NC 27708, USA; telephone: (919) 684-2173.

RICHDEMO

Purpose

To predict whether an arms race will lead to a war or to a time when the two opposing parties are driven to increase mutual threats but are constrained from further arms increases by economic or other factors.

Description

Lewis F. Richardson developed the famous Richardson Arms Race model in 1919. His work went largely unnoticed until the early 1970s. Since then scholars and researchers have applied his model to a number of historic and current situations. Professor Philip A. Schrodt, author of the RICHDEMO model, has also written a description of the Richardson model and its historic development (*BYTE*, July 1982, pp. 109-134).

Theory and Assumptions

The major assumptions are: (a) nation Y feels threatened by the arms of its opponent, nation X; (b) the more arms Y has, the more arms X will want to acquire; (c) nation X must meet basic social needs and cannot devote its entire economy to producing weapons, so that the more arms it has, the fewer additional arms it will be able to acquire; (d) past grievances affect the overall arms level and are unaffected by the current arms levels; and (e) the assumptions (a-d) above also apply to country Y.

These assumptions are expressed mathematically in two difference equations:

$$X(t + 1) = kY(t) - aX(t) + g$$
$$Y(t + 1) = mX(t) - bY(t) + h$$

The functions $X(t)$ and $Y(t)$ are the values of the arms levels at time t; $X(t + 1)$ and $Y(t + 1)$ are those values at time t plus one increment of time. The parameters k, a, g, m, b, and h are chosen to fit a particular situation. Parameters k, m, a, and b are all positive; g and h are either positive or negative depending on whether the two nations are basically hostile or basically friendly toward each other.

Evaluation

The Richardson model is the basic structure behind most modern models of the arms race. Professor Schrodt's RICHDEMO provides an excellent introduction to the theory and dynamics of the Richardson model formulation.

Hardware and Software Requirements

IBM PC/XT/AT with a PASCAL compiler or interpreter, or Apple II with Apple PASCAL.

Source

Prof. Philip A. Schrodt, Political Science Department, Northwestern University, Evanston, IL 60201, USA; telephone: (312) 491-2642; bitnet: SCHRODT@NUACC.

Prisoner's Dilemma

Purpose

To simulate the decision-making situation in the "prisoner's dilemma" by allowing the user to play against a computer-generated opponent.

Description

The program is based on the classic prisoner's dilemma scenario. Two people suspected of committing a crime together are arrested, separated, and interrogated. There are four possible outcomes; both prisoners can confess, both can remain silent, or either one can confess while the other remains silent.

The dilemma arises because their sentences depend on the decisions they both make, and they cannot confer. For example: if both confess, they each receive nine years of imprisonment; if only one confesses, that one is jailed for just two years, while the other is jailed for twelve years; if neither confesses, they both go to jail for four years.

Each prisoner will be tempted to confess, since doing so will reduce the sentence regardless of whether the other prisoner confesses or not. But on the other hand, if the prisoners have enough mutual trust to keep silent, they will get a lower collective sentence.

Theory and Assumptions

In the game, the computer takes the role of one prisoner and the user that of the other prisoner. The game goes through many rounds, with the computer keeping statistics on which side is sentenced to the longest number of years in prison.

Some political scientists argue that here is an analogy between the prisoner's dilemma and the dilemma of an arms race in which each country wishes to dominate the other. While it is unrealistic to think that each nation can continue increasing its weapons indefinitely, each is afraid to quit. Here is the dilemma. For disarmament or arms reduction to occur in this situation, it is necessary for the nations to act in such a way that neither gains superiority. Each nation faces the choice between cooperation, reducing its arms to benefit both itself and the rival nation, or betrayal, adding to its own weapons stockpile to benefit itself alone.

There is a great deal of literature (some of which is listed in the documentation) describing alternative strategies to employ when playing the prisoner's dilemma game. Four of the basic ones are used by the computer-generated opponent. These are: (a) responding randomly, (b) always being trusting and cooperative, (c) always being distrusting and combative, and (d) always acting tit for tat, i.e., imitating the other side. The user can play against all of these strategies and develop new ones to test against the standards.

Evaluation

This is an interesting package, but it falls short in a number of ways. First, the documentation is very limited. While it explains the mechanics of using the program, there is very little discussion of the theory behind the prisoner's dilemma. Second, there is no discussion of the strategies that players might use. The players must figure these out themselves. Finally, there is no way to analyze the results of alternative strategies. The program should be able to focus attention on the pattern of moves and their significance.

The package is very easy to use and install, but the program is easily disrupted if the operating instructions are not followed exactly.

Hardware and Software Requirements

IBM PC/AT/XT or compatible or Apple II/II+/IIe.

Source

National Collegiate Software, Duke University Press, 6697 College Station, Durham, NC 27708, USA; telephone: (919) 684-2173.

Tragedy of the Commons

Purpose

To illustrate Garrett Hardin's principle of the Tragedy of the Commons—that increased exploitation of a common resource is desirable in the short term for each individual in a community, but disastrous in the long term to the whole community.

Description

In Tragedy of the Commons, the user takes on the role of a sheep herder in medieval England. As was the case at that time, all shepherds in the program's simulated world share a common pasture for grazing their flocks. The objective of each shepherd is to maximize

profit. Profits fall far below maximum if the common pasture is destroyed through overgrazing.

Theory and Assumptions

In each round, the program calculates the potential profit, actual profit, and overgrazing factor. This information is presented in a chart (see Figure 9-5) and is used by the shepherd to make the next set of decisions.

Initially, the user and the other, computer-generated shepherds have no sheep. At this point, the economic incentive to increase flock size is great. As the shepherds buy sheep, the pressure on the resources of the commons increases. As more forage is demanded from the commons, the land becomes decreasingly productive and can be damaged beyond its ability to recover. While the marginal return to individual investment decreases with increased use of the commons, an addition to the flock always brings a positive marginal return for the shepherd who owns it.

Evaluation

The Tragedy of the Commons model is a good method for illustrating the need for regulation over common areas. It is easy to use and understand, it makes its point well, and it is suitable for training and instruction.

```
ROUND 4

Round:                               1      2      3      4

Potential profit per head            30     30     30     30
Previous overgrazing factor          0      2      4      5
Actual profit per head               30     28     26     25
Previous # of cattle owned           1      2      3      3
Income for round                     30     56     78     75
Carryover monetary units             90     35     6      39
Accumulated wealth                   120    91     84     114
Cost of living                       -45    -45    -45    -45
Net operating funds                  75     46     39     69
# of cattle bought this round        1      1      0      0
Cost per head                        40     40     40     40
Expenditures for cattle              40     40     0      0
Monetary units remaining             35     6      39     69
```

Figure 9-5: Chart presenting the results through round four of Tragedy of the Commons.

Unfortunately, the program does not provide for the analysis of alternative regulation strategies. After one or two runs, the user has learned all there is to learn from it. The model could be improved by the addition of some exercises based on management of common resources in the world today.

Hardware and Software Requirements
IBM PC/XT/AT or compatible; BASIC. A printer is also recommended, but not essential.

Source
National Collegiate Software, Duke University Press, 6697 College Station, Durham, NC 27708, USA; telephone: (919) 684-2173.

10. Rural and Urban Development

Introduction

Rural and urban development are critically important in the future of almost every nation, and the complexities of these processes are enormous. Taxation, transportation, education, law enforcement, population growth, land tenure, and competition between cities and rural areas are among the many factors involved. The models described here can help policy makers understand and cope with some of these complexities.

The CITY GROWTH model addresses the causes of urban growth and decay, which in itself is a matter of national significance. This model has additional potential, however. By duplicating the model's structure, introducing suitable linkages between the two duplicate models, and initializing the two versions to represent urban and rural areas, a user could apply CITY GROWTH usefully to a wide range of questions about relationships between urban and rural areas.

The model titled Housing Needs Assessment (HNA) can be applied on either a national or regional basis. The model analyzes current housing stocks and future needs for housing relative to the projected ability of the people to pay for that housing. This model can be very helpful in identifying housing problems at an early stage and in estimating the costs of housing programs.

The Bertaud Affordability Model also addresses housing needs but does so on a smaller scale and with more detailed attention to construction costs.

MAHA is a dynamic systems model of the long-term development of a river basin. Its initial application was to a very large development project on the Mahaweli River of Sri Lanka. This model brings together the many diverse factors that influence the ultimate effectiveness of such a development project.

The Tropical Coastal Resources Model (TCRM) also deals with large-scale development planning. This model is addressed specifically to the impact of upland land-use decisions on the viability of coastal and nearshore ecosystems.

The Urban Database Management System (UDMS) is a mapping and data management system for application to urban areas. This system is particularly useful in selecting optimum locations for public facilities.

Every nation must count on the leadership of its cities and provinces to make wise planning decisions. There is nothing the leaders of a jurisdiction can do that has a higher potential for difficulties then making those decisions without understanding their fiscal implications. The Municipal Impact Evaluation System (MUNIES) provides a means of analyzing in some detail the fiscal implications of major planning and policy decisions in even large urban areas. The spreadsheet programs that come with the *Microcomputers, Fiscal Analysis, and Municipal Budgeting Manual (MFAMBM)* provide, at a low cost, similar capabilities for towns and villages.

Throughout the world, urban areas are struggling with massive problems of solid waste disposal. The Dynamics of Solid Waste Generation Model explores the systems nature of the solid waste problem. The Co-Composting Spreadsheet provides an analytical tool for detailed studies of solid-waste composting plants of various sizes.

Half of the world's population lives in small agrarian villages, and efforts to help such villages develop have met with only mixed success. The Agrarian Economy Systems (AES) model is a dynamic synthesis of rural economic development theory that offers new insights into effective rural development strategies and new clues as to why some rural development strategies have failed. VILL1, another dynamic model, represents the many interrelated processes at work in a single rural village—including changing aspirations and migrations. It provides a means of estimating the long-term impact of specific village-development programs.

CITY GROWTH

Purpose
To simulate the growth and development of a city under alternative management policies.

Description
CITY GROWTH is a dynamic model of the processes that affect the growth and decay of cities. The model is addressed to a number of questions, including: "What makes cities degenerate? What can be done to revitalize stagnant urban areas? Are present urban-management programs effective?"

The CITY GROWTH model can be used in two modes. In the growth mode, the model simulates the life cycle of an urban area from its founding through a period of growth to a state of

stagnation and decay after a period of 250 years. The other mode begins with the resulting depressed situation and is used to examine alternative policies that might improve conditions over the next fifty years.

CITY GROWTH and *Urban Dynamics*, the book in which the model is described, grew out of a series of conversations between Professor Jay W. Forrester, Sloan School of Management, Massachusetts Institute of Technology, and Mr. John M. Collins, former Mayor of Boston.

Theory and Assumptions
The simulated city in CITY GROWTH (see Figure 10-1) has land devoted to housing and industry. The population is represented by three classes: managerial-professional, labor, and underemployed. Movement among the classes is

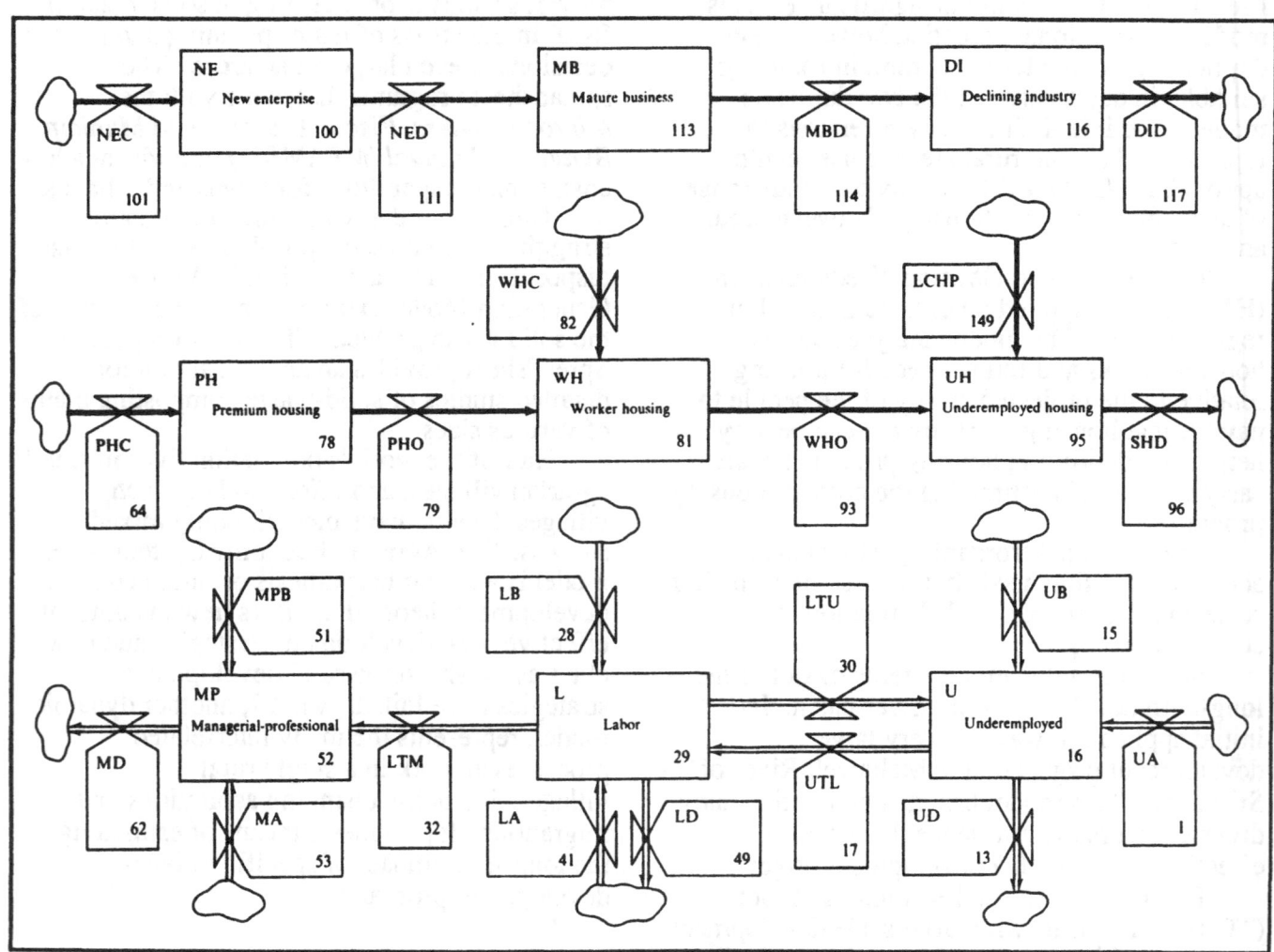

Figure 10-1: The major levels (rectangles) and rates (valve symbols) for the CITY GROWTH model.

simulated. Business and housing both mature and depreciate. The city is surrounded by an infinite *environment* to and from which people migrate in response to the attractiveness of conditions in the city. The projections typically cover a period of fifty years.

Evaluation

While much can be learned from CITY GROWTH in its present form, the model has been criticized by urban planners because it has no detailed representation of the suburbs surrounding a city. It would be a relatively simple task to replace the so-called environment surrounding the city with a suburban or rural sector that had the same structure as the present CITY GROWTH model. If this additional structure were added, the model would be a powerful tool for analyzing issues relating to rural-urban migration and other interactions between rural and urban areas.

Hardware and Software Requirements

IBM/PC/XT/AT or compatible and Professional DYNAMO Plus or DYSMAP2.

Source

A detailed description of the model and the equations are included in J. W. Forrester, *Urban Dynamics* (Cambridge, Mass.: MIT Press, 1969). The address of the press is: MIT Press, Massachusetts Institute of Technology, Cambridge, MA 02142, USA. The price is US $30.

Housing Needs Assessment (HNA) Model

Purpose

To project a nation's housing needs and capital requirements over a twenty-year period.

Description

The Housing Needs Assessment (HNA) model uses data describing a country's current housing stock, demographics, and family income to compute a twenty-year projection of the nation's housing needs and the amount of capital the government will have to contribute to satisfy those needs. The model determines the government's contribution by calculating the gap between the total cost of the necessary housing improvements and the ability of citizens to meet that cost.

Theory and Assumptions

The HNA model (see Figure 10-2) projects housing needs by determining different components of total housing need and then combining them. Five components are considered: housing required to end present overcrowding, housing required to upgrade presently unacceptable housing, construction required to upgrade housing to the minimum acceptable level, housing required to accommodate population growth, and housing required to replace units that become uninhabitable.

For costing purposes, construction is divided into renovation, building from nothing to an acceptable level, and building from nothing to an unacceptable level. Capital estimates include the costs of materials, land, labor, and infrastructure. To take into account the fact that construction costs vary throughout a country, the model provides for three different levels of costs.

After completing the estimate of total cost, the model calculates the capital that the population can reasonably be expected to contribute toward housing costs. Current family income is derived from income surveys after adjustment for underreporting. Urban and rural family incomes are assumed to increase in proportion to gross domestic product.

Finally, the model determines the capital that will have to be provided by the government or by development agencies, by calculating the difference between what is needed and what the population can provide.

Evaluation

This is a very well thought-out model that could aid tremendously in planning the housing of a nation. While the model cannot predict with great accuracy how many homes will have to be built in any given year, it can definitely indicate the trends. The model could also be used to test how housing needs and availability change under various scenarios—different economic growth rates and interest rates, altered minimal standards for housing, and so forth.

Potential users should be warned that it takes a great deal of time and effort to collect all of the detailed information necessary for running the program.

The documentation is excellent and includes a background book and a user's manual. Both books contain a description of the model. The background book details many of the model's assumptions and provides a number of helpful diagrams. The user's manual contains many of the actual equations used in the program.

The program needs a better data-editing system. Currently, entering data is painfully slow because each data cell must be addressed by its column and row number. A system employing a mouse would be much better, and even a full screen editor making use of the cursor would be an improvement.

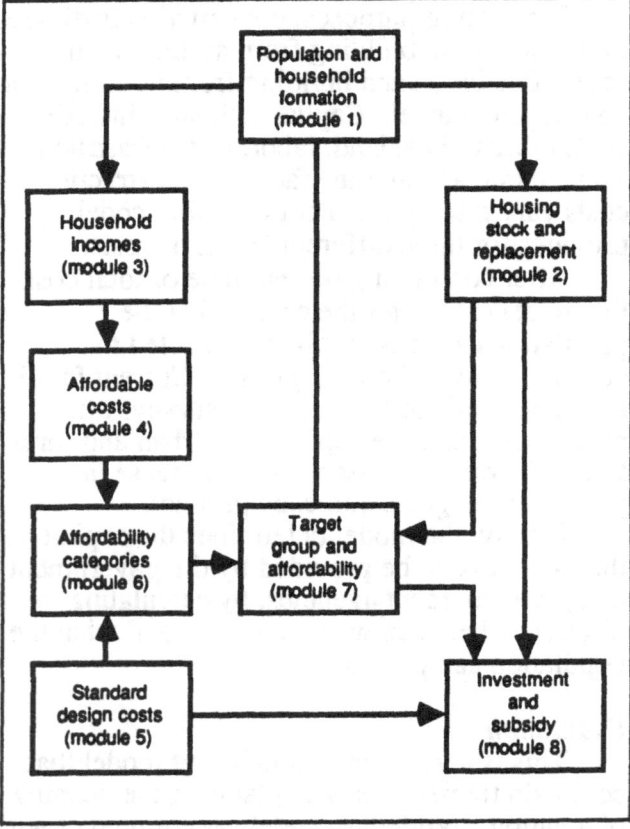

Figure 10-2: The main components of the Housing Needs Assessment (HNA) model.

Hardware and Software Requirements
    IBM PC/XT/AT or compatible, 128 KB RAM, BASIC.

Source
    Mr. R. J. Struyk, The Urban Institute, 2100 M Street, NW, Washington, DC 20037, USA; or U.S. Agency for International Development, Office of Housing and Urban Problems, Washington, DC 20523, USA. No fixed price

has been set for the software. Under some circumstances it might be available at only a nominal cost.

Bertaud Affordability Model

Purpose
    To assist policy makers, planners, and user groups to analyze trade-offs between physical characteristics of housing projects and the financing available to target groups.

Description
    The Bertaud Affordability Model was developed to simplify the task of designing affordable and acceptable housing for low-income populations. The model is a mathematical representation of the interrelationships among the physical and financial characteristics of a shelter project. It can be used to see how changes in the physical characteristics of a shelter project affect: site-acquisition costs, site-layout and land-use characteristics, infrastructure standards and costs, shelter unit options and costs, financing terms, timing of project expenditures and revenues, and the developer's financing arrangement.

Theory and Assumptions
    The Bertaud Affordability Model consists of seven components. (See Figure 10-3.) The land and development costs component calculates direct and indirect costs for the project.
    The component on land use and pricing of non-residential land combines the output of the land and development costs component with additional data (describing site areas and proposed sales prices for units) and produces an estimate of the cost that must be recovered per square meter of marketable land.
    The component regarding pricing and affordability of residential plots compares the costs of a project's shelter units with housing payments that target group families can afford.
    The cost recovery component uses the outputs of the other components to calculate the land development costs that must be recovered if the project is to break even.
    The component on alternatives to break even calculates "break-even" values for nine important project variables. Substitution of any one of these values for the previous value will

eliminate any surplus or deficit for the whole project.

The component on percentage of circulation calculates the percentage of site area required for traffic circulation from inputs of plot frontage, access road width, collector road width, and number of plots per block.

The component on project cost and cash flow uses outputs from other components to calculate the internal rates of return and the return on invested equity for the project.

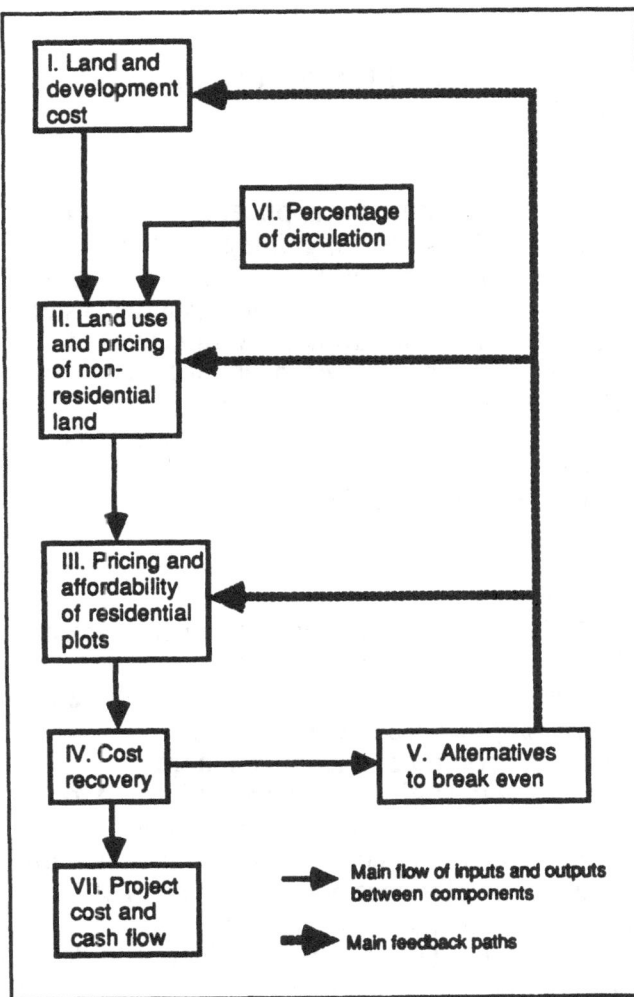

Figure 10-3: The main relationships among the seven components of the Bertaud Affordability Model.

Evaluation
The Bertaud model would be useful to shelter-financing and shelter-providing agencies, policy makers, technical staff, beneficiary and external assistance agencies. It can be used in all stages of the project cycle, from project identification to project evaluation.

The documentation for the Bertaud Affordability Model entitled *A Model for the Preparation of Physical Development Alternatives for Urban Settlement* was prepared by Planning and Development Collaborative International (PADCO) for the World Bank's Economic Development Institute. This documentation details how to apply the model and describes its limitations.

Hardware and Software Requirements
IBM PC/XT/AT or compatible, or Apple II, or Sharp 1250A Pocket Computer.

Source
Planning and Development Collaborative International, 1834 Jefferson Place, NW, Washington, DC 20036, USA; telephone: (202) 296-0004; telex: 248529; cable: PADCO. Pricing information was not available at the time of this review.

MAHA

Purpose
To provide development planners with a suitable tool for applying systems analysis in the development planning process.

Description
Development planners have been frustrated by the poor performance of many development projects. All too often unanticipated effects reduce the benefits the projects were expected to provide. In an effort to improve the planning of development projects, the U.S. Agency for International Development (USAID) sponsored an exercise to explore the usefulness of an interdisciplinary systems approach to planning. A group of experts in agriculture, forestry, socioeconomics, demographics, and wildlife met for a week to structure a model of the Mahaweli River Basin Project in Sri Lanka. The MAHA model is the result of this group effort and of further elaboration of the model since the initial meeting.

While the data in the model are specific to the Mahaweli River basin, much of the structure is generic. The model could easily be adapted for use elsewhere by changing the parameters.

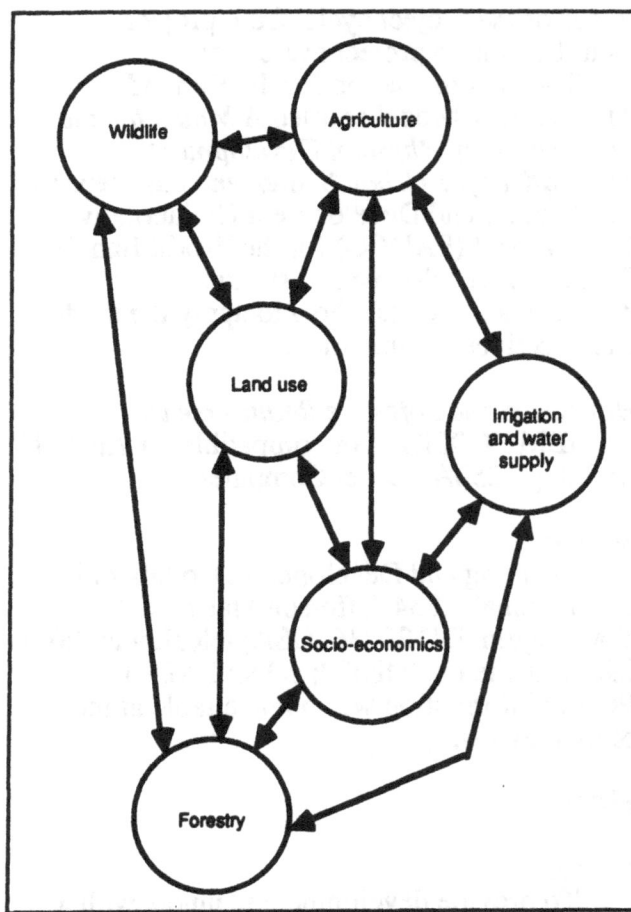

Figure 10-4: An overview of the MAHA model showing the main submodels and their linkages.

Theory and Assumptions

The model (see Figure 10-4) encompasses many sectors of the Mahaweli Project, including agriculture, forestry, farm and non-farm population, infrastructure, and wildlife. There are almost a thousand active equations in the model with extensive feedback within and between sectors.

Evaluation

The MAHA model has proved to be useful and realistic. As a result of this modeling exercise, changes were made in the USAID-sponsored part of the Mahaweli Project.

It should be noted that, although non-technical members of the modeling group were able to interpret the results with only a little coaching from the modelers, the MAHA model is large, complex, and not easily used by modeling novices. Thus, although

documentation of MAHA is available, some consulting or training is recommended to potential users.

Hardware and Software Requirements

IBM PC/XT/AT or compatible, 640 KB RAM, Professional DYNAMO Plus or perhaps DYSMAP2.

Source

Mr. Paul Faeth, WRI/IIED, 1709 New York Ave. NW, Washington, DC, 20006, USA. The price had not yet been determined at the time of this review.

Tropical Coastal Resources Model (TCRM)

Purpose

To demonstrate the applicability and use of systems analysis for: (a) gaining a better understanding of the systemic interactions of the various components of multiple resource systems in the coastal humid tropics and of effects of human activity on ecosystem stability, and (b) bridging the communication gap between research scientists and development assistance planners and/or decision makers who are required to conceptualize system elements and linkages.

Description

TCRM was developed by Nora Berwick out of a conviction that most project planners—unaware of interdisciplinary systems analytic approaches to development planning—continue to employ a largely economic and engineering perspective and to focus on the specific spatial area involved. Thus, in the case of coastal regions, the planning process generally does not incorporate the upland-use linkages to the nearshore environments. The increasing evidence of the effects of terrestrial land-use practices on coastal ecosystems called for a broader approach to development planning.

Theory and Assumptions

TCRM simulates the "downstream" effects of catchment land use and coastal-based development activities on selected coastal resources. Specifically, the model is designed to illustrate the general dynamics of watershed catchment linkages to and interactions among the three major tropical coastal ecosystems—mangroves, seagrasses, and coral reefs. Alteration of baseline sediment and nutrient levels are specifically represented.

TCRM is divided into four sectors (mangroves, seagrasses, coral reefs, and nearshore fisheries) with sector-specific state variables (or levels), their associated rate equations, and the auxiliaries that define the rates. There are about four hundred active equations in the current version with extensive feedback within and between the sectors. The model structure is generic, and the parameters can be adjusted for site-specific use. Continued model development and site-specific field testing are currently under way. Documentation is available through Conservation Systems.

Evaluation
TCRM is important as a tool for understanding the linkages between upland developments and nearshore ecosystems. There is little prospect for protecting nearshore ecosystems until these linkages are better understood and predictive tools are available for use by development planners.

In its current form, TCRM is based on descriptions in the literature of the linkages between upland developments and the conditions of the nearshore ecosystems at Kaneohe Bay, Hawaii. To become a respected, predictive model, TCRM will need to be applied to other specific areas. The easy adaptability of the model will facilitate applications to other settings.

Hardware and Software Requirements
IBM PC/XT/AT or compatible, 640 KB RAM, two floppy disk drives, DOS 2.0 or later; Professional DYNAMO Plus, LAMDA, or perhaps DYSMAP2.

Source
Ms. Nora L. Berwick, Conservation Systems, 102 Seventh Street, NE, Washington, D.C. 20002, USA; telephone: (202) 544-4222. The price had not yet been determined at the time of this review.

Urban Database Management System (UDMS)

Purpose
To store, analyze, and display geographical data, in order to provide computer-generated maps for planning and managing human settlements.

Description
UDMS was originally developed at the United Nations Centre for Human Settlements for demonstrating how computers can be applied to human-settlements planning and management. It is a mapping system used to store and analyze demographic characteristics of a region, such as the distribution of population, the income levels of various regions, and the optimum locations for public facilities.

Theory and Assumptions
The UDMS system consists of six BASIC programs, each dealing with a particular aspect of geographic data management. These programs can work with up to thirteen different types of data files representing defined regions, thematic maps of regions, networks, distance matrices, and other information. Most information is entered in the form of rectangular coordinates via a standard ASCII file created with a spreadsheet or word-processing program.

UDMS performs many types of statistical analysis such as linear regression, location of points within a defined region, discovery of optimum locations for facilities, gravity modeling, and the formation of shortest-path networks between facilities. Projections can be further modified by interaction matrices and by varying the weights of points and junctions.

UDMS offers eight different types of maps, each with zoom and pan features. Print-outs can be made, but the program may have to be modified to suit certain printers.

Evaluation
UDMS is an impressive program with extensive mapping routines. It has an interactive menu, and its calculation and mapping routines run very fast for a BASIC program. Various overlays may be placed on the maps to define regions, grids, optimum locations, networks, or any other set of data defined by the user.

Unfortunately, UDMS also has its flaws. For one thing, it seems to have been written by several people who did not coordinate their efforts. The first title screen in the program lists the version as 5.0; the second lists it as 5.2; the program listing describes it as version 5.1.

Furthermore, the manual is confusing and not well structured. It explains very little about the actual process of data entry, concentrating instead on explanations of the different types of data files and the variables within them. While technical assistance is available in theory, the documentation does not encourage one to think that assistance would be readily available or particularly helpful.

To apply UDMS fully, a user would have to be patient, persistent, and relatively skilled in programming. With more complete documentation, support, and coordination among the people creating UDMS, the program could be made more accessible to a wider range of users.

Hardware and Software Requirements

IBM PC/XT/AT or compatible, PC/MS-DOS, Microsoft BASIC or equivalent, two 360 KB disk drives, and a minimum of 256 KB RAM. IBM CGA graphics or equivalent are required for the mapping routines, and an Epson printer is needed for hard copy print-outs.

Source

The United Nations Centre for Human Settlements (HABITAT), P.O. Box 30030, Nairobi, Kenya; telephones: 333930, 520600, 520320; telex: 22996. Pricing information was not available at the time of this review.

Municipal Impact Evaluation System (MUNIES)

Purpose

To analyze in advance the fiscal impact of major planning decisions that a city might make.

Description

MUNIES calculates the fiscal impact of public service demands on departmental and municipal budgets, revenue rates, bonding capacity, and other financial indices resulting from demographic, land-use, cost or other changes in the community. It can be used to assess in advance the fiscal implications of major

planning decisions such as alternative growth policies, land use policies, infrastructure planning, rezoning cases, annexations, and leveraging public dollars. MUNIES projects for up to twenty periods of time (usually years).

Theory and Assumptions

MUNIES (see Figure 10-5) contains two stages: a needs analysis stage and a fiscal analysis stage. In Stage 1, the needs analysis, MUNIES calculates staffing and capital facility requirements for each operating department or subsystem identified by the user.

In Stage 2, the fiscal analysis, MUNIES calculates budgets for each subsystem or department. It also calculates a budget summary for the jurisdiction, such as a city, county, or state or provincial government, or for a private developer. Finally, it provides fiscal impact summaries, which show assessed values of properties, the tax rate required to balance total revenues and expenses, bonding information, and the surplus or deficit based on the existing tax rate.

MUNIES can also be linked to two other programs, the Fiscal Analysis System (FISCALS) and the Capital Improvements Programming System (CIPS). FISCALS calculates a needs forecast for each operating department or subsystem. CIPS forecasts a jurisdiction's annual capital-facility needs, both for new and replacement infrastructure, and provides a needs analysis, capital-facility requirements, available capacity, excess capacity, facility cost, amortization payments, and associated operating costs for each subsystem or department identified by the user.

Evaluation

MUNIES enables users to understand the fiscal implications of planning decisions before the decisions are made. With MUNIES, users can vary critical assumptions about population, employment, land use, costs, tax rates, assessment rates, market values, bonding terms and service levels. The user can then determine the effect of varying any one or several of these factors of the jurisdiction's budget. By comparing the calculated results for the different scenarios or assumptions, the MUNIES and FISCALS user is able to make a well-informed decision about the issue of concern.

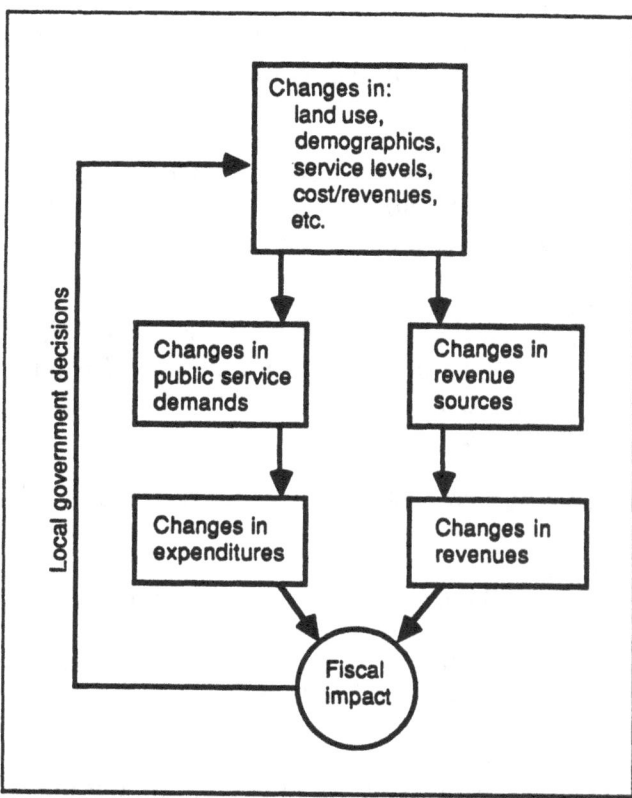

Figure 10-5: Procedural steps involved in applying the Municipal Impact Evaluation System (MUNIES).

Hardware and Software Requirements
IBM PC XT/AT and compatibles.

Source
Tischler and Associates, Inc., 5631 Leesburg Pike, Suite 100, Falls Church, VA 22041; telephone: (703) 578-0777 or (800) 424-4318. MUNIES is available for lease or purchase. Consulting services are also available. Contact the source for details.

Microcomputers, Fiscal Analysis, and Municipal Budgeting Manual (MFAMBM) Spreadsheets

Purpose
To provide towns and communities with an effective, inexpensive tool for analysis of the local economic base, revenues, expenditures, capital costs, public service fees, and other matters related to budgeting for a town.

Description
The MFAMBM provides fourteen spreadsheets for fiscal analysis and budgeting. Two are example spreadsheets; twelve are general purpose templates into which numbers can be entered for towns meeting the assumptions of the spreadsheets. (A template is a data-ready spreadsheet into which formulas have already been entered.)

The MFAMBM spreadsheets enable the communities to develop a budget process that will result in full analysis of costs, revenues, and expenditures for the past, present, and future. Policy makers involved in strategic planning find the spreadsheets helpful in understanding the community's revenue and expenditure limitations and in establishing goals and objectives. The spreadsheets make it possible to establish fiscal controls, to analyze alternatives, and to identify financial opportunities. The spreadsheets also make it possible to provide taxpayers with complete budget information at budget and town meetings.

The equations and formulas in the spreadsheets are designed specifically for the tax laws and support programs of the state of Massachusetts in the United States, but the spreadsheets could be applied with relatively minor changes to towns and villages in most countries.

The MFAMBM spreadsheets were prepared by M. K. Smith, W. A. Kennedy, J. D. Nutting, and D. H. Warren at the Massachusetts Municipal Association with funding from Massachusetts Executive Office of Communities and Development.

Theory and Assumptions
The thirteen templates (see Figure 10-6) include four dealing with revenues, three dealing with costs, one integrating costs and revenues, one for calculating tax rates, and four for trend projections.

The revenue templates relate to local receipts, general state assistance (cherry sheet), state school support (Chapter 70), and property taxes (tax levy). The expenditure templates (budget, capital schedule, and capital replacement) together cover future capital and debt expenditures, costs of repairing or replacing capital equipment, and operating costs. Both revenues and expenditures are brought together in the profile template. The tax rate template

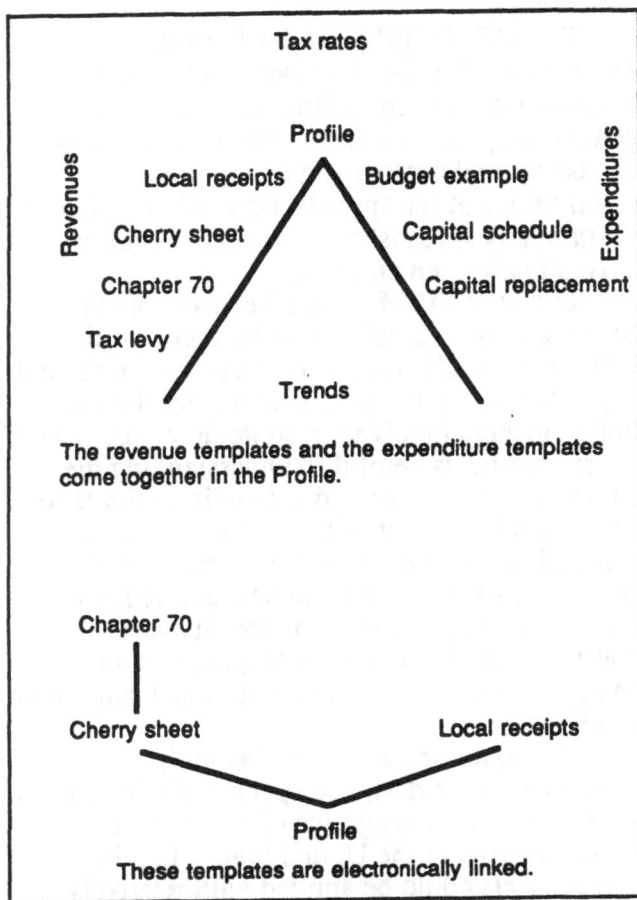

Figure 10-6: Interrelationships among the templates in Microcomputers, Fiscal Analysis, and Municipal Budgeting Manual (MFAMBM) spreadsheets.

determines the impact of net appropriations on the property tax rate. It is useful in setting the tax rates for different classes of property. The four statistical trends templates provide projections based on either three or five years of historic data in either nominal or real (adjusted for inflation) terms.

Evaluation
The MFAMBM (what a name!) disk comes with an excellent user's manual. Each template is described in terms of its purpose, what goes in, what comes out, how it should be used, the equations on which is it based, and sample source documents.

The MFAMBM package can definitely be applied to municipalities other than those in Massachusetts. Some of the equations and parameters unique to Massachusetts will need to be changed, but the overall structure of these

spreadsheets should be relevant almost anywhere. In fact, the MFAMBM package must be one of the best bargains available to town managers everywhere.

Hardware and Software Requirements
Apple Macintosh computer with either the Excel or Multiplan spreadsheet software.

Source
Massachusetts Municipal Association, Field Services Division, Sixty Temple Place, Boston, MA 02111, USA; telephone: (617) 426-7272. The price is US $35.

Dynamics of Solid Waste Generation

Purpose
To find the best policy for reducing the amount of solid waste and conserving natural resources, without sacrificing manufacturing profits or the standard of living.

Description
A major problem for cities throughout the world today is the disposal of solid waste. The average U.S. citizen, for example, discards annually 188 pounds of paper, 250 metal cans, 133 bottles and jars, and 388 caps and crowns.

The Dynamics of Solid Waste Generation is a model of the social and economic mechanisms involved in the creation of the solid waste. The model is capable of simulating the consequences of a wide range of hypothetical policies.

The user chooses among alternative policies and sets specific parameters, such as the recycling rate and consumption rate. The program simulates the consequences of the chosen policies for a period of several decades and presents the results in graphs or tables.

Rather than providing specific value predictions, the model gives a general idea of how the solid waste system changes over time in response to policy changes. Information reported includes the natural resources used, the number of products in use, the amount of solid waste produced, the pollution produced, the recycling rate, and an indicator of manufacturer's profit.

Theory and Assumptions
The Dynamics of Solid Waste Generation model (see Figure 10-7) looks at the solid waste

system in terms of natural resource stocks, their conversion into products, and the ultimate deterioration of products into solid waste. Rather than simulating the entire waste-production system of a nation, the model focuses on a single commodity, copper, as representative of the many resources in the resource-product-waste system.

Three interconnected feedback loops provide the foundation of the model. The first loop is a simple model of resource depletion. As the resource is depleted, it becomes more difficult to produce, costs of production increase, price increases, and the rate of utilization decreases.

The second loop is a simple model of the complex processes through which an economy converts resources into products and "stores" the resources as products. This loop adjusts the resource production rate and the price of processed resources to satisfy the current demand.

The third loop represents depreciation of products, waste generation, reuse, and recycling. Recycling returns resources to the economy for use in other products. Reuse extends the useful life of products. Waste is the final state of products that are neither recycled or reused.

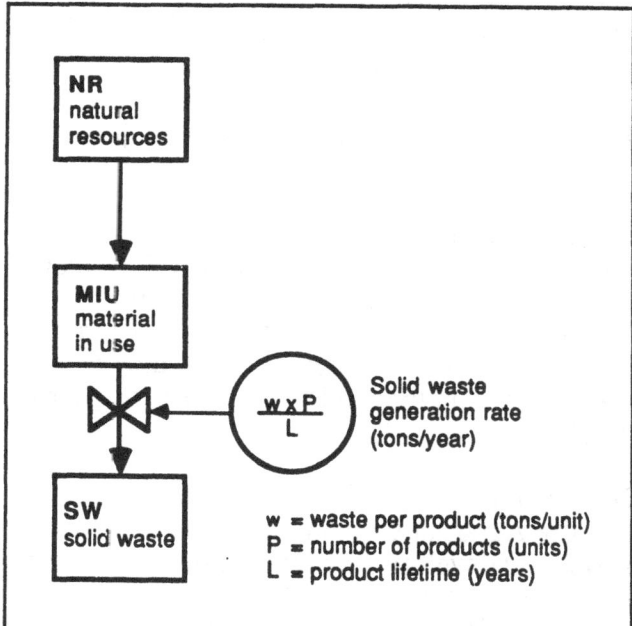

Figure 10-7: The flow of resources to waste in the Dynamics of Solid Waste Generation.

Evaluation

This program would be useful for anyone interested in reducing solid waste and conserving of natural resources. The results of the simulation suggest a wide range of policies that should be given consideration.

The documentation is very thorough. All variables, tables, and constants are labeled and explained. The text makes clear which parameters can be used in representing specific policies.

A listing of the model is included in the documentation. Some knowledge of dynamic simulation methods is helpful, since the model equations must be entered and various policy-related parameters set.

Hardware and Software Requirements

IBM PC/XT/AT or compatible; Professional DYNAMO Plus or perhaps DYSMAP2. Or, a Macintosh and the STELLA modeling language.

Source

The program is presented in *Toward Global Equilibrium: Collected Papers*, edited by Dennis and Donella Meadows. The book, published originally by Wright-Allen Press, Inc., is now being sold by: MIT Press, Massachusetts Institute of Technology, Cambridge, MA 02142, USA. The price is US $40.

Co-Composting Spreadsheet

Purpose

To help municipalities, planning commissions, and other agencies determine the feasibility and costs of running a plant for co-composting garbage (organic solid wastes) and human waste (night soil and/or sewage sludge) as a safe alternative to landfill dumping or other means of disposal.

Description

The Co-composting Spreadsheet is a template designed to analyze the economics of four types of municipal co-composting plants that have different capacities and different methods of composting. It allows the user to input pertinent data and use predefined formulas and structures to manipulate that data. The four plant types are represented by four separate models, which are described below.

Model A is for a plant having a capacity of three tons per eight-hour day, using a windrow style on an unpaved site of 500 square meters, and operating exclusively with manual labor. It can handle the organic solid waste from 10,000 people plus night soil from 160 people, or sludge from 1,900 people.

Model B is for a plant having a capacity of fifty tons per eight-hour day, and using a two-hectare paved site with windrowing. It is a mechanized operation that can handle the organic solid waste from 160,000 people plus night soil from 2,500 people, or sludge from 30,000 people.

Model C is for a plant that has a capacity of 150 tons per sixteen-hour day, uses a windrow-style of composting on an 18.5-hectare paved site, and is highly mechanized. It can handle the organic solid waste from 500,000 people plus night soil from 8,500 people, or sludge from 93,000 people.

Model D is for a plant similar to the one addressed by Model C but with twice the equipment and throughput.

Theory and Assumptions

All the models in the spreadsheet take the form of a simple line-item budget covering a twenty-year period, which is computed linearly to form the projection. The models assume replacement of equipment after ten years with no salvage value, and no resale of the land or landfill area.

The user may choose between two different modes of projection: a simple financial projection and a method employing "shadow prices." Through the shadow prices it is possible to include the estimated value of the compost's effect on agricultural output, the effects on the environment (both positive and negative) of processing the waste, and other such values that have no market price.

Evaluation

The Co-Composting Spreadsheet is a thorough model for evaluating the feasibility of running a composting plant and is applicable to both profit and non-profit operations. It is suitable for the large-scale needs of municipalities and the small-scale ones of villages. It offers enough diversity for use by corporations considering becoming involved in commercial compositing operations.

The model comes with a 100-page, English language document entitled *Co-Composting of Domestic Solid and Human Waste*. Most of this document is devoted to a discussion of different types of composting plants. The instructions for use of the spreadsheet occupy less than twenty pages scattered through the report. While there is a table of contents, it does not distinguish between the descriptive material and the program documentation. As a result, the instructions are difficult to locate and, once found, are rather inexplicit. Furthermore, they assume the user to be thoroughly familiar with Lotus 1-2-3. Also, while the alternative assumptions of the models are explained, there are no instructions on how to modify those assumptions to different situations.

The template for this model is well designed and versatile enough to be useful to a very wide range of people. The setup of the model within the Lotus framework is straightforward, but Lotus training is required to interpret the poor documentation.

Hardware and Software Requirements

IBM PC/XT/AT or compatible, two floppy disk drives, and Lotus 1-2-3 release 1A, or a more recent release.

Source

Mr. Frederick Wright, The World Bank, 1818 H Street, NW, Washington, DC 20005, USA. The pricing policy had not yet been established at the time of this review.

Agrarian Economy Systems (AES)

Purpose

To synthesize and modify economic development theory into a dynamic model that: (a) displays a strong resilience to significant change when the development policies of the past few decades are applied and (b) allows the testing of alternative policies for their long-term effectiveness.

Description

The Agrarian Economy Systems (AES) model was developed by Dr. Khalid Saeed for a doctoral dissertation at the Massachusetts Institute of Technology. Dr. Saeed was interested in what seemed to him to be a major failing in development economics, namely, that the policies and programs that emerge from development economics have failed after several decades to produce a significant change in agrarian economies.

For his thesis research Dr. Saeed decided to synthesize economic development theory into the dynamic AES model and to compare the model's behavior to the development experience of Pakistan. He found that a model based on accepted development theory predicted far more rapid development than had actually occurred in Pakistan.

Dr. Saeed then developed a second version of his AES model. For the second version, he started with the original model and replaced some of the basic assumptions of development theory with information derived from microeconomic analysis of actual situations in Pakistan. Ultimately, Dr. Saeed was able to make the second version of his model replicate the development experience of Pakistan over the past eighty years.

Dr. Saeed feels that the second AES model better represents the processes at work within most agrarian societies in developing countries than does classical economic development theory. He argues that his second AES model provides a laboratory within which a wide range of development policies can be tested for their long-term effectiveness.

Theory and Assumptions

The second AES model (see Figure 10-8) uses a two-part structure to represent the agrarian economy of developing countries. One part consists of the self-employed or wage-earning peasant sector; the other part consists of the worker-hiring or land-leasing capitalist sector.

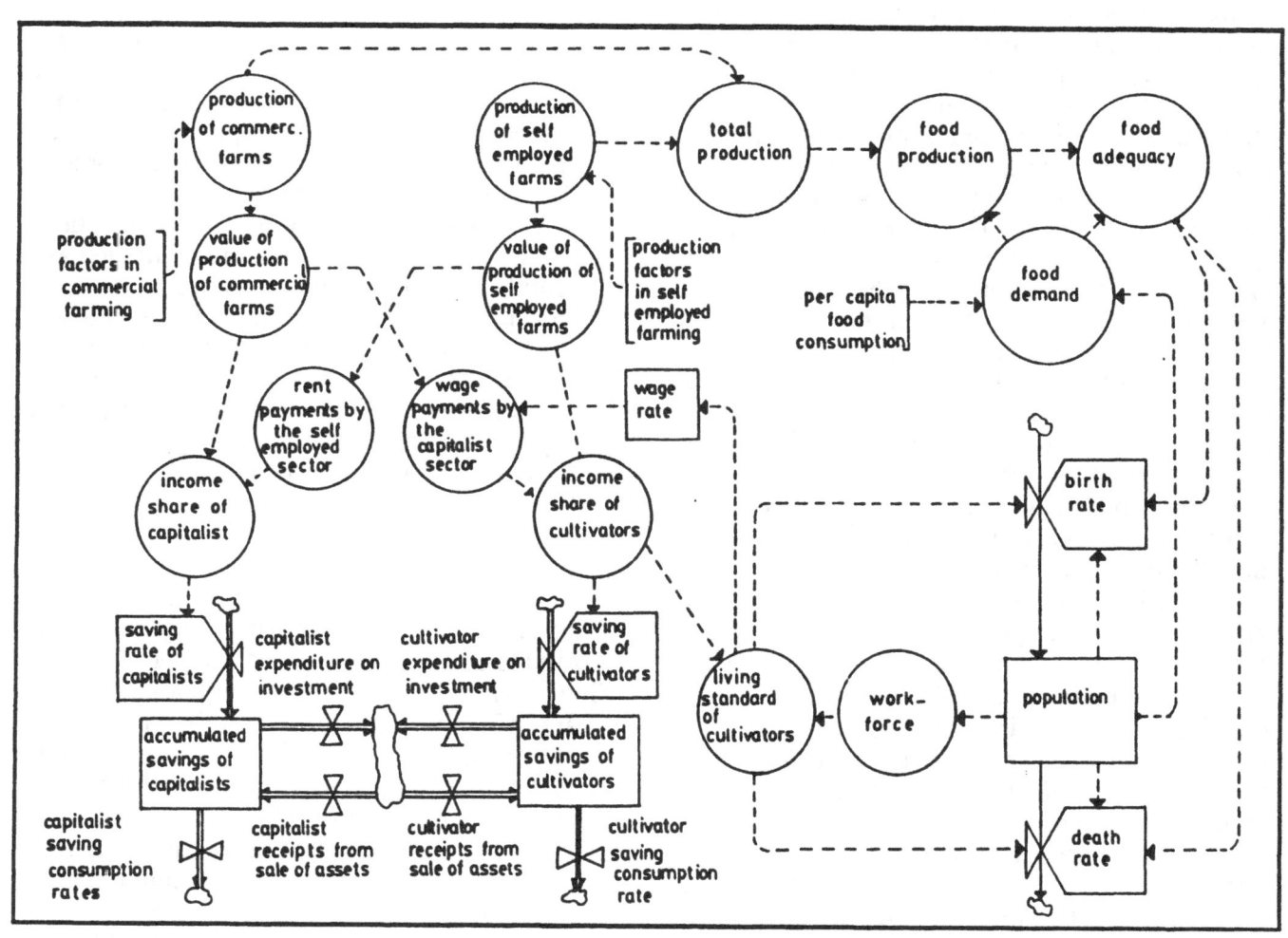

Figure 10-8: Overview of the Agrarian Economy Systems (AES) model.

The peasants, whether tilling their own or rented land or employed for wages, are the sole suppliers of labor. As a group, they share the objective of maximizing consumption. The capitalist sector, on the other hand, strives to maximize profit.

The capital sector of the model specifically includes both traditional and modern capital. Land ownership and income distribution are represented. Production factors are allocated between the peasant or traditional sector and the capitalist or modern sector in response to rational decisions by producers, consumers, and suppliers of production factors. The value of production is shared by households on the basis of the quantity of production factors they contribute and their bargaining strength.

The model was developed first by representing market forces as described by the assumptions of neoclassical economic theory. When the resulting model failed to be as resistant to change as developing countries are observed to be, the neoclassical assumptions were gradually modified. Three major changes were needed to make the model structure correspond to actual conditions in developing countries. These three changes relate to assumptions concerning the transfer of land ownership, the factors determining wage rates, and the factors determining savings rates. With these changes in assumptions, the model simulates an economy in which there is a strong internal tendency toward concentration of resources in the capitalist sector, a tendency that is observed in most developing countries.

The AES model is certainly not based on mainstream development thought, but it addresses an issue very much on the minds of most professionals in the field: "How can development theory be improved?"

Whether or not one agrees with all of the AES models' assumptions, the models make several important contributions: (a) The first model synthesizes classical economic development theory into a single dynamic model; (b) the first and the second models incorporate both the traditional and modern sectors (and their interactions) into a single model; (c) the second model is capable of simulating an eighty-year period of economic history of a developing country; and (d) both models focus attention on the systems nature of the development problem.

The models' greatest contribution may be in drawing attention to the many ways in which development policies and programs can be defeated by structural feedbacks within a developing country's economy and society. In simulating alternative policies and programs with the AES models, Dr. Saeed found that many conventional approaches do not lead to rapid development or even to significant improvement. These unsuccessful approaches include policies aimed at increasing food production (even when supplemented with food aid and food assistance), policies aimed at limiting population, and policies intended to help the poorest of the poor. This pattern, he argues, has also been the experience of most developing countries:

> [T]he source of the model's resistance to well-intended policies...arises from the powerful feedbacks which dominate the behavior of [agrarian economies]... [T]he efficacy of a policy depends on how effectively it changes the relative strength of those feedbacks. Unless the internal goals of the system are changed, any direct effort to increase food supply, change population, or help the poor will be resisted by the forces embodied in the feedback loops...
>
> It would be fair to say that the solutions to hunger and poverty attempted in the past and being attempted now have a phenomenological perspective that addressed the symptoms instead of the organizational [feedbacks] that create those symptoms. Hence, these policies could easily be defeated by the powerful tendencies created by those [feedbacks] which remain intact.

Evaluation

On the basis of analysis with his model, Dr. Saeed identifies two promising entry points for efforts to counter poverty and hunger. Specifically, he advocates changing income shares of the workers and the ambient cereal food consumption per capita. The leap from the model results to the details of some of his recommendations, especially the recommendation that meat be a primary dietary component, may need further examination. Nevertheless, Dr. Saeed's emphasis on "mobilization of internal forces of the system rather than countering system tendencies through direct intervention" is a refreshing perspective.

Hardware and Software Requirements

IBM PC/XT/AT or compatible, 640 KB RAM, graphics card, monochrome monitor, printer. DOS, Professional DYNAMO Plus or perhaps DYSMAP2. Or, after some rewriting of the equations, Apple Macintosh computer with the STELLA modeling language.

Source

The original AES model is presented in Dr. Khalid Saeed's 1980 doctoral thesis, "Rural Development and Income Distribution: The Case of Pakistan," which is available from: Thesis Reproduction Center, Massachusetts Institute of Technology, Cambridge, MA 02139, USA. Several additional papers and the current version of the model are available from: Dr. K. Saeed, Asian Institute of Technology, Rajapark Building, 163 Asoke Road, Bangkok 10110, Thailand; telex: 20666 RAJAPAK TH. The additional papers and the model are free to researchers.

VILL1

Purpose

To provide an analytical tool for evaluating the long-term effects of alternative strategies for the development of rural agricultural villages.

Description

VILL1 is a dynamic, multisectoral model of the long-term development of an agricultural village under the influence of a variety of external development programs. In addition to the usual demographic and economic sectors, VILL1 includes sectors representing migration and aspirations. Decisions on migration and changes of aspirations are known to have a major impact on the dynamics of village development but are rarely included specifically in models.

VILL1 was developed by Dr. D. H. Meadows while she was a professor at Dartmouth College in New Hampshire.

Theory and Assumptions

In VILL1 the village system is represented by four interlocking sectors (see Figure 10-9). The fertility-mortality sector accounts for changing birth and death rates as a function of

the economic situation and the goals and aspirations of the villagers. The migration sector calculates migration rates from the same inputs. The economic sector represents the village's resource base and its productivity as determined by land, labor, capital, and agricultural technologies. In the aspirations sector, the dynamics of value changes, rising material goals, and changing social norms are represented. These norms and goals then influence decisions made in all other sectors of the system—whether to have a child, to invest in capital, or to migrate. Each of the sectors receives inputs from and generates outputs to the other sectors.

Evaluation

VILL1 paints only a very broad-brush portrait of the village, trying to emphasize only the most important interconnections that

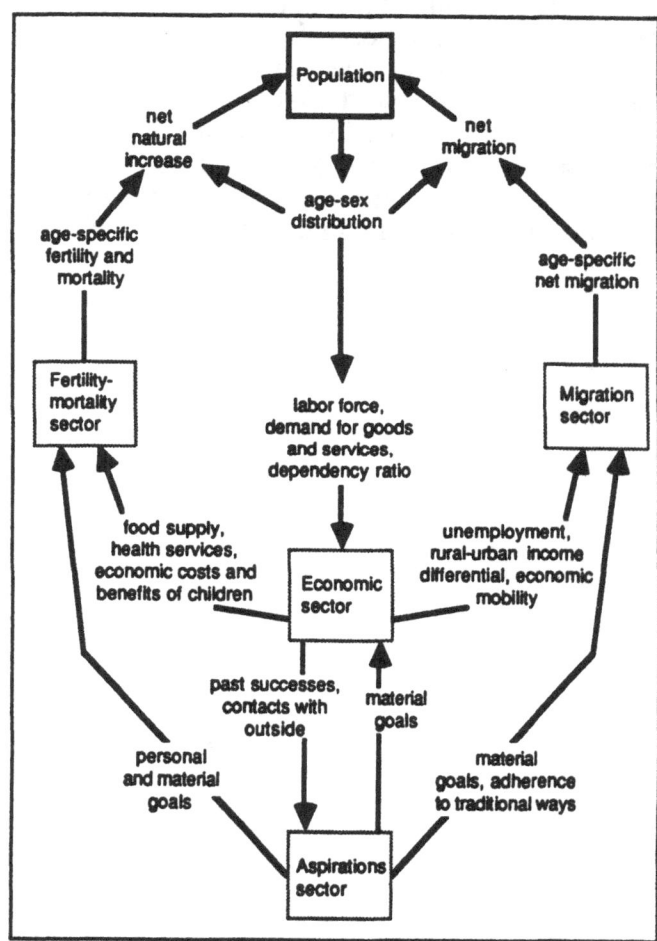

Figure 10-9: Interactions among the sectors of the Village Model (VILL1).

dominate long-term village development. The broad-brush portrait, however, is quite interesting.

Runs explore the response of the village to a number of policy interventions including: improved health care, improved fertility control (family planning), food aid, decreased migration costs, raised aspirations (through education), and capital aid. The village changes very little in response to any single one of these outside interventions.

Multiple interventions from outside the system, however, can produce radically different outcomes. The village can become very rich and nearly depopulated, or, with little change in population, its income can be raised temporarily or permanently. It can undergo a complete demographic transition, or it can shift to an equilibrium not very different from the traditional one. Under the right conditions its own internal change mechanisms may be just as effective as those imposed from outside.

A model as simple as VILL1 can provide a basic, holistic framework that can be understood and discussed fairly easily. However, it is so aggregated that it cannot deal with many important aspects of the village that require more detailed and complicated representation, for example, income distribution changes, trade-offs between traditional and modern capital, or the effects of out-migration on the age structure of the labor force. VILL1 has therefore been expanded into two more complex and disaggregated models, VILL2, which contains a complete age-structure representation, and VILL3, which expands the economic sector and represents two economic classes and the transactions in land, credit and labor between them. VILL2 and VILL3 serve as illustrations of how the basic conceptual structure of VILL1 can be elaborated and of how the elaborations affect the general policy recommendations derived from the simple model.

Hardware and Software Requirements
IBM PC/XT/AT, 640 KB RAM, Professional DYNAMO or perhaps DYSMAP2; or, with some rewriting of the equations, Apple Macintosh computer with the STELLA simulation language.

Source
Papers describing VILL1, VILL2, and VILL3 are available from: Dr. D. H. Meadows, Box 58, Plainfield, NH 03781, USA. The price is US $20 for the set.

11. Transportation and Communication

Introduction

Transportation and communication are two very broad topics, and the software pieces reviewed here do not begin to cover the wide range of programs now available on these subjects. What is here, however, should give a sense of the possibilities and identify a few places for interested readers to begin making inquiries.

The most common theme of transportation software is highways, and we have included four examples. MOTORS is a comprehensive package for planners and decision makers concerned with all phases of highway and transit planning. The Quick Benefit-Cost Procedure for Evaluating Proposed Highway Projects (QBCP) is a simple, quick methodology for initial evaluation of proposed highway projects. Unfortunately, it does not include environmental factors or an adequate link to land-use decisions, but two other programs do. These are the spreadsheet program Intersection and Roadway, which is designed specifically to examine the environmental implications of highway improvement projects, and TRACS, which analyzes the effects that new developments will have on street and highway congestion.

Street, highway, and transit management have unique aspects in urban areas, and software is available to assist with these special needs. The program Fire Router facilitates the evaluation of alternative routes that emergency vehicles can use in an urban area. The RTD Pivot Point Logit Model is used to project the effect that fare changes will have on ridership in urban transit systems. The Arterial Analysis Package (AAP) can help create an efficient urban transportation system by optimizing the timing of traffic signals.

Out of the many microcomputer programs now available in the communications field, we have chosen Computer Aided Translator (CAT) programs, which promote communication among persons who read and write different languages. MicroCAT, for example, translates English into Spanish, French, German, Italian, and Portuguese and Japanese, Spanish, and French into English.

MOTORS

Purpose

To provide comprehensive tools for highway and transit planning.

Description

MOTORS is a collection of forty separate but compatible programs designed to cover all phases of highway and transit analysis. The programs in MOTORS can model both small traffic management projects and large ones covering whole transportation corridors, cities, regions, or even entire countries. The programs are capable of modeling systems with 400 zones, 2,000 nodes, and 6,000 links.

MOTORS was developed by M. M. Dillon, Ltd., one of Canada's leading traffic and transportation consultancies, and has been used extensively in North America, Europe, and the Far East.

Theory and Assumptions

For convenience, the MOTORS programs are divided into five categories: demand modeling programs, matrix programs, highway network programs, transit programs, and utility programs. Most of these programs can be linked by output of one being used as input to another. (See Figure 11-1.)

The demand modeling programs produce trip matrices for highway and transit systems. The programs are: land-use database organizer, regression analysis, zonal trip ends, trip rate calculator, trip-end file merger, gravity model, Fratar model, trip-cost frequency tabulator, and modal split.

The matrix programs are designed so that the user can input a trip matrix generated by the demand modeling programs or can direct MOTORS to generate one from individual trip survey records. There are also programs that perform matrix arithmetic.

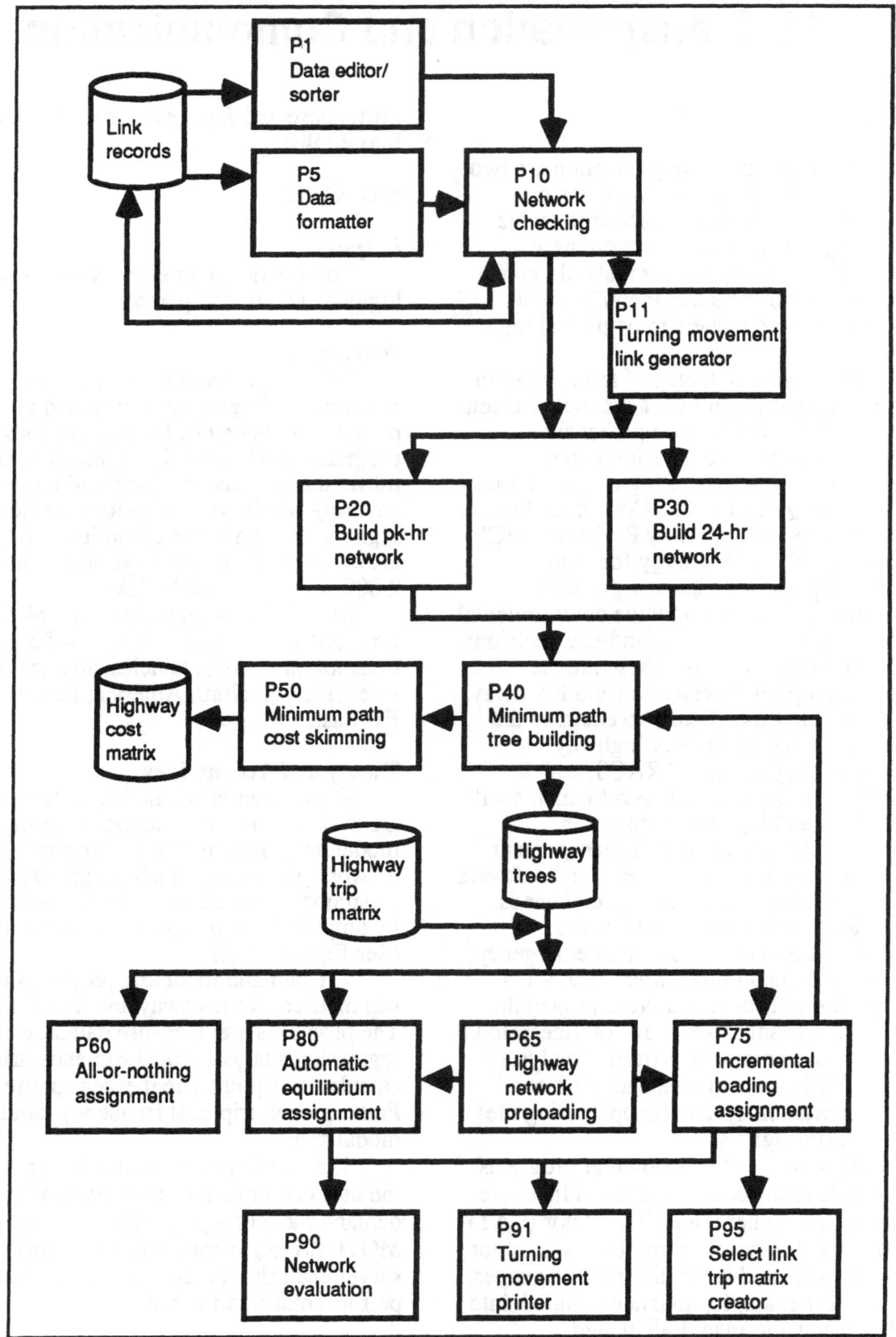

Figure 11-1: Example of the MOTORS programs linked together to undertake highway analysis.

The highway network programs are used to simulate highway networks using link-and-node formats, to find minimum paths, and to carry out operational evaluations on networks. Inputs to the highway network programs include: travel time, link length, link speed, link capacity, capacity class, percentages of peak volume, link classification, and link jurisdiction. The programs are: highway data editor/sorter, highway data formatter, highway network checking, turning movement link generator, highway network building (peak hour), highway network building (twenty-four-hour), highway minimum path tree building, highway minimum path cost skimming, highway all-or-nothing assignment, highway network preloading, highway automatic incremental loading assignment, highway automatic equilibrium assignment, highway network evaluation, turning movement printer, and select link assignment trip matrix creator.

The transit network programs simulate transit networks using up to 128 routes instead of links. These programs are: transit network building, transit minimum path tree building, transit minimum path cost skimming, transit route assignment, transit link assignment.

There are two utility programs. The data file header reader displays the headers of files for identification purposes; the network file printer either prints or displays the network files produced by MOTORS.

Evaluation

MOTORS is a comprehensive collection of professional-level programs for use by analysts in transportation planning. The programs are relatively easy to use, and the documentation is good.

Hardware and Software Requirements

IBM PC/XT/AT or compatibles, 256 KB RAM, two floppy disk drives, dot matrix printer; MS-DOS 2.0 or later.

Source

Mr. Robert J. Lewis, Senior Associate, M. M. Dillon Ltd., Box 1850, Station A, Willowdale, Ontario M2N 6H5, Canada; telephone: (416) 229-4646; telex: 064-7540. The programs are available in groups, and the price varies with the number of programs included. The Basic Highway Package is US $1,000; The Complete Highway Package is US $2,000; The Complete Highway and Transit Package is US $3,000; The MOTORS-PLOT Network Graphic Enhancement is US $700.

Quick Benefit-Cost Procedure for Evaluating Proposed Highway Projects (QBCP)

Purpose

To provide transportation officials with a preliminary screening tool for use in evaluating proposed highway projects.

Description

Every year transportation officials around the world receive proposals for many more highway projects than can be constructed with available funds. The proposals often come with estimates of the costs, but generally not with quantitative estimates of the benefits. The Quick Benefit-Cost Procedure (QBCP) calculates rough estimates of both the benefits and costs to be expected from a proposed highway project and compares the two.

QBCP was developed by the New York State Department of Transportation. In its 1981 implementation, it was a manual procedure based on nomograms. In 1984 John H. Lemmerman and Cheryl Richter wrote programs to put the procedure on microcomputers.

Theory and Assumptions

QBCP estimates the benefits of a proposed highway project as the difference between projected operating and travel-time costs under conditions before and after construction of the project. Costs associated with increased delays during construction are not considered. The impact of the project on accident rates, environmental quality, maintenance costs, and traffic growth are not considered in the model and must be treated separately.

The key factor used in the program to determine operating and travel-time costs is the annual average daily traffic (AADT). AADT is projected with an elasticity model in which the future AADT is obtained by multiplying present AADT by a linear function of projected changes in the number of automobiles owned in the area, the number of households, and the population. Separate equations are provided for minor arterials, principal arterials, and large freeways such as interstates.

QBCP relies primarily on the assumption that savings on transportation costs result from increased running speed and decreased congestion. The program assumes that most highway projects will result in faster moving traffic and fewer traffic jams, at least for current levels of traffic. The possibility that a new highway may increase traffic—rather than simply expediting existing traffic—is not considered.

Evaluation

QBCP is potentially useful where large numbers of highway proposals need preliminary analysis. It is no substitute, however, for more detailed analysis, since it is capable of dealing neither with the costs of accidents, environmental damage, and maintenance, nor with the possible traffic-stimulation effects of highway projects.

The program is suited better to rural than to urban applications. For use in areas other than New York state, the equations in the elasticity model would have to be re-estimated.

The program itself is easy to use. The prompts are clear; inappropriate entries are not accepted. There is ample opportunity to go back and correct errors. The documentation, which comes on the disk, is thorough and well written. The output is well organized on the screen and easy to understand.

Hardware and Software Requirements

IBM PC/XT/AT or compatible, or an Apple II/II+/IIe with 48 KB RAM. BASIC.

Source

Mr. Nathan S. Erlbaum, Senior Transportation Analyst, Transportation and Statistics and Analysis Section, Department of Transportation, 1220 Washington Avenue, State Campus, Building 4, Albany, NY 12232, USA; telephone: (518) 457-2967. The program is free.

Intersection and Roadway

Purpose

To predict vehicular emissions along roadway segments and at signalized intersections before and after various levels of improvement.

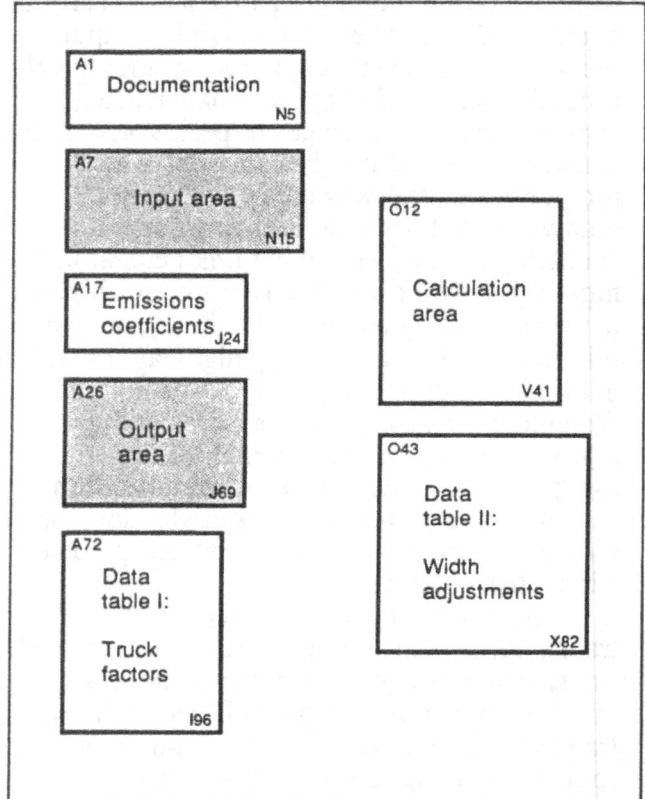

Figure 11-2: Template map for Roadway AQ.

Description

Intersection and Roadway is a package of two spreadsheet-template programs: Intersection AQ and Roadway AQ. Both provide predictions for a base year and any two future years. A template map for Roadway AQ is shown in Figure 11-2. The programs can assist analysts to redesign transportation networks in such a way that air quality is improved through reduced emissions of carbon monoxide, hydrocarbons, and oxides of nitrogen.

Theory and Assumptions

In the Roadway AQ program, both the existing roadways and proposed improvements are specified in terms of the number and width of travel lanes, vehicle volumes, roadside characteristics (obstructions and shoulder width), and shoulder type. To begin the calculations, a relationship is computed between the volume of traffic on a segment of highway and the capacity of that road. This relationship is then used to calculate emissions in grams per vehicle mile using functions derived from the large MOBILE2 program, which was developed by the U.S. Environmental Protection Agency.

Intersection AQ is designed much like Roadway AQ but applies to four-legged signalized intersections. It requires that each approach to the intersection be specified in terms of width of approach, number of sides for parking, percent turns, green time, percent trucks, number of directions of travel, and vehicle volumes. The capacity of each approach is calculated from these data using the guidelines from the *Highway Capacity Manual*, published by the U.S. Department of Transportation in 1965. The ratio of volume to capacity is calculated by dividing peak hour volumes by the capacity value. This ratio is then used to calculate emissions using functions derived from the MOBILE2 computer program.

Evaluation

Both Intersection AQ and Roadway AQ are easy to use for anyone familiar with spreadsheets. Both calculate the projected emissions figures quickly. A split screen effect allows the input to be at the top of the monitor, while the output is at the bottom. The emissions coefficients table, the portion of the template that is most likely to be changed, is easily found in the input and output areas.

The documentation is complete and well written. It includes detailed directions for running the programs, a listing of the equations, and a sample run.

While these programs are easy to use and install, users should already be familiar with spreadsheets, air pollution terminology, and the basics of highway design.

Hardware and Software Requirements

IBM PC/XT/AT or compatible, 192 KB RAM, two floppy disk drives; MS-DOS 1.1 or later; Lotus 1-2-3. Or, Apple II/II+/IIe, 64 KB RAM, and a disk drive; DOS 3.3 and VisiCalc. The templates can be transferred to another spreadsheet program if desired, making the program operable on many systems.

Source

National Center for Microcomputers in Transportation, University of Florida, 346 Weil Hall, Gainesville, FL 32611, USA; telephone: (904) 392-0378. The price is US $10.

TRACS

Purpose

To analyze the implications that changes in land use will have on traffic.

Description

TRACS was designed to analyze the effect that new developments in an area would have on traffic flows in the local street system. The program can also be used to investigate the effectiveness of proposed solutions to traffic problems arising from development.

Theory and Assumptions

TRACS begins with existing traffic counts and intersection geometries and adds to them information about land use, trip generation, trip distributions, and travel paths. (See term definition-screen in Figure 11-3.) The program uses information on gateways, streets, intersections, and new zones of development in order to calculate volume, capacity, and service levels for each intersection of interest. From these inputs, a service level—the number of vehicles that will have to be accommodated by the system—is projected for the future. Once this level is established, the program can be used to find the best way to manipulate the current system to handle the new traffic load.

TRACS can handle up to fifty intersections, gateways, and zones. The program allows the user to configure the map, so there are no limits on the shape of the analysis area or the positioning of the streets and connectors. Finally, it is easy to visualize the different zones and intersections, since everything is displayed on the screen in its correct relative position.

Evaluation

TRACS will be of interest to anyone either setting up new traffic systems or revising old ones. Since all of the data can be changed so easily, the program lends itself to "what if?" analysis. Scenarios can be tested almost as quickly as the inputs can be made. Also, since data on different factors are stored in different files, it is easy to test scenarios based on combinations of changes.

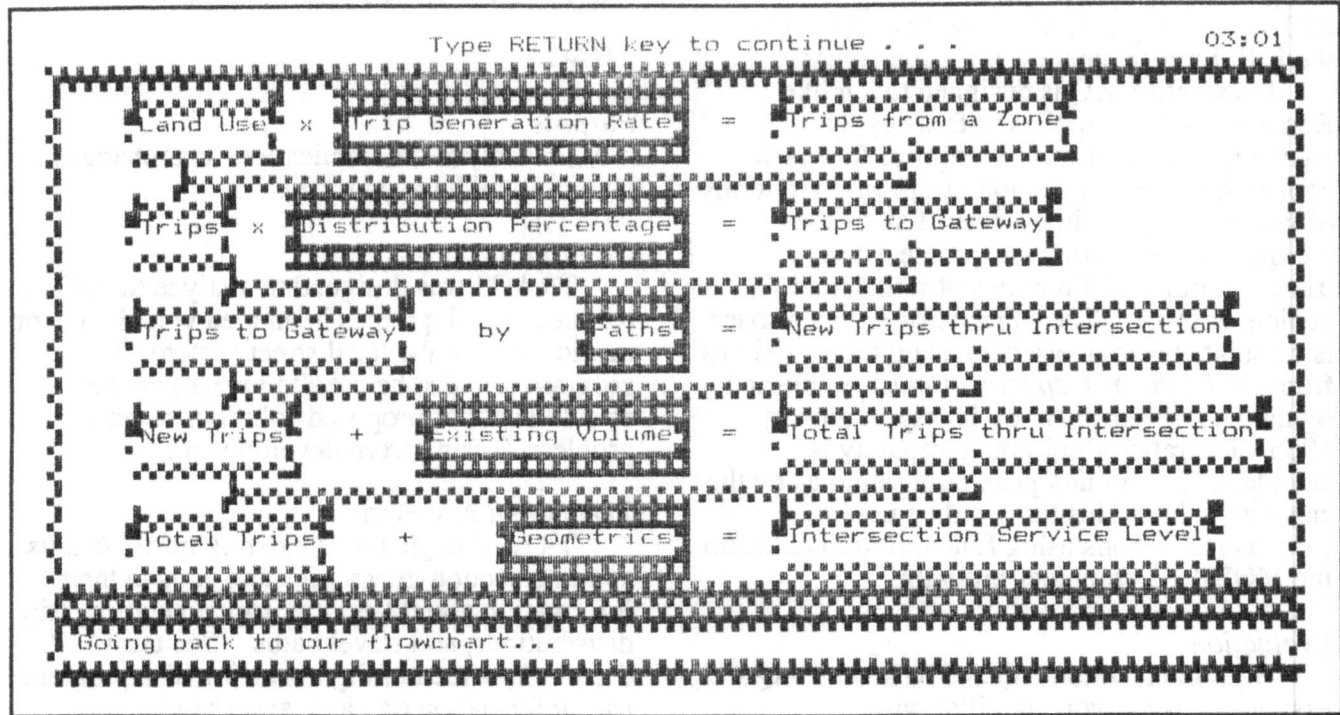

Figure 11-3: A term-definition screen from TRACS.

TRACS is user friendly. The screen setup is easily understood. All editing is done with a mouse. Turns, lane configurations, and the geographical layout are visually represented, a feature that makes the program easy to learn and helps the user keep track of changes.

Hardware and Software Requirements

IBM PC/AT/XT or compatible, 384 KB RAM (448 KB RAM is recommended), two floppy disk drives (or a hard disk), a mouse, and a serial port.

Source

DKS Associates, 1419 Broadway, Suite 700, Oakland, CA 94612-2069, USA; telephone: (415) 763-2061. The price is US $1,000 for a single-address site license.

Fire Router

Purpose

To establish the most efficient placement of fire stations and other emergency service facilities.

Description

Fire Router is a tool to aid urban planners in placing fire stations and other emergency service centers in the optimal position for serving an area's protection needs. It is a group of interrelated programs (see Figure 11-4) used to manipulate data and prepare a street map that can be used to calculate traveling time and distance from a planned or existing firehouse to any point on the map. Through these calculations, the program can determine the best route, as defined by the user. Fire Router can also be used to plan out the best sequence of stations to be called in the event of a multiple-alarm fire.

Theory and Assumptions

The program requires detailed street information, including individual intersections. The space being analyzed must be divided into fire zones, the discrete service areas allotted to the individual fire houses. Within each fire zone, every viable transportation route is coded. Streets where fire trucks cannot travel are left out of the map.

Each street segment is coded as a link in the program, and each intersection is coded as a node. For each link, two of the following parameters must be defined: speed, distance, or time. Since each street segment and intersection is considered individually, it is possible to compute quite accurate travel times along the various routes.

Evaluation

Fire Router is an excellent program that has an important practical application. It can save many hours of trial-and-error experimentation and can provide more accurate results than manual methods.

To produce meaningful results, users must have a good understanding of the capabilities and requirements of fire vehicles. Impassable roads must be excluded, and estimates of transit times must be realistic. For best results, the team using the model should include both a planner and a fireman.

The program is not hard to use, although skills in the use of computers and maps are helpful. The program's output is given by route number, so the user must relate the information back to a map. Nonetheless, the results are easily understood. The documentation is well written, although lengthy.

Hardware and Software Requirements

IBM PC/XT/AT or compatible, 256 KB RAM, dot matrix printer.

Source

Mr. Robert J. Lewis, Senior Associate, M. M. Dillon, Ltd., Box 1850, Station A, Willowdale, Ontario M2N 6H5, Canada; telephone: (416) 229-4646; telex: 064-7540.

RTD Pivot Point Logit Model

Purpose

To project changes in transit ridership after a modification of fares or service level.

Description

The RTD Pivot Point Logit Model was designed to help planners anticipate how the ridership of a mass transit system would be affected by a change of fare or a change in level of service. The actual changes that can be addressed by the model are: fare, headways, in-

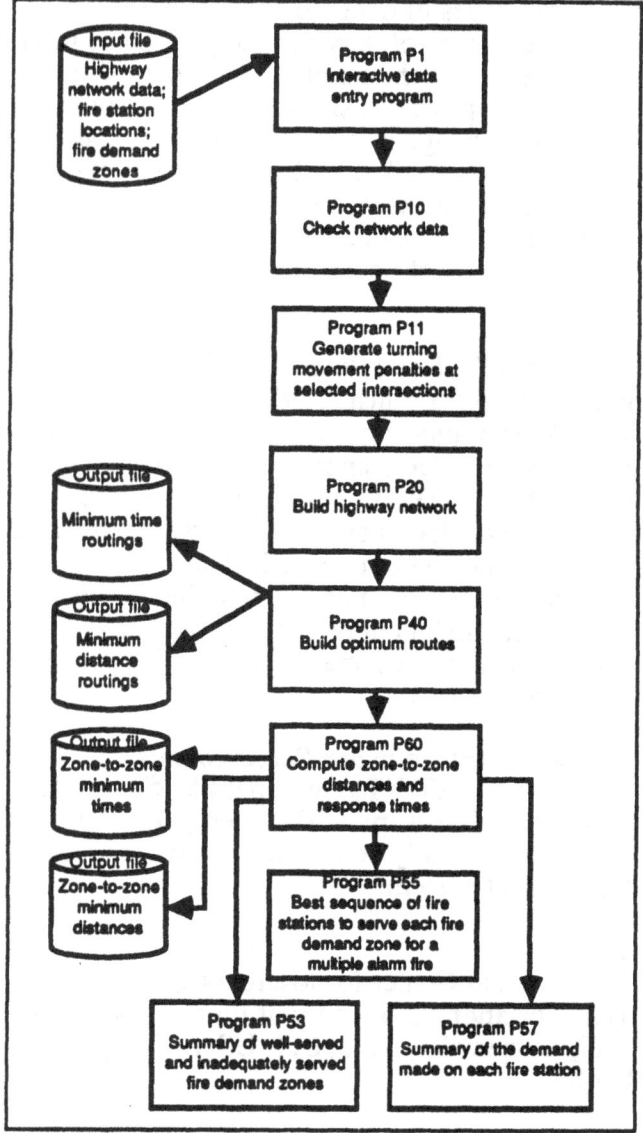

Figure 11-4: The sequence of operations involved in using Fire Router.

vehicle travel times to and from the area of service, and travel time of alternative modes of transportation.

Theory and Assumptions

The model is based on the pivot-point logit model developed by Cambridge Systematics Inc. for the Federal Energy Administration in 1976. The default coefficients for the Regional Transportation District (RTD) version were developed by the Denver Regional Council of Governments in its Unified Travel Patterns Model. These coefficients can be changed in the template to reflect local conditions.

Two types of data are needed: base-mode shares and level-of-service changes. Base-mode shares represent the number of people using a particular type of transit for a particular purpose before the change in policy occurs (e.g., people commuting to work by subway). Level-of-service changes refer to the policy options being considered (e.g., increased parking prices or different hours of operation).

Evaluation

The RTD Pivot Point Logit Model is a good planning aid for transportation officials charged with determining service policy and setting fare levels. Given some knowledge of how a spreadsheet works, this is an easy model to operate. The documentation is terse but provides the basic information needed. The documentation does not describe the theory behind the model but refers to two other documents that presumably provide further technical information.

Hardware and Software Requirements

IBM PC/AT/XT or compatible; SuperCalc 3. Because it is a spreadsheet template, the model could easily be rewritten to run on any spreadsheet system.

Source

National Center for Microcomputers in Transportation, University of Florida, 346 Weil Hall, Gainesville, FL 32611, USA. The price is US $5.

Arterial Analysis Package (AAP)

Purpose

To help traffic engineers determine the most efficient timing pattern for signals in complex street systems.

Description

The Arterial Analysis Package (AAP) allows traffic engineers to use interactively three of the most powerful tools available for managing signal lights on streets and highways: Signal Operations Analysis Package (SOAP-84), Progressive Analysis and Signal System Evaluation Routine (PASSERII-84), and TRANSYT-7F.

AAP uses the strengths of each of these component modules to design and analyze

arterial signal timing. SOAP-84 is used to plan signal controls at individual intersections, PASSER II-84 to develop the optimal signal progression on a linear arterial highway, and TRANSYT-7F to determine the optimum signal timing for an entire network of interconnected streets and highways.

SOAP was originally developed in 1979 by the U.S. Department of Transportation's Federal Highway Administration. It has since undergone a number of modifications and revisions to produce the current version entitled SOAP-84. The Progressive Analysis and Signal System Evaluation Routine (PASSERII) was originally developed in 1973 by Dr. Carol Messer of the Texas Transportation Institute at Texas A&M University and has been revised and updated several times by Dr. Messer and others. The original version of TRANSYT was developed in 1967 in the United Kingdom by Dennis I. Robertson and has undergone seven major revisions.

Theory and Assumptions

AAP is the integrating framework for SOAP-84, PASSER II-84, and TRANSYT-7F. Solutions may emerge from analysis with an individual program or from the use of the programs in support of each other (see Figure 11-5). All three modules require similar inputs, and AAP includes a preprocessor that routes the same data, in proper format, to all three of the component models. The shared inputs include: geometric and traffic control parameters of the traffic system, traffic volumes, saturation flow rates, and minimum phase times. In addition, AAP provides the following: input data reports, performance evaluation summaries, timing design summaries, graphic displays or plots, special tables, and diagnostic messages beyond those provided by the individual modules.

SOAP-84 evaluates the input design relative to a specified pretimed design. The module determines the timing sequence that sensing controllers could be expected to generate and designs and evaluates the timing for pretimed controllers. SOAP-84 can also optimize designs in various ways. The program can analyze up to forty-eight time periods of between five and sixty minutes each. Outputs include: vehicle hours of delay, percent of vehicles stopped, gallons of excess fuel consumed, the number of vehicles forced to make excess left turns, the

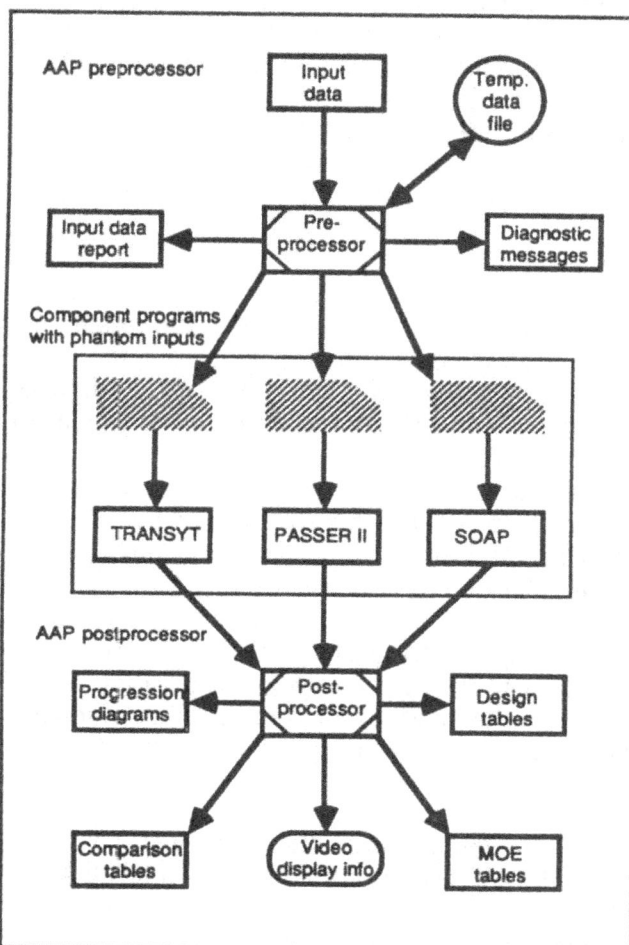

Figure 11-5: The multiple solution method of using the three submodels of the Arterial Analysis Package (AAP).

maximum queue length, and the volume-to-capacity ratio.

PASSERII-84 is a macroscopic, deterministic optimization model designed to maximize band width on a linear arterial highway. It optimizes cycle length, phase sequences, offsets, and progression speeds by applying a time series search-and-find optimization routine to the input data. It calculates delay by using the highway capacity equation contained in the U.S. Federal Highway Administration's *Highway Capacity Manual*. Queue clearance is found using Miller's method. Random and saturation delays are determined using the method of the U.S. National Cooperative Highway Research Program. The

outputs include a best-solution report and time-space diagrams.

TRANSYT-7F uses the link and node system of simulating traffic flows. The nodes represent intersections; links are one or more lanes of traffic. The actual analysis is based on a macroscopic, deterministic, simulation and optimization model. This means that platoons of vehicles rather than individual vehicles are considered. A platoon dispersion algorithm is used to simulate the spreading out of platoons as they travel through the system. Delay is simulated using Webster's method. Outputs include: a traffic performance table, a detail report on controller timing settings, a stopline flow profile plot report, time-space diagrams, and a cycle length evaluation summary.

Evaluation

The AAP framework allows for the easy handling of both single-intersection, multi-period problems and multi-intersection single-period problems. Multi-intersection, multi-period problems are beyond the capabilities of AAP.

The individual modules also have various limitations. SOAP-84 does not differentiate between through traffic and right turns, which can be a problem if there is heavy pedestrian traffic. To make the development of the TRANSYT-7F model manageable, some constituents of the traffic system were omitted. These omissions include traffic congestion, vehicle type mix, and the gradient, curvature, surface quality, and temperature of the roads. While the module is useful in many situations, these limitations must always be kept in mind.

The AAP user manual is extremely well written. It includes a number of sample runs that lead the user through design applications. The manual details the limitations of each module and the areas where the modules conflict. Strategies for overcoming limitations and conflicts are provided.

Traffic planners in any country would find AAP useful in reducing the delays caused by poorly synchronized traffic controls.

Hardware and Software Requirements

IBM PC/XT/AT and compatibles, 256 KB RAM (512 KB RAM if using a RAM disk), two 360 KB floppy disk drives (or one 360 KB floppy disk drive and a hard disk), monochrome or color monitor, printer; DOS 2.0 or higher. A math coprocessor chip is recommended, but not required.

Source

McTrans Center, National Center for Microcomputers in Transportation, University of Florida, 346 Weil Hall, Gainesville, FL 32611, USA; telephone: (904) 397-0378.

Computer Aided Translator (CAT) Programs

Purpose

To prepare translations efficiently, rapidly, and inexpensively and to improve the productivity of translators.

Description

The performance of mainframe computers translating from one human language into another has been advancing steadily for a decade or more, and recently several computer aided translator (CAT) programs for microcomputers have become available. The program described here, MicroCAT, translates English into Spanish, French, German, Italian, or Portuguese and also translates Spanish, French, and Japanese into English. Many of the features of MicroCAT also apply to other computer aided translator programs.

MicroCAT is capable of generating up to eight thousand words of rough translation per hour. With the assistance of MicroCAT, some professional human translators are able to complete as much as eight hundred words of finished text per hour. Some users report MicroCAT has cut translation expenses by as much as 70 percent.

Theory and Assumptions

The original text may be entered from a keyboard, diskette, optical scanner, magnetic tape, modem, or interface to a word processor. After entry, the text is rapidly scanned by the computer for words not in the thirteen-thousand-word MicroCAT dictionary. A human translator

can quickly add these words to the dictionary. MicroCAT then makes the translation, analyzing and restructuring the text according to the rules of the target language. When the translated text appears beside the source text on the word processor screen, the human translator goes to work creating accurate, consistent translations.

Evaluation

The MicroCAT system makes good use of the human translator's time. With the rough translation completed by the computer, the translator's skills and talents are used to edit and polish. A high-quality text can thus be produced quite rapidly.

While translations produced by computers may never reach the quality attained by a professional human translator, programs like MicroCAT can definitely facilitate translation work. Furthermore, the quality of translations by microcomputer programs is likely to increase markedly in the next few years as parallel processing techniques and artificial intelligence methods are applied using the new thirty-two-bit microprocessors.

Hardware and Software Requirements

IBM AT or compatible with 640 KB RAM, a hard disk, a printer supported by the particular software package, and DOS 3.1 or later.

Source

Computer aided translation software for microcomputers is available from several sources. MicroCAT is available from: Weidner Communications Corporation, 40 Skokie Boulevard, Northbrook, IL 60062, USA; telephone: (800) 323-4945; telefax: (312) 564-8138; telex: 753629. A similar software product is available from: Automated Language Processing Systems, 295 Chipeta Way, P.O. Box 8719, Salt Lake City, UT 84108, USA; telephone: (801) 584-3000; telefax: (801) 584-3010; telex: 453195 ALPS PROVO. The price varies but is approximately US $10,000 per language per direction of translation.

Part Two: Integrated Models

12. Multisectoral National Models

Introduction

Most models in this book address only small parts of the overall area with which the leaders of nations are concerned. Certainly national leaders must give consideration to individual problems related to energy, health, environment, and other sectors, but they also must integrate, at least mentally, a large number of such sectors as they consider alternative courses of action for their nations.

It is good news, therefore, that modelers have begun developing multisectoral models that are providing increasingly integrated pictures of the conditions and options of nations. Such models are reviewed in this chapter. The GLOBUS model (reviewed in the "Global Models" chapter) also contains a multisectoral national submodel that, with only minor changes, can be made to represent virtually any nation. Furthermore, the GLOBUS national submodel is the only multisectoral national model available that specifically includes domestic politics.

The first model reviewed in this chapter was developed by Dr. Francisco Sagasti and his colleagues in the course of the Peruvian 21st Century Study. Dr. Sagasti, now Chief of Strategic Planning for the World Bank, observed that "we live in a spreadsheet culture" and decided to put his whole thirteen-sector national model on interrelated spreadsheets to make it more accessible. The Peru 21st Century Model is one of the finest national models now available.

Although the Peruvian model will be understood by professionals, it is too complex and technical to be useful in introducing general audiences to the multisectoral issues that confront all nations. STRATAGEM-1 is the ideal tool for such nontechnical groups. This small yet complex model is the basis for a game in which players take on roles as government ministers, thereby gaining experience and insights into the complex task of managing a nation.

Resources for the Awareness of Population Impacts on Development (RAPID) is by far the most widely used multisectoral model. This model, which has excellent graphics, has been used to promote family planning programs in more than fifty countries. Unfortunately the model behind the elaborate graphics is rather trivial and oversimplifies many important aspects of development planning.

Bachue-International (BI) is a well-integrated model comparable in complexity to the Peruvian spreadsheet model. It focuses especially on issues related to employment.

The model entitled Life Cycle of Economic Development (LCED) explores the dynamic processes of national growth and development over periods of approximately two and a half centuries. The model is primarily economic but includes a more explicit representation of resources than do most economic models.

The SAHEL model is a multisectoral representation of a nation that has a traditional (i.e., non-industrialized) economy. The model includes many factors that are generally agreed to be critically important to the development of nations but are usually not included in development models.

The Enhancing Carrying Capacity Options (ECCO) models are based on the resource accounting methodology rather than on traditional economic methods. Traditional economic models use price as the common indicator of value among incommensurable goods and services, but the ECCO models use energy instead. National studies with ECCO produce insights often missed in traditional analyses.

MAYA, the Mayan collapse model, is a multisectoral model of the history of a civilization. This innovative, interdisciplinary model merges history, anthropology, and systems analysis. Many new insights can be expected as more models of this sort are built and such disciplinary integration develops.

Peru 21st Century Model

Purpose

To identify and evaluate future development options for Peru.

Description

There are a number of methods 21st Century Study teams can use to get the software they need to do their research. They can buy programs, hire others to write them, or write them themselves. Grupo de Análisis para el Desarrollo (GRADE) chose the last course when they carried out the Peruvian 21st Century Study (formally entitled the Analysis of Long-term Options for Peruvian Development Project).

The team wrote the interrelated sectoral submodels using popular spreadsheet software. They chose the spreadsheet software because, unlike sophisticated modeling languages, the methodologies used in spreadsheet modeling can be understood by almost anyone. The ease with which a model can be understood by decision makers is critically important in policy analysis. If decision makers cannot understand a model, they are unlikely to accept policy recommendations derived from it.

Theory and Assumptions

There are thirteen spreadsheet submodels within the Peru 21st Century Model. Ten of these spreadsheets estimate future values for variables in individual sectors: population, employment, education, housing, health, agriculture, nutrition, mining, energy, and industry. The three remaining spreadsheets are cross-sectoral consistency submodels that estimate future values for gross domestic product, investment, and foreign trade. The structure of the education sector is illustrated in Figure 12-1.

The population submodel is based on a simplified version of the standard United Nations demographic model. It requires user-supplied fertility and mortality rates to estimate the aggregate population and male to female ratio for a twenty-year period. Output generated by the population submodel is used as input to the housing, health, employment, education, and agriculture submodels.

The employment submodel calculates the future work force and the number of additional jobs that will be required to employ the workers.

The education submodel calculates, on the basis of estimated student attendance, the number of teachers and classrooms needed for the next twenty years. Using these figures, it then estimates the number of additional schools required and the level of investment needed for their construction.

The submodel on housing divides the population into urban and rural sectors and calculates the number of new housing units that will be needed by each sector and the level of investment that will be required to build them.

The health submodel calculates the number of doctors, nurses, and hospital beds needed for each of the twenty-five regional divisions of Peru. It also estimates the costs associated with acquiring those additional resources and with carrying out general vaccination campaigns.

The agricultural submodel is used to determine the production level that must be achieved for the twelve most important crops in order to provide adequate food for the country's growing population. It also calculates the effect that different crop distributions, changes in land productivity, and various percentages of land used for agriculture would have on total agricultural production.

The nutrition submodel assigns each Peruvian a "basket of food" that contains all the food necessary to meet basic nutritional needs. It then calculates the total amount of food needed to provide these baskets for the entire population. Food surpluses or shortages are then calculated on the basis of outputs from the population and agricultural submodels.

The mining submodel projects future production levels of copper, lead, zinc, silver, gold, and iron. It uses a series of econometric equations to produce these projections.

The energy submodel estimates the supply and demand of energy by sectors. It uses a series of econometric regressions to predict energy surpluses or shortages.

The industry submodel uses a series of econometric relations and input-output matrices to calculate future requirements for investment, imports, employment, and exports.

Evaluation

Because all of the submodels that make up the Peru 21st Century Model are spreadsheets, they are extremely easy to use and to understand. Anyone who has worked with spreadsheets will

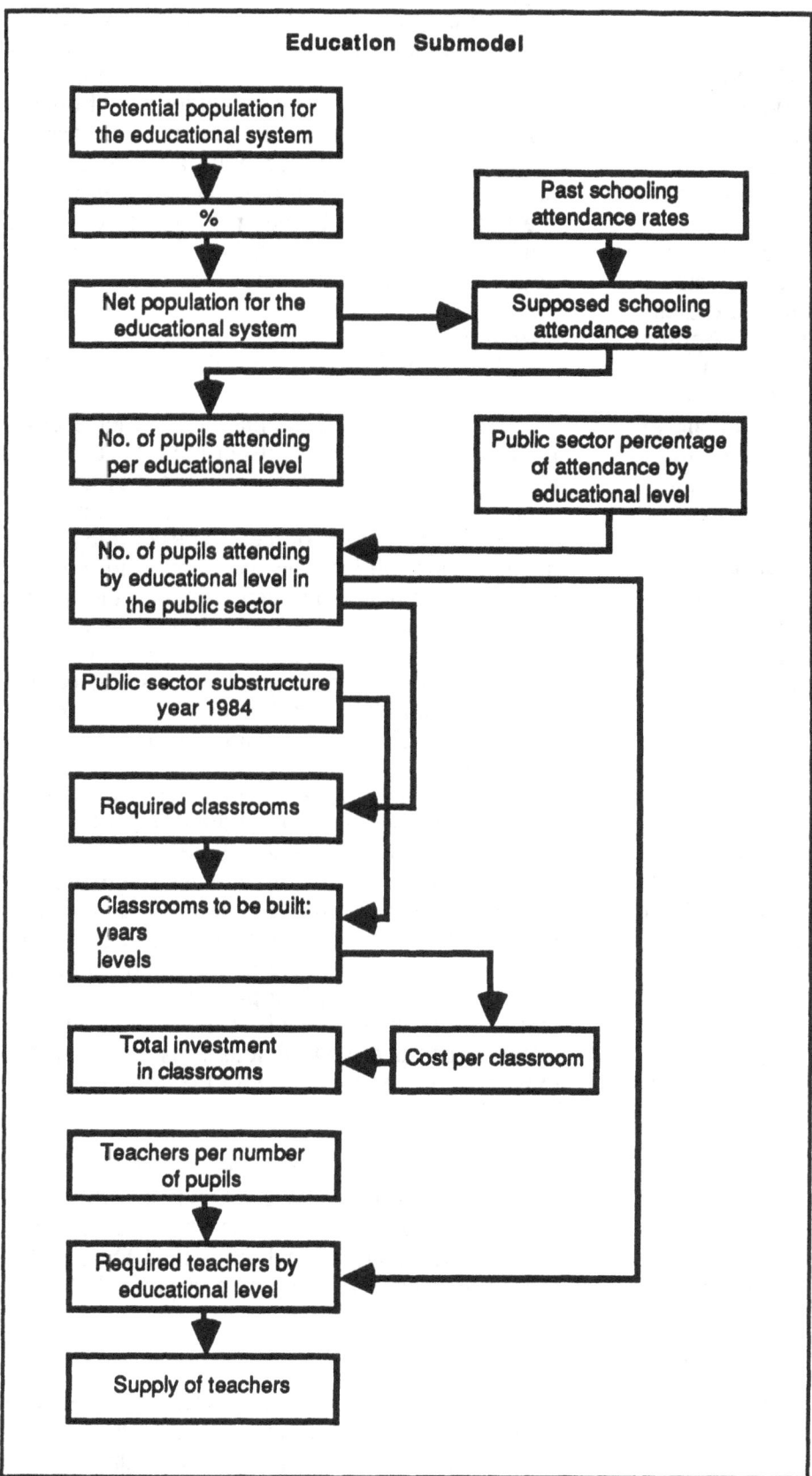

Education Submodel

Potential population for the educational system

%

Net population for the educational system

Past schooling attendance rates

Supposed schooling attendance rates

No. of pupils attending per educational level

Public sector percentage of attendance by educational level

No. of pupils attending by educational level in the public sector

Public sector substructure year 1984

Required classrooms

Classrooms to be built:
years
levels

Total investment in classrooms

Cost per classroom

Teachers per number of pupils

Required teachers by educational level

Supply of teachers

Figure 12-1: The structure of the education sector of the Peru 21st Century Model.

have no problem using these submodels. More importantly, they will have no problem understanding the methodologies underlying the outputs.

The documentation, in Spanish or English, is extensive and is illustrated with structure charts that make the models even easier to understand.

The success of the Peru 21st Century Model shows that serious modeling work can be done without the use of sophisticated modeling languages. This is good news not only to model builders, who must explain their work to non-experts, but also to decision makers, who often must judge and evaluate models.

Hardware and Software Requirements
　　IBM PC/XT/AT or compatibles, Symphony; or Apple II-E, VisiCalc.

Source
　　Mr. Gonzalo H. Garland, GRADE, Apartado 18-0572, Miraflores, Lima 18, Peru and Institute for 21st Century Studies, 1611 North Kent St., Suite 610, Arlington, VA 22209, USA. The price is to be determined.

STRATAGEM-1

Purpose
　　To simulate the management of a nation over a fifty-year period, including the effects of policy decisions regarding population, energy, nutrition, debt, material consumption, and environment.

Description

STRATAGEM-1 is a combination board game and computer simulation. The board is illustrated in Figure 12-2. The players take the roles of ministers in an imaginary country. They make decisions on policy and the allocation of tax revenues, and the computer simulates the results.

STRATAGEM-1 was created in 1983 by Dennis Meadows and his staff when he was director of the Integrative and Special Studies Project at the International Institute for Applied Systems Analysis (IIASA). At the time, the International Institute for Environment and Development (IIED) was looking for an energy and environment game that could be used in training, and the IIASA team set out to build one. The original model was written very quickly by Dennis and Donella Meadows as an outgrowth of some of their earlier work. Developing the game itself, including a game board, took a few months. Since its creation, the game has been played in many countries by students, academicians, businessmen, civil servants, and national leaders.

Theory and Assumptions

In STRATAGEM-1, a group of five to ten players controls policy decisions in a mythical developing country through a fifty-year period. Initially, the country has a small population, fair food consumption, low death rates (18/1,000 per year), high birth rates (41/1,000 per year), and 2.3 percent annual population growth.

The game is not designed to model any particular country. It concentrates instead on situations requiring decisions in all developing nations. There are three possible outcomes for any STRATAGEM-1 game. Balanced growth leading to a high quality, sustained state is considered a win. Players lose if their country ends up in a state of stagnation, or if it grows too rapidly and is forced into decline.

There are five sectors in STRATAGEM-1, and each player or team of players is in charge of one. The sectors are: population and household consumption; energy production and energy efficiency; food production and environmental protection; goods production and human services; and international finance, exports, imports, and debt.

The game progresses in cycles that represent five real-time years. In each cycle, players must allocate the total available capital among the various sectors. Their goal is to do this in a way that promotes balanced growth. There are a number of different ways to achieve the highest quality of development. Players may choose to concentrate on one sector, hoping to create surpluses that can be sold on the international market. Alternatively they may decide to invest equally in all of the sectors in order for the country to become self-sufficient.

Evaluation

The game is useful for training and instruction.

During the game the players, in their roles as government ministers, must come to a consensus about how to allocate money to the various sectors and about whether or not to borrow money from foreign sources. These policy decisions are put into the computer, and the program calculates the outcomes, i.e., the results of the decisions, for the beginning of the next cycle. Print-outs of the outcomes showing the new conditions in the country are distributed to the players and become the basis for the next allocations. The process continues in this manner over ten cycles.

Players are advised of the cause and effect relationships in the model at the outset of the game, so that they can coordinate their efforts and investments to achieve the desired balanced growth. The problem in the game, as in the real world, is that the mental models of the decision makers are inadequate for handling all aspects of even a relatively simple representation of a nation. Furthermore, each of the roles brings a different perspective to discussions about what must be done, and when, with the country's limited resources.

Hardware and Software Requirements

The STRATAGEM-1 kit comes with the game board, game money, playing pieces, and the computer program, which is in BASIC and can be adapted to run on any computer that can run BASIC.

Source

Prof. Dennis L. Meadows, Director, Institute for Policy and Social Science Research, University of New Hampshire, Murkland Hall, Durham, NH 03824, USA; telephone: (603) 862-2186.

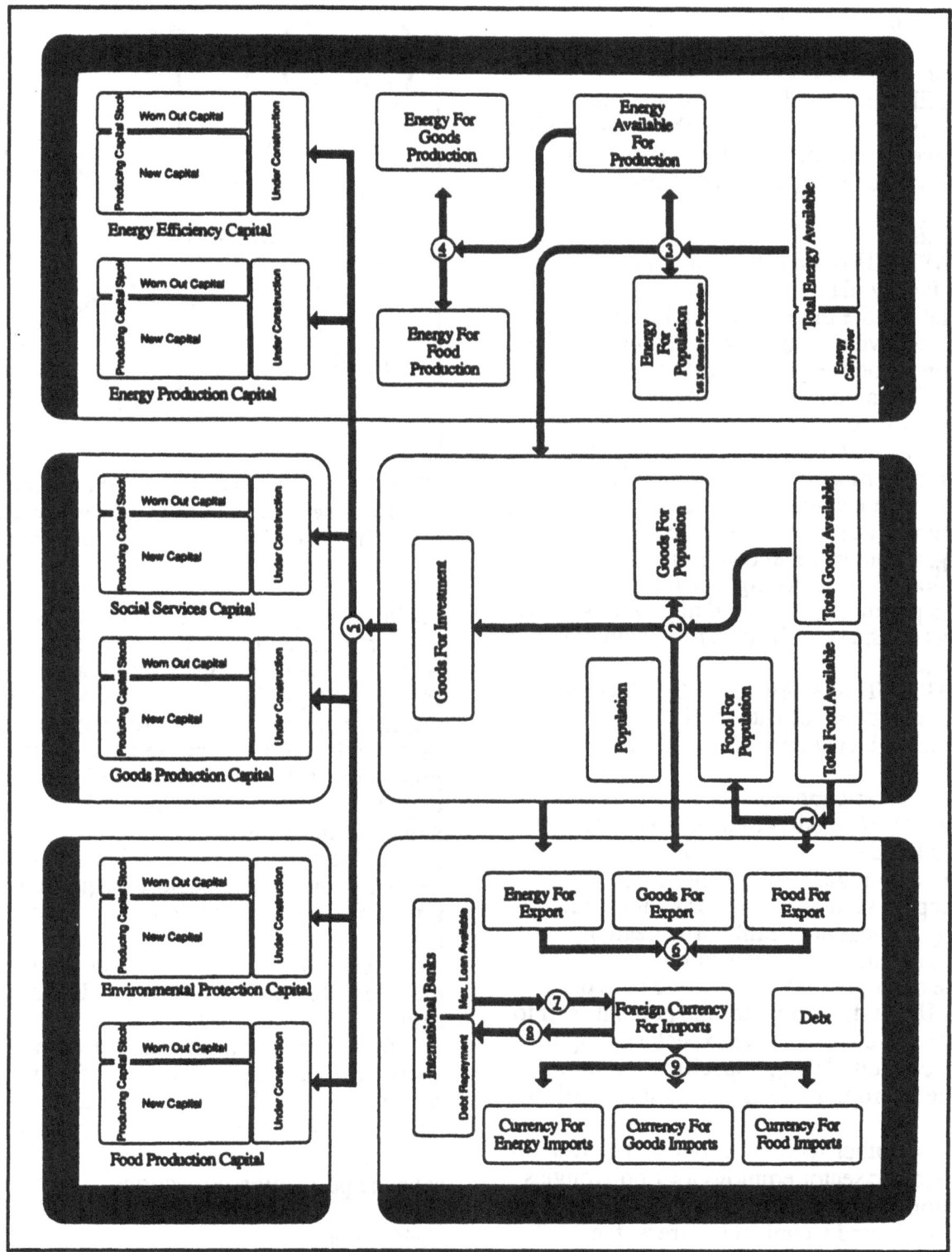

Figure 12-2: Illustration of the game board for STRATAGEM-1.

Resources for the Awareness of Population Impacts on Development (RAPID III)

Purpose

To illustrate for decision makers in developing countries how the ability of a nation to achieve its economic and social goals is adversely affected by population growth.

Description

RAPID III is a multisectoral model for selling family planning programs. During a presentation, the model can quickly calculate answers to "what if" questions and present the results in attractive pie charts, bar charts, or graphs. The model is easily configured to represent a specific country.

The RAPID program is fundamentally a demographic model. In addition to demographic projections, it calculates simple indicators of the economic, educational, health, urbanization, housing, and nutritional consequences of population growth. Its high-quality color graphics permit dramatic and highly persuasive briefings on the benefits of family planning programs.

RAPID III was developed by The Futures Group under contract with the U.S. Agency for International Development (USAID).

Theory and Assumptions

RAPID III consists of seven sectoral modules linked in an open-loop, star-shaped structure (see Figure 12-3) centered on the demographic sector. The other sectors are: economy, education, health, urbanization, housing, and agriculture-nutrition.

The demographic sector is the core of RAPID III. It disaggregates the population into five-year age cohorts. Life expectancy input data are converted to age-specific mortalities using the appropriate Coale-Demeny model life table.

The six other sectors operate as follows: (a) The economic sector employs a Cobb-Douglas production function to relate output to labor, capital stock, and technical progress; the economic sector may be replaced with exogenous economic projections; (b) the education sector totals the school-age cohorts and calculates the percentage of the school-age population actually attending schools; (c) the

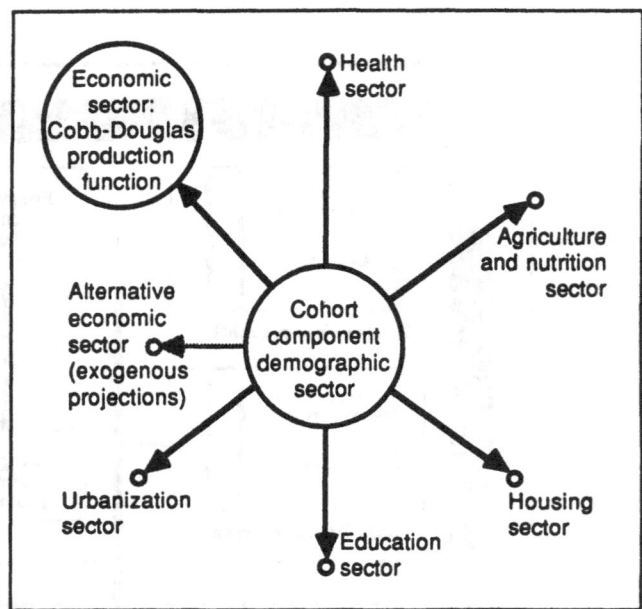

Figure 12-3: Relationships among the sectors of the RAPID model. Size of circles provides a rough indication of the complexity of the individual sectors.

health sector projects the numbers of doctors and hospital beds required to attain the desired ratios of each to the total population; it also calculates the size of high risk groups such as children under the age of five and mothers; (d) the urbanization and housing sector calculates urban population, urban rooms required, size of largest city, number of households and their size, and new housing requirements; and (e) the agriculture-nutrition sector calculates people per hectare of arable land, calorie requirements for a typical family, and supply and demand of a major food community.

Functionally, RAPID III consists of four modules. The presentation module displays the results of runs in either tabular or graphic format. The defaults module is used to customize the analysis, e.g., to set the number of regions and sectors. The database module is used to input data for a specific nation. The demographic projection module is used to create, modify, and save the population projections.

Evaluation

RAPID III and its predecessors are possibly the most influential and widely used models of development. The Futures Group estimates that the model is currently in use in forty to forty-five countries.

From their inception, the RAPID models were designed for brief, dramatic presentations on the implications of population growth for development prospects. An implicit objective has always been to persuade top national leaders to institute and support family planning programs.

RAPID presentations have been very effective in selling family planning. The benefits of family planning are presented clearly and persuasively. The high-quality color graphics provide a sharpness and vividness to the presentations, conveying a sense of competence and authority.

RAPID III is far less sophisticated, however, than its graphics might lead one to believe. The demographic sector is well developed and so is the economic sector (when it is actually used and not replaced with exogenous projections). Most of the other sectors are far less robust. Those on health, housing, education, urbanization, and agriculture-nutrition are quite lacking in complexity, in some cases involving little more than the ratio of two numbers. There is a danger that the extremely simple structure of these sectors is not recognized by the audiences that see RAPID III presentations.

Such criticisms of RAPID are generally answered in three ways: (a) RAPID is for awareness raising, not planning; (b) presentations for top-level decision makers must be kept simple; and (c) the structure of RAPID is described in the Futures Group's publication *Description of the RAPID Socioeconomic Model*.

Such answers are not satisfying and ignore the realities: (a) RAPID has in fact been used for planning; (b) the decision makers of any nation can understand model assumptions if these assumptions are presented clearly and in non-technical terms; and (c) the description of the structure of RAPID in *Description of the RAPID Socioeconomic Model* is presented not in easily understood diagrams, but rather in abstract mathematical equations.

A simple, attractive, on-screen description of the model's assumptions and structure could be developed and used to introduce every RAPID presentation. Such an introduction would, however, draw attention to the simplistic nature of the model's assumptions and might reduce the effectiveness of the family-planning sales pitch.

There is no question that family planning would benefit many parts of the world and that tools are needed for effectively presenting the benefits of family planning. It is a mistake, however, to sell family planning deceptively through overly simplistic models, and RAPID III is such a model.

The development community needs a model that incorporates the presentational polish of RAPID III with a balanced, robust treatment of economics, education, health, urbanization, housing, agriculture, and nutrition. The original RAPID program was an excellent start in this direction. It is unfortunate that nearly a decade of funding has produced so little improvement in the substantive quality of RAPID.

Hardware and Software Requirements
IBM PC/XT/AT or compatible computers, 640 KB RAM, hard disk, color monitor (CGA, EGA, or VGA) or monochrome monitor (with Hercules graphics adapter), IBM or Epson compatible dot matrix printer, DOS version 2.0 or higher.

Source
Mr. John Stover, Vice President, The Futures Group, 76 Eastern Boulevard, Glastonbury, CT 06033-1264, USA; telephone: (203) 633-3501; or Dr. John Crowley, Office of Population, USAID, Science and Technology/POP/PDD, SA-18, Room 711, Washington, DC 20523, USA. The program is free.

Bachue-International (BI)

Purpose
To serve as a framework for a country- or region-specific model of the interactions among population, employment, income distribution, and economic development.

Description
Bachue-International is a generic country model that is used both as a tool for teaching about sectional linkages and as a framework for developing country-specific models. Country models have been developed for Mauritania, India, and Kenya. The model takes its name from Bachue (Ba'chue), the Colombian goddess of love, fertility, and harmony between nature and man.

In the mid-1970s, the International Labour Organization (ILO) developed a family of large-scale economic and demographic models for mainframe computers as part of its World Employment Programme. The first of this family of Bachue models was built for the Philippines. It was followed by models for Kenya, Brazil, and Yugoslavia.

The country-specific Bachue models are large and complex. They require enormous amounts of computer time to run. They are costly and difficult to build and use, and their outputs are not easily related to policy issues.

The Bachue-International (BI) model is an attempt to derive some of the benefits from the larger models while avoiding the problems of their size. Although BI is less disaggregated than the Bachue mainframe models, it preserves the essential relationships found in the mainframe versions.

The Bachue models, both mainframe and microcomputer, distinguish themselves from other economic-demographic models in several ways. They do not use optimization algorithms. They are disequilibrium models that are solved recursively. A large number of their variables are endogenous. They include extensive feedbacks between income distribution, demographic variables, and economic variables. They are highly disaggregated and include a large amount of demographic detail. Their projections are typically for a thirty-year period.

Theory and Assumptions

As illustrated in Figure 12-4, the BI model contains three subsystems: (a) demographic, (b) economic, and (c) employment and income distribution. The demographic subsystem has a direct impact on the economic subsystem through investment and demand for goods and services. The demographic subsystem influences income distribution through labor supply. The economic system affects income distribution through labor demand and earnings distribution. Income distribution influences demographics through education, migration, births, and deaths.

The demographic subsystem uses the Coale-Demeny life tables to estimate fertility rates and other exogenous variables. The module projects population by age, sex, rural or urban location, education level, and labor force participation.

Significant demographic assumptions include the following: Opportunity costs are a useful indicator of women's decisions on how many children to have; the same types of factors affect fertility rates in both urban and rural areas; constraints on women's time during education and labor force participation affect fertility rates; and education indirectly improves the distribution of income.

The economic subsystem is based on an input-output model with ten sectors: agriculture, mining, food processing, textiles, chemicals, metal manufacturing, miscellaneous

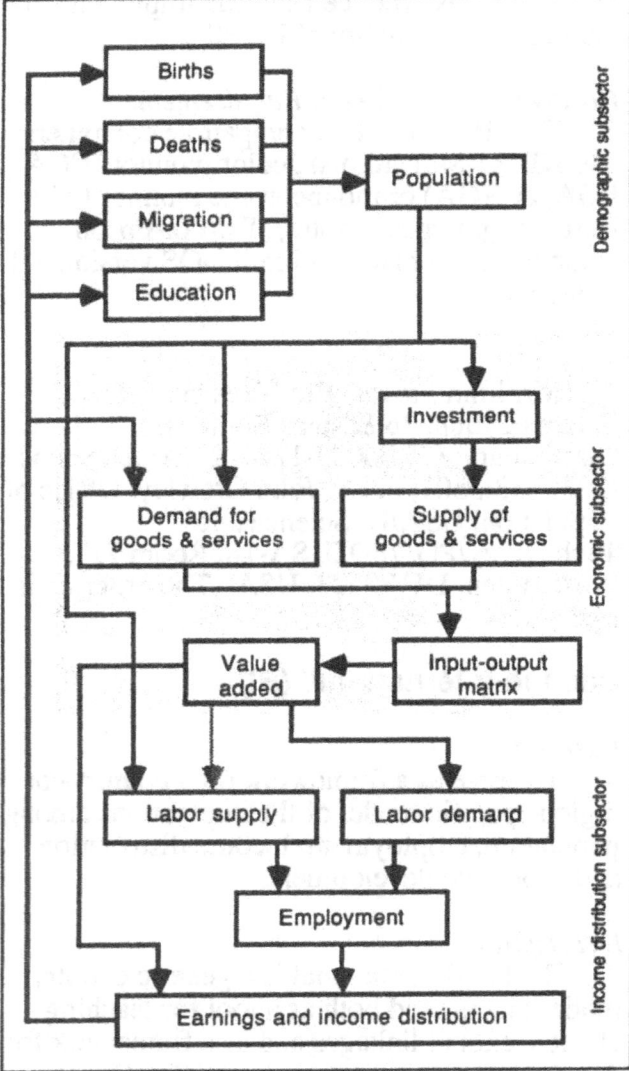

Figure 12-4: The principal relationships among the three major sectors of Bachue-International. Note that the model's treatment of government intervention has been omitted for sake of simplicity.

manufacturing, construction, energy, and services. Agriculture and mining are considered to be rural industries; the remaining eight are regarded as urban.

Assumptions inherent in the economy subsystem include: Skilled workers exist only in urban areas; growth in employment is proportional to growth in output; and all imports are competitive with local industries. Investment is an endogenous variable. No inventories are accumulated.

The income distribution subsystem simulates rural and urban per capita incomes, employment by sector, skill level by sector, distribution of earnings by decile, and government tax revenues. Unemployment benefits are the only government transfer payments. Government employment is determined by the government's salary budget. Government tax revenues come from taxes on profits and on personal earnings.

Significant assumptions in the income distribution subsystem include: Employers and self-employed individuals are skilled workers; employees move promptly to areas where jobs are available; there is a neo-classical labor market, i.e., unemployment rates are influenced by changes in the demand and supply for labor; and labor demand is linked to the desired output levels of firms.

Evaluation

Bachue-International is the best generic multisectoral model we have found that focuses on employment and income distribution. The model could be very useful in many countries where employment and income distribution need to be given special attention. The documentation for the original mainframe version is provided in R. S. Moreland, *Population, Development and Income Distribution—A Modelling Approach* (New York: St. Martin's Press, 1984). Unfortunately, the book is out of print, but photocopies may be available from Dr. Moreland or from ILO. While the book presents the theoretical basis for both the mainframe and microcomputer versions of the model, it is definitely not a user's guide. To our knowledge there is no user's guide for either the mainframe or the microcomputer version of the model.

A second drawback to this model is one associated with any large, complex package: the need for extensive data. Converting the generic

BI Model into a country-specific model based on the appropriate data would require several months of work by a well-trained economist. Support from the original modelers would be very helpful, and consulting services can probably be arranged.

Many nations would benefit from studies based on Bachue-International. The model would be far more useful if it were rewritten in a higher-level programming language (e.g., DYNAMO) to facilitate data entry and graphic output. Even in its current form, however, this model deserves much more attention than it has received.

Hardware and Software Requirements

IBM PC/XT/AT or compatible, 640 KB RAM, two floppy disk drives, math coprocessor chip. BASIC and Ryan-McFarlain FORTRAN.

Source

Mr. Richard Anker, EPPB, Employment and Development Department, ILO, Geneva 22, Switzerland; or Dr. Scott Moreland, Research Triangle Institute, P.O. Box 12194, Research Triangle Park, NC 27709-2194, USA; telephone: (919) 541-7228.

Life Cycle of Economic Development (LCED)

Purpose

To describe the dynamic processes through which nations grow to power, loose vitality, and stagnate, and to apply the knowledge gained to the case of a modern industrialized nation.

Description

History books are filled with examples of the rise, stagnation, and decline of nations and empires. Generally the process occurs over a few hundred years. A period of rapid expansion, growth, and accumulating power gives way to dissolution and degeneration as the problems associated with growth require increasing amounts of attention and energy.

As illustrated in Figure 12-5, the LCED model links classical economic structures into a fully dynamic feedback structure. The model runs over a 250-year period to show how pressures latent in the growth phase can emerge later to suppress growth.

The model was designed as part of a study focused on the 100-year transition phase from growth to either decay or vibrant equilibrium. A key part of this transition process involves the shifting allocation of labor and capital among major production sectors to balance the changing needs of the population over the life cycle of development. Throughout the process, capital accumulation in each sector is determined by the relative marginal productivities of capital and labor.

The model illustrates several different possibilities for the life cycle of a nation's development. Growth can be halted by limits on food, space, and resources. A dynamic, prosperous, active equilibrium is also possible.

LCED was developed to represent Canada, but it can be applied to any nation. The model provides a laboratory in which to examine the implications of various policies on the life cycle of a nation's development.

Theory and Assumptions

The LCED model represents the economy with five production sectors all linked through population into a dynamic structural framework. The agricultural sector uses labor, capital, and land as inputs to food production. The activities represented in the agricultural sector include farming, fishing, food processing, and the production of short-life goods used in food production, such as fertilizers, pesticides, and seeds.

The goods sector produces durable goods that are used or operated by the consumer public. Labor, capital, and processed resources are used to produce the goods. The activities of the goods sector include production of housing, cars, clothing, and recreational facilities.

The services sector uses direct labor and capital to produce services for the population. The activities in the service sector include work in health, government, education, arts, banking, transportation, communication, and hotels and restaurants, as well as repairs and personal services. The services sector is assumed to have no resource input except indirectly through the resources in its capital.

The capital sector uses labor, capital, and processed resources to produce capital for all five production sectors including itself. Capital is any form of output with a long lifetime that is used as an input to production. Both capital

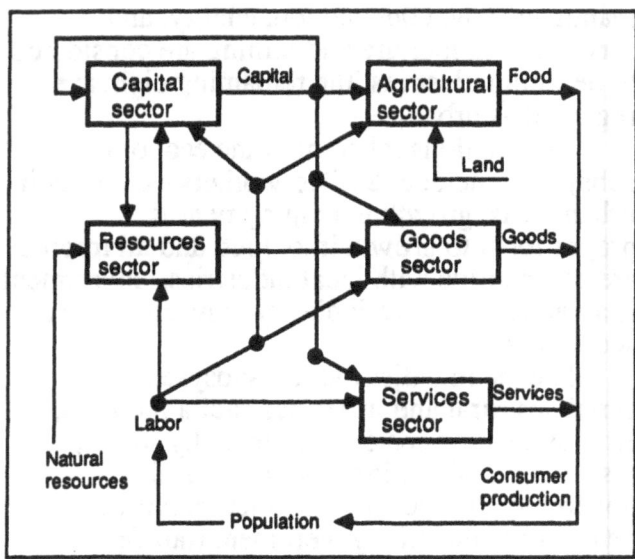

Figure 12-5: The linkages among the five sectors of the LCED model.

goods and knowledge of productive techniques are classified as capital in the model. The average lifetime of capital is approximately twenty-five years. The activities in the capital sector include research and development, manufacture of machinery, professional training, and construction of productive structures such as factories, roads, and dams.

The resources sector uses labor, capital, and natural resources to produce processed resources for the goods and capital sectors. The activities in the resources sector include production of metals, chemicals, plastics, building materials, plus oil and other forms of energy. The natural resources tapped by the resources sector are nonrenewable inputs from nature.

The model has a circular structure. The two secondary sectors—capital and resources—support the consumer sectors. Output from the three consumer sectors—food, goods, and services—supports the population. Labor from population supports all five productions sectors. The only factors of production that lie outside the circular flow pattern are the environmental production inputs—natural resources and land.

Evaluation

In a sense, there is little new in the LCED model. Virtually all of the structures are derived from classical economics. What is new is the linkage of the classical structures into an overall dynamic framework.

There is one significant omission in the model: waste. The five sectors perform their functions effectively over 250 years and produce no trash, toxic chemicals, or pollutants. One might argue that disposal space is a resource and therefore is depleted along with the other resources. It would be preferable, however, to have waste represented explicitly, since it presents problems that are quite different from those of normal resource management.

As the model's author notes, LCED as it stands is not suitable for detailed policy analysis. Nonetheless, the model deals with issues that are vitally important to the whole of societies. It could be very useful to anyone interested in the long-term welfare of a nation or people, including farsighted and thoughtful government leaders who are seeking policies that will address present problems without reducing future options.

Hardware and Software Requirements

IBM PC/XT/AT or compatible, 640 KB RAM, hard disk, printer. Color monitor recommended, but not required. Professional DYNAMO Plus or perhaps DYSMAP2. It might also be possible to use an Apple Macintosh Plus, SE, or II and the STELLA simulation software, but the equations would have to be rewritten somewhat.

Source

The model equations are presented in N. B. Forrester, *The Life Cycle of Economic Development* (Cambridge, Mass.: MIT Press, 1973). The address of the press is: MIT Press, Cambridge, MA 02142, USA. The price of the book is US $15.00, subject to change.

SAHEL

Purpose

To analyze alternative policies and programs that might provide a lasting solution to the periodic famines that plague Sahelian Africa.

Description

SAHEL is a dynamic simulation of the interaction of population growth, soil conditions, range condition, herd size, economy, and values in the nomadic cultures that inhabit the Sahelian

zone of Africa. The model allows users to evaluate a wide range of policies and programs that might be pursued by development and humanitarian organizations to alter long-term trends in desertification, emigration, malnutrition, and famine.

The SAHEL model was developed in the mid-1970s by Dr. Anthony C. Picardi at the Massachusetts Institute for Technology with funding from the U.S. Agency for International Development (USAID) and the United Nations. The development of this model was part of a large emergency project to assess what the development community could and should do to respond to the massive famines and rapid desertification of the Sahelian region.

The model suggests that most forms of assistance now being employed (drilling and maintenance of wells, and veterinary, public health, family planning, and sanitation programs) are generally ineffective and in most cases counter productive.

On the other hand, the model indicates that one set of policies, programs, and value changes could produce dramatically improved conditions by the year 2070. The programs involve rapidly reducing herds down to levels that can be sustained by the land over long periods (the long-term average sustained yield). A supplemental feed program maintains stocks at this level during periodic droughts. The primary value change is a diminished social importance of herd size.

Within the model, this approach produces many long-term benefits including range recovery, increased offtake potential, reduced human death rates, generally increased nutritional status, reduced population growth, and a substantial decline in migration out of the area.

Theory and Assumptions

SAHEL (see Figure 12-6) consists of five sectors that are interlinked with many dynamic feedback loops: (a) The demographic sector projects how the human population will change in response to food availability and the economic utility of children; (b) the livestock sector projects the size of the livestock population on the basis of the forage available and the offtake rate; (c) the rangeland sector projects soil conditions and available forage from the stocking rate and exogenous rainfall projections;

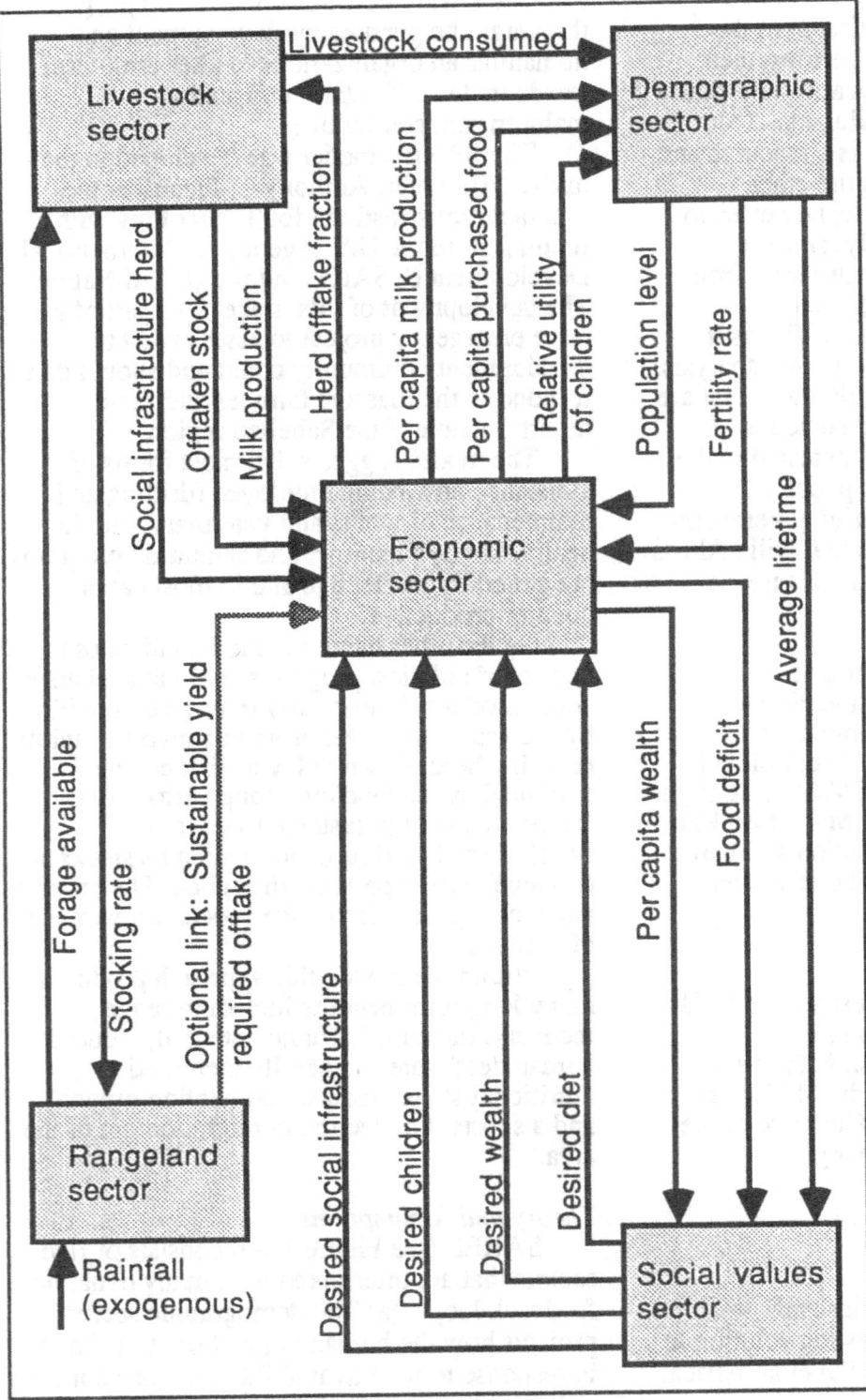

Figure 12-6: The causal flow diagram for the SAHEL model.

(d) the economic sector projects income, wealth, food availability, and the economic utility of children on the basis of herd offtake, milk production, socioeconomic goals, population levels, and fertility rates; a Cobb-Douglas production function is used in the calculations; and (e) the social values sector projects socioeconomic goals (desired wealth, diet, children, and social infrastructure) on the basis of per capita wealth, food availability, and life expectancy.

Evaluation

Value change is one of the most profound factors in the economic development of a nation or region. Yet few long-term development models explicitly include value change. SAHEL does, and for this reason (among many others) it deserves much more attention than it has received.

One might think that because SAHEL successfully integrated ecological, agricultural, economic, demographic and values issues into a single well-documented, well-researched model, it would have been enthusiastically received. What has happened is exactly the opposite. SAHEL raised fundamental questions about the long-term effectiveness of much of the development and relief work in Africa, and officials at both USAID and the UN were consequently unwilling to encourage serious discussion of the findings. The history of the model's development and hostile reception has been recorded by D. H. Meadows and J. R. Robinson in their book *The Electronic Oracle* (New York: Wiley, 1985).

In a recent conversation, Dr. Picardi remarked, "USAID didn't want our study published. They gave us money to print only a half dozen copies. They forbid MIT to publish it with Institute funds and refused to send it to the USAID field offices in Africa.

"There were several reasons given, some obviously false. My personal opinion is that they wanted a study that recommended a quick fix. Preferably something high-tech that U.S. businesses could supply. Cattle breeding technology or the use of satellites, maybe.

"The message of SAHEL is that there is no quick, technical fix. The problems in the Sahel are all interconnected in a complex socio-political-ecological system. The only solutions are long-term. Instead of `quick, high-tech fixes' what is needed is a number of well-educated, systems-oriented people who are willing to go live there and the institutional commitment to support them for a decade or two. That wasn't what USAID or the UN wanted to hear."

SAHEL continues to have much relevance and utility. While it does not cover all aspects of African development, it includes more issues relevant to the Sahel then any other model we have discovered.

Hardware and Software Requirements

Either IBM PC/XT/AT or compatible, 640 KB RAM, hard disk, printer, and Professional DYNAMO Plus or perhaps DYSMAP2; or, after a rewriting of the equations, Apple Macintosh Plus, SE, or II, printer, and STELLA software.

Source

The 400-page thesis in which the model is presented is available from: Thesis Reproduction Center, Massachusetts Institute of Technology, Cambridge, MA 02139, USA. The thesis, two articles on the model, and a disk containing the model equations are also available from: Dr. Anthony C. Picardi, 58 Washburn Avenue, Wellesley, MA 02181, USA. The prices are US $50 for the thesis and US $50 for the disk. Both prices are subject to change.

Enhancing Carrying Capacity Options (ECCO)

Purpose

To evaluate and compare long-term policies for sustainable development that take into account the carrying capacity of the region and the interactions among population, resources, environment, and development.

Description

The ECCO models (see Figure 12-7) test the outcome of a wide range of policy options such as altering birth rates, attaining self-sufficiency in food and energy, altering fiscal policies and interest rates on loans, discovering and exploiting natural resources, and making alternative choices about land use. The aim is to present the decision maker with a quantified measure of the long-term outcomes of chosen policy options.

The ECCO models were written by Professor Malcolm Slesser at the Energy Studies Unit of Strathclyde University under contract from the Population Division of UNESCO and with funding from UNFPA, FAO, and Mr. John A. Harris, IV. The original ECCO model, begun in 1980, required a mainframe computer. Since then a smaller microcomputer version, Micro-ECCO, was developed as a demonstration version of the original program ECCO. A generic version of ECCO written in DYNAMO for IBM PCs and compatibles is nearing completion at the time of this writing.

Theory and Assumptions

The ECCO models are based on the resource accounting methodology. These models measure the activity of each component of the economy in terms of the energy resource it consumes rather than in terms of monetary units. Slesser argues that by using energy accounting (rather than the traditional methods of monetary accounting) in tracing flows of goods and services, ECCO moves beyond the "perpetual motion" model of classical economics and develops projections that are more reliable over longer periods of time than those developed with traditional economic models.

The major assumptions of the ECCO models are: (a) All economic processes may be quantified in terms of energy; (b) if any economic activity is traced back in time, all

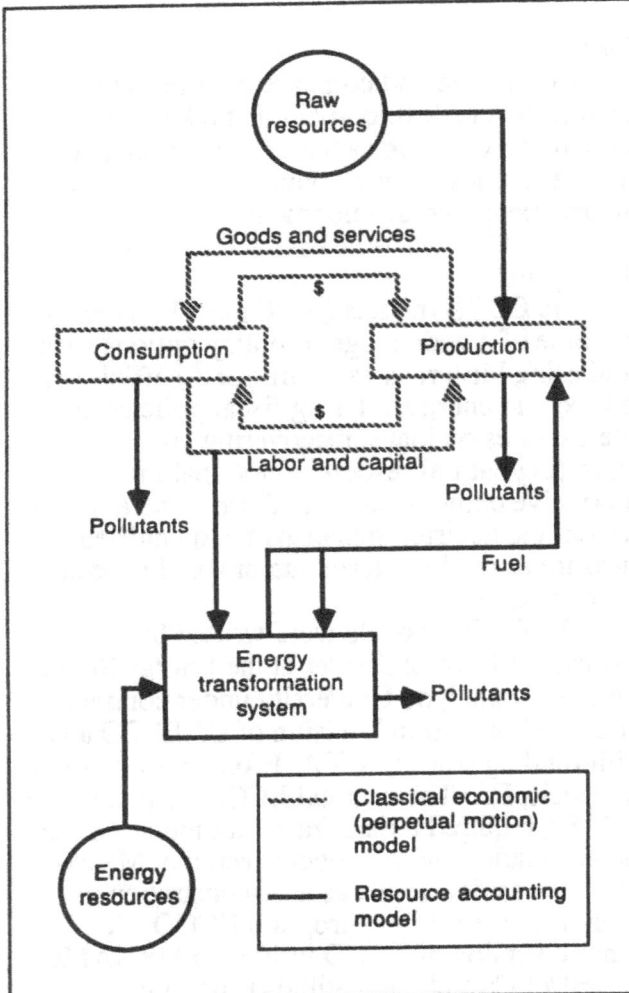

Figure 12-7: The overall structure of the ECCO models. The parts drawn with dashed lines represent the "perpetual motion" model of classical economics.

inputs to production can be reduced to prior and current labor, prior and current energy, and resources in the ground; (c) resources in the ground serve no purpose until extracted; and (d) in developing countries labor is not constrained by quantity, but possibly by quality.

Many interacting calculations are made in ECCO. Capital is allocated to the food sector according to the degree of self-sufficiency desired by the user. A similar approach is used in allocating capital to the energy sector. A minimum nutritional level is met by importing (if necessary); alternative policies can be superimposed. Wherever balance-of-payments presents a constraint on expansion, the user can explore the effect of increased aid or borrowed funds. The future population is calculated and compared with the present population that may be fed from indigenous food supplies.

Evaluation

Given the difficulties that traditional economic models have in developing reliable projections for even the short term, new approaches are needed. ECCO, in using the resource accounting methodology, is definitely a new approach. How effective it will be remains to be seen.

Studies using one or another of the ECCO models are under way or completed in Mauritius, the United Kingdom, Thailand, and Kenya and are being considered in Peru and Sri Lanka. The Mauritius study is farthest advanced.

The only validation study possible so far has been on the United Kingdom. The ECCO-U.K. model was able to forecast 1984 conditions from 1974 initial data with what Slesser terms "a useful degree of accuracy."

Documentation for the ECCO models has been difficult to obtain and less clear than is needed. The documentation for the original ECCO model is published as a separate appendix to the main report, and UNESCO does not send the appendix with the model unless specifically requested to do so. The documentation for the smaller Micro-ECCO is incomplete. The manual includes: (a) an informative introductory discussion of the resource accounting methodology and how it compares to traditional economic accounting, (b) a general diagram of the model, and (c) a general description of the interrelationships among the model's elements. The equations, however, are not listed. As a result, the user can never really know how the data are being manipulated. The documentation for the new Generic ECCO is expected to be more thorough and complete.

Even complete documentation is unlikely to be sufficient for the development of a country-specific model from Generic ECCO unless the modeler is already familiar with energy accounting. Some training from UNESCO and consulting with Professor Slesser are recommended. Potential users should also be aware that extensive data collection is required before the model can be applied to a specific nation.

Hardware and Software Requirements

Generic ECCO requires an IBM PC/XT/AT or compatible with 512 KB RAM, hard disk, and printer; Professional DYNAMO Plus or perhaps DYSMAP2. Micro-ECCO comes in compiled BASIC. The mainframe version of ECCO is written in the NDTRAN-2 dynamics language.

Source

Micro-ECCO and the new Generic ECCO are available from: Prof. Malcolm Slesser, Resource Use Institute, 12 Findhorn Place, Edinburgh 9, Scotland; telephone: 44-31-031-667-0052.

The older mainframe version of ECCO is available from: UNESCO, Population Division, 7, Place de Fountenoy, 75700, Paris, France; telephone: 33-14-568-3741. Request Malcolm Slesser et al., *Carrying Capacity Assessment for Kenya: A Report to UNESCO and FAO*, (KEN—13/297.21.02, 13.12.84) and Appendix A (a separate volume).

Training and assistance are available in English from UNESCO, Population Division. Consultation is available from Prof. Slesser.

MAYA

Purpose

To help elucidate the course of the collapse of the Mayan civilization using systems analysis.

Description

The collapse of the Mayan civilization is a recurring nightmare for every national leader who knows the story. Living in what is now southern Mexico, Guatemala, Belize, and Northern Honduras, the Mayas had the highest civilization in the New World during the first millennium C.E. No other pre-Columbian civilization in Mesoamerica or South America was as manifestly literate or as proficient in mathematics or astronomy. The artistic and architectural achievements of the Mayas rank among the very best in the history of the hemisphere. Yet in little more than a century, this unrivaled civilization went from power and prosperity to ruin. Nine-tenths of the population disappeared.

How could such an advanced civilization disappear so quickly and so completely? Until

this question is answered, leaders throughout the world will continue to wonder: "Could it happen again? Could it happen here?"

MAYA, the Mayan collapse model, applies the methods of systems analysis to the enormous amount of anthropological data now available on events during the Mayan collapse. The author, Dr. John W. G. Lowe, is an anthropologist with a strong background in systems analysis, physics, and mathematics. He concludes that given certain assumptions about increased population, decline in per capita productivity, growing needs for regulation, and regulation's expanding costs, classic Mayan politics would be expected to become progressively destabilized until a critical point was exceeded and the system of states began to support a self-sustaining chain reaction of breakdowns. This chain reaction was not a sociopolitical eclipse, but rather a profound social and demographic catastrophe of the cultural system. Ultimately cultural systems reside in the heads of individuals, and perpetuation of cultural systems depends on replication of mental templates from one individual to another and from one generation to the next. There would seem to be a critical ratio of replacement below which cultural collapse occurs. Consequently, demographic catastrophe can precipitate cultural collapse of an especially profound nature. It is this sort of transformation that appears to characterize the Mayan collapse.

Theory and Assumptions

Dr. Lowe reviews the archaeological data on the Mayan collapse and the simple causal models that have been proposed. He then describes twelve systemic models of societal collapse. Drawing on these systemic models, he describes the Mayan civilization in terms of the ecology, settlement patterns, hierarchy, and trade. After comparisons with historical parallels in Mesopotamia and Greece, he develops his own model.

MAYA (see Figure 12-8) is analogous to an epidemiological model. Population, trade, agriculture, and administrative activities are concentrated at many different sites within the civilization. As the collapse progresses, unaffected sites catch the "disease" and go into a crisis mode. Some recover; some collapse. There is essentially no recovery from collapse.

The model consists of a set of coupled differential equations linking the common population, elite population (administrators), and food production. A combination of population pressure, ecological factors, and administrative overhead develop in a way that produces positive feedback (a vicious circle) driving the system into collapse.

Evaluation

Dr. Lowe had made a major contribution in applying dynamic analysis to the historic question of the Mayan collapse. His book is not as well balanced, however, as it might be. Its strengths are the overview chapters covering the archaeological data and earlier theories and models. It is weakest on explaining the author's own model and what is learned from that model.

While the documentation describes the model in terms of differential equations and programming equations, the link between the two descriptions is missing. A set of causal diagrams linking the two would help enormously.

The author dismisses out of hand several plausible causal structures that have been proposed to explain the Mayan collapse. A more persuasive approach would have been to include the hypothesized structures in the model to determine whether or not they were the key factors in the collapse.

For someone wanting to learn from the Mayan experience, the weakest point in the presentation is that only one scenario is presented. The emphasis seems to be on convincing archaeologists that the MAYA model explains the major features of the collapse. Other readers are left wondering: "Could the collapse have been avoided? Were there other alternatives open to the Mayan leaders? If this particular set of feedbacks had not caused collapse, were there others that would have? What is to be learned from the Mayan experience?" The model does not—but could—answer these questions.

While it could be improved, the MAYA model is an important step in the synthesis of systems analysis and anthropology, and in time more can be expected from this synthesis. Already Dr. Lowe has moved his model from GASP IV modeling language to the more widely available and user-friendly STELLA language. The STELLA language will automatically

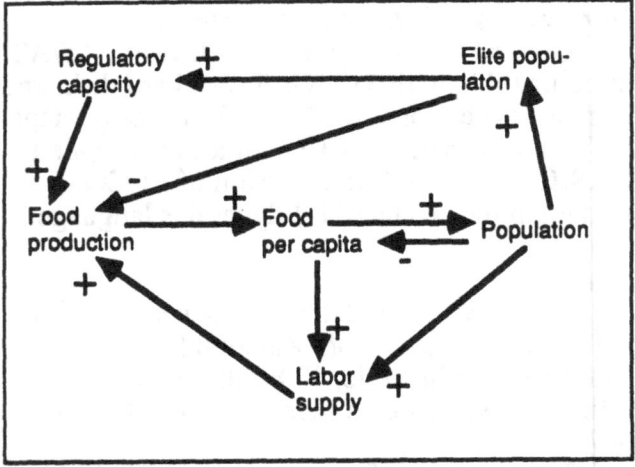

Figure 12-8: Linkages among the major variables in the MAYA model.

provide the much-needed causal diagrams and will facilitate experimentation with more complex structures and alternative policies.

The methods used by Dr. Lowe could be applied to many historic situations of interest to the leaders of nations. For example, these methods could be used to model the decline of the Roman Empire or the rise and fall of the Third Reich. The causal assumptions of historians can be expressed as differential equations and integrated with a modeling language like STELLA. These techniques open up the possibility of developing computerized case histories on the management of nations.

Hardware and Software Requirements

Apple Macintosh Plus or SE; the STELLA modeling language.

Source

The original GASP IV version of the model is presented in John W. G. Lowe, *The Dynamics of Apocalypse* (Albuquerque: University of New Mexico Press, 1985). Address for the press is: University of New Mexico Press, Journalism Building, Suite 220, Albuquerque, NM 87131, USA. The STELLA version of the model is available from: Dr. John W. G. Lowe, 1285 Longfellow Avenue, Teaneck, NJ 07666, USA. The book is US $22.50. No price had been set for the STELLA version of the model at the time of this review.

13. Global Models

Introduction

Nations are linked inseparably to each other in many ways, including trade, finance, migration, climate, rivers, pollutant flows, communication, transportation, and treaties. These linkages must be taken into account when a nation is exploring alternative development strategies. For a decade or more, global background scenarios have been the primary means for including such linkages in the analysis of alternative strategies. Such scenarios are written statements about assumed future changes in the various linkages among nations and in the general global situation.

Internal consistency presents a persistent problem in the development of global scenarios. For example, in a global scenario the sum total of grain imports for individual nations must not exceed total world grain production. Similarly, projected steel exports for all nations should not exceed the global total of steel imports. Simple and obvious as these examples may seem, developing global scenarios that are both detailed and internally consistent is difficult.

Global models offer a new, important tool for the development of scenarios. Unfortunately, most of the first dozen or so global models operated on large mainframe computers that were expensive and inaccessible, but microcomputer versions of global models are now becoming available.

WORLD3, the model behind the famous *The Limits to Growth*, can now be operated on a microcomputer. This classic model stimulated the creation of a number of additional global models, many of which can now be used on microcomputers also.

One of the first models stimulated by *The Limits to Growth* was the World Integrated Model (WIM). A major contribution of WIM was to provide an explicit representation of regions of the world rather than a total world average. Although WIM has yet to be adapted for use on microcomputers, one member of the original study team has developed a global model inspired in part by WIM. The new model,

International Futures Simulation (IFs), has the world represented in nine regions.

Another major response to *The Limits to Growth* was SARUM, the global econometric model designed by Peter Roberts at the British Department of the Environment, London. This modeling effort was terminated by budget cuts that came after the model was developed but before SARUM could be used for any major analyses or studies. The model was adopted by many other research teams, however, and a group in the Netherlands decided to put the model on a microcomputer. The resulting World Economic Model (WEM) is a powerful global econometric research tool that is much less expensive than any comparable analytical tool.

Until very recently all of the global models omitted any explicit representation of domestic and international political processes. The newest global model, GLOBUS, incorporates political processes and reasonably detailed trade flows, although it does not include either a resources sector or an environmental sector. GLOBUS is likely to become the basis of a new line of global models.

A quite different approach to global analysis was pioneered by the late Buckminster Fuller in what he called World Game. Participants in World Game sessions employed relatively simple mental models to explore the implications of a large assembly of global data. The disciples of Buckminster Fuller have now assembled much of the original World Game framework into a software package called Global Data Manager (GDM). The framework provided by GDM is quite useful in helping groups expand their mental global models.

WORLD3

Purpose

To simulate over periods of 100 years or more the dynamic global interaction of population, arable land, agricultural capital, industrial capital, service capital, non-renewable resources, and pollution.

Description

WORLD3 was the first global model commissioned by the Club of Rome. It was designed by D. L. Meadows, D. H. Meadows, J. Randers, R. F. Naill, E. K. O. Zahn, and W. W. Behrens, III and was the basis for D. H. Meadows et al., *The Limits to Growth* (New York: Universe Books, 1972).

Because of the wide attention given to *The Limits to Growth*, the WORLD3 model has been disseminated around the world and is probably the best known of all the global models. It is an expansion of the WORLD2 model, which Professor Jay W. Forrester used in writing his book *World Dynamics* (Cambridge, Mass.: MIT Press, 1971).

The thesis of *The Limits to Growth* was a shock to the world. The authors asserted that growth in population, resource consumption, and pollution could not continue indefinitely, since such growth would create conditions that would increase human mortality rates, thus checking population growth. The model projected that the limits to growth would be encountered around the middle of the 21st century.

The book also observed that a vibrant steady-state condition was possible in which human health and welfare could be maintained at a high level for long periods of time. A vibrant steady-state situation was found to be more easily achieved if the transition to it were begun sooner rather than later.

WORLD3 and *The Limits to Growth* raised a very fundamental moral issue. Underlying the relations among nations had been the assumption that there is no injustice inherent in some nations being far more wealthy than others. As long as everyone believed that through hard work each nation could make its "piece of the global economic pie" arbitrarily large, the fact that some nations have more than others did not necessarily imply an unjust situation. If, however, there is an upper limit to the size of the total global economic pie, as *The Limits to Growth* says, then questions of justice begin to arise.

The political implications of the book are enormous, and political leaders responded strongly. The reactions of leaders in the industrialized, developing, and centrally planned nations are reported by W. L. Oltmans in *On Growth* (New York: G. P. Putnam's Sons, Inc.,

1974) and *On Growth Two* (New York: G. P. Putnam's Sons, Inc., 1975). The fact that President Ronald Reagan felt compelled to assert in his 1985 State of the Union Address that there "...are no limits to growth..." suggests that the controversy raised by the WORLD3 model has not yet been fully resolved.

Theory and Assumptions

WORLD3 employs the system dynamics methodology to analyze the interaction of five sectors of the world socio-economic system (see Figure 13-1). The sectors are population, capital, agriculture, resources, and pollution. The world is represented as a single global aggregate; that is, there is no regional disaggregation. There is extensive feedback among the many endogenous variables.

The model has been criticized because it does not include explicit representation of price and technology. However, although price is not an explicit variable, feedback mechanisms similar to market forces do slow resource consumption as high-grade resources are consumed. While change in technology is not represented explicitly, it can be introduced by changing various parameters at the beginning of or during simulation runs.

Evaluation

WORLD3 is the model that made global modeling a high-visibility field of study. It is a classic that everyone interested in global models should know. WORLD3 is also among the easiest of global models to use. The documentation is extensive and of excellent quality, and the concepts are easily understood.

Users should familiarize themselves with the criticisms of the model. An extensive overview and list of references to reviews and critiques is available in Chapter 25 of G. O. Barney, ed., *The Global 2000 Report to the President*, Vol. 2, (Oxford: Pergamon Press, 1980).

Hardware and Software Requirements

IBM PC/XT/AT or compatible, 640 KB RAM, hard disk, color monitor; Professional DYNAMO Plus, or perhaps DYSMAP2. With some rewriting of the equations, the model could also be run on an Apple Macintosh computer using the STELLA simulation language.

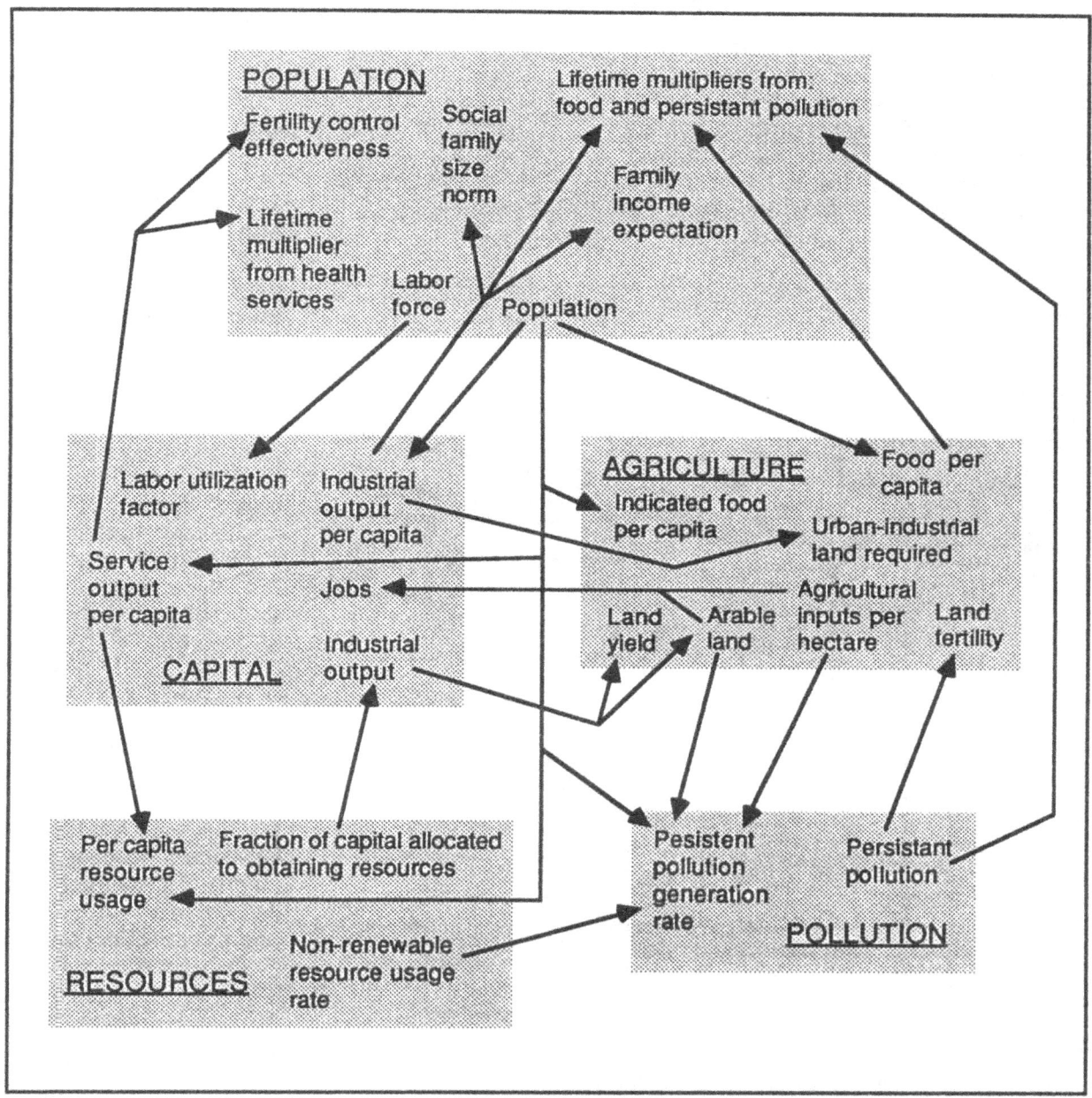

Figure 13-1: Interactions among the five basic sectors of WORLD3.

Source
The model is listed in Appendix A of D. L. Meadows et al., *The Dynamics of Growth in a Finite World* (Cambridge Mass.: MIT Press, 1974). The analysis of the implications of WORLD3 are presented in D. H. Meadows et al., *The Limits to Growth* (New York: Universe Books, 1972). Price for *The Dynamics of Growth in a Finite World* is US $50.

International Futures Simulation (IFs)

Purpose
To provide a framework for evaluating the widely different public statements made about the workings of the global development system and about probable global futures.

Description

IFs is a tool for "if..., then..." analysis. Users describe alternative assumptions (if statements) about future global and national policies. The consequences of the assumed policies and programs (then statements) are calculated by the model out to the year 2030. The model projects fifty different variables in the areas of population, economics, agriculture, and energy. The projections may be global or may be disaggregated to cover up to eight regions. Variables can be changed to create new scenarios and test alternative policies and assumptions.

IFs was developed for use in advanced secondary schools and universities. When it is utilized in unstructured study, IFs can give students a general exposure to major global data and trends. Structured lessons based on IFs can help students examine the assumptions inherent in some of the major global studies and the issues that these studies raised. In either situation, IFs encourages students to ask several questions: "What kind of world can we expect in the future? What uncertainties and problems are to be faced? What kind of a world do we want to help create?"

IFs was developed by Professor Barry B. Hughes at the Graduate School of International Studies, University of Denver. Hughes had worked on the development of the World Integrated Model with Professor Mihajlo D. Mesarovic at Case Western Reserve University. When he came to the University of Denver, Hughes built a large IFs model for research on a mainframe. Later he designed a simplified microcomputer version of the mainframe IFs for teaching purposes. The large research version of IFs is now being converted to run (at about twenty minutes per run) on an IBM AT or compatible. The smaller teaching version of IFs is the model being reviewed here.

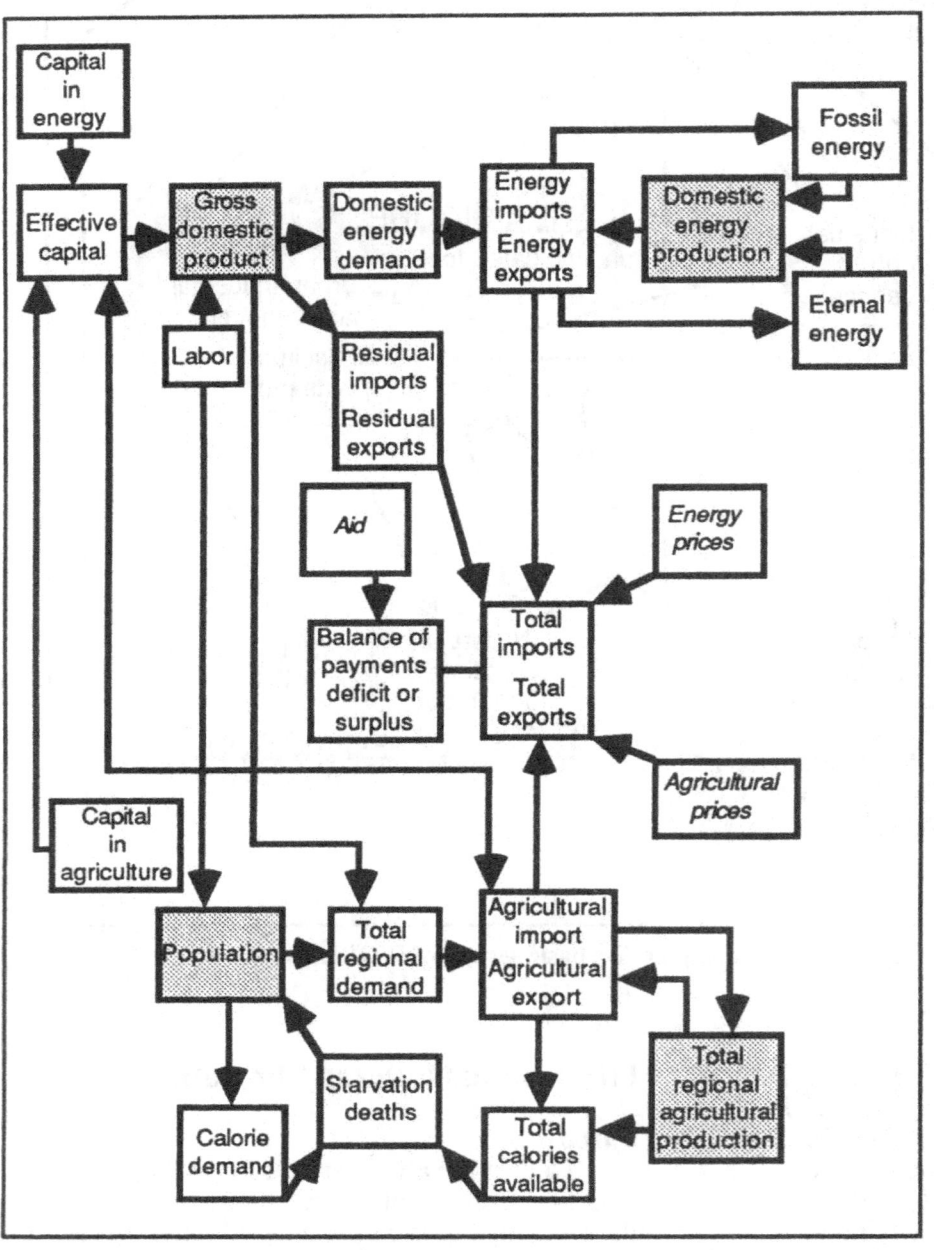

Figure 13-2: Linkages among variables in the IFs model. Linkages among the variables in italics are exogenous.

Theory and Assumptions

The IFs model is a dynamic global model in which the nations of the world are represented as nine regions: (a) United States, (b) western Europe, (c) other developed nations, (d) countries belonging to the Organization of Petroleum Exporting Countries, (e) Latin America, (f) Africa, (g) South Asia, (h) China and other centrally planned developing countries, and (i) all other countries.

The model (see Figure 13-2) contains four interlinked submodels. The economic submodel centers on gross domestic product. The two most important variables influencing it are labor and effective capital. Labor is linked directly to population. Effective capital is total capital stock less capital expenditures in energy and agriculture. Aid also has an impact on gross domestic product.

The population submodel centers on total population. It responds to exogenous population growth rates and to a global population growth factor. The calorie need factor (calories per capita needed to avoid starvation) and the population size together determine the total calorie needs for the region. Population is also the basis of agricultural demand, although that demand can be affected exogenously by assumptions about technology or conservation.

The key variable in the energy submodel is energy production. It is compared with energy demand from the economic submodel. Energy production is a sum of two types of production, fossil fuel production and "eternal" (renewal and inexhaustible) energy production. Fossil fuel production is dependent on assumptions about remaining resource levels. Fossil fuel and eternal fuel production depend on exogenously specified fuel growth rates. The energy capital requirement, the amount of capital devoted to producing energy, depends on the production levels and the capital costs per unit produced of fossil and so called eternal (renewable and inexhaustible) fuels. The utilization of inexhaustible fuel is exogenously specified; the utilization of renewable fuels increases as fossil resources diminish.

A key variable in the agricultural submodel is agricultural production. It is a product of yield and land under cultivation. Yield is productivity per unit of land (e.g., metric tons per hectare). Yield depends on an exogenously specified growth rate and a "global factor." The capital

cost of yield (corresponding to farm buildings, tractors, etc.) is a function of the yield level and a capital cost coefficient. The total agricultural capital requirement is simply the sum of the capital costs of yield and of land.

Most of the linkages among submodels are based in trade. The agricultural export and import levels depend on total regional demand and production. Trade levels and domestic production determine total calories available. The balance between this variable and calorie demand may result in deaths due to starvation. Energy imports supplement domestic energy production to meet domestic energy demand. A global surplus or deficit affects fossil and eternal energy production in a negative feedback loop. Residual imports and residual exports are a function of gross domestic product. Energy prices convert energy trade to dollar terms, as do agricultural prices for agricultural trade. Summing dollar energy, dollar agricultural, and residual exports and imports (already dollar-terms) gives total exports and imports. The trade and aid levels determine the balance of payments deficit or surplus. Shortages in balance of payments restrain agricultural imports and economic growth via effective capital.

There are some important submodel linkages besides those involving trade. Population size determines labor force size. Economic size affects agricultural demand. Capital in energy and in agriculture influences effective capital levels in the economic submodel.

Much of the behavior of IFs is dominated by two positive feedback loops. One is part of the economic submodel and centers on growth in capital and in gross domestic product. The other, within the population submodel, centers on population growth. All other loops act to constrain the growth of these two.

Evaluation

The teaching version of IFs is a surprisingly complex model given its small size (192 KB) and its nine-region trading structure. It is quite straightforward to operate after it is installed. (There are a few tricks to the installation, however.) Support is available from CONDUIT, the supplier.

The documentation is neatly presented and well suited for instruction. An introductory chapter explains many of the historic issues in global studies and leads students into using the model to develop their own opinions on some of the issues. Background material for the instructor is also included. Unfortunately, although the documentation does include a general description of the model, it does not include the model equations. These are not even available from Professor Hughes. As a result, neither teachers nor students have any idea of the detailed structure and assumptions of the teaching version of IFs; it is simply a black box model. This is unfortunate, since one important lesson that students should learn about models is that they should never use one that they cannot examine in detail. The model would be much more useful and would inspire greater confidence if the equations were made available.

The equations for Research IFs, the original version of the model, will be available from Professor Hughes as soon as he completes the adjustments necessary for its use on an IBM AT or compatible. Research IFs should be a useful tool for both research and advanced training.

Hardware and Software Requirements

IBM PC/XT/PCjr or compatible; DOS 2.10, 192 KB RAM, one disk drive, color graphics card.

Source

CONDUIT, The University of Iowa, Oakdale Campus, Iowa City, IA 52242, USA; telephone: (319) 335-4100. The price is US $95.

World Economic Model (WEM)

Purpose

To offer a consistent quantitative framework for carrying out prospective analysis and policy design exercises in the area of international economic relations.

Description

The WEM structure is based largely on SARUM, the mainframe, global econometric model developed by the Systems Analysis Research Unit, the British Department of Environment, London. The WEM program is designed in a very general way, so that decisions concerning regional coverage, sectoral definition, and choice of relationships are determined through the specification of the database, rather than through actual coding.

The WEM model is intended to perform analyses extending over a long time horizon, typically for a target interval between ten and fifty years beyond the chosen base year. For this reason, the model is most reliable when: (a) a shorter term model is available for calibrating WEM behavior during the time period extending from the base year to the beginning of WEM's target interval, and (b) the user has access to current qualitative forecasts regarding the future development of WEM's exogenous variables during the target period.

WEM is being developed by Dr. A. R. Gigengack at the Faculty of Economics, State University of Groningen, The Netherlands.

Theory and Assumptions

The WEM model is based on the assumption that over the long-term the economic and political system tends to behave in a homeostatic manner. In other words, it will tend, unless subjected to shocks, to move toward a stable behavior pattern. This does not mean that the system is expected to be stable. In fact, one purpose of scenario design is to define both the form and magnitude of the shocks to which the system will be exposed in the future. It does mean, however, that it is assumed that pressure will arise within the system to dampen the effects of shocks. This dampening effect is achieved within the model by resorting to the ideas and concepts of neoclassical economics, i.e., the working of prices, costs, etc., to alter economic decision making.

The model is cast in the form of a set of non-linear differential equations and is iteratively solved as simulation time progresses. The data required consists of: (a) base year magnitudes, (b) estimates of parameters for functional relationships, and (c) projections of exogenous variables extending from the base year to the end of the simulation period. The latter can consist of point estimates, postulated rates of change, or approximations by piece-wise linear functions.

Evaluation

WEM is based on the mainframe global model SARUM, which has attracted much attention and stimulated the formation of several independent research projects. The availability of a microcomputer version of WEM will substantially advance this type of global modeling.

Version 0 of WEM, (WEM-0), has been tested and found to produce output essentially identical to the mainframe SARUM. The only differences between the mainframe and microcomputer versions have to do with input, output, and file handling. Therefore, a reasonably accurate description of the theory behind WEM-0 is already available in *The SARUM 76 Global Modelling Project* and *The SARUM Handbook*, both published jointly by the Department of the Environment and the Department of Transport, British Government, London. WEM-0 will be operational and available sometime in 1990.

Hardware and Software Requirements

IBM PC/XT/AT, 640 KB RAM, 20 MB hard disk, and Color Graphics Adapter. A math coprocessor chip is recommended. Professional Turbo-Pascal (including the programmer's toolboxes), version 5.0.

Source

Dr. A. R. Gigengack, World Model Project, State University of Groningen, P.O. Box 800, 9700 AV Groningen, The Netherlands; telefax: 31-50-633720; telephone: 31-50-633733.

GLOBUS

Purpose

To provide a nation-based, political world model based on empirical data, with which to investigate the dynamics of the world's political, economic, social, and cultural system.

Description

GLOBUS is a computer simulation model of many important macropolitical and macroeconomic relationships within and among twenty-five prominent contemporary nations plus a rest-of-the-world entity. It is designed and used to explore possible solutions to long-term global problems. The model simulations run for a period of forty years.

The model was originally begun on a Cray supercomputer. The run time on the Cray was short, but the queue time was long. Ultimately the research team moved the model to microcomputers using the Intel 80386 central processing unit. Run time on the microcomputer was found to be comparable to the queue time for the Cray.

The GLOBUS model can be used for evaluating a broad range of problems. Examples include the long-term political and economic implications of changes in East-West tensions; the long-term effects of alternative defense policies pursued by one nation or a group of nations; the benefits and costs of increasing protectionism in trade policies; changes in domestic politics resulting from economic and political trends, as well as the international implications of such changes; and changes in national economic performance that might lead to shifts in existing political relations.

The GLOBUS model was developed at the Wissenschaftszentrum Berlin under the general direction of Karl W. Deutsch. Stuart A. Bremer was Research Group leader. The project grew from Deutsch's conviction that national leaders—and informed citizens—need global models to help them understand how their nation relates to the rest of the world and vice versa. Bremer quotes Deutsch's thoughts that guided the GLOBUS project through more than a decade of work:

No country in the world today can completely disregard world conditions in making its national policies. A world model, therefore, which one might think of as the last priority of a busy national decision maker, turns out actually to be a serious precondition unless economic and political plans of nations are to become largely exercises in fantasy. The framework that a good world model can provide is not the same as giving exact predictions. Yet, there are major plans and trends which, if they can be identified and the degree of their interdependence and the expectable extent of their interactions be ascertained, allow one, through the use of modern technology, statistics, data files, and computers, to keep track of more detail than any particular decision maker could.

Theory and Assumptions

The fundamental, underlying assumption of GLOBUS is that to understand current and future global problems it is vital to see: (a) that economics and politics cannot be divorced from one another (as they usually are in the disciplinary structure of social sciences) and (b)

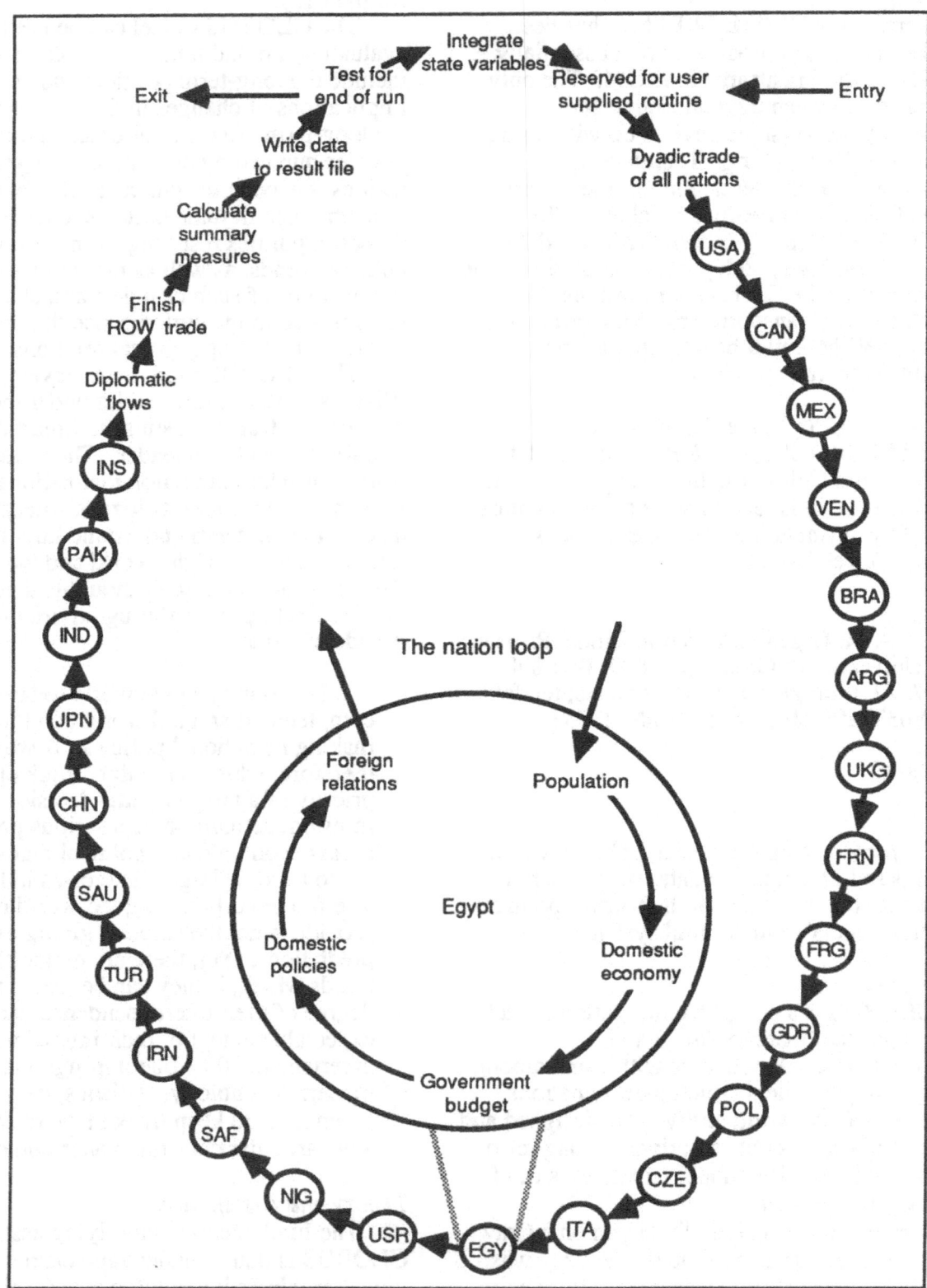

Figure 13-3: The simulation loop linking the 25 national submodels and the other submodels of the GLOBUS model.

that nations do not exist in isolation from one another and are not able to determine their destinies independently. Together the countries of the world constitute a web of interdependence in which national political and economic conditions affect international political and economic relations and vice versa.

The GLOBUS model is dynamic (as opposed to static or equilibrium), recursive (involving feedback processes), continuous (having simulation time that is continuous rather than discrete), and regionally disaggregated (instead of globally averaged). The simulation loop linking the 25 national submodels and the other submodels is shown in Figure 13-3. The national submodels include: Argentina, Brazil, Canada, China, Czechoslovakia, East Germany, Egypt, France, India, Indonesia, Iran, Italy, Japan, Mexico, Nigeria, Pakistan, Poland, Saudi Arabia, South Africa, Soviet Union, Turkey, United Kingdom, United States, Venezuela, and West Germany. Each national submodel includes specific sectors on foreign relations, domestic politics, government budget, domestic economy, and population. The model does not explicitly represent natural resources or the environment.

The unique feature and major contribution of GLOBUS is its explicit modeling of domestic political processes and international political processes. The domestic political model focuses on indicators of political stability, support and opposition to the government, and government performance. It is based in part on the political theory of David Easton.

The international political model is based on 650 directed dyads, and given this large number, it is necessary to keep the individual dyadic models relatively small. GLOBUS uses two variables—cooperation and conflict—derived from the scale of inter-nation events developed by Edward Azar for use in his Conflict and Peace Data Bank. The model then follows the *interaction approach* in which the behavior sent by nation A to nation B is determined in large part by the behavior nation A has received recently from nation B.

Evaluation

The GLOBUS model is an enormous advance in global modeling. It is the first and only global model to represent explicitly domestic politics and international relations,

necessary components of a truly useful global model. While this daring move will doubtless be criticized by some political scientists, many global models of the future will trace their ancestry to GLOBUS.

GLOBUS is indeed far from perfect. The authors point out that they had insufficient data on income distribution and income groups for the economic and political sub-models. The model does not include wars, only different levels of international tension. Domestic political considerations should influence government budgets, but do not.

The most serious weakness in GLOBUS is that it lacks both resource and environment sectors. Given all that has been learned over the past two decades about the importance of natural resources and the environment, a global model should incorporate an explicit representation of these factors.

It must be noted, however, that the developers of GLOBUS faced a choice: with limited funds they could either model domestic and international politics or they could model resources and environment, but not both. Unquestionably they made the best choice and the greatest contribution by building the first major global model with significant representation of domestic and international politics.

Because it was developed by public funds in West Germany, the model and its source are available at a modest price intended to recover the cost of just the disks and printing. Several national governments are already showing interest in obtaining the model.

The documentation includes the *Micro GLOBUS User's Manual* and the more detailed book, *The GLOBUS Model*. Neither of these documents contains the source code, but algebraic equations are provided in the book. Users wishing to modify or extend the model will need to obtain the source code.

Overall, GLOBUS is an important new contribution to global modeling. Much further work could be done with the model, and it is to be hoped that some governments and international organizations will continue where the GLOBUS authors were forced to stop for lack of funds.

Hardware and Software Requirements
    IBM AT or compatible with 640 KB RAM, 20 MB hard disk, 1.2 MB floppy drive, DOS Version 2.1 or higher, IBM Professional or Ryan McFarland FORTRAN. Recommended: math coprocessor chip, graphics adapter, color monitor, and Norton Utilities. Run time for an Olivetti M-24 8 MHz using the Intel 8086 and 8087 chips is 6.1 hours; for a Compaq 386 running at 16 MHz using Intel 80386 and 80287 chips, the run time is about 4.3 hours.

Source
    The model (compiled or source code) and user's manual are available from: GLOBUS Research Group, Wissenschaftszentrum Berlin, Steinplatz 2, 1000 Berlin 12; telephone: (030) 3-13-40-81; telex: 183584 WZB D. The book is available from: Westview Press, 5500 Central Avenue, Boulder, CO 80301, USA and from: Campus Verlag, Myliusstrasse 15, D-6000, Frankfurt 1, West Germany.

Global Data Manager (GDM)

Purpose
    To integrate into one system a complete set of global data and to make those data easily accessible to government policymakers, corporate executives, media personnel, researchers, teachers, students, and the general public.

Description
    Global Data Manager (GDM) is a framework that makes data gathered from the United Nations, the World Bank, the World Health Organization, the Population Reference Bureau, World Priorities, and the Stockholm International Peace Research Institute accessible on a microcomputer. While it is not a global model, GDM is an excellent domain in which to exercise one's mental global model.
    GDM is a product of World Game Projects, Inc., a nonprofit, non-partisan research and educational organization founded in 1971. The purpose of the organization is to develop further the World Game problem-solving tool pioneered by the late Buckminster Fuller.
    The staff of World Game Projects, Inc. are currently developing models to be used with GDM. The models will work as games, and

GDM will be the game board. FAMINE, the first model, will focus on the African and Ethiopian food systems.

Theory and Assumptions
    The Global Data Manager is a spreadsheet for displaying, manipulating, and comparing data on the world, 8 continents, and 192 countries. The data include: energy, food, population, agriculture, shelter, health care, education, communications, transportation, materials, recreation, economics, environment, military, government services, industry, and general background information.
    GDM is an excellent framework within which to develop and test theories about global issues. The user can easily compare data country by country, continent by continent, or compare country and continent data with world averages. The GDM's ability to store, retrieve, sum, sort, add, subtract, divide, multiply, plot, graph, and derive new data makes it an ideal framework within which to develop simple models.

Evaluation
    GDM is easy to use and install. The data of interest are chosen from a number of menus; the program automatically creates a spreadsheet from the chosen data. The data can then be manipulated using the spreadsheet. The sources are reliable, and the range of data provided is very large.

Hardware and Software Requirements
    IBM PC/XT/AT, 360 K RAM, at least one 360 KB floppy disk drive, Color Graphics Adapter, monochrome or color monitor. DOS 2.1 or higher.

Source
    Medard Gabel, World Game Projects, Inc., University City Science Center, 3508 Market Street, Philadelphia, PA 19104, USA; telephone: (215) 387-0220. The price of Global Data Manager 2.0 is US $95, of Basic World Data Disk, US $50. Ten additional data disks are in preparation on energy, country background, demographic, food, minerals, military weapons and expenditures, education, and culture. A set of these data disks will cost between US $50 and US $125. An annual report, *World Game Report*, is available for US $25 per year.

Part Three: Tools

14. A Skeptic's Guide to Computer Models

This chapter was written by Dr. John D. Sterman, Associate Professor, Sloan School of Management, Massachusetts Institute of Technology, 50 Memorial Drive, Cambridge, MA 02139, USA. Copyright © John D. Sterman, 1988. An earlier version of this paper also appeared in Foresight and National Decisions: The Horseman and the Bureaucrat *(Grant 1988). It is printed here with permission. The author wishes to acknowledge that many of the ideas expressed here emerged from discussions with or were first formulated by, among others, Jay Forrester, George Richardson, Peter Senge, and especially Donella Meadows, whose book* Groping in the Dark *(Meadows, Richardson, and Bruckmann 1982), was particularly helpful.*

But Mousie, thou art no they lane
In proving foresight may be vain;
The best-laid schemes o' mice an' men
    Gang aft a-gley,
An lea'e us nought but grief an' pain,
    For promis'd joy!
          Robert Burns, "To a Mouse"

The Inevitability of Using Models

Computer modeling of social and economic systems is only about three decades old. Yet in that time, computer models have been used to analyze everything from inventory management in corporations to the performance of national economies, from the optimal distribution of fire stations in New York City to the interplay of global population, resources, food, and pollution. Certain computer models, such as *The Limits to Growth* (Meadows et al. 1972), have been front page news. In the U.S., some have been the subject of numerous congressional hearings and have influenced the fate of legislation. Computer modeling has become an important industry, generating hundreds of millions of dollars of revenues annually.

As computers have become faster, cheaper, and more widely available, computer models have become commonplace in forecasting and public policy analysis, especially in economics, energy and resources, demographics, and other crucial areas. As computers continue to proliferate, more and more policy debates—both in government and the private sector—will involve the results of models. Though not all of us are going to be model builders, we all are becoming model consumers, regardless of whether we know it (or like it). The ability to understand and evaluate computer models is fast becoming a prerequisite for the policymaker, legislator, lobbyist, and citizen alike.

During our lives, each of us will be faced with the result of models and will have to make judgments about their relevance and validity. Most people, unfortunately, cannot make these decisions in an intelligent and informed manner, since for them computer models are *black boxes*—devices that operate in completely mysterious ways. Because computer models are so poorly understood by most people, it is easy for them to be misused, accidentally or intentionally. Thus there have been many cases in which computer models have been used to justify decisions already made and actions already taken, to provide a scapegoat when a forecast turned out wrong, or to lend specious authority to an argument.

If these misuses are to stop and if modeling is to become a rational tool of the general public, rather than remaining the special magic of a technical priesthood, a basic understanding of models must become more widespread. This paper takes a step toward this goal by offering model consumers a peek inside the black boxes. The computer models it describes are the kinds used in foresight and policy analysis (rather than physical system models such as NASA uses to test the space shuttle). The characteristics and capabilities of the models, their advantages and disadvantages, uses and misuses are all addressed. The fundamental assumptions of the major modeling techniques are discussed, as is the appropriateness of these techniques for foresight and policy analysis. Consideration is also given to the crucial questions a model user should ask when evaluating the appropriateness and validity of a model.

Mental and Computer Models

Fortunately, everyone is already familiar with models. People use models—mental models—every day. Our decisions and actions are based not on the real world, but on our mental images of that world, of the relationships among its parts, and of the influence our actions have on it.

Mental models have some powerful advantages. A mental model is flexible; it can take into account a wider range of information than just numerical data; it can be adapted to new situations and be modified as new information becomes available. Mental models are the filters through which we interpret our experiences, evaluate plans, and choose among possible courses of action. The great systems of philosophy, politics, and literature are, in a sense, mental models.

But mental models have their drawbacks also. They are not easily understood by others; interpretations of them differ. The assumptions on which they are based are usually difficult to examine, so ambiguities and contradictions within them can go undetected, unchallenged, and unresolved.

That we have trouble grasping other peoples' mental models may seem natural. More surprising, we are not very good at constructing and understanding our own mental models—or using them for decision making. Psychologists have shown that we can take only a few factors into account in making decisions (Hogarth 1980; Kahneman, Slovic, and Tversky 1982). In other words, the mental models we use to make decisions are usually extremely simple. Often these models are also flawed, since we frequently make errors in deducing the consequences of the assumptions on which they are based.

Our failure to use rational mental models in our decision making has been well demonstrated by research on the behavior of people in organizations (e.g., families, businesses, the government). This research shows that decisions are not made by rational consideration of objectives, options, and consequences. Instead, they often are made by rote, using standard operating procedures that evolve out of tradition and adjust only slowly to changing conditions (Simon 1947, 1979). These procedures are determined by the role of the decision makers within the organization, the amount of time they have to make decisions, and the information available to them.

But the individual perspectives of the decision makers may be parochial, the time they have to weigh alternatives insufficient, and the information available to them dated, biased, or incomplete. Furthermore, their decisions can be strongly influenced by authority relations, organizational context, peer pressure, cultural perspective, and selfish motives. Psychologists and organizational observers have identified dozens of different biases that creep into human decision making because of cognitive limitations and organizational pressures (Hogarth 1980; Kahneman, Slovic, and Tversky 1982). As a result, many decisions turn out to be incorrect; choosing the best course of action is just too complicated and difficult a puzzle.

Hamlet exclaims (perhaps ironically) "What a piece of work is a man, how noble in reason, how infinite in faculties...!" But it seems that we, like Hamlet himself, are simply not capable of making error-free decisions that are based on rational models and are uninfluenced by societal and emotional pressures.

Enter the computer model. In theory, computer models offer improvements over mental models in several respects:

They are explicit; their assumptions are stated in the written documentation and open to all for review.

They infallibly compute the logical consequences of the modeler's assumptions.

They are comprehensive and able to interrelate many factors simultaneously.

A computer model that actually has these characteristics has powerful advantages over a mental model. In practice, however, computer models are often less than ideal:

They are so poorly documented and complex that no one can examine their assumptions. They are black boxes.

They are so complicated that the user has no confidence in the consistency or correctness of the assumptions.

They are unable to deal with relationships and factors that are difficult to quantify, for which numerical data do not exist, or that lie outside the expertise of the specialists who built the model.

Because of these possible flaws, computer models need to be examined carefully by potential users. But on what basis should models be judged? How does one know whether a model is well or badly designed, whether its results will be valid or not? How can a prospective user decide whether a type of modeling or a specific model is suitable for the problem at hand? How can misuses of models be recognized and prevented? There is no single comprehensive answer, but some useful guidelines are given on the following pages.

The Importance of Purpose

A model must have a clear purpose, and that purpose should be to solve a particular problem. A clear purpose is the single most important ingredient for a successful modeling study. Of course, a model with a clear purpose can still be incorrect, overly large, or difficult to understand. But a clear purpose allows model users to ask questions that reveal whether a model is useful for solving the problem under consideration.

Beware the analyst who proposes to model an entire social or economic system rather than a problem. Every model is a representation of a system—a group of functionally interrelated elements forming a complex whole. But for the model to be useful, it must address a specific problem and must simplify rather than attempting to mirror in detail an entire system.

What is the difference? A model designed to understand how the business cycle can be stabilized is a model of a problem. It deals with a part of the overall economic system. A model designed to understand how the economy can make a smooth transition from oil to alternative energy sources is also a model of a problem; it too addresses only a limited system within the larger economy. A model that claims to be a representation of the entire economy is a model of a whole system. Why does it matter? The usefulness of models lies in the fact that they simplify reality, putting it into a form that we can comprehend. But a truly comprehensive model of a complete system would be just as complex as that system and just as inscrutable. The map is not the territory—and a map as detailed as the territory would be of no use (as well as being hard to fold).

The art of model building is knowing what to cut out, and the purpose of the model acts as the logical knife. It provides the criterion about what will be cut, so that only the essential features necessary to fulfill the purpose are left. In the example above, since the purpose of the comprehensive model would be to represent the entire economic system, few factors could be excluded. In order to answer all questions about the economy, the model would have to include an immense range of long-term and short-term variables. Because of its size, its underlying assumptions would be difficult to examine. The model builders—not to mention the intended consumers—would probably not understand its behavior, and its validity would be largely a matter of faith.

A model designed to examine just the business cycle or the energy transition would be much smaller, since it would be limited to those factors believed to be relevant to the question at hand. For example, the business cycle model need not include long-term trends in population growth and resource depletion. The energy transition model could exclude short-term changes related to interest, employment, and inventories. The resulting models would be simple enough so that their assumptions could be examined. The relation of these assumptions to the most important theories regarding the business cycle and resource economics could then be assessed to determine how useful the models were for their intended purposes.

Two Kinds of Models: Optimization Versus Simulation

There are many types of models, and they can be classified in many ways. Models can be static or dynamic, mathematical or physical, stochastic or deterministic. One of the most useful classifications, however, divides models into those that optimize versus those that simulate. The distinction between optimization and simulation models is particularly important since these types of models are suited for fundamentally different purposes.

Optimization

The Oxford English Dictionary defines *optimize* as "to make the best of most of; to develop to the utmost." The output of an optimization model is a statement of the best way to accomplish some goal. Optimization models do not tell you what will happen in a certain situation. Instead they tell you what to do in order to make the best of the situation; they are normative or prescriptive models.

Let us take two examples. A nutritionist would like to know how to design meals that fulfill certain dietary requirements but cost as little as possible. A salesperson must visit certain cities and would like to know how to make the trip as quickly as possible, taking into account the available flights between the cities. Rather than relying on trial and error, the nutritionist and the salesperson could use optimization models to determine the best solutions to these problems.

An optimization model typically includes three parts. The *objective function* specifies the goal or objective. For the nutritionist, the objective is to minimize the cost of the meals. For the salesperson, it is to minimize the time spent on the trip. The *decision variables* are the choices to be made. In our examples, these would be the food to serve at each meal and the order in which to visit the cities. The *constraints* restrict the choices of the decision variables to those that are acceptable and possible. In the diet problem, one constraint would specify that daily consumption of each nutrient must equal or exceed the minimum requirement. Another might restrict the number of times a particular food is served during each week. The constraints in the travel problem would specify that each city must be visited at least once and would restrict the selection of routes to actually available connections.

An optimization model takes as inputs these three pieces of information—the goals to be met, the choices to be made, and the constraints to be satisfied. It yields as its output the best solution, i.e., the optimal decisions given the assumptions of the model. In the case of our examples, the models would provide the best set of menus and the most efficient itinerary.

Limitations of Optimization

Many optimization models have a variety of limitations and problems that a potential user should bear in mind. These problems are: difficulties with the specification of the objective function, unrealistic linearity, lack of feedback, and lack of dynamics.

Specification of the Objective Function: Whose Values? The first difficulty with optimization models is the problem of specifying the objective function, the goal that the model user is trying to reach. In our earlier examples, it was fairly easy to identify the objective functions of the nutritionist and the salesperson, but what would be the objective function for the mayor of New York? To provide adequate city services for minimal taxes? To encourage the arts? To improve traffic conditions? The answer depends, of course, on the perspective of the person you ask.

The objective function embodies values and preferences, but which values, whose preferences? How can intangibles be incorporated into the objective function? How can the conflicting goals of various groups be identified and balanced? These are hard questions, but they are not insurmountable. Intangibles often can be quantified, at least roughly, by breaking them into measurable components. For example, the quality of life in a city might be represented as depending on the rate of unemployment, air pollution levels, crime rate, and so forth. There are also techniques available for extracting information about preferences from interviews and other impressionistic data. Just the attempt to make values explicit is a worthwhile exercise in any study and may have enormous value for the clients of a modeling project.

It is important that potential users keep in mind the question of values when they examine optimization models. The objective function and the constraints should always be scrutinized to determine what values they embody, both explicitly and by omission. Imagine that a government employee, given responsibility for the placement of sewage treatment plants along a river, decides to use an optimization model in making the decision. The model has as its objective function the cheapest arrangement of plants; a constraint specifies that the arrangement must result in water quality standards being met. It would be important for the user to ask how the model takes into account the impacts the plants will have on fishing, recreation, wild species, and development potential in the areas where they are placed. Unless these considerations are explicitly incorporated into the model, they are implicitly held to be of no value.

Linearity. Another problem, and one that can seriously undermine the verisimilitude of optimization models, is their linearity. Because a typical optimization problem is very complex, involving hundreds or thousands of variables and constraints, the mathematical problem of finding the optimum is extremely difficult. To render such problems tractable, modelers commonly introduce a number of simplifications. Among these is the assumption that the relationships in the system are linear. In fact, the most popular optimization technique, linear programming, requires that the objective function and all constraints be linear.

Linearity is mathematically convenient, but in reality it is almost always invalid. Consider, for example, a model of a firm's inventory distribution policies. The model contains a specific relationship between inventory and shipments—if the inventory of goods in the warehouse is 10 percent below normal, shipment may be reduced by, say, 2 percent since certain items will be out of stock. If the model requires this relationship to be linear, then a 20 percent shortfall will reduce shipments by 4 percent, a 30 percent shortfall by 6 percent, and so on. And when the shortfall is 100 percent? According to the model, shipments will still be 80 percent of normal. But obviously, when the warehouse is empty, no shipments are possible. The linear relationship within the model leads to an absurdity.

The warehouse model may seem trivial, but the importance of non-linearity is well demonstrated by the sorry fate of the passenger pigeon, *Ectopistes migratorius*. When Europeans first colonized North America, passenger pigeons were extremely abundant. Huge flocks of the migrating birds would darken the skies for days. They often caused damage to crops and were hunted both as a pest and as food. For years, hunting had little apparent impact on the population; the prolific birds seemed to reproduce fast enough to offset most losses. Then the number of pigeons began to

decline—slowly at first, then rapidly. By 1914, the passenger pigeon was extinct.

The disappearance of the passenger pigeons resulted from the non-linear relationship between their population density and their fertility. In large flocks they could reproduce at high rates, but in smaller flocks their fertility dropped precipitously. Thus, when hunting pressure was great enough to reduce the size of a flock somewhat, the fertility in that flock also fell. The lower fertility lead to a further decrease in the population size, and the lower population density resulted in yet lower birth rates, and so forth, in a vicious cycle.

Unfortunately, the vast majority of optimizations models assume that the world is linear. There are, however, techniques available for solving certain non-linear optimization problems, and research is continuing.

Lack of Feedback. Complex systems in the real world are highly interconnected, having a high degree of feedback among sectors. The results of decisions feed back through physical, economic, and social channels to alter the conditions on which the decisions were originally made. Some models do not reflect this reality, however. Consider an optimization model that computes the best size of sewage treatment plants to build in an area. The model will probably assume that the amount of sewage needing treatment will remain the same, or that it will grow at a certain rate. But if water quality improves because of sewage treatment, the area will become more attractive and development will increase, ultimately leading to a sewage load greater than expected.

Models that ignore feedback effects must rely on *exogenous variables* and are said to have a narrow boundary. Exogenous variables are ones that influence other variables in the model but are not calculated by the model. They are simply given by a set of numerical values over time, and they do not change in response to feedback. The values of exogenous variables may come from other models but are most likely the product of an unexaminable mental model. The *endogenous variables*, on the other hand, are calculated by the model itself. They are the variables explained by the structure of the model, the ones for which the modeler has an explicit theory, the ones that respond to feedback.

Ignoring feedback can result in policies that generate unanticipated side effects or are diluted, delayed, or defeated by the system (Meadows 1982). An example is the construction of freeways in the 1950s and 1960s to alleviate traffic congestion in major U.S. cities. In Boston it used to take half an hour to drive from the city neighborhood of Dorchester to the downtown area, a journey of only a few miles. Then a limited access highway network was built around the city, and travel time between Dorchester and downtown dropped substantially.

But there's more to the story. Highway construction led to changes that fed back into the system, causing unexpected side effects. Due to the reduction in traffic congestion and commuting time, living in outlying communities became a more attractive option. Farmland was turned into housing developments or paved over to provide yet more roads. The population of the suburbs soared, as people moved out of the center city. Many city stores followed their customers or were squeezed out by competition from the new suburban shopping malls. The inner city began to decay, but many people still worked in the downtown area—and they got there via the new highways. The result? Boston has more congestion and air pollution than before the highways were constructed, and the rush-hour journey from Dorchester to downtown takes half an hour, again.

In theory, feedback can be incorporated into optimization models, but the resulting complexity and non-linearity usually render the problem insoluble. Many optimization models therefore ignore most feedback effects. Potential users should be aware of this when they look at a model. They should ask to what degree important feedbacks have been excluded and how those exclusions might alter the assumptions and invalidate the results of the model.

Lack of Dynamics. Many optimization models are static. They determine the optimal solution for a particular moment in time without regard for how the optimal state is reached or how the system will evolve in the future. An example is the linear programming model constructed in the late 1970s by the U.S. Forest Service, with the objective of optimizing the use of government lands. The model was enormous, with thousands of decision variables and tens of thousands of constraints, and it took months just

to correct the typographical errors in the model's huge database. When the completed model was finally run, finding the solution required full use of a mainframe computer for days.

Despite the gigantic effort, the model prescribed the optimal use of forest resources for only a single moment in time. It did not take into account how harvesting a given area would affect its future ecological development. It did not consider how land-use needs or lumber prices might change in the future. It did not examine how long it would take for new trees to grow to maturity in the harvested areas, or what the economic and recreational value of the areas would be during the regrowth period. The model just provided the optimal decisions for a single year, ignoring the fact that those decisions would continue to influence the development of forest resources for decades.

Not all optimization models are static. The MARKAL model, for example, is a large linear programming model designed to determine the optimal choice of energy technologies. Developed at the Brookhaven National Laboratory in the U.S., the model produces as its output the best (least-cost) mix of coal, oil, gas, and other energy sources well into the next century. It requires various exogenous inputs, such as energy demands, future fuel prices, and construction and operating costs of different energy technologies. (Note that the model ignores feedbacks from energy supply to prices and demand.) The model is dynamic in the sense that it produces a "snapshot" of the optimal state of the system at five-year intervals.

The Brookhaven model is not completely dynamic, however, because it ignores delays. It assumes that people, seeing what the optimal mix is for some future year, begin planning far enough in advance so that this mix can actually be used. Thus the model does not, for example, incorporate construction delays for energy production facilities. In reality, of course, it takes time—often much longer than five years—to build power plants, invent new technologies, build equipment, develop waste management techniques, and find and transport necessary raw materials.

Indeed, delays are pervasive in the real world. The delays found in complex systems are especially important because they are a major source of system instability. The lag time required to carry out a decision or to perceive its effects may cause overreaction or may prevent timely intervention. Acid rain provides a good example. Although there is already evidence that damage to the forests of New England, the Appalachians, and Bavaria is caused by acid rain, many scientists suspect it will take years to determine exactly how acid rain is formed and how it affects the forests. Until scientific and then political consensus emerges, legislative action to curb pollution is not likely to be strong. Pollution control programs, once passed, will take years to implement. Existing power plants and other pollution sources will continue to operate for their functional lifetimes, which are measured in decades. It will require even longer to change settlement patterns and lifestyles dependent on the automobile. By the time sulfur and nitrogen oxide emissions are sufficiently reduced, it may be too late for the forests.

Delays are a crucial component of the dynamic behavior of systems, but—like non-linearity—they are difficult to incorporate into optimization models. A common simplification is to assume that all delays in the model are of the same fixed length. The results of such models are of questionable value. Policymakers who use them in an effort to find an optimal course of action may discover, like the proverbial American tourist on the back roads of Maine, that "you can't get there from here."

When To Use Optimization

Despite the limitations discussed above, optimization techniques can be extremely useful. But they must be used for the proper problems. Optimization has substantially improved the quality of decisions in many areas, including computer design, airline scheduling, factory siting, and oil refinery operation. Whenever the problem to be solved is one of choosing the best from among a well-defined set of alternatives, optimization should be considered. If the meaning of *best* is also well defined, and if the system to be optimized is relatively static and free of feedback, optimization may well be the best technique to use. Unfortunately, these latter conditions are rarely true for the social, economic, and ecological systems that are frequently of concern to decision makers.

Look out for optimization models that purport to forecast actual behavior. The output of an optimization model is a statement of the best way to accomplish a goal. To interpret the

results as a prediction of actual behavior is to assume that people in the real system will in fact make the optimal choices. It is one thing to say, "in order to maximize profits, people should make the following decisions," and quite another to say "people will succeed in maximizing profits, because they will make the following decisions." The former is a prescriptive statement of what to do, the latter a descriptive statement of what will actually happen.

Optimization models are valid for making prescriptive statements. They are valid for forecasting only if people do in fact optimize, do make the best possible decisions. It may seem reasonable to expect people to behave optimally—after all, wouldn't it be irrational to take second best when you could have the best? But the evidence on this score is conclusive: real people do not behave like optimization models. As discussed above, we humans make decisions with simple and incomplete mental models, models that are often based on faulty assumptions or that lead erroneously from sound assumptions to flawed solutions. As Herbert Simon puts it,

> The capacity of the human mind for formulating and solving complex problems is very small compared with the size of the problem whose solution is required for objectively rational behavior in the real world or even for a reasonable approximation to such objective rationality. (Simon 1957, p. 198)

Optimization models augment the limited capacity of the human mind to determine the objectively rational course of action. It should be remembered, however, that even optimization models must make simplifying assumptions in order to be tractable, so the most we can hope from them is an approximation of how people ought to behave. To model how people actually behave requires a very different set of modeling techniques, which will be discussed now.

Simulation

The Latin verb *simulare* means to imitate or mimic. The purpose of a simulation model is to mimic the real system so that its behavior can be studied. The model is a laboratory replica of the real system, a *microworld* (Morecroft 1988). By creating a representation of the system in the laboratory, a modeler can perform experiments that are impossible, unethical, or prohibitively expensive in the real world.

Simulations of physical systems are commonplace and range from wind tunnel tests of aircraft design to simulation of weather patterns and the depletion of oil reserves. Economists and social scientists also have used simulation to understand how energy prices affect the economy, how corporations mature, how cities evolve and respond to urban renewal policies, and how population growth interacts with food supply, resources, and the environment. There are many different simulation techniques, including stochastic modeling, system dynamics, discrete simulation, and role-playing games. Despite the differences among them, all simulation techniques share a common approach to modeling.

Optimization models are prescriptive, but simulation models are descriptive. A simulation model does not calculate what should be done to reach a particular goal, but clarifies what would happen in a given situation. The purpose of simulations may be *foresight* (predicting how systems might behave in the future under assumed conditions) or *policy design* (designing new decision-making strategies or organizational structures and evaluating their effects on the behavior of the system).

In other words, simulation models are "what if" tools. Often such "what if" information is more important than knowledge of the optimal decision. For example, during the 1978 debate in the U.S. over natural gas deregulation, President Carter's original proposal was modified dozens of times by Congress before a final compromise was passed. During the congressional debate, the Department of Energy evaluated each version of the bill using a system dynamics model (Department of Energy 1979). The model did not indicate what ought to be done to maximize the economic benefits of natural gas to the nation. Congress already had its own ideas on that score. But by providing an assessment of how each proposal would affect gas prices, supplies, and demands, the model generated ammunition that the Carter administration could use in lobbying for its proposals.

Every simulation model has two main components. First it must include a representation of the physical world relevant to the problem under study. Consider for example a model that was built for the purpose of understanding why America's large cities have continued to decay despite massive amounts of aid and numerous renewal programs (Forrester 1969). The model had to include a representation of the physical components of the city—the size and quality of the infrastructure, including the stock of housing and commercial structures; the attributes of the population, such as its size and composition and the mix of skills and incomes among the people; flows (of people, materials, money, etc.) into and out of the city; and other factors that characterize the physical and institutional setting.

How much detail a model requires about the physical structure of the system will, of course, depend on the specific problem being addressed. The urban model mentioned above required only an aggregate representation of the features common to large American cities. On the other hand, a model designed to improve the location and deployment of fire fighting resources in New York City had to include a detailed representation of the streets and traffic patterns (Greenberger, Crenson, and Crissey 1976).

In addition to reflecting the physical structure of the system, a simulation model must portray the behavior of the actors in the system. In this context, behavior means the way in which people respond to different situations, *how* they make decisions. The behavioral component is put into the model in the form of decision-making rules, which are determined by direct observation of the actual decision-making procedures in the system.

Given the physical structure of the system and the decision-making rules, the simulation model then plays the role of the decision makers, mimicking their decisions. In the model, as in the real world, the nature and quality of the information available to decision makers will depend on the state of the system. The output of the model will be a description of expected decisions. The validity of the model's assumptions can be checked by comparing the output with the decisions made in the real system.

An example is provided by the pioneering simulation study of corporate behavior carried out by Cyert and March (1963). Their field research showed that department stores used a very simple decision rule to determine the floor price of goods. That rule was basically to mark up the wholesale cost of the items by a fixed percentage, with the value of the markup determined by tradition. They also noted, however, that through time the traditional markup adjusted very slowly, bringing it closer to the actual markup realized on goods when they were sold. The actual markup could vary from the normal markup as the result of several other decision rules: When excess inventory piled up on the shelves, a sale was held and the price was gradually reduced until the goods were sold; if sales goals were exceeded, prices were boosted. Prices were also adjusted toward those of competitors.

Cyert and March built a simulation model of the pricing system, basing it on these decision-making rules. The output of the model was a description of expected prices for goods. When this output was compared with real store data, it was found that the model reproduced quite well the actual pricing decisions of the floor managers.

Limitations of Simulation

Any model is only as good as its assumptions. In the case of simulation models, the assumptions consist of the descriptions of the physical system and the decision rules. Adequately representing the physical system is usually not a problem; the physical environment can be portrayed with whatever detail and accuracy is needed for the model purpose. Also, simulation models can easily incorporate feedback effects, non-linearities, and dynamics; they are not rigidly determined in their structure by mathematical limitations as optimization models often are. Indeed, one of the main uses of simulation is to identify how feedback, non-linearity, and delays interact to produce troubling dynamics that persistently resist solution. (For examples see Sterman 1985, Morecroft 1983, and Forrester 1969.)

Simulation models do have their weak points, however. Most problems occur in the description of the decision rules, the quantification of soft variables, and the choice of the model boundary.

Accuracy of the Decision Rules. The description of the decision rules is one potential trouble spot in a simulation model. The model must accurately represent how the actors in the system make their decisions, even if their decision rules are less than optimal. The model should respond to change in the same way the real actors would. But it will do this only if the model's assumptions faithfully describe the decision rules that are used under different circumstances. The model therefore must reflect the actual decision-making strategies used by the people in the system being modeled, including the limitations and errors of those strategies.

Unfortunately, discovering decision rules is often difficult. They cannot be determined from aggregate statistical data, but must be investigated first hand. Primary data on the behavior of the actors can be acquired through observation of actual decision making in the field, that is, in the boardroom, on the factory floor, along the sales route, in the household. The modeler must discover what information is available to each actor, examine the timeliness and accuracy of that information, and infer how it is processed to yield a decision. Modelers often require the skills of the anthropologist and the ethnographer. One can also learn about decision making through laboratory experiments in which managers operate simulated corporations (Sterman 1989). The best simulation modeling draws on extensive knowledge of decision making that has been developed in many disciplines, including psychology, sociology, and behavioral science.

Soft Variables. The majority of data are soft variables. That is, most of what we know about the world is descriptive, qualitative, difficult to quantify, and has never been recorded. Such information is crucial for understanding and modeling complex systems. Yet in describing decision making, some modelers limit themselves to hard variables, ones that can be measured directly and can be expressed as numerical data. They may defend the rejection of soft variables as being more scientific than "making up" the values of parameters and relationships for which no numerical data are available. How, they ask, can the accuracy of estimates about soft variables be tested? How can statistical tests be performed without numerical data?

Actually, there are no limitations on the inclusion of soft variables in models, and many simulation models do include them. After all, the point of simulation models is to portray decision making as it really is, and soft variables—including intangibles such as desires, product quality, reputation, expectations, and optimism—are often of critical importance in decision making. Imagine, for example, trying to run a school, factory, or city solely on the basis of the available numerical data. Without qualitative knowledge about factors such as operating procedures, organizational structure, political subtleties, and individual motivations, the result would be chaos. Leaving such variables out of models just because of a lack of hard numerical data is certainly less "scientific" than including them and making reasonable estimates of their values. Ignoring a relationship implies that it has a value of zero—probably the only value known to be wrong! (Forrester 1980)

Of course, all relationships and parameters in models, whether based on soft or hard variables, are imprecise and uncertain to some degree. Reasonable people may disagree as to the importance of different factors. Modelers must therefore perform sensitivity analysis to consider how their conclusions might change if other plausible assumptions were made. Sensitivity analysis should not be restricted to uncertainty in parameter values, but should also consider the sensitivity of conclusions to alternative structural assumptions and choices of model boundary.

Sensitivity analysis is no less a responsibility for those modelers who ignore soft variables. Apparently hard data such as economic and demographic statistics are often subject to large measurement errors, biases, distortions, and revisions. Unfortunately, sensitivity analysis is not performed or reported often enough. Many modelers have been embarrassed when third parties, attempting to replicate the results of a model, have found that reasonable alternative assumptions produce radically different conclusions. (See the discussion below of the experiment conducted by the Joint Economic Committee with three leading econometric models.)

Model Boundary. The definition of a reasonable model boundary is another challenge for the builders of simulation models. Which factors will be exogenous, which will be endogenous? What feedbacks will be incorporated into the model? In theory, one of the great strengths of simulation models is the capacity to reflect the important feedback relationships that shape the behavior of the

system and its response to policies. In practice, however, many simulation models have very narrow boundaries. They ignore factors outside the expertise of the model builder or the interests of the sponsor, and in doing so they exclude important feedbacks.

The consequences of omitting feedback can be serious. An excellent example is provided by the Project Independence Evaluation System (PIES) model, used in the 1970s by the U.S. Federal Energy Administration and later by the U.S. Department of Energy. As described by the FEA, the purpose of the model was to evaluate different energy strategies according to these criteria: their impact on the development of alternative energy sources, their impact on economic growth, inflation, and unemployment; their regional and social impacts; their vulnerability to import disruptions; and their environmental effects (Federal Energy Administration 1974, p. 1).

Surprisingly, considering the stated purpose, the PIES model treated the economy as exogenous. The economy—including economic growth, interest rates, inflation, world oil prices, and the costs of unconventional fuels—was completely unaffected by the U.S. domestic energy situation—including prices, policies, and production. The way the model was constructed, even a full embargo of imported oil or a doubling of oil prices would have no impact on the economy.

Its exogenous treatment of the economy made the PIES model inherently contradictory. The model showed that the investment needs of the energy sector would increase markedly as depletion raised the cost of getting oil out of the ground and synthetic fuels were developed. But at the same time, the model assumed that higher investment needs in the energy sector could be satisfied without reducing investment or consumption in the rest of the economy and without raising interest rates or inflation. In effect, the model let the economy have its pie and eat it too.

In part because it ignored the feedbacks between the energy sector and the rest of the economy, the PIES model consistently proved to be overoptimistic. In 1974 the model projected that by 1985 the U.S. would be well on the way to energy independence: energy imports would be only 3.3 million barrels per day, and production of shale oil would be 250,000 barrels per day. Furthermore, these developments would be accompanied by oil prices of about $22 per barrel (1984 dollars) and by vigorous economic growth. It didn't happen. In fact, at the time this paper is being written (1988), oil imports are about 5.5. million per day, and the shale oil industry remains a dream. This situation prevails despite the huge reductions in oil demand that have resulted from oil prices of over $30 per barrel and from the most serious economic recession since the Great Depression.

A broad model boundary that includes important feedback effects is more important than a great amount of detail in the specification of individual components. It is worth noting that the PIES model provided a breakdown of supply, demand, and price for dozens of fuels in each region of the country. Yet its aggregate projections for 1985 weren't even close. One can legitimately ask what purpose was served by the effort devoted to forecasting the demand for jet fuel or naphtha in the Pacific Northwest when the basic assumptions were so palpably inadequate and the main results so woefully erroneous.

In fairness it must be said that the PIES model is not unique in the magnitude of its errors. Nearly all energy models of all types have consistently been wrong about energy production, consumption, and prices. The evidence shows clearly that energy forecasts actually lag behind the available information, reflecting the past rather than anticipating the future (Department of Energy 1983). A good discussion of the limitations of PIES and other energy models is available in the appendix of Stobaugh and Yergin (1979).

Overly narrow model boundaries are not just a problem in energy analysis. *The Global 2000 Report to the President* (Barney 1980) showed that most of the models used by U.S. government agencies relied significantly on exogenous variables. Population models assumed food production was exogenous. Agriculture models assumed that energy prices and other input prices were exogenous. Energy models assumed that economic growth and environmental conditions were exogenous. Economic models assumed that population and energy prices were exogenous. And so on. Because they ignored important intersectoral feedbacks, the models produced inconsistent results.

Econometrics

Strictly speaking, econometrics is a simulation technique, but it deserves separate discussion for several reasons. First, it evolved out of economics and statistics, while most other simulation methods emerged from operations research or engineering. The difference in pedigree leads to large differences in purpose and practice. Second, econometrics is one of the most widely used formal modeling techniques. Pioneered by Nobel Prize-winning economists Jan Tinbergen and Lawrence Klein, econometrics is now taught in nearly all business and economics programs. Econometric forecasts are regularly reported in the media, and ready-to-use statistical routines for econometric modeling are now available for many personal computers. And third, the well publicized failure of econometric models to predict the future has eroded the credibility of all types of computer models, including those built for very different purposes and using completely different modeling techniques.

Econometrics is literally the measurement of economic relations, and it originally involved statistical analysis of economic data. As commonly practiced today, econometric modeling includes three stages—specification, estimation, and forecasting. First the structure of the system is specified by a set of equations. Then the values of the parameters (coefficients relating changes in one variable to changes in another) are estimated on the basis of historical data. Finally, the resulting output is used to make forecasts about the future performance of the system.

Specification
Specification is the description of the model's structure. This structure consists of the relationships among variables, both those that describe the physical setting and those that describe behavior. The relationships are expressed as equations, and a large econometric model may have hundreds or even thousands of equations reflecting the many interrelationships among the variables.

For example, an econometric model of the macroeconomy typically will contain equations specifying the relationship between GNP and consumption, investment, government activity, and international trade. It also will include behavioral equations that describe how these individual quantities are determined. The modeler may expect, for instance, that high unemployment reduces inflation and vice versa, a relationship known as the Phillips curve. One of the equations in the model will therefore express the Phillips curve, specifying that the rate of inflation depends on the amount of unemployment. Another equation may relate unemployment to the demand for goods, the wage level, and worker productivity. Still other equations may explain wage level in terms of yet other factors.

Not surprisingly, econometrics draws on economic theory to guide the specification of its models. The validity of the models thus depends on the validity of the underlying economic theories. Though there are many flavors of economics, a small set of basic assumptions about human behavior are common to most theories, including modern neoclassical theory and the "rational expectations" school. These assumptions are: optimization, perfect information, and equilibrium.

In econometrics, people (economic agents, in the jargon), are assumed to be concerned with just one thing—maximizing their profits. Consumers are assumed to optimize the "utility" they derive from their resources. Decisions about how much to produce, what goods to purchase, whether to save or borrow, are assumed to be the result of optimization by individual decision makers. Non-economic considerations (defined as any behavior that diverges from profit or utility maximization) are ignored or treated as local aberrations and special cases.

Of course, to optimize, economic agents would need accurate information about the world. The required information would go beyond the current state of affairs; it also would include complete knowledge about available options and their consequences. In most econometric models, such knowledge is assumed to be freely available and accurately known.

Take, for example, an econometric model simulating the operation of a firm that is using an optimal mix of energy, labor, machines, and other inputs in its production process. The model will assume that the firm knows not only the wages of workers and the prices of machines and other inputs, but also the production attainable with different combinations of people and machines, even if those combinations have never been tried. Rational expectation models go so far as to assume that the firm knows future prices, technologies, and possibilities, and that it can perfectly anticipate the consequences of its own actions and those of competitors.

The third assumption is that the economy is in or near equilibrium nearly all of the time. If disturbed, it is usually assumed to return to equilibrium rapidly and in a smooth and stable manner. The prevalence of static thinking is the intellectual legacy of the pioneers of mathematics and economics. During the late nineteenth century, before computers or modern cybernetic theory, the crucial questions of economic theory involved the nature of the equilibrium state for different situations. Given human preferences and the technological possibilities for producing goods, at what prices will commodities be traded, and in what quantities? What will wages be? What will profits be? How will a tax or monopoly influence the equilibrium?

These questions proved difficult enough without tackling the more difficult problem of dynamics, of the behavior of a system in flux. As a result, dynamic economic theory—including the recurrent fluctuations of inflation, of the business cycle, of the growth and decline of industries and nations—remained primarily descriptive and qualitative long after equilibrium theory was expressed mathematically. Even now, dynamic behavior in economics tends to be seen as a transition from one equilibrium to another, and the transition is usually assumed to be stable.

The rich heritage of static theory in economics left a legacy of equilibrium for econometrics. Many econometric models assume that markets are in equilibrium at all times. When adjustment dynamics are modeled, variables are usually assumed to adjust in a smooth and stable manner toward the optimal, equilibrium value, and the lags are nearly always fixed in length. For example, most macroeconometric models assume that capital stocks of firms in the economy adjust to the optimal, profit-maximizing level, with a fixed lag of several years. The lag is the same whether the industries that supply investment goods have the capacity to meet the demand or not. (See, for example, Eckstein 1983 and Jorgenson 1963).

Yet clearly, when the supplying industries have excess capacity, orders can be filled rapidly; when capacity is strained, customers must wait in line for delivery. Whether the dynamic nature of the lag is expressed in a model does make a difference. Models that explicitly include the determinants of the investment delay will yield predictions significantly different from models that assume a fixed investment lag regardless of the physical capability of the economy to fill the demand (Senge 1980). In general, models that explicitly portray delays and their determinants will yield different results from models that simply assume smooth adjustments from one optimal state to another.

Estimation

The second stage in econometric modeling is statistical estimation of the parameters of the model. The parameters determine the precise strengths of the relationships specified in the model structure. In the case of the Phillips curve, for example, the modeler would use past data to estimate precisely how strong the relationship between inflation and unemployment has been. Estimating the parameters involves statistical regression routines that are, in essence, fancy curve-fitting techniques. Statistical parameter estimates characterize the degree of correlation among the variables. They use historical data to determine parameter values that best match the data themselves.

All modeling methods must specify the structure of the system and estimate parameters. The use of statistical procedures to derive the parameters of the model is the hallmark of econometrics and distinguishes it from other forms of simulation. It gives econometricians an insatiable appetite for numerical data, for without numerical data they cannot carry out the statistical procedures used to estimate the models. It is no accident that the rise of econometrics went hand in hand with the quantification of economic life. The development of the national income and produce accounts by Simon Kuznets in the 1930s was a major advance in the codification of economic data, permitting consistent measures of

economic activity at the national level for the first time. To this day all major macroeconometric models rely heavily on the national accounts data, and indeed macroeconomic theory itself has adapted to the national accounts framework.

Forecasting

The third step in econometric modeling is forecasting, making predictions about how the real system will behave in the future. In this step, the modeler provides estimates of the future values of the exogenous variables, that is, those variables that influence the other variables in the model but aren't themselves influenced by the model. An econometric model may have dozens of exogenous variables, and each must be forecast before the model can be used to predict.

Limitations of Econometric Modeling

The chief weak spots in econometric models stem from the assumptions of the underlying economic theory on which they rest: assumptions about the rationality of human behavior, about the availability of information that real decision makers do not have, and about equilibrium. Many economists acknowledge the idealization and abstraction of these assumptions, but at the same time point to the powerful results that have been derived from them. However, a growing number of prominent economists now argue that these assumptions are not just abstract—they are false. In his presidential address to the British Royal Economics Society, E. H. Phelps-Brown said:

> The trouble here is not that the behavior of these economic chessmen has been simplified, for simplification seems to be part of all understanding. The trouble is that the behavior posited is not known to be what obtains in the actual economy. (Phelps-Brown 1972, p. 4)

Nicholas Kaldor of Cambridge University is even more blunt:

> ...in my view, the prevailing theory of value—what I called, in a shorthand way, "equilibrium economics"—is barren and irrelevant as an apparatus of thought... (Kaldor 1972, p. 1237)

As mentioned earlier, a vast body of empirical research in psychology and organizational studies has shown that people do not optimize or act as if they optimize, that they don't have the mental capabilities to optimize their decisions, that even if they had the computational power necessary, they lack the information needed to optimize. Instead, they try to satisfy a variety of personal and organizational goals, use standard operating procedures to routinize decision making, and ignore much of the available information to reduce the complexity of the problems they face. Herbert Simon, in his acceptance speech for the 1978 Nobel Prize in economics, concludes:

> There can no longer be any doubt that the micro assumptions of the theory—the assumptions of perfect rationality—are contrary to fact. It is not a question of approximation; they do not even remotely describe the processes that human beings use for making decisions in complex situations (Simon 1979, p. 510).

Econometrics also contains inherent statistical limitations. The regression procedures used to estimate parameters yield unbiased estimates only under certain conditions. These conditions are known as *maintained hypotheses* because they are assumptions that must be made in order to use the statistical technique. The maintained hypotheses can never be verified, even in principle, but must be taken as a matter of faith. In the most common regression technique, ordinary least squares, the maintained hypotheses include the unlikely assumptions that the variables are all measured perfectly, that the model being estimated corresponds perfectly to the real world, and the random errors in the variables from one time period to another are completely independent. More sophisticated techniques do not impose such restrictive assumptions, but they always involve other a priori hypotheses that cannot be validated.

Another problem is that econometrics fails to distinguish between correlations and causal relationships. Simulation models must portray the causal relationships in a system if they are to mimic its behavior, especially its behavior in new situations. But the statistical techniques used to estimate parameters in econometric models don't prove whether a relationship is causal. They only reveal the degree of past correlation between the variables, and these correlations may change or shift as the system evolves. The prominent economist Robert Lucas (1976) makes the same point in a different context.

Consider the Phillips curve as an example. Though economists often interpreted the Phillips curve as a causal relationship—a policy trade-off between inflation and unemployment—it never did represent the causal forces that determine inflation or wage increases. Rather, the Phillips curve was simply a way of restating the past behavior of the system. In the past, Phillips said, low unemployment had tended to occur at the same time inflation was high, and vice-versa. Then, sometime in the early 1970s, the Phillips curve stopped working; inflation rose while unemployment worsened. Among the explanations given by economists was that the structure of the system had changed. But a modeler's appeal to "structural change" usually means that the inadequate structure of the model has to be altered because it failed to anticipate the behavior of the real system!

What actually occurred in the 1970s was that, when inflation swept prices to levels unprecedented in the industrial era, people learned to expect continuing increases. As a result of the adaptive feedback process of learning, they learned to deal with high inflation through indexing, COLAs, inflation-adjusting accounting, and other adjustments. The structure, the causal relationships of the system, did not change. Instead, causal relationships that had been present all along (but were dormant in an era of low inflation) gradually became active determinants of behavior as inflation worsened. In particular, the ability of people to adapt to continuing inflation existed all along but was not tested until inflation became high enough and persistent enough. Then the behavior of the system changed, and the historical correlation between inflation and unemployment broke down.

The reliance of econometric estimation on numerical data is another of its weaknesses. The narrow focus on hard data blinds modelers to less tangible but no less important factors. They ignore both potentially observable quantities that haven't been measured yet and ones for which no numerical data exist. (Alternatively, they may express an unmeasured factor with a proxy variable for which data already exists, even though the relationship between the two is tenuous—as when educational expenditure per capita is used as a proxy for the literacy of a population.)

Among the factors excluded from econometric models because of the hard data focus are many important determinants of decision making, including desires, goals, and perceptions. Numerical data may measure the results of human decision making, but numbers don't explain how or why people made particular decisions. As a result, econometric models cannot be used to anticipate how people would react to a change in decision-making circumstances.

Similarly, econometric models are unable to provide a guide to performance under conditions that have not been experienced previously. Econometricians assume that the correlations indicated by the historical data will remain valid in the future. In reality, those data usually span a limited range and provide no guidance outside historical experience. As a result, econometric models are often less than robust: faced with new policies or conditions, the models break down and lead to inconsistent results.

An example is the model used by Data Resources, Inc. in 1979 to test policies aimed at eliminating oil imports. On the basis of historical numerical data, the model assumed that the response of oil demand to the price of oil was rather weak—a 10 percent increase in oil price caused a reduction of oil demand of only 2 percent, even in the long run. According to the model, for consumption to be reduced by 50 percent (enough to cut imports to zero at the time), oil would have to rise to $800 per barrel. Yet at that price, the annual oil bill for the remaining 50 percent would have exceeded the total GNP for that year, an impossibility (Sterman 1981). The model's reliance on historical data led to inconsistencies. (Today, with the benefit of hindsight, economists agree that oil demand is much more responsive to price than was earlier believed. Yet considering the robustness of the model under extreme conditions could have revealed the problem much earlier.)

Validation is another problem area in econometric modeling. The dominant criterion used by econometric modelers to determine the validity of an equation or a model is the degree to which it fits the data. Many econometrics texts (e.g., Pindyck and Rubinfeld 1976) teach that the statistical significance of the estimated parameters in an equation is an indicator of the correctness of the relationship. Such views are mistaken. Statistical significance indicates how well an equation fits the observed data; it does not indicate whether a relationship is a correct or true characterization of the way the world works. A statistically significant relationship between variables in an equation shows that they are highly correlated and that the apparent correlation is not likely to have been the result of mere chance. But it does not indicate that the relationship is causal at all.

Using statistical significance as the test of model validity can lead modelers to mistake historical correlations for causal relationships. It also can cause them to reject valid equations describing important relationships. They may, for example, exclude an equation as statistically insignificant simply because there are few data about the variables, or because the data don't contain enough information to allow the application of statistical procedures.

Ironically, a lack of statistical significance does not necessarily lead econometric modelers to the conclusion that the model or the equation is invalid. When an assumed relationship fails to be statistically significant, the modeler may try another specification for the equation, hoping to get a better statistical fit. Without recourse to descriptive, micro-level data, the resulting equations may be ad hoc and bear only slight resemblance to either economic theory or actual behavior. Alternatively, the modelers may attempt to explain the discrepancy between the model and the behavior of the real system by blaming it on faulty data collection, exogenous influences, or other factors.

The Phillips curve again provides an example. When it broke down, numerous revisions of the equations were made. These attempts to find a better statistical fit met with limited success. Some analysts took another tack, pointing to the oil price shock, Russian wheat deal, or other one-of-a-kind events as the explanation for the change. Still others argued that there had been structural changes that caused the Phillips curve to shift out to higher levels of unemployment for any given inflation rate.

These flaws in econometrics have generated serious criticism from within the economic profession. Phelps-Brown notes that because controlled experiments are generally impossible in economics "running regressions between time series is only likely to deceive" (Phelps-Brown 1972, p. 6). Lester Thurow notes that econometrics has failed as a method for testing theories and is now used primarily as a "showcase for exhibiting theories." Yet as a device for advocacy, econometrics imposes few constraints on the prejudices of the modeler. Thurow concludes:

> By simple random search, the analyst looks for the set of variables and functional forms that give the best equations. In this context the best equation is going to depend heavily upon the prior beliefs of the analyst. If the analyst believes that interest rates do not affect the velocity of money, he find a 'best' equation that validates his particular prior belief. If the analyst believes that interest rates do affect the velocity of money, he finds a 'best' equation that validates this prior belief. (Thurow 1983, pp. 107-8)

But the harshest assessment of all comes from Nobel laureate Wassily Leontief:

> Year after year economic theorists continue to produce scores of mathematical models and to explore in great detail their formal properties; and the econometricians fit algebraic functions of all possible shapes to essentially the same sets of data without being able to advance, in any perceptible way, a systematic understanding of the structure and the operations of a real economic system. (Leontief 1982, p. 107; see also Leontief 1971.)

But surely such theoretical problems matter little if the econometric models provide accurate predictions. After all, the prime purpose of econometric models is short-term prediction of the exact future state of the economy, and most of the attributes of econometrics (including the use of regression techniques to pick the "best" parameters from the available numerical data and the extensive reliance on exogenous variables) have evolved in response to this predictive purpose.

Unfortunately, econometrics fails on this score also; in practice, econometric models do not predict very well. The predictive power of econometric models, even over the short-term (one to four years), is poor and virtually indistinguishable from that of other forecasting methods. There are several reasons for this failure to predict accurately.

As noted earlier, in order to forecast, the modeler must provide estimates of the future values of the exogenous variables, and an econometric model may have dozens of these variables. The source of the forecasts for these variables may be other models but usually is the intuition and judgment of the modeler. Forecasting the exogenous variables consistently, much less correctly, is difficult.

Not surprisingly, the forecasts produced by econometric models often don't square with the modeler's intuition. When they feel the model output is wrong, many modelers, including those at the "big three" econometric forecasting firms—Chase Econometrics, Wharton Econometric Forecasting Associates, and Data Resources—simply adjust their forecasts. This fudging, or add factoring as they call it, is routine and extensive. The late Otto Eckstein of Data Resources admitted that their forecasts were 60 percent model and 40 percent judgment ("Forecasters Overhaul Models of Economy in Wake of 1982 Errors," *Wall Street Journal*, 17 February 1983). *Business Week* ("Where Big Econometric Models Go Wrong," 30 March 1981) quotes an economist who points out that there is no way of knowing where the Wharton model ends and the model's developer, Larry Klein, takes over. Of course, the adjustments made by add factoring are strongly colored by the personalities and political philosophies of the modelers. In the article cited above, the *Wall Street Journal* quotes Otto Eckstein as conceding that his forecasts sometimes reflect an optimistic view: "Data Resources is the most influential forecasting firm in the country...If it were in the hands of a doom-and-gloomer, it would be bad for the country."

In a revealing experiment, the Joint Economic Committee of Congress (through the politically neutral General Accounting Office) asked these three econometric forecasting firms (DRI, Chase, and Wharton) to make a series of simulations with their models, running the models under different assumptions about monetary policy. One set of forecasts was "managed" or add factored by the forecasters at each firm. The other set consisted of pure forecasts, made by the GAO using the untainted results of the models. As an illustration of the inconsistencies revealed by the experiment, consider the following: When the money supply was assumed to be fixed, the DRI model forecast that after ten years the interest rate would be 34 percent, a result totally contrary to both economic theory and historical experience. The forecast was then add factored down to a more reasonable 7 percent. The other models fared little better, revealing both the inability of the pure models to yield meaningful results and the extensive ad hoc adjustments made by the forecasters to render the results palatable (Joint Economic Committee 1982).

Add factoring has been criticized by other economists on the grounds that it is unscientific. They point out that, although the mental models used to add factor are the mental models of seasoned experts, these experts are subject to the same cognitive limitations other people face. And whether good or bad, the assumptions behind add factoring are always unexaminable.

The failure of econometric models have not gone unnoticed. A representative sampling of articles in the business press on the topic of econometric forecasting include the following headlines:

"1980: The Year The Forecasters Really Blew It." (Business Week, 14 July 1980).

"Where The Big Econometric Models Go Wrong." (Business Week, 30 March 1981).

"Forecasters Overhaul Models of Economy in Wake of 1982 Errors." (Wall Street Journal, 17 February, 1983).

"Business Forecasters Find Demand Is Weak in Their Own Business: Bad Predictions Are Factor." (Wall Street Journal, 7 September 1984).

"Economists Missing The Mark: More Tools, Bigger Errors." (New York Times, 12 December 1984).

The result of these failures has been an erosion of credibility regarding computer models—all models no matter what their purpose, not just econometric models designed for prediction. This is unfortunate. Econometric models are poor *forecasting* tools, but well-designed simulation models can be valuable tools for *foresight* and *policy design*. Foresight is the ability to anticipate how the system will behave if and when certain changes occur. It is not forecasting, and it does not depend on the ability to predict. In fact, there is substantial agreement among modelers of global problems that exact, point prediction of the future is neither possible nor necessary:

> ...at present we are far from being able to predict social-system behavior except perhaps for carefully selected systems in the very short term. Effort spent on attempts at precise prediction is almost surely wasted, and results that purport to be such predictions are certainly misleading. On the other hand, much can be learned from models in the form of broad, qualitative, conditional understanding—and this kind of understanding is useful (and typically the only basis) for policy formulation. If your doctor tells you that you will have a heart attack if you do not stop smoking, this advice is helpful, even if it does not tell you exactly when a heart attack will occur or how bad it will be. (Meadows, Richardson, and Bruckmann 1982, p. 279)

Of course, policy evaluation and foresight depend on an accurate knowledge of the history and current state of the world, and econometrics has been a valuable stimulus to the development of much-needed data gathering and measurement by governments and private companies. But econometric models do not seem well-suited to the types of problems of concern in policy analysis and foresight. Though these models purport to simulate human behavior, they in fact rely on unrealistic assumptions about the motivations of real people and the information available to them. Though the models must represent the physical world, they commonly ignore dynamic processes, disequilibrium, and the physical basis for delays between actions and results. Though they may incorporate hundreds of variables, they often ignore soft variables and unmeasured quantities. In real systems the feedback relationships between environmental, demographic, and social factors are usually as important as economic influences, but econometric models often omit these because numerical data are not available. Furthermore, econometrics usually deals with the short term, while foresight takes a longer view. Over the time span that is of concern in foresight, real systems are likely to deviate from their past recorded behavior, making unreliable the historical correlations on which econometric models are based.

Checklist for the Model Consumer

The preceding discussion has focused on the limitations of various modeling approaches in order to provide potential model consumers with a sense of what to look out for when choosing a model. Despite the limitations of modeling, there is no doubt that computer models can be and have been extremely useful foresight tools. Well-built models offer significant advantages over the often faulty mental models currently in use.

The following checklist provides further assistance to decision makers who are potential model users. It outlines some of the key questions that should be asked to evaluate the validity of a model and its appropriateness as a tool for solving a specific problem.

What is the problem at hand? What is the problem addressed by the model?

What is the boundary of the model? What factors are endogenous? Exogenous? Excluded? Are soft variables included? Are feedback effects properly taken into account? Does the model capture possible side effects, both harmful and beneficial?

What is the time horizon relevant to the problem? Does the model include as endogenous components those factors that may change significantly over the time horizon?

Are people assumed to act rationally and to optimize their performance? Does the model take non-economic behavior (organizational realities, non-economic motives, political factors, cognitive limitations) into account?

Does the model assume people have perfect information about the future and about the way the system works, or does it take into account the limitations, delays, and errors in acquiring information that plague decision makers in the real world?

Are appropriate time delays, constraints, and possible bottlenecks taken into account?

Is the model robust in the face of extreme variations in input assumptions?

Are the policy recommendations derived from the model sensitive to plausible variations in its assumptions?

Are the results of the model reproducible? Or are they adjusted (add factored) by the model builder?

Is the model currently operated by the team that built it? How long does it take for the model team to evaluate a new situation, modify the model, and incorporate new data?

Is the model documented? Is the documentation publicly available? Can third parties use the model and run their own analyses with it?

Conclusions

The inherent strengths and weaknesses of computer models have crucial implications for their application in foresight and policy analysis. Intelligent decision making requires the appropriate use of many different models designed for specific purposes—not reliance on a single, comprehensive model of the world. To repeat a dictum offered above, "Beware the analyst who proposes to model an entire social or economic system rather than a problem." It is simply not possible to build a single, integrated model of the world, into which mathematical inputs can be inserted and out of which will flow a coherent and useful understanding of world trends.

To be used responsibly, models must be subjected to debate. A cross-disciplinary approach is needed; models designed by experts in different fields and for different purposes must be compared, contrasted, and criticized. The foresight process should foster such review.

The history of global modeling provides a good example. The initial global modeling efforts, published in *World Dynamics* (Forrester 1971) and *The Limits to Growth* (Meadows et al. 1972) provoked a storm of controversy. A number of critiques appeared, and other global models were soon developed. Over a period of ten years, the International Institute for Applied Systems Analysis (IIASA) conducted a program of analysis and critical review in which the designers of global models were brought together. Six major symposia were held, and eight important global models were examined and discussed. These models had different purposes, used a range of modeling techniques, and were built by persons with widely varying backgrounds. Even after the IIASA conferences, there remain large areas of methodological and substantive disagreement among the modelers. Yet despite these differences, consensus did emerge on a number of crucial issues (Meadows, Richardson, and Bruckmann 1982), including the following:

Physical and technical resources exist to satisfy the basic needs of all the world's people into the foreseeable future.

Population and material growth cannot continue forever on a finite planet.

Continuing "business as usual" policies in the next decades will not result in a desirable future nor even in the satisfaction of basic human needs.

Technical solutions alone are not sufficient to satisfy basic needs or create a desirable future.

The IIASA program on global modeling represents the most comprehensive effort to date to use computer models as a way to improve human understanding of social issues. The debate about the models created agreement on crucial issues where none had existed. The program helped to guide further research and provided a standard for the effective conduct of foresight in both the public and private sectors.

At the moment, model-based analyses usually take the form of studies commissioned by policymakers. The clients sit and wait for the final reports, largely ignorant of the methods, assumptions, and biases that the modelers put into the models. The policymakers are thus placed in the role of supplicants awaiting the prophecies of an oracle. When the report finally arrives, they may, like King Croesus before the Oracle at Delphi, interpret the results in accordance with their own preconceptions. If the results are unfavorable, they may simply ignore them. Policymakers who use models as black boxes, who accept them without scrutinizing their assumptions, who do not examine the sensitivity of the conclusions to variations in premises, who do not engage the model builders in dialogue, are little different from the Delphic supplicants or the patrons of astrologers. And these policymakers justly alarm critics, who worry that black box modeling abdicates to the modelers and the computer a fundamental human responsibility (Weizenbaum 1976).

No one can (or should) make decisions on the basis of computer model results that are simply presented, "take 'em or leave 'em." In fact, the primary function of model building should be educational rather than predictive. Models should not be used as a substitute for critical thought, but as a tool for improving judgment and intuition. Promising efforts in corporations, universities, and public education are described in Senge 1989; Graham, Senge, Sterman, and Morecroft 1989; Kim 1989; and Richmond 1987.

Towards that end, the role of computer models in policymaking needs to be redefined. What is the point of computer modeling? It should be remembered that we all use models of some sort to make decisions and to solve problems. Most of the pressing issues with which public policy is concerned are currently being handled solely with mental models, and those mental models are failing to resolve the problems. The alternative to continued reliance on mental models is computer modeling. But why turn to computer models if they too are far from perfect?

The value in computer models derives from the differences between them and mental models. When the conflicting results of a mental and a computer model are analyzed, when the underlying causes of the differences are identified, both of the models can be improved.

Computer modeling is thus an essential part of the educational process rather than a technology for producing answers. The success of this dialectic depends on our ability to create and learn from shared understandings of our models, both mental and computer. Properly used, computer models can improve the mental models upon which decisions are actually based and contribute to the solution of the pressing problems we face.

References

Barney, Gerald O., ed. 1980. *The Global 2000 Report to the President.* 3 vols. Washington, D.C.: U.S. Government Printing Office.

Business Forecasters Find Demand Is Weak in Their Own Business: Bad Predictions Are Factor. *Wall Street Journal*, 7 September 1984.

Cyert, R., and March, J. 1963. *A Behavioral Theory of the Firm.* Englewood Cliffs, N.J.: Prentice Hall.

Department of Energy. 1979. *National Energy Plan II.* DOE/TIC-10203. Washington, D.C.: Department of Energy.

_____. 1983. *Energy Projections to the Year 2000.* Washington, D.C.: Department of Energy, Office of Policy, Planning, and Analysis.

Eckstein, O. 1983. *The DRI Model of the US Economy.* New York, McGraw Hill.

Economists Missing the Mark: More Tools, Bigger Errors. *New York Times*, 12 December 1984.

Federal Energy Administration. 1974. *Project Independence Report.* Washington, D.C.: Federal Energy Administration.

Forecasters Overhaul Models of Economy in Wake of 1982 Errors. *Wall Street Journal*, 17 February, 1983.

Forrester, Jay W. 1969. *Urban Dynamics.* Cambridge, Mass.: MIT Press.

_____. 1971. *World Dynamics.* Cambridge, Mass.: MIT Press.

_____. 1980. Information Sources for Modeling the National Economy. *Journal of the American Statistical Association* 75(371):555-574.

Graham, Alan K.; Senge, Peter M.; Sterman, John D.; and Morecroft, John D. W. 1989. Computer Based Case Studies in Management Education and Research. In *Computer-Based Management of Complex Systems*, eds. P. Milling and E. Zahn, pp. 317-326. Berlin: Springer Verlag.

Grant, Lindsey, ed. 1988. *Foresight and National Decisions: The Horseman and the Bureaucrat.* Lanham, Md.: University Press of America.

Greenberger, M., Crenson, M. A., and Crissey, B. L. 1976. *Models in the Policy Process.* New York: Russell Sage Foundation.

Hogarth, R. M. 1980. *Judgment and Choice.* New York: Wiley.

Joint Economic Committee. 1982. *Three Large Scale Model Simulations of Four Money Growth Scenarios.* Prepared for subcommittee on Monetary and Fiscal Policy, 97th Congress 2nd Session, Washington, D.C.

Jorgenson, D. W. 1963. Capital Theory and Investment Behavior. *American Economic Review* 53:247-259.

Kahneman, D., Slovic, P., and Tversky, A. 1982. *Judgment Under Uncertainty: Heuristics and Biases.* Cambridge: Cambridge University Press.

Kaldor, Nicholas. 1972. The Irrelevance of Equilibrium Economics. *The Economic Journal* 82:1237-55.

Kim, D. 1989. Learning Laboratories: Designing a Reflective Learning Environment. In *Computer-Based Management of Complex Systems*, P. Milling and E. Zahn, eds., pp. 327-334. Berlin: Springer Verlag

Leontief, Wassily. 1971. Theoretical Assumptions and Nonobserved Facts. *American Economic Review* 61(1):1-7.

_____. 1982. Academic Economics. *Science* 217:104-107.

Lucas, R. 1976. Econometric Policy Evaluation: A Critique. In *The Phillips Curve and Labor Markets*, K. Brunner and A. Meltzer, eds. Amsterdam: North-Holland.

Meadows, Donella H.; Meadows, Dennis L.; Randers, Jorgen.; and Behrens, William W. 1972. *The Limits to Growth*. New York: Universe Books.

Meadows, Donella H. 1982. Whole Earth Models and Systems. *CoEvolution Quarterly*, Summer 1982, pp. 98-108.

Meadows, Donella H.; Richardson, John; and Bruckmann, Gerhart 1982. *Groping in the Dark*. Somerset, N.J.: Wiley.

Morecroft, John D. W. 1983. System Dynamics: Portraying Bounded Rationality. *Omega* II:131-142.

_____. 1988. System Dynamics and Microworlds for Policy Makers. *European Journal of Operational Research* 35(5):301-320.

1980: The Year The Forecasters Really Blew It. *Business Week*, 14 July 1980.

Phelps-Brown, E. H. 1972. The Underdevelopment of Economics. *The Economic Journal* 82:1-10.

Pindyck, R., and Rubinfeld, D. 1976. *Econometric Models and Economic Forecasts*. New York: McGraw Hill.

Richmond, B. 1987. *The Strategic Forum*. Lyme, New Hampshire (13 Dartmouth College Highway, Lyme, NH 03768, USA): High Performance Systems, Inc.

Senge, Peter M. 1980. A System Dynamics Approach to Investment Function Formulation and Testing. *Socioeconomic Planning Sciences* 14:269-280.

_____. 1989. Catalyzing Systems Thinking Within Organizations. In *Advances in Organization Development*, F. Masaryk, ed., forthcoming.

Simon, Herbert. 1947. *Administrative Behavior*. New York: MacMillan.

_____. 1957. *Models of Man*. New York: Wiley.

_____. 1979. Rational Decisionmaking in Business Organizations. *American Economic Review* 69:493-513.

Sterman, John D. 1981. The Energy Transition and the Economy: A System Dynamics Approach. Ph.D. dissertation, Massachusetts Institute of Technology, Cambridge.

_____. 1985. A Behavioral Model of the Economic Long Wave. *Journal of Economic Behavior and Organization* 6(1):17-53.

_____. 1989. Modeling Managerial Behavior: Misperceptions of Feedback in a Dynamic Decision Making Experiment. *Management Science* 35(3):321-339.

Stobaugh, Robert and Yergin, Daniel. 1979. *Energy Future*. New York: Random House.

Thurow, Lester. 1983. *Dangerous Currents*. New York: Random House.

Weizenbaum, J. 1976. *Computer Power and Human Reason: from Judgment to Calculation*. San Francisco: W. H. Freeman.

Where The Big Econometric Models Go Wrong. *Business Week*, 30 March 1981.

15. Sources of Data

This chapter was prepared by Mr. Daniel Tunstall, who is now a Senior Associate at the World Resources Institute, 1709 New York Avenue, NW, Suite 700, Washington, DC 20006, USA.

Introduction

Modelers, like other data analysts, spend a large part of their time looking for, selecting, compiling, and documenting data. How many projects have floundered because the data collection effort took too much time and too much money, or because the data collection effort was slighted? What is needed, when looking for good data, is a place to start and a path to follow.

This chapter provides a brief review of the principal sources of basic national-level statistics that are available to the public in the following areas: population and health, economics, politics and security, transportation, energy, water, land use, food and agriculture, forestry, fisheries, and environmental quality.

The selection of subjects and topics reflects the growing importance of renewable resources in understanding and measuring sustainable development. More attention is given in this review to environmental quality, water resources, land use, forests, fisheries, and transportation than to social and economic topics, since data on these latter subjects are easier to find and they are covered in more detail in other reviews. See, for example, *Sourcebook of Global Statistics* published by Facts on File Publications and *Index to International Statistics: A Guide to Statistical Publications of International Intergovernmental Organizations* published by the Congressional Information Service.

Sources have been chosen with a number of criteria in mind, namely, the coverage of countries, comparability, availability, documentation, computerization, and timeliness. In *ideal* cases the sources contain statistics for all countries of the world or at least all major countries, the statistics are adjusted to international standards and definitions, the sources are readily available to the public at a reasonable price, the sources contain definitions of terms and information on how the data were collected, the data are available in machine-readable as well as published form, and the data series are updated regularly.

Not all the sources selected meet all six criteria. Many data series compiled by agencies of the United Nations, for example, are computerized but are not yet available in a form that can be used on a personal computer. Also, data distributed by the major international organizations often are not timely. It takes six to nine months to compile data after the reference year, and as much as a year or more to prepare the publications and release them to the public. Usually there is a trade-off: the more countries covered in a given source, the longer it takes to compile and publish the data.

In the last section of this chapter a few key bibliographies and other reviews are identified that will help the reader locate additional sources and will provide a guide to the latest materials available.

At the end of the chapter, the full name and address is given for each of the principal institutions and publishers producing international statistics.

Population and Health

There are three principal organizations concerned with the collection and analysis of demographic statistics. The United Nations and the U.S. Bureau of the Census compile independent estimates of population and the major determinants of population growth for all countries of the world. The two organizations share internal studies and other information on methodologies so their published data are quite similar. The Population Reference Bureau, located in Washington D.C., is a source of timely and authoritative studies on how and why populations are changing.

International demographic statistics can be acquired on computer diskette from the Population Reference Bureau. Data are available on tape from the Center for International Research of the U.S. Bureau of the Census and from the U.N. Department of International Economic and Social Affairs (UNDIESA).

Size and Growth of Population; Age and Sex Composition; Urban and Rural Distribution

There are two basic sources of population statistics published by the United Nations: estimates and projections prepared by the U.N. Population Division and official statistics collected by the U.N. Statistical Office; both of these units are part of UNDIESA.

Every two years the Population Division of UNDIESA produces an updated set of population estimates and projections for all major countries, regions, continents, and the world. The 1986 report, *World Population Prospects: Estimates and Projections as Assessed in 1984* (ST/ESA/SER.A/98), contains tables by subject covering: total population and annual rates of change, crude birth and death rates, total fertility rates, and life expectancy and infant mortality. Data are provided for three population projection alternatives or variants: high, medium, and low, covering five-year intervals from 1950 to 2025. A fourth alternative based on constant fertility is not shown in the tables, but the data for it are available on tape, along with the entire database.

Geographic coverage includes estimates and projections for the world, the developed and less-developed regions, 8 areas, 24 regions, and 210 countries. Key series by country include estimates and projections for total population, male and female, major age groups, births and deaths, fertility rates, infant mortality, urban and rural population, and life expectancy.

For estimates and projections of urban and rural populations by country and statistics on the world's largest cities, see *Estimates and Projections of Urban, Rural, and City Populations, 1950-2025: The 1982 Assessment* (ST/ESA/SER.R/58) and *The Prospects of World Urbanization, Revised as of 1984-85* (ST/ESA/SER.A/101). These publications are also produced by the U.N. Population Division and are available on tape.

Official national sources are compiled by the Statistical Office of the U.N. Department of International Economic and Social Affairs and are published in the annual *Demographic Yearbook*. Updates are released in the quarterly *Population and Vital Statistics Report*. Each edition of the *Yearbook* contains tables titled: world summary, population, natality, fetal mortality, infant and maternal mortality, and general mortality. Statistics are also included on special topics such as marriage and divorce (1982) and the population census (1983).

The Center for International Research of the U.S. Bureau of the Census produces country, regional, and world demographic data that are similar in coverage to those of the U.N. but give a clearer indication of the sources and methods used to prepare the estimates. See, for example, *World Population, 1985: Recent Demographic Estimates for the Countries and Regions of the World*.

International Migration

Finding good statistics on international migration is very difficult. For a review of historical data, see the U.N. Department of International Economic and Social Affair's *Trends and Characteristics of International Migration Since 1950* (ST/ESA/SER.A/64), published in 1979. It contains an extensive review and analysis of migration by region, including political migrations and refugee movements. Tables on immigrants and emigrants and data on foreign-born populations are prepared for selected countries. A revised edition of this publication is being prepared. For the estimates of international migration by country that are used to prepare total population projections, see *World Population Prospects*. Refugees are by definition temporary migrants and are therefore not counted in migration statistics. The monthly periodical *Refugees*, published by the U.N. High Commissioner for Refugees (UNHCR), is a useful source of current information on refugee movements.

Life Expectancy; Mortality; Disease

World Health Statistics Annual, published by the World Health Organization (WHO), is a principal source of international statistics on health. It contains official statistics, analysis of problems and trends, and a review of policies and plans. The 1986 edition includes sections on vital statistics and life tables, causes of death by country (with data for only one African country,

Mauritius), a global overview, and an evaluation of the WHO global health strategy. *World Health Statistics Quarterly*, also published by WHO, provides current updates and analyses of disease outbreaks and selected programs.

World Population Prospects is a better source than *World Health Statistics Annual* for time series data on life expectancy and infant mortality.

Economics

Since economics is so dominant in the field of public-use statistics, there are many sources of data on the topic. The sources do differ, and it is not always apparent where the statistics have originated. Nor is it always clear what modifications and adjustments have been made to data to make them comparable over time and among countries.

The list of sources given below is biased toward governmental and intergovernmental institutions because these organizations produce statistics for most countries of the world, provide documentation on how the data have been modified, and usually have professional staff available to help with questions by mail, phone, or in person. Even among governmental institutions (national, regional, and global), data will vary in terms of time periods covered, units of measure, currencies, deflators, estimating procedures used for non-reporting countries, and many other factors.

This section focuses on basic economic statistics and indicators, not analysis and projections, although many of the sources identified will include analysis of conditions and trends as well as providing data tables. Basic sources of national-level economic statistics are described first. For additional detail, see subsequent sections.

General
Probably the single most useful source of national economic statistics is *International Financial Statistics* (*IFS*) prepared and published by the International Monetary Fund in twelve monthly issues and an annual yearbook. The data cover 137 countries, with regional and world aggregates. In the annual yearbook, data are given for the past twenty to twenty-five years, together with estimates for 1950, 1955, and 1960 when available.

While the table layout is the same for all countries, some countries obviously submit considerably more detailed data than others. As a result, many series are specific to a given country. The basic annual table for Egypt, for example, includes 173 statistical series covering exchange rates, money and banking, interest rates, prices, international transactions (exports, imports, and balance of payments), government finance, and national accounts (GDP, public and private consumption, GNP, GDP in constant prices, GDP deflator, etc.). The major sources for the data are listed in the monthly report. Again using Egypt as the example, they are the *Economic Review* prepared by the Central Bank of Egypt and the *Monthly Bulletin of Foreign Trade* prepared by the Central Agency for Public Mobilization and Statistics. All data series in *IFS* are coded, allowing the user to make country comparisons. *IFS* is available on a computer tape, which is updated monthly and has annual supplements.

Another basic source is the U.N. *Statistical Yearbook* (*SY*). Published annually by the U.N. Statistical Office, it contains a wider selection of data tables than *IFS*, including national accounts, wages, prices and consumption, government sector statistics, balance of payments, finance, and development assistance. However, it is not as timely. Tables in *SY* are organized by topic, not by country as in *IFS*.

The U.N. Statistical Office also produces the *Monthly Bulletin of Statistics*, which provides the latest available figures on many of these same economic factors.

For key economic indicators of development, see the section on World Development Indicators in the World Bank's annual *World Development Report*, which is available both from the World Bank and from the publisher, Johns Hopkins University Press. It contains data for 128 countries. Included are statistics on GNP; inflation; growth and structure of production, consumption, and investment; structure of demand, manufacturing, trade, debt, debt service, and borrowing; development assistance; government expenditure; income distribution; and interest rates. Most indicators are given in terms of ratios, percentages, and growth rates. These tables are now available on diskette for use on a personal computer.

National Accounts

The basic source for national accounts statistics is *National Accounts Statistics: Main Aggregates and Detailed Tables*. It is an annual publication, compiled by the U.N. Statistical Office in New York City and released to the public about three or four years after the reference year. It contains detailed national income and product account balances by country for the previous ten to twelve years. Statistical data include final consumption expenditures by type; production, income/outlays, and capital formation accounts by institution; and production by type of activity. Data are available in current and constant prices, and monetary values are expressed in national currencies.

The World Bank develops its own measure of gross national product. These data are reported, with very helpful documentation, in the *World Development Report* (*WDR*) and in the *World Bank Atlas*. The *WDR* and the *Atlas* are available from the World Bank; the *WDR* is also available from the publisher, Johns Hopkins University Press.

Debt

Perhaps the single most difficult economic problem of the 1980s is the rapid growth in public and private debt. As a result, there is rapid development of the statistics in this area, with new data series and new and expanded publications. *World Debt Tables: External Debt of Developing Countries* is prepared annually by the International Finance Division, International Economics Department of the World Bank. *World Debt Tables* contains both a statistical compendium and an analysis of the debt situation. Data are compiled through the Bank's Debt Reporting Service. Statistics are reported on long-term public debt for sixty-nine countries. The Bank compiles preliminary data or makes its own estimates for thirty-six countries. Supplements to *World Debt Tables* are published throughout the year.

The data series in *World Debt Tables* are organized by country. Statistics include debt outstanding, commitments, disbursements, principal repayments, net flows, interest payments, net transfers, total debt service, and principal ratios or indicators such as debt outstanding as a percentage of GNP and total debt service as a percentage of GNP. For many

countries, data on the amount of projected public debt and total debt service are also provided, and some countries provide data on private non-guaranteed debt as well. Data on computer tape are available for historical series from 1970-1986 and projected payments on long-term debt for 1987-1996.

The Organization for Economic Cooperation and Development (OECD) prepares the *External Debt of Developing Countries* and *Geographical Distribution of Financial Flows to Developing Countries*. Both provide statistics on the flow of funds from countries that are members of OECD's Development Assistance Committee. Included are statistics on official development assistance and total resource flows for more than a hundred developing countries.

Prices and Trade

To monitor and analyze international trade, it is necessary to have data on the type and amount of goods traded (exported and imported) and the prices at which the transactions are made. From this information, the value of trade can be calculated, summed, and compared with other economic variables.

Commodity Trade and Price Trends is prepared annually by the Commodity Studies and Projections Division of the World Bank. It provides price indices in current and constant U.S. dollars for fifty-five commodities covering foods, non-food agricultural products, fuels, metals, and minerals. More than one price index is given for many of these commodities. The deflator used is the manufacturing unit value index, which provides an approximation of the true purchasing power of primary commodities over time.

Basic international trade statistics are found in Volume I (*Trade by Country*) and Volume II (*Trade by Commodity*) of the *International Trade Statistics Yearbook*, compiled by the U.N. Statistical Office in the Department of International Economic and Social Affairs. Volume I contains statistical time series for traded commodities, organized by country for 154 countries for the years 1975-1984. In the latest edition, the table on Egypt, for example, contains data on the value of trade between Egypt and its major trading partners and on the amount (by weight and value) of major imports and exports. The commodities listed are classified by the Standard International Trade

Classification (SITC). Volume II contains commodity tables that indicate world trade in selected commodities, at the three-, four-, and five-digit SITC. Computerized data on trade for a given set of countries and a given set of commodities can be purchased on tape directly from the U.N. Statistical Office.

A third source, which provides summary indicators for trade and prices, is the *Yearbook of International Commodity Statistics*, compiled by the U.N. Conference on Trade and Development. It provides disaggregated time series at the world, regional, and country levels for trade in principal agricultural commodities and minerals. Part I provides data on the share of primary commodities as a percentage of all merchandise trade (exports and imports) for all countries. Part II includes data on the quantity and value of imports and exports, in current U.S. dollars, for all countries.

For additional trade data, see sections in this chapter on agriculture, forestry, fisheries, and energy.

Labor

The International Labour Organization (ILO) in Geneva, Switzerland, provides a detailed set of estimates and projections for the economically active population in all countries of the world. These data are compiled in a five-volume set entitled *Economically Active Population Estimates and Projections, 1950-2025*. The latest edition, the third in a series, was completed in 1985. The volumes contain statistics on all the employed and unemployed and those looking for work for the first time. Included in the data are employers, self-employed, salaried employees, wage earners, unpaid family workers, members of producer's cooperatives, and members of the armed forces. For each country, details are provided on the sex composition and age (at five-year intervals) of the labor force. Volume I covers Asia; Volume II, Africa; Volume III, Latin America; and Volume IV, Northern America, Europe, Oceania, and the U.S.S.R. Volume V is a world summary. A computer tape for the entire database can be ordered directly from ILO.

The annual *Yearbook of Labour Statistics* from the ILO provides updated information on employment issues and unemployment.

Industry

The *Industrial Statistics Yearbook* is published annually by the U.N. Statistical Office. Volume I, *General Industrial Statistics*, contains data on more than ninety countries for five recent years. Principal series are: number of establishments, number of employees, wages and salaries, output, costs, value added, capital, inventories, and index numbers of industrial production. All monetary series are given in local currency. Detail at the three- and four-digit level are given for all mining and quarrying, manufacturing, and electricity industries. Volume I also provides index numbers of industrial production and employment worldwide.

Volume II, *Commodity Production Statistics*, gives world production figures for a standard list of 530 commodities, with coverage of up to 200 countries.

Other Sources

There are a number of other sources of basic economic statistics and indicators that may be more timely, cheaper, easier to find, and more detailed than the summary tables produced by the U.N. Statistical Office and other U.N. agencies.

Each of the regional U.N. Economic Commissions prepares a statistical yearbook that, in addition to providing considerable detail, contains listings of national sources. See, for example, the *Statistical Yearbook for Asia and the Pacific*, compiled by the Economic and Social Commission for Asia and the Pacific. Comparable yearbooks are available from the Economic Commissions for Latin America and the Caribbean, for Western Asia, for Asia and the Pacific, for Europe, and for Africa.

The *Handbook of Economic Statistics: A Reference Aid* is prepared by the U.S. Central Intelligence Agency and is particularly useful for finding economic indicators of the major communist countries: U.S.S.R., Bulgaria, Poland, East Germany, Hungary, Rumania, China, Albania, Cambodia, Cuba, Laos, North Korea, Vietnam, and Yugoslavia.

The Organization for Economic Cooperation and Development provides data in published and computerized form about national accounts, labor force, foreign trade, industrial activity, and short-term indicators for the major industrialized countries.

Politics and Security

For information on politics and security, public authorities are not always the best source. They are reluctant to report accurate and timely figures on political demonstrations, riots, strikes, armed attacks, civilian and military fatalities, and military advisors and armed forces stationed abroad. Yet, because military and related expenditures are such an important component of central government budgets, organizations that monitor government expenditures, such as the International Monetary Fund, are able to collect some reliable data on these matters. These figures can be used to indicate the extent to which a nation's economy is dominated by the military sector. Other statistics, such as deaths in war and even the number and extent of armed conflicts, are collected by the press, historians, political scientists, and peace and defense groups. The sources listed and described below come from all of the above groups.

For the past couple of decades, the single most authoritative source of data and analysis on military affairs has been *World Armaments and Disarmament*, prepared by the Stockholm International Peace Research Institute in Stockholm, Sweden, and published by Oxford University Press. Recent editions contain review articles and data tables on nuclear and space weapons, chemical and biological warfare, military expenditures and the arms trade (with time series data on military expenditures as a percentage of gross domestic product), and developments in arms control. Topics are not treated consistently from year to year, so the reader has to consult the readers' guide and other indexes to find related statistics.

World Military Expenditures and Arms Transfers is an annual publication of the U.S. Arms Control and Disarmament Agency. It is a particularly good source for time series and complete country coverage. Tables provide data for the world, regions, and all countries on military expenditures and armed forces. Also included are indicators of military expenditures on a per capita basis as a percentage of gross national product and central government expenditures. Other tables cover arms transfers, both imports and exports, and arms as a

percentage of total imports. A separate table provides data on the value and type of equipment sold to each country by each of the world's major arms suppliers.

The most popular source of data and analysis in this field is *World Military and Social Expenditures*, prepared by Ruth Leger Sivard and colleagues at World Priorities. She compares the costs of producing, maintaining, and using military hardware with unmet social needs around the world. Current statistics are provided in the following areas: (a) military forces abroad for both the United States and allies and the Soviet Union and allies; (b) the nuclear powers, nuclear weapons capability, and nuclear power reactors; (c) official violent repression against citizens, with countries rated by none, some, and frequent; and limitations on the right to vote, with countries rated by none, some, and no vote; (d) wars by number of deaths of 100,000 or more: the 1985 edition provides a listing of all wars in the 20th century, with the number of civilians, military personnel, and total killed; and (e) military expenditures, including the number of armed forces, cost of military, arms imports, and international peace keeping; and foreign assistance.

A fourth source is the *World Handbook of Political and Social Indicators*. The third edition was prepared by Charles Lewis Taylor and David Jodice and published by Yale University Press. Volume I, *Cross-National Attributes and Rates of Change*, contains interesting and controversial data such as a political rights index compiled and maintained by Freedom House. Countries are coded with scores ranging from one (highest degree of liberty) to seven (lowest degree of liberty) and based on seven different indicators of a country's political system. (Among the factors considered are these: Does the system give persons an opportunity to participate in the electoral process? Does the system permit the leader to be voted out of office? Does the system permit citizens to elect their own leaders and representatives? Does the constitution support democratic elections?) Included are a civil rights index, measures of political and economic discrimination, potential separatism, voter turnout, and other statistics.

Volume II, *Political Protest and Government Change*, contains less subjective data but is just as valuable. Tables with data that rate and rank countries are given on the following topics: protest and regime-support demonstrations, political strikes, riots, armed attacks, assassinations, political executions, and transfers of executive power. Also included are more traditional statistics on national elections. A valuable feature of the *World Handbook* is the extensive and careful presentation of how the data were compiled, coded, and analyzed. Although the statistics are presented in a way that appeals to more professional political scientists than to a general audience, these volumes are virtually the only source of summarized information on these topics.

Transportation

Although transportation is usually treated in national economies as a single sector, the actual statistical information comes from the individual modes—roads, airways, railways, waterways, and pipelines—with considerable diversity in the kinds of data collected and the methods of collection used for each mode. This diversity is evident at the international level as well. Despite these differences, statistical coverage for most countries is available on basic transportation facilities and functions: extent of the infrastructure, number and type of vehicles in operation, the number and amount of passengers and freight transported, transportation safety (usually measured in the accident rate), and finances and taxes related to transportation.

For those modes of transportation for which there is a strong international governmental organization, it is relatively easy to locate reliable data because that organization will have a mandate to collect and distribute basic statistics. An example is the information on aviation compiled by the International Civil Aviation Organization. When such an organization is not present, as is the case in railroad transportation, the data are more difficult to find and more limited in country and topic coverage.

The U.N. *Statistical Yearbook* contains a useful section on transportation. It provides summary statistics for up to a hundred countries on railway traffic, motor vehicles in use, shipping fleets, goods loaded and unloaded, and civil aviation. For many countries, the U.N. Statistical Office publishes summary statistics

based on original data collected by the U.N. regional economic commissions from national governments and private sources. More detailed and more timely coverage of national data is often available in the annual and biannual *Statistical Yearbook*s produced by these commissions.

Other useful sources of basic transportation statistics are the Area Handbook series prepared by the Foreign Area Studies program of American University and sold by the U.S. Government Printing Office. A more timely source is the Country Profile series supported by the Office of Foreign Disaster Assistance of the U.S. Agency for International Development. This series, however, covers only about fifty USAID-assisted countries.

Airways
Civil Aviation Statistics of the World is produced annually by the International Civil Aviation Organization (ICAO), located in Montreal. This volume is the principal source of statistics for aircraft (number in operation, size, hours flown, manufacturer and type, number produced and on order), pilots (number of active licenses), safety (number of accidents and fatalities), airline fleets (names and size by country), traffic (passenger-kilometers, ton-kilometers), and finance (airline revenues and expenditures). Data are included on non-scheduled operations as well as scheduled flights, but not for military air activities. The statistics are arranged by regions and individual countries and by major airlines within countries.

Over a hundred individual countries plus seventeen countries with multinational carriers regularly report statistics to the ICAO. Most series are available for the last ten years. Statistics back to 1946 can be requested. The ICAO also publishes the *Digest of Statistics*, which contains considerably more detail on traffic, finances and personnel, airport traffic, etc. A data tape at this level of detail is available from the ICAO.

A separate publication entitled *World Air Transport Statistics* is compiled annually by the International Air Transport Association, the airline industry group. It provides more information on member airlines than the ICAO does, but country coverage is not as extensive.

Roadways

The International Road Federation (IRF), located in Geneva and Washington, D.C., annually prepares *World Road Statistics*. Principal statistics included are: networks (extent and type of roadways—superhighways, highways, paved roads, unpaved roads); production and export of vehicles (cars, buses, trucks, tractors); vehicles in use (cars, buses, trucks, tractors, two-wheel vehicles); road traffic (volume in million kilometers traveled per year); accidents (number of accidents, persons injured and killed); and taxes and expenditures (cost of road construction and maintenance, import taxes, and local assessments). Data are available for more than a hundred countries for the past five years. More detailed statistics are available for the industrialized countries in Europe and North America from the Economic Commission for Europe in *Statistics of Road Traffic Accidents in Europe* and the *Annual Bulletin of Transport Statistics for Europe*.

Railways

For statistics on length of public railways, see Jane's *World Railways*. Data are included for almost all countries. Information is also given for the number of engines and freight and passenger cars in use. For statistics on railway traffic (millions of passenger-kilometers and millions of ton-kilometers), see Table 174, in the 1982 U.N. *Statistical Yearbook*, released in 1985.

Waterways

The Defense Mapping Agency in Washington, D.C. prepares the *World Port Index*, which provides basic information on the location, characteristics, facilities, and services of all major ports, shipping facilities, and oil terminals throughout the world. Port data listings are organized in geographic sequence following major coast lines and in alphabetical order by name of the port. The ports are not listed separately by country, and it can be a tedious operation to compile national statistics.

Lloyd's of London compiles data on the world's merchant shipping fleet. These data are included in Table 176 of the 1982 U.N. *Statistical Yearbook*. Data are organized by country (flag of registration), region, and the world for the total fleet and for oil tankers and ore and bulk carriers.

For statistics on the amount of material and goods transported and the number of vessels entering and clearing ports, see tables in the U.N. *Statistical Yearbook*. The total amount of goods loaded and unloaded is categorized as petroleum (crude and products) and dry cargo and is reported in thousand metric tons for countries, regions, and the world. Estimates are based on data collected from external trade statistics. The number of vessels entering and clearing ports is given in thousand net registered and includes the sum of foreign and domestic merchant vessels entering with cargo and those cleared with cargo to a foreign port. Both tables include data for approximately eighty to a hundred countries and cover the years 1979-82 and 1970-82 respectively.

Energy

After the oil embargo of 1973-74, a number of important changes occurred in the development and dissemination of energy statistics. Governments and international organizations became much more involved in collecting and distributing data about energy. In the United States, the Department of Energy established the Energy Information Administration, which greatly expanded the publication of domestic and international energy statistics and forecasts. During the late 1970s and early 1980s, they established the *Annual Energy Review*, the *Monthly Energy Review*, and the *International Energy Annual*. The U.N. Statistical Office in New York continued to produce its *Energy Statistics Yearbook* and became much more aggressive at preparing estimates for countries when official data were not available or were inconsistent. The International Energy Agency (a part of the Organization for Economic Cooperation and Development), the European Communities, and the regional commissions of the United Nations (ECE, ECLA, ECA, ECWA, and ESCAP) also greatly expanded their collection and publication efforts. During the 1980s increased efforts have been made toward making these data sets more consistent.

Industry went in the opposite direction. Prior to 1973-74, all the major oil companies (Shell, Exxon, BP, Texaco, etc.) produced estimates of world and regional energy production and consumption, and a few produced projections to 1990, 2000, and beyond. Now, though, only British Petroleum continues to produce and distribute a global review of energy in its *BP Statistical Review of World Energy*. The industry associations and major publishers, such as the American Petroleum Institute, PennWell Publishers, and Gulf Publishers, focus their attention more directly on fuel-specific information, leaving the global estimates and projections to governments and various research institutes. The American Petroleum Institute continues to produce its timely *Basic Petroleum Data Book*, and PennWell Publishers produces the weekly *Oil and Gas Journal*, the *Oil and Gas Journal Data Book: Annual Statistics, Surveys, Indicators, and Index*, and its annual *International Petroleum Encyclopedia*. However, these publications appeal more to analysts working on specific problems of finding and producing energy resources than they do to those who study energy consumption or overall national and international energy policies.

There are three sources for international energy statistics that can be used to meet most basic needs: the *BP Statistical Review of World Energy* (*BP-SRWE*), prepared annually by British Petroleum; the *International Energy Annual* (*IEA*), prepared annually by the U.S. Energy Information Administration; and the *Energy Statistics Yearbook* (*ESY*), prepared annually by the U.N. Statistical Office in New York.

The *BP Statistical Review of World Energy* contains sections on oil, natural gas, hydroelectricity, nuclear energy, coal, and primary energy consumption. Unfortunately it does not list sources of information, but it does contain conversion factors and definitions. It provides ten years of data, covers only the most important producing and consuming countries, and is the most timely of the three publications.

The *International Energy Annual* contains sections on: world primary energy production in BTUs and in physical units; world petroleum supply, dispositions, and refining capacity; international petroleum prices; world natural gas supply and disposition; world coal supply and disposition; and energy reserves. A complete list of sources, a table of conversion factors, and a glossary are also provided. The *IEA* goes somewhat beyond the *BP-SRWE* in country coverage and statistical detail. It also lists the

names of staff to call for help. A computer tape is available but contains only the published data from recent *IEA* publications.

The U.N. *Energy Statistics Yearbook* is by far the most comprehensive of the three sources. It contains detailed statistics for more than 180 countries, 7 regions, and the world as a whole. Obviously, data are not available for all variables for all countries. The *ESY* gathers data from all national governments but also uses data from the Food and Agriculture Organization, the International Atomic Energy Agency, the International Energy Agency and Nuclear Energy Agency of the OECD, the Organization of Petroleum Exporting Countries, the Economic Commission for Europe, the U.S. Department of Energy, and the World Energy Conference. Statistics are available for the most recent four years, and each edition of the *ESY* contains revisions and updates for the previous four to five years. For political reasons the U.N. usually accepts the data submitted by a country, and as a result some figures are erroneous.

Tables in the *ESY* cover the following topics: (a) commercial energy: production, trade, and consumption, given in physical and scientific units, with a separate column for total requirements, including estimates for traditional fuels such as fuelwood, dung, bagasse, and other biomass; (b) solid fuels: production, trade, and consumption of coal, hard coal, lignite, coke, briquettes, peat, and fuelwood; (c) liquid fuels: production, trade, and consumption of crude petroleum, aviation gasoline, motor gasoline, kerosene, jet fuels, gas-diesel, and residual fuels; (d) gaseous fuels: production, trade, and consumption of natural gas; (e) electrical energy: installed capacity of electricity, trade and consumption of electricity, production of steam and hot water; and (f) nuclear fuels, energy resources, and prices: uranium production; fossil fuel, nuclear, and hydrologic resources; and crude petroleum prices.

Each edition contains definitions, conversion factors, and, in the 1986 edition (1984 *ESY*), a complete bibliography of national data sources. A computer tape by the same name is available from the United Nations Statistical Office. It contains more detailed data than found in the printed *ESY*, with time series going back to 1950. A big advantage of this and other United Nations sources is that they provide longer time series than other sources.

Consistency, though, can be a problem because of the annual revisions of the data.

Resources and Reserves

The principal source for updated estimates of coal, petroleum, natural gas, hydroelectric, and uranium reserves and resources is the World Energy Conference. For summarized data, see the *BP-SRWE*, the *IEA*, and the *ESY*. PennWell's *Oil and Gas Journal* compiles country-by-country estimates annually for petroleum and natural gas reserves. *World Oil*, published by Gulf Publishers, produces annual worldwide estimates of petroleum and natural gas reserves, including ones in the Eastern bloc countries.

Production, Trade, and Prices

For summary data, see the *BP-SRWE*, the *IEA*, and the *ESY*. The Energy Information Administration also produces *International Energy Prices*. The International Energy Agency of the OECD produces *Quarterly Oil and Gas Statistics, Annual Oil and Gas Statistics and Main Historical Series*, and *Energy Prices and Taxes*.

OECD's Nuclear Energy Agency produces *Uranium: Resources, Production and Demand* and *Nuclear Power and Fuel Cycle Data in OECD Member Countries: Summary Report*. For data on nuclear power generation in all countries, see the International Atomic Energy Agency's annual *Nuclear Power Reactors in the World* and *Operating Experience with Nuclear Power Stations in Member States*.

The Food and Agriculture Organization of the United Nations (FAO) has produced detailed country estimates of fuelwood in its Forestry Paper no. 42, *Fuelwood Supplies in Developing Countries*.

The best single source of statistics and summary information on petroleum exploration, drilling, transportation, and processing for all major producing countries is the *International Petroleum Encyclopedia* from PennWell Publishers.

Consumption

On the topic of energy consumption, the *ESY*, the *IEA*, and the *SRWE* are again the best sources. For estimates of energy use by sector, see *Energy Balances of OECD Countries* and *Energy Balances of Developing Countries*, both

published irregularly by the International Energy Agency. A relatively new publication, *Energy Balances for Latin America*, was compiled by the Latin American Energy Organization (OLADE) in 1985 and covers twenty-five countries in the region. This report updates to 1982 and backdates to 1970 materials covered in a previous volume published by OLADE.

Water

There is no single international governmental organization whose purpose it is to collect, analyze, and report information, in a timely manner, on the world's water resources and their use. The UNESCO Division of Water Sciences comes closest to filling this role, but its focus is more on studies than on provision of up-to-date, country-specific data. As a result, international water statistics are often problematic. Information may be difficult to compare or interpret because of variation in definitions, data collection methods, and time periods of observation. Furthermore, trend statistics on some topics, such as water withdrawal and use, are rarely available from countries other than the industrialized nations.

There are three basic published sources of statistics and studies on international and global water resources and water use: M. I. L'vovich, *World Water Resources and their Future* (Mysl' P. H. Moscow, 1974), English translation ed. Raymond L. Nace (American Geophysical Union, 1979); Frits van der Leeden, *Water Resources of the World, Selected Statistics* (Water Information Center, Inc., 1975); and *World Water Balance and Water Resources of the Earth* (U.S.S.R. Committee for the International Hydrological Decade, 1974), English translation (UNESCO Press, 1978). A fourth source, J. Forkasiewicz and J. Margat, "Tableau Mondial de Donnees Nationales D'economie de l'Eau, Resources et Utilisation" (Orleans, France: Departement Hydrogeologie, 1980) is an unpublished monograph in French that provides a summary of statistics on water availability, withdrawal, and use by sector and includes recent estimates for individual countries. For access to these data, see *World Resources* reports published by the World Resources Institute. Alternative national sources of data for water resources, availability, withdrawal, and use are listed in van der Leeden's publication.

Water Resources

Basic statistics on the following aspects of the world's water balance can be found in the indicated tables in L'vovich: the hydrosphere, Table 1; fresh water of the hydrosphere (glaciers, groundwater, lakes and reservoirs, soil moisture, water vapor, and rivers), Table 2; annual world water balance (precipitation, runoff, and evapotranspiration), Table 9; water balance of river basins (area, precipitation, runoff, and evapotranspiration), Table 13; and water balance and freshwater resources of the continents, Table 20.

In Table 25, L'vovich provides detailed estimates of freshwater resources of the principal countries in the world. Information is given on area, population, precipitation, total, groundwater, and surface runoff (in cubic kilometers per annum), evapotranspiration, and transit streamflows for 156 countries and regions. In Figures 40 and 41, L'vovich provides estimates for the total and groundwater runoff per capita for all major countries. Figures are given in thousands of cubic meters per year. These figures were used in G. O. Barney, ed., *The Global 2000 Report to the President*, (Washington, D.C.: U.S. Government Printing Office, 1980) to project the adequacy of freshwater.

See the UNESCO publication of the U.S.S.R. Committee report for detailed data on the water cycle and water balances by continent and the world as a whole.

Water Availability and Use

Water availability is usually measured in terms of stable streamflow or stable runoff. It excludes flood waters and water stored in deep aquifers but includes both internal and transit flows. Withdrawal is a measure of water taken from a surface or underground source and conveyed to the place of use. *World Resources 1987* and *World Resources 1988-89*, published by World Resources Institute and the International Institute for Environment and Development, provide statistics on total and per capita availability and total and per capita withdrawal by country. Data are also given on sectoral use: by the public in homes and commercial establishments, by self-supplied industry, by electricity generation facilities for cooling, and by agriculture for irrigation. Most of these statistics were compiled by J. Forkasiewicz and J. Margat from various national and international studies.

Land Use

Demand for global, regional, and national land-use and land-cover statistics is growing. Added to traditional needs for such information for national security and food production are new needs for global climate modeling, deforestation and desertification monitoring, biological conservation, coastal development, and the exploration of resources—renewable and non-renewable—across the earth and below the seas. Unfortunately, currently available, published statistics do not meet these needs very well.

One problem is that the statistics on land use, particularly year-to-year estimates, can be very unreliable. Accuracy of the data depends on the timeliness of agricultural censuses and other land-use and land-cover surveys conducted by national governments, but in some cases these surveys may be ten or more years out of date. The integration of remotely sensed data with administrative and survey statistics should lead to major improvements in the next few years.

The Food and Agriculture Organization (FAO) in its annual *Production Yearbook* compiles a set of land-use statistics for all countries, continents, and the world for seven land-use categories: total area, total land area, arable land, permanent crops, permanent pasture, forest and woodlands, and other land. Inland water can be estimated as the residual between total area and total land area, but this figure is not always very reliable. The last category, other land, is a catchall and includes urban areas, roads and ports, national parks and other protected areas, deserts, tundra, wetlands, etc. Statistics are given in thousand hectares for the most recent year and selected previous years. Data for all years from 1960 through 1985 are available on a tape by the same name from FAO. The *Production Yearbook* is available from Unipub and from Bernan-Unipub.

Elaine Matthews in "Global Vegetation and Land Use: New High Resolution Data Bases for Climate Studies," *Journal of Climate and Applied Meteorology* 23 (1983): 474-487, provides estimates from pre-agricultural times to the present for forest, woodland, shrubland, tundra, grassland, and desert, using the UNESCO classification of 225 vegetative types. Data in the paper are given in percentage of land changed to cultivation, but estimates of actual area are available from the author.

R. A. Houghton et al., in "Changes in the Carbon Content of Terrestrial Biota and Soils between 1860 and 1980, A Net Release of Carbon Dioxide to the Atmosphere," *Ecological Monographs* 53 (1983): 235-262, has prepared decade-by-decade estimates for forests and woodlands, grasslands and pasture, and croplands for ten continental regions. Data are given in million hectares.

Recent trends in land use have been calculated from FAO and U.S. Department of Agriculture statistics by Francis Urban and Thomas Vollrath. Their publication, *Patterns and Trends in World Agricultural Land Use* (FAER-198), is available from the U.S. Government Printing Office.

James Tucker and colleagues at NASA's Goddard Space Flight Center have used the NOAA satellite AVHRR data (Advanced Very High Resolution Radiometer) to develop a vegetative index that discriminates global changes in vegetative cover from season to season and from year to year. Statistics showing trends by country and subregion for the years 1980-85 are in the process of being analyzed for future publication. When they are available they will appear in the World Resources Institute's *World Resources* reports, published by Basic Books.

World Resources 1988-89, available from the World Resources Institute and Basic Books, contains summary tables on land use from most of the above sources.

Information about statistics of specific land-use topics is included in other sections of this chapter. See "Forestry" for sources of statistics on tropical forests, "Environmental Quality" for data sources on protected areas, and "Food and Agriculture" regarding more detailed statistics on irrigated areas.

Food and Agriculture

There are two principal sources of agricultural statistics: the U.N. Food and Agriculture Organization (FAO) in Rome and the U.S. Department of Agriculture (USDA) in Washington, D.C. A study comparing the two data sources was published in 1980 by the International Food Policy Research Institute. The report, prepared by L. A. Paulino and S. S. Tseng, is entitled *A Comparative Study of FAO and USDA Data on Production, Area, and Trade of Major Food Staples.* The major differences discerned between the two sources are: country coverage for production (161 for FAO, 124 for USDA); time reference period (calender year for FAO, split or harvest year for USDA); and procedures for modifying official country statistics (FAO is more likely to accept official statistics; USDA is more likely to adjust country statistics that are assessed as unreliable or historically inconsistent).

The choice of which source to use depends on a user's specific needs and the availability of the data. Because FAO provides data for more countries and for more topics, its publications and data tapes are given more attention in this review than are USDA materials.

In addition to FAO and USDA, the United Nations regional commissions, OECD, and the European Communities publish detailed statistics on agricultural production, trade, prices, and inputs.

Perhaps the single most useful volume of agricultural statistics is the annual FAO report *Country Tables: Basic Data on the Agricultural Sector.* This important publication is not one of FAO's standard yearbooks, and it is often omitted from reading lists. *Country Tables* provides key indicators for 150 countries, regions, and world totals, covering the period 1961-86. Indicators include agricultural, fish, and forest production, measured in thousand metric tons per annum; population and agricultural labor force; exports and imports in U.S. dollars; major commodities; trade indices; food supply and consumption in calories, protein, and fats, and calories as a percentage of requirements; means of production (tractors in use, fertilizer used); and agricultural gross domestic product as a percentage of total gross domestic product. Two-page country tables are surprisingly complete and up to date. They contain the latest figures available and annual rates of change for the periods 1961-70, 1971-80, and 1981-85.

Production and Trade

The FAO *Production Yearbook*, prepared annually by the Statistics Division, provides detailed figures for the latest ten years for 160 countries, major geographic regions, and the world. Included are annual estimates by weight for over seventy separate crops (e.g., wheat, rice, barley, bananas) and livestock (number of animals slaughtered and dressed weight). Also included are index numbers of agricultural production (total, crop, livestock, total cereals) and of per capita production. Prices and index numbers are included in Table IX. The *Production Yearbook* is also available on computer tape and contains values for all years back to 1961.

Data on agricultural production and trade are also available in *Prices of Agricultural Products and Selected Inputs in Europe and North America, 1985/86*, ECE/FAO Price Review no. 36 (United Nations, 1987). For longer time series and more detailed statistics, the best sources are individual reports on crops and commodities from FAO, USDA, and industry associations. Examples are the *Sugar Yearbook* from the International Sugar Organization, the International Tea Committee's *Annual Bulletin of Statistics*, and *World Wheat Statistics* from the International Wheat Council.

The *FAO Trade Yearbook*, also an annual publication, provides statistics on quantity and value for 120 commodities over the past six years. Also included are data on trade of inputs (tractors, fertilizers, and pesticides). Separate country tables are available for imports and exports, measured in physical quantities and valued in current U.S. dollars. A separate data tape by the same name is available from FAO.

Inputs

No single publication provides full statistical coverage of fertilizers, pesticides, machinery, land, irrigation, labor, and food chemicals, but data on specific agricultural inputs can be found in a number of sources.

Fertilizers: FAO produces a separate report on one important input, fertilizers. The *FAO Fertilizer Yearbook* provides annual statistics on production, trade, consumption, and available supply of nitrogenous, phosphate, and potash fertilizers. Coverage in thousand metric tons is available for about 180 countries. Data are given as consumption per hectare of agricultural area,

arable land, and permanent cropland, and as consumption per capita. Separate country tables provide statistics on fertilizer production, imports, exports, and consumption. Table VI provides information on prices and subsidies. A data tape of the *Fertilizer Yearbook* is available from FAO.

Pesticides and Machinery: Table VII of the *Production Yearbook* gives statistics on tractors in use and pesticide consumption by major type, such as chlorinated hydrocarbons and carbamates. Coverage of pesticide consumption is limited to a few countries.

Land, Irrigation, and Labor: Table I of the *Production Yearbook* is a good source for data on land and irrigated land, given in thousand hectares, as is Table II for data on population living on farms and farm labor. For detailed statistics on land tenure and land holdings, collected from national agricultural censuses, see the *Compendium of Social Statistics*, released about every four years by the U.N. Statistical Office in New York. The *World Resources* reports from World Resources Institute summarize the latest agricultural land distribution statistics for 146 countries.

Food Chemicals: The U.S. Food and Drug Administration's Center for Food Safety and Applied Nutrition has compiled a computer database of what might be described as "everything added to food in the United States." It also has a great deal of information about what is added to foods in other countries.

The database contains an inventory of 3,000 items including 300 direct-addition food additives, over 70 natural and synthetic color additives, 400-500 natural herbs and spices, 1,200 synthetic flavoring substances, 400 substances "Generally Recognized as Safe" (GRAS), and a number of processing aids and other miscellaneous food chemicals. The list at this time excludes environmental contaminants, pesticides, and chemicals migrating to food from food packaging.

For each of the entries, information is given on the preferred chemical name, synonyms, a Chemical Abstracts Service (CAS) Registry Number for unique identification, the Council of Europe (COE) identification number, the U.K. identifying designation, and—for natural herbs and spices—the Latin binomial name. The database also includes for each substance the number of any regulation (under Title 21 of the

U.S. Code of Federal Regulations) that authorizes use of that substance.

For a subset of 1,600 substances, the data base contains additional information on chemical structure, an FDA "minimum testing level," an inventory of international toxicological studies performed on the substance using animals, a highly condensed summary of the evaluated toxicological data, and the lowest dose level shown to cause adverse effects in animal studies.

The database project group has developed time series data on the number of pounds of each substance disappearing annually into the U.S. food supply. The statistics are collected from industry by the U.S. National Academy of Sciences under contract to the FDA. The primary database contains the current year information; a related database maintained by the Academy contains data for both current and previous years.

Comparison studies between U.S. per capita consumption and the per capita consumption in other industrialized countries have been made for selected substances. These studies suggest that, for a majority of substances, the U.S. consumption figures are good indicators of per capita consumption in the industrialized countries of both Europe and Asia.

The relative safety margins of many food additives in use in many countries can be evaluated by comparing the consumption data in the database (or more detailed consumption data from individual countries) with the threshold doses in the database.

FDA has published documentation in a paper entitled "FDA's Priority-Based Assessment of Food Additives: I. Preliminary Results" and in a handout describing the technical details of the field specifications for the database. Two additional papers have been published analyzing and summarizing these data. Printouts of parts of the database are made regularly. Reprints of the publications and printouts are available on request and for a modest fee.

Public access to magnetic tape copies of the database has not yet been regularized, but access is possible if the requesting letter states that "the request is being made under the provisions of the Freedom of Information (FOI) Act." Specialized printouts or magnetic tapes can be prepared for a

fee that depends on the amount of time and effort required.

Consumption

Consumption data, measured in terms of average food supply (calories, protein, fats, and calories consumed as a percentage of requirements), are available in Table VII of the FAO *Production Yearbook*. Complete definitions and detailed estimates of food consumption by type of food are published in FAO's *Food Balance Sheets 1979-81 Average*. Included are average amounts consumed per year (in kilograms) and per day (in grams) for cereals, roots and tubers, sugars, pulses, nuts and oilseeds, vegetables, fruit, meats, eggs, fish and seafood, milk, oils and fats, spices, and coffee, tea, and cocoa.

Other Agricultural Topics

In 1983 the Land and Water Division of FAO released a technical report entitled *Potential Population Supporting Capacities of Lands in the Developing World*. This study, carried out in cooperation with the International Institute for Applied Systems Analysis and the U.N. Fund for Population Activities, was an attempt to relate agricultural land, agricultural systems, and food production to food needs of the world's fastest growing populations. Chapter 3 of the summary report provides country and regional estimates and projections of population supported at different levels of food production with different levels of technology.

Agricultural policies and statistics on food aid are reviewed in *State of Food and Agriculture*, prepared annually by FAO, and *World Food Needs and Availabilities*, prepared annually by USDA with support from the U.S. Agency for International Development.

FAO produces a number of technical paper series that include important agricultural statistics. Among the series are: Animal Production and Health; Soils Bulletin; Plant Production and Protection Papers; Irrigation and Drainage Papers; Agricultural Services Bulletin; Food and Nutrition Papers; Fisheries; and Forestry. Single copies of papers from these series are often available free of charge from FAO. Another nice feature is that the complete list of titles for the past three to five years is listed on the back cover of each report.

Forestry

There are two major kinds of forestry data available, data about the forest itself and figures on production and trade.

Forest Land

The annual *Production Yearbook* of the Food and Agriculture Organization of the United Nations (FAO) contains estimates for forest land in hectares. These figures are derived indirectly as residuals from agricultural censuses and are most appropriate for use in analyzing long-term trends in forest land. However, because of the growing concern for the loss of tropical moist forest, particularly in developing countries, a number of attempts have been made in the past fifteen years to inventory forest land in more depth and with greater accuracy.

The most comprehensive effort has been the Tropical Forest Resource Assessment Project completed by FAO in 1980. Data for seventy-six tropical countries were originally published in the *Tropical Forest Reserves*, FAO Forestry Paper no. 30, (Rome: FAO, 1982). Areal statistics, given in hectares, included the extent of all forests and woodlands, managed closed forests (those with a management plan), and protected forests, as well as the extent of deforested land. Among the other data reported were the estimated rates of deforestation for the 1980s and the estimated rates of reforestation. Similar statistics on forests in temperate climatic zones were published in *Forest Resources 1980* (Rome: FAO, 1985).

Recent statistics on forest conditions such as wildlife, hunting, recreation, and watershed protection are available in *Forest Resources of the ECE Region (Europe, the U.S.S.R., North America)*, published in 1985 by the U.N. Economic Commission for Europe and FAO.

For a detailed critique of the FAO data on tropical forests and comparisons with other data collection efforts, see Alan Grainger, "Quantifying Changes in Forest Cover in the Humid Tropics: Overcoming Current Limitations," *Journal of World Forest Resource Management* 1 (1984): 3-23.

The FAO Forestry Resource Division has continued to release data for individual tropical countries as assessments and updates are completed. The most convenient source for this new material is Part IV, World Resource Data Tables, in the World Resources Institute's *World Resources 1988-89*, published by Basic Books.

Papers by Matthews and Houghton, referred to in the "Land Use" section of this chapter, also contain other estimates of long-term trends in forest land.

FAO and national governments are making increasing use of remote-sensing technologies to estimate forest cover and deforestation. For an overview of the use of remote sensing systems for monitoring changes in tropical forests, see Armand T. Joyce and Steven A. Sader, "The Use of Remotely Sensed Data for the Monitoring of Forest Changes in Tropical Areas" (Paper presented at the Twentieth International Symposium on Remote Sensing of the Environment, Nairobi, Kenya, December 4-10, 1986).

Forest Products

The annual FAO *Yearbook of Forest Products* is the principal source of time series statistics on production and trade of forest products. The 1984 *Yearbook*, released in 1986, includes annual data for twelve years, 1973-84, covering about 150 countries for forest products and between 50 and 80 countries for trade of each product.

Production statistics are given in thousand cubic meters of roundwood, fuelwood and charcoal, industrial roundwood, sawlogs and veneer logs, pulpwood and particles, wood resides, and other. Statistics are also available on processed timber (wood commodities) for sawn-wood, panels, paper, newsprint, etc. Imports and exports are measured both in quantity and value. All values are given in U.S. current dollars, along with exchange rates for local currencies. A standard computer tape entitled Yearbook of Forest Products can also be obtained from FAO.

The FAO also produces a biannual report on prices, *Forest Products Prices*. The latest edition was released in 1985 and covers the years 1965-1984. Recent projections of consumption and production of forest products have been published in *Forest Products: World Outlook Projections*, Forestry Paper no. 73 (Rome: FAO, 1986).

Fisheries

The principal source of statistics on fish catch, commodities, and trade is the Food and Agriculture Organization of the United Nations (FAO). The FAO Marine Resource Service compiles data from national governments, industry, and, most importantly, regional fishery organizations and makes this information available to the public in two volumes published annually, *Yearbook of Fishery Statistics: Catches and Landings* and *Yearbook of Fishery Statistics: Fishery Commodities*. While FAO is the most important source for fish catch statistics, information on marine and coastal resources is collected, compiled, and reported by many other organizations. Only references to a few sources of statistics on living resources are given in this brief review.

Fish Catch and Commodities

Catches and Landings provides ten years of data for nominal fish catch in metric tons per annum. Catch statistics are given for fifty-two species groups for twenty-seven fishing areas or fisheries around the world, including inland and marine waters, and for countries, regions, and the world. Data cover fin fish, crustaceans, molluscs, and aquatic plants. Separate country tables include data on catch for the most important species of the country. The U.S. National Marine Fishery Service (NMFS) also presents summary tables of world fish catch in its annual publication *Fisheries of the United States*.

Fishery Commodities provides country and region statistics on production, imports, and exports during a four-year period. Data are included for weight in metric tons per annum and for economic value in current U.S. dollars. Fish commodities include fish (fresh/frozen/smoked/etc.), crustaceans, fish oils, and fish meals. A separate table provides data on the average per capita consumption of fish by country and region over several years.

Living Marine Resources

Most fish are caught in coastal waters. Data on jurisdictional claims to these waters are published by the Office of the Special Representative of the U.N. Secretary General for the Law of the Sea in *Law of the Sea Bulletin*, no. 2 (March 1985). Statistics on length of coast line are given in the Central Intelligence Agency's *The World Factbook 1987*. For estimates of near-shore living resources (mangrove forests, coral reefs, and sea grass beds) and statistics on marine mammals (original abundance and current population counts and catch, covering both threatened and non-threatened species), see *World Resources 1986* and *World Resources 1987*, published by Basic Books.

Environmental Quality

Despite all the interest in and support for environmental policies and programs over the past two decades, the publication of international environmental statistics has been neglected. In the past two years, however, this situation has changed with the release of a number of reports and compendia by governmental and non-governmental organizations.

The most important of these is the *Environmental Data Report* (*EDR*), prepared for the United Nations Environment Programme (UNEP) by the Monitoring and Assessment Research Centre in London and published by Basil Blackwell. Released in June 1987, the *EDR* makes available to the public for the first time some of the key statistical data and trends from UNEP's Global Environmental Monitoring System (GEMS). GEMS is a collective effort among international organizations to monitor the world's environment in order to protect human health and conserve valuable natural resources. It provides coordination and some financial support to WHO, WMO, FAO, UNESCO, IUCN, and others who actually collect and analyze data.

The *EDR* is the first of a proposed biennial series. Topics covered include: environmental pollution, climate, natural resources, population/settlements, human health, energy, transport/tourism, wastes, natural disasters, accidents, national security, and international cooperation. Each section contains a brief analysis and detailed tables. Because environmental statistics are drawn from so many different sources, the compilers wisely have included detailed sources, definitions, and data qualifications.

The *World Resources* reports, prepared jointly by the World Resources Institute (WRI) and the International Institute for Environment and Development (IIED) and published by Basic Books, include a section titled "World Resource Data Tables." The strength of *World Resources 1986*, *World Resources 1987*, and *World Resources 1988-89* is the breadth of their coverage on renewable natural resources and on developing countries. When available, the compilers have included time series data for 146 countries, organized by region and continent. Sections include: basic economic indicators, population and health, human settlements, land use and cover, food and agriculture, forests and rangelands, wildlife and habitat, energy and minerals, fresh water, oceans and coasts, atmosphere and climate, and policies and institutions. Like the *EDR*, the *World Resources* reports contain extensive references and technical notes.

In 1985, in addition to its annual *State of the Environment Report*, the Organization for Economic Cooperation and Development (OECD) released an *Environmental Data Compendium 1985*. An update, *Environmental Data Compendium 1987*, followed two years later. It is expected that other volumes will be released every two years. Conceptually, the *Compendium* is organized into three sections: the state of the environment (air, inland waters, marine environment, land, forest, wildlife resources, solid waste, noise, risks, and radioactivity); pressures on the environment (energy, transport, industry, agriculture); and managing the environment (responses, general data). Coverage is for the twenty-four westernized, industrial countries of Europe, North America, and Asia that make up OECD's membership. Text and technical notes are in French and English.

Another source is *Environment Statistics in Europe and North America: An Experimental Compendium*, Statistical Standards and Studies Series, no. 39 (Economic Commission for Europe, 1987). It includes sections on environmental resources, generation and treatment of waste residuals, concentration of pollutants in environmental media, topical issues, and climate and selected background information. There is a brief section on protecting freshwater lakes, with Lake Baikal of the Soviet Union given as an example. The publication of these environmental statistics, although limited in scope, may be another example of the growing willingness on the part of authorities in the Soviet Union and East European countries to share information with the public.

Obtaining access to national reports on environmental statistics is difficult. No current list of titles, publishers, and prices exists. *World Resources 1987* contains a list of countries that have produced either reports on the state of the environment, environmental statistics, or environmental profiles. In 1981, the U.N. Statistical Office prepared a *Directory of Environment Statistics*, which listed available statistical reports covering 150 countries, but it is now considerably out of date.

Air Quality and Climate

Air pollution statistics are of two principal types: emission estimates and ambient concentrations. Further disaggregations for emissions include sources (stationary and mobile; background or natural and human generated), and location (indoor and outdoor). Further disaggregations for ambient concentrations focus primarily on effects (human health, ecological, economic, and aesthetic). Both emission estimates and ambient conditions can be aggregated from sampling sites to urban, regional, national, international, and global levels. Some individual pollutants, such as sulfur dioxide, may be monitored, analyzed, and reported for all of the above categories, whereas others, such as radon, are usually reported for background sources and indoor ambient levels only.

The best sources for air pollution statistics are the *EDR* and the OECD *Compendium*. The *EDR* includes tables on the following specific pollutants: carbon dioxide (global carbon dioxide emissions, atmospheric concentrations); chloroflurocarbons (production and release in atmosphere, CFCs in the troposphere); ozone (surface ozone and total ozone); sulfur dioxide (global emissions, emissions and deposition in Europe, emissions by country, ambient concentrations for sixty-two cities in forty-one countries, including many developing countries); suspended particulates (ambient concentrations in air by city, with coverage comparable to sulfur dioxide); nitrogen oxides (emissions in selected countries, concentrations in the troposphere); and precipitation chemistry (concentrations of sulfates and nitrates, pH).

Additional data are given in the OECD *Compendium* on the following: emissions (totals and by source) of nitrogen oxides, sulfur oxides, hydrocarbons, and carbon monoxide; concentrations of sulfur dioxide, nitrogen dioxide, suspended particulates, nitrates, and sulfates; and pH.

Very few internationally comparable statistics are available on health and ecological impacts of air pollution, and information on indoor air pollution is even more limited.

Statistics on surface temperature changes (global and hemispheric), snow cover, sea-ice, mass balance fluctuation of glaciers, and sea level are available in the *EDR*.

Water Quality

Data on water pollution are collected from freshwater rivers, streams, and lakes, coastal waters, and deep ocean environments. The statistics are of two basic types: discharges (point and non-point sources) and in-stream concentrations. Most discharge data are collected in ways that make useful comparisons virtually impossible, so they are not referenced here. Comparable data on in-stream concentrations are more readily available, but rarely in time series that can be used to analyze trends.

Very few statistics from the GEMS water data program, located at the Canadian Centre for Inland Waters, have been published. Both the *EDR* and the *World Resources* reports, however, contain tables of unpublished GEMS water data for major rivers. Tables in the *EDR*, for example, provide data on physical characteristics (temperature, pH, dissolved oxygen, electrical conductivity, suspended solids, and dissolved Ca, Na, and Cl) and on nutrients and pollutants (biological oxygen demand, chemical oxygen demand, nitrogen, phosphorous, cadmium, mercury, lead, and fecal coliforms). The *EDR* statistics cover 130 rivers in forty-two countries, though the coverage is spotty. Median values are given for measurements made in the years 1979-81. No information is provided that would allow the user to compare measured concentrations with criteria used to monitor and control water quality for human health and ecological safety.

Statistics on the number of people and the percentage of the population in developing countries with access to safe drinking water and sanitation are available from the World Health Organization (WHO) in *The International Drinking Water Supply and Sanitation Decade: Review of National Baseline Data: December 1980* and *The International Drinking Water Supply and Sanitation Decade: Review of Mid-Decade Progress (as of December 1985)*. See *World Resources 1988-89*, Table 15.4, for more recent figures. The table includes totals for 127 countries. In most cases, urban and rural percentages are shown for 1980 and 1985.

Toxic Substances and Hazardous Wastes

In recent years, a few internationally comparable statistics have begun to appear on environmental toxins and waste disposal. The best data on toxic substances pertain to their production (e.g., metals and pesticides). Some information on toxic contamination of food, animal and human tissue is also available. The best data for wastes come from situations in which wastes are separated and processed in some way—reutilized, recovered, or recycled.

Selected statistics on heavy metal and pesticide contaminants in food and animal tissue are found in *EDR*. Hazardous wastes produced, stored, and disposed of are monitored in a few countries, and those data are reproduced in the OECD *Compendium*.

Wildlife: Species and Habitat

Statistics on threatened and endangered species are available from the International Union for Conservation of Nature and Natural Resources (IUCN) in their Red Data Book series. Most of these reports are compiled by the Species Conservation Monitoring Unit of the World Conservation Monitoring Centre. These publications include Red Data Books on birds of Africa, invertebrates, amphibia and reptilia, swallowtail butterflies, mammals, and plants. Statistics include: the number of species known and the number threatened with extinction, habitat, threats to survival, conservation measures, and population trends. Year and species coverage depend on field work in individual countries. For additional data on plants, see IUCN's *Plants in Danger: What do We Know?* published in 1986.

Statistics on protected habitats and protected areas in general are available from the Protected Area Data Unit of the World Conservation Monitoring Centre in the *1985 United Nations*

List of National Parks and Protected Areas. Statistics cover all countries and all major biogeographical realms and provinces. Data include number and size of protected areas, habitat classification, and date established.

General References

A growing number of general references and bibliographies can help the statistics user, even the experienced professional user, find better international statistics.

World Tables, published by the World Bank, provides 115 up-to-date economic, demographic, and social indicators for 137 countries for 21 years. Furthermore, the Bank now compresses these data using the new STARS data compaction program and makes them available on 5.25 or 3.5 inch diskettes. The data can be decompressed and read out formatted for Lotus 1-2-3, Javelin Plus, or ASCII text.

Sourcebook of Global Statistics, published biannually by Facts on File Publications, is a "user's guide to statistical information." Written by George Kurian, it contains 209 entries listing major statistical books and reports from both governmental and private sources. The book provides reputable data for the business community and is strong on commodities and other internationally traded goods and services. It provides excellent coverage of traditional sources, including all the major U.N. statistical reports, and it is indexed.

A more detailed and more costly source is *Index to International Statistics: A Guide to the Statistical Publications of International Intergovernmental Organizations (IIS)*. It is compiled and published by the Congressional Information Service, which also publishes the *American Statistics Index*. The *IIS* provides detailed indices to statistical information by subject, author, geographic area, sources, titles, and publication number. Abstracts are organized by a source-specific publication number so that all abstracts from an organization, e.g., World Bank, are together. The abstracts are more informative than those in the Kurian book. The *IIS* does not cover private publications or computerized databases. Try to find it in a library because it is expensive.

Although quite dated, the *Directory of International Statistics*, Volume I, prepared by the U.N. Statistical Office, is the only directory that cross-references statistical series to the producing agency. Agriculture, forestry, and fisheries statistics, for example, are given by type (agricultural area, land under crops, wood or forest cover, etc.) and then referenced to the relevant report, in this case the Food and Agriculture Organization's *Production Yearbook*. Multiple sources are given for many series, but only U.N. sources are referenced.

From time to time the United Nations Advisory Committee for the Co-ordination of Information Systems (ACCIS) prepares reference guides to statistical and other information sources by subject. The 1987 *ACCIS Guide to United Nations Information Sources of Food and Agriculture* and the 1988 *ACCIS Guide to United Nations Information Sources on The Environment* provide brief reviews of statistical holdings by each U.N. agency and major private organizations. The index cross-references both sets of entries. Separate entries are given by subject. Regional and national sources are listed. Because the focus of these publications is on general information, not statistics, they should be used after the FAO, World Resource Institute, and UNEP sources referenced previously. For a detailed listing of all United Nations databases, see the 1985 publication, *Directory of United Nations Databases and Information Systems*, also compiled by ACCIS. The United Nations in New York sells all three of these sources.

To find services available through computer networks, see the *Directory of Online Databases* by Cuadra Associates. Another good source is the *Data Base Directory*, prepared semiannually by Knowledge Industry Publications.

A user faced with the task of finding statistics quickly and easily for many different topics for many different countries should first try the U.N. *Statistical Yearbook* and Europa Publications' *Europa Yearbook*. The *Europa Yearbook* contains a country-by-country review of the recent economic and political situation and a set of tables with data on major economic, social, demographic, trade, energy, and natural resources. Both of these basic sources are found in libraries and are updated frequently.

Cited Sources

Official International Organizations
Economic and Social Commission for Asia
 and the Pacific
United Nations Building
Rajadamnern Avenue
Bangkok 2, Thailand

Economic Commission for Africa
P.O. Box 3001
Addis Ababa, Ethiopia

Economic Commission for Europe
Palais des Nations
CH-1211 Geneva 10, Switzerland

Economic Commission for Latin America and
 the Caribbean
Washington Office
1735 Eye Street NW, Suite 809
Washington, DC 20006, USA
or
Economic Commission for Latin America and
 the Caribbean
Distribution Unit
Documents and Publications Service
UN CEPAL
Casilla 179-D
Santiago, Chile

Economic Commission for Western Asia
P.O. Box 27
Baghdad, Iraq

European Communities
European Communities Information Service
2100 M Street, NW
Washington, DC 20037, USA
or
Office of Official Publications of the
 European Communities
5, rue du Commerce
L-2985 Luxembourg, Luxembourg

Food and Agriculture Organization of the
 United Nations
Via delle Terme di Caracalla
00100 Rome, Italy
or

Unipub
P.O. Box 1222
Ann Arbor, MI 48106, USA

International Atomic Energy Agency
Vienna International Center
P.O. Box 100
A 1400 Vienna, Austria

International Bank for Reconstruction and
 Development (World Bank)
Publications Unit
600 19th Street, NW
Washington, DC 20433, USA

International Civil Aviation Organization
 (ICAO)
1000 Sherbrooke Street West
Suite 400
Montreal, Quebec H3A 2R2, Canada

International Energy Agency
Organization for Economic Cooperation
 and Development (OECD)
OECD Publications and Information Center
1750 Pennsylvania Avenue, NW
Washington, DC 20006, USA

International Labour Organization
ILO Publications
CH-1211 Geneva 22, Switzerland
or
International Labour Organization
Washington Office
1750 New York Avenue, NW
Washington, DC 20006, USA

International Monetary Fund
700 19th Street, NW
Washington, DC 20431, USA

Latin American Energy Organization
(OLADE)
Casilla 6413 C.C.I.
Quito, Ecuador

Nuclear Energy Agency
38 Boulevard Sucrat
F-75016 Paris, France
or

Nuclear Energy Agency
Organization for Economic Cooperation
 and Development (OECD)
Publications and Information Center
1750 Pennsylvania Avenue, NW
Washington, DC 20006, USA

Organization for Economic Cooperation
 and Development (OECD)
Publications and Information Center
1750 Pennsylvania Avenue, NW
Washington, DC 20006, USA

Special Representative of the
 U.N. Secretary General for
 the Law of the Sea
Ocean Affairs, Law of the Sea
Room DC2-0432
New York, NY 10017, USA

United Nations
United Nations Publications
2 U.N. Plaza
Room DC2-0853
New York, NY 10017, USA

United Nations Advisory Committee for the
 Co-ordination of Information Services
 (ACCIS)
ACCIS Newsletter
ACCIS Secretariat
Palais des Nations
1211 Geneva 10, Switzerland

United Nations Conference on Trade and
 Development
Liaison Office
Secretariat Building, Room 927
United Nations, NY 10017, USA
or
United Nations Conference on Trade and
 Development
Editorial and Documents Section
Palais des Nations
CH-1211 Geneva 10, Switzerland

United Nations Department of International
 Economic and Social Affairs (UNDIESA)
2 U.N. Plaza
New York, NY 10017, USA

United Nations Education, Scientific
 and Communication Organization
UNESCO Press
7, Place de Fontenoy
5700 Paris, France

United Nations Environment Programme
 (UNEP)
P.O. Box 30552
Nairobi, Kenya

United Nations High Commissioner for
 Refugees
Washington Office
1785 Massachusetts Avenue, NW
Washington, DC 20036, USA

United Nations Population Division
Attention: Chief, Estimates and
 Projections Section
Department of International
 Economic and Social Affairs (UNDIESA)
Room DC2-1934
New York, NY 10017, USA

United Nations Statistical Office
Statistical Services Branch
United Nations Department of International
 Economic and Social Affairs (UNDIESA)
2 U.N. Plaza
Room DC2-1620
New York, NY 10017, USA

World Bank
Publications Unit
600 19th Street, NW
Washington, DC 20433, USA

World Health Organization (WHO)
Publications Center USA
49 Sheridan Avenue
Albany, NY 12210, USA

U.S. Government Agencies
 Goddard Space Flight Center
 U.S. National Aeronautics and Space
  Administration (NASA)
 Greenbelt Road
 Greenbelt, MD 20771, USA

U.S. Agency for International Development
(USAID)
Office of Foreign Disaster Assistance
320 21st Street, NW
Washington, DC 20523, USA

U.S. Arms Control and Disarmament Agency
Office of Public Affairs
320 21st Street, NW
Washington, DC 20451, USA

U.S. Bureau of the Census
Customer Services
Data User Services Division
Washington, DC 20233, USA

U.S. Central Intelligence Agency
Photoduplication Service
Library of Congress
Washington, DC 20540, USA

U.S. Defense Mapping Agency
U.S. Department of Defense
Directorate for Information Operations and
 Reports
Suite 1204, 1215 Jefferson Davis Highway
Arlington, VA 22202, USA

U.S. Department of Agriculture
Economic Research Service
Washington, DC 20250, USA

U.S. Energy Information Administration
U.S. Department of Energy
National Energy Information Center
Washington, DC 20585, USA

U.S. Food and Drug Administration
Center for Food Safety and Applied Nutrition
200 C Street, SW, (HFF-1)
Washington, DC 20204, USA

U.S. Government Printing Office
Superintendent of Documents
Washington, DC 20402, USA

U.S. National Marine Fisheries Service
Public Affairs, Page Two Bldg
3300 Whitehaven Street, NW
Washington, DC 20236, USA

Private Publishers and Associations
American Geophysical Union
2000 Florida Avenue, NW
Washington, DC 20009, USA

American Petroleum Institute
1220 L Street, NW
Washington, DC 20005, USA

Basic Books, Inc.
10 East 53rd Street
New York, NY 10022, USA

Basil Blackwell
432 Park Avenue South, Suite 1503
New York, NY 10016, USA

Bernan-Unipub
4611-F Assembly Drive
Lanham, MD 20706, USA

British Petroleum Company
Britannic House, Moor Lane
London EC2Y 9BU, United Kingdom

Congressional Information Service, Inc.
4520 East-West Highway
Bethesda, MD 20814, USA

Cuadra Associates, Inc.
2001 Wilshire Boulevard, Suite 305
Santa Monica, CA 90403, USA

Europa Publications Limited
18 Bedford Square
London WC1B 3JN, United Kingdom

Facts on File Publications
460 Park Avenue, South
New York, NY 10016, USA

Gulf Publishers
P.O. Box 2608
Houston, TX 77252, USA

International Air Transport Association
(IATA)
P.O. Box 160
26 chemin de Joinville
1216 Cointroin
Geneva, Switzerland

International Food Policy Research Institute
1776 Massachusetts Avenue, NW
Washington, DC 20036, USA

International Road Federation
525 School Street, SW
Washington, DC 20024, USA

International Sugar Organization
28 Haymarket
London SW1Y 4SP, United Kingdom

International Tea Committee
Sir John Lyon House
5 High Timber Street
London EC4V 3NH, United Kingdom

International Union for the Conservation of
 Nature and Natural Resources
IUCN Publications Services
219 (c) Huntingdon Road
Cambridge C83 ODL, United Kingdom

International Wheat Council
Haymarket House
28 Haymarket
London SW1Y 4SS, United Kingdom

Jane's Publishing Co., Ltd.
1340 Braddock Place, Suite 300
P.O. Box 1436
Alexandria, VA 22313, USA

Johns Hopkins University Press
701 West 40th Street, Suite 275
Baltimore, MD 21211, USA

Knowledge Industry Publications, Inc.
701 Westchester Avenue
White Plains, NY 10604, USA

Oxford University Press
Customer Service Department
1600 Pollitt Drive
Fairlawn, NJ 07410, USA

PennWell Publishers
1421 South Sheridan Road
P.O. Box 1260
Tulsa, OK 74101, USA

Population Reference Bureau
777 14th Street, NW, Suite 800
Washington, DC 20005, USA

Water Information Center, Inc.
44 Sintsink Drive East
Port Washington, NY 11050, USA

World Conservation Monitoring Centre
219 (c) Huntington Road
Cambridge C83 ODL, United Kingdom

World Energy Conference
34 St. James Street
London SW1A 1HD, United Kingdom

World Priorities
3013 Dumbarton Avenue, NW
Washington, DC 20007, USA

World Resources Institute
1709 New York Avenue, NW, Suite 700
Washington, DC 20006, USA

Yale University Press
92A Yale Station
New Haven, CT 06520, USA

16. Modeling Languages

Introduction

Beyond the models and simulations described in this book, there are many that could be developed and would be of use to nations. In fact, governmental administrators are regularly commissioning new models and simulations.

Advanced simulation languages can increase the productivity of time and funds devoted to developing new models and simulations, and this chapter provides information on the languages now available.

The information that follows was assembled by the editors of *Simulation*, a monthly publication of the Society for Computer Simulation. The information is copyrighted by *Simulation* and is reprinted here with permission. Readers interested in subscribing to *Simulation* or in obtaining annual updates to the following information should write to: Society for Computer Simulation International, P.O. Box 17900, San Diego, CA 92117, USA.

The following list is not limited to programs that operate on a microcomputer. While some of the programs do operate on a microcomputer, others require a minicomputer, a mainframe computer, or in a few cases, a supercomputer.

The modeling languages are of two types, those that are used in general purpose simulations and those that address specific areas and specific types of problems.

The general purpose modeling languages deal with: interactive and non-interactive continuous systems, networks, queues, interactive and non-interactive discrete events, algebraic equations, ordinary and partial differential equations, distributed systems, linear and non-linear systems, and many-body systems.

The general purpose languages cover the following methodologies: linear and non-linear programming, system dynamics, econometric analysis, input-output analysis, harmonic analysis, frequency analysis, transient analysis, two- and three-dimensional animation, parametric analysis, regression analysis, uncertainty propagation, and real-time analysis.

The simulation languages addressed to specific areas and specific types of problems are even more diverse than the general purpose languages. The specific areas and problems addressed include: factory operations (materials routing, scheduling, inventory analysis, warehouse systems, and batch and integrated manufacturing), pipeline management, shovel-truck systems in open pit mining, gas and oil refining, fossil-fuel and nuclear power plants, missile system engagements, chemical processes (distillations and combustion), wastewater treatment, communications systems (digital communications, digital signal processing, and microwave systems), computer systems, control systems, electronic circuits, hydraulic systems, transportation systems, social systems, economic systems, database analysis, street, utility line, and stream networks, mass and energy balance, energy optimization, thermodynamics, pharmacokinetics, pharmacodynamics, respiratory physiology, cardiovascular physiology, robot design, and robot dynamics.

The list that follows is far from complete, but it is an indication of the range and diversity of the modeling languages available. It is also a place to begin for those who are looking for a modeling language to meet a specific need.

Modeling Languages for use on
Microcomputers, Minicomputers, and Mainframes

Item	Brief description	Contact	Computer(s)	Operating system/ other software required	Approximate cost
AC-2, SST, FRNC-5, REFORMER, FURCRAK, ACPC, PREDICTOR	Programs for the step-wise checkrating of heat exchangers.	David F. Itten An der Bleiche 47 6370 Oberursel 5 West Germany Phone: (06171)-7 48 90	IBM, CYBER or others		Cost available upon request
ACHILLES	A discrete event simula-tion for dynamic factory operation management.	Mark A. Pool In-Motion Technology 444 Castro Street Mountain View, CA 94041 Phone: (415) 966-8448	Any	FORTRAN	Cost available upon request.
ACSL	Models and analyzes continuous systems.	John Rodrigues MGA, inc. 73 Junction Square Dr. Concord, MA 01742 Phone: (508) 369-5115	APOLLO, Apple, Concurrent, CDC CONVEX, CRAY DEC, ELXSI, Gould, Harris, HP, IBM, Prime, Silicon Graphics, Sun, UNISYS	ALL/FORTRAN	$5,000-$25,000
ACSL/PC	Models and analyzes continuous systems.	John Rodrigues MGA, inc. 73 Junction Square Dr. Concord, MA 01742 Phone: (508) 369-5115	IBM PC or compatible	DOS/FORTRAN	$2,300
ACSL/PC Utilities	Utilities that facilitate use of ACSL/PC. Includes interfaces between ACSL and PC-MATLAB, Com-mand file build, interac-tive help and on screen plots while ACSL is exe-cuting, utility for reading an ACSL RRR file.	Philip S. Bartells SIMTECH Services 102 Woodbrook Lane Forest, VA 24551 Phone: (804) 525-8406	IBM PC or compatible	DOS / ACSL/PC	$200 - $360
ADAPT II	Pharmacokinetic and pharmacodynamic modeling and data analysis.	Biomedical Simulations Resource School of Engineering Univ. of Southern California Los Angeles, CA 90089-1451 Phone: (213) 743-3648	VAX	VMS 4.4 or later	No charge to the biomedical community for non-commercial use
Adaptable Equation Solver	Solves a user selectable set of equations.	Harry W. Townes 514 N. 10th Ave. Bozeman, MT 54715 Phone: (406) 994-6297	Any	Needs only a C compiler	Freeware $20 (suggested)
ADSIM	A continuous systems simulation language including compiler, utilities, interactive en-vironment and large libraries.	Applied Dynamics, International 3800 Stone School Road Ann Arbor, MI 48104 Phone: (313) 973-1300	SYSTEM 100	VAX VMS and FORTRAN 77	$17,500

Item name	Brief description	Contact	Computer(s)	Operating System/ other software required	Approximate cost
ADSIM for VAX	All functional capabilities of ADSIM are preserved except for input/output handling. Compiles and executes on the VAX.	Applied Dynamics, International 3800 Stone School Rd. Ann Arbor, MI 48108 Phone: (313) 973-1300	SYSTEM 100	VAX VMS and FORTRAN 77	$7,500
Animation	Enables entities to travel through the network and build up in queues.	MicroAnalysis and Design, Inc. 9132 Thunderhead Drive Boulder, Colorado 80302 Phone: (303) 442-6947	IBM PC or compatible	Micro SAINT 2.2 or higher; EGA recommended	$1,495
APE+ : ACSL Program Enhancer+	Workstation environment for ACSL/PC, EASE+ACSL and PC-MATLAB.	Philip S. Bartells SIMTECH Services 102 Woodbrook Lane Forest, VA 24551 Phone: (804) 525-8406	IBM PC or compatible	DOS / ACSL/PC	$800 - $1800
ASPEN PLUS	Simulates chemical process flowsheets for proposed or operating plants.	Aspen Technology, Inc. 251 Vassar Street Cambridge, MA 02139 Phone: (617) 497-9010	Most major hardware manufacturers	FORTRAN	Please contact Aspen Tech for cost details
AutoCode	Generates machine independent, real-time source code from engineering block diagrams.	Juli Jensen 2500 Mission College Blvd. Santa Clara, CA 95054-1215 Phone: (408) 980-1500	VAXstation Apollo	VMS, Aegis	
AutoCode PC	Generates machine independent, real-time source code from engineering block diagrams.	Juli Jensen 2500 Mission College Blvd. Santa Clara, CA 95054-1215 Phone: (408) 980-1500	IBM XT/AT or compatible	MS-DOS, PC-DOS, math coprocessor, hard disk, graphics adapter	
AWARENESS Neural Networks	Interactively demonstrates qualities and capabilities of four neural network paradigms.	Neural Systems Inc. 2827 West 43rd Ave. Vancouver, B.C., Canada V6N 3H9 Phone: (604) 263-3667	IBM PC or compatible	Graphics Card	$275
BATCHES	Simulator for multiproduct and multipurpose batch/semicontinuous chemical processes.	Girish S. Joglekar Batch Process Technologies, Inc. P.O. Box 2001 W. Lafayette, IN 47906 Phone: (317) 463-6473	FORTRAN 77 compiler	None	Cost available upon request
BATCHFRAC	Batch distillation simulation program that solves unsteady state heat and material balance equations.	Aspen Technology Inc. 251 Vassar Street Cambridge, MA 02139 Phone: (617) 497-9010	Most major hardware manufacturers	FORTRAN	Please contact AspenTech for cost details
BEAM (Background and Enhanced Animation for MAST)	Color graphics animation of MAST results. Includes all motion, with graphic display of current statistics.	John E. Lenz CMS Research, Inc. 600 South Main Street Brooklyn Center Oshkosh, WI 54901 Phone: (414) 235-3356	IBM PC, VICTOR 9000	DOS 3.1 or higher; IBM ColorGraphics Board	$6500 package (SPAR, MAST, BEAM); $900 academic

Item name	Brief description	Contact	Computer(s)	Operating System/ other software required	Approximate cost
BEST-NETWORK	Network simulation tool for throughput and connectivity analysis/design. No programming necessary.	Eric N. Best Best Consultants 21450 Chagall Rd. Topanga, CA 90290 Phone: (818) 340-1146	All major computers that run ANSI FORTRAN	FORTRAN compiler	$4,500
BETH	14 modules that calculate physical properties, evaluate performance and plot information relative to power plants.	Ron Griebenow P.O. Box 736 Idaho Falls, ID 83402 Phone: (208) 529-1000	IBM PC/XT or true compatible	MS-DOS 2.0 or above	$400 per module, discounts available upon multiple purchase
BORIS	Building-blocks-oriented interactive modeling and simulation system.	M. Mrva Siemens AG, ZTI SOF 3 Otto-Hahn-Ring 6 D-8000 Munich 83, F.R.G.	Siemens 7000 series	BS 2000 Pascal-BS2000	Cost available upon request; discounts for universities
BOSS: Block Oriented Systems Simulator	An integrated software package for simulation, analysis, and design of communication systems.	K. Sam Shanmugan STAR Corporation P.O. Box 3385 Lawrence, KS 66046	VAXstation II	VMS, FORTRAN, LISP	$9,750
BWR Dynamic Models	Full scope BWR plant system dynamic models, all written in FORTRAN 77. BWR 3, 4, & 5 versions available.	Var S. Tashijan Simulation Technologies, Inc. P.O. Box 898 Naperville IL 60566-0898	Gould/SEL or compatible. IBM AT or compatible	MPX, FORTRAN 77, DOS/MSDOS, PROFORT	Contact STI for details
CADmotion	Interactive general-purpose discrete event simulation system featuring concurrent color animation.	Simulation Software Systems 2107 North First Street, Suite 680 San Jose, CA 95131 Phone: (408) 436-8300 Fax: (408) 436-8376	IBM PC/XT/AT, PS/2, or true compatible	DOS 2.1 and later, External Processor feature uses any language, can use CGI/VDI drives	$4900 includes 30 day return policy and 1 free year of updates
CAMP (Computer Aided Modeling Program)	CAMP derives system differential equations from bond graphs, block diagrams, and their combination and delivers them to ACSL.	Jose J. Granada CADSIM ENGINEERING 2536 Lafayette Dr. Davis, CA 95616 Phone: (916) 758-8432 or 756-8288	DEC, CDC, IBM, PRIME, APOLLO, MICROVAX	All/FORTRAN	One time license charge of $5000; university discounts
CANDLE	Computer Aided Natural Design Language for Engineering.	David S. Stauffer 1106 Brookmeade Huntsville, AL 35816 Phone: (205) 539-0541	IBM PC or compatible (other machines upon request)	DOS 2.0 or higher	$750
CANPAC-Controls Analysis Package	Provides a windowed menu environment for performing many standard controls analysis tasks.	Philip S. Bartells SIMTECH Services 102 Woodbrook Lane Forest, VA 24551 Phone: (804) 525-8406	IBM PC or compatible	DOS / PC-MATLAB with the Controls Toolbox option	$420
CAPDET-PC	Computer-Assisted Procedure for the Design and Evaluation of waste-water Treatment alternatives.	Hydromantis, Inc. 22 Pearl St., South Hamilton, Ontario L8P 3W5 Canada Phone: (416) 529-1121	IBM-PC or compatible	MS-DOS or PC-DOS	$800

Item name	Brief description	Contact	Computer(s)	Operating System/ other software required	Approximate cost
CESNAP	Combustion, Engineering, Simulator, Neutronics, Analysis Program.	Albert T. Shesler Combustion Engineering, Inc. 1000 Prospect Hill Road CEP# 9422-0425 Windsor, CT 06095 Phone: (203) 285-4179	IBM PC or compatible	DOS 2.0 or higher	Cost available upon request
CHALLENGE! Version 4.0	Computer assisted interactive simulation of mass casualty incident management.	Rodger D. Kelley P.O. Box 3402 San Clemente, CA 92672 Phone: (714) 492-4748	IBM compatible only 2.1 DOS 264K	2.1 or greater DOS IBM	$600
Cinema	Simulation and animation system that enables the user to create a real-time, dynamic model that accurately represents the simulated system.	Calder Square, P.O. Box 10074 State College, PA 16805 Phone: (814) 238-5919	IBM PC/XT/AT or compatible, Micro VAX II, SUN	MSDOS, VMS, UNIX	$14,000-28,000
CIRCUITS	Simulation of power electronics systems with interactive graphic input/output.	CEDRAT Zirst Meylan, France 38240 Phone: (+)33 (76)905045	Macintosh		$5,000
COMBIF	Modeling and identification of multidimensional dynamic fields.	Dr. Wieslaw Golsz Eng. Wojciech Adamowicz ul. Powstancow 42/19 31-422 KRAKOW POLAND	IBM PC/XT/AT or compatible	DOS	$400
COMBIS	Modeling and structural identification of continuous systems and control processes. Heuristic self-organization method.	Dr. Wieslaw Golsz Eng. Wojciech Adamowicz ul. Powstancow 42/19 31-422 KRAKOW POLAND	IBM PC/XT/AT or compatible	DOS	$400
CSSL-IV	Continuous System Simulation Language-version four.	R.N. Nilsen 20926 Germain Street Chatsworth, CA 91311 Phone: (818) 998-7824	Wide variety of micros and mainframes	FORTRAN-77	$12,500 (university discounts available)
CTRL-C	Interactive language for computer-aided control engineering and simulation.	Carol Michaels Systems Control Technology, Inc. 2300 Geng Road Palto Alto, CA 94303 Phone: (415) 494-2233	VAX/VMS and UNIX systems, Sun, Gould, Apollo, IBM VM/CMS	VMS, UNIX, or VM/CMS	Cost available upon request
CVSAD- Cardiovascular Systems & Dynamics	An interactive simulation for teaching cardiovascular physiology.	Command Applied Technology, Inc P.O. Box 511 Pullman, WA 99163-0511 Phone: (509) 334-6145	IBM PC/XT/AT or compatible	MS-DOS compatible 5.25 inch floppy disk	$150 (discount in quantity)
CYPROS, Micro CYPROS	Input/output of data, data analysis, modeling, simulation, and design of control systems.	Martin Albert Camo, Inc. 31368 Via Collinas, Ste. 102 Westlake Village, Ca 91362 Phone: (818) 991-5295	IBM PC/XT/AT or compatible/ DEC VAX	DOS, (for add-on modules: RM FORTRAN)/ VMS	$2300/module, $8900 complete

Item name	Brief description	Contact	Computer(s)	Operating System/ other software required	Approximate cost
DARE P	Runs in FORTRAN IV, similar to CSSL language specs.	John V. Wait ECE Dept., Bldg. 104 University of Arizona Tucson, AZ 85721 Phone: (602) 621-2434 or (602) 621-2160	Any that runs FORTRAN IV	VMS VAX, CDC, etc.	$3,600, 50% discount to universities
DARE-INTER-ACTIVE	Interactive simulation of continuous systems with enhanced run-time experimentation facilities and interactive color graphics.	Francois E. Cellier Dept. of Elect. & Comp. Engr. University of Arizona Tucson AZ 85721 Phone: (602) 621-6192	VAX	VMS	$3500; $1800 academic
Decision Support Modeling System (DSM)	Highly flexible, open loop simulation of non-linear systems.	Robert Associates, Inc. 34 Hereford Place Ottawa, Ontario K1Y 3S5 Canada	Apple Macintosh II	None	Contact vendor
DESCTOP (DESIRE/VAX)	Direct-executing simulation, 400 state variables (50 if stiff), FFTs, screen editor, sub-models.	G. A. Korn 6801 Opatas Street Tucson, AZ 85715 Phone: (602) 298-7054	VAX, MICROVAX	VMS, MICRO-VMS	$1800 (MICROVAX) $2400 (VAX) educ. discounts
DESIRE/387/287	Direct-executing simulation, 1,000 state variables, FFTs. screen editor, sub-models.	G. A. Korn 6801 Opatas Street Tucson, AZ 85715 Phone: (602) 298-7054	80386 with 80387 80286 or 80386 with 80287	PC-DOS, MS-DOS	$595; also site license
DSL/VS	Dynamic Simulation Language/VS.	Tyson N. Howell, IBM 355 South Grand Avenue Los Angeles, CA 90060 Phone: (213) 621-5810	IBM mainframes: S/370, 43XX, 30XX	VS FORTRAN/ FORTRAN 77, PL/1 Transient Library, MVS/TSO or VM/CMS	$10,000 or will rent to universities for $454/month
DSNP - Dynamic Simulator of Nuclear Power plants	A simulation language for analyzing thermal hydraulic transients.	John T. Madell P.O. Box 199 Western Springs, IL 60558 Phone: (312) 246-0640	Micro to mainframe	Any system supporting FORTRAN-77	Call for specific information
DSS/2	A transportable FORTRAN 77 code for the numerical integration of systems of ordinary and partial differential equations.	W.E. Schiesser Whitaker No. 5 Lehigh University Bethlehem, PA 18015 Phone: (215) 861-4264	Any computer with a FORTRAN 77 compiler	None	$1000 for source code on nine track tape
DYNAMO III/F+ (Plus)/370	Continuous simulation packages for IBM S/370 computers.	Kip Cooper Pugh-Roberts Associates 5 Lee Street Cambridge, MA 02139 Phone: (617) 864-8880	Any mainframe supporting FORTRAN, IBM S/370	FORTRAN, MVS/TSO or CMS	$2,500-$12,000 education discounts, site licenses available
DYSMAP	System dynamics simulations of non-linear systems using syntax identical to DYNAMO.	Brian Dangerfield Department of Business and Management Studies University of Salford Salford M5 4WT United Kingdom Phone: (44) 061-736-5843 Extension 7278 or 7074	IBM PC/XT/AT or compatible; also micros based on the Intel 80386 chip	PC/MS DOS	£995 (pounds sterling) for the PC version; more for the 80386 version.

Item	Brief description	Contact	Computer(s)	Operating system/ other software required	Approximate cost
DYSYS	System dynamics simulation of ecological, social, and economic systems.	Michael Machel Te-Wi Verlag Theo-Prosel-Weg 1 D 8000 München 40 Federal Republic of Germany	IBM PC/XT/AT or compatible, Commodore 64/128, Apple II, Sinclair Spectrum, Epson HX-20	None	Contact Vendor
EASE+ACSL	Derives nonlinear state equations from block diagrams and delivers same to ACSL.	Bruce Powell EXPERT-EASE Systems 1301 Shoreway Rd. Belmont, CA 94002 Phone: (415) 593-3200	IBM/PC or compatible	DOS	$1500 PC, $4500 VAX
EASY5	A software package which simulates dynamic response and performs control system analysis.	George S. Duleba P.O. Box 24346 MS 7W-26 Seattle, WA 98124-0346 Phone: (206) 644-6285	Cyber, Cray, VAX, IBM, APOLLO	Standard operating systems for indicated hardware	$15,000-$70,000
ENHANCED DESIRE (DESIRE/386)	Direct-executing simulation, 100 state variables, FFTs, screen editor, sub-models.	G.A. Korn 6801 Opatas Street Tucson, AZ 85715 Phone: (602) 298-7054	IBM PC/XT/AT with 8087, 80287; also 80386/7	PC-DOS, MS-DOS	$495; also site license
ENPORT-7	Simulation of nonlinear dynamic systems modeled with bond graphs and block diagrams.	ROSENCODE Associates, Inc. 200 North Capital Building Lower Level Lansing, MI 48933 Phone: (517) 483-3216	Most major hardware	ANSI 77 FORTRAN	$7500 (inquire about educational discount)
ESL	An advanced CSSL which provides both translator and interpreter execution.	J.L. Hay ISIM SIMULATION Salford University Business Services Ltd. Business House University Rd. Salford M5 4PP U.K. Phone: (44) 061-736-8921	PRIME, SEL, VAX, IBM PC-AT	FORTRAN 77 compiler	$10,000
Extend	Interactive continuous and discrete event simulation	Imagine That, Inc. 7109 Via Carmela San Jose, CA 95139 Phone: (408) 365-0305	Macintosh	None	$495 (Educational discounts available.)
EXCON	Expert system to construct control strategies for material routing.	B.-D. Becker IPA-FhG Schlosstr. 68 D-7000 Stuttgart 1 West Germany Phone: (0711) 61915-53	IBM XT/AT or compatible	MS-DOS, windows	$2,000
EZQ equation solver	Solves differential, difference and algebraic equations.	G.L. Gottlieb P.O. Box 6126 Evanston, IL 60204 Phone: (312) 942-6412	Apple II+, e, c, gs Macintosh and IBM PC (2nd quarter 87)	None	$150
FACTOR	Simulation of production systems	FACTROL. Inc. 2801 Kent Ave. P.O. Box 2569 West Layfayette, IN 47906 Phone: (317) 463-3637	DEC VAX, HP 9000/800, IBM PC, IBM 9370	VMS, UNIX, MS DOS, VM	$35,000 to $155,000

Item	Brief description	Contact	Computer(s)	Operating system/ other software required	Approximate cost
FAD	Determination of number of vehicles and buffer sizes for material flow planning.	Bernd Noche SDZ GmbH Emil-Figge-Str. 75 4600 Dortmund 50 West Germany Phone: (0231/7549-139)	VAX, IBM PC or compatible	VMS, BS2000/SIMULA	$15,000
General Algebraic Modeling System (GAMS)	Linear programming based on easily comprehendible algebraic notation for formulas and data. Developed at the World Bank.	The Scientific Press 540 University Ave. Palo Alto, CA 94301	IBM PC/XT/AT or compatible	PC/MS DOS	Contact Vendor
GEMS-II	Network-based discrete-event language. General purpose, with manufac-turing orientation.	Lodestone II, Inc. 3833 Texas Ave., Suite 460 Bryan, TX 77802 Phone: (409) 846-4171	IBM PC/XT/AT or true compatible, most main-frames, and minis	MS-DOS, MS-FORTRAN to include user-written routines, FORTRAN 77 compiler	Contact vendor
Generic Visual System (GVS)	For visual simulation ap-plications. Land, flight, space and ground-based simulations.	John L. Archdeacon Gemini Technology Corp. 11770 Warner Ave., Ste. 116 Fountain Valley, CA 92708 Phone: (714) 966-8455	Silicon Graphics, SUN, GX4000, E&S PS300	VAX/VMS, UNIX	$5000 and up. Contact vendor
GENETIK	General-purpose visual interactive simulation en-vironment providing direct model access and execution.	Insight International Ltd. 2 Robert Speck Parkway, Suite 750 Mississauga, Ontario L4Z 1H8 Canada Phone: (416) 896-0515	IBM PC/XT/AT or PS2, VAX and Apollo	DOS 3.0, VAX VMS	Available upon request
GPSM™	A graphical front-end to IRA's Performance Analyst's Workbench System (PAWS™).	Doug Neuse Information Research Associates 911 West 29th Street Austin, Texas 78705 Phone: (512) 474-4526	IBM PC or compatible, Sun, Apollo, DEC VaxStations.	MS-DOS, Unix, VMS	$3,000
GPSS	Company offers several implementations of GPSS for various equipment.	Simulation Software Ltd. 760 Headley Drive London, Ontario N6H 3V8 Canada Phone: (519) 657-8229 Telex: 064-78585 LDN	VAX, MicroVAX, SUN-3, PYRAMID, MV/ECLIPSE, ELXSI	Varies	Varies
GPSS/H	Powerful, flexible, easy-to-learn language and environment; superset of well-known GPSS V.	Wolverine Software Corp. 7630 Little River Turnpike, Suite 208 Annandale, VA 22003 Phone: (703) 750-3910	IBM PC/XT/AT, PS2; IBM 370; Apollo, Sun, and other work stations	MS-DOS; VM/PC; UNIX	Contact vendor; volume, network, and academic pricing available
GPSS/H	Powerful, flexible, easy-to-learn language and environment; superset of well-known GPSS V.	Wolverine Software Corp. 7630 Little River Turnpike, Suite 208 Annandale, VA 22003 Phone: (703) 750-3910	IBM; VAX; NCR Tower; Apollo, Sun, and other workstations	VM, MVS; VMS, Ultrix; UNIX	$9900-$29,700, or $3000-$9000/yr lease; volume, net-work, and academic pricing available
GPSS/PC™	Full power implementa-tion of GPSS, interactive graphics and animation.	Minuteman Software P.O. Box 171 Stow, MA 01775 Phone: (508) 897-5662 or (800) 223-1430	IBM PC/XT/AT/386 or compatible	PC- or MS-DOS 2.0 or later	$995 educational pricing, which includes student version; site license available.

Item	Brief description	Contact	Computer(s)	Operating system/ other software required	Approximate cost
GPSS/PC Animator™	CAD based animation post processor with rendering option for use with the GPSS/PC™ simulation environment.	Minuteman Software P.O. Box 171 Stow, MA 01775 Phone: (508) 897-5662 or (800) 223-1430	IBM PC/XT/AT/386 or compatible	PC- or MS-DOS 2.0 or later, AutoCAD 9.0 with ADE-3	$995, educational pricing available
GPSSR/PC	Mainframe-style GPSS with animation, interactive debugging and report browsing.	Simulation Software Ltd. 760 Headley Drive London, Ontario N6H 3V8 Canada Phone: (519) 657-8229 Telex: 064-78585 LDN	IBM PC/XT/AT or compatible	PC-DOS 2.0, MS-DOS 2.0 or later	$750, educational price $250. (One time charge)
GRAPH	Expert system for scientific research in graph theory and its applications.	Zoran Radosavljevic Faculty of Electrical Eng. University of Belgrade 11000 Belgrade Bulevar, Revolucije 73 Yugoslavia	VAX, easily adaptable to other computers	VMS, GKS for FORTRAN	$3,000
Graphical Programming of Simulation Models (GPSM)	A graphical front end to the Performance Analysts's Workbench System (PAWS™).	Doug Neuse Information Research Associates 911 West 29th Street Austin, TX 78705 Phone: (512) 474-4526	IBM PC/XT/AT, APOLLO workstations	None	$5,000
GRD1 (Grid Refinement for Differential systems, Version 1)	A transportable FOR-TRAN 77 code for the numerical integration of nonstiff/stiff ODEs.	W.E. Schiesser Whitaker No. 5 Lehigh University Bethlehem, PA 18015 Phone: (215) 861-4264	Any computer with a FORTRAN 77 compiler	None	$1000 for source code on nine track tape
HASP	Hydraulics System Simulation	Cambridge Control Limited High Cross Madingley Road Cambridge CB3 0HB, UK	VAX	VMS	Available on request
HEI Real Time Computer Simulator	Automated factory/ warehouse simulation, emulation and diagnostics.	Kathy Cornell HEI Corporation 350 E. Randy Rd. Carol Stream, IL 60188	IBM PC/XT/AT, COMPAQ 386	MS-DOS	$1,500
HEXTRAN Program	An essential tool for engineers involved in heat and recovery and energy optimization for the chemical processing industry.	David G. Smiley, V.P. Sales Simulation Sciences, Inc. 1051 W. Bastanchury Rd. Fullerton, CA 92633 Phone: (714) 879-9180	IBM/3000, 4000, PRIME, VAX, Data General	OS/MVS, VM/CMS, Primos	Cost available upon request
HIT System	Operator training system combining microcomputer technology and interactive video.	Roy Lucas 5201 Langfield Rd. Houston, TX 77040 Phone: (713) 460-4460	DEC Professional 380	None	$35,000+
HOCUS Simulation System	Discrete and continuous process simulation system requiring no programming, and having no model size or complexity limitations.	P-E Inbucon Modeling Division 4118 Murphy's Run Ct. Hampstead, MD 21074 Phone: (301) 239-3372	Most 286/386 micros, Sun, Apollo, Vax, Prime, DG, IBM RT, etc.	Xenix/Unix on 286/386 micros, and native O/S on all other computers.	Contact vendor

Item	Brief description	Contact	Computer(s)	Operating system/ other software required	Approximate cost
HOST	A framework for integrating submodels and data based on Turbo Pascal. Output is in a spreadsheet format.	Center for Development Policy Research Triangle Inst. P.O. Box 12194 Research Triangle Park, NC 27709-2194	IBM PC/XT/AT or compatible	PC/MS DOS and Turbo Pascal 3.0 or later	Contact Vendor
HULLCURV	Simulation for determination of envelope functions for AGVS or monorails.	Bernd Noche SDZ GmbH Emil-Figge-Str.75 4600 Dortmund 50 West Germany Phone: (0231/7549-139)	IBM PC or compatible	MS-DOS/PASCAL	$15,000
HYSAN™	Hydraulic system analysis modeling and solution software.	Hugh C. Morris Hydrasoft Corporation 914 E. Dunne Morton, IL 61550 Phone: (309) 266-9906	IBM PC/XT/AT, PS/2 or compatible	MS-DOS	$2,000
HYSIM™	A comprehensive and complete process flowsheet simulator for gas processing or oil refining.	T. Vysniauskas Hyprotech Ltd. 1700 Varsity Estates Dr. NW Calgary, Alberta T3B 2W9 Canada Phone: 1-800-661-8696	Any ordinary IBM compatible PC, most mainframes	MS-DOS 2.1 or higher for PCs	$15,000 for PCs
IFS (International Futures)	Global forecasting model (8 regions) for population, food, energy and economics.	Peter Trotter CONDUIT The University of Iowa Oakdale Campus Iowa City, IA 52242 Phone: (319) 335-4100	IBM PC/XT/AT or compatible	MS-DOS	$100
INSIGHT	Discrete-event simulation.	Mary Ann Flanigan SysTech, Inc. P.O. Box 509203 Indianapolis, IN 46250 Phone: (317) 842-6586	All major micro, mini, and mainframe computers	Any system that supports FORTRAN	Lease for $5,000 per year.
Interactive INSIGHT	Interactive discrete-event simulation.	Mary Ann Flanigan SysTech, Inc. P.O. Box 509203 Indianapolis, IN 46250 Phone: (317) 842-6586	IBM PC/PS2 or compatible, mainframes.	PC/MS DOS, OS2, UNIX, or any system with C and FORTRAN	$1,900 (Complete)
Interactive Simulation Language	Direct-executing simulation with on line editor, 100+ state variables.	R.D. Benham 5312 W Tucannon Kennewick, WA 99336 Phone: (509) 783-3829	PDP-11/data general 16-bit computers; Apple II series, C64/C128	RT-11/RDOS; Apple DOS/Commodore DOS	$250-$2400 (educational discounts available)
Inter-SIM	Discrete-event simulation package with animation facilities.	B.D. Krause Milo (Consult. Eng.) Riverview House London Road, Basing, Basingstoke RG24 OJL, UK	IBM PC or compatible, VAX	PC/MS DOS; UNIX; VMS	£750 (pounds sterling) (IBM) £3500 pounds sterling (VAX)
INTERWORK II™ Concurrent Programming Toolkit	A "C" language software package for distributed simulation providing a global object name space, lightweight processes, and a global time base.	Block Island Technologies 13563 NW Cornell Road, Suite 230 Portland, OR 97229 Phone: (503) 241-8971	Intel iPSC™ Concurrent Computer System	Supplied with iPSC	$25,000

Item	Brief description	Contact	Computer(s)	Operating system/ other software required	Approximate cost
ISIM	A continuous system simulation program and language.	Tony Griffith Simulation Systems Ltd. The Gables, North End, Yatton Bristol, BS19 4AS, UK Phone: 0-934-838803	Any machine with FORTRAN IV, 66 or 77; 60K bytes RAM and disk	All standard	£495 to £2000 (pounds sterling) depending on self install, educ./ind.
ISIM	Interactive continuous system simulation language.	Crosbie Hay & Associates P.O. Box 943 Chico, CA 95927 Phone: (916) 894-8255	IBM PC or compatible	MS-DOS/PC-DOS	$600 (multiple systems & educational discounts available)
JADE 3.0, Distributed Programming Environment	An integrated multi-lingual environment for specifying implementing and testing distributed systems.	Jade Simulations International Corporation #80, 1833 Crowchild Trail, NW Calgary, Alberta, T2M 4S7 Canada Phone: (403) 282-5711	Sun workstations via TCP/IP protocols	UNIX	$15,000
LASER	Portable artificial intelligence programming environment.	Ramana Reddy 768 Augusta Avenue Morgantown, WV 26505 Phone: (304) 293-3607	VAX, IBM/AT and 68000 based computers	UNIX and VMS	$10,000 to $20,000
Libra™	Performs harmonic-balance simulation by combining linear frequency-domain and nonlinear time-domain analysis in a single tool.	EEsof, Inc. 5795 Lindero Canyon Rd. Westlake Village, CA 91362 Phone: (818) 991-7530	IBM PC or compatible, DEC VAX series, Hewlett-Packard 9000 series, Apollo and Sun workstations	None	Contact vendor
Linear System Modeling and Analysis Program (LSMP)	Microcomputer software for modeling and analyzing linear system dynamics using Laplace transform techniques (frequency and transient response analysis).	R. Wade Allen Systems Technology, Inc. 13766 S. Hawthorne Blvd. Hawthorne, CA 90250 Phone: (213) 679-2281	IBM PC or compatible	MS-DOS	$3,000
LYSIS	Modeling of linear and non-linear dynamic systems and time-series data.	Biomedical Sim. Res. School of Engineering Univ. of Southern Cal. Los Angeles, CA 90089-1451 Phone: (213) 743-3648	VAX II Workstation	VMS	No charge to the biomedical community for non-commercial use
MAC II-MATLAB	Performs matrix computation, control design analysis, digital signal processing, parametric modeling, and engineering graphics.	The MathWorks, Inc. 21 Eliot Street South Natick, MA 01760 Phone: (508) 653-1415	IBM PC or compatible	DOS 2.0 or above	$895
MANIP	Interactive modelling and simulation system for thermal engineers.	A. Symons / R. Kool BSO/Aerospace P.O. Box 8055 1180 LB Amstelveen The Netherlands Phone: 20-476161	32-bit super-minis/ workstations	UNIX	Varies depending upon configuration

Item	Brief description	Contact	Computer(s)	Operating system/ other software required	Approximate cost
MAP/1	A modeling and analysis program for batch manufacturing.	Michael F. Quigley Pritsker & Associates, Inc. 1305 Cumberland Ave. P.O. Box 2413 West Lafayette, IN 47906 Phone: (317) 463-5557 or 800-423-7636	Virtually machine independent. (DEC, IBM, Apollo, Sun, etc.)	FORTRAN compiler	Dependent on machine class
MAST (Manufacturing System design Tool)	Simulation language for the study of integrated manufacturing.	John E. Lenz CMS Research, Inc. 600 South Main Street Brooklyn Center Oshkosh, WI 54901 Phone: (414) 235-3356	IBM PC/AT VAX, any mainframe w/ FORTRAN 77 compiler	DOS 3.1 or higher on PC; wide variety including UNIX on mainframe	$6500 package (SPAR, MAST, BEAM); $900 academic
MATRIXx/Plus	Integrated environment for block diagram modeling, simulation, control design and analysis.	Juli Jensen 2500 Mission College Blvd. Santa Clara, CA 95054-1215 Phone: (408) 980-1500	DEC, VAX, IBM, VAXstation, Apollo	VMS, VM MVS, Aegis	Contact vendor
MC-PWR	An enhanced dynamic model for two-phase analysis of PWR nuclear power plant on a microcomputer.	Dr. Parveen K. Jain S. Levy Incorporated 3425 South Bascom Ave. Campbell, CA 95008 Phone: (408) 377-4870	IBM PC/XT/AT or compatible	MS-DOS or PC-DOS	$24,000
MDOF	Missile system engagement simulation with multiple degrees-of-freedom.	James B. Morrison 401 Wynn Drive Huntsville, AL 35805 Phone: (205) 837-6000	Computer system independent	FORTRAN IV compiler	$150,000-$200,000
Micro-DSS	Micro-DSS is an IBM-AT version of DSS/2 with color graphics.	W.E. Schiesser Whitaker No. 5 Lehigh University Bethlehem, PA 18015 Phone: (215) 861-4264	Any computer that is IBM AT compatible	Ryan-McFarland (professional) FORTRAN 77	$1,000
Micro-DYNAMO/DOS	Continuous simulation package for education, nonlinear dynamic systems.	Kip Cooper Pugh-Roberts Associates 5 Lee St. Cambridge, MA 02139 Phone: (617) 864-8880	IBM PC/XT/AT or compatible	DOS 2.0 or later	$195 professor's copy, student copy discount
microENPORT	Microcomputer version of ENPORT.	ROSENCODE Associates, Inc. 200 North Capital Building, Lower Level Lansing, MI 48933 Phone: (517) 483-3216	IBM XT/AT or compatible	MS-DOS	$495 (educational licensing available)
micro PASSIM	A development package to implement combined discrete and continuous simulation in Pascal.	Claude C. Barnett Walla Walla College College Place, WA 99324 Phone: (509) 527-2881	IBM PC/XT/AT	MS-DOS/Turbo Pascal	$125
Micro SAINT 3.1	Easy-to-use task network modeling system. Menu-driven, help screens, no coding! Very powerful. Graphics.	Micro Analysis and Design, Inc. 9132 Thunderhead Drive Boulder, CO 80302 Phone: (303) 442-6947	IBM PC or compatible	MS-DOS, PC-DOS, or TI DOS	$1,495

Item	Brief description	Contact	Computer(s)	Operating system/ other software required	Approximate cost
Microwave SPICE™	Non-linear, time-domain circuit simulation program tailored specifically for microwave and RF engineers, providing an in-depth analysis of the non-linear aspects of a circuit.	Maria VanderKolk EEsof, Inc. 5795 Lindero Canyon Rd. Westlake Village, CA 91362 (818) 991-7530	IBM PC or compatible	None	
MIC-SIM	General purpose, discrete-event simulation package. Menu-driven with extensive modeling capabilities. Supports 10,000 activities per model.	Integrated Sytems Technologies, Inc. 312-B East Broad Street Cookeville, TN 38501 Phone: (615) 528-5280	IBM PC/XT/AT, PS/2 or compatible	PC/MS-DOS	Working Demo Pkg $25. $450-$1750 with University/Site/ Corporate licenses available
MIC-SIM VIEW	Animation add-on package for MIC-SIM. Provides high resolution graphic animation during a simulation execution. Icon and layout editors included.	Integrated Systems Technologies, Inc. 312-B East Broad Street Cookeville, TN 38501 Phone: (615) 528-5280	IBM PC/XT/AT, PS/2 or compatible with EGA or VGA monitor.	PC/MS-DOS, MIC-SIM	$2,000
MIDGET	Program generator for special-purpose operating systems (simulation language environments).	Magnus Rimvall Institute of Automatic Control ETH-Zentrum CH-8092 Zurich Switzerland Phone: (+41) 1-256-2842	VAX	VMS	$600 profit org.; $200 universities
Mini-Dynamo	Continuous simulation package for 16-bit minicomputers.	Kip Cooper Pugh-Roberts Associates 5 Lee Street Cambridge, MA 02139 Phone: (617) 864-8880	Any 16-bit minicomputer supporting FORTRAN (VAX/VMS)	FORTRAN (VAX/VMS)	$3,000, $1,500 for education, site licenses available
MIRANIM	Director-oriented and extensible three-dimensional computer animation system.	N. Magnenat-Thalmann 5255 Decelles Montreal H3T 1V6 Canada Phone: (514) 340-6616	DEC	VAX VMS	$1,500
MMS-EASE	A graphics-based pre & post processor for all versions of the Modular Modeling System (MMS)	Roger L. Trent Babcock & Wilcox, NPD 3315 Old Forest Road Lynchburg, VA 24506-0935 Phone: (804) 385-2236	IBM PC or compatible	DOS/None	Quote available on request
MMS-EASE+	Automates the preparation of MMS models and input decks.	Ross D. Schaack P.O. Box 10935 Lynchburg, VA 24506-0935 Phone: (804) 385-2584	IBM PC/XT/AT or compatible	DOS 2.0 or higher	$5,500
MMS/PC	A modular code for modeling and dynamic simulation of fossil and nuclear power plants using an interactive PC Workstation environment.	Roger L. Trent Babcock & Wilcox, NPD 3315 Old Forest Road Lynchburg, VA 24506-0935 Phone: (804) 385-2236	IBM PC or compatible	DOS / ACSK, FORTRAN	Quote available upon request

Item	Brief description	Contact	Computer(s)	Operating system/ other software required	Approximate cost
Model-C™	A graphical tool for modeling general non-linear dynamic systems.	Carol Michaels Systems Control Technology, Inc. 1801 Page Mill Road Palo Alto, CA 94304 Phone: (800) 227-1910 or (415) 494-2233	VAXstation II	uVMS 4.4, VWS 3.0	Contact vendor
Modular Modeling System (MMS)	A modular code for modeling and dynamic simulation of fossil and nuclear power plants.	Roger L. Trent Babcock & Wilcox, NPD 3315 Old Forest Road Lynchburg, VA 24506-0935 Phone (804) 385-2236	CRAY, CDC, IBM, AMDAHL, HP9000, DEC/VAX, and others that support ACSL	ALL/ACSL, FORTRAN	Quote available upon request
Monte Carlo Simulations Advanced Version	Integrated system with statistical analysis, simulation, and long-term projection.	Actuarial Micro Software 8025 North Point Blvd., Suite 215E Winston-Salem, NC 27106 Phone: (919) 773-1313	IBM PC, Macintosh	No special OS required	$600
MULTI.SIM	Simulates a multi-level marketing channel.	Walter Maner Computer Science Dept. BGSU Bowling Green, OH 43403 Phone: (419) 352-0411	DEC-20	Simula	TBA
Network	System for analyzing networks such as streets, utility lines, streams, etc.	S.J. Camarata, Jr. 380 New York Street Redlands, CA 92373 Phone: (714) 793-2853	Prime, DEC VAX, Data General	Primos, VMS, AOS VS	Available from ESRI
Network II.5	A design aid to build models of computer systems.	Paul Gorman CACI 3344 N. Torrey Pines Ct. La Jolla, CA 92037 Phone: (619) 457-9681	IBM PC, IBM mainframe, VAX, MicroVAX all other versions	None	$13,500 PC; $29,500 (free trial available)
OMNISYS™	Simulates microwave systems	Maria VanderKolk EEsof, Inc. 5795 Lindero Canyon Road Westlake Village, CA 91362 Phone: (818) 991-7530	IBM PC or compatible, DEC VAX series, HP9000, Apollo and Sun workstations.		Contact vendor
OPTIK	A suite of visual interactive modeling tools including animated discrete-event simulation and data base facilities.	Insight International Ltd. 2 Robert Speck Parkway, Suite 750 Mississauga, Ontario L4Z 1H8 Canada Phone: (416) 896-0515	VAX, APOLLO, IBM PC AT or equivalent and Compaq 386	DOS 3.0, FORTRAN 77	Cost available upon request
OPTISIM	Combined interactive simulation and optimization of continuous systems (e.g., parameter estimation).	Jan Spriet Kardinaal Mercierlaan 92 B-3030 Heverlee, Belgium	IBM PC XT/AT, IT or compatible; also Macintosh	MS DOS 2.0, PC DOS. Requires 256K, 8087 optional color and Hercules graphics	$750; educational discount
PASION	Pascal-related general purpose simulation language. Process/event structure, can be applied to discrete and continuous models.	Stanislaw Raczynski P.O. Box 22-783 14000 D.F. Mexico City, Mexico	IBM PC	A Pascal compiler	$70

Item	Brief description	Contact	Computer(s)	Operating system/ other software required	Approximate cost
PAWS™ Performance Analyst's Work bench System	High-level, declarative discrete-event simulation language for perfor- mance modeling of com- puter, communication, manufacturing, and elec- tronics systems.	Doug Neuse Information Research Associates 911 West 29th Street Austin, TX 78705 Phone: (512) 474-4526	All major com- puters with an ANSI FORTRAN compiler and 1 MB of user address space	FORTRAN compiler	$18,000
PC-GRASP	Color computer graphics simulation of robotic workcells.	Stephen Derby RD 3, Box 233A Troy, NY 12180 Phone: (518) 279-9414	IBM PC/AT	None	$1,500
PC-MATLAB	Performs matrix computation control design analysis, digital signal processing, parametric modeling, and engineering graphics.	The MathWorks, Inc. 21 Eliot Street South Natick, MA 01760 Phone: (508) 653-1415	IBM PC or compatible	DOS 2.0 or above	$695
PCModel	A highly interactive, general purpose discrete- event simulation system featuring concurrent col- or graphic animation.	Simulation Software Systems 2107 North First Street, Suite 680 San Jose, CA 95131 Phone: (408) 436-8300	IBM PC/XT/AT, PS/2 or true compatible	DOS 2.1 and later	$399, $975, $1850, $4900 includes 30 day return policy, 1 year of free updates
PCModel/GAF (Graphic Animation Facility)	A general-purpose modeling and simulation system with high resolu- tion graphic animation.	Simulation Software Systems 2470 Lone Oak Drive San Jose, CA 95121 Phone: (408) 270-2300	IBM PC/XT/AT, PS/2 or true compatible	DOS 2.1 and later	$7,500, includes 1 year of free updates and training.
PC-SOL Release 4.0	General Purpose interac- tive discrete simulation system, using SOL language (extension to PASCAL).	H. Ulfers Systems Simulation Consultants 11051 Ring Road Reston, VA 22090 Phone: (703) 437-5887	IBM PC/XT/AT or compatible	DOS 2.0 and up; TURBO Pascal 4.0	$500 (institutional discount)
Personal Com- puter Engineering Simulation Program	Continuous system simulation on the IBM PC family, with graphics on color displays.	IBM 2077 Gateway Place San Jose, CA 95110 Phone: (408) 288-4113	IBM PC/XT/AT, PS/2 family	DOS 2.0 or higher, FORTRAN 2.0 or professional FORTRAN	$400
PIPEPHASE Program	Simulates the steady state flow of single and multiphase fluids in pipelines and piping networks.	Mr. David G. Smiley Simulation Sciences, Inc. 1051 W. Bastanchury Rd. Fullerton, CA 92633 Phone: (714) 879-9180	IBM/3000 & 4000, CDC Cybernet/6000, 7000, 172 & 174, PRIME, CRAY, VAX, Micro VAX, and Sperry	OS/MVS, VM/CMS, NOS, PRIMOS	Cost available upon request
PITSIM2	A time incrementing simulator for shoveltruck systems in open pit mines.	E. Koniaris or P.N. Calder Queen's University Dept. of Mining Eng. Kingston, Ontario K7L 3N6 Canada Phone: (613) 545-6366	IBM 3081, HP1000	FORTRAN 77 compiler	Contact Dept. of Mining Eng.
PKFIT	For the simulation and analysis of pharmacoki- netic data.	Keith T. Muir USC School of Pharmacy 1985 Zonal Avenue Los Angeles, CA 90033 Phone: (213) 224-7527	IBM PC or compatible	PC-DOS/MS-DOS 256K RAM color graphics adapter	$50

Item	Brief description	Contact	Computer(s)	Operating system/ other software required	Approximate cost
PLOT4U.EXE	For the analysis of experimental and simulated pharmacodynamic data.	Michael B. Bolger USC School of Pharmacy 1985 Zonal Avenue PSC 700 Los Angeles, CA 90033 Phone: (213) 224-7111	IBM PC/XT/AT or compatible	DOS 2.0 and up	$50
PML-Pulmonary Mechanics Laboratory	An interactive simulation for teaching respiratory function physiology.	Command Applied Technology, Inc P.O. Box 511 Pullman, WA 99163-0511 Phone: (509) 334-6145	IBM PC/XT/AT or compatible	MS-DOS compatible 5.25 inch floppy disk	$150 (discount in quantity)
Policy/Goal Percentaging. Also known as Best Choice.	Designed to process a set of goals and alternatives for achieving them.	Stuart S. Nagel 1720 Park Haven Drive Champaign, IL 61820 Phone: (217) 359-8541	IBM DOS	Tencore	$45
Process Quality Simulator	To evaluate the quality of parts being made by a manufacturing process.	David A. Narone 2116 Waterloo Stockton, CA 95205 Phone: (209) 941-2669	IBM PC, Apple II family	None	$135
PROCESS Simulation Program	Performs rigorous mass and energy balances. Unit operation modules are incorporated for simulation of process units.	David G. Smiley Simulation Sciences, Inc. 1051 W. Bastanchury Rd. Fullerton, CA 92633 Phone: (714) 879-9180	IBM/3000, 4000, 360 & 370 CDC Cybernet 6000, 7000, 172 & 174 Univac/Sperry PRIME, Hewlett Packard, CRAY, VAX and MicroVAX	MVS, DOS, CMS, NOS1 & 2 VE, VMS Unix, Primos, COS, NOS	Cost available upon request
Professional DYNAMO (PLUS)	Continuous simulation packages, with Gaming Framework, linear- analysis/optimization add-on.	Kip Cooper Pugh-Roberts Associates 5 Lee Street Cambridge, MA 02139 Phone: (617) 864-8880	IBM PC/XT/AT or compatible	None	$500-$2,000 (educ. disc., site licenses available)
PRO-MATLAB	Performs matrix computation, control design and analysis, digital signal processing, parametric modeling, and engineering graphics.	The MathWorks, Inc. 21 Eliot Street South Natick, MA 01760 Phone: (508) 653-1415	Sun, Apollo, VAX, Gould, Ardent	Unix, VMS, Ultrix	Contact vendor
PROMISE (Process Oriented, Machine Independent, Simulation Environment)	Modelling of communicating parallel processes.	A.A.C.M. Klaasse National Aerospace Lab. NLR P.O. Box 90502 1006 BM AMSTERDAM The Netherlands	All major hardware with at least 32-bit words	ANSI FORTRAN 77 compiler	Depending on configuration and application
Promula	Simulation of dynamic, non-linear systems with the ability to integrate submodels written in FORTRAN, Pascal, and BASIC.	Mindware Corporation 3620 North High Street Suite 301 Columbus, OH 43214 Phone: (614) 263-5454	IBM PC/XT/AT or compatible	PC/MS DOS	$750
PROPUN	Uncertainty propagation of the arbitrary function of several different random variables using Monte Carlo simulation method.	Julius Goodman CSULB, Dept. of Eng. 1250 Bellflower Blvd. Long Beach, CA 90840 Phone: (213) 498-5638	IBM PC/XT/AT or compatible	PC DOS	Negotiable

Item	Brief description	Contact	Computer(s)	Operating system/ other software required	Approximate cost
PROTOBLOCK	A symbolic menu- and icon-driven control system design tool that supports transparent interaction with PRO-MATLAB and ACSL.	John Rodriguez, MGA, Inc. 73 Junction Drive Concord, MA 01742 Phone: (508) 369-5115	Sun, Apollo, and VAX workstations, VAX mainframes	VMS, UNIX, and AEGIS	$7,000
PSP	Interactive process simulator for oil and gas process engineering.	James McAuliffe Southwestern Computing Service, Inc. 1631 South Boston Tulsa, OK 74119 Phone: (918) 587-3321	Most mainframes, minis and micros; PC's using Unix/Zenix	Unix or Zenix on PC's	$12,500 and up; available for purchase, lease, or timesharing
Q+	Discrete-event simulation for analysing performance of computers, communication, and manufacturing systems.	C. Janczewski AT&T Bell Labs. Crawfords Corner Rd. Room 3M-328 Holmdel, NJ 07733 Phone: (201) 949-0678	SUN workstation or AT&T 630	SUN OS3.5 or later; UNIX® System V Host processor.	Cost available on request
ROBCAD	Engineering tool for design and real-time graphic simulation of robots, kinematic mechanisms, and systems.	Mary Jo Cartwright Tecnomatix, Inc. 30200 Telegraph Rd., Suite. 179 Birmingham, MI 48010 Phone: (313) 258-3900	Silicon Graphics, Sun, Prime	Unix	Cost available upon request; discounts for universities
ROSI	Robot dynamics/ Mechanisms Simulation	Cambridge Control Limited High Cross Madingley Road Cambridge CB3 0HB, UK	VAX	VMS	Available upon request
RTVOS	Provides a low-overhead environment with fast I/O path, high resolution frequency-based scheduler performance modeling and multi-language process data recording.	W.J. Marlow Harris Computer Systems Division 2101 W. Cyress Creek Rd. Ft. Lauderdale, FL 33309 Phone: (305) 974-1700	Harris H-Series	RT-VOS	Contact vendor
SACDA	Steady-state simulation for engineering	SCADA, Inc. 343 Dundas St. Suite 500 London, Ontario Canada N6B 1V5 Phone: (519) 679-6570			Contact SCADA
SAMOA	A discrete event simulation package including statistics collection and event tracing written in Ada.	Jade Simulations International Corporation #80, 1833 Crowchild Trail, NW Calgary, Alberta T2M 4S7 Canada Phone: (403) 282-5711	VAX under UNIX	UNIX	$10,000
SAMOC	General purpose, object-oriented simulation package in C++.	Jade Simulations International Corporation #80, 1833 Crowchild Trail, NW Calgary, Alberta, T2M 4S7 Canada Phone: (403) 282-5711	VAX under UNIX	UNIX	$10,000

Item	Brief description	Contact	Computer(s)	Operating system/ other software required	Approximate cost
Saint Plus	MicroSAINT's VAX version. Easy to use task network modeling system. Menu driven, help screens, graphics.	Mitchell and Gauthier, Inc. 73 Junction Square Drive Concord, MA 01742 Phone: (508) 369-5115	VAX	VAX,VMS	Price available upon request
SANDYS	For time simulation of dynamic systems.	Bertil Ohlsson ASEA Research and Innovation S-721 78 Vasteras Sweden	HP9000, VAX, IBM 3084	UNIX, VMS, VM/CMS	Cost Available upon request
SAPS-II	Ctrl-C function library for qualitative simulation forecasting structural identification.	Francois E. Cellier Dept. of Electr. & Comp. Eng. University of Arizona Tucson, AZ 85721 Phone: (602) 621-6192	VAX	VMS	$500; $300 academic
SCoP	Interactive simulation system. Menu driven; graphic output; includes numeric library and optimizer.	J. Mailen Kootsey National Biomed. Sim. Resource Box 3709 Duke University Medical Center Durham, NC 27710 Phone: (919) 681-3049	IBM PC/XT/AT or compatible; VAX; UNIX systems	IBM DOS; VMS, UNIX requires C compiler	$25 DOS; $100 VMS or UNIX
SD/FAST	Writes explicit, efficient, nonlinear equations of motion for multibody systems in FORTRAN or ADSIM.	Dan Rosenthal Symbolic Dynamics, Inc. 928 Wright Ave. Suite 108 Mountain View, CA 94043 Phone: (415) 960-1532	VAX, Sun, Apollo, ELXSI. Any Computer can execute the generated equations.	All/FORTRAN	$20,000 - $40,000
SEE WHY	Visual interactive simulation system for general purpose discrete-event modeling. Animated, integrated color graphics; full simulation capabilities. Models or submodels can be linked to WITNESS.	ISTEL Incorporated 60 Mall Road Burlington, MA 01803 Phone: (617) 272-7333	IBM PC/XT/AT, PS/2; DEC VAX	PC-DOS, MS-DOS;VMS	Contact vendor
SIGMUS	Simulation software generator for multiprocessor systems,based on their structure and their instruction set.	M. Mrva Siemens AG ZT1SOF3 Otto-Hahn-Ring 6 D-8000 Munich 83, F.R.G.	Siemens 7000 series	BS 2000 FORTRAN 77	Cost available upon request, discounts for universities
SIM++ (Distributed)	Library of tools for discrete event simulation in C++ which can be run across a network of workstations or on microcomputers.	Jade Simulations International Corporation #80, 1833 Crowchild Trail NW Calgary, Alberta T2M 4S7 Canada Phone: (403) 282-5711	Sun workstations, BNN Butterfly	UNIX	Contact vendor
SIM++ (Sequential)	Library of tools for discrete event simulation in C++ which are compatible with SIM++ (Distributed).	Jade Simulations International Corporation #80, 1833 Crowchild Trail NW Calgary, Alberta T2M 4S7 Phone (403) 282-5711	Sun workstations	UNIX	$5,000

Item	Brief description	Contact	Computer(s)	Operating system/ other software required	Approximate cost
SIMBOL	Integrated Simulation Control and Design	Cambridge Control Limited High Cross Madingley Road Cambridge CB3 0HB, UK	IBM PC or compatible (requires EGA/CGA)	MS-DOS	£895 (pounds sterling)
SIMAN	General-purpose language with special features for modeling manufacturing systems.	Systems Modeling Corp. The Park Building 504 Beaver Street Sewickley, PA 15143 Phone: (412) 741-3727	MS-DOS compatible computers and any with 77 FOR-TRAN compiler	MS-DOS, OS/2, FORTRAN 77	Contact vendor
SIMFACTORY	An analysis tool for factory planning and production analysis.	Ken Tumay CACI 3344 N. Torrey Pines Ct. La Jolla, CA 92037 Phone: (619) 457-9681	IBM XT/AT or compatible	MS DOS	$13,500 (free trial available)
SIMIS III	Discrete-event modeling and analysis program with animation for manufacturing and material flow systems.	Bernd Noche SDZ GmbH Emil-Figge-Str.75 4600 Dortmund 50 West Germany Phone: (0231/7549-139)	VAX, APOLLO, IBM PC or compatible	VMS, MS-DOS, UNIX/PASCAL	$15,000-$60,000
SIMKIT	Knowledge-based simulation and model environment based on KEE.	Fred Cummins 1975 El Camino Real West Mountain View, CA 94040 Phone: (415) 965-5627	Symbolics, TI Explorer	LISP	$26,500 without KEE (which is required)
SIMNET	General Purpose network-based language with interactive debugging and execution capabilities.	SimTec, Inc. P.O. Box 3492 Fayettville, AR 72702 Phone: (501) 575-6031	MS-DOS compatible computer with FORTRAN 77 compiler	Micro: MS-DOS, Mainframe/Mini: FORTRAN 77	Contact vendor
SIMNON	Simulates nonlinear dynamical systems described by differential and difference equations.	Tomas Schonthal Dept. of Automatic Control Lund Inst. of Technology Box 118 S-221 00 Lund, Sweden	IBM PC, VAX, DEC 10/20, Sperry 1100, etc.	Various	$700-$8,000
SIMONE	Simulation of dynamic processes in gas transporting pipeline systems.	J. Zavorka UTIA-CSAV Pod vodarenskou vezi 4, 182 08 Praha 8 Czechoslavia	IBM PC or compatible; math coprocessor	DOS/FORTRAN	Contact vendor
SIMPLE	Interactive simulation package for manufacturing.	B.-D. Becker IPA-FhG Schlosstr. 68 D-7000 Stuttgart 1 West Germany Phone: (0711) 61915-53	IBM XT/AT or compatible	MS-DOS, windows	$12,000
Simple_1 Simulation Environment	For discrete and continuous simulation, with built in animation.	Philip T. Cobbin Sierra Simulations & Software 303 Esther Avenue Campbell, CA 95008 Phone: (408) 378-6374	IBM PC/XT/AT or true compatible such as AT&T PC6300	MS- OR PC-DOS level 2.1 or higher	$750, $150 (academic) $45 (student)

Item	Brief description	Contact	Computer(s)	Operating system/ other software required	Approximate cost
SIMSCRIPT II.5	A high level, structured simulation language that can support complex models.	Rick Crawford CACI 3344 North Torrey Pines Ct. La Jolla, CA 92037 Phone: (619) 457-9681	IBM PC, IBM main-frame, VAX, MicroVAX, SUN, Gould, Sperry, CDC, Prime, Data General	None	$13,500 PC; $29,500 all other versions (free trial available)
SIMSMART	A user friendly real-time and faster-than-real-time dynamic simulator for continuous process industries.	E.R. Siedlak Applied High Technol. Ltd. 2 Plourde Street, Ste. 205 Charlemagne, Quebec, J5Z 3E8 Canada Phone: (514) 582-1461	Hardware Independent. Presently operating on MOD-COMP 32/85	"C" compiler	$150,000 (Canadian dollars)
SIMULA	General purpose pro-gramming language em-bodying the concepts of obect-oriented programming.	Simula a.s. Postbox 4403 Torshov N-0402 Oslo 4 Norway Phone: (472) 156710	CDC, DEC, IBM, ND-500, SPERRY, PRIME, VAX, IBM PC or com-patible, 68000 machines, Data General & others	None	Contact vendor
SIMULAP	Parametric simulation system.	B.-D. Becker IPA-FhG Schlosstr. 68 D-7000 Stuttgart 1 West Germany Phone: (0711) 61915-53	IBM XT/AT or compatible	MS-DOS, windows	$10,000
SimuSolv	Simulates behavior, op-timizes performance and estimates phenomenological parameters.	John Rodrigues MGA, Inc. 73 Junction Square Drive Concord, MA 01742 Phone: (508) 369-5115	DEC, IBM	All/FORTRAN	$45,000
SLAM II	Comprehensive simula-tion language permitting discrete event, con-tinuous, and network modeling.	Michael F. Quigley Pritsker & Associates, Inc. 1305 Cumberland Ave. P.O. Box 2413 West Lafayette, IN 47906 Phone: (317) 463-5557 or 800-423-7636	Virtually machine independent (DEC, IBM, Apollo, SUN, etc.)	FORTRAN compiler	Dependent on machine class
SLAM II/PC Animation System	General-purpose simula-tion modeling language and graphics/animation system.	Michael F. Quigley Pritsker & Associates, Inc. 1305 Cumberland Ave. P.O. Box 2413 West Lafayette, IN 47906 Phone: (317) 463-5557 or 800-423-7636	IBM PC or compatible	None	$9,500 (Special graphics adapter and mouse: $500)
SOLON	Simulation of demand/ supply interactions in transportation systems.	Y.J. Stephanedes Gamma Institute, Inc. 467 Woodlawn Ave. St. Paul, MN 55105 Phone: (612) 625-1305	IBM PC/XT/AT	DOS	$450-$5,000
SPAR (System Planning of Aggregate Requirements)	For evaluation of in-tegrated manufacturing gross capabilities. Will generate data for use in the MAST language.	John E. Lenz CMS Research, Inc. 600 South Main Street Brooklyn Center Oshkosh, WI 54901 Phone: (414) 235-3356	IBM PC or compatible, VAX	DOS 3.1 or higher; VMS	$6500 package (SPAR, MAST, BEAM); $900 academic

Item	Brief description	Contact	Computer(s)	Operating system/ other software required	Approximate cost
SPSS/PC+	Interactive data analysis package. Options available.	SPSS Inc. 444 North Michigan Ave. Chicago, IL 60611 Phone: (312) 329-3500	IBM PC/XT/AT or compatible	PC-DOS (MS-DOS 2.0 or higher)	Contact vendor
STELLA (Structural Thinking Experimental Learning Laboratory with Animation)	Animated simulation of dynamic, non-linear social and physical systems.	High Performance Systems, Inc. 13 Dartmouth College Highway Lyme, NH 03768 Phone: (603) 795-4122	Macintosh	None	$500
SYSL/M	Continuous and sampled-data system simulation.	E consulting P.O. Box 1182 Poway, CA 92064 Phone: (619) 578-4057	IBM PC/XT/AT or compatible; PS-2	DOS FORTRAN	$395 (academic discounts available)
SYSMOD	A general-purpose discrete/combined/continuous simulation language.	Systems Designers Software, Inc. 101 Main Street Cambridge, MA 02142 Phone: (617) 499-2000	IBM range and VAX range	None	$20,000
SYSTEM_BUILD	Graphical, block diagram tool for interactive modeling and simulation of dynamic systems.	Juli Jensen 2500 Mission College Blvd. Santa Clara, CA 95054-1215 Phone: (408) 980-1500	DEC VAX, IBM, VAXstation, Apollo	VMS, VM MVS, Aegis	Contact vendor
SYSTEM_BUILD/PC	Graphical, block diagram tool for interactive modeling and simulation.	Juli Jensen 2500 Mission College Blvd. Santa Clara, CA 95054-1215 Phone: (408) 980-1500	IBM XT/AT or compatible	MS-DOS, PC-DOS Math coprocessor, hard disk, graphics adapter	Contact vendor
System for Controllable Parameter Evaluation (SCOPE)	Provides current power plant performance evaluations to plant operators and results engineers.	Juan M. Cajigas Gilbert Services, Inc. P.O. Box 1498 Reading, PA 19603 Phone: (215) 775-2600	IBM XT/AT or compatible	DOS	$3000-$8000
TARA	Real-time efficient simulation of dynamic systems including stiff and lightly damped highly oscillatory systems.	Eclipse Real-Time Scientific S/W 316 Pettis Avenue Mountain View, CA 94041 Phone: (415) 964-2127	All except PCs and Workstations	ALL/FORTRAN	Computer/configuration dependent
TC-PROLOG	PROLOG based discrete/continuous simulation and problem solving system.	LOGICWARE 5000 Birch St., Suite 3000 The West Tower Newport Beach, CA 92660	IBM, VAX, M68000 based systems, IBM PC/XT/AT/discrete version only	CMS, OS; VMS, UNIX; UNIX, UNOS; PC-MSDOS	$800-$24,000
TESS	An integrated interactive simulation support system with relational database management and graphics capabilities.	Michael F. Quigley Pritsker & Associates, Inc. 1305 Cumberland Ave. P.O. Box 2413 West Lafayette, IN 47906 Phone: (317) 463-5557 or 800-423-7636	DEC VAX; IBM 30xx, 43xx; Apollo DN series, SUN 3 series, PRIME 2250 and higher; ASCII	VMS; VM/CMS and MVS/TSO; AGGIS; UNIX; PRIMOS	Dependent on machine class

Item	Brief description	Contact	Computer(s)	Operating system/ other software required	Approximate cost
The Cash Flow Simulator	Creates histograms of Net Present Worth values.	Debra Di Biase c/o DRT Associates 4686 Alex Drive San Jose, CA 95130 Phone: (408) 379-2158	IBM PC/XT/AT or compatible with 256K memory	None	$50 (introductory price)
The Inventory Simulator	Simulates cost and performance measures of inventory.	Debra Di Biase c/o DRT Associates 4686 Alex Drive San Jose, CA 95130 Phone: (408) 379-2158	IBM PC/XT/AT or compatible with 256K memory	None	$50 (introductory price)
Thermal Improvement Program (TIP)	A diagnostic tool for use in the control room of a coal-fired, steam power plant.	Joe Nasal or Cliff Price General Physics Corporation 111 Main Street Lockport, NY 14094 Phone: (716) 433-2592	IBM/PC or compatible	PC/DOS or MS/DOS	$25,000-$50,000
Touchstone®	Touchstone provides a highly interactive design environment for the analysis, simulation, and optimization of linear microwave/RF devices and circuits.	Maria VanderKolk EEsof, Inc. 5795 Lindero Canyon Road Westlake Village, CA 91362 Phone: (818) 991-7530	IBM PC or compatible, DEC VAX series, HP9000, Apollo and Sun workstations	None	Contact vendors
TUTSIM	Models and analyses of non-linear systems.	Walter Reynolds TUTSIM Products 200 California Ave. Suite 212 Palo Alto, CA 94306			$500.00 Academic discounts available
TSIM	General non-Linear Dynamic Simulation	Cambridge Control Limited High Cross Madingley Road Cambridge CB3 0HB, UK	VAX, Apollo, SUN	VMS, UNIX, AEGIS	£7,095- £11,660 (pounds sterling)
TurboSim IV	Turbo Pascal based discrete-event simulation. Source included.	Micro Simulation 37 William J. Heights Framingham, MA 01701 Phone: (617) 875-6098	IBM PC/XT/AT or compatible, MS-DOS	Borland International Turbo Pascal ver. 4.0	$100
UniFit	Fits probability distributions (e.g. normal gamma, etc.) to observed system data.	Averill M. Law Simulation Modeling & Analysis Company P.O. Box 40996 Tucson, AZ 85717 Phone: (602) 299-8441	IBM PC or compatible	None	$900
Venturer	Interactive and tolerant program on a microcomputer for appraisal of risk.	SAR Investment Properties 1 Laygarth Sq. Rothwell, Leeds England LS26 OTU Phone: 0532-829633	IBM PC or compatible	None	$695
WASTEPCK	An interactive dynamic simulation of a duel fired natural circulation balanced draft boiler.	B.W. Surgenor Queen's University Kingston, Ontario K7L 3N6 Canada Phone: (613) 545-2568	IBM PC or compatible (MSDOS) or APPLE IIe (DOS or ProDOS)	Demonstration copy available upon request	$2,950 (Cdn) 1st copy

Item	Brief description	Contact	Computer(s)	Operating system/ other software required	Approximate cost
WITNESS	Visual interactive simulation system designed especially for modeling manufacturing operations. Menu driven; animated, integrated color graphics; full simulation capabilities.	ISTEL Corporation 60 Mall Road Burlington, MA 01803 Phone: (617) 272-7333	IBM PC/AT, PS/2; DEC VAX	PC-DOS, MS-DOS, OS/2; VMS	Contact vendor
WORKSTATION Communications Simulator	Software for design, analysis, and simulation of digital communication links.	J.W. Modestino Symcom, Inc. 48 Ford Ave. Troy, NY 12180 Phone: (518) 274-7711	IBM PC, workstations	All/ FORTRAN	$4500 - $8000
Workstation interactive communications simulator	Software system for simulation of point-to-point digital communications systems.	Rensselaer Communications Consultants, Inc. 48 Ford Avenue Troy, NY 12180 Phone: (518) 274-3985	VAX		Contact Vendor
XCELL+	Interactive graphic model building for quick prototyping of manufacturing systems.	Michael F. Quigley Pritsker & Associates, Inc. 1305 Cumberland Ave. P.O. Box 2413 West Lafayette, IN 47906 Phone: (317) 463-5557 or 800-423-7636	IBM PC/AT, HP Vectra or compatible	MS-DOS	$8,000 XCELL: limt'd version w/mono chrome graphics $4,000

17. Geographic Information Systems

Much of the material in this chapter is adapted with permission from "An Overview of Geographic Information Systems for Archaeological Research and Data Management," by Dr. Kenneth L. Kvamme, Arizona State Museum, University of Arizona, Tucson, AZ 85721, USA. The article appeared originally in Microcomputers in Archeology, *published in 1986 by the Society for American Archeology, 808 17th Street, NW, Washington, DC 20006, USA; telephone: (202) 223-9774.*

Introduction

The effective utilization and development of geographically distributed resources is a major part of the task of managing a nation. Cities, transportation systems, ecosystems, agricultural areas, water resources, mining areas, and communications systems are all interlinked geographically as well as economically. Until recently, hand-drawn maps have been the primary tool for analyzing geographically distributed management problems. Now, geographic information systems (GIS) make it possible to integrate maps with databases about the objects and features represented on the maps. Remote sensing from satellites provides additional capabilities that only recently have become available at moderate costs.

There is enormous potential for GIS technology to improve the management and administration of nations. Governments have hardly begun to make use of the existing capabilities, and vastly enhanced capabilities are on the way.

In this chapter we make no attempt at a comprehensive exploration of GIS, but rather provide a brief introduction to the topic with suggestions on where the interested reader can turn for further information and assistance.

It should also be noted here that the chapter on "Catalogs, Books, and Newsletters" includes a description of a report designed for governments and other groups wanting to establish their own GIS facility. The report, *A Survey of Geographic Information Systems for Natural Resources Decision Making*, is quite comprehensive and applies to virtually every aspect of land-use planning.

While this chapter does not review particular GIS application programs, some of the other chapters review software applications in which GIS technology is an essential part. The "Agriculture" chapter describes the Famine Early Warning System in which GIS software is used to provide decision makers with maps and satellite images on which impending famine areas can be noted from changes in vegetative cover. The "Rural and Urban Development" chapter describes the UDMS system, which generates maps useful in planning urban settlements.

Geographic information systems are computer-based means for assembling, analyzing, and storing varied forms of data corresponding to specific geographical areas, with the spatial locations of the areas forming the basis of the system. Because they combine the data with the spatial location, geographic information systems are able to compare automatically a variety of socioeconomic, environmental, and land-use data sets for the same point on the ground. Many synergisms result from this capability.

To deal with both spatially related information and associated locational identifiers, a geographic information system must have the means for: (a) converting pictorial images into digital data (encoding) and recording spatial data (data entry); (b) maintaining, editing, and updating the data (database management); (c) retrieving and analyzing data (manipulation); and (d) displaying the products of analysis (inventory and map generation).

In a GIS, graphic output (e.g., a map) represents only one mode of data retrieval and only a subset of the system functions, which may include a wide range of spatial and non-spatial data manipulations. Thus, as illustrated in Figure 17-1, geographic information systems are not simple graphics-mapping systems but are

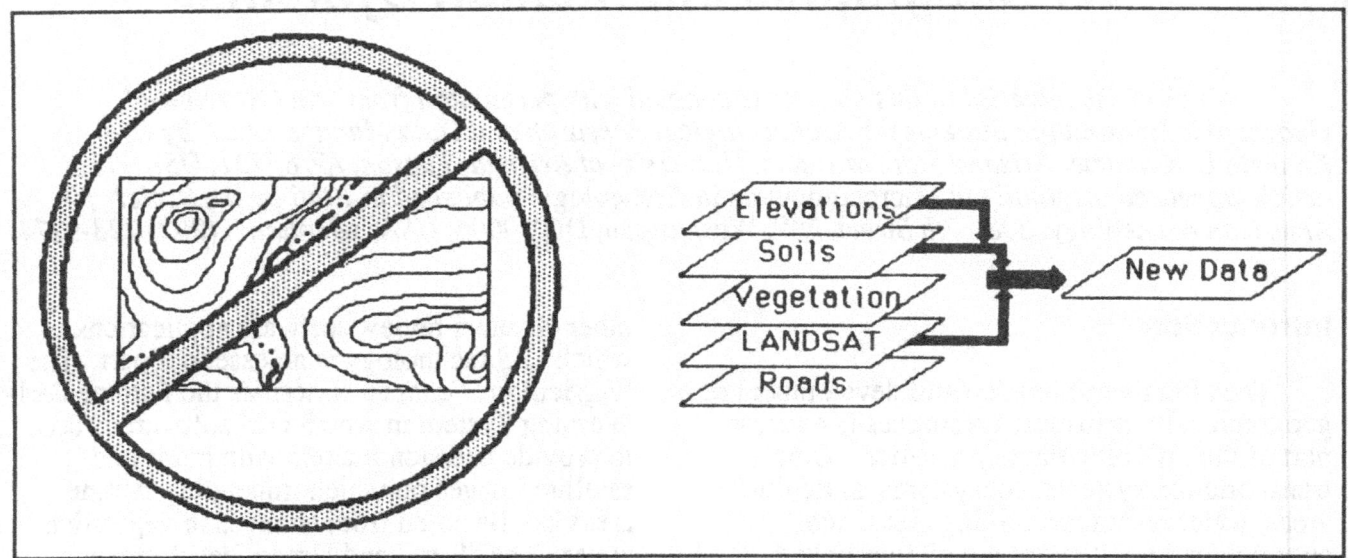

Figure 17-1: A geographic information system does not just produce maps, as computer graphics and cartography do, but rather interrelates data, manipulates data, analyzes data, and creates new data.

systems that interrelate, manipulate, and analyze a variety of geographically distributed data, in addition to mapping.

The Components of GIS

Geographic information systems include equipment and software for data capture or encoding, analysis, storage, retrieval, and display of cartographic data in the form of both maps and statistical summaries (e.g., charts, histograms). Examples of the components of a GIS and their interrelations are illustrated in Figure 17-2.

As indicated in Figure 17-2, the computer integrates and controls the wide range of equipment involved in a GIS. Of course, the computer alone is insufficient to make a GIS. Software is also needed. Software packages are available that process remote sensing images and maps into geographic data sets; manipulate, print, and perform statistical analyses of the geographic data; control input devices; and control special output devices. Some mapping packages also act like GIS programs. For information about companies selling GIS software for microcomputers, see "Sources" at the end of this chapter.

The Two Basic Types of GIS

As illustrated in Figure 17-3, there are two fundamental types of geographical information systems designs: cell-based (raster) and vector based. These two types—and their respective advantages and disadvantages—are described below.

Cell-based or raster GIS superimpose a regular grid, containing rows and columns of cells, over a region and then assign a numeric value to each cell to represent a particular on-the-ground feature within the area encompassed by the cell. Raster systems are well suited to analysis and quantitative manipulations because of their numeric structure and data organization. Data can be manipulated by rows or columns, a process that is fairly easy for computers to do. These systems are ideal for continuously varying data (e.g., elevations, slopes) since a number can be stored in each cell, but they can also encode discrete data (e.g., soil classes). Furthermore, new types of map data are easy to derive using raster systems.

On the other hand, cell-based or raster systems do have some disadvantages. They take relatively large amounts of storage (a number typically must be stored for each cell), although recent advances in mass storage and high-resolution display devices are reducing this problem. Another drawback is low precision of representation and display (e.g., a tendency toward a stair-step effect), particularly when large cell sizes are used. Again, recent advances are reducing this disadvantage.

Vector-based GIS focus on discrete map features that can be digitized and encoded as points, lines, or polygons. Vector-based systems are ideal for information management systems dealing with traditional (discrete) map features. Digitized polygon coordinates for such map features as a political boundary, a soil class, or an archaeological site can be stored and retrieved in much the same way as other types of information in a relational database system.

Compared to raster systems, vector-based systems take relatively little storage even for complex shapes, since only the (x, y) coordinates of the digitized points are stored. They also are

characterized by greater precision of display, since polygons, lines, and points can closely represent map features. Vector-based systems also have the advantage that they can be converted to raster type data of virtually any cell size.

One of the disadvantages of vector-based geographic information systems is that they involve complex software and more complicated encoding. Furthermore, many types of analysis are difficult to perform with these systems. Usually the data must be converted to raster form before analyses can be done. Finally, although vector-based systems are ideal for discrete (nominal- or ordinal-level) data, continuous information (e.g., elevation, slope) is more difficult to display and must be done through contouring.

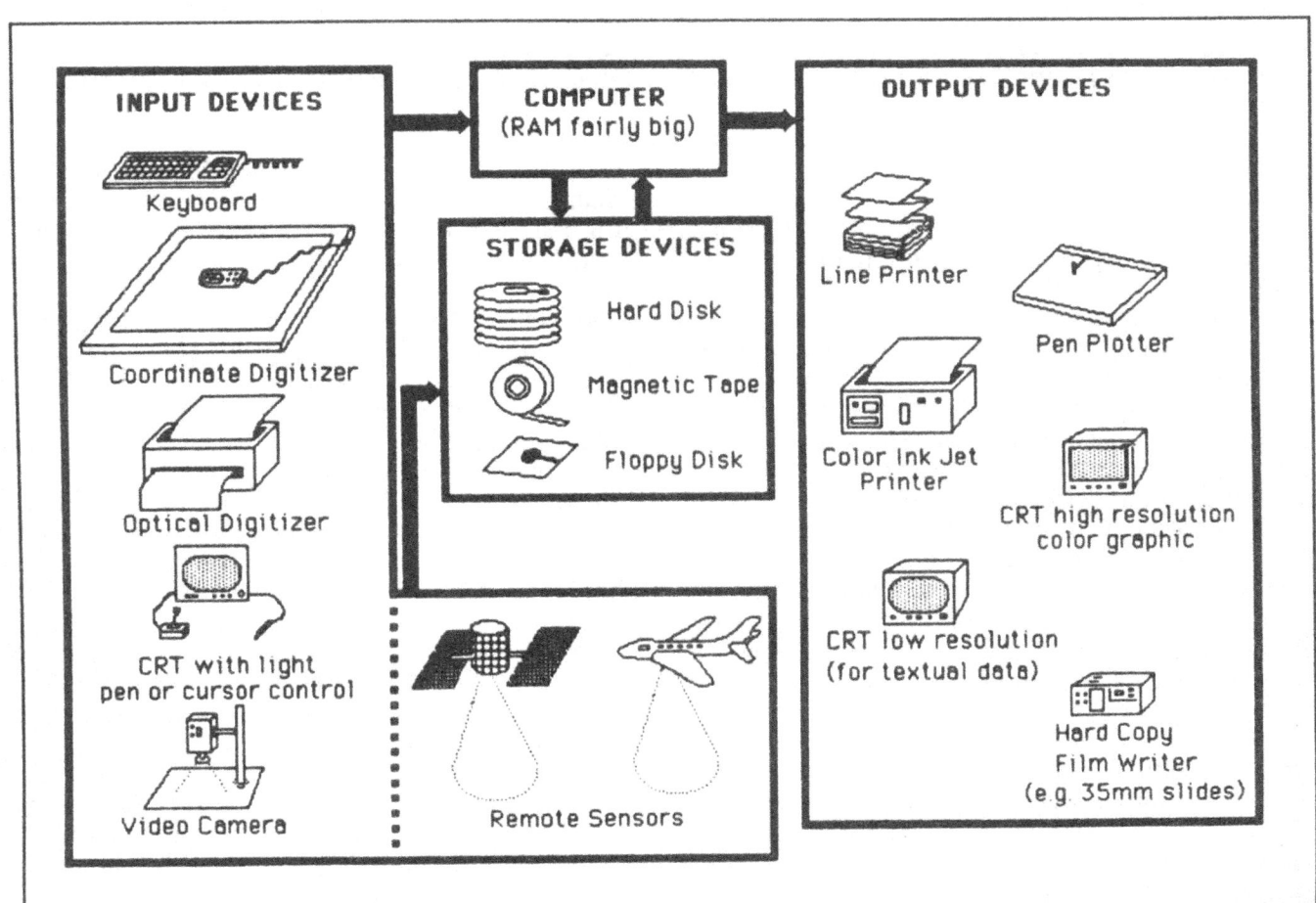

Figure 17-2: Hardware associated with many geographic information systems.

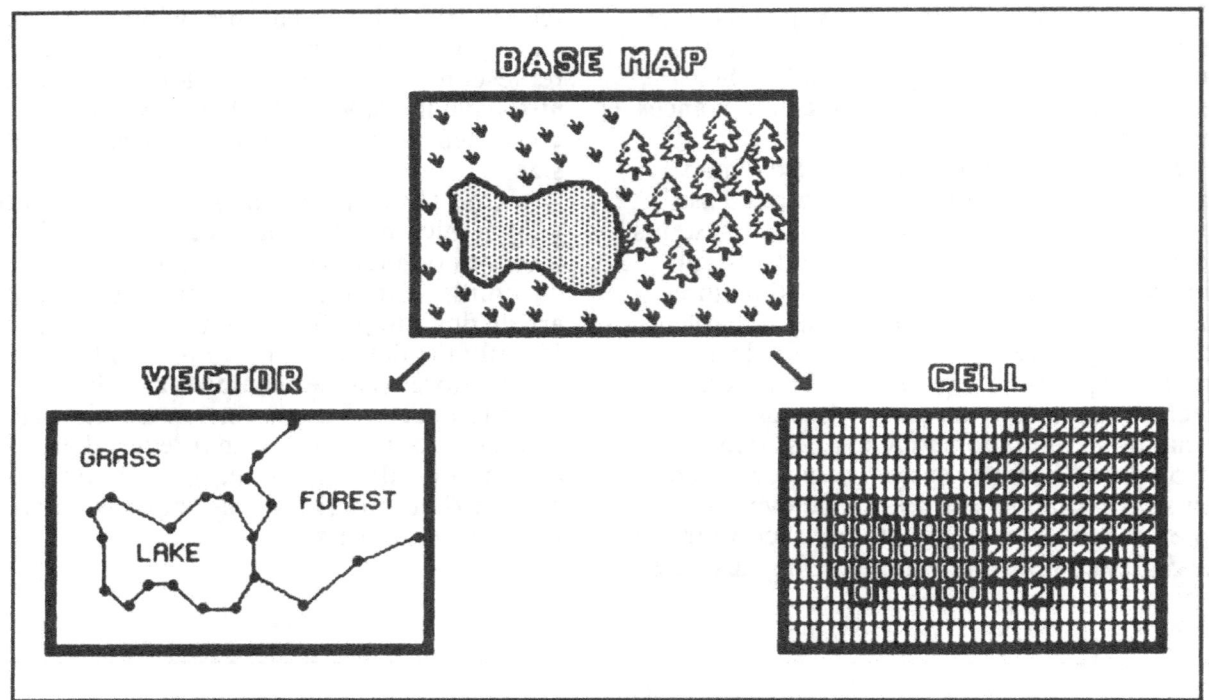

Figure 17-3: The difference between vector-based and cell-based (raster) geographic information systems.

Encoding Devices

To use a geographic information system, it is necessary to have computer-compatible geographical data. Some databases of this sort are available commercially, and these are described below. In addition, there are a number of devices and technologies available that encode geographically distributed or map-type information into computer-compatible form. Among these are the coordinate digitizer, the optical digitizer, and the video camera.

A coordinate digitizer includes a mouse or cursor that typically contains cross-hairs and a series of input keys. The use of a coordinate digitizer is illustrated in Figure 17-4. The cursor is connected to a special tablet which is available in sizes up to 48 inches x 64 inches (120 centimeters x 160 centimeters). Maps or other graphics are affixed to the tablet and the cursor is used manually to trace features of interest such as contour lines, streams, or soil unit boundaries. The tablet typically has one million addressable (x, y) coordinates per square inch. As the cursor is moved along the tablet surface, the feature being traced is translated into numerous

coordinates which the computer is able to manipulate. Specific features can be identified, for example, with a "O" for permanent streams or a "1" for semipermanent streams. See "Sources" at the end of this chapter for companies manufacturing coordinate digitizers.

Optical digitizers (scanners) are an up-and-coming digitizing technology. They use a light-sensitive head, such as a photo light head or a charge-coupled device (CCD), that moves back and forth over the printed map surface, greatly reducing the need for manual intervention. The head records reflected light as it moves across each scan line, providing a means to recognize lines and other printed graphics on a map. (See Figure 17-5). Resolution can be extremely high, from several hundred to over a thousand points per inch. This technology is inherently raster, composed of rows (scan lines) and columns of pixels (picture elements).

A disadvantage of some digitizers is that unwanted textual information—elevation values, village names, etc.—also are digitized by the light-sensitive head, creating the need for subsequent manual editing to remove the unwanted data.

For addresses of companies selling optical digitizers, see "Sources" at the end of this chapter.

Digital video-type cameras also can be used to digitize map or other pictorial information, including photographs. (See Figure 17-6.) The raster image that results contains rows and columns of pixels (picture elements) of virtually any resolution. Each pixel contains a number or gray-value on a scale representing darkness to lightness in terms of reflectance properties. These numbers then can be digitally manipulated by a computer to recognize lines or other map features. "Sources" at the end of this chapter gives addresses of companies selling video cameras for digitizing.

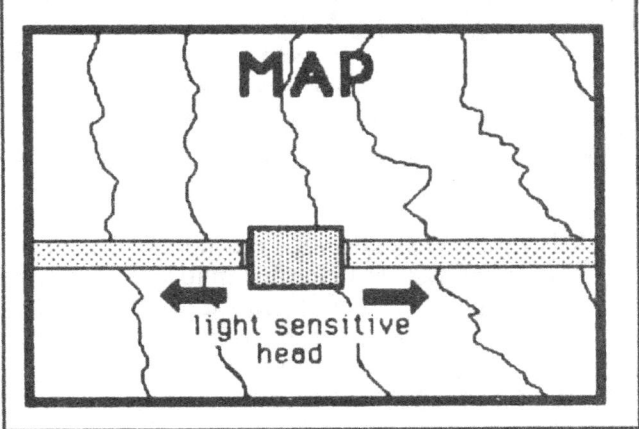

Figure 17-5: An optical digitizer (scanner) in operation.

Commercially Available Digital Databases

It is not always necessary to encode data for a GIS from maps and other images, since a number of digital geographic databases are available commercially. The U.S. Geological Survey (USGS) provides a variety of environmental and other information in digitally encoded form on computer tape or even floppy disks. Additionally, many private surveying or aerial photograph/reconnaissance companies now provide geographic information, such as elevation data, in computer-compatible format. Some of the important data files available for the United States and other parts of the world are described below. See "Sources" for the appropriate addresses.

Defense Mapping Agency Digital Terrain Data. Originally produced by the Defense Mapping Agency Topographic Center and now available through the U.S. Geological Survey (USGS), these data consist of

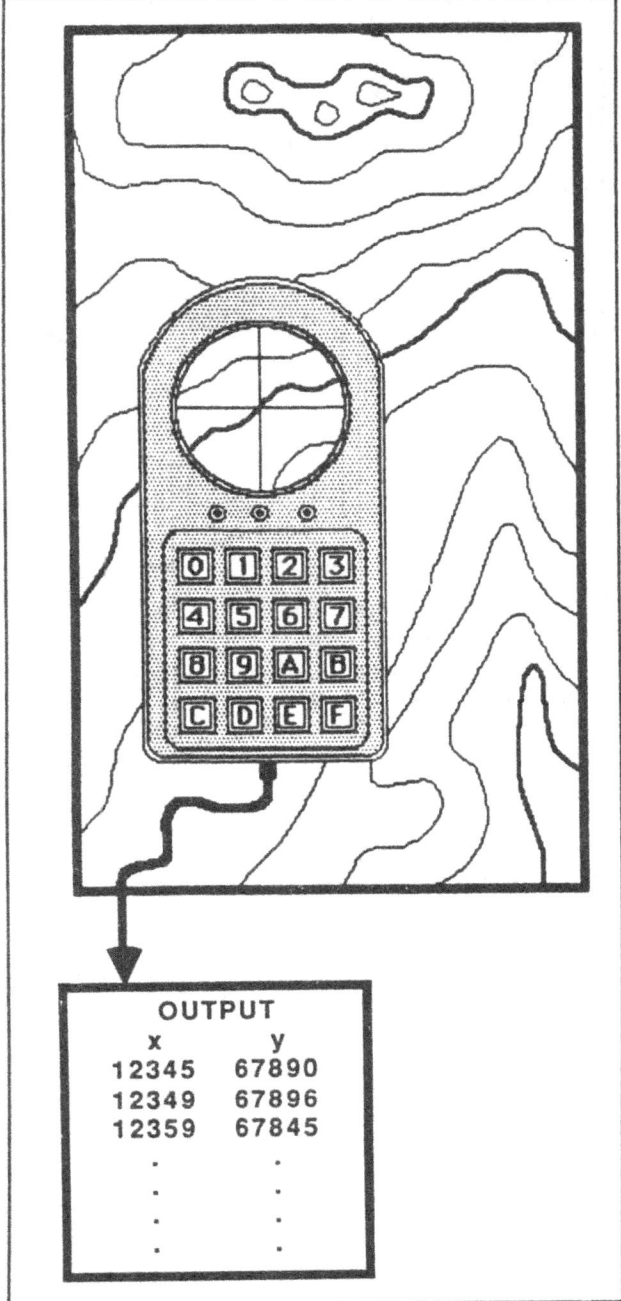

Figure 17-4: The use of a coordinate digitizer for obtaining computer-compatible geographical data from existing maps.

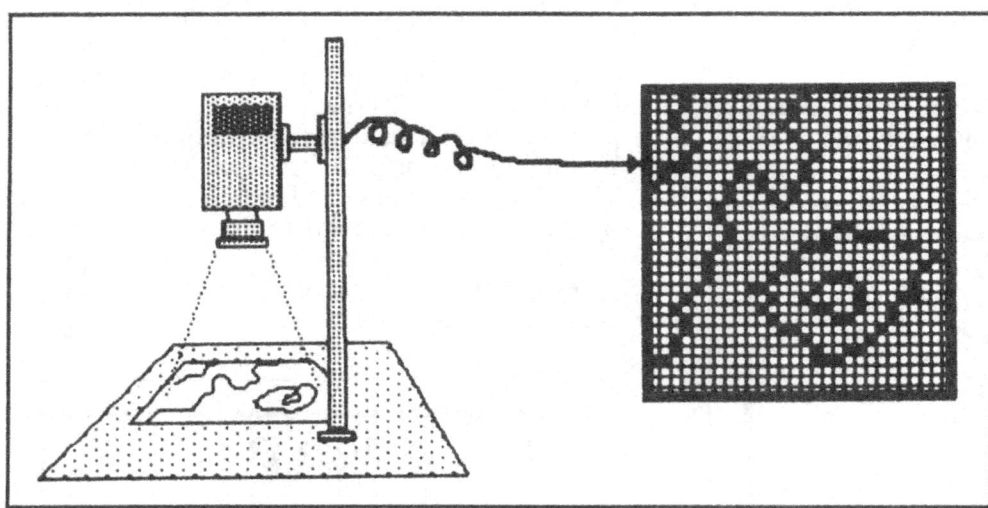

Figure 17-6: The use of a digital video camera to digitize information from a map.

Pattern recognition and image classification procedures can be used to identify vegetation cover type, soil classes, etc., which then can be input to a geographic information system.

Global Environmental Monitoring System (GEMS) and the associated Global Resource Information Database (GRID) described in the "Sources of Data" chapter of this book, in the section entitled "Environmental Quality."

elevation data obtained through digitization of the 1:250,000 scale series maps. Accuracy at this scale is not sufficient for applications dealing with micro-terrain features, since small ridges or drainage systems tend to be underportrayed.

Digital Elevation Models (DEM). Produced by USGS at a scale of 1:24,000 from existing maps or through aerial photogrammetry, these data files correspond to the areas of the 7.5 minute series maps. An elevation value is available every thirty meters across the map area.

Digital Line Graphs (DLG). Produced by USGS, these data include line or vector type information such as roads, political boundaries, hydrology. These data are available at 1:24,000 or 1:250,000 scale.

U.S. GeoData. These data are available at a scale of 1:2,000,000. Three basic types of map information are available: (a) boundaries (state and county, federally administered lands), (b) transportation (roads, railroads, airports), and (c) hydrographic (streams, water bodies).

LANDSAT or other remotely sensed imagery. Features in high altitude or outer space photographs can be digitized using devices discussed above. These data also are available in digital form on computer tape.

Sources

Sources of Microcomputer Software for Geographic Information Systems
Environmental Systems Research Institute
380 New York Street
Redlands, CA 92373, USA
Software: PA ARC/INFO for PC compatibles and Sun

MicroImages, Inc.
201 North 8th, Suite 15
Lincoln, NE 68508-1347, USA
Software: MIPS (Map and Image Processing System) for PC compatibles and Compaq 386

ERDAS, Inc.
Advanced Technology Development Center
430 Tenth Street, NW, Suite N206
Atlanta, GA 30318, USA
Software: Earth Resources Data Analysis System (ERDAS) for PC compatibles

Prof. Duane F. Marble
Department of Geography
Ohio State University
Columbus, OH 43210-1361, USA
Software: OSU MAP-for-the-PC for PC compatibles

Dr. Craig Zum Brunnen
Department of Geography
University of Washington
Seattle, WA 98195, USA
Software: Soviet Union Microcomputer
Geographic Information System (SUMGIS)
for Apple III

ITD Space Remote Sensing Center
Building 1103, Suite 118
Stennis Space Center, MS 39529, USA
Software: Geographic Resource Analysis
Support System (GRASS) for Macintosh II,
Compaq 386, and Sun

Clark University
Graduate School of Geography
Worcester, MA 01610, USA
Software: IDRISI for PC compatibles

*Sources of Mapping Software Packages with
Some GIS Capabilities*
Telos Software Products
3420 Ocean Park Boulevard
Santa Monica, CA 90405, USA
Software: Filevision/Business Filevision for
Macintosh

MapInfo Corp.
200 Broadway
Troy, NY 12180, USA
Software: MapInfo for PC compatibles

Quantitative Systems
P.O. Box 462
Cayucos, CA 93430, USA
Software: Graphic Mapping System (GMS)
for PC compatibles

Strategic Mapping, Inc.
4030 Moorpark Avenue, Suite 250
San Jose, CA 95117, USA
Software: Atlas Advanced Mapping Package
(AMP) for PC compatibles

Sources of Coordinate Digitizers
ALTEK Corporation
2150 Industrial Parkway
Silver Spring, MD 20904, USA

CALCOMP
2411 West La Palma Avenue
Anaheim, CA 92801, USA

GTCO Corporation
1055 First Street
Rockville, MD 20850, USA

Houston Instrument
8500 Cameron Road
Austin, TX 78753, USA

Summagraphics Corporation
777 State Street Extension
P.O. Box 781
Fairfield, CT 06430, USA

Sources of Optical Digitizers (Scanners)
The Complete PC
521 Cottonwood Drive
Milpitas, CA 95035, USA

Thunderware, Inc.
21 Orinda Way
Orinda, CA 94563, USA

Diamond Flower Electric Instrument Co., Inc.
2544 Port Street
West Sacramento, CA 95691, USA

Caere Corporation
100 Cooper Court
Los Gatos, CA 95030, USA

Palantir Corporation
2500 Augustine Drive
Santa Clara, CA 95054, USA

Kurzweil Computer Products, Inc.
185 Albany Street
Cambridge, MA 02139, USA

*Sources of Digital Video Cameras for Digitizing
Pictorial Material*
New Image Technology, Inc.
10300 Greenbelt Road, Suite 104
Seabrook, MD 20706, USA

Spectral Data Corporation
1595B Ocean Avenue
Bohemia, NY 11716, USA

ERDAS, Inc.
Advanced Technology Development Center
430 Tenth Street, Suite N206
Atlanta, GA 30318, USA

Chinon America, Inc.
660 Maple Avenue
Torrance, CA 90503, USA

Sources of Digital Geographic Data
United Nations Environment Programme
Global Environment Monitoring System
P.O. Box 30552
Nairobi, Kenya
Data: Digital geographic data from the Global
Resource Information Database (GRID)

National Geophysical Data Center
325 Broadway
Boulder, CO 80303, USA
Data: Worldwide elevation, gravitic,
geologic, and other data

U.S. Geological Survey
National Cartographic Information Center
507 National Center
Reston, VA 22092, USA
Data: LANDSAT, DEM, DLG, Defense
Mapping Agency Digital Terrain Data

U.S. Geological Survey
EROS Data Center
User Services Section
Sioux Falls, SD 57198, USA
Data: LANDSAT

U.S. Geological Survey
U.S. GeoData
MS 507-GD3A
Reston, VA 22092, USA
Data: Hydrography, transportation, and
boundaries

World Digital Coordinates, Inc.
11770 Warner Avenue, Suite 107
Fountain Valley, CA 92708, USA
Data: Hydrography, transportation, public
land survey, DEM, DLG

18. Artificial Intelligence: Present and Future Significance for Governments

This chapter was prepared by Dr. Margee M. Ensign, School of International and Public Affairs, Columbia University, 420 North 118th Street, #1432, New York, NY 10027, USA. Some of the research described in this chapter was supported by a grant from the Ford Foundation.

Introduction

Research in artificial intelligence (AI) began in the 1950s, and by the early 1970s significant strides had already been made in understanding and modeling human intelligence. Over the coming decade, the technology of AI will change profoundly the economy, defense, and government operations of nations throughout the world. The National Research Council (1988) has identified the following expected developments: (a) in sensory computing: machine understanding of speech and visual images; (b) in expert systems: machine-based representations of expert human knowledge in specialized professional domains; (c) in cognitive systems: machines that can plan, reason, and learn from practice; and (d) in robotics: intelligent machines that can interact purposefully with the physical world.

The many already-existing applications plus those under development make it essential that national leaders understand the trends and implications of artificial intelligence. Fortunately there are now some excellent reports available on the topic, and a selection of these is given in the reference list for this chapter. General sources include Gardner (1985), Barr and Feigenbaum (1981), Cohen and Feigenbaum (1982), Feigenbaum and McCorduck (1984), and Charniak and McDermott (1985). The subject was reviewed in "Artificial Intelligence: The Second Computer Age Begins," *Business Week*, 8 March 1982, pp. 66-75. Interested readers should also investigate such journals as *PCAI*, *AI Magazine*, *AI Expert*, and *Artificial Intelligence*.

Expert Systems

This chapter focuses on just one AI application that may prove extremely important for governments—expert systems. These computer models are attempts to mimic the way human experts solve problems. An expert system for medical diagnosis, for example, contains the knowledge that medical personnel have about diseases and the reasoning procedures used by a doctor in evaluating symptoms, deciding on a diagnosis, and choosing a treatment. Such an expert system allows its user to type information about a patient's symptoms into a computer and then provides one or more alternative diagnoses and recommendations for treatment.

The goal of the designers of expert systems is to structure programs that solve problems and make decisions as well as human experts would. But how do humans make decisions? One of the advances coming out of cognitive science research in recent decades is a better understanding of how human decision making actually operates. In certain fields (economics, for example), it had been assumed that this behavior was rationally based. But according to AI research, humans in fact rely on heuristics or "rules of thumb" in making choices (Lenat 1981) and act as information processors rather than as rational maximizers (Dyson and Purkitt 1986).

Therefore, an effective expert system must include both the factual knowledge the human expert has about a certain field and the reasoning procedures that the human expert uses to process information about the current situation, form hypotheses, and develop possible solutions. These reasoning procedures include both the rules of thumb mentioned above and an inference mechanism.

Until recently, extracting and structuring the factual and judgmental knowledge of human experts into an expert system has been difficult, time consuming, and expensive, but the process is now becoming more accessible and less costly. Natural language interfaces and "shells" are even allowing people who are not AI specialists to prepare expert systems, and shells appropriate for small projects now cost as little as fifty dollars. As these developments proceed, the technology of expert systems will become even more readily available to the public and to policy makers (Freedman 1987).

More information about expert systems can be obtained in Hayes-Roth, Waterman, and Lenat (1983); Duda and Shortliffe (1983); Shurkin (1983); Buchanan and Shortliffe (1984); and Wolfgram, Dear, and Galbraith (1987). Other general sources include the journals *AI Expert*, *PCAI*, and *AI Magazine*, and the proceedings from the annual conference of the American Association for Artificial Intelligence (AAAI) and from the bi-yearly meeting of the International Joint Conference on Artificial Intelligence (IJCAI). Feigenbaum and McCorduck (1984) and Schoen and Sykes (1987) provide discussions of anticipated future developments in expert systems.

Expert Systems Useful to Governments

Among the numerous expert systems that have been developed, many have utility in providing government services, formulating policy, and supporting economic development. The following examples include programs that should be of interest to government officials and other public leaders.

Ministers of health will certainly find uses for expert systems, since one important application of these programs is to medical diagnosis, particularly in situations where medical specialists are scarce. The Expert Diagnosis and Treatment Modules (reviewed in the "Demography, Health, and Education" chapter of this book) work on microcomputers and provide a second opinion for mid-level health practitioners working in remote areas of developing countries. In China, where doctors

with advanced training are still scarce, expert systems are being developed for use in community hospitals (National Research Council 1986).

There are also more specialized medical expert systems. The system called MYCIN assists in diagnosis of infectious blood diseases and provides an explanation of the way in which the diagnoses are reached; the program was developed at Stanford University in 1972. Several other specialized expert medical diagnostic systems have been developed since. For example, CASNET, developed at Rutgers University, is an expert system on glaucoma.

Government ministers responsible for mineral resources now have several expert systems available. PROSPECTOR, developed for the U.S. Geological Survey by SRI International, can aid in evaluating and managing a nation's mineral resources. PROSPECTOR has been credited with helping geologists in the discovery of a million-dollar molybdenum deposit in Washington State; the story is reported in "Recognition of a Hidden Mineral Deposit by an Artificial Intelligence Program," *Science* 217 (1982):927-929. MUDMAN, another program, assists in the diagnosis of drilling operations.

A wide range of expert systems already exist that should be of special interest to ministers of industry and to industrial leaders. Expert systems are in use that monitor and schedule large industrial operations, handle personnel planning, and increase productivity in the manufacturing sector. There are various programs related to construction, including, for example, one on designing foundations for bridges and buildings. Programs are also available that help to diagnose failures in data processing equipment, computer boards, and electronic controls. Some of the industrial programs are extremely specialized: the Colorado School of Mines has developed WELDSELECTOR, which assists welders in choosing the best materials for welding, and the Campbell Soup company has produced an expert system that can be used in repairing hydrostatic cooking equipment.

Much of the early funding for AI research came from the U.S. Department of Defense, so it is not surprising that many expert systems have been developed in the national security area. Among the expert systems of use to ministers of defense are ones that analyze images, simulate battlefields, analyze intelligence data, and manage logistics. One security-related expert system has been described by Lusher (1988).

Ministries dealing with financial matters can benefit from expert systems on foreign exchange management, insurance risk estimation, analysis of creditworthiness, and other financial analyses. Sophisticated financial planning systems are also available. More information about financial expert systems is available in Wolfgram, Dear, and Galbraith (1987) and in Pau (1986).

Education ministries may choose among numerous instructional expert systems. One of the most important applications is "intelligent" computer assisted instruction (ICAI), which analyzes where individual students are making mistakes and diagnoses precisely what the students must learn to avoid making the same mistakes. Examples of such programs include SOPHIE, which teaches electronics; SCHOLAR, a geography program; WEST for elementary mathematics; and BUGGY, which pinpoints misconceptions about arithmetic. The pedagogical orientation underlying many of these programs is explained in volume II of Barr and Feigenbaum (1982); Anderson (1983); Anderson, Boyle, and Yost (1985); Wenger (1987); and the "AI and Education" sections of the proceedings of the bi-yearly International Joint Conference on Artificial Intelligence (IJCAI). Specific applications are discussed in the journal *AI and Education*.

VIEWPOINTS: An Expert System in Detail

In this section, a specific expert system will be described to help readers better understand how these systems operate. The system, VIEWPOINTS, is an instructional program dealing with foreign policy. It is being developed by the author and will be available during 1990. Readers wanting further information should write Dr. Ensign at the address given at the beginning of this chapter.

In the field of foreign policy, as in other areas, computer simulations can be used effectively as educational tools—to clarify the content of various issues and their underlying cause and effect relationships, to develop strategic thinking, and to promote inquiry. However, to date, most modeling work on foreign policy has concentrated on representing

one of three major topics: individual belief systems, specific foreign policy events, and single countries operating as unitary actors (Ensign 1988). VIEWPOINTS goes beyond that by representing all of the following simultaneously in a single system: (a) a number of actors involved in the same issue, (b) the specific belief systems of the actors, and (c) the political and economic rules that shape their decision making.

The VIEWPOINTS system deals with three important development issues (debt, foreign assistance, and hunger) in four developing countries (Jamaica, Egypt, Kenya, and Nigeria). Major actors (the country's top development leader, the World Bank, the International Monetary Fund, and for some countries the U.S. Agency for International Development) are specifically represented in the system. The system simulates the interactions among the actors and allows the user to explore the implication of various problem-solving strategies.

The VIEWPOINTS knowledge base is being constructed from content analysis of both primary and secondary materials, including political speeches, government publications, memoirs, and newspaper articles. On the basis of this information, decision rules combining both qualitative and quantitative statements are developed for each of the actors.

Using VIEWPOINTS, a student or actual policy maker can learn more about issues such as debt, assistance, and hunger. Even more importantly, VIEWPOINTS helps the user understand the different perceptions that various actors have about the same problems and the different "solutions" they pursue as a result. The assumption and belief systems of all of the actors are included, so the user can view issues from many different perspectives and try out alternative solutions as the simulated consequences unfold.

The workings of VIEWPOINTS are illustrated in Figure 18-1. The user is first asked to select an issue area (e.g., debt) and a country (e.g., Jamaica). The user then chooses a role and becomes an actor. The situation in the country is described using a scenario, and the actor is asked to respond to the situation. Additional background may be obtained by examining "state of the world" information available within VIEWPOINTS.

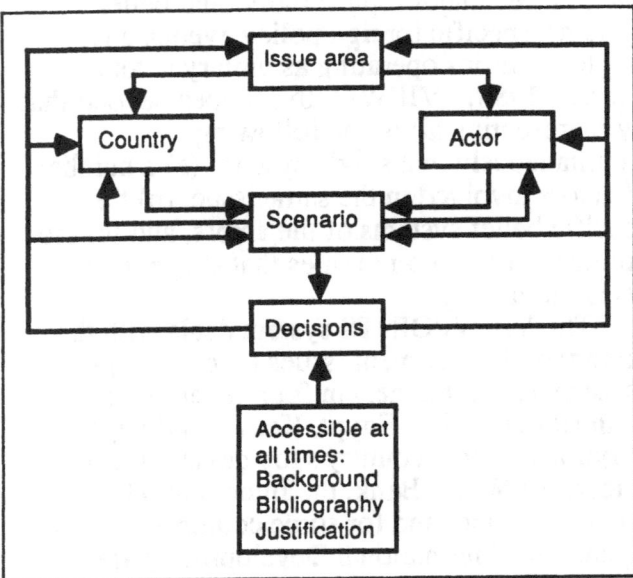

Figure 18-1: Interactions among the components of VIEWPOINTS.

When ready, the actor enters a decision. VIEWPOINTS then calculates and exhibits the consequences of that decision on the development of the scenario. After observing how one set of policy decisions affect the situation, the user can try a different policy approach or can even choose to examine the problem from a different perspective by taking on the role of a different actor.

VIEWPOINTS differs from most expert instructional systems, which typically pinpoint and correct the misunderstandings that are leading to the student's mistakes. In VIEWPOINTS, as in actual foreign policy, there are no clearly "correct" answers. Instead, VIEWPOINTS instructs by providing, at all times, a transparent trace of the causal relationships that lead to changes in the simulated situation. At the end of the simulation, the user's choices can be compared with those of actual actors who have been involved in the real-world issues.

The users of VIEWPOINTS discover that their policy interventions can produce a wide range of responses from the other actors within the system, depending on the value systems (decision rules) of those actors. In turn, these actors develop their perceptions of problems, their values, and their decision rules from experience. Thus, ultimately, it is the overall domestic and international context that determines the response the users receive to their initiatives.

Conclusion

During the agricultural and industrial phases of economic history, the wealth of nations depended on land, labor, and capital. In the future, it will depend increasingly on information, knowledge, and intelligence. As Feigenbaum and McCorduck (1984) have pointed out, access to and control over knowledge may become the new wealth of nations.

Practical applications of artificial intelligence have already been found in many sectors of society, and more are on the way. Japan's multi-billion dollar Fifth Generation Projects have been undertaken with the expectation that increases in productivity and efficiency will more than justify the expense of this AI research. Given such major investments, major breakthroughs in AI are to be expected. These developments are likely to be very important to the functioning of national economies and the delivery of government services.

While the new AI technologies will have impacts on almost every sector of the economy, some of these effects may be negative. For example, the mixed evidence available to date suggests that introduction of expert systems into banking, insurance, and other service industries leads to reductions in employment—not a positive step in the many countries of the world where unemployment is already a serious problem. There have been surprisingly few systematic studies of the impact of AI on employment and of its other possible social implications, although Boden (1977) gives a preliminary discussion of these issues.

Government leaders and others in positions of power should seriously consider the possible usefulness of AI in their particular fields. However, they should also remember that, like any other new technology, AI needs to be evaluated for both its positive and negative potential impacts, rather than being adopted uncritically.

References

Anderson, J. R. 1983. *The Architecture of Cognition.* Cambridge, Mass.: Harvard University Press.

Anderson, J. R.; Boyle, C. Franklin; and Yost, Gregg. 1985. The Geometry Tutor. *Proceedings of the Ninth International Joint Conference on Artificial Intelligence, Los Angeles, California, 18-23 August 1985.*

Artificial Intelligence: The Second Computer Age Begins. *Business Week*, 8 March 1982, pp. 66-75.

Barr, Avron and Feigenbaum, Edward. 1981. *The Handbook of Artificial Intelligence.* Vol. 1-2. Los Altos, California: William Kaufmann.

Boden, Margaret. 1977. *Artificial Intelligence and Natural Man.* New York: Basic Books.

Buchanan, Bruce and Shortliffe, Edward. 1984. *Rule-Based Expert Systems: The MYCIN Experiments of the Stanford Heuristic Programming Project.* Reading, Mass.: Addison-Wesley Publishing Co.

Charniak, Eugene and McDermott, Drew. 1985. *Introduction to Artificial Intelligence.* Reading, Mass.: Addison-Wesley Publishing Co.

Cohen, P. and Feigenbaum, Edward. 1982. *The Handbook of Artificial Intelligence.* Vol. 3. Los Altos, Calif.: William Kaufmann.

Duda, Richard and Shortliffe, Edward. 1983. Expert Systems Research. *Science* 220:261-267.

Dyson, J. W. and Purkitt, H. 1986. An Experimental Study of Cognition Processes and Information in Political Problem Solving. Final Report to the National Science Foundation, Florida State University and U.S. Naval Academy.

Ensign, Margee M. 1988. *Images and Behavior of Private Bank Loans to the Developing Countries.* New York: Gordon and Breach.

Feigenbaum, E. A. and McCorduck, P. 1984. *The Fifth Generation: Artificial Intelligence and Japan's Computer Challenges to the World.* Reading, Mass.: Addison-Wesley Publishing Co.

Freedman, Roy. 1987. Evaluating Shells. *AI Expert* September 2(9):69-74.

Gardner, Howard. 1985. *The Mind's New Science. A History of the Cognitive Revolution.* New York: Basic Books.

Hayes-Roth, Frederick; Waterman, Donald; and Lenat, Douglas, eds. 1983. *Building Expert Systems.* Reading, Mass.: Addison-Wesley Publishing Co.

Lenat, Douglas B. 1981. The Nature of Heuristics. *Artificial Intelligence* 19:189-249.

Lusher, Elaine. 1988. An Expert System for Logistics Management. *AI Expert*, September 1988, pp. 46-53.

National Research Council. 1986. *Microcomputers and their Applications for Developing Countries.* Boulder, Colo.: Westview Press.

National Research Council. 1988. *The National Challenge in Computer Science and Technology.* Washington: National Academy Press.

Pau, L. F., ed. 1986. *Artificial Intelligence in Economics and Management.* New York: Elsevier Publishing Co.

Recognition of a Hidden Mineral Deposit by an Artificial Intelligence Program. 1982. *Science* 217:927-929.

Schoen, Sy and Wendell Sykes. 1987. *Putting Artificial Intelligence to Work.* New York: John Wiley and Sons.

Shurkin, Joel. 1983. Expert Systems: The Practical Face of Artificial Intelligence. *Technology Review*, November/December 1983, pp. 73-78.

Wolfgram, Deborah; Dear, Teresa; and Galbraith, Craig. 1987. *Expert Systems for the Technical Professional.* New York, John Wiley and Sons.

Wenger, Etienne. 1987. *Artificial Intelligence and Tutoring Systems: Computational and* *Cognitive Approaches to the Communication of Knowledge.* Los Altos, California: Morgan Kaufmann Publishers Inc.

19. Catalogs, Books, and Newsletters

Introduction

While searching for relevant software for this book, we have examined several hundred books, journals, catalogs, and newsletters. In many cases we found these publications to be rich sources of information about software programs that have applications to national governance but are too specialized to be reviewed in this book. This chapter describes a number of publications that deal with such software. While the listing is by no means comprehensive, it does cover many valuable resources that are currently familiar to only small circles of experts.

The first categories cover many of the same topics addressed by the sectoral chapters of this book and include: agriculture, industry, energy, environment, natural resources (water, forestry, and fisheries), demography, health, education, urban development, national security, and transportation. The remaining categories are: planning in general, mathematics, modeling, geographic information systems, microcomputers and software in development, microcomputers and society, and free, public domain, and government software.

Agriculture

Texas Agricultural Extension Service Software Catalog

This excellent catalog describes about 150 microcomputer programs in the following categories: irrigation, entomology, financial, livestock, machinery, home economics, wildlife and fisheries, weather, and utility. The reviews are short and to the point; each clearly describes the purpose of the piece and the software and hardware needed to run it. An index by name and topic is included. The software listed here would be very useful to ministries of agriculture, their field workers, and the agriculture departments in universities.

The source is: Texas Agricultural Extension Service, Extension Computer Technology Group, Attention: Catalog Request, College Station, TX 77843-2468, USA; telephone: (409) 845-3929. The catalog is free on request.

Industry

Engineering and Industry Software Directory

Microcomputer programs with industrial applications are listed in the *Engineering and Industry Software Directory*, which is published by the non-profit group Engineering Information.

The source for the directory is: Engineering Information, Inc., 345 East 47th Street, New York, NY 10017, USA.

Energy

National Energy Software Center

The U.S. Department of Energy operates a National Energy Software Center, which collects microcomputer software related to energy and also acts as a distributor of these programs.

The source is: National Energy Software Center, Argonne National Laboratory, 9700 South Cass Avenue, Argonne, IL 60439, USA.

EPRI GUIDE: Computer Programs and Databases

The Electric Power Research Institute (EPRI) is a research institution funded by member electric power companies. EPRI has developed a large amount of software for use in the electric utility industry, and the *EPRI GUIDE* describes the software and ordering information. Software specifically for IBM PCs and compatible computers is listed in a separate section. Only member organizations may order software from EPRI.

The source is: National Energy Software Center, Argonne National Laboratory, 9700 South Cass Avenue, Argonne, IL 60439, USA.

Environment

Groundwater Codes

Concern about thermal and toxic pollution of groundwater supplies has resulted in numerous groundwater codes being developed.

Many of the codes were originally developed on mainframe computers and have since been converted to microcomputers. The sources cited below cover the topics of hazardous waste migration, aquifer thermal energy storage, unsaturated zone processes, and siting of high-level radioactive wastes.

C. T. Kincaid, J. R. Morrey, and J. E. Rogers, *Geohydrochemical Models for Solute Migration*, volume 1; *Process Description and Computer Code Selection* (Palo Alto, Calif.: Electric Power Research Institute, 1984)

J. W. Mercer, C. R. Faust, W. J. Miller, and F. J. Pearson, Jr., "Review of Simulation Techniques for Aquifer Thermal Storage (ATES)," in *Advances in Hydroscience*, V. T. Chow, ed. (New York N.Y.: Academic Press, 1982).

C. A. Oster, *Review of Ground-Water Flow and Transport Models in the Unsaturated Zone* (Washington, D.C.: U.S. Nuclear Regulatory Commission, 1982).

S. D. Thomas, B. Ross, and J. W. Mercer, *A Summary of Repository Siting Models* (Washington, D.C.: U.S. Nuclear Regulatory Commission, 1982).

Most of the codes described in these summaries are available both from the original developers and from several distribution centers. One such distribution center is the National Water Well Association, a professional society that produces software programs. The Association's address is: 6375 Riverside Drive, Dublin, OH 43017, USA. Another distribution center is the International Ground Water Modeling Center (IGWMC). The IGWMC is a good source of codes for microcomputers and offers numerous short courses. The U.S. office is sponsored, in part, by the U.S. Environmental Protection Agency. The IGWMC has offices at two locations: Holcomb Research Institute, Butler University, Indianapolis, Indiana 46208, USA, and TNO-DGV Institute of Applied Geoscience, P.O. Box 285, 2600 AG Delft, The Netherlands.

PC Disk-based Citation Files of Published Environmental Simulation Models

This is an extensive collection of files on 5.25-inch or 3.5-inch disks containing approximately three thousand references from the past twenty years to articles and other publications from the world's professional literature describing simulation models in the fields of agriculture generally, crops, forests, livestock, rangelands, arid lands, and wildlands. The references describe models of crop growth, meteorological relations, soil relations, pest dynamics, wildlife populations, ecosystem functioning, and other relationships.

The source is: Micro-Computer Software and Consulting Service, Attention: Mr. Ronald N. Kickert, 4151 Northwest Jasmine Place, Corvallis, OR 97330, USA; telephone: (503) 758-0070.

"Environmental Software Review" in Pollution Engineering

The journal *Pollution Engineering* publishes an annual review of environmental software in its January issue. Each review includes a brief description of the software and gives its source. The 1988 issue described seventy-six programs pertaining to air pollution, water pollution, comprehensive environmental management, and hazardous substances.

The source is: *Pollution Engineering*, Pudvan Publishing Company, 1935 Shermer Road, Northbrook, IL 60062, USA; telephone (312) 498-9840. Prices of subscriptions and issues depend on the country to which they are mailed.

Assessment of Measurement Methods and Predictive Models for Hazardous Substances

The Research Triangle Institute's report *Assessment of Measurement Methods and Predictive Models for Hazardous Substances* includes reviews of models related to the accidental release of hazardous substances into the air. The chapter reviews the physics, chemistry, and mathematics of the problem, and lists and compares fifteen frequently used models.

The source is: Research Triangle Institute, P.O. Box 12194, Research Triangle Park, NC 27709, USA. The publication number is RIT/3889/00-01F, March 1988.

Water

Groundwater Management: The Use of Numerical Models

Groundwater models have been used for the last several decades to manage and study water supply problems. Several attempts have been made to summarize available models. The most complete summary is provided in: P. van der Heijde et al., *Groundwater Management: The Use of Numerical Models*, 2nd ed., Water Resources Monograph (Washington, D.C.: American Geophysical Union, 1985).

The source is: American Geophysical Union, 2000 Florida Avenue, NW, Washington, DC 20009, USA.

Forestry

The Directory of Forestry and Wood Products Computer Software

The Forest Resources Systems Institute (FORS) is a nonprofit, international organization devoted to promoting the use of computers in forestry and related industries.

Regular FORS publications include *The Compiler* (a bimonthly magazine) and *The Directory of Forestry and Wood Products Computer Software*, a collection of reviews of forestry-related software. In addition, FORS puts out special publications on BASIC, MS-DOS, Lotus 1-2-3, and dBASE III. They also run an electronic bulletin board, distribute some computer programs, and sponsor meetings and workshops.

The *Directory* reviews programs on economics, forest protection, harvesting, marketing and accounting, operations research, mensuration and biometry, networks and databases, recreation, soils and hydrology, utilities, wildlife and fisheries, engineering and mapping, and wood products. The reviews are excellent and comprehensive, and the four indices provide quick access. Most of the programs are for microcomputers, but some are designed for larger computers. This impressive directory is a must for anyone involved in forestry-related activities.

The source is: Forest Resources Systems Institute, 122 Helton Court, Florence, AL 35630, USA; telephone: (205) 767-0250. The price is US $80.

Fisheries

Selected Computer Programs in FORTRAN for Fish Stock Assessment

This publication, FAO Fisheries Technical Paper no. 259 (Rome, 1985), includes eighteen fishery programs. Each description gives the purpose of the program, explains how to input data, briefly describes the methodology, and gives the full listing of the program in FORTRAN. Included are programs that fit growth curves and models to different types of data, that do virtual population analysis or cohort analysis, and that predict mortality rates, stock size, and catch by age group and year.

The language used is very technical and specific to fisheries work. The descriptions of methodology are usually limited to three or four sentences defining the variables, and evaluations of the programs are not included. This is a unique resource for the fisheries field, but it will be useful only to well-trained fisheries experts who can do their own assessments of the models.

The sources are: FAO Fisheries Department, Food and Agriculture Organization, Via delle Terme di Caracalla, 00100 Rome, Italy; and the editor of the book: S. Eugene Sims, Consultant, Department of Mathematics and Statistics, Louisiana Tech University, Ruston, LA, USA.

Computer Uses in Fish and Wildlife Programs

This three hundred-page report contains papers from a 1983 conference on the use of microcomputers in fish and wildlife management. The papers are addressed to the management of fish and wildlife data, to examples of national databases, and to examples of data analysis procedures.

The source is: Prof. Gerald Cross, Virginia Polytechnic Institute and State University, Department of Fisheries and Wildlife Sciences, 100 Cheatum Hall, Blacksburg, VA 24061, USA; telephone: (703) 961-7348.

Multi-State Fish and Wildlife Information Systems

This newsletter is designed to provide training and technical assistance to states and agencies interested in efforts to develop and use computerized fish and wildlife information systems and to coordinate such efforts.

The source is: Department of Fisheries and Wildlife Sciences, Virginia Polytechnic Institute and State University, Blacksburg, VA 24061, USA; telephone: (703) 961-7348.

Demography

POPLAC NEWS

This is an excellent quarterly, thirty-two-page newsletter published by Population in Latin America and the Caribbean (POPLAC), a nonprofit, professional organization. A recent issue contains articles on a new Canadian economic-demographic model, new spreadsheet demographic programs from the U.S. Bureau of the Census and from the University of Pennsylvania, a review of new survey software, a review of a new release of a popular database program, tips on using desktop publishing software in preparing demographic reports, a story on the experiences of an Asian developing country in introducing microcomputers in its family planning offices, a report on improvements in the Retrieval of Data for Small Areas by Microcomputer (REDATAM) system, evaluations of recently released microcomputer hardware for demography, tips on using a modem to obtain demographic data, and current information on POPLINE—the population information online service operated by POPLAC.

The source is: Population in Latin America and the Caribbean (POPLAC), Executive Secretary, c/o Social Development Center, 1313 East 60th Street, Chicago, IL 60637, USA; telephone: (312) 947-2010; telex: 206021. The newsletter is US $25 for persons in industrialized countries and US $15 for persons in developing countries.

Microcomputer Software for Population and Development Planning: Proceedings of a Workshop

This thirty-four-page report of a 1988 conference covers demographic models, sectoral models, training models, and multipurpose packages. It also assesses general issues in applying microcomputer software to demographic and development work and outlines directions for future progress.

The source is: Committee on Population, National Research Council, National Academy of Sciences, 2101 Constitution Avenue, NW, Washington, DC 20418, USA.

Health

[Food and Nutrition] Microcomputer Software Collection

The U.S. Department of Agriculture operates a Food and Nutrition Information Center. As one of its services the Center publishes a catalog entitled *Microcomputer Software Collection*. This thirty-page report lists over a hundred microcomputer software programs relating to food and nutrition. Vendors of the programs are also identified.

The Center's own collection is available for public inspection and trial, but the Center does not loan the software or allow it to be copied.

The source is: Food and Nutrition Information Center, National Agricultural Library, Room 304, 10301 Baltimore Boulevard, Beltsville, Maryland 20705, USA. The catalog is free.

Management Information Systems and Microcomputers in Primary Health Care

This is the report of a conference organized by the Aga Khan Foundation, Aga Khan University, and Portugal's National School of Public Health. The conference, held at the Gulbenkian Foundation Conference Centre, Lisbon, Portugal in November 1987, was addressed to five topics: the use of management information systems in the administration of community-based primary health care, management information support for district health systems based on primary health care, cost analysis in primary health-care management information systems, microcomputers and alternative data management techniques, and microcomputers in primary health-care planning and management decision modeling.

The source is: Aga Khan Foundation, P.O. Box 435, 1211 Geneva, Switzerland.

[Public Health] Software Exchange

Public health professionals have organized the Computer and Communications Applications in Public Health Users Group (CCAPH), which distributes public domain software relating to public health and publishes a newsletter, *Software Exchange*, listing the software available from CCAPH.

The source is: CCAPH, 6006 28th Street, NW, Washington, D.C. 20015, USA. There is an annual fee of US $10 for the newsletter and participation in the software exchange.

"A Directory of Medical Software Companies" in M.D. Computing

The journal *M.D. Computing* regularly publishes "A Directory of Medical Software Companies" in one of its issues. The 1988 version was the fifth annual directory and listed over a thousand programs. The listings are primarily for office management applications, but they do include programs related to many other aspects of medicine.

The source is: *M.D. Computing*, Springer-Verlag New York, Inc., 44 Hartz Way, Syracuse, NY 07096-2491, USA. The price is US $6 for single issues of the journal.

Education

Microcomputer Applications in Education and Training for Developing Countries

The U.S. National Academy of Sciences has assembled an expert panel on the use of microcomputers for education in developing countries. This valuable collection of articles written by the panel members covers the topics of teacher training, software, primary and secondary education, special education, advanced education, and future developments. It includes not only theoretical papers, but also actual case studies of microcomputers being used in education. Both school administrators and officials in education ministries would find this book helpful.

The source is: Westview Press, 5500 Central Avenue, Boulder, CO 80301, USA.

CONDUIT Catalog of Educational Software

CONDUIT is a nonprofit group that publishes educational software for the secondary and university levels. Its catalog covers programs in biology, chemistry, economics, education, futures/forecasting, languages, mathematics, music, physics, psychology, science, political science, sociology, and statistics. A section on multidisciplinary tools is also included. The reviews are clear, and the index sorts models by discipline and type of microcomputer. All of the packages are user friendly, and the documentation is excellent. Free classroom previews are available for educational institutions. This is an important

resource for instructors interested in using microcomputers in teaching.

The source is: The University of Iowa CONDUIT, Oakdale Campus, Iowa City, IA 52242, USA. The catalog is free.

CONDUIT Author's Guide

CONDUIT has prepared a guide for authors who are developing computer-based instructional materials. The principal target audience is college instructors who are experienced in teaching but new to instructional computing. The book covers design, development, style, packaging and reviewing. Flow diagrams in each chapter illuminate the stages, and examples are given using actual models. The reference sections, summaries, and index are especially useful. This is an excellent tool for the designing of educational software in any field and at any level.

The source is: The University of Iowa, CONDUIT, Oakdale Campus, Iowa City, IA 52242, USA. The price is US $10.

Wheels for the Mind

Wheels for the Mind is a quarterly publication that provides up-to-date information on interesting uses of the Macintosh microcomputer, with special emphasis on "creative thinking through creative computing" and on education. The magazine reports, for example, on how the Macintosh is being used in projects in specific academic disciplines and gives examples of particularly innovative university programs involving Macintosh. *Wheels for the Mind* is the best source of innovative Macintosh software and is highly recommended for everyone using a Macintosh computer, especially in an educational setting.

The source is: Apple Computer, Inc., Wheels for the Mind, P.O. Box 1834, Escondido, CA 92025, USA. The price for a one-year subscription is US $12; for two years, US $21.

Urban Development

Operational Urban Models: An Introduction

Operational Urban Models: An Introduction (London: Methuen and Co., 1981) is a practical guide to operational urban modeling. The author, David Foot, describes and evaluates three types of spatial models (gravity, linear, and optimizing mathematics), using examples of actual British urban studies. Both models of the overall urban system and models of small subsystems are included. Many of the models are mathematical, but the level of mathematics is basic algebra. An extensive bibliography is provided that could be used to locate specific urban models.

The source is: Methuen and Co., Ltd., 11 New Fetter Lane, London EC4P 4EE, UK; or: Methuen, Inc., 733 Third Ave., New York, NY 10017, USA.

[Urban Management] Software Reference Guide

The *Software Reference Guide* is published by the International City Management Association (ICMA) and is designed for urban managers and planners. This handy reference includes a catalog of software by program area, a sampling of current software used by local governments, and a description of relevant publications and databases. ICMA also publishes a newsletter, *MicroSoftware News*.

The source is: Software Information Clearinghouse, ICMA, 1120 G Street, NW, Washington, DC 20005, USA. The price is US $35, subject to change.

National Security

Catalog of War Gaming and Military Simulation Models

This comprehensive catalog reviews 363 models being used in the Western defense community. Each description includes input, output, time requirements, limitations, necessary hardware and software, security classification, source, and current users. Pieces range from very small-scale models (e.g., on troop placement in transport planes) to very large-scale ones (e.g., on ICBM exchanges). When the catalog was published in 1982, none of the models ran on microcomputers such as the IBM-PC, and some were not available to the public for security reasons. Many of the programs require large quantities of data, and some involve more than a year's worth of setting-up work.

The catalog was produced by the Organization of the Joint Chiefs of Staff, Studies, Analysis, and Gaming Agency;

Technical Support Division, The Pentagon, Room 1D 940, Washington, DC 20301, USA. The catalog can be ordered from: National Technical Information Service, 5285 Port Royal Road, Springfield, VA 22161, USA. The publication number is AN# ADA115950. The price is about US $58.

Transportation

Microcomputers in Transportation: The Software Source Book

This useful publication lists microcomputer software, references, and training programs in the field of transportation. Topics covered include transit operations, paratransit planning and operations, traffic engineering, and transportation planning. The software reviews are well written, although they do not include evaluations. A noteworthy feature of the book is its discussion of public domain transportation software available for IBM computers and compatibles.

The source is: Technology Sharing Program (I-30SS), Office of the Assistant Secretary for Governmental Affairs, U.S. Department of Transportation, Washington, DC 20590, USA. A copy is free upon request.

McTrans Catalog and Newsletter

McTrans (National Center for Microcomputers in Transportation) is run for the U.S. Federal Highway Administration by the Transportation Research Center (TRC). McTrans distributes a wide range of transportation software internationally, provides technical assistance, serves as a site for information exchange, and puts out various publications, including the *McTrans Catalog* and the *McTrans Newsletter*. The *McTrans Catalog* is the most complete listing available of transportation software. The reviews are informative, and the prices of the software are reasonable. Anyone involved with microcomputers in transportation would benefit from the McTrans publications.

The source is: Charles Wallace, Director, McTrans Center, University of Florida, 512 Weil Hall, Gainesville, FL 32611, USA; telephone: (904) 392-0378; electronic bulletin board: (305) 554-2145.

Planning in General

Planning Software Survey

This catalog includes software for many topics of interest to planners: administration and program monitoring, demographics, environment and natural resources, fiscal management, infrastructure and transportation, land use, mapping and graphics, statistical analysis, survey analysis, and systems analysis. Some of the models listed would be hard to find except through this particular network of planners. The reviews do not include evaluations of the software; otherwise, however, they are quite comprehensive. Some reviews provide sample output or descriptions of particular planning applications.

The source is: American Planning Association, 1313 East 60th Street, Chicago, IL 60637, USA.

InfoTEXT

This quarterly newsletter for planners is published by the Information Technology Division of the American Planning Association (APA). It contains current information on computer applications in planning and related fields. It also provides information on obtaining the public domain, shareware, and freely copyable demonstration software of interest to public sector employees.

The source is: InfoTEXT, Center for Urban Studies, University of Akron, Akron, OH 44325, USA; telephone: (216) 375-7616. The price is US $15 for APA members and US $25 for non-members; an additional fee of US $5 is charged for overseas memberships to cover the cost of extra postage.

Mathematics

Sources and Development of Mathematical Software

This book, edited by Wayne R. Cowell, gives an overview of current mathematical software. After a discussion of the history of mathematical modeling, it gives in-depth reviews of four specific software packages produced at the Mathematics and Computer Science Division of Argonne National Laboratory, where Cowell works. This is followed by general descriptions of types of mathematical models, including issues to be

considered in software. Actual programs are used as case histories to illustrate certain points, but real-life modeling applications are not discussed. The final section contains complete information on five commercial mathematics software libraries.

This is a solid reference tool, but it differs from many of the resources reviewed here in that it is not a quick reference guide for purchasing software. Despite the technical content, the writing itself is fairly jargon-free and will be clear to a person with the appropriate mathematical background.

The source is: Prentice-Hall, Inc., Englewood Cliffs, NJ 07632, USA.

Modeling

System Dynamics Review

The *System Dynamics Review*, published twice each year by the System Dynamics Society, contains papers on research, applications, methodology, generic structures, and other significant topics in system dynamics. This excellent, well written journal contains descriptions of many pieces of software that could be useful to national decision makers, particularly to anyone who uses or develops models for policy analysis.

The source is: System Dynamics Society, MIT Room E40-294, Cambridge, MA 02139, USA. The annual subscription price is US $60 for individuals, US $75 for libraries.

Modeling and Simulation on Microcomputers

The Society for Computer Simulation sponsors annual conferences on how microcomputers are, and could be, used in simulation. *Modeling and Simulation on Microcomputers* contains the papers from those annual conferences. The articles are generally well written; many are at the cutting edge of modeling. Contributors include experts in virtually all fields of modeling. Any serious student of the use of computers in simulation would benefit from the proceedings and the Society's other publications.

The source is: Society for Computer Simulation International, Simulation Councils, Inc., P.O. Box 17900, San Diego, CA 92117-7900, USA; telephone: (619) 277-3888.

The price varies by year; the 1988 price was US $28.

The Electronic Oracle: Computer Models and Social Decisions

The following is an abridgement of a review by Professor J. G. Krishnayya, Director, Systems Research Institute, Poona, India. The review was published originally in the Institute's newsletter, *The ICDM Newsletter.*

The Electronic Oracle: Computer Models and Social Decisions by D. H. Meadows and J. M. Robinson attempts to describe the state of the art of social systems modeling, especially at the national planning level.

The approach the authors have taken is to present a detailed description and evaluation of nine specific models, embedded within a general discussion of modeling. The models were selected from a large sample, to meet the criteria of being mature, well-documented, and highly-regarded in their fields and to represent a variety of techniques and countries of application within the category of national-level policy models.

The plan of the book is as follows. It starts with a brief introduction, followed by an overview of four important modeling techniques (system dynamics, econometrics, input-output analysis, and optimization). The authors describe these as modeling paradigms, in the sense of Thomas Kuhn's well-known *The Structure of Scientific Revolutions*. The presentations are lucid, and the paradigm concept turns out to be an illuminating approach to understanding the strengths and weaknesses of the techniques (and of the particular models).

Part III, by far the lengthiest section, contains detailed descriptions of the models. Each model is presented in a uniform way, with coverage of its institutional setting, purpose, method, boundaries, structure, data, testing, conclusions, computer requirements, implementation, and documentation. The models are:

SAHEL: a system dynamics model of inter-relationships among human population, livestock, and grazing range in the Sahel region of Africa.

RFF: an input/output model to investigate the impact of population growth on environment and resources in the U.S. over fifty years.

SOS: an economic-demographic model for a developing country; it has been applied to several countries, including India, Nepal, and Indonesia.

TEMPO II: another economic-demographic simulation model, with special emphasis on the effects of population growth on economic development; the model as been adapted to represent many countries, including Peru, Venezuela, Chile, Tanzania, Taiwan, and others.

LTSM: another economic-demographic simulation with special emphasis on agriculture; the model has been applied to Egypt and Pakistan.

Bachue: a comprehensive economic-demographic simulation model, making use of econometrics and input/output methods; the Philippines version is described; several other national versions have been constructed.

KASM: a comprehensive model of the Korean agricultural sector to be used for the government's five-year plans over a fifteen-year period.

Mexico V: an econometric forecasting and policy model for Mexico, developed at the Wharton School of Finance.

CHAC: an optimizing model for Mexican agriculture.

All these models were developed during the mid-1970s, but the comparative analysis and the critique remain valid.

Part IV evaluates the models comparatively along the three major dimensions of model content, model quality, and implementation (i.e., policy impact). In the analysis of model content, several factors are considered; these include population growth, production and product allocation, technological change, migration and labor allocation, and environment and natural resources. Many illustrative figures present the causal and feedback loops perceived by the authors in the models. Finally, Part V discusses modeling and modelers as an institutional system and makes a few prescriptions.

The Electronic Oracle is an important book. If you were limited to just one book on policy modeling, this is the one we would recommend, even if you are not particularly interested in any of these individual models. Meadows and Robinson have made a special effort to present each model fairly, and, being modelers themselves, have been sensitive to the problems and difficulties modelers face. The language is always clear and easy to understand, and there are many insightful comments.

Geographic Information Systems

A Survey of Geographic Information Systems for Natural Resources Decision Making

This report of approximately 150 pages was developed in an attempt to provide local decision makers with affordable, cost-effective, easy-to-use geographic information systems (GIS) in the expectation that this technology can significantly improve the quality of land-use decisions in rural areas and small communities. This survey documents the attributes of sixty-four GIS software packages, describes what decision makers in rural areas should seek in a GIS system, and lists the analytical functions required to implement the Land Evaluation and Site Assessment (LESA) model recommended by the authors.

The source is: American Farmland Trust, 1717 Massachusetts Avenue, Suite 610, Washington, DC 20036, USA; telephone: (202) 332-0769. The price is US $19.95.

Microcomputers and Software in Development

"Public Domain Software for Development" in Microelectronics Monitor

This brief article provides information on about a dozen software packages for use in various aspects of development. All of the packages are either free or available at only nominal cost. Dr. Robert Schware, who wrote the article, is Senior Information Technology Specialist at the World Bank. He is becoming one of the key persons—if not *the* key person—at the Bank on matters relating to the application of microcomputers in development work.

The source is: Development and Transfer of Technology Division, Department for Industrial Promotion, UNIDO, P.O. Box 300, A-1400 Vienna, Austria (request: *Microelectronics Monitor*, No. 24, 1987/IV); or Dr. Robert

Schware, The World Bank, 1818 H Street, Washington, DC 20433, USA.

Guidelines for Managing Automation Assistance in A.I.D. Development Projects

This handbook was developed for people—especially those working for the U.S. Agency for International Development (USAID)—who design, manage, or evaluate development projects with an automated data processing (ADP) component. The manual considers issues that should be considered in projects that involve ADP and identifies sources of additional information. The manual is keyed to the normal USAID project cycle and covers automation strategy and planning, applications analysis, technical analysis, acquisition, institutionalization, and evaluation. The document is rather bureaucratic in tone and approach, but it does include some useful ideas.

The source is: Agency for International Development, M/SER/IRM/SA-14, Washington, DC 20523, USA.

Microcomputers and their Applications for Developing Countries

This book was prepared by the Board on Science and Technology for International Development of the U.S. National Academy of Science with funding from the U.S. Agency for International Development. It is not a catalog, but rather an overview of the implications of microcomputer technology for international development.

The book addresses the potential problems and social questions associated with the transfer of microcomputer technology to developing nations and reviews applications of microcomputers to information and communication management. The structure and uses of computer-based information systems are described, as well as their applications in the fields of agriculture, health, energy, and municipal management. Examples from developing countries, including one in-depth case study, are included. There are useful appendices, graphs, tables, and an overview of relevant software.

This book is a valuable, well-written resource tool for policy makers in developing nations who are contemplating the introduction of microcomputers.

The source is: Westview Press, 5500 Central Avenue, Boulder, CO 80301, USA.

Microcomputers in Development: A Manager's Guide

Microcomputers in Development: A Manager's Guide (2nd ed., Elizabeth Shay, ed.) explains how microcomputers can be used to fulfill management functions in development and gives development managers comprehensive information on the use of microcomputers in developing countries.

The book discusses such topics as hardware and software characteristics associated with user-friendliness and the factors to consider in choosing a microcomputer for sustained use in development projects. Information is provided on popular software pieces and their application to development management and on major microcomputer brands and their track records in development projects. Other sections cover training, supplies, installation, and maintenance. The final chapter discusses the lessons to be learned from the use of microcomputers in specific development projects. There are numerous helpful charts, tables, and appendices.

This is a first-rate resource on microcomputers in development. It covers every aspect of using microcomputers in development projects and developing countries, and it does so in an understandable, comprehensive, and accurate way.

The source is: Kumarian Press, 630 Oakwood Avenue, Suite 119, West Hartford, CT 06110, USA.

Guide to Software for Developing Countries

The *Guide to Software for Developing Countries* describes software relevant to developing nations. It consists mainly of very brief reviews of models in the areas of agriculture, economic and social resources, physical infrastructure, and administration. Also included are descriptions of hardware, support software (e.g., word-processing programs and spreadsheets), systems software, and relevant literature. The reviews are rather limited and do not include evaluations. The book is an IBM publication: only software for IBM machines or compatibles is reviewed, and only IBM machines are included in the hardware section.

The source is: Communications and External Programs Manager, IBM Area South, 190, Avenue Charles de Gaulle, 92523 Neuilly sur Seine, France.

Newsletters

There are now at least three newsletters devoted specifically to the application of computers in the economic development process. The newsletters and their sources are:

> *Computers in Development and Relief Newsletter*, Attention: Mr. Roger Knott, 106 Park Road, Loughborough, Leics LE11 2HH, UK

> The UK Council for Computing Development, Attention: J. L. Bogod, Charles Clore House, 17 Russell Square, London WC1, UK

> *The ICDM Newsletter*, Center for Development Policy Modeling, Systems Research Institute, Attention: Vinod Menon, 17A Gultekdi, Poona 411 037 India

In addition, there is a regular article on computing in development in the periodical *South*. The source is: South Publications Ltd., 230 Park Avenue, Suite 932, New York, NY 10169, USA.

Microcomputers and Society

The Computer Professionals for Social Responsibility (CPSR) Newsletter

CPSR is a non-profit organization of computer professionals concerned about society's use of computer technology. CPSR is concerned that as societies become increasingly dependent on computers, they become vulnerable as well, particularly in such vital areas as air traffic control, communications, nuclear power plant operation, and national security. CPSR distributes articles, books, and videotapes pertaining to the social implications of computing. *The CPSR Newsletter* reports on a wide range of issues that should be of concern to national leaders.

The source is: Computer Professionals for Social Responsibility, P. O. Box 717, Palo Alto, CA 94301, USA. The price is US $30 for the newsletter and general membership.

Social Science Computer Review

The *Social Science Computer Review* is edited by the Social Science Research and Instructional Computing Laboratory of North Carolina State University and published by Duke University Press. It includes general articles and reports on issues, applications, and activities germane to microcomputers and the social sciences. Each issue includes a large number of small reviews on relevant software, news of recent software releases, and in-depth evaluation of a few important pieces of soft sciences software. This is a major resource for people applying computer technology in the social sciences.

The source is: Duke University Press, Box 6697 College Station, Durham, NC 27708, USA. The annual subscription price is US $56 for libraries, US $28 for individuals.

Free, Public Domain, and Government Software

GNU Bulletin

The *GNU Bulletin* is the semi-annual newsletter of the Free Software Foundation. The Foundation is dedicated to eliminating restrictions on copying, redistribution, understanding, and modifying computer programs. To this end the Foundation is promoting the development and use of free software in all areas of computer use through a "copyleft" agreement—a legal agreement that gives everyone the freedom to copy a program as long as the persons receiving the copies get them with the freedom to distribute further copies and the freedom to understand and modify the program—which means that they must receive the source code. The last provision makes it impossible for a person whom the Foundation calls a "bad citizen" to obtain a program free, produce compiled binary code (which cannot be understood or modified), and sell the binary code with a no-copy license. The Foundation's major project is the development of a complete integrated software system called, recursively, GNU's Not Unix (GNU) that will be upwardly compatible with the Unix operating system. The Foundation also maintains a computer bulletin board on which it provides information on other sources of free software. The Foundation recommends particularly the following sources:

Austin Code Works
11100 Leafwood Lane
Austin, TX 78750, USA
telephone: (512) 258-0785

Boston Computer Society
One Centre Plaza
Boston, MA 02108, USA
telephone: (617) 367-8080

C User's Group
2120 West 25th Street, Suite B
Lawrence, KS 66046, USA
telephone: (913) 841-1631

DEC User's Society (DECUS)
219 Boston Post Road (BP02)
Marlborough, MA 01752, USA
telephone: (508) 480-3259

The TEX Program
Attn.: Pierre Mackay
Department of Computer Science
University of Washington
Seattle, WA 98195, USA
telephone: (206) 545-2386

The source is: Free Software Foundation, Inc., 675 Massachusetts Avenue, Cambridge, MA 02139, USA; telephone: (617) 876-3296; electronic mail: gnu@prep.ai.mit.edu.

DYNACOMP Catalog

DYNACOMP, Inc. has collected together a large number of useful programs that are in the public domain, i.e., programs that are not copyrighted but are also not copylefted (see review of the *GNU Bulletin*, above). These programs are available from DYNACOMP at nominal costs.

The source is: DYNACOMP, Inc., DYNACOMP Office Building, 178 Phillips Road, Webster, NY 14580, USA; telephone: (800) 828-6772 or (716) 265-4040.

NTIS NewsLine

This quarterly newsletter published by the U.S. Government's National Technical Information Service (NTIS) includes a regular column on microcomputer and mainframe software and on data that have been prepared by the government and are now available for sale through the NTIS.

The source is: Promotions Department, National Technical Information Service, 5285 Port Royal Road, Springfield, VA 22161, USA; telephone: (703) 487-4812.

Directory of Computer Software: A Practical Approach to Obtaining Federally-Developed Computer Programs

The U.S. Government develops an enormous amount of software, and much of it ultimately becomes available at a small fraction of the cost of the original development. Unfortunately, it is also true that much of the software is of very limited utility to anyone other than the agency that originally developed the software. As a result, it is often a frustrating task to find government software that might be of use in other countries and other situations. The *Directory of Computer Software: A Practical Approach to Obtaining Federally-Developed Computer Programs* is probably the most useful single source of information on such software now available.

The source is: National Technical Information Service, 5285 Port Royal Road, Springfield, VA 22161, USA. Order publication number PB88-190962/LAA, and ask if a later edition has been prepared. The price is US $55.

Appendix

Appendix

The Institute for 21st Century Studies

The Institute for 21st Century Studies, an independent, nonprofit, charitable, and educational organization, assists both industrialized and developing nations to carry out 21st Century Studies, i.e., studies that explore alternative strategies for achieving sustainable economic and ecologic development and national security.

Leaders around the world—both in and out of government—have come to realize that a special approach is needed to identify effective, long-term national strategies, and many are establishing task forces to explore alternative national futures and to identify strategies for achieving desirable futures. The teams, which may work within the government or be based at a university, an independent institute, or an academy of science, characteristically include professionals from many different fields. The studies they carry out provide detailed factual information about the current status of the country, describe possible and probable national futures, and help identify strategic choices that can lead to desired futures.

By the Institute's definition, a national futures studies is a 21st Century Studies if it:

• is led by the nation's own experts rather than by foreign consultants;

• examines multiple sectors, including trade, foreign debt, demography, natural resources, environment, technology, health, education, security, and other key areas;

• integrates the sectoral analyses, focusing attention on the linkages among the sectors;

• adopts a perspective of two to three decades rather than concentrating on short-term issues.

• identifies national strategies that work well in the short-term without creating unwanted consequences in the long-term; and

• considers the impact the nation will have on global economy, environment, and security and the impact the global situation will have on the nation.

The following nations and regions have projects that meet or approximate the Institute's definition of a 21st Century Study: Africa, Australia, Brazil, Canada, Chile, Colombia, Costa Rica, Ecuador, El Salvador, Europe, Finland, France, Great Britain, Latin America and the Caribbean, Iceland, India, Indonesia, Ireland, Israel, Japan, Mauritius, Mexico, the Netherlands, Nigeria, Norway, the Pacific Islands, People's Republic of China, Peru, Poland, Portugal, South Korea, southern Africa, Sub-Saharan Africa, the Soviet Union, Taiwan, Thailand, and Turkey. In addition, there are global 21st Century Study projects completed or underway in Canada, the United States, and the Soviet Union. Both the World Council of Churches and His Holiness the Dalai Lama have related projects in progress.

Origin of the Institute

The Institute for 21st Century Studies is one of the many results of the U.S. government's *The Global 2000 Report to the President*. This classic analysis of the economic, demographic, resource, and environmental future of all nations was commissioned by President Jimmy Carter and directed by Dr. Gerald O. Barney.

Immediately following the 1980 publication of the *Global 2000* report, Dr. Barney began receiving requests for help from people around the world who were interested in launching wide-scope future studies for their own nations. It soon became apparent that there was a need for an organization devoted to assisting teams carrying out studies on long-term possibilities for their countries. Recognition of this need led to the establishment in 1983 of the Institute for 21st Century Studies.

The Institute's Mission

The principal mission of the Institute is to provide support for the growing international network of 21st Century Study teams. The support provided includes:

• assisting potential study team leaders in beginning a 21st Century Study;

• providing methodological training for the study team members;

• participating in the design and analysis stages of some of the studies;

• providing information about alternative strategies in specific sectors;

• facilitating contacts with organizations and consultants capable of helping with particular aspects of the studies;

• gathering, analyzing, and passing on to the teams, tools (such as microcomputer models) that will be useful in their work;

• assisting teams in the publication and international distribution of their reports; and

• helping to assure that the study reports receive high-level national attention.

The International Meetings on 21st Century Studies

The Institute has sponsored two international meetings on 21st Century Studies. The first was held in Mexico City in 1985 and was co-sponsored by the Mexican 21st Century Study team; eight projects were reported. The second was held in Washington, DC in 1989; fifty projects were reported. Proceedings of the first meeting have been published by the Fundación Javier Barros Sierra in Mexico City. Proceedings of the second meeting will be published by the Institute in late 1990.

The Institute's Board of Directors

Members of the Institute's Board include: Dr. Antonio Alonso C., Director, Foro México 2010; Dr. Daniel Gómez-Ibáñez, Chairman, Council for a Parliament of the World's Religions; Ms. Patricia Maimon-Music, artist; Dr. Alan Rulis, Chief, Regulatory Food Chemistry, U.S. Food and Drug Administration; Mr. Peter Aykroyd, Deputy Assistant Minister, Transport Canada (Ret.); Dr. Katherine C. Esty, organizational development expert; and Ms. Michaela Walsh, President, Women's World Banking.

Advisory Council members include: Mr. Lester R. Brown, President, Worldwatch Institute and The Honorable Steingrímur Hermannsson, Prime Minister, Iceland.

The Institute's Support

The Institute is supported by fees charged for its services and by grants. Support has been received from many of the study teams, from many U.S. foundations (especially the Rockefeller Brothers Fund), UNESCO, the World Bank, and several individuals, corporations, and religious institutions.

The Institute's Offices

The Institute has offices in North America and in Europe. The North American office is headed by Dr. Gerald O. Barney, the Institute's founder and Executive Director. The European office is headed by Dr. Martha J. Garrett.

Further information on 21st Century Studies and on the Institute can be obtained by writing to either the North American or the European office. The addresses are as follows:

Institute for 21st Century Studies
1611 North Kent Street
Suite 610
Arlington, VA 22209-2111, USA.

Institute for 21st Century Studies
Svealiden 15B
S-431 39 Mölndal, Sweden.

Indexes

Index of Publications

See also reference lists on pages 12-13, 228-229, 291-292.

Index of Individuals and Institutions

Index of Models

This index includes models, linked systems, expert systems, programming and modeling languages, databases, and selected general software. *See also* tables on pages 255-277.

Index of Topics

Pieces of software that have a sector as their main theme are listed without parentheses; those that include the sector among their components are given in parentheses. *See also* page 255 for modeling language functions and applications.

Kondratiev wave; software 64-65

Labor and employment: software (19-22, 28-30, 59-63, 76-79, 80-82, 144-146, 154-155, 160-161, 164-168, 182-183, 186-191, 193-196, 199-202); data sources 235, 243

Land and land use: software 93 (IPT), 173, 193, (19-20, 23-25, 27-31, 77-79, 138-141, 155-158, 160-161, 173-174, 193-195, 197-199, 301); data sources 241-244, 247, 299. *See also* Agriculture, Marine and coastal. resources, Rangelands, Rural development, Urban development

Libraries; 9-10

Linear programming: 213, 214; software 21, 28-30, 37

Linearity; 213

Livestock: software 25-26, 93-94, 150-151 (26-27, 30-31, 191-194); data sources 243, 244; software sources 293, 294

Macroeconomics. *See* Economics.

Mainframe computers; 6-9, 44, 114, 178, 188, 189, 193, 195, 197, 200, 202, 203

Maize; software 35

Manufacturing. *See* Industry.

Mapping: software 103-104, 159-160, 174-175, 285; software sources 295, 299. *See also* Geographic information systems.

Marine and coastal resources: software 93 (IPT), 158-159; data sources 246-247

Mass transit. *See* Transit.

Material transport: software 94-98; software source 294

Materials requirements planning (MRP); software 71-72

Mathematical software; source 299

Mayan civilization; software 195-196

Mediation model; software 138-140

Medicine: software 47-54, 288; software sources 296-297. *See also* Health care.

Mental models; 184, 195, 197, 210, 215, 225, 226, 227

Microcomputers, advances and implications; 5-11, 302-303

Microprocessors, advances in; 7-9

Migration: software (19-22, 39-41, 42-46, 167-168, 187-189); data sources 232

Military. *See* Arms and arms race, Civil conflict, Combat, National security, War games.

Mineral resources: software 288; data sources 206, 234, 247

Mining: software 188, 189,(182-183); data sources 235

Model boundary; 218-219

Model purpose; 211

Modeling: 209-229; software sources 299-301; languages 255-277.

Movable-type press, effects of; 9

Multicriterial, multiobjective analysis; software 138-140

Multisectoral national models; software 181-196

Municipalities: software 159-164; data sources 247

National accounts: software (58-59, 74-79, 182-183); data sources 233, 234

National Energy Plan (U.S.); 74

National microcomputer resource centers; 11

National security: software 127-136, 288-289, (141-143, 206); data sources 236-237, 246; software source 298

National 21st Century Studies. *See* 21st Century Studies.

Natural disasters; data sources 246. *See also* Emergency services.

Natural resources: software 108-125, (162-163, 189-191, 193-195, 197-199); data sources 246, 249. *See also* Environment and ecology, Fisheries, Forestry, Land and land use, Water availability and use, Wildlife.

Nelder and Mead algorithm; 111

New ideas; software 146-147

Newsletters; 293-304

Newton-Raphson method; 111

Non-equilibrium models; software 22-23, 59-65, 65, 187-189, 202-203

Non-linear programming; software 21

Normalized difference vegetation index (NDVI); 31

Nuclear energy: software (76-79, 138-140); data sources 236, 239-240

Nuclear war and weapons: software 133-134; data sources 236. *See also* Arms and arms race, Combat, National security, War games.

Nuclear waste; software (138-140). *See also* Radioactive materials.

Nutrition. *See* Food and food needs.

Object-oriented programming; 8

Oil: software; 218, (74-79, 83-85, 133-134, 138-140); data sources 238-240

Operating systems, advances in; 6, 8

Optimization: 211-215; software 28-30, 35, 87, 174-175, 176-178, 188; software source 300-301

Pastures. *See* Rangelands.

Pesticides. *See* Agricultural inputs, Hazardous materials.

Peterson equation; 122